Fallen Giants

CLIMBING
MT. EVEREST

UNDER THE AUSPICES OF THE MT EVEREST COMMITTEE
THE CINEMATOGRAPH RECORD OF THE
MOUNT EVEREST EXPEDITION of 1922
Programme Price Sixpence.

Fallen Giants

A History of Himalayan Mountaineering
from the Age of Empire to the
Age of Extremes

Maurice Isserman and Stewart Weaver

With Maps and Peak Sketches by
Dee Molenaar

YALE UNIVERSITY PRESS   NEW HAVEN AND LONDON

Designed by James J. Johnson and set in Adobe Garamond and Linotype Egyptian 505
by Duke & Company, Devon, Pennsylvania.
Printed in the United States of America.

Library of Congress Cataloging-in-Publication Data

Isserman, Maurice.
Fallen giants : a history of Himalayan mountaineering from the age of empire to the age of extremes /
Maurice Isserman and Stewart Weaver ; with maps and peak sketches by Dee Molenaar.
p.   cm.
Includes bibliographical references and index.
ISBN 978-0-300-11501-7 (cloth : alk. paper)
1. Mountaineering—Himalaya Mountains—History. 2. Himalaya Mountains—Description and travel.
I. Weaver, Stewart Angas. II. Molenaar, Dee. III. Title.
GV199.44.H55I87 2008
796.522095496   2007044696

A catalogue record for this book is available from the British Library.

The paper in this book meets the guidelines for permanence and durability of the Committee on
Production Guidelines for Book Longevity of the Council on Library Resources.

10 9 8 7 6 5 4 3 2 1

Frontispiece: The program cover for John Noel's film of the 1922 British Mount Everest expedition.
Reprinted by permission of the Royal Geographical Society.

For Ruth, David, Cea, *and* Henry

"Onward and Upward"

If an account of the climbing of Everest is ever written, I take leave to doubt whether it will be as widely read as have been the stories of successive failures. For, say what one may, when the summit is reached some of the mystery and grandeur surrounding a peak hitherto untrodden by man is lost; and a book recounting the fall of one of the giants will be bought—or by mountaineers more likely borrowed—with misgiving and read with loathing.

H. W. TILMAN, *The Ascent of Nanda Devi* (1937)

Contents

Preface: A Fallen Giant   ix

ONE. When Men and Mountains Meet   1

TWO. The Age of Empire, 1892–1914   33

THREE. "Because It Is There":
       George Mallory and the Fight for Everest, 1921–1924   83

FOUR. "A Random Harvest of Delight," 1929–1933   127

FIVE. "Himalayan Hey-Day," 1934–1939   165

SIX. The Golden Age Postponed, 1940–1950   223

SEVEN. "Don't Be a Chicken-Hearted Fellow": Everest, 1950–1953   254

EIGHT. The Golden Age of Himalayan Climbing, 1953–1960   295

NINE. New Frontiers, New Faces, 1961–1970   350

TEN. The Age of Extremes, 1971–1996   398

Notes   455

Bibliography   539

Index   565

Preface
A Fallen Giant

Shortly before noon on May 1, 1999, the American climber Conrad Anker stood amid the downward-sloping shale slabs of the North Face of Mount Everest at an altitude of 27,000 feet. Suddenly he caught a glimpse of something white—not snow white but marble white—about 100 feet away. Walking over to investigate, he found himself staring at the frozen remains of a man, obviously long dead, lying facedown on the mountain. The man's right leg looked broken, as did his right elbow. His hands were gloveless and extended before him, as if in the act of reaching out to arrest a fall. Circling his waist and tangled around one shoulder was an old cotton rope. One foot lay bare, and the other wore a hobnailed boot. Most of the man's clothing had been ripped from the back of his body by the wind, but what remained—wool, cotton, and silk—was of a fashion not seen on the mountain for many decades. The collars of the shirts and jackets he'd worn on the day of his fall remained around his neck. And stitched inside one of the collars was a nametag that read "G. Mallory." Nearly seventy-five years after the June day in 1924 when George Mallory and Andrew Irvine had disappeared en route to the summit of Mount Everest, Mallory had been found.

As a group, mountaineers display a deep reverence for the history of their endeavor, and it was both reverence and historical curiosity that prompted the 1999 search expedition that led to the discovery of Mallory's body. Though they would be criticized by some for photographing his remains and for removing relics from his pockets, Anker and his comrades gave Mallory a decent burial to the best of their ability. They covered his body with rocks and recited over him Psalm 103: "As for man, his days are as grass. . . ."

Mountaineering history is enshrined in a rich literature, including Anker and David Roberts's 1999 account of the discovery of Mallory's body, *The Lost Explorer.* Many mountaineers date their decision to take up the sport from an encounter with a good book on the subject. A striking feature of this literature is that for the most part it has been written by the climbers themselves. Mountain climbing is a sport without spectators and, particularly in the Himalaya, the climbers are almost always the only ones on the scene to witness and record their triumphs and tragedies. Fortunately for their readers, some of the best Himalayan mountaineers have also proven to be gifted writers.

All of which gave two historians pause before they decided to take on the challenge of writing their own history of Himalayan mountaineering. Despite sharing a background of climbing and trekking experiences that stretch over decades and many mountain ranges (including the Himalaya), neither of us, alas, can claim to be mountaineers of anywhere near the caliber of those whose exploits we will consider in this book. Doubtless we would have written a better book if, between the two of us, we could claim the ascent of at least one 8,000-meter peak. We have instead relied on the generous and informed advice of a number of those who enjoy that distinction to minimize our errors and misjudgments. This book could not have been written without their contributions. We would like to think, however, that our training and perspective as historians will bring something of unique value to this first attempt at a comprehensive history of Himalayan mountaineering since Kenneth Mason's classic *Abode of Snow* appeared in 1955.

This book chronicles the evolution of Himalayan mountaineering from the age of empire to the age of extremes (to use the terms coined by British historian Eric J. Hobsbawm)—that is to say, from the late-nineteenth century to our own time. Unlike Kenneth Mason, we do not—and indeed could not—attempt to include a description of every major Himalayan climb in our account. Mason wrote his book in an era when, in a good year, half a dozen expeditions might set out to climb peaks scattered throughout the 1,500-mile swath of the Himalaya. We write in an era when that many expeditions might attempt in a single season to climb a single mountain by a single route. Our book will not compete with the existing mountaineering encyclopedias or databases, and a good many worthy expeditions will necessarily either go unmentioned or be relegated to endnotes. (Those interested in a more detailed listing of climbs on Nepalese peaks should consult Richard Salisbury, *The Himalayan Database: The Expedition Archives of Elizabeth Hawley,* published by the American Alpine Club in 2004. For climbs throughout the region, see "The Himalayan Index," the Web site listing maintained by the Alpine Club in London, at http://www.alpine-club.org.uk.) Out of a vast catalogue of climbers and climbs, we have selected for inclusion in this book those that we believe are either particularly notable in their own right or particularly revealing of the time and place from which they emerged.

The British historian Arnold Toynbee once denounced the view that history consisted of "one damn thing after another." In that same spirit, we would argue that mountaineering history can be more than the record of "one damn peak after another." Mountain climbing is an endeavor that takes place above but not apart from the world at large. The terrain we seek to explore consists not only of glaciers, ridgelines, and mountain faces, but also the cultural values, expectations, and conflicts that have marked Himalayan climbing over the course of its roughly 150-year history.

Throughout we have attended not just to the actual records of who climbed what mountain when and by which route, but also to what we are calling the "expeditionary cultures" that defined and sustained these efforts. In short, we have looked beyond the two traditional sources for mountaineering history, climbing journals and expedition books, and tried to uncover and interpret a much wider array of sources, including whenever possible the personal correspondence of climbers. Our climbers are historical actors on and off the slopes, shaped by the world they inhabit as much as any of the statesmen, politicians, clerics, soldiers, artists, or artisans whose stories are told in more conventional genres of political, intellectual, cultural, and social history. George Mallory, for instance, for all his idiosyncrasies, was in many respects typical of the late-Victorian middle-class establishment. A product of Winchester and Cambridge, he considered himself a gentleman in the traditional (and exclusive) English sense of the word and took the privileges accruing to his social class very much for granted. And though he himself famously disavowed any motive in climbing Mount Everest beyond the fact that it was there, the expeditions he joined in the 1920s followed the high colonial imperative of exploring, surveying, and ultimately subduing the Himalayan frontier. Throughout this book, these are the sorts of associations we have drawn in order to situate the arcane activity of Himalayan mountaineering fully in the context of its times.

The expeditionary culture of the age of empire, perhaps best exemplified by the Everest expeditions of Mallory's day and some years thereafter, was a paradoxical thing. It was bound up with visions of imperial destiny that assumed the rule of white Europeans over darker-skinned Asians and drew many of its conventions from the hierarchical order of the English public school and the British Army. At the same time, it harbored individual climbers who were often misfits in their own societies, romantic rebels who found a spiritual purpose and freedom in the mountains unavailable to them through conventional pursuits at home. At its worst, accordingly, expeditionary culture fostered colonial arrogance and quasi-military hubris. But at its best, it nurtured some genuinely admirable qualities, including a strong sense of fellowship and responsibility to others in the pursuit of common goals in the face of danger. To the extent that this book traces the eclipse of those qualities by the hypertrophied commercial individualism of the age of extremes, it is a tale of decline, a story of fallen giants in more than one sense.

Two notes on style may prove helpful to those reading this account. One has to do with the matter of spelling, which can be quite variable in Indian and Himalayan contexts. Bill Tilman, who was in the first party of Westerners ever to visit the Buddhist monastery that sits below Mount Everest on its Nepalese side, refers to it in his 1952 *Nepal Himalaya* as "Thyangboche." By 1963, when Americans first climbed Everest, the spelling had evolved to "Thangboche" in their official expedition account. Today most writers use "Tengboche," and that is the version we use here, in keeping with our general preference for contemporary forms (except when quoting from historical accounts). On the other hand, we have chosen to preserve traditional spellings and place-names when we felt that the contemporary (and linguistically correct) variants would seem anachronistic or perhaps unfamiliar to the reader: thus we retain "Bombay" for Mumbai, "Calcutta" for Kolkata, "Simla" for Shimla, and so on.

Another variable in the literature of Himalayan mountaineering is the altitude given for mountain summits. When Mount Everest first fell to a British expedition in 1953, its height was thought to be 29,002 feet above sea level; ten years later, when the Americans climbed it, the estimate of its height had jumped to 29,028 feet; today, its height is usually given as 29,035 feet, or 8,850 meters. To avoid confusion, when naming a mountain for the first time we will give its altitude in both feet and meters, either in full or abbreviated parenthetically: thus on first mention we will refer to the world's second-tallest mountain as "K2 (28,250ft/8,611m)." Thereafter, for simplicity's sake, we will describe routes, features of the mountain, and details of climbs in terms of feet alone. Our altitude estimates are the most recent available and drawn from either the American Alpine Club's Himalayan Database or the British Alpine Club's Himalayan Index.

Many people have helped us in writing this book, including some of the chief protagonists in its pages. We have called repeatedly on three climbers in particular—Charlie Houston, Tom Hornbein, and Nick Clinch—and we welcome this chance to thank them for their generous interest in our project. In addition, we are grateful for help provided by the climbers George Band, Arlene Blum, Bob Cormack, Ed Douglas, Norman Dyhrenfurth, John Evans, Andy Harvard, M. S. Kohli, Peter Lev, Molly Loomis, Tom Lyman, Jim McCarthy, Mike Mortimer, Tamotsu Nakamura, Bill Putnam, Lizzy Scully, Phil Trimble, Chris Warner, and Jim Whittaker. In Dee Molenaar we have not only a renowned mountain cartographer but a veteran of one of the most dramatic climbs we describe: the 1953 American attempt on K2. We are especially grateful for his willingness to collaborate with us on this book.

Other knowledgeable people who advised us on climbing history and literature include Bill Buxton, Greg Glade, Jim Lester, A. D. Moddie, Harriet Tuckey, Bill Ullman, John B. West, and Fritz W. Wintersteller. Celia Applegate helped with our research at the German Alpine Club in Munich and generously served as our German translator throughout.

Apart from climbers and climbing historians, our greatest debt is to archivists and librarians. We are grateful to the staffs of our home institutions, the Hamilton College and University of Rochester libraries, plus all those who assisted us in our research at the Appalachian Mountain Club, the British Library, Cambridge University Library, the German Alpine Club (Munich), the Himalayan Club Library at the India International Center (Delhi), Magdalene College (Cambridge) Library, the National Geographic Society, the Oxford University School of Geology Library, the Royal Geographical Society, and the Scottish National Library. And, in particular, we are grateful to Margaret Ecclestone, Yvonne Sibbald, Barbara Grigor-Taylor, and Anna Lawford at the Alpine Club Library in London and to Bridget Burke, Fran Hill, and Gary Landeck at the American Alpine Club Library in Golden, Colorado.

CHAPTER ONE

When Men and Mountains Meet

The Abode of Snow

One hundred and twenty million years ago, the geologists tell us, the Indian landmass broke free of the colossal Mesozoic continent of Gondwana and began to drift northward at the astonishing average speed of sixteen centimeters a year. About 45 million years ago it crossed the equator and collided with the submerged edge of Eurasia along a front of about 1,500 miles. Much of the dense ocean floor north of India plunged into the earth's mantle and disappeared beneath a line of now-extinct volcanoes. But as the inexorable collision continued and completely closed the intervening sea, the lighter sedimentary rocks of India and Tibet had nowhere to go but up. In effect, the edges of two tectonic plates collided and buckled and by the process that geologists call orogeny created the youngest and highest mountain range on earth: the Himalaya. The name, properly used always in the singular, is an ancient Sanskrit compound meaning "abode of snow" (*Himā,* snow; *alāya,* abode), and it applies most strictly to that 1,500-mile-long range bounded by the Indus and Brahmaputra rivers, by the peaks of Nanga Parbat in the west and Namcha Barwa in the east. But the tectonic buckling of Asia extends more widely than that, roughly from Afghanistan to Burma, and it is not over. To this day India plows into Tibet at the breakneck speed of five centimeters a year and lifts the Himalaya by as much as a centimeter. At its present height of 29,035 feet (8,850 meters), Mount Everest (locally Chomolungma and officially, in Nepal, Sagarmatha) remains the world's highest mountain. But Nanga Parbat at the far western extremity of the Himalaya is the fastest rising and may one day stand preeminent. Nothing grows on these mountains that rise halfway to the Earth's stratosphere, but in a geological sense they are very much alive.[1]

In its entirety, and taken to include the closely adjoining ranges of the Karakoram and the Hindu Kush, the Himalaya is the greatest geophysical feature of the earth. Though not the longest mountain range—that distinction goes to the Andes of South

America—it is easily the highest, averaging 6,000 meters along its northern rampart and claiming all fourteen of the world's 8,000-meter peaks. The highest mountain in the Western Hemisphere, Argentina's Aconcagua (22,841ft/6,962m), would not even make the top 200 in the Himalaya, where more than thirty mountains exceed 25,000 feet. Aptly named, the abode of snow boasts the world's largest subpolar glacial systems and its deepest land gorges. It is the source of three of the world's great riverine systems—the Indus, the Ganges, and the Brahmaputra—and enfolds one-sixth of the world's people in its watershed. But for the Himalaya there would be no fertile soil on the Indo-Gangetic Plain, nor any life-affirming rain. Small wonder, then, that Hindus especially revere the Himalaya as the abode not just of snow but of the gods. "In a hundred ages of the gods I could not tell thee of the glories of Himachal, where Shiva lived and where the Ganges falls from the foot of Vishnu like the slender thread of the Lotus flower," runs a well-known verse in the Skanda Purana, an ancient Vedic text. "As the dew is dried up by the morning sun, so are the sins of mankind by the sight of Himachal."

South to north, the Himalaya proper measures from 150 to 200 miles in width and comprises three parallel curvilinear thrusts or ranges, arranged by elevation and geological age. Of these, the youngest and lowest is the Shivalik Range or, in Nepal, the Churia, a dusty brown sierra that runs more or less continuously west-northwestward from the Brahmaputra to the Indus at a modest average elevation of 3,500 to 4,000 feet. Composed entirely of eroded Miocene to Pleistocene sediments from the higher elevations, the Shivaliks are the sub-Himalayan foothills. In Hindu mythology they are the eaves of the roof of Shiva's home in the Himalaya: thus the name, Shivalik, "belonging to Shiva." Once densely forested and home to innumerable tigers, leopards, elephants, and bears, they are now largely denuded and empty of wildlife except in those few sanctuaries and forest preserves that the Indian and Nepalese governments have established here over the years, beginning with Jim Corbett National Park in Kumaon in 1936. Often separated from the higher mountains by a broad plain, or *dun* (as, for instance, at Dehra Dun in Uttarakhand), the Shivaliks afforded the essential vantage points from which William Lambton, George Everest, and other officers of the Great Trigonometrical Survey of India triangulated the Himalayan rampart in the early to mid-nineteenth century. Though subject to severe flooding and erosion, they are extensively farmed and home to the many new towns that service the relatively recent and reckless economic development of the mountains.

Next, and usually across a twenty- to thirty-mile intervening plain, comes what geologists call the Lesser or Middle Himalaya, an older, more complex range contorted by uplift and composed of Proterozoic to Lower Cenozoic sediments from the Indian plate margin. Though aligned geologically parallel to the Shivaliks (west-northwest), the Lesser Himalaya is so carved and cut through by mountain torrents that it takes the surface form of an intricate series of radial southern spurs or ridges supporting the Great Himalayan crest. The Lesser Himalaya is quite high as world mountains go, averaging 7,000 to 13,000 feet in elevation and featuring summits of over 16,000 feet (higher, that is, than Europe's

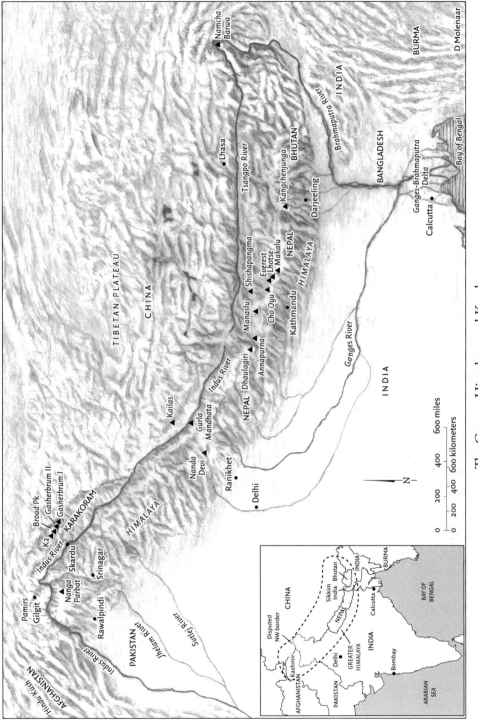

The Greater Himalaya and Karakoram.

Mont Blanc or anything in the contiguous forty-eight United States). But because of the protecting rampart above and the abundance of warm spring rains, a tree line seldom occurs and the climate is temperate. For this reason, the British built their famous summer hill stations here at elevations ranging from 5,000 to 7,000 feet and thus unknowingly provided what would become the essential points of access for those intending to climb the higher mountains. Simla, Mussoorie, Ranikhet, Almora, Nainital, and Darjeeling, once the quiet mountain sanatoria of a colonial elite, are now the noisy urban centers of a densely populated and ruthlessly exploited mountain zone. Terraced farms and concrete villages cling everywhere to the once thickly forested slopes of the Lesser Himalaya, presenting the Indian and Nepalese governments with a critical and much-discussed environmental and ecological challenge. Even so, to follow the Singalila Ridge out of Darjeeling through ancient alpine meadows and past countless hilltop shrines to the remote border village of Sandakphu and then look across the mist-filled valleys to Kangchenjunga, Makalu, and the Everest massif is still to sense the sacred timelessness of the Lesser Himalaya and its power of resistance to the degrading influence of civilization.[2]

Finally, then, beyond Sandakphu and the many villages like it, lies the Great Himalayan axis, the crystalline core of the whole system, composed mainly of intruded granites and gneisses but sometimes mixed with metamorphosed sediments from the bed of the ancient Tethyan Sea. This is a sparsely populated and largely lifeless region of ice, snow, and rock dominated by the stupendous mountain crest that falls short of 18,000 feet only where it is cleaved by the south-rushing rivers of the Tibetan Plateau. Taken as a whole, the Great Himalaya defies easy description, and most geographers have resorted to a convenient six-part subclassification first devised by Sir Sidney Burrard of the Survey of India in 1907 and then amended by Kenneth Mason for the purposes of his pioneering history of Himalayan exploration in 1955.[3]

This begins, in the west, with the Punjab Himal, a roughly rectangular mountain region defined geographically by the Indus and Sutlej rivers and now divided politically into India (Himachal Pradesh), Pakistan (Northwest Frontier Province), and the disputed mountain province of Jammu and Kashmir. Here rise four of the eponymous five rivers of the Punjab (literally the "land of five rivers"): the Jhelum, the Chenab, the Ravi, and the Beas, as well as the eastern tributaries of the Indus, the mighty river for which India itself is named (though it now flows for most of its 1,800-mile course through Pakistan). The pride of the Punjab Himal is Nanga Parbat, at 26,659 feet (8,126 meters) the ninth-highest mountain in the world and, when viewed from the west, where it rises near-sheer from the bed of the Indus for 23,000 feet, among the most spectacular. From Nanga Parbat, the western anchor of the entire system, the Himalayan crest extends southeast to the Nun Kun massif in Kashmir and thence across northern Himachal Pradesh to the Sutlej and the Indo-Tibetan border. North of the crest in the Punjab Himal is the subsidiary Zanskar range featuring, most notably, Leo Pargial (22,279ft/6,791m), a remote, round-headed massif on the disputed Indo-Chinese frontier and the scene in 1817 of one of the first true

Nanga Parbat and the Rakhiot Glacier from Fairy Meadow, 1932.
Reprinted by permission of the German Alpine Club.

Himalayan climbing efforts. South of the crest is the Pir Panjal, the westernmost range of the Lesser Himalaya that extends from the famous Vale of Kashmir to the once lovely, now despoiled valley of the Beas in Kulu, where one of the authors spent two weeks of many a childhood summer.

Some 80 to 100 miles north of the main crest of the Punjab Himal and running roughly parallel to it across the Indus River valley is the Karakoram, an 80,000-square-mile mountain fastness named for the millions of tons of black fallen rock (*kara,* black; *koram,* rock or gravel) that lie strewn about its countless glaciated valleys. Strictly speaking, the Karakoram is a trans-Himalayan range, insofar as it rises to the north of the Indus and (unlike the Himalaya) forms the watershed between the Indian Ocean and the deserts of Central Asia. It is, however, a product of the same tectonic collision of the Indian and Eurasian plate boundaries, and given its proximity to the Punjab Himal and its shared geopolitical history, most geographers and mountaineers assimilate it to the Himalaya for purposes of argument, a practice we will follow here.

Taken alone, the Karakoram is the highest mountain range in the world, with an average elevation of 20,000 feet (6,100 meters) along a continuous rampart of over 300 miles. Of the seventy-five peaks that exceed 24,000 feet in height in the Himalaya, fully thirty-three are in the Karakoram, as are four of the fabled fourteen eight-thousanders: Gasherbrum I, or "Hidden Peak" (26,469ft/8,068m); Gasherbrum II (26,361ft/8,035m); Broad Peak (26,400ft/8,047m); and the uniquely named K2 (28,250ft/8,611m), the second-highest mountain in the world. Besides the highest mountains, the Karakoram claims the world's largest subpolar glaciers, among them the Hispar, the Braldu, the Biafo, the Baltoro (with its famous Concordia junction with the Godwin-Austen beneath K2), and the heavily disputed (by India and Pakistan) Siachen, which even in these days of global warming is an astonishing forty-five miles long. Early explorers and surveyors divided the Karakoram into glacial sections known as *muztagh* (from the Turkic *muz,* ice; *tagh,* mountain), each with its own mountain group. Thus, the Batura Muztagh is the westernmost section of the Karakoram drained by the Batura Glacier, the Hispar Muztagh is the entire section from the Hunza Gorge east to the Panmah Glacier, the Baltoro Muztagh is the high central section that forms the continental divide and claims all four of the 8,000-meter peaks, and so on. For the sake of convenience, geographers also divide the range latitudinally into the Greater and Lesser Karakoram, the latter comprising massifs of shorter, southward alignment but still considerable height, most notably Rakaposhi (25,550ft/7,788m) and the twin peaks of Masherbrum (25,659ft/7,821m) in the southern Baltoro Muztagh. Of all the Himalayan ranges, the Karakoram was once the most remote and inaccessible. But with the completion of the Karakoram Highway in 1978 it has been laid open to the world and annually infested by thousands of trekkers and mountaineers.[4]

Continuing southeast from that part of the old Punjab that is now Himachal Pradesh, the Great Himalaya enters the historic district of Garhwal-Kumaon in the new

A column of Balti porters attached to the Duke of the Abruzzi's 1909 Karakoram expedition marches along the Godwin-Austen Glacier beneath the great pyramid of K2. Photograph by Vittorio Sella. © 2005—Fondazione Sella, Biella, Italy. Courtesy, Fondazione Sella, Biella, Italy.

Indian state of Uttarakhand. Here rise all the infant tributaries of the Jumna (Yamuna) and Ganges (Ganga) rivers, and the mountains, consequently, are supremely holy among Hindus. The holiest of holies, Kailas (21,850ft/6,660m), the very throne of Shiva and the center of the world, lies to the north across the Niti Pass in Chinese-occupied Tibet. But Nanda Devi (25,642ft/7,816m), here in Kumaon, is almost equally revered as the throne of Shiva's consort, Parvati, and the Kedarnath, Bhagirathi, Satopanth, and Chaukhamba groups in western Garhwal preside monumentally over some of the most visited pilgrim shrines in India.

Of all the regions of the Great Himalaya, Garhwal-Kumaon is the only one that the British ruled directly (as the Kumaon Division of the United Provinces of Agra and Oudh), and it remains the most redolent of the Raj. This was Jim Corbett country, Rudyard Kipling country. Here on the outlying lesser range of the Nag Tibba are the old hill stations of Simla (the British summer capital), Chakrata, and Mussoorie (once the home of Sir George Everest and the podium from which he conducted the trigonometrical survey of the Himalaya between 1833 and 1843). Farther east is the old Raj cantonment of Ranikhet, still home to the Indian Army's renowned Kumaon Regiment and long the staging town for mountaineering expeditions in Garhwal. Nearby Nainital, named for the emerald green eyes (*naina*) of Parvati, was the summer capital of the United Provinces, and though "emerald green" no longer describes either the town or its famous freshwater lake, Naina (formerly China) Peak, just a few miles up the Upper Cheena Mall, still affords on a clear day a breathtaking 120-mile panorama of "the Snows," from Kedarnath (22,768ft/6,940m) in the west to Api (23,398ft/7,132m) inside the border of Nepal in the east. The centerpiece, and from Naina Peak the nearest point on the crest, is Nanda Devi, the highest and loveliest mountain in India, and one uniquely defended by an awesome encircling rampart averaging 20,000 feet in height. On the rampart itself Trisul (23,359ft/7,120m), Changabang (22,519ft/6,864m), Maiktoli (22,319ft/6,803m), and Dunagiri (23,182ft/7,066m) stand sentinel over the sanctuary of the blessed goddess; just beyond it to the east are Nanda Kot (22,509ft/6,861m) and the magnificently five-peaked Panch Chuli (20,846ft/6,354m), or "five hearths," the last earthly resting place of the five Pandavas—epic heroes of the Mahabharata—before they ascended to heaven. To the northwest of Nanda Devi, Kamet (25,445ft/7,756m) and Abi Gamin (24,130ft/7,355m) bestride the Kumaoni continuation of the subsidiary Zanskar Range, which here forms the effective border of India and Tibet. Taken as a whole, with its sharply defined, unusually elegant and approachable mountains, its fragrant pine and deodar forests, its flowered meadows and hospitable villages, Garhwal-Kumaon is the most alpine in character of Himalayan regions. The British felt very much at home here and more easily tempted than elsewhere into mountain exploration and ascent.

From Garhwal-Kumaon the Himalayan crest crosses the Kali River into Nepal, a perfectly rectangular kingdom about the size of England and Wales together and divided latitudinally into the Terai, or southern lowlands, and the Himal, the northern highlands.

Three river systems drain the Nepal Himal, the Karnali, the Gandaki, and the Kosi, and geographers commonly divide it into three corresponding sections. The Karnali section in the west features the Api-Saipal mountain group, drained by the tributary Seti River; the outlying peak of Gurla Mandhata (25,242ft/7,694m) on the Zanskar crest in southern Tibet; the Kanjiroba Himal; and, most famously, the Dhaulagiri massif, a dense and dramatic cluster of giants that culminates in the sixth-highest peak on earth, Dhaulagiri (26,794ft/8,167m), or "White Mountain." Just to the east, the deep gorge of the Kali Gandaki separates Dhaulagiri from the Annapurna massif, easily admired from the lowland town of Pokhara, and the central Gandaki section of the Nepal Himal. Beyond Annapurna I (26,544ft/8,091m) and the pilgrim shrine of Muktinath, the Peri Himal and the Larkya Himal continue the eastward line and support, on a subsidiary north-south ridge, Manaslu (26,781ft/8,163m), the world's seventh-highest mountain, and Himalchuli (25,895ft/7,893m). Finally, in the east, the Kosi and its tributaries (Bhote Kosi, Tamba Kosi, Dudh Kosi, Arun, and Tamur) drain an enormous broken rampart that runs from Shishapangma (26,397ft/8,046m) in Tibet to Kangchenjunga (28,168ft/8,586m) on the Nepalese border of Sikkim. In between these two massifs, towering above the valleys of Dudh Kosi and the Arun, is the unsurpassable Mahalangur Himal featuring, from west to east, four of the world's six highest mountains: Cho Oyu (26,905ft/8,201m), Everest, Lhotse (27,939ft/8,516m), and Makalu (27,765ft/8,463m).

In sum, Nepal is a mountain kingdom almost beyond imagining, but for all the long years of British rule in India, it was strictly closed to foreigners, and with the exceptions of Everest and Kangchenjunga (both of which were partially and occasionally approachable from outside), its highest mountains remained inaccessible to climbers until the fall of the xenophobic Rana regime in 1950. Before then, Nepal's main significance to the history of mountaineering was that it was home to the Sherpas, the "people of the east," the ethnically Tibetan people of the Solu Khumbu who from early in the twentieth century proved indispensable to Western comprehension and possession of the Himalaya.

Eighty miles east of Everest, the Himalayan crest passes into Sikkim, long a quasi-independent princely state and now a quasi-autonomous province of the Republic of India. The Sikkim Himalaya is much the smallest section of the range, traversing less than half a degree of longitude and essentially amounting to Kangchenjunga and its many satellites. Of all the great Himalayan peaks, Kangchenjunga, the "five treasures of the snows" (so named for its five distinct summits that, according to Sikkimese legend, guard the five treasures of salt, gems, grain, armor, and holy scripture), is the only one that displays its glories to the world at large, as the English mountaineer Frank Smythe once put it.[5] Everest and K2, its only superiors, ask a fair amount of those who would so much as look at them, so cloistered are they in the remote fastnesses of the Khumbu and the Karakoram. But Kangchenjunga, not for nothing the guardian deity of Sikkim, rises to its staggering heights forty-four miles from the Bengali hill town of Darjeeling, rewarding the most casual traveler with an intimate sense of the infinite. It is an unusually independent mountain, no mere peak or eminence, but a mighty mountain massif thrust twelve miles south of the main Himalayan chain. Gathered around on its radial ridges are many proud vassals, notably Jannu (25,294ft/7,710m), Kabru (24,258ft/7,394m), and to the east across the Zemu Gap, the exquisite Siniolchu (22,594ft/6,887m), said by many to be the most beautiful mountain in the world. Because of its proximity to civilization and its relative political accessibility, the Kangchenjunga massif was, like Garhwal and Kumaon, the scene of much early exploration and ascent, though the main summit defied all comers until 1955.

East of Kangchenjunga and across the Lachen tributaries of the Tista River, the modest Dongkya Ridge runs due south from the outlying peak of Pauhunri (23,375ft/7,125m) and forms the border of Sikkim and Tibet. East of Pauhunri a notably wide break occurs in the Himalayan crest, the Chumbi Valley, once the high road to Lhasa and also the high (though roundabout) road to Everest for the early British expeditions. Here the long southeastern alignment of the Abode of Snow ends. From the holy peak of Chomolhari (23,999ft/7,315m), which stands sentinel over the Chumbi Valley opposite Pauhunri, the Eastern or Assam Himalaya proceeds due east for 150 miles across northern Bhutan and then slightly northeast for another 150 miles along the McMahon Line—the disputed frontier between the Tibet Autonomous Region of China and the Indian state of Arunachal Pradesh—to Namcha Barwa (25,465ft/7,762m) on the Tsangpo River, where it makes its dramatic hairpin turn south to the Brahmaputra. Given its long-standing cultural isolation and its political sensitivity, the Eastern Himalaya was the last of the six sections to be explored and it remains the least familiar, perhaps because it features none of the much-fetishized eight-thousanders and sustains a relatively modest average elevation above sea level. Lately, however, Bhutan has entered aggressively into the modern world and discovered for good and ill the foreign revenue value of its mountains. Farther east on the McMahon Line, the Pachaksiri and Kangto ranges of the Assam Himalaya, still terra incognita as late as 1980, have finally yielded their summits, and in 1992, thirty-nine years after the ascent of Nanga Parbat at the western extremity of the Great Himalaya, a combined Chinese and Japanese team climbed Namcha Barwa at the eastern, thus completing, by one measure at least, the conquest of the world's highest heights.

Early Encounters and Exploration

The Himalaya has been a place of encounter between East and West since the middle centuries of the second millennium B.C., when nomadic clans of Caucasian origin variously described as Aryans, Indo-Aryans, or Indo-Europeans began migrating across the Iranian Plateau and over the Hindu Kush into India, displacing the "dark" (*dasa*) indigenous peoples of the subcontinent and bringing with them their own Vedic system of gods and goddesses, to whom (like their Greek and Roman cousins) they assigned a mythic home in the mountains. The nature, timing, and extent of this Aryan migration remain matters of considerable scholarly controversy, but that it happened at all was a fact of considerable significance to the British, who used it to justify their colonial rule in the name of Indo-European reunion. The Germans had no colonial standing in India, but they above all others became obsessed in the 1930s with the alleged Aryan origins of Indo-European civilization, so much so that in 1938 Heinrich Himmler dispatched a pseudo-scientific expedition under SS-Untersturmführer Ernst Schäfer to Tibet to find evidence of his wayward kin (and perhaps to undermine the British relationship with the Tibetan ruling elite). German mountaineers came to the Himalaya by way of the Caucasus, and in their minds they somehow elided these two Eurasian ranges and claimed both as their ancestral own. The Himalaya, as the German mountaineer Willy Merkl would later put it, was the homeland (*heimat*) of the Indo-Germanic peoples, the place where mountains had entered into their blood and shaped their cultural destiny.[6]

Such fond and self-serving imaginings aside, knowledge of the Himalaya first came to Europe by way of Alexander the Great, whose Macedonian army forced the Khyber Pass and penetrated the Punjab as far as the Hyphasis (the modern Beas) in 326 B.C. How far north Alexander himself ventured beyond Aornos (today's Pir-Sar) on the Indus is uncertain, but the existence of the town of Sikanderabad in the Hunza Valley speaks to some form of contact, perhaps with adventurous Greeks following in the army's wake. "Skardu," the name of the staging village for K2 on the Gilgit Road in Baltistan, allegedly recalls "Iskandaria," a Balti rendering of "Alexander," and local legend attributes the barge by which the early K2 expeditions crossed the Indus at Skardu to the Macedonian prince; it is "Alexander's Barge." Indian nationalists are as uncomfortable with the Macedonian invasion as they are with the Aryan migration. To them it was a mere raid that made no impression historically or politically on India. But the excavations of Sir Aurel Stein, superintendent of the Indian Archaeological Survey from 1910 to 1929, proved the wide Alexandrian influence in the mountain regions, and in 1913 the Mir of Hunza proudly told Kenneth Mason of the Indian Survey that he was a direct descendant of the Macedonian prince by a peri (sprite or fairy) of the Hindu Kush. Alexander must have left some cultural impression, then, and his presence, however fleeting, gave the Himalaya a Hellenistic association that would capture the imagination of the first generation of classically educated mountaineers.[7]

In A.D. 997, almost thirteen centuries after Alexander, Mahmud of Ghazni stormed down the Khyber Pass on the first of his seventeen blood-and-plunder raids that introduced Islam to the subcontinent and thus permanently complicated the demographic and political disposition of the mountains. Mahmud's own hard-won kingdom in Kashmir and the Punjab did not survive his death in 1030. But he was the harbinger of centuries of Muslim migration and conquest that were to culminate in the founding of the great Mughal Empire under Babur in 1526. From their twin capitals at Delhi and Agra, Babur's Mughal successors mostly looked south to add to their dominion; the mountains they left in the haphazard keeping of Hindu rajas, many of them descended of Rajasthani noblemen who had fled the earlier Muslim conquests and established tribal kingdoms in the north. At its height under Aurangzeb (r. 1658–1707), however, the Mughal Empire claimed vast stretches of the Lesser and Greater Himalaya from Sikkim to Afghanistan. Once established, its vassal states in the mountain regions of Kashmir and the Punjab survived across the centuries to yield their disputed authority to the new Islamic state of Pakistan at the partition of the subcontinent in 1947. And though, unlike Hinduism, Islam confers no particular cosmological significance on the mountains, its cultural orientation westward, toward Mecca, Arabia, and the Levant, brought their existence to the attention of Europe and thus hastened their eventual "discovery" and exploration.

Marco Polo crossed the Central Asian highland of the Pamirs and may even have skirted just north of the Karakoram en route to China in 1272 or 1273. But the first European known to have seen the Himalaya, and the first person, so far as anyone knows, to attempt to render it on a map was Father Antonio Monserrate, a Spanish missionary to the court of Akbar, in 1590. Thirteen years later, intrigued by persistent reports of Christian communities in Cathay, another Spanish Jesuit, Benedict de Goes, accompanied a trading caravan from Lahore to Kabul and thence through the Pamirs to Yarkand, thus becoming the first European to travel overland from India to China. The first Europeans to cross (rather than circumvent) the Himalaya were Father Antonio de Andrade and Brother Manuel Marques, who set out from Agra in March 1624 and four months later reached Chabrang (Tsaparang) on the upper Sutlej by way of the perilous Mana Pass (18,400ft) in Garhwal. Andrade established the first Jesuit mission in Tibet the following year and it briefly flourished, drawing a succession of priests over the Mana and later the Rohtang Pass (13,050ft) in Kulu. To the east, meanwhile, two Portuguese Jesuits, John Cabral and Stephen Cacella, had crossed the mountains by way of the Chumbi Valley and the Tang La (15,219ft) and established a second mission at Shigatse on the Tsangpo that survived until 1631. Thirty years later, Johann Grueber, an Austrian Jesuit, and Albert d'Orville, a Belgian, traveled overland from Beijing to Agra by way of Lhasa and Kathmandu. How they crossed the Nepal Himalaya they did not say, but if, as seems likely, they followed the Po Chu to the frontier village of Nyenam, where it breaks through the mountains between Shishapangma and Cho Oyu to become the Bhote Kosi, they were almost certainly the first Europeans to see Mount Everest and evidently the last to be unmoved by it: nowhere in his diary does Grueber make even the briefest mention of the mountains, an interesting commentary in itself on the seventeenth-century (or the Jesuit) sensibility.[8]

The last of the priestly pioneers, the Italian Ippolito Desideri, crossed from Srinagar to Leh, in the trans-Himalayan region of Ladakh, by way of the Zoji La (11,578ft) in May 1714 and proceeded on to Lhasa, where he remained until the Jesuit mission to Tibet ended in 1721.[9] Thereafter, the initiative in Himalayan exploration passed from the servants of God to the servants of Mammon in the shape of the British East India Company. Founded by royal charter in December 1600, the Governor and Company of Merchants of London, as it was then formally known, established its first trade enclave in India at Surat on the River Tapti in 1612. It acquired Bombay from the Portuguese in 1674 and Madras, then a mere fishing village, from a tributary raja of the Coromandal in 1639. Initially the company had no interest in territorial aggrandizement in India; it was there by the authority of the Mughal emperor simply to trade for the spices and textiles of the East. Over time, however, as Mughal authority waned in India and trade rivalry with the French increased, the East India Company found itself drawn into local dynastic struggles from which it often emerged with surrogate governing authority. The date often (and somewhat arbitrarily) taken to mark the dawn of "British India" is June 23, 1757, when by a deft combination of military bravura and diplomatic intrigue Robert Clive defeated the army of Siraj-ud-daula at the "Mango Grove" of Plassey and established himself (in fact if not in name) as the ruling power in Bengal. Calcutta, the modest trading post established by Job Charnock on the Hooghly River in 1690, became from 1772 the capital of British India, the seat of the governor-general, and the essential northern vantage point from which, over time, the British were to comprehend and control the Himalaya.[10]

Before leaving India in 1767, Clive appointed Captain James Rennell of the Bengal engineers to the post of surveyor-general of Bengal, an appointment often taken roughly to mark the foundation of the Indian Survey. Rennell's brief was "to set about forming a general Map of Bengall with all Expedition," and this he did, mainly by compiling the route surveys of military officers in the field. He did little surveying himself, and none in the mountains, but he did travel north as far as the border with Bhutan, saw what was probably Chomolhari, and guessed that the Himalaya were "among the highest mountains of the old hemisphere." A few years later Clive's successor, Warren Hastings, sent the twenty-eight-year-old Scotsman George Bogle on a diplomatic mission to Tibet in hopes of opening trade relations with China. After considerable delay in Bhutan, Bogle and his companion, Alexander Hamilton, crossed the Tang La in late October 1774, thus becoming the first Britons to cross the Himalaya onto the Tibetan plateau. Barred from entering Lhasa, where the Dalai Lama was still in his minority, they made their way eventually to Shigatse (Xigaze), where Bogle took a Tibetan wife and won the friendship of the Sixth Panchen Lama, Lobsang Palden Yeshé, then ruling in the Dalai Lama's stead as regent. He won little in the way of commercial advantage for the East India Company, however, and nine years later Hastings sent a second emissary, his cousin Samuel Turner, who reached Shigatse only to find that the Panchen Lama had died of smallpox on a visit to Beijing. Bogle and Turner were intrepid travelers and astute cultural observers, but neither had been accompanied by a trained surveyor, and apart from the course of the Tsangpo River their missions added little to geographical knowledge. When James Rennell published the second edition of his pioneering *Map of Hindoostan* in 1792, everything north of the outer foothills remained terra incognita, a wide space filled with random lines of peaks taken straight out of Ptolemy.[11]

Tibetan annoyance at the refusal of Hastings's successor, Lord Cornwallis (of Yorktown fame), to come to their aid during a war with the Gurkhas in 1788, together with rising Chinese influence in Lhasa, led to the closing of the Tibetan frontier in 1792.

Apart from an occasional trespasser, no Englishman would again cross the Tang La until Francis Younghusband reopened Anglo-Tibetan relations at gunpoint in 1904. The Kingdom of Nepal briefly tolerated a British resident at Kathmandu between 1801 and 1803, thus affording the surveyor Charles Crawford a tantalizing glimpse of the mountains, the heights of which he put variously at "11,000–20,000 feet above stations of observation."[12] But soon thereafter the Anglo-Nepalese treaty of friendship lapsed, the resident withdrew, Crawford's calculations and drawings were lost, and a veil of obscurity once again descended on the central Himalaya. Not until 1950 would foreign travelers return to the Kosi region of eastern Nepal that Crawford had crudely begun to survey in 1802.

In India, meanwhile, company aggression against the Maratha Confederacy had by 1805 ostensibly extended British territory as far north as Delhi, and where the army went, the surveyors followed, struggling to keep this fast-expanding empire within Calcutta's cartographic grasp. Robert Colebrooke, Rennell's successor as surveyor-general of Bengal, took to the field himself (along with his wife, two children, four elephants, five camels, thirty-six assorted servants, and an escort of fifty sepoys) in 1807 determined to find the sources of the Ganges. From Patna in Bihar he pushed up the tributary rivers Gogra and Rapti to Gorakhpur, where he took his first series of observations of the Nepal Himal. Leaving his family in the keeping of the European community at Lucknow, he then pushed northwest through the Terai to Pilibhit in the sub-Himalayan region of Rohilkhand. From here, having taken a second series of observations of mountains that were, he now felt confident, "without doubt equal, if not superior, in elevation to the Cordilleras of South America," he meant to proceed surreptitiously into Garhwal-Kumaon, then still part of the Kingdom of Nepal. But in early 1808 he went down with malarial dysentery and sent his assistant, Lieutenant William Webb of the Tenth Bengal Native Infantry, to "survey the Ganges from Hurdwar to Gungoutri (or the Cow's Mouth) where the river is stated by Major Rennell to force its way through the Hymalaia Mountains by a Subterranean Passage."[13]

Accompanied by Captain F. V. Raper (also of the Tenth Bengal) and the colorful Anglo-Indian mercenary Hyder Young Hearsey, Webb made it as far as Raithal on the upper Bhagirathi, forty miles from the glacial source of the Ganges. He then followed the Alaknanda tributary as far as Badrinath, and the Dhauli as far as Tapoban, where he climbed the Kuari Pass (12,140ft) and became the first European to behold the entire Garhwal Himal. Everything he saw convinced Webb that these were the highest mountains in the world, but he had no hard evidence until 1810, when he fixed the mountain known to him as Dhaulagiri from four survey stations in the plains and came up with a height of 26,862 feet. He was right within 68 feet. But back in Europe, where geographers had long since settled that the Andes were the world's highest mountains, Webb's findings were generally dismissed as the fevered imaginings of the East. Not until George Everest brought the Great Trigonometrical Survey of India to the north in the 1830s would the preeminent stature of the Himalaya be put beyond dispute.[14]

In December 1808, shortly after William Webb's pioneering foray into Garhwal and Kumaon, the English veterinary surgeon William Moorcroft arrived at Pusa in Bengal as the East India Company's new superintendent of stud. Finding the equine stock in a lamentable state, he set off on a 1,500-mile journey to the outer reaches of British India, buying horses, gathering information, and generally acquainting himself with the peoples and places of the northwest frontier. He returned to Pusa convinced that the answer to the company's stud problems lay beyond the mountain passes, and in April 1812 he set off again, on dubious authority and in the questionable company of Webb's old friend Hyder Young Hearsey. Disguised as Hindu sadhus and under the assumed names of Mayapoori and Hargiri, the two men crossed into Kumaon and traced the Ramganga to its source east of Nanda Devi. Finding no breach in the rampart there, they retraced Webb's route to Josimath, went up the Dhauli, and crossed the Niti Pass (16,628ft) east of Kamet into the Gartok region of western Tibet. There they found few horses but plenty of valuable pashmina wool and (still more interesting to Moorcroft) some evidence of recent Russian presence in the region. "I have little doubt that Buonaparte has received important infor-mation respecting the condition of countries never pressed by the foot of an Englishman though within thirty-four days journey of the Company's Provinces," Moorcroft wrote in alarm to Charles Metcalfe in Delhi, not knowing at the time (July 1812) that France and Russia were no longer allied, that Napoleon, indeed, had crossed the River Niemen and invaded Russia.[15] But if behind on his news, Moorcroft was ahead of his time in perceiving Russian interest in the trans-Himalayan regions, and his unlicensed journey of 1812, the first of many that he was to make before his death in Afghanistan in 1825, anticipates a century-long obsession with the tsarist bogey that decisively influenced the nature of Great Britain's colonial encounter with the Himalaya.

Servants of the Map

Company annexation of Garhwal-Kumaon following the Anglo-Nepali War of 1814–16 —a war ostensibly provoked by Gurkha encroachment on company territory—for the first time brought a complete cross-section of the Himalaya "within the reach of British research and enterprise," as the governor-general's office put it. Once a matter of scientific curiosity, the heights of the mountains now became a matter of government inquiry, and as soon as the region was "settled"—reduced and reconciled to British rule, that is—the surveyors took to the field. By 1819 James Herbert, who had succeeded John Hodgson as "Surveyor of the north-west mountain provinces," had established at Saharanpur the first Himalayan baseline, the first definitive line of measurement by which the position and altitude of the peaks could be precisely fixed. No one, as yet, had any thought of climbing the peaks, the highest of which, "A2" (Nanda Devi), came in for the moment at the frightening (and almost accurate) figure of 25,749 feet. But in 1830 G. W. Traill, the first deputy commis-sioner of Kumaon, crossed the Great Himalayan axis between Nanda Devi and Nanda Kot, from the Pindari Valley to the Milam, that is, by way of the difficult snowbound pass that still bears his name. The 17,700-foot ascent was notable for its time, and indeed has seldom been repeated since. According to local legend it so aroused the wrath of the goddess that she struck Traill snow-blind and would not relent until he made a repentant offering at the temple in Almora. "The story may not be strictly accurate," the English mountaineer Bill Tilman once remarked, "but only a pedant would have it otherwise."[16]

To the south, meanwhile, George Everest had succeeded William Lambton as superintendent of the Great Trigonometrical Survey and was steadily bringing the Arc of the Meridian—the benchmark series of triangulated positions that measured the earth's spheroid along the 78th degree of longitude—north toward the mountains. It was dangerous, expensive, and painstaking work, frequently interrupted by heat, illness, and all sorts of political and technological obstructions, but by the time he retired in 1841 Everest had taken the arc to its terminus at Dehra Dun and begun a parallel meridional (north-south) series based on Joseph Olliver's Calcutta Longitudinal (east-west) of 1825–31. These, the eastern bars of Everest's famous "grid-iron" of Indian surveys, in turn formed the basis of the North-East Longitudinal (c. 1840–50), a 750-mile chain of triangles that ran parallel to the Himalaya from Dehra Dun all the way to Assam. And the North-East Longitudinal, from where it intersected the Calcutta Meridional at Sonakhoda in northern Bengal, finally made possible the definitive measurement of the eastern mountains from the late 1840s.

"The western peak of Kangchenjunga attains an elevation of no less than 28,176 feet above the sea, which far exceeds what has hitherto been conjectured," wrote Andrew Waugh, Everest's successor as superintendent of the survey, on having triangulated this most conspicuous of Himalayan giants from Darjeeling in 1847. It was an astounding discovery, yet Waugh neither publicized it nor claimed for Kangchenjunga the title of the world's highest mountain, for in November 1847, from the top of Tiger Hill, a famous prominence outside of Darjeeling, he had spotted at a distance of 120 miles a shy and indistinct summit that he suspected might be higher. For now he simply called it "gamma" and left it to his assistants, John Peyton and James Nicholson, to take its bearings from various angles over several succeeding seasons. By 1850 gamma had become Peak XV and the focus of much excited attention in Calcutta. But not until March 1856 would Waugh announce its existence to the world. The famous story that has Radhanath Sikdhar, the trigonometrical survey's chief computer, rushing into Waugh's office exclaiming, "Sir, I have discovered the highest mountain in the world" is, alas, a nationalist fiction. The "discovery" of Peak XV and the fixing of its height at 29,002 feet above sea level was the work of many hands—Sikdhar's certainly among them—over many years, both in the field and in the office. And though the Great Trigonometrical Survey is obviously implicated in that minute elaboration of knowledge by which the British laid hold of India, chain by chain, its officers and surveyors were in fact normally scrupulous in adhering to local names for topographical features. Only in the exceptional case of Peak XV did Waugh presume to ignore conflicting reports of local nomenclature and name the mountain in honor of his revered predecessor, George Everest.[17]

Of the many naturalists who traveled either hard on the heels or just ahead of the surveyors in the Himalaya, easily the most important was Joseph Dalton Hooker (1817–1911), friend, collaborator, and protégé of Darwin, who having just accompanied James Clark Ross on the Antarctic voyage of the *Erebus* went out to India at Treasury expense in 1847 and spent the better part of the next two years in Sikkim and eastern Bengal. His main interests were botanical; his first book, *Rhododendrons of the Sikkim-Himalaya* (1849–50), led to the nineteenth-century rhododendron craze among British gardeners. But Hooker was a sometime geologist as well, and his famous *Himalayan Journals* (1854), which he dedicated to Darwin, contain some of the first and still most compelling descriptions of "Chumulari," "Kinchin-junga," and other notable peaks, whose general aspects and profiles he and his illustrators finally brought home to an enthralled reading public. Though no surveyor, Hooker spent enough time making maps to arouse the reasonable suspicions of the raja of Sikkim and his chief minister, the *diwan,* and in November 1849 he was seized and detained at Tumlong, north of Gangtok, along with Archibald Campbell, the British agent. The East India Company secured the two men's release by threatening invasion and then annexed a portion of southern Sikkim just for good measure, thus bringing the Raj that much closer to the battlements of Kangchenjunga.[18]

After Hooker, the most prominent scientific explorers of the Himalaya at mid-century were Hermann, Adolf, and Robert Schlagintweit, three of five Bavarian brothers —sons of an eminent eye surgeon—who in 1854, having made their names with a study of the physical geography of the Alps, came to India under the joint sponsorship of the king of Prussia and the East India Company to undertake a study of the earth's magnetic field. From Calcutta, where they arrived in March 1855, having already completed an arduous cross-country trek from Bombay to Madras, Hermann set off alone for Darjeeling, hoping to follow the Singalila Ridge north to Kangchenjunga. The hostile disposition of the Sikkimese government having frustrated these plans, he went east to Assam and made his way up the Brahmaputra as far as Dibrugarh. Adolf and Robert, meanwhile, made their way to the recently established hill station of Nainital in Kumaon, from where Adolf undertook the second crossing of Traill's Pass—having first made a propitiatory offering to the goddess in Almora—and continued on to Milam on the Tibetan frontier.

Disguised as Buddhist lamas, Adolf and Robert (who had traveled separately by the trade route to Milam) then slipped into Tibet, escaped detention, and were the first Europeans since Moorcroft to reach Gartok. On their return, they ascended the Abi Gamin Glacier and made an outright attempt on what they thought was Kamet, or "Central Ibi Gamin," as they called it, but was probably Abi Gamin (24,130ft/7,355m), the nearest adjoining peak to the north. As far as anyone can tell, this was the first sporting ascent in the Himalaya, the first attempt to get to the top of a mountain just for the sake of it, and not surprisingly it failed, though not before the Schlagintweits and eight courageous porters had spent ten nights above 17,000 feet and reached an estimated height of 22,239 feet, a record that stood for nine years. A year later, out of Simla, Hermann and Robert traveled separately over the Great Himalaya to Leh, in Ladakh, and thence endlessly north, becoming the first Europeans to cross the Karakoram and the Kunlun ranges from India to Turkestan.[19]

Foiled in their bid to secure an Afghan buffer against the Russian bear in 1841, the British turned first to Sind and then to the Punjab for compensatory conquest. By 1848 huge tracts of the once-proud kingdom of Ranjit Singh, the "lion of the Punjab," including Kashmir, Jammu, and Ladakh, had fallen to the East India Company or its puppets and thus lay open to exploration and survey, the inevitable accompaniment to territorial aggression. One intrepid Englishman, Godfrey Thomas Vigne, had traveled extensively in these remote northwestern regions between 1835 and 1838, seen Nanga Parbat—"the most awful and magnificent sight in all the Himalayas"—reached the snout of the Chogo Lungma Glacier, and followed the Saltoro Valley out of Khapalu until he stumbled unexpectedly on the impassable rampart of the Karakoram, which he was the first European to describe.[20]

Otherwise, this was still largely unknown country when Lieutenant Thomas George Montgomerie of the Royal Engineers brought the Great Trigonometrical Survey to Kashmir in 1855. Neither he nor his several assistants were mountaineers in the conventional sense of the term. They carried no ice axes, they wore no crampons, they knew nothing of alpine rope or points of belay. Even so, for the purposes of the Kashmir survey they lugged their theodolites and heliotropes and plane tables and signal poles to very considerable heights, to the 15,000- to 20,000-foot summits, even, of the outer mountains, where they would sometimes camp for weeks, cold, exhausted, and hungry, waiting for the clear line of sight on which all their intricate trigonometrical calculations depended. How much climbing Montgomerie himself did is open to question. According to one disgruntled assistant, he "got his honours and made a name for himself with as little personal hardship as any man in the Indian Survey." But it was indisputably from the 16,872-foot summit of Haramukh, above the Vale of Kashmir, that Montgomerie in 1856 first saw at a distance of 140 miles "two fine peaks standing very high above the general range" and for the moment designated them in his notebook "K1" and "K2," for Karakoram 1 and Karakoram 2. K1 turned out subsequently to have a local name and as per survey custom went on to the maps as "Masherbrum." But K2 had none that the British could ever find and authenticate, and thus K2 it remained, and remains, in cryptic cartographic homage to the unsung climbers of the Indian Survey.[21]

The outbreak of the Great Mutiny in 1857 brought sporadic violence to Kashmir, but thanks largely to Montgomerie's personal influence with the aged Maharaja Gulab Singh and his successor Ranbir Singh, the survey went on, though Montgomerie himself withdrew more or less permanently to the safety of Srinagar. In his place in the field emerged the outstanding figure of Henry Haversham Godwin-Austen, surveyor, explorer, artist, geologist, and in the informed estimation of Kenneth Mason, "probably the greatest mountaineer of his day."[22] Born at Teignmouth in 1834, the eldest son of a well-known geologist, Godwin-Austen entered Sandhurst in 1848, where he studied topographical drawing in the old French pictorial school. Commissioned in the Twenty-fourth Foot in 1851 and posted to Burma, he served first as aide-de-camp to his grandfather, Major General Henry Thomas Godwin, commander of the British forces during the Second Burmese War. His wholly original maps of the Irrawaddy delta brought him to the attention of Andrew Waugh, then surveyor-general of India, and in 1856, on Waugh's recommendation, Godwin-Austen was attached to the Great Trigonometrical Survey and transferred to Kashmir. The mutiny found him in the lesser ranges of the Kazi Nag and Pir Panjal where, near the village of Jammu, he was evidently set upon and beaten so seriously that he had to be invalided back to England for a year. When precisely he returned to India is unclear, but by 1860 he was back in Kashmir, surveying the Shigar and Saltoro valleys of the Lesser Karakoram.

By this time, the British had identified the Karakoram as the logical northern frontier of Kashmir, the logical border, that is to say, between British India (as of 1858 a crown colony no longer in the keeping of the East India Company) and the unknown hinterlands of Central Asia. Godwin-Austen's charge, in effect, was to make known this border, to establish it, fix it, and put it on the map. He had no authority actually to cross the Karakoram, but in 1861 his explorer's enthusiasm got the better of him and, accompanied by some sixty porters, guides, and assistants he set off from Askole up the Panmah Glacier in hopes at least of reaching the Muztagh, the formidable 18,000-foot icebound pass over the Great Karakoram just twenty miles west of K2. After two days' tramp up the glacier in poor visibility, and a miserable last night on the ice, he chose eight men from among his crew and ventured up through a frightening labyrinth of shifting crevasses. "I tried with our ropes to sound the depths of some of these fissures, but all of them tied together only made up 162 feet, which was not long enough," Godwin-Austen later recalled. "The snow lay up to the edges of the crevasses, and traveling became so insecure that we had to take to the ropes, and so, like a long chain of criminals, we wound our way along." Late afternoon found the party within a mile and 500 vertical feet of the Muztagh, but threatening clouds had descended, the glacier was making disagreeable noises—"crunching, splitting, and groaning to an awful extent"—and Godwin-Austen wisely chose retreat, leaving the glory of the first European crossing to Francis Younghusband in 1887.[23]

But he was not half done with the Karakoram. Retracing his footsteps to Askole, Godwin-Austen and his crew proceeded east up the Braldu Valley toward Paiju and the snout of the Baltoro Glacier. Just beyond lay the innermost sanctum of the western trans-Himalaya, a vast canyon of rock-strewn ice and snow that enfolds ten of the world's thirty highest mountains. Godwin-Austen was the first European to ascend the Baltoro, the first to measure and map its course, the first to climb on the "monumental spires and buttresses of orange granite that tower above the north side like the nave of some vast cathedral."[24] His main objective was to fix the height and position of K2, to determine whether it lay north or south of the Karakoram watershed and thus within Kashmir or without. Fifteen

Henry Haversham Godwin-Austen
(1834–1923). Reprinted by permission
of the Royal Geographical Society.

miles up the Baltoro he drew level with Masherbrum and the Muztagh Glacier to the north. Sixteen miles straight ahead, he could see "K3" and the Gasherbrum group in all its glory, but K2 thus far had eluded him, and unwilling in the face of dwindling food to drive his porters any farther, he grabbed his plane table and notebook and with a few Balti guides started to climb an outlying spur of Masherbrum in hopes of a better view.

Two thousand feet above the glacier—a notable climb—a distant bit of ice and rock came tantalizingly into view above the nearer snow line. Encouraged, Godwin-Austen pushed on to the very summit of the spur, and there, "with not a particle of cloud to hide it, stood the great Peak K 2 on the watershed of Asia!—the worthy culminating point of a range whence those waters have their sources which drain such vast regions." While his guides busied themselves building up a cairn, Godwin-Austen sketched the conical mass of K2, fixed its height and position, and in effect claimed it for his queen. For K2, he had discovered, was on the watershed; its glaciers drained south to the Indus. It was, therefore, as far as he was concerned, in India and thus part of the British Empire. Adding a final stone to his guides' cairn, Godwin-Austen descended, satisfied, to the Baltoro.[25]

Happily, General James Walker's late-century effort to impose the name Mount Godwin-Austen on K2 foundered, and Everest remains the only great Himalayan peak to suffer such colonial indignity. Maps still recognize the glacier that flanks K2 to the east as the Godwin-Austen Glacier, however, in postcolonial tribute to the greatest of the Karakoram surveyors. No such feature great or small honors the memory of William Henry Johnson, a lesser-born contemporary of Godwin-Austen who rose through the civil ranks of the survey to become Montgomerie's assistant in Kashmir, yet in simple mountaineering terms his were arguably the most notable achievements of these years. Already a veteran of Kumaon when he came to Kashmir in 1857, Johnson soon proved an indispensable point man, a tireless commander of the advance guard whose job it was to find and secure the survey's preliminary observation stations. It was he, in fact, who placed the station on Haramukh from which Montgomerie later triangulated and sketched K2. Back in Kumaon, a quarter of a mile east of the Nela Pass, he had already placed a triangulation station on the Himalayan crest at 19,069 feet, then a survey record, and now, in Kashmir, year by year he surpassed himself, placing stations at 19,600 feet, 19,900 feet, 20,600 feet, and higher. By 1862 he had placed nine stations above 20,000 feet. Of these, four remained the world's highest for the next sixty years.[26]

As an Indian-born, humbly educated civil assistant who had never been to England, let alone Oxford or Sandhurst, Johnson hardly existed in the intensely status-conscious eyes of the Raj, and as he himself (unlike Godwin-Austen) did little of the all-important topographical and cartographic work, his remarkable climbing achievements went all but unnoticed. But at least we know his name. Climbing along with him (and with Montgomerie and Godwin-Austen and all the other sahibs of the survey) were unknown numbers of native assistants, the humble *khalasis,* paid about six rupees a month to lug the essential signal poles and theodolites and plane tables to rarefied heights unimaginable in Europe. The famous story that attributes the world's height record to one such khalasi, said to have carried a signal pole to the 23,064-foot summit of Shilla in 1860, has, alas, been discredited (at least insofar as Shilla turned out to be only 20,048 feet high). But it ought to be recalled anyway, in recognition of the considerable mountaineering achievements of these anonymous servants of the map without whose tireless assistance Godwin-Austen and company would have achieved nothing.

The Great Game

With the completion of the Kashmir Series in 1864, the Great Trigonometrical Survey had staked out a British Indian Empire that roughly corresponded to the line of the mountains and closely abutted in the northwest on Chinese and Russian Central Asia. Officially, the government of India in Calcutta now forbade any further trespass for fear of unsavory political repercussions. Unofficially, it remained eager to know what was going on in the ill-defined kingdoms beyond the passes and, specifically, how closely Russian influence was impinging on India's mountain frontiers. The phrase "the Great Game," often mistakenly attributed to Kipling, actually derives from a letter of Arthur Connolly, a young captain of the Sixth Bengal Native Light Cavalry, who had been dispatched by Lord Ellenborough, president of the Board of Control, to reconnoiter the political no-man's-land between the Caucasus and the Khyber Pass in 1831. Even then, the British had been alarmed about Russia's Asian ambitions and their potentially unsettling effects on India, so much so that they invaded Afghanistan in 1839 in order to install a ruler favorable to their interests. As adapted by Kipling, however, and thus commonly understood, "the Great Game" evokes the cold war of espionage and intrigue that raged along the Himalayan frontier in the late nineteenth century, from the completion of the Kashmir survey to Francis Younghusband's military mission to Lhasa in 1904. Its significance to the history of Himalayan mountaineering is tangential and indirect: nowhere in *Kim* does anyone climb for climbing's sake. Yet the metaphor, notably, is a sporting one and suggests at least some historical relation between espionage and ascent. Like the Indian Survey, the Great Game involved a considerable bit of spontaneous mountaineering, more than many histories of mountaineering let on, and in the culminating figure of Younghusband especially, it merged seamlessly into the romantic quest for the highest heights. Out of the political and military struggle for control of the colonial frontier, that is to say, ultimately came the thought of conquering the summits.

By one logic, the Great Game might be said to have begun in July 1863, when a Muslim traveler named Abdul Hamid (or Mohamed-i-Hameed) left Leh, the Kashmiri capital of Ladakh, for the fabled city of Yarkand in Chinese Turkestan (now the Xinjiang Uygar Autonomous Region). Though dressed as a simple *munshi* (teacher or learned one), Hamid was in fact a clerk in the Indian Survey who had been trained in the use of sextant and compass and sent over the mountains to gather topographical and political intelligence for the British. He was the first of the "pundits," as they came to be known, native explorers attached to the survey explicitly for the purpose of espionage on and beyond the Himalayan frontier. The idea of employing Indians in such a capacity was Thomas Montgomerie's. When surveying in Ladakh in 1860, this real-life inspiration for Kipling's Colonel Creighton had noticed that "natives of Hindostan" traveled freely through areas forbidden to Europeans and wondered why they should not therefore be put to the work of clandestine exploration. "If a sharp enough man could be found he would have no difficulty in carrying a few small instruments amongst his merchandize, and with their aid . . . good service might be rendered to geography," Montgomerie suggested, at first casually to the Asiatic Society of Bengal and then officially, in May 1862, to the government of India in Calcutta. The late mutiny had created an atmosphere of racial mistrust in India, and Calcutta initially greeted the idea of native spies with wary skepticism. But the failure in quick succession of two British-led attempts to enter Tibet in 1861 and 1862 eventually settled the issue in Montgomerie's favor. By 1863, needed money in hand, he was back in

WHEN MEN AND MOUNTAINS MEET

Kashmir teaching Abdul Hamid how to fix latitude with a pocket sextant and estimate altitude from the temperature of boiling water. Before long, the student had "acquired tolerable proficiency," Montgomerie recalled, and set off for Leh inconspicuously equipped with sextant, compass, artificial horizon, two thermometers ("all of the smallest size procurable"), two "plain silver watches," a copper jug and oil lamp for boiling water, a small tin lantern for reading instruments by night, pen and ink, two notebooks, and spare paper.[27]

Hamid himself, alas, never returned: he survived an arduous crossing of the Karakoram Pass and a severe winter in Yarkand only to die of wild rhubarb poisoning while on his way back to Leh. The ubiquitous Johnson, then in the field in Ladakh, somehow recovered the dead man's books and instruments, however, and Montgomerie declared the "experimental expedition" a success, one that gave some idea of "the enormous width of the Himalayan Range"—400 miles at the narrowest point—and amply confirmed the presence of Russians in Chinese Turkestan. Both encouraged and alarmed, the surveyors now took up the clandestine exploration of Central Asia in earnest. From the village of Milam, northeast of Nanda Devi, Montgomerie recruited two cousins, Nain Singh (hereafter known as the Pandit, or Pandit No. 1) and Mani Singh, and brought them to the headquarters of the Indian Survey at Dehra Dun. Here, for two years, the cousins studied the mysterious arts of secret surveillance and distance measurement by rosary bead and prayer wheel before setting out on their remarkable careers as itinerant spies. From Kathmandu, Nain Singh crossed the Himalaya in 1865 and surveyed as far east as the forbidden city of Lhasa, where he even managed an audience with the Dalai Lama without arousing suspicion. Two years later, accompanied by his cousin and his brother, Kalian Singh (alias G. K.), Nain Singh crossed the Mana Pass out of Badrinath and undertook the first systematic survey of western Tibet. In 1873, with yet another cousin, Kishen Singh (alias A. K.), he joined T. Douglas Forsyth's famous mission to Kashgar, an elaborate affair that featured six military officers, several scientists, four Indian surveyors, 350 porters, and 550 pack animals. The purpose of the Forsyth mission, headed by the commissioner of the Punjab, was to establish friendly diplomatic and commercial relations with Yakub Beg, the recently self-proclaimed emir of Kashgaria, the southern, predominantly Muslim half of Chinese Turkestan. In this it largely failed. Yet it successfully provided cover for a great deal of clandestine travel in the trans-Himalaya and was, in scale and overall style, the prototype of those future mountaineering expeditions that awkwardly combined military surveillance, scientific research, and climbing pure and simple.[28]

By the time Nain Singh retired from active service on a government pension in 1875, he was one of about twenty native explorers in the pay of the Indian Survey. Of these, the most famous is probably Sarat Chandra Das (alias the Babu) for the simple reason that he inspired Kipling's "Hurree Babu." But from a mountaineering point of view, the most important of the pundits was Hari Ram, or "No. 9," of whom little is known other than that he was a Hindu of Kumaon who entered the service of the survey in 1868. Whether it was he who, that same year, penetrated the country north of Everest as far as the Tingri

Maidan is uncertain; no account of this furtive expedition—the first in the direction of Everest—survives. But it was certainly Hari Ram who in the summer of 1871 left Darjeeling in the guise of a physician, passed through Sikkim and over the Tipta La (16,740ft) to Shigatse in Tibet, and then moved eastward across the Tibetan Plateau to Tingri, later the staging town for expeditions to the North Face of Everest. From here, the known road ran northwest to Jongkajong and then south to Kirong and Kathmandu but, being a trespasser, Hari Ram could not risk it and instead followed the Bhote Kosi over the hair-raising Thong La (Kuti Pass), sixty miles west of Everest, where at one point the path consisted of slabs of stone laid over iron pegs driven into the vertical wall of the chasm 1,500 feet above the river. In January he arrived safely in Kathmandu and returned thence to Darjeeling, thus achieving—though always at a considerable distance—the first known circuit of the Everest group. Two years later, from his home village of Pithoragarh in Kumaon, Hari Ram crossed the Kali on a single rope span and traversed northern Nepal from west to east as far as the Kali Gandaki, the tributary torrent that cleaves the mountains between the Dhaulagiri and Annapurna massifs. And in 1885 he returned from a long retirement to lead a furtive expedition up the Dudh Kosi to the Solu Khumbu region of northeastern Nepal, where he lingered for a month before braving the Nangpa La (18,753ft), a high glacial pass over the Himalayan crest and into Tibet between Cho Oyu and Gaurishankar (23,405ft/7,134m). Though he could not see Everest off to the east, at fifteen miles he was nearer to it than any trained observer to date, and the route survey he brought back constitutes the crude foundation of all subsequent British efforts to comprehend the Everest region.[29]

The fifth and final journey of Hari Ram to Nepal and Tibet in 1892–93 was the last known exploit of the Indian pundits. The Great Game was not over. In fact, with the Russian annexation of the ancient transcaspian city of Merv in 1883 and the subsequent Anglo-Russian standoff at the Afghan village of Pandjeh in 1885, it had entered its decisive phase. But the British no longer felt obliged to play the game by stealth or in secret. Tsarist encroachment on India, more real now than imagined, had put them in a fighting mood, especially in Simla, where Sir Charles MacGregor, quartermaster-general of the Indian Army and founder of its new Intelligence Department, urged on the viceroy a "Forward Policy" of open confrontation and strategic annexation. From London, things looked altogether less dire and as long as it lasted the Liberal government of William Gladstone exercised a gently restraining hand. But in June 1886 a disaffected lobby of Liberal imperialists led by Joseph Chamberlain rebelled in the House of Commons against Gladstone's policy of home rule for Ireland (and, by extension, over his relative indifference to empire in general). The Liberal government fell, and following the July election the Conservatives came in under the Marquess of Salisbury, a convinced imperialist with an ardent faith in England's civilizing mission. The hour of the Forward Policy had arrived, and on the Himalayan frontier it became manifest in the oddly diminutive person of Francis Edward Younghusband.

Soldier, explorer, geographer, brigand, patriot, mystic: Younghusband was the last great imperial adventurer, and he more than anyone evokes the colonial context in which Himalayan mountaineering developed. Born in the Punjabi hill station of Murree in 1863, he was the son of Major General John William Younghusband and the nephew of Robert Shaw, a well-known mountain explorer who had forsaken the tea trade to become the British political agent at Yarkand. Following the customary rite of passage through English boarding school and the Royal Military College, Sandhurst, Younghusband took a commission in the King's Dragoon Guards and returned to India, where he soon won a reputation as a "thruster"—an eager, adventure-seeking officer, that is, with an insatiable taste for patrol work and reconnaissance, for "proving ahead of the main body into the blue." Yet he was also an introspective romantic with a sympathetic interest in Eastern spirituality, and together these two qualities—his adventurism and his mysticism—compelled him continually toward the mountains.[30]

Through his uncle Robert, probably, Younghusband came to the notice of the Indian Intelligence Department, and in May 1885, in the immediate aftermath of the Pandjeh Incident, he was summoned to Simla to undertake the revision of the military gazetteer of Kashmir. Here he came across a copy of *The Defence of India* (1883), Charles MacGregor's controversial and confidential exposé of the impending Russian menace, and somehow got it into his head that the fate of the Raj rested on Manchuria, an obscure corner of the Chinese Empire lodged between Mongolia, Siberia, and Korea. The geopolitical logic of this eluded even the readily Russophobic MacGregor, but he agreed to Younghusband's request for six months' leave and sent him off on what ultimately became an epic nineteen-month journey across Central Asia, from Manchuria and Beijing to Kashgar and Yarkand and then south over the Karakoram to Kashmir. It was all highly original, pioneering stuff, but the highlight for posterity was the crossing of the Karakoram, for under orders from Colonel Mark Bell, then head of the Intelligence Department, Younghusband eschewed the conventional caravan route over the Karakoram Pass and crossed the Muztagh, the difficult 18,000-foot pass just west of K2 that had defeated Godwin-Austen in 1861. He thus became the first European to see K2 from the north, and, more significantly still, with no mountaineering experience and no alpine equipment—"not even a pair of nailed boots, still less an ice-axe," he recalled—he and his Balti guide Wali managed what the great Swedish explorer Sven Hedin later described as "the most difficult and dangerous achievement in these mountains to date." However limited its value from a strategic or scientific point of view, this crossing of the Muztagh opened an era in the history of mountaineering and confirmed Younghusband in his self-appointed role of Himalayan ambassador to the West.[31]

In 1889 Younghusband—now the youngest elected fellow of the Royal Geographical Society—returned to the Karakoram to investigate recent tribal raids on trade caravans and to counter Russian and Chinese overtures toward the rogue Kashmiri dependency of Hunza. Though an Anglo-Russian Boundary Commission had settled the Afghan frontier along the Hindu Kush in 1885, the Kashmiri frontier along the Pamirs and the Karakoram remained hopelessly ill defined, from the British point of view, and vulnerable to unfriendly

Colonel Sir Francis Younghusband, ca. 1903,
shortly before his armed mission to Tibet.
Reprinted by permission of the
Royal Geographical Society.

incursion. In 1888 a minor frontier war had led to the permanent establishment of a British
agency at the strategically sensitive crossroads of Gilgit, some 100 miles north of Srinagar.
Younghusband's job now was to extend the Gilgit Agency's control north and east through
the mountains. Accompanied by a small escort of men from the Fifth Gurkha Rifles, he
crossed the Karakoram Pass out of Leh and undertook the first systematic exploration of
the trans-Himalayan Shaksgam Valley. He then moved west toward the Pamirs, crossed the
Mintaka Pass into Hunza, and followed the Hunza Valley south past Rakaposhi to British-
administered Gilgit. What precisely he accomplished by all this mountain roaming is difficult to say. Younghusband simply was, as one biographer has said, "the trekking arm of
empire in the border zones of British India, Russia, China, and Afghanistan."[32] Moreover,
he was the figure in whom the political and strategic exigencies of the Great Game inspired
a spiritual and artistic appreciation of Himalayan travel for its own sake. His notable descent
of the Muztagh aside, Younghusband was not himself truly a Himalayan mountaineer; he
did not aspire to the summits. But his well-known mountain journeys between 1886 and

1891, besides contributing to the essential preliminary "pacification" of the border country, were the direct inspiration, in 1892, for the first large-scale Himalayan mountaineering expedition. With Younghusband, then, the colonial prologue concludes; with William Martin Conway, art historian and Alpinist par excellence, the climbing history begins.

The Playground of Europe

And yet, to allude to Martin Conway and his 1892 expedition to the Karakoram—generally reckoned the first Himalayan mountaineering expedition—is to invite a brief Alpine digression. Just as Younghusband was in many respects the culminating figure in a long preliminary history of Western encounters with the Himalaya, so Conway was, in 1892, the culminating figure in a long preliminary history of mountain climbing. Himalayan mountaineering began, that is to say, at the intersection of two distinct developments: the colonial exploration and appropriation of the Indian frontier and the largely (though not exclusively) British invention of climbing as a form of recreation, sport, and fellowship back in Alpine Europe. Unlike the conquest of the Himalaya, the conquest of the Alps is a thrice-told tale and needs little elaboration here. It does need review, however, if only fully to set the stage for the higher drama to come. Himalayan climbing was at the outset an organized extension of a cultural practice deeply rooted in Alpine experience. In many respects its history began not in trans-Himalayan Kashmir but in those Alpine borderlands of France, Italy, and Switzerland that Leslie Stephen famously called "the playground of Europe."[33]

Histories of mountaineering conventionally begin with some attempt to account for the mountain aesthetic, for how and why a topographical feature long derided as a malignant excrescence on the earth's spherical perfection came to be admired as the beginning and end of all natural scenery. No doubt some ancients revered the heights just as some moderns have reviled them, but the general change in Western attitudes from "mountain gloom" to "mountain glory" is indisputable and clearly traceable by various routes to the mid- to late eighteenth century. With the gothic revival, for instance, came a corresponding appreciation of the gothic landscape of the Alps; with the cult of the picturesque came a fashionable interest in rugged mountain scenes. In 1757 Edmund Burke gave classic definition to the aesthetic distinction between the Beautiful—the regular, the proportioned, the visually predictable—and the Sublime—the dramatic, the unexpected, the awe inspiring—and thus provided for those who read his work a ready vocabulary for the novel experience of mountain wonder. Jean-Jacques Rousseau most notably added the romantic idealization of the Alpine peasant and by extension his Alpine environment. Besides being magnificent and sublime in and of themselves, mountains for Rousseau were the seats of republican virtue where man yet lived in an uncivilized and therefore uncorrupted state of nature. They were also, as the Scottish geologist James Hutton, among others, discovered, ever in gradual motion and thus evidence (against the biblical literalists) of the

earth's unfathomable age. Hutton was no romantic, but somewhere at the late-eighteenth-
to early-nineteenth-century intersection of the romantic sensibility, uniformitarian geology,
and the railroad—for what good is love of mountains if one cannot get to them?—there
developed a modern affection for mountains and mountain travel that continues unabated
to this day.[34]

The new love of mountains and the new opportunity for mountain travel cannot
alone account for the advent of mountaineering, however, if only because neither necessarily
encouraged thoughts of climbing. John Ruskin was indisputably the culminating prophet of
the mountain aesthetic, yet he condemned mountaineering as fatuous and irreverent. "You
have despised nature [and] all the deep and sacred sensations of natural scenery," he once
told the climbing fraternity of the British Alpine Club in 1865. "The French revolutionists
made stables of the cathedrals of France; you have made racecourses of the cathedrals of the
earth. . . . The Alps themselves, which your own poets used to love so reverently, you look
upon as soaped poles in bear gardens, which you set yourselves to climb and slide down
again, with 'shrieks of delight.'" Just what accounted for the regrettable climbing impulse
Ruskin did not say, but his remark dripped with class condescension, and those studying
the subject closely have of late associated early Alpine mountaineering with the brash and
commercially assertive ethos of the professional middle class.[35]

Mountain climbing, the argument runs, was at root about self-improvement and
character building. It was a form of athletic recreation suited to the aggressive posturing
of the self-made man. Small wonder then that the British, despite having no reckonable
mountains of their own, should have taken the lead in this Alpine enterprise. Of all Europeans, the argument further runs, they were the most entrepreneurial and globally ambitious. "The road to success may be steep to climb, and it puts to the proof the energies
of him who would reach the summit," Samuel Smiles had written in *Self-help* (1859), his
enormously popular Victorian treatise on the art of social mobility, and it seems to have
been under the influence of this banal metaphor as much as Burkean or Ruskinian aesthetics
that increasing numbers of English tourists set out to climb the mountains.[36] Darwin's *On
the Origin of Species* appeared in the same year as *Self-help* and put still more premium on
the notion of struggle against natural adversity as a basic fact of life and the key to cultural
survival. How closely one should associate these familiar currents in Victorian thought
with the advent of mountain climbing is open to question. But mountain climbing is a
cultural practice like any other; it has a social and political background, a historical setting
and context. And at its origin, it was undeniably an outward expression of mid-Victorian
middle-class life.

Others had, of course, climbed mountains long before the mid-Victorians. Inspired
by Livy's account of the ascent of Mount Haemus by Philip of Macedon (Alexander the
Great's father), the poet Petrarch famously scrambled up Mont Ventoux in the Vaucluse in
April 1336 and was the first man to comprehend and write about his summit experience
in recognizably romantic terms. Under orders from his king, Charles VIII of France (and

with technically precocious resort to "subtle means and engines"), Antoine de Ville, Lord
of Dompjulien and Beaupré, climbed Mont Aiguille, a daunting 6,880-foot rock tower in
the Dauphiné, just south of Grenoble, in the epochal year of 1492: a climb not repeated
until Jean Liotard soloed it in 1834. In 1555 Conrad Gesner, a professor at the University
of Zurich, climbed 7,000-foot Pilatus on the shores of Lake Lucerne very much for the
thrill of the thing and to feel his consciousness drawn to the lofty contemplation of the
Great Architect. Nineteen years later his countryman Josias Simler, also of the University
of Zurich, published *Vallesiae Descriptio et de Alpibus Commentarius* (1574), the first known
mountaineering manual. Simler was writing largely for those travelers forced to cross the
Alps, however, not for avocational climbers, and with the waning of the earthly and hu-
manistic spirit of the Renaissance—Leonardo too had been an early mountaineer—the
climbing impulse faded in Europe, to be revived only in 1741, when a young English
expatriate named William Windham led the curate Richard Pococke and a small party
of fellow countrymen on an excursion out of Geneva to the village of Chamonix in the
Haute Savoie.[37]

    Now a sprawling tourist metropolis and the unrivalled mountain-climbing capital
of Europe, Chamonix was in 1741 a remote and backward farming village of no interest to
anyone but a few crystal collectors and chamois hunters. The fantastic tangle of mountains
and glaciers that dominated its surrounding valley was generally reviled as ugly and fear-
some, the icy realm of witches and dragons. But Windham and company, to their surprise,
found the Chamonix Valley "rather agreeable," the mountains and glaciers fascinating, and
on arriving at the village they hired a few local peasants to escort them onto the Mer de
Glace, the "sea of ice" that in those days descended from the North Face of Mont Blanc (or
"Mont Maudit," the cursed mountain, as the Chamoniards knew it) right to the edge of the
village. But "that did not satisfy our curiosity," Windham later wrote, "and we discovered
that we had come too far simply to stop." Against their guides' advice, the party pressed on
for four hours to Montenvers, a small plateau above the Mer de Glace. From here, having
marveled a while at the "terrible havock" made by avalanches and gaped at the panoramic
views, they descended once more onto the glacier, where they fired off their pistols for
the sake of the echoes and toasted good health to Admiral Vernon—the naval hero of the
hour—and success to British arms. Lacking the necessary instruments, they made no formal
scientific observations, they took no altitude measurements; but they did note the absence of
any witches or dragons, and Windham's subsequent account of this first touristic excursion
into the Chamonix Valley had the immediate effect of encouraging others to follow
and complete the investigations he and his companions had most haphazardly begun.[38]

    Of the many travelers who followed Windham and Pococke into the Chamonix
Valley, by far the most important to the history of Alpine mountaineering was Horace
Bénédict de Saussure (1740–99), a wealthy Genevan geologist and botanist who on the
occasion of his first visit in 1760 not only climbed the Brévant, a pinnacle in the Aiguilles
Rouges, but also offered a sizable reward to the first person successfully to climb Mont

Blanc, the dominating massif of the Chamonix Valley and (as far as he knew) the highest mountain in Europe. He got no immediate takers, but the publicity surrounding the offer got the Chamoniards to thinking, and in 1775 four local men climbed as far as the subsidiary Dôme du Goûter (14,120ft/4,304m). Several failures followed in quick succession before Michael-Gabriel Paccard, a local doctor, and Jacques Balmat, a local chamois hunter, reached the main summit in 1786 and then promptly fell out over who had taken the leading role. The ascent of Mont Blanc quickly became the stuff of controversy and legend, and it remains as much today. For our purposes, its significance lies in the spur it gave to Alpine mountaineering generally. De Saussure's *Voyages dan les Alpes* (1779) had already brought the marvels of Chamonix home to readers in Geneva, Paris, and London, but now, with Paccard's and Balmat's ascent, and even more with de Saussure's own successful repetition of the ascent in 1787, no vicarious account would do. The public came to see the Chamonix Valley for itself, and this once-remote village quickly became the crowded center of a novel form of middle-class recreation.[39]

In 1787 Mark Beaufoy became the first Englishman to climb Mont Blanc. Three years later William Wordsworth included the Alps in his tour of revolutionary France and found in them a potent source of poetic inspiration. From 1795 to 1815 war with France inhibited English travel to Europe, but not consistently: both Samuel Taylor Coleridge and J. M. W. Turner took advantage of the short-lived Peace of Amiens in 1802 to visit the Alps. Coleridge's "Hymn before Sunrise in the Vale of Chamouni," first published in the *Morning Post* in September 1802, sealed the English romantic identification with the place, and the paintings that Turner produced from his Alpine sketchbook (as championed by Ruskin) eventually defined the image of mountain beauty for the nineteenth century. Meanwhile, Marie Paradis in 1808 became the first woman to climb Mont Blanc (if being pushed, pulled, and carried to the top by Jacques Balmat and a crew of guides counts as a climb). In 1811 Johann Rudolf and Hieronymus Meyer climbed the Jungfrau in the Bernese Oberland, the first notable climb outside the Chamonix Valley. The Peace of 1815 brought English tourists back to Chamonix in ever-increasing numbers, and though Mont Blanc itself could still move the young Percy Bysshe Shelley to poetic raptures in 1816— "I never knew—I never imagined what mountains were before"—Chamonix itself, with its swarms of landlords, guests, and guides, left him cold: it was already ruined. The deaths of three guides in an avalanche on Mont Blanc threw a pall over the valley in 1820, but only momentarily, and the organized, institutional history of mountaineering may be said to have begun three years later, in 1823, when the king of Sardinia (then the nominal ruler of Haute Savoie) proclaimed the founding of the Syndicat des guides de Chamonix, a local guild dedicated to the service of shepherding foreign visitors up the mountains.[40]

For roughly thirty years thereafter, Alpine mountaineering largely answered to the scientific imperative. The romantics remained content to admire the peaks from below; the climbers (most notably the Swiss-born American Louis Agassiz and the Scotsman James David Forbes) were sober-minded geologists and naturalists concerned above all with

mountain formation and the mysterious movements of glaciers. The Englishman Albert
Smith, on the other hand, was a natural born showman, the author of many lowbrow
plays, burlesques, and stage parodies who in 1851, having already profited by public interest in his travels to the east, decided to climb Mont Blanc for the sake of spectacle. His
subsequent mixed-media stage show, *The Ascent of Mont Blanc,* complete with pasteboard
Swiss chalet, plaster mountains, rolling dioramas, and Saint Bernard dogs, ran for six years
at the Egyptian Hall, Piccadilly, took in £30,000, and made Albert Smith the world's first
climbing celebrity: "the man of Mont Blanc." It also, in Great Britain anyway, helped displace the romantic and scientific impulses surrounding Alpine travel in favor of the simple
urge for adventure. Smith popularized, some would say vulgarized, mountain climbing.
He unleashed "Mont Blanc Mania" in the public, middle-class mind, and to that extent,
many have argued, effectively invented the modern sport of mountaineering.[41]

The year 1854, the second year of Albert Smith's theatrical run (no coincidence),
saw the first large-scale British invasion of the Alps. Mont Blanc remained the main attraction. But it is Alfred Wills's ascent of the Wetterhorn from Grindelwald on September 17,
1854, that historians take (somewhat arbitrarily) to mark the beginning of the legendary
"golden age" of Alpine climbing. Over the next decade, 140 virgin summits fell, most of
them to British climbers whose energy and possessive zeal reflected both their middle-class
origins and their sense of national entitlement. Leslie Stephen, John Ball, John Tyndall,
A. W. Moore, Edward Whymper, preeminently among many others, became the founding
fathers of a sport that only in these years came to be known as "mountaineering." Being
English, they soon felt the need for a social forum in which to share and discuss their
elevated experiences, and December 1857 saw the founding in London of the world's first
Alpine Club. *Peaks, Passes, and Glaciers,* the Alpine Club's first anthology of members'
climbing narratives, appeared to great public acclaim in 1859; the first number of the
Alpine Journal, the world's first periodical record of mountain adventure (*and* scientific
observation, the subtitle half-heartedly promised), was published four years later in 1863.
From the start, the Alpine Club was an exclusive society open only to those with considerable means and a certified record of climbing achievement. Of the 823 members admitted
between 1857 and 1890, not one hailed from outside the university-educated middle class.
In its hidebound social exclusiveness, the club eventually retarded the growth and development of mountaineering in England. Initially, however, its members were indisputably the
leading climbers of their day, though they almost invariably relied on local guides to lead
them up to their summits. For the most part, the storied golden age came about through
a cooperative working relationship between the Alpine Club and a small group of elite,
professional guides.[42]

The simultaneously triumphant and tragic climax of the golden age of Alpine
mountaineering came on July 14, 1865, with Edward Whymper's first ascent of the Matterhorn and the deaths that same day, on the descent, of four of his companions: Lord Francis
Douglas, Rev. Charles Hudson, Douglas Hadow, and Michel Croz, a great Chamonix

guide. Many years later, the great Victorian Alpinist W. A. B. Coolidge recalled "the sort of palsy that fell upon the good cause after that frightful catastrophe," particularly among English climbers, who now "went about under a sort of dark shade, looked on with scarcely disguised contempt by the world of ordinary travelers."[43] But even before the disaster, those veteran climbers for whom a virgin summit was the be-all and end-all of mountaineering had begun to think the Alps played out, and now, with the last great prize claimed under such demoralizing circumstances, they not surprisingly began to look farther afield. In 1868 Douglas Freshfield (then at the beginning of a long and distinguished career of mountain exploration), A. W. Moore, and Comyns Tucker undertook the first notable expedition to the Caucasus, explored the range from end to end, and nearly reached the summit of Elbruz, at 18,510 feet (5,642 meters) the highest mountain in Europe. Four years later William Cecil Slingsby made the first of many pioneering visits to the mountains of Norway, which, though lower than the Alps, were arguably as dramatic (rising as they do from near sea level) and challenging. And in 1879–80 the great Edward Whymper, after two unsatisfactory trips to Greenland, led a successful expedition to Chimborazo and other peaks in the Ecuadorean Andes that set the organizational standard for many a Himalayan expedition to come.[44] Whymper in fact had hoped to go to the Himalaya himself in 1874. Had he done so—only obscure political considerations prevented it—he might very well, as his biographer Frank Smythe believed, have met with success and anticipated by many years the pioneers (like Smythe himself) who first groped their uneasy way up the Himalayan glaciers and ridges. Or, more likely, he might have found that neither Mont Blanc nor the Matterhorn nor even Chimborazo approximated the scale and challenge of a great Himalayan peak and that all his vast experience availed him little. Between the Playground of Europe and the Abode of Snow lay differences of degree and kind, and for a generation at least after Whymper, the great Alpinists of the day, one after another, would flail and falter before them.

CHAPTER TWO

The Age of Empire
1892–1914

The first experienced Alpinist to visit the Himalaya was the Hungarian Maurice de Déchy, who went out to Sikkim in 1879 equipped—in what became a standard practice before the "discovery" of the Sherpas—with a Swiss guide, Andreas Maurer of Meiringen. He hoped to climb some great peak in the vicinity of Kangchenjunga. But no sooner had he reached the prominence of Phalut on the Singalila Ridge than he contracted malaria and had to withdraw, thereafter to content himself with the Alps and the Caucasus. Thus it fell to the English barrister William Woodman Graham, whose Alpine record embraced almost every notable pass and summit, to make the first trip to the Himalaya for purely climbing purposes, "more for sport and adventures," as Graham himself unapologetically put it, "than for the advancement of scientific knowledge." From Bombay, where he embarked with the guide Josef Imboden of St. Niklaus on February 20, 1883, he proceeded via Agra to Calcutta and thence by way of the recently opened narrow-gauge railway to Darjeeling, the Queen of the Hills. After some delay "pending the arrival of guns"—an odd narrative detail that reveals something about the frontier atmosphere of early Himalayan mountaineering—he set off in late March for the Kangchenjunga massif. From the remote stone hut of Dzongri on the Rathong Chu—then home to summer herdsmen, now home to summer trekkers—he crossed the Singalila Ridge into forbidden Nepal and surreptitiously climbed an unnamed peak of (he claimed) over 20,000 feet. The next day, again from Dzongri, he struck north over the Goecha La to the Talung Glacier and was evidently contemplating a circuit of Kangchenjunga (which he innocently thought he could complete in nine days) when cold, illness, and the inadvertent burning of his climbing boots got the better of him. April 10 found him back in Darjeeling, somewhat worse for wear but pleased at having seen up close both northern flanks of the great mountain.[1]

The following June (less Imboden, who had gotten "a touch of fever and diarrhœa" and returned, homesick, to Switzerland), Graham set off with Emil Boss and Ulrich Kaufmann (the Swiss hotelier and guide, respectively, who together had climbed Mount

Cook in the New Zealand Alps the previous year) for Garhwal in British India. From the village of Josimath on the Alaknanda he proceeded up the Rishi Ganga, hoping to climb Nanda Devi but settling instead, when the sanctuary of the goddess proved impenetrable, for a game but failed attempt on the outlying peak of Dunagiri. He next climbed with "no great difficulties" what he thought was Changabang, the "shining mountain" then known simply as A21, but judging from his vague description and the alleged ease of ascent was more likely Hanuman (19,930ft/6,075m), a southern subsidiary of Dunagiri. Graham's entire itinerary, in fact, is shrouded in considerable mystery and controversy. He had no accurate maps, his aneroid barometers were pitifully unreliable when it came to fixing altitude, he misread his compass points on occasion, and he had an unfortunate tendency, in his subsequent accounts, to skimp on vital topographical details. Back in Sikkim for a second time in September, for instance, he allegedly climbed Kabru, Kangchenjunga's 24,258-foot neighbor, with no great difficulty and without feeling the ill effects of altitude in a mere three days. If genuine, this was an astonishing technical and physiological feat that announced the arrival of high Himalayan mountaineering, but quite apart from the basic improbability of it, Graham's description of the climb makes little topographical sense and neither the Indian Survey nor the Alpine Club ever credited it—in part, it should be said, because Graham was not one of their own. His status as a pioneer, as one of the first Europeans to climb in the Himalaya purely for pleasure, is indisputable; his actual record of Himalayan achievement is not. And most chroniclers have therefore given pride of place to William Martin Conway (later Baron Conway of Allington).[2]

Conway in the Karakoram

Conway was in every respect the more characteristic figure of late-Victorian England. Born in 1856, Martin (as he was always called) was the only son of William Conway, a well-known evangelical churchman and canon of Westminster Abbey. Educated at Repton School and Trinity College, Cambridge, he took an undistinguished third-class degree in history in 1879 and thereafter, at the fatherly encouragement of Henry Bradshaw, the university librarian, pursued a quasi-scholarly interest in woodcuts and early printed books. From 1879 to 1882 he traveled extensively in the Low Countries gathering material for *Woodcutters of the Netherlands in the Fifteenth Century* (1884), the first and most learned of his roughly thirty books of art, art history, and art criticism. In 1885, on the strength of his book, his connections, and three years of teaching under the auspices of the Cambridge University Extension movement, he became the first Roscoe Professor of Art at University College, Liverpool, where between ill-attended lectures and worshipful visits to the aged John Ruskin at Coniston, he took the lead in founding the National Association for the Advancement of Art and its Application to Industry. Turned down for the Slade Professorship at Cambridge (Ruskin's old chair) in 1887 but unable any longer to abide the provincial life, he resigned his post at Liverpool in 1888 and moved to London, where he lived off the considerable

(William) Martin Conway, Baron Conway
of Allington (1856–1937), by Bassano, 1895.
Reprinted by permission of the National
Portrait Gallery, London.

fortune of his American wife, Katrina Lambard, daughter of Charles Lambard, the builder
of the Chesapeake and Ohio Railway, and (more significantly still) stepdaughter of Manton
Marble, former editor and owner of the *New York World.*

Meanwhile, from the childhood day he first climbed Worcester Beacon in the
Malvern Hills, Conway had developed an instinct for mountains and mountain travel.
Here too, of course, Ruskin was a heady influence, and by the time he graduated from
Cambridge, Conway had several Alpine seasons to his credit and had already been elected
to the Alpine Club. Though he knew and admired Whymper and the great A. F. Mummery
(the Hobsonian economist who had become by the late 1880s the best-known climber
of his generation) he was never, himself, much of a peak-bagger; rather, like Eric Shipton
and Bill Tilman after him, he favored the icy cols and passes that led from one valley
to the next. In the great late-nineteenth-century Alpine debate between "centrists" and
"ex-centrists"—between, that is, those who stayed in one place and bagged every summit
within reach and those who wandered randomly about roughing it from place to place,
Conway stood preeminently for the latter. In 1881 he published the *Zermatt Pocket Book,*

the successful model for an original and influential series of Alpine climbing guides that he was ultimately to edit with W. A. B. Coolidge. Already by then, however, the conquest of every summit and the resolution of every last topographical problem had dispelled for him the charm and wonder of the Alps. Alpine knowledge and achievement, it turned out, came at an imaginative price: "I think it was that discovery that drove me from the Alps to the mountain ranges of Asia, Spitsbergen, and South America," Conway later wrote. "There at any rate the wonder and the mystery returned in full measure, in spite of all Alpine knowledge and experience."[3]

By the turn of the decade, two years after resigning his Liverpool post and having finally published a long-projected book on Albrecht Dürer, Conway was very much at loose ends, idly dividing his time between his house in Clanricarde Gardens, the Savile Club, the Alpine Club, the British Museum, and University College, London, where he attended lectures on prehistory and classical archaeology. It was in some ways a fulfilling life, but one better suited to a middle-aged dilettante than to a young married man of thirty-four, and sometime in March or April 1890 (inspired, perhaps, by the example of his friend Robert Louis Stevenson, who had recently set off for the South Seas), Conway hit on the vague plan of finding fame in the exploration of the Himalaya. His wife disapproved as did, initially, her stepfather, Manton Marble, to whom Conway had applied for sponsorship. "'Tis not quite relevant to your art-career to be climbing mountains," Marble wrote. At the same time, however, he perceived that "Himalayan supereminence may be the corner-stone of artistic eminence" in that it would "provoke readers of all sorts—would give you an audience, would 'get your kit up,'" and on Grand Prix Day 1891 he agreed to underwrite Conway's expedition provided it were made under the auspices of both *The Times* and the Royal Geographical Society.[4]

Founded under the patronage of King William IV in 1830 and subsequently charged by Queen Victoria with "the advancement of geographical science" and "the improvement and diffusion of geographical knowledge," the Royal Geographical Society from its modest original quarters at 1 Savile Row had become over the years a sort of scientific broker of nineteenth-century British imperial expansion. It had sponsored, promoted, and publicized the legendary African explorations of David Livingstone, Sir Richard Burton, and John Speke as well as the Arctic explorations of Sir John Franklin and Sir George Nare. Up to now it had taken no direct interest in the Himalaya, though it had provided by way of its journal (first called the *Journal of the Royal Geographical Society*, then the *Proceedings of the Royal Geographical Society*, and finally the *Geographical Journal*) a popular but also quasi-official and authoritative public forum for Godwin-Austen, Younghusband, Graham, and other early Himalayan explorers. Douglas Freshfield, one of Great Britain's leading mountaineers in the generation after Whymper, had been a fellow of the society since 1869 and honorary secretary since 1881. He was also the rising president of the Alpine Club, and it was probably through his sympathetic agency that Conway obtained a hearing with the council of the society in June 1891. The council had no interest in a mere climbing expedition like Graham's. But in the end it voted Conway a provisional grant of £200 pending some satisfactory sort of scientific return. The director of the Royal Botanical Gardens at Kew similarly promised a grant pending the delivery of "high-level plants which are interesting in themselves, easy to collect and easy to dry." Thus encouraged, Conway made for Switzerland to hone his climbing skills and turned his mind to the critical question of companions.[5]

He thought first, not surprisingly, of Albert Frederick Mummery, a reasonably well-known political economist who had overcome both his modest social background and congenital physical disabilities to become a brilliant mountaineer, the best, in fact, of the late-Victorian generation. Born at Dover in 1855, the son of a tanner-*cum*-mayor, Mummery first visited Switzerland in 1871, too late to claim any major virgin summits but in good time to join the scramble for innovative and original routes. Between 1879 and 1881 he made a number of notable ascents—including the Zmutt Ridge of the Matterhorn—with his guide, Alexander Burgener, but thereafter, his apprenticeship served, Mummery became the leading advocate of guideless climbing as well as climbing for its own unscientific, purely athletic sake. "The essence of the sport lies not in ascending a peak," Mummery wrote, "but in struggling with and overcoming difficulties." The romantic traditionalists disagreed, and in 1880 they blocked Mummery's election to the Alpine Club, partly out of jealousy, partly because he was "in trade" and therefore unsuitable social material, but also because they regarded him as a mere gymnast who recklessly courted risk. Later, Mummery's first ascent of Dykh Tau (17,074ft/5,204m) in the Caucasus, together with his important technological innovations (including the famous lightweight, silken tent that bears his name), made his election unavoidable. But he remained an outsider at the Alpine Club, which was at that time dominated by Oxbridge graduates and landed gentlemen. Martin Conway was the consummate insider, but he respected Mummery, who "knew mountains as some men know horses," he said. When he heard that Mummery too had Himalayan ambitions, he proposed joining forces. In fact, both Freshfield and Mummery met with Conway at the Royal Geographical Society in April 1891 and agreed to join him in Darjeeling the following September for an attempt on Kangchenjunga.[6]

That intervening summer—Freshfield having dropped out owing to the sudden death of his son—Conway and Mummery made some experimental climbs together in the Graian Alps. "The more I knew of him the more I liked him," Conway wrote, "and the more evident it became that his attitude toward mountains was fundamentally different from mine." Conway was at heart a mountain wanderer. When the Kangchenjunga proposal fell through for obscure political reasons, he quickly identified K2 in the Karakoram as the lofty object of his ambition. What he really had in mind though, it soon became clear, was not an assault on a great peak but an elaborate regional reconnaissance. "I wanted to cover as much ground as possible and to find out what the whole district was like," Conway later explained. "I intended to take an artist along, and to bring back such a sketch-survey as circumstances permitted, to make scientific collections also, and to engage in all the scientific investigations which could be pursued under the circumstances." The purist in Mummery had no interest in all this. He wanted to find K2 and climb it, and in late August, having determined that Conway's party was neither strong enough nor fast enough to grapple with such a mountain, he reluctantly withdrew from it. "Had I only to face average difficulty in leaving home I should certainly come," he wrote to Conway. "But it is a very serious matter to me and nothing but the feeling that K2 was fairly within our grasp would stir me to the necessary effort."[7]

Failing Mummery, Conway turned for mountaineering expertise to Oscar Eckenstein, a British-born son of a German political exile who had climbed extensively in Switzerland and Wales and whose sister Lina had collaborated with Conway on his book on Albrecht Dürer. Like his father, O. E. (as he was known) was an outspoken socialist given to disparaging remarks about the British Empire and, worse, the Alpine Club (which he regarded as a priggish collection of self-promoting quacks). His Alpine climbing record was perfectly respectable, but Eckenstein—a mathematician and engineer by profession—was always interested more in the puzzles and tools of climbing, in its techniques and arcane equipment, than in personal achievements in the ordinary mountaineering sense. His claim to fame rests on his innovative method of "balance climbing" on rock and on his invention of the ten-point crampon. Physically he was short and sturdily built. "He did not know the meaning of the word 'fatigue' [and] could endure the utmost hardship without turning a hair," one acquaintance recalled. But he had a quarrelsome temperament and did not submit easily to the kind of gentlemanly authority that Conway meant to wield. Nor did he want to play the role of amateur scientist that Conway evidently intended for him. The two did not get along, in short, and were to part company before the expedition was anywhere near its end.[8]

Sponsors and climbers aside, the "most important requisite" of any expedition, in Conway's conventional view, was "a first-rate guide," and this he found in the person of Mattias Zurbriggen, a Swiss-Italian who had climbed extensively with Eckenstein, as it happened, and who would later make the first ascent (solo) of Aconcagua (22,841ft/6,962m), the highest mountain in the Western Hemisphere. Aesthete that he was, Conway also wanted an artist in the party, but none of name had the money or inclination to join him and he ultimately settled on A. D. McCormick, a young, unknown watercolorist who had never so much as seen a mountain but who had a wealthy benefactor willing to pay his share of the expenses. Heywood Roudebush, a Conway in-law (and friend of McCormick) came along in an undefined, all-purpose capacity, as did, briefly, one Lieutenant Colonel Lloyd-Dickin, an amateur ornithologist and hunter. The most notable addition, however, from the point of view of Himalayan history, was Charles Granville Bruce of the Fifth Gurkha Rifles, a mountain regiment quartered at Abbottabad that had played a conspicuous part in recent "pacification" campaigns on the northwest Indian frontier. Bruce's father, Lord Aberdare of Glamorgan, was a prominent Liberal peer and former president of the Royal Geographical Society: facts that no doubt commended this young subaltern to Conway's favorable notice. He had a modest Alpine record of his own and, more to the point, some experience of the mountain regions through which Conway meant to travel. In just three years, in fact, and at the still-tender age of twenty-five, Bruce had already acquired some mastery of the mountain vernaculars and that uncanny understanding of the "native mind" for which he was later (and somewhat dubiously) celebrated. Though it was Francis Young-husband who first recruited the famed Gurkhas (Nepali soldiers in the service of the British Indian army) to the work of mountain exploration and travel, it was Bruce who first fully recognized their potential value as climbers and native guides, as local alternatives to the hitherto indispensable Swiss imports. In time, the Sherpas of eastern Nepal proved more lastingly suited to this adjunct role. But the history of native participation in Himalayan mountaineering began in 1891, when Charles Bruce persuaded Martin Conway to attach Parbir Thapa and three other Gurkhas of his regiment to the Karakoram expedition.[9]

His party assembled, Conway devoted the remaining months of 1891 to the purchase and packing of stores, to preparatory study at the Royal Geographical Society and the Natural History Museum, and to securing the needed approval of the government of India. In October M. E. Grant-Duff, then president of the Royal Geographical Society, wrote to the Marquess of Lansdowne, then viceroy of India, introducing him to Conway and his "expedition for the exploration of the high glacier regions of the Karakoram." Their object, Grant-Duff explained, "will be to explore and map the upper glacial area; to ascend the most lofty summits attainable, beginning with the peak Mango Gusor, the central position of which makes it especially valuable as a point of view for topographical purposes; to make a thorough study of the Great Baltoro and Biafo glaciers, and afterwards to attempt to reach the top of the R Jong La and descending westwards and southwards down the Nagar glacier to cross the Nushik La to Arundu." Lansdowne raised no objection to this rough itinerary but referred Conway for final approval to the Indian Intelligence Department, the Indian Army, and the Indian Survey at Dehra Dun. Eckenstein, Bruce, and Parbir Thapa, meanwhile, met with Zurbriggen in Zermatt for two weeks' training on the Unter Gabelhorn, the Rimpfischorn (where after "a terrific wallow in snow" they were "completely beaten"), and the Kleine Matterhorn. Zurbriggen pronounced the relatively inexperienced Bruce "a first-rate mountaineer." The party having reassembled in London, each member agreeing to publish no account of the expedition in advance of Conway's promised presentation to the Royal Geographical Society, the expedition left for India from Fenchurch Street station on February 5, 1892.[10]

Five weeks' passage via Dover, Gibraltar, Port Said, Aden, Karachi, Lahore, and Rawalpindi brought the expedition safely to Abbottabad, garrison of the Fifth Gurkhas and staging town for the 14,000-foot Babusar Pass west of Nanga Parbat. Here, having outrun their ponderous baggage train, Conway and company suffered Bruce's hospitality for two weeks before moving on to Srinagar, the capital of princely Kashmir, on March 28. From here Conway originally meant to make directly for Skardu, Askole, the Baltoro Glacier, and K2 (the climbing of which was still his half-avowed intention), but now, being still well ahead of the climbing season, he decided instead on a more roundabout approach via Astor and the Gilgit Road. He evidently had some thought of climbing Rakaposhi, the great western sentinel of the Karakoram. But one look at it from the vicinity of Bunji on the upper Indus sufficed to erase this ambition. "The south-south-west arête seemed to offer an easy route to the summit," Conway recalled in his expedition account, "but we presently discovered that all access to the ridge was cut off by an unbroken series of avalanche slopes. Our hopes of beginning with this ascent were thus not a little damped."[11]

In fact, the more Conway saw of the Himalaya, the less interested he seemed in climbing as opposed to exploring, sketching, and surveying. Having finally reached Gilgit, the last effective outpost of British authority, on May 5, he then gave an entire month over to an exploration of the Bagrot Valley, a glacial ravine that drains the southeastern flanks of Rakaposhi and joins the Gilgit River about fourteen miles below the town. This was a wholly original bit of survey travel, and it included several minor ascents and a halfhearted attempt (by Bruce, Conway, and Zurbriggen) on the reckonable "Emerald," now Miar Peak (22,388ft/ 6,824m). But it did not feel like the climbing expedition that Eckenstein had signed on to, and he, for one, increasingly groaned under Conway's seemingly aimless itinerary.

On June 8, the expedition moved north out of Gilgit into the Hunza Valley. Just a year earlier this had been the scene of a dramatic British military campaign that ended in the suppression of the tribal fiefdoms of Hunza and Nagar and the effective imposition of (indirect) British rule, but in his lavish expedition account, Conway makes little mention of this, preferring to leave the impression that he and his party were entering unknown ground. A good month then went into the exploration of the northern flanks and valleys of the Rakaposhi Range before finally, in early July, the expedition approached the inner Karakoram by way of the Hispar Glacier. "Here, indeed, was a highway into another world with which man had nothing to do," Conway later recalled in his characteristically romantic vein. "It might lead into a land of dragons, or giants, or ghosts. The very thought of man vanished in such surroundings, and there was no sign of animal life. The view was like seen music." The walking, however, at least in Eckenstein's telling, was abominable, an endless and tedious scramble over glacial moraine and scree. By now the expedition was low on supplies, and on July 3 Conway dispatched Bruce, Eckenstein, two Gurkhas (Amar Singh and Karbir), and eight Nagar porters over the Nushik La (which Godwin-Austen had reached from the south but had not crossed in 1861) to the village of Arandu at the foot of the Chogo Lungma Glacier. He and Zurbriggen, meanwhile, proceeded up the Hispar to the Hispar Pass and "Snow Lake," the great mountain basin at the head of the Sim Kang and Biafo Glaciers. Passing under the prominent aiguille that Conway named the Ogre (Uzum Brakk), they then followed the Biafo along its course through the Latok and Meru groups to its terminus in the Braldu Valley, thus completing the longest subpolar glacial passage in the world.[12]

For reasons he never fully explained, Conway now decided to send Eckenstein back to England. For his part, Eckenstein later said that "there had been a good deal of

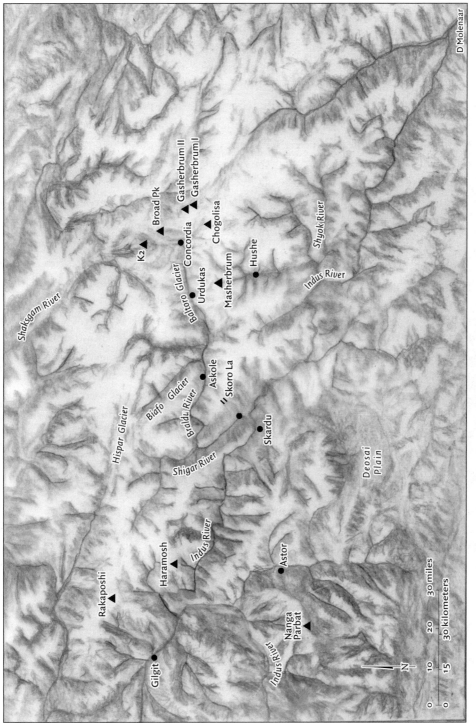

The Greater Karakoram.

friction from time to time, and that, as we had now been some two and a half months in the mountains without making a single ascent of importance, having only crossed two previously known passes, I was not anxious to go on." But this scarcely did justice to the depth of the falling-out. The truth as Bruce described it privately to his father was that Eckenstein, for all his mountaineering ability, had turned out to be "a useless burden to the party; expensive and incapable." Whether Eckenstein's outspoken socialism and hostility to empire influenced this ungenerous assessment is hard to say. What is certain is that Eckenstein had lost all interest in Martin Conway's endlessly meandering "Pilgrimage of Romance." He wanted to attempt a first-class Himalayan peak, and though Conway had never directly ruled this out and still hoped, in fact, to set a height record, he appeared too little in earnest to ease Eckenstein's anxieties. On July 27, therefore, at a general meeting of the expedition at Askole, the little village below the Biafo that Conway expected one day to be the Zermatt of the Karakoram, the two agreed to part ways, Conway for the Baltoro Muztagh, Eckenstein for Srinagar and home.[13]

That same day, July 27, Conway composed the first of his promised *Times* dispatches: a novel feature of this expedition that for the first time catered directly to rising public interest in Himalayan exploits. It boasted "the first definitely recorded passage of the Hispar Pass—the longest glacier pass in the world." It made no mention of Conway's painstakingly gathered scientific collections, but these were "advancing apace," he privately assured his mother-in-law, Abigail Lombard. "We have over 300 different kinds of flowers, over 200 geological specimens, some 40 butterflies, not many beetles, two human skulls which we risked our lives to pilfer from the Nagyr graveyard, native musical instruments, and all manner of other odd stuff, besides a quantity of big horns which will ultimately grace our dining-room." Conway's precious map, meanwhile, was now nearly two yards long, every square half inch of it the faithful representation of a square mile of country, most of it higher than Mont Blanc and all of it previously unsurveyed. "If only we can find an easy peak and climb higher than men have previously done the whole expedition will have been a great success," he wrote home, and it was with that vague final design in mind that his whole elaborate caravan, now eighty men and 103 loads strong, lumbered up the Baltoro in early August.[14]

Two years earlier a little-known Italian named Roberto Lerco had ventured up the Baltoro to the foot of K2 and may even have climbed a little way up the mountain's famous southeast, or "Abruzzi" Spur. He left no record of his journey, however, and Conway in fact was altogether unaware of Lerco's still quite shadowy existence. He knew, of course, that both Godwin-Austen and Younghusband had traversed the lower Baltoro before him, and he had taken pains to consult with both before leaving London, but as far as he knew he was the first European to trace the mighty glacier to its head and to see for the first time the most magnificent mountain amphitheater in the world. Straight ahead, above the broad glacial junction that Conway named Place de la Concorde after a similar junction at the head of the Aletsch Glacier in Switzerland, rose the Gasherbrum group, four mighty conjoined summits, the highest of which, Gasherbrum I, Conway named Hidden Peak, because it came into view only as he moved south along the upper Baltoro. To the north, a few miles up the tributary glacier that Conway named for Godwin-Austen, stood the "Great Pyramid" of K2, never before seen (as far as Conway knew) in full profile base to summit. An equal distance to the south, at the head of the glacier that Conway named for Godfrey Vigne, the intrepid Englishman who had stumbled on the Karakoram in 1838, stood K6, Conway's "Bride Peak," better known today as Chogolisa (25,157ft/7,668m). Already behind him, awesomely above the central Baltoro, stood the Masherbrum group, and opposite it, to the north, the incomparable monolith of Muztagh Tower (23,874ft/7,284m), Conway's "Watch-Tower" or "Guardian." Still ahead of him, filling the space between K2 and the Gasherbrum group, was the huge massif that he named Broad Peak after the triple-summited Breithorn of the Zermatt Valley. Altogether the sight was one to challenge even Conway's considerable powers of romantic description and it marked a definitive moment in European comprehension of the scale of the Himalaya. "Name of a Brigand!" was all that Zurbriggen could say. "They don't know what mountains are in Switzerland!"[15]

Which one of these monumental peaks to attempt was now the sobering question. Conway had pinned his most recent hopes on the Gasherbrum peaks, "but Zurbriggen declared that it frightened him to look at them," Bruce reported to his father, and that was that. K2 and Broad Peak were similarly terrifying, Masherbrum "most uncompromisingly inaccessible," and despite the inspiring scenery the whole company fell into defeatist despond until from the scattered stone slopes of Crystal Peak—a minor summit on the north bank of the Baltoro that Conway, Bruce, Zurbriggen, Harkbir, Amar Singh, and Parbir climbed for purposes of reconnaissance on August 10 and named for the fine crystals they found on top—Conway saw away to the southeast at a distance of fifteen miles "a rounded mountain mass" to which he gave the name Golden Throne, for it was "throne-like in form" and had traces of gold in its volcanic substance. "It was this, the most brilliant of all the mountains we saw, that had been rising into view with our ascent, and now, in the dim dawn, smote upon our delighted eyes when we turned round," Conway later wrote. "With one consent we cried out, 'That is the peak for us; we will go that way no other.'"[16]

No doubt Conway's rapturous enthusiasm for the Golden Throne, a relatively inconspicuous and undramatic mountain known today as Baltoro Kangri (23,864ft/7,274m), was considerably influenced by the thought that he might actually climb it, that of all the high peaks in the Baltoro region, this one alone offered a reasonable chance of success. Even so, it defeated him, though only because he never actually found it: an added challenge of Himalayan mountaineering in the early days. On August 24, having laid siege to the mountain in what became the approved Himalayan style, Conway, Bruce, Zurbriggen, Parbir Thapa, and Harkbir strapped on Eckenstein's crampons—climbing irons, Conway called them—and clawed their way up what looked to them like a ridge leading to the Golden Throne only to find themselves on a separate prominence well below the summit and utterly cut off from it by an intervening chasm. It was a disappointing climax to the expedition, but Conway made the most of it by christening his high point Pioneer Peak and generously assigning it an altitude of over 23,000 feet. Satisfied, then (or at least determined to maintain), that he had established a height record, Conway broke out the cognac and cigars brought for the purpose from London and declared the expedition a success. "All recognized that the greatest we were going to accomplish was done, and that henceforward nothing remained for us but downwards and homewards."[17]

Nothing remained, that is, but a fair bit of promotion and publicity. "Do all you can to show how much more Alpine climbers can do than the ordinary Anglo-Indian explorer," Douglas Freshfield had written to Conway on the very day he stood atop Pioneer Peak, and now, back in London (where he happened to arrive just in time for the annual Alpine Club dinner), Conway obliged, taking great pains to draw public attention to his exploits. He lectured all over England, attended dinners and receptions in his honor, granted interviews in the newspapers, and held forth ceremoniously at the Royal Geographical Society and the Alpine Club. The acclaim was considerable, but when Conway thought of extending his lecture tour to the United States, Manton Marble advised against it. "I do not overlook the climbing, the immense glaciers, the tip-top mark, etc.," Marble wrote discouragingly from New York, "but nobody here has heard of anything but Mt. Everest, not of your K2." From Fisher Unwin Conway accepted a generous contract—£1,000 plus royalties—for a popular and lavishly illustrated book, *Climbing and Exploration in the Karakoram-Himalayas,* which on its appearance in 1894 set the important precedent of the "official" expedition narrative. Reviews were mostly favorable, but one discerning critic in the *National Observer* noted that "in spite of armies of coolies, drafts of Ghoorkas, Swiss guides, the aid of the Royal Society, the Geographical Society and the British Association, [Conway] succeeded only in getting up a single second-rate peak of a paltry 22,000 feet or so, from which he surveyed the real Himalayas . . . very much as we may gaze at the Matterhorn from the top of the Riffelhorn."[18]

In fact, Conway's mountaineering achievements were not inconsiderable: he had made sixteen climbs of over 16,000 feet, crossed the Hispar Pass, climbed Crystal Peak, and made a notable first attempt on Baltoro Kangri. Thanks to Eckenstein he had introduced the use of crampons in the Himalaya, and thanks to Bruce he had hit on the enduring idea of native mountaineering support. But it was above all in the matter of expeditionary design and style that Conway set an original standard. He was the first to secure official sponsorship, the first to negotiate exclusive press contracts, the first to take along an expedition artist, the first to write an expedition history. Though small by subsequent standards, his expedition established the large-scale tradition in Himalayan mountaineering and (through the linking figure of Bruce especially) decisively influenced the British approach to Everest. Conway himself never returned to the Himalaya (though he evidently contemplated doing so in 1896). Raised to knighthood by the Earl of Rosebery in 1895 for his "remarkable work as a traveler," he stood unsuccessfully as a Liberal for Bath in the general election of that year, and thereafter concentrated increasingly on art and politics.[19] As former president of

A. F. Mummery, his wife, Mary, and daughter, Hilda, ca. 1892.
Reprinted by permission of the British Library.

the Alpine Club (1902–4) and holder of the Founders Medal of the Royal Geographical Society (1905) he remained, however, a prominent public authority on the Karakoram and the grand old man of British mountaineering until his death at age eighty-one in 1937.

The Death of Mummery

Mummery, meanwhile, having declined the chance to accompany Conway to the Karakoram in 1892, had focused his own Himalayan ambitions on Nanga Parbat, the great "naked mountain" that looms starkly over the Indus Valley at the far western end of the Himalaya proper. Though as worthy and awesome an object of attention as any in Asia—at 26,659 feet it is the ninth-highest mountain in the world—Nanga Parbat is unusually accessible, rising as it does just eighty miles north of the Kashmiri capital of Srinagar. Thus its appeal, in part, to Mummery, who in sharp distinction to Conway had limited resources at his disposal and no interest in assembling an elaborate or long-haul expedition. He neither wanted nor sought any form of sponsorship and he proudly disdained any scientific or exploratory purpose: "To tell the truth, I have only the vaguest ideas about theodolites, and as for plane tables, their very name is an abomination," he shockingly confessed.[20] His one ambition was to climb a great Himalayan peak by the most direct means possible and in the select company of two or three reliable friends. Such an approach had worked for him in the Caucasus (where he had climbed Dykh Tau, the second-highest mountain in Europe, with just one rope-mate, Heinrich Zurfluh of Meiringen), and he saw no reason why it would not work again even in the rarified air of the Himalaya.

In 1894 Mummery applied for and received permission to enter the quasi-autonomous province of Kashmir with a small party that initially included only Geoffrey Hastings, one of the pioneering new breed of Lakeland crag climbers, and John Norman Collie, an eminent chemist who had cut his climbing teeth on the Cuillin Hills of Skye and was, in some people's judgment, the most versatile climber of his generation. Together with Cecil Slingsby, Ellis Carr, and Lily Bristow, Hastings and Collie constituted the core of a new guideless climbing fraternity that Mummery had drawn around himself in the early 1890s and with whom he had made a notable series of Alpine ascents, featuring the Dent du Requin, the West Face of the Aiguille du Plan, the Col des Courtes, and the first guide-less ascent of the Brenva Spur on Mont Blanc. But how they would fare in the Himalaya remained very much to be seen, at least as far as Mummery's detractors in the Alpine Club were concerned. "[Mummery] is undoubtedly a very fine gymnastic rock climber, but I doubt that he has much 'sense of the mountain' or capacity as an explorer," W. E. Davidson, one such naysayer, wrote to Whymper. "I cannot recall any climb of first rate importance in which he has led (as he always does lead) that he had not previously made with guides on the one hand, or which on the other required powers of path-finding as opposed to climbing. He is not going to take any guides and will therefore have to rely entirely on his own resources, since his companion Collie merely walks after him—though I believe he is a satisfactory 'Herr' in this respect. I don't fancy either that Mummery can spare the time or the money requisite for success in such a difficult and distant field for exploration and therefore do not anticipate any results of importance from it."[21]

On June 20, 1895, just one week after the publication of Mummery's *My Climbs in the Alps and Caucasus,* a book that shortly took its place alongside Whymper's *Scrambles amongst the Alps* as an abiding classic of mountaineering literature, the "three musketeers," as they were known—Collie, Hastings, and Mummery—sailed for India. From Bombay, where they embarked two weeks later, they made straight for the mountain via the British cantonments of Rawalpindi and Murree, where the monsoon broke, and where Mummery met with the commanding general and arranged for the attachment of two Gurkhas to his party. At Baramula in the Vale of Kashmir, he unexpectedly ran into Charles Bruce, now a major in the Fifth Gurkhas, who had come over from Abbottabad to arrange the party's pony transport and portage. Knowing of the yeomanlike work Bruce had done for Conway, Mummery urged him to join his party as well, but Bruce for the moment was bound to his regiment and returned to Abbottabad to agitate for leave. The three musketeers, meanwhile, their party considerably augmented by twelve ponies, a cook, an unnamed headman, and an unspecified number of porters ("coolies," Mummery called them, in the demeaning language of the day) proceeded north across Wular Lake and over the Kamri Pass (13,368ft) to Tarshing, a large and prosperous village in the Rupal Valley, some ten miles off the Gilgit Road. They pitched Base Camp on July 16 in a picturesque meadow three miles above the village alongside the Rupal Gah. Collie's barometer read 10,000 feet.

Above them reared the 15,000-foot Rupal Face of Nanga Parbat. It is one of the

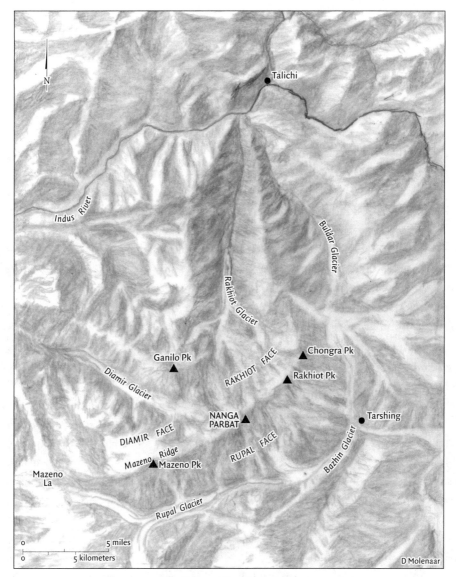

The Nanga Parbat massif.

great mountain walls in the world, but Mummery was initially unimpressed, or at least unintimidated. "I don't think there will be any serious mountaineering difficulties on Nanga, and the peak is much freer from hanging glaciers than I had expected," he wrote optimistically to his wife, Mary (herself a reckonable mountaineer), on July 17. "I fancy the ascent will be mainly a question of endurance." Collie, on the other hand, was skeptical, doubtful of the possibility of establishing camps on the Rupal Face, and (scientist that he was) more conscious than Mummery of the likely effects of the altitude. When what was supposed to have been a mere "training climb" of an outlying southern peak (Collie's

"Chiche Peak") faltered at 16,000 feet on July 18, Mummery accepted that he was in no condition to storm the Rupal Face and agreed to reconnoiter alternate routes.[22]

Accordingly, on July 20, Hastings, Mummery, and Collie crossed the Mazeno La (17,586ft), a well-known trading route west of Nanga Parbat, into the uninhabited Diamir Valley. Here, on the northwest or Diamir Face of the mountain, they saw an interconnected series of steep rock ribs (now known as the Mummery Ribs) that seemed to offer a direct route to the glistening snowfields below the summit. Deciding at once to remove their efforts here, they then attempted what they hoped would be a more direct pass back to their base in the Rupal Valley, only to find themselves stranded at 21,000 feet on the wrong side of the Mazeno Ridge. Collie sensibly vetoed Mummery's suggestion of a provision-less bivouac, and there followed a harrowing overnight trek back the way they had come. For all that he was an incomparable climber, Mummery, by virtue of his shortsightedness and his overall physical weakness, was a poor and reluctant trekker: a fact that was to play a significant part in the tragedy to come. By the time he straggled, last of the three, into the camp at Tarshing, he was "pretty well done up," having been going for over forty-eight hours on little or no food. But his powers of recovery were remarkable and his certainty in having found "an absolutely safe way up Nanga" unshaken. "I feel fairly confident of getting up," he wrote to his wife from Tarshing, "and you need feel no anxiety of any sort."[23]

On July 27 and 28, joined now by Charles Bruce (who had managed to secure leave) and two Gurkhas of his regiment, Ragobir Thapa and Goman Singh (neither of whom had any climbing experience), the company made a halfhearted attempt on a north-eastern prominence they named Chongra Peak (22,388ft/6,824m), but "laziness was in the air," as Collie put it, and the effort expired at about 17,000 feet. Three days later an attempt to climb the Mazeno Ridge and cross directly into the Diamir Valley also failed and ended in a miserably ill-provided bivouac at 19,000 feet. A clear-sighted leader might have paused now to consider whether he was in over his head, whether the Himalaya was not conceived on an entirely different scale from those Alps to which he was accustomed, and whether it did not, therefore, require some other, more deliberate and sustained approach. But, as Davidson had prophesied, Mummery seemed to have little overall sense of the mountain; he remained convinced that the challenge was negligible and that Nanga would yield to direct alpine assault. On August 1, having barely survived the bivouac, he, Collie, Hastings, Bruce, and Ragobir retreated from the Mazeno Ridge and trudged once more over the Mazeno La (where Ragobir nearly expired for want of food) to Lubar and the Diamir Valley. Here they established a sort of advanced base at the head of the Diamir Glacier (14,500ft) and began their reconnaissance of what Bruce later described as "the most uncompromising mountain face it is possible to conceive."[24]

Mummery's plan called for placing a camp at about 18,000 feet at the top of what he described as "a nice little ridge of rock leading up between two glaciers" (the Mummery Ribs). From here a relatively gentle snowfield led to the northern summit ridge. If he could place a second camp with two days' provisions on this snowfield at 22,000 feet,

Mummery thought, the summit would be his. Unfortunately, Bruce's leave had expired—he was unwell in any case—and Hastings had injured his ankle in the cursed crossing of the Mazeno La. This reduced the climbing party to four: too few for a serious first attempt on the ninth-highest mountain in the world. But again, Mummery was thinking only in terms of objective climbing difficulties, not of the vast scale of the mountain, and these did not worry him. The "little ridge of rock" was similar in standard of difficulty to the Chamonix aiguilles, he thought, and therefore (it followed) climbable.[25]

And it was climbable. Beginning at midnight on August 5, leaving Collie and Goman Singh to explore the Diamir Glacier between the outlying Ganilo Peak and Nanga Parbat, Mummery and Ragobir—much the better climber of the two Gurkhas—reached a height of 17,000 to 18,000 feet above the second rib and returned most encouraged, having also found a suitable site for a tent. Thereafter things bogged down as the weather turned against them and the altitude took its inevitable (though then dimly understood) toll. "We find Nanga a tough nut to crack," Mummery wrote home on August 9, in a new pessimistic strain. "The way up is easy enough, but it is very difficult to get our camps fixed, and the air certainly does affect one." The Gurkhas were first rate, "quite up to the average Swiss guide in style," he reported, and "as steady as possible." But they were not able to carry much, and thus it fell to Collie and Mummery (who was not much of a carrier himself) to ferry the heavy loads. On August 8 they carried twelve pounds of chocolate, twelve pounds of Huntley and Palmer's biscuits, and a quantity of "Brand's soups and essence" to about 17,000 feet and felt every foot of it. "The air is so baffling," Mummery reported to his wife, "and the sun is almost worse; it regularly takes all the strength out of one after 10 A.M." In short, Mummery was learning the hard way about the subjective difficulties of Himalayan climbing. "Of mountaineering, as we know it in the Alps, there is little or none," he now conceded and retreated to Base Camp to await a change in the weather.[26]

On August 11, while Hastings and Goman Singh hiked out to Astor to buy fresh provisions, Mummery, Collie, Ragobir, and a Kashmiri hunter named Lor Khan made a sporting ascent of "Diamirai Peak," a 19,000-foot prominence on a northwestern spur of the Mazeno Ridge. The effort of this, though successful, sufficed to convince Collie that Nanga was beyond them, and he began quietly to counsel retreat. Mummery, on the other hand, found the success encouraging, and on August 15, after two precious days spent foraging for food in the Bunar Valley, the attack on the Diamir Face resumed. Collie succumbed almost at once to diarrhea and headache and returned to Base Camp with the hunchbacked porter he called Richard III. Supported only by Lor Khan, Mummery and Ragobir persisted for a few more days and might have reached the summit, Mummery naively believed, had Ragobir not finally broken down at 20,000 feet on August 18.

With some difficulty, Collie now persuaded Mummery to abandon the Diamir Face. This left the northern Rakhiot Face as the only remaining possibility, and Collie reluctantly agreed to a quick reconnaissance of it. The logical route of access lay down the Diamir Valley to the Bunar Gah and then east along the Indus over the intervening ridges to the Rakhiot Valley, but Mummery wanted no part of such a roundabout trek. He proposed, rather, to force the high glacial pass (if pass the Diamir Gap could be called) under the outlying Ganilo Peak and descend the northwestern flank of Nanga Parbat directly into the Rakhiot Valley. Leaving Collie and Hastings to shepherd the porters the long way around, he set off with Ragobir Thapa and Goman Singh on August 24 and was never seen again.

Three days later, looking up from the safety of the Rakhiot Valley toward the Ganilo Peak, Collie saw that any descent from that quarter was inconceivable and hoped that Mummery and the two Gurkhas had thought better of it and decided on the long route after all. When after two more days they had not appeared, he sent Hastings back to the Diamir Valley to look for them. Hastings found the Diamir camps (which had been left provisioned against just this eventuality) untouched and reluctantly deduced that the three men had somehow perished. Collie meanwhile had alerted the assistant British agent at Astor, one Captain Stewart, who at once ordered a extensive search of the lower valleys. This availed nothing, and on September 8, with snow falling heavily and avalanches threatening the upper glaciers, Collie sadly gave the three men up for lost.

What precisely had happened to them remained unknown. "We think he must have been caught by some avalanche (started by previous snowfall), one masked from view by upper slopes until it was on the top of them," Hastings wrote from Astor to Mummery's bereaved brother. "The Ghoorkas were both of them very good men, one equal in steadiness and sureness of foot with the best Swiss guides. It is exceedingly unlikely it was owing to a slip on their part. Mummery had said that if the pass was bad, he would return and follow us round. The weather is more or less broken; the nights high up, very cold, so our chances of finding the traces, if avalanches has been the cause, are very slight, but you may rest assured we will do our utmost."[27]

Charles Bruce (though long removed from the scene) also thought it unlikely that Mummery had fallen; he was simply too good a mountaineer. Collie, on the other hand, quietly kept his counsel and for years afterward had little to say about Mummery. His expedition account, published in 1902, paid every appropriate tribute. Between the lines, however, one senses his disapproval of Mummery's recklessness, and forty years later he expressed it openly (albeit privately) to Geoffrey Winthrop Young. No doubt Mummery was a splendid rock climber and "*by far* the finest *ice climber* amongst *all amateurs.*" But he was "*not* a good mountaineer," Collie said. "He was not good in knowing what was the best way up a mountain or the safest. Once he was started on a route it was almost impossible to get him to turn back from difficulties and dangers."[28] What particular difficulties and dangers Mummery finally faced on the Ganilo Ridge on August 24, 1895, will never be known. But very likely they were of a Himalayan dimension that he did not understand, and in taking his life and the lives of two others, they made for the first mortal tragedy in the history of Himalayan mountaineering.

Votes for Women

Up to the death of Mummery in 1895, the Himalayan heights had been largely a British preserve. Apart from the khalasis and "pundits" employed by the Indian Survey and the Gurkhas attached to Conway's and Mummery's expeditions, few native hill men (as far as we know) had strayed purposefully from the valley settlements, unless to high pasturage or those icy passes that served as traditional trade routes. In the 1850s, as we have seen, the three Schlagintweit brothers had explored and climbed in Sikkim and Garhwal as well as the Karakoram, and in 1879 the Hungarian mountaineer Maurice de Déchy made a faint gesture in the direction of Kangchenjunga. With these exceptions (and those of our distant Jesuit missionaries), Himalayan exploration and mountaineering to date had functioned as an extension of the British colonial state. Mummery, to be sure, as opposed to Young-husband or even Conway, would have proudly disclaimed any explicit colonial purpose. He carried no flag and he did not think of his attempt on Nanga Parbat as extending the vertical margins of the Raj. But his very presence in the still-disputed region, aided and abetted as it was by the agents of empire from the viceroy on down—"The Viceroy, we find, has instructed the Resident that we are coming, and our progress will be regal!" Mummery had written to his wife en route to Nanga Parbat—testified to the continuing vitality of the British territorial imperative.[29] Himalayan mountaineering, whether Mummery would have it so or not, was an exclusively British and masculine enterprise, and so it remained until 1898 when, quite unexpectedly and unbidden, an American woman arrived on the scene.

Her name was Fanny Bullock Workman, and at thirty-nine years of age she was a force to be reckoned with, a proud and imperious New England heiress whose father, Alexander Hamilton Bullock, had been one-time Republican governor of the Commonwealth of Massachusetts. Born in Worcester and raised by a succession of governesses and tutors, Fanny Bullock (as she then was) attended Miss Graham's Finishing School in New York and then lived independently in Paris and Dresden, where she mastered French and German and accommodated herself comfortably to the ways of the European gentry. She returned to Worcester in 1879 and, two years later, married William Hunter Workman, a Yale- and Harvard-educated surgeon twelve years her senior. William introduced Fanny to climbing, first in the White Mountains of New Hampshire and then in the Alps, where she was among the earliest women to climb the Matterhorn, Mont Blanc, and the Jungfrau. In 1889 William resigned his medical practice on grounds of ill health and moved his small family (which now included a daughter, Rachel) to Germany for the sake of its musical and intellectual culture. Thanks to John Dunlop's invention of the pneumatic tire in 1888, the bicycle was just then coming into vogue as a recreational form of transport, and between operas and museum outings the Workmans took to it with relish. For five years they punctuated their expatriate routine with cycling tours of Scandinavia, France, and Italy. And then, in 1893 (having safely stashed young Rachel in a boarding school), they gave up the settled life altogether for one of sustained exploration and travel, first awheel in Algeria, Spain, Indochina, and India, and then almost exclusively on foot in the Karakoram Himalaya.

Algerian Memories, the first of the Workmans' eight travel books, appeared in New York and London in 1895 and despite its manifest literary failings won for them a lasting and loyal readership. Just who had taken the leading hand in writing it is impossible to say, but to read it or any of the books that followed leaves no doubt as to who was the dominant force in this famous collaboration. Fanny Bullock Workman (as she always called herself, in defense of her independent identity) was a strong-willed, outspoken exponent of the rights of women. Where organization, administration, or itinerary were concerned, she deferred to no one, least of all her aging and ailing husband, but rather used their combined travels as a living demonstration of her own capabilities. She was not the most culturally sensitive or observant of travelers. From the lead seat of the tandem bicycle, she brandished whip and revolver to clear her path and ward off extortionate or impudent natives. She did, as her latter-day admirers never fail to note, always attend carefully to the condition of women wherever she happened to be. But her general hostility to Asian culture derived less from female solidarity than from a conventional sense of the deference due to her as a rich white American.

After their tour of the Iberian Peninsula in 1897, the Workmans sailed east "with the purpose of seeing something of the treasures of Buddhist, Hindu, and Mohammedan Architecture and Art."[30] They hit Cape Comorin at the tip of the Indian subcontinent in early 1898 and from there bicycled north, duly noting every town, monument, and ruin that they passed. Come May, to escape the heat of the plains, they made for Srinagar, dismounted, and trekked through the mountains of Ladakh as far as the Karakoram Pass. Of all the vast and varied landscapes of India, the mountains alone finally captured their imagination, and in September, sparing no expense, they ordered tents and mountaineering equipment from London, summoned no less a guide than Rudolf Taugwalder from Zermatt, and set off for Sikkim to make an attempt on Kangchenjunga. How far out of Darjeeling they got before, in their routine telling, native intransigence and political obstruction stopped them is hard to say: not far. But the Workmans were somehow sufficiently encouraged to hazard the Himalaya over and over again. June 1899 found them back in Srinagar, fresh from a six-month cycling tour of Cambodia and Indonesia and poised to begin the first of their seven long expeditions to the Karakoram.

With them this time came Mattias Zurbriggen, the Italian guide who had been with Conway in the Karakoram in 1892, four "camp servants," and what the Workmans characteristically described as "a motley flock of loud mouthed Baltis."[31] Their route took them north from Srinagar to Skardu, up the Shigar Valley and over the Skoro La to Askole on the Braldu. From here they simply traced Conway's footsteps in reverse and ascended the Biafo Glacier to the Hispar Pass. Weather permitting, they had meant to try for a summit somewhere in the vicinity of Snow Lake, the peerless glacial cirque at the head of the Biafo.

But Zurbriggen, who had been feeling poorly for several days, declared himself unequal to the task and instead they all retreated somewhat bitterly to Askole. A week later, amply equipped with a fresh corps of thirty porters, they returned to the wide cirque under the Skoro La (on their maps the "Skoro La Glacier") and climbed two moderate peaks, one of which they pompously named Mt. Bullock Workman. The high point of the expedition then came on August 25 with the first ascent of Koser Gunge (20,997ft/6,400m), a formidable outlying massif overlooking the Shigar Valley. As was their wont—and aneroid instruments being what they were in those days—the Workmans overestimated its height, but by any measure Koser Gunge was a difficult climb, especially in woolen skirts and hobnailed boots, and in summiting it Bullock Workman claimed her third successive altitude record for women.

In 1902 the Workmans returned to India with Zurbriggen and Karl Oestreich of Frankfurt, topographer, and undertook an aggressive exploration of the twenty-eight-mile long Chogo Lungma Glacier at the bifurcation of the Rakaposhi and Haramosh ranges in the Lesser Karakoram. Godwin-Austen had been in this vicinity in 1862, and a few years later the British traveler Frederick Drew had ventured some miles onto the Chogo Lungma itself. But the Workmans were the first Westerners to climb it to its 19,000-foot head beneath "Indus Nagar Watershed Peak No. 2" (now Malubiting), and the mountain they called Pyramid Peak (long Yengutz Har and now Spantik). A year later, accompanied this time by Joseph and Laurent Petigax of Courmayeur, they returned to the Chogo Lungma and claimed to have reached—William, not Fanny—23,394 feet on Pyramid Peak, but as this height well exceeds that of the summit (which they generously put at 24,500 feet), it is impossible to say with any certainty where they were or whether William had, as he thought, bested Conway's height record on Baltoro Kangri (which was itself hardly definitive). In truth, all of the Workmans' itineraries are shrouded in considerable topographical mystery and controversy. Kenneth Mason, author of the first authoritative history of Himalayan mountaineering, was an old Indian Survey hand and anti-American to boot, so his assertions that the Workmans "lacked a sense of topography," that "their surveyors were too much hustled," that "they often misidentified the fixed points on which their maps should have been based," can be to some degree discounted. The fact remains, however, that when the German geodesist and climber Wilhelm Kick surveyed the Chogo Lungma in 1954 he found it difficult to reconcile the actual terrain with the Workmans' confused narrative. That the Workmans were intrepid explorers and climbers none could possibly doubt, but they were also aggressive self-promoters who in their eagerness for recognition and honors sometimes exaggerated the originality and significance of what they had done.[32]

After two years spent largely on the lecture circuit in Europe—Fanny in 1905 became only the second woman ever to storm the masculine citadel of the Royal Geographical Society—the Workmans returned to Kashmir for a thorough exploration of the Nun Kun massif, a tight cluster of mountains on the Great Himalayan axis some 120 miles southeast of Nanga Parbat. Though situated in a fairly well-known and well-traveled region—the

William Hunter Workman and Fanny Bullock
Workman in the Karakoram in 1902.
From Fanny Bullock Workman and
William Hunter Workman, *Ice-Bound Heights
of the Mustagh: An Account of Two Seasons
of Pioneer Exploration and High Climbing in
the Baltistan Himalaya* (London: Archibald
Constable, 1908). Courtesy of the Trustees
of the Boston Public Library.

Workmans themselves had passed close by on their return from northern Ladakh in 1898—
Nun Kun itself remained a compelling mystery. Charles Bruce and F. G. Lucas had taken
a training party of sixteen Gurkhas there and done a bit of preliminary reconnaissance in
1898. Arthur Neve, a medical missionary who with his brother Ernest had climbed many
modest mountains in the Pir Panjal, had visited Nun Kun twice, once reaching 18,000 feet
on the eastern flanks above the Shafat Glacier. And in 1903 the Dutch climber H. Sillem had
discovered the high névé plateau between the great twin peaks of Nun (23,408ft/7,135m)
and Kun (23,218ft/7,077m). Otherwise the whole massif lay untouched by foreigners when
the Workmans clamorously descended on it in 1906.[33]

  With them this time came not only an Italian guide, Cyprien Savoye of Courmayeur, but a whole crew of Italian porters recruited through Ettore Canzio of the Turin

Alpine Club. After four summers in the Himalaya, the Workmans had evidently despaired of those local "coolies" who, in their hostile judgment, lived only to obstruct and harass their otherwise certain progress. To be fair, the "wily native" is a stock figure of Himalayan literature from Conway on down, a persistent narrative import from the colonial repertoire. But the Workmans enlarge this stock figure to extravagant dimensions. Their otherwise invaluable books read like one long, anguished harangue against the lazy, lying, thieving, mutinous cheats on whom they unhappily depended for local support. Needless to say the British, who prided themselves on their deft paternal touch, seized on this as an easy point of criticism. "They were too impatient and rarely tried to understand the mentality of their porters and so did not get the best out of them," Kenneth Mason, for one, observed condescendingly of the Workmans. This too is straight out of the colonial cupboard, but it is nonetheless telling for that. "Almost alone of Victorian travelers, the Workmans had absolutely no sympathy or even common-sense understanding of the local people, into whose poor and remote villages they burst with trains of followers demanding service and supplies," the geographer Dorothy Middleton rightly wrote. The "efficacy of kind treat-ment" was in their frank New England view "sentimental nonsense," and to the end of their mountain days they persisted in a commanding and commandeering approach that over time has diminished their reputation even as it then diminished their achievement.[34]

Which achievement was, nevertheless, on Nun Kun considerable, though typi-cally not quite as considerable as the Workmans themselves let on. From the large Ladakhi trading center of Kargil, where they recruited sixty local porters to supplement their six Italians (whom they meant to reserve for high altitudes), they moved south to Suru and then east along the Suru River to Tashi-Tongze, a small, dust-covered hamlet three miles above the monastery town of Rangdum. Here they forded the Suru River—no mean feat in early July—and made for the Shafat Nala, the drainage valley of the Shafat Glacier and the only possible line of approach to the relatively accessible southeastern flank of the Nun Kun massif. At "Morraine Camp" three miles up the valley, their Kargil recruits deserted en masse, leaving them with just the Italian "porters" and the twenty or so local "coolies" they had impressed at Suru. But the Workmans were accustomed to such logistical setbacks by now, and on July 17, undaunted, they carried on five miles up the glacier and made a Base Camp at 15,000 feet opposite the dramatic outlying peak still known simply as Z1 (20,278ft/6,181m). After a week's acclimatization and leisurely exploration of the Shafat basin, they pushed up onto a dazzling white snowfield or plateau, some three miles long by one and one-half miles wide and completely encircled by a sparkling tiara of six or eight great peaks. The Workmans were not, as they claimed, the first to see this distinc-tive topographical feature of the Nun Kun massif—Sillem in fact had photographed it in 1903—but they were the first to make camp on it and establish its height, thus claiming, as they did so, the record for the highest measured point to date at which mountaineers had spent the night.[35]

From this allegedly record-setting "Camp America" (as they patriotically called it),

Bullock Workman launched her successful attempt on what she thought was the second-highest but was in fact the third-highest point on the massif, her "Pinnacle Peak" (22,735ft/6,930m). That she overestimated its height by some 565 feet should not detract from this, her greatest mountaineering achievement. Pinnacle Peak is by any measure a formidable Himalayan mountain: high, ice-clad, and as steep as its name implies. To be sure, Cyprien Savoye did all the laborious step-cutting that the ascent demanded, and an unnamed porter carried all the memsahib's gear. But that Bullock Workman climbed the mountain at all, without benefit of modern equipment and encumbered by her voluminous skirts, speaks to both her ability and her resolve. Though the climb did not, as she repeatedly claimed, win for her "a place with Dr Workman in the small band of mountaineers who have reached a height of over 23,000 feet," it did set an altitude record for women that would stand until Hettie Dhyrenfurth's ascent of Sia Kangri C, formerly Queen Mary Peak (23,861ft/7,273m) in the Karakoram in 1934.[36]

From their Base Camp on the Shafat Glacier, the Workmans next ventured west into the Fariabad watershed, crossed the Barmal La under "D41" to the Barmal Glacier, crossed the Sentik La to the village of Tongul and thence to Suru, thus completing the first full circuit of the Nun Kun massif. In simple mountaineering terms, this was their most notable expedition, but the map they produced was so patently flawed that they did not get much credit for it in the preserves of the Royal Geographical Society or the Indian Survey. Nor did their 1908 expedition to the Hispar Glacier in the Karakoram win much notice. Conway had already been there in 1892, and though the Workmans' itinerary was more complex than his and included several minor ascents, it added little to their reputations as either explorers or mountaineers.[37]

Their exploration of the Siachen Glacier in the eastern Karakoram in the successive summers of 1911 and 1912, on the other hand, added greatly to their reputations and was in fact the crowning achievement of their careers. For the Siachen was not only the longest and widest subpolar glacier in the world; it was also, in their day, the least explored and least accessible. After a wholly original reconnaissance of the southern and western approaches in the summer of 1911, they returned to the Siachen proper in 1912 and traced it to its distant sources on the Shaksgam and Baltoro watersheds. Along the way they penetrated the glacier's many tributaries and climbed several mountains, most notably Tawiz, a 21,000-foot (7,500-meter) prominence on the western wall opposite Apsarasas (23,769ft/7,245m). At the head of the glacier they climbed the "Indira Col" (so named after the goddess Laxmi) and from there looked north to the utterly unknown mountains of Turkestan. From a western tributary they called the West Source Glacier, they crossed the Sia La (c. 18,700ft) onto the Kondus Glacier and thus became the first people to approach Baltoro Kangri (Conway's "Golden Throne") from the southeast. From another western tributary, they climbed to around 20,000 feet on the giant then known simply as Peak 36 and now known as Saltoro Kangri (25,396ft/7,507m). But the literal and rhetorical high point of the expedition was a 21,000-foot plateau beneath the conical mountain they named (in deference to Conway) the Silver Throne (21,653ft/7,502m). Here, in a moment immortalized by her ever-ready Kodak, Fanny unfurled neither a star-spangled banner nor a Buddhist prayer flag but a suffragette broadside, thus casting her own distinctively feminist mantra—VOTES FOR WOMEN—onto the Himalayan winds.[38]

It was a fitting climax to her and her husband's travels. Now aged fifty-four and sixty-five respectively, they had finally pushed themselves to the limits of their physical endurance. Once back in Germany they surrendered themselves to the lecture circuit and the collaborative writing of *Two Summers in the Ice-Wilds of Eastern Karakoram,* their masterpiece. When war broke out in 1914, delaying by several years the appearance of their book, they left Germany for Cannes, where Fanny fell ill and died in 1925. William, whose reputed illness had occasioned their lives of travel in the first place, then returned to Massachusetts, where he lived on to the age of ninety-one.[39]

Honors poured in on the Workmans at the end, but their legacy to Himalayan mountaineering was a decidedly mixed one. They had logged more miles and climbed more peaks than anyone to date; they had produced five sumptuously illustrated and widely read expedition volumes; and by simple virtue of her sex Fanny of course had set an invaluable Himalayan precedent. But the Workmans were not great mountaineers. At their best they were vigorous and competent patrons who followed capably in the hard-won steps of their Italian guides. At their worst they were, as one critic has written, "forerunners of the archetypal tourist: impatient, critical, often at odds with their porters and local inhabitants, self-important and at times unscrupulous."[40] They were also, of course—and merely by coincidence, one hopes—American. For good and ill, they more than anyone broke the exclusive British claim on the Himalaya and introduced a novel element of national competition.

The Great Beast 666

An odd fact of the Workmans' otherwise impressive résumé is that they never visited the Baltoro Muztagh, the inner sanctum of the Karakoram and home to its highest mountains. Whether they thought Conway had done it justice in 1892—unlikely, since they had been perfectly content to follow in his footsteps on the Hispar and the Biafo—or whether they quietly judged even its lesser peaks beyond their abilities they did not say. The Baltoro simply did not engage their interest, and as a result they ended their days without ever having seen K2 from a distance of under 100 miles. Nor had anyone else, after Conway, so much as approached the world's second-highest mountain until 1902, when Oscar Eckenstein (who had fallen out with Conway and gone home from Askole in 1892) returned to Kashmir with the expressed intention of climbing it. With him came two Austrian climbers, Heinrich Pfannl and Victor Wessely; a Swiss physician, Jules Jacot-Guillarmod; a young undergraduate from Trinity College, Guy Knowles; and, as deputy leader, the most colorful and eccentric character ever to cross the crowded stage of Himalayan history: Aleister Crowley, aka "the Great Beast 666."

Born Edward Alexander Crowley in Leamington Spa, Warwickshire, on October 12, 1875, Aleister (as he called himself in deliberate repudiation of his given name) was the eldest child of two evangelists for the Plymouth Brethren, a fanatic Protestant sect that believed in the literal truth of the Bible and the imminence of the Second Coming. As a boy, Aleister strove to be a perfect apostle, but as he grew older and resistant to his parents' moral tyranny, he found himself increasingly drawn to the False Prophet of Revelation, the Beast whose number is 666. It was his mother who in her despair took to calling him "the Great Beast," but Aleister thereafter claimed the sobriquet for his own, declaring himself a Satanist. From Malvern College and Tonbridge School, he went up to Trinity College, Cambridge, ostensibly to read for the Natural Sciences Tripos but really to indulge himself in a congenially medieval setting. In October 1897 a fevered (and probably drug-induced) vision convinced him of the worthlessness of all earthly pursuits and the power of the supernatural. Abandoning the natural for the occult sciences, he left Cambridge without taking a degree in 1898 and joined the London temple of the Hermetic Order of the Golden Dawn, a covert cabalist society that then counted among its practicing initiates one William Butler Yeats.

From here, as one biographer has said, Crowley's life unwound as a long series of "ecstasies, abominations, and bizarreries." First from a flat in Chancery Lane (where he styled himself Count Vladimir Svareff) and then from his Oratory on the shores of Loch Ness (where he styled himself the Laird of Boleskine), he dabbled by frenzied turns in drugs, free love, black magic, hatha yoga, tantric Buddhism, Rosicrucianism, astrology, and pornography, thus earning himself a reputation as "the Wickedest Man in the World" (and ultimately a hallowed place on the cover of the Beatles' *Sgt. Pepper's Lonely Hearts Club Band*). What all this had to do with mountaineering he never coherently said, but this too was among Crowley's passions, the physical expression of his quasi-Nietzschean philosophy of "overcoming," and already by the time he left Cambridge he had climbed extensively in Switzerland, Cumberland, and Wales. Over Easter 1898 he met Oscar Eckenstein at Wastdale Head in the Lake District and found in him not only a congenial climbing partner with a like-minded contempt for the old fogeys of the Alpine Club but something like both brother and father figure. Older by sixteen years, Eckenstein taught Crowley the principles of balance and visualization on rock; he encouraged Crowley to approach climbing more as a mental and visual art than a physical sport. At a time when, as Crowley later recalled it, he had been wandering the lakes in despair and crying to the universe for someone to teach him the truth, Eckenstein appeared in the smoke of his own pipe, as if conjured by magic, and the Great Beast immediately clung to him. Within days of meeting the two men had struck what Crowley called "a sort of provisional agreement to undertake an expedition to the Himalayas when occasion offered."[41]

Meanwhile, Crowley went off to Mexico to study the art of incorporeality—the art, that is, of making himself invisible. After a few months of concentrated prayer and incantation, satisfied that his reflection in the mirror had become faint and flickering, he summoned Eckenstein, and together they climbed Popocatapetl and Ixtaccihuatl, the beautiful twin volcanoes that the Aztecs had venerated as gods. Eckenstein then returned to London to organize their Himalayan expedition. Crowley carried on westward to San Francisco, Hawaii (where he indulged in a brief affair with the wife of an American lawyer), Japan, Sri Lanka (where with the help of an old friend from the Golden Dawn he took up meditation and apparently reached the middle metaphysical state of *Dhyana*), and finally India (where he wandered as a mendicant and developed a lifelong devotion to Shiva, the Hindu god of destruction). In March 1902 he met Eckenstein by prior arrangement in Delhi and proceeded with him to Rawalpindi, then the exclusive staging town for Kashmir and the Karakoram. There they met Knowles, a young Englishman who "knew practically nothing of mountains," Crowley said, but "had common sense enough to do what Eckenstein told him," Jacot-Guillarmod, a Swiss doctor who "looked and behaved like Tartarin de Tarascon [and] knew as little of mountains as he did of medicine," and Pfannl and Wessely, two Austrians whose climbing credentials were impeccable—two years earlier Pfannl had made the first ascent of the Géant by the North Ridge and North-West Face—but whose irremediable foreignness and "international jealousy" ultimately contributed, in Crowley's xenophobic mind, to the failure of the expedition.[42] On March 29, unreasonably burdened by three tons of luggage, the party set out on their ten-week trek for the Baltoro and the highest mountain then accessible to Westerners, the mountain that Crowley alone among early climbers unfailingly called Chogo Ri.

Just one day later, at Tret, the deputy commissioner of Rawalpindi intercepted the expedition and refused Eckenstein right of entry into Kashmir. Crowley immediately assumed that Martin Conway had somehow poisoned the official waters, that "the incident," as he put it, "was the result of unmanly jealousy and petty intrigue . . . complicated by official muddle."[43] More likely Eckenstein's name had aroused suspicion among those ever on the alert for Prussian spies. At any rate, the rest of the expedition proceeded under Crowley's acting command while Eckenstein appealed over one head after another all the way to the viceroy, Lord Curzon, who begrudgingly accepted Crowley's testimonials on behalf of the leader's Englishness and rescinded his detainment. Thus delayed by three weeks, Eckenstein caught Crowley at Srinagar, and the reunited party marched without further incident over the Zoji La into Baltistan. They reached Skardu, the provincial capital on the Indus, on May 14 and Askole, the last settlement before the Baltoro, remarkably ahead of schedule on May 26.

Here, at Askole, Eckenstein and Crowley quarreled over the several-volume library that the latter intended to haul onto the glacier. Eckenstein not unreasonably objected to the superfluous weight, but Crowley had read enough Joseph Conrad to know what happened to those who let go of their hold on civilization in the wild: the library stayed. The two Austrians, meanwhile, fed up with Eckenstein's suffocating discipline and evidently forgetting they were not in the Alps, suddenly thought to pack three days' provisions in their rucksacks and go off to climb K2 on their own. Faced with Eckenstein's strenuous objections, they gave in, but not happily. K2 was not even in sight yet, but it was already a fractured and sullen party that lumbered up the glacier toward it in early June.

June 15 found the expedition at the dramatic glacial junction below the Gasherbrum group that Conway had named Concordia. The next day, ahead of the others, Crowley moved north up the tributary Godwin-Austen Glacier ("where man had never yet trodden," he mistakenly claimed). K2 was now in full view, and after studying it through his field glasses "all day and all night," Crowley breezily concluded that one would have "no difficulty in walking up the snow slopes on the east-south-east to the snowy shoulder below the final rock pyramid."[44] This was far too optimistic an assessment; hard experience would later prove the last 2,000 feet of K2's Southeast Ridge to be as difficult a summit push as any in the Himalaya. And Crowley as yet had no conception of the difficulties *below* these distinctive snow slopes on the east-southeast. But he had indeed perceived the route by which K2 would ultimately be climbed. June 16 found him camped at 16,500 feet under the South Face of the mountain, more or less at the site of most subsequent Base Camps. From here he pushed on up the Godwin-Austen to the foot of a subsidiary southeastern spur that struck him as vaguely promising and would indeed (as the Abruzzi Spur) one day yield the Southeast Ridge and the summit.

Eckenstein, meanwhile, hoped for a better route. On July 1, after two weeks of debilitating storms, he dispatched Pfannl and Wessely to reconnoiter the northeastern ridge that falls from the summit parallel to the glacier in the direction of Skyang Kangri, Crowley's "Staircase Peak" (24,786ft/7,555m). Inexplicably—for the Northeast Ridge is a long and tortuous knife-edge that would yield only in 1978 and then with extreme difficulty—the Austrians pronounced it climbable, and on July 7, over Crowley's objections, Eckenstein ordered a general removal to a new Base Camp seven miles up the glacier. From here, the expedition's Camp XI at 19,450 feet, Crowley claims to have climbed on his own to over 22,000 feet on July 9, but no account other than his makes any mention of this and it is difficult to credit. That night, in any case, he succumbed to fever, chills, and vomiting and withdrew to his tent for the duration. The next day, July 10, Jacot-Guillarmod and Wessely climbed to about 21,500 feet on the Northeast Ridge before ruling it out as a reasonable line of approach. The two Austrians next suggested a consolation attempt on Skyang Kangri by way of "Windy Gap" (Skyang La), the distinctive col at the northeastern head of the glacier that they had reconnoitered a few days earlier and named Grenzsattel (Frontier Col), but this Eckenstein rigidly vetoed as outside the expedition's brief. Whether he authorized Pfannl's and Wessely's last-ditch effort to reach the notch in the Northeast Ridge between Skyang Kangri and the outlying "Pt. 22,380" is not clear; at any rate it expired at around 21,000 feet when Pfannl collapsed with what would now be recognized as pulmonary edema. By the time Pfannl had been evacuated with great difficulty to the grassy oasis of Urdukas on the Baltoro, a semidelirious Crowley had threatened Knowles with a revolver, Knowles had delivered a disarming knee to Crowley's stomach, Wessely had stolen the emergency rations and been expelled from the expedition, Pfannl's mind had quite gone, the weather had worsened, and cholera had broken out in the Braldu Valley. In short, the 1902 K2 expedition dissolved in rancorous disorder.[45]

The Great Beast returned home and resumed his sorcery. In 1903 he surprisingly married one Rose Edith Skerett (the widowed sister of the painter Gerald Kelly), and through her involuntary trances entered into supernatural communication with his guardian angel, a certain Aiwass, who dictated to him *The Book of the Law,* the gospel text of a new Zarathustrian faith that Crowley called *thelema* after the Greek for "will." "Do what thou wilt shall be the whole of the Law," Crowley proclaimed in his new persona as the reincarnation of a pharaonic priest named Ankh-f-n-khonsu. In 1904 he became the proud father of Nuit Ma Ahathoor Hecate Sappho Jezebel Lilith Crowley and looked to be settling down as Laird of Boleskine when the Swiss doctor, Jacot-Guillarmod, arrived in April 1905 to propose a return engagement to Kangchenjunga in Sikkim. Crowley thought he had done with mountains, but he still yearned after the world's height record and agreed to come on the understanding that he, and not Eckenstein, would be leader.

He need not have worried: Eckenstein wanted no part of the climb; nor did Guy Knowles, who had seen quite enough of the wrong end of Crowley's revolver. In their places Jacot-Guillarmod recruited two of his countrymen, Alexis Pache and Charles Reymond. Crowley meanwhile hurried out to India to secure needed permissions and to organize the supply caravan. On his arrival in Darjeeling, he foolishly recruited his hotelkeeper, a young Italian named Alcesti C. Rigo de Righi, as transport officer, "not foreseeing that his pin brain would entirely give way as soon as he got out of the world of waiters." The three Swiss arrived on July 31, accepted in writing Crowley's sole and supreme authority in "all matters respecting mountain craft," and by August 8 they were off: five Europeans, three Kashmiri servants (the same three who had accompanied Eckenstein's K2 expedition), and some 230 local porters.[46]

Six years earlier, the British mountaineer and explorer Douglas Freshfield had come out to Sikkim and against great political and topographical odds completed the first circumnavigation of the Kangchenjunga massif. With him came Edmund Garwood, surveyor, and the great Vittorio Sella (of whom more later), photographer. Crowley thus had at his disposal not only Freshfield's descriptive narrative but a reliable map and an incomparable portfolio of mountain photographs. Never one to doubt his own superior instincts, however, he chose to ignore Freshfield's suggestion that the western face of Kangchenjunga afforded the mountaineer the likeliest line of attack and chose instead to attempt the great Southwest Face by way of the Yalung Glacier (which Freshfield had not explored, though it would eventually prove the line of first ascent). Leaving Darjeeling by the Singalila Ridge, he crossed the Chumbab La westward into Nepal and the Yalung Chu. At Tseram, a small village just below the snout of the glacier, he was to await an envoy of the Diwan of Nepal but chose to ignore this political nicety and proceeded unescorted toward the mountain. Already the party was at sixes and sevens, Jacot-Guillarmod convinced of the impossibility of the Southwest Face, Reymond generally sullen and reluctant, and de Righi (if Crowley's account is to be believed) "half insane with the fear that comes to people of his class in the absence of a chat-tering herd of his fellows, and in the presence of the grandeur of nature." Pache at least was "making extremely good," Crowley said, and Crowley himself was in fine fettle—fine enough to lay into his porters with his customary vigor, anyway—and fully confident of success when the party pitched Camp III at the head of the glacier at about 18,000 feet.[47]

From here Crowley evidently intended a westward traverse of the mountain toward the outlying summit of Kangbachen (25,928ft/7,903m). The advantage of such a line was that it skirted the great ice fall that tumbled dangerously down from the distinctive shelf under the main summit; the disadvantage was that it led to a point about three quarters of a mile away from the main summit and thus assumed a difficult high traverse of the West Ridge. But of course it never came to that. By the time Crowley reached Camp IV on a sharp snow ledge above the glacier, his party was in open revolt. Jacot-Guillarmod especially was appalled at Crowley's high-handed leadership and brutal treatment of the shockingly barefooted porters. For his part, Crowley had evidently decided that Jacot-Guillarmod was mentally unbalanced and therefore beneath any notice. Somehow he drove everyone on to Camp V at about 20,400 feet, and on September 1 he, Pache, and Reymond even climbed 1,000 feet higher before a small avalanche unnerved their porters and forced a perilous retreat. The next morning Jacot-Guillarmod and de Righi convened a durbar at Camp V and attempted to depose Crowley from the expedition leadership. The day's excited argument ended inconclusively, however, and at 5:00 P.M. Jacot-Guillarmod decided to withdraw for the night to the main base of Camp III. Crowley cautioned him against such a steep snow descent in the heat of the day (or so he later claimed), but the doctor (again, in Crowley's telling) was beyond appeals to reason. The descent proceeded with Jacot-Guillarmod leading de Righi, Pache, and four unnamed porters on a single rope. Just whose fall precipitated the tragedy remains unknown, but in the ensuing avalanche, Pache and three of the porters were crushed and killed.

Up at Camp V, Reymond and Crowley heard "frantic cries," and Reymond at least immediately descended to help. But Crowley remained in his tent, cool and collected: "A mountain 'accident' of this sort is one of the things for which I have no sympathy what-ever," he wrote that very evening in a self-exculpatory letter to the *Pioneer* (Calcutta). The next day he descended without pause past the site of the accident ("without even knowing if our comrades would be found," Jacot-Guillarmod later wrote) and left on his own for Darjeeling, where he seized control of the expedition funds (most of which had been put up by the doctor). Back in Calcutta, he wrote highly tendentious accounts of the expedi-tion for the *Pioneer* and the *Daily Mail* and used the tragedy as occasion to attack the "old women" of the Alpine Club, whose intrigue against him had somehow, in his disturbed mind, led to the tragedy. Jacot-Guillarmod and de Righi, meanwhile, were airing their own version of events in the press and threatening Crowley with legal action. When Crowley called this bluff, Jacot-Guillarmod turned to blackmail and threatened to make public some of Crowley's pornographic verse. Thus cornered, Crowley paid over "a small sum for certain items which had been overlooked" and went off big game hunting in Orissa with his Nepalese mistress and the maharajah of Moharbhanj.[48]

So ended in sordid recrimination the strange mountaineering career of the Great Beast 666. From Calcutta, Crowley had written to Eckenstein proposing a return to Kangchenjunga (without foreigners) in 1906, but not surprisingly this came to nothing, and Crowley, now thirty years old, gave himself over entirely to sex, drugs, and black magic. He retained a strong interest in the Himalaya, however, and through the years continued to offer acid commentary on the follies and vanities of other, more elaborate expeditions. In 1921, when Everest was much in the news thanks to the official British reconnaissance, he conceived a bold plan whereby he and an American disciple, one William Seabrook, would fly tents and provisions to a "high alp or level glacier S.E. of Everest" and from there "rush the mountain" and thus claim the summit for themselves.[49] Needless to say, this too came to nothing, but in light of today's hurried ascents of the great mountain, it was not altogether ridiculous. Aleister Crowley was in obvious respects a deluded and demented man. But no less an authority than Tom Longstaff (who had met him in Switzerland in 1899) praised him as a fine if unconventional climber of uncommon daring. From far outside the privileged purlieus of the Alpine Club and the Royal Geographical Society (who between them did in fact conspire to diminish or even erase Crowley's achievement), he found his way to the world's second- and third-highest mountains and somehow discerned and reconnoitered the routes by which they would first be climbed.

A Right Royal Mountaineer

In the summer of 1938, a young Columbia medical student named Charles Houston led a small American Alpine Club expedition to the Karakoram in hopes of climbing K2. After discouraging investigations of the Northwest and Northeast ridges, the team decided to attempt the Southeast Ridge by way of the subsidiary spur that Crowley had noticed hopefully from below in 1902. On June 23, while reconnoitering the lower part of the spur with his friend Bill House, Houston was startled to find a few small sticks of wood strewn about a little col some 1,000 feet above the Godwin-Austen Glacier. Needless to say, the great Himalayan mountainsides were not then the indiscriminate trash heaps that they have since become; such relics as these—bits of a packing crate, by the look of them— were unusual and easy to account for. As the Eckenstein expedition had not attempted the Southeast Spur in 1902, but proceeded on up the glacier to the foot of the Northeast Ridge, there was, in fact, only one possibility: these had to be traces of the 1909 Italian expedition of the Duke of the Abruzzi.[50]

Luigi Amedeo Giuseppe Maria Ferdinando Francesco di Savoia-Aosta, il Duca d'Abruzzi, was, as the elaborate name might suggest, "a right royal mountaineer." The grandson of Victor Emmanuel II, king of Italy, and the son of Amadeo, the Duke of Aosta and (briefly) the king of Spain, he was born in Madrid in January 1873, one month before his father's abdication and the proclamation of the first Spanish republic. Thus deprived of one royal inheritance, he retained a remote claim on another, the throne of Italy, and came of age in the ancient city of Turin (Torino) every inch a prince. His grandfather was a keen sportsman, an ibex and chamois hunter, and on school holidays young Luigi often visited the royal game preserves of the Gran Paradiso, a rugged region of the Graian Alps just thirty miles from Monte Cervino (as the Italians know the Matterhorn). Most of the members of the ruling house of Savoy were mountain enthusiasts, not surprisingly, but one, the beautiful Princess Margherita di Savoia (niece of the king and wife of the heir to the throne) was especially keen; it was she, evidently, who instilled in the young Prince Luigi a passion for mountaineering. He climbed Punta Levanna in the Graian Alps in 1892 and never thereafter looked back. Within a year (despite the onerous demands of his naval commission) he had accumulated an impressive record of Alpine ascents, including Gran Paradiso, Mont Blanc, and Monte Rosa. In 1894 a chance encounter with A. F. Mummery, his climbing idol, led to an unlikely friendship, and late that summer the prince and the commoner teamed up (with Norman Collie) for the second ascent of the Zmutt Ridge of the Matterhorn. The duke then set out on a two-year naval cruise aboard the *Cristoforo Colombo* that took him, among other places, to Calcutta, where he seized the chance to venture inland as far as Darjeeling for a look at Kangchenjunga. Already the Himalaya beckoned, and when, en route for home, he learned of Mummery's death on Nanga Parbat, he vowed to go to Kashmir himself and climb the "naked mountain" in his late friend's honor.[51]

Alas, no sooner had the duke set his sights on Nanga Parbat than plague and famine struck the Punjab and the government of India closed all access to the Himalaya. As an alternative, the duke boldly chose Mount Saint Elias (18,008ft/5,489m), an unclimbed massif not twelve miles from the sea in the lower Alaskan Yukon. Though neither terribly high nor technically demanding, Saint Elias is a remote, storm-swept, inaccessible, and altogether inhospitable mountain that even today remains a serious undertaking. Five attempts had failed before the duke's succeeded and made him a national hero, the acknowledged heir to the New World crown of Columbus. For his next trick and the greater glory of Italy, the duke decided in 1900 to go for the North Pole, the Holy Grail of modern exploration, and though he did not reach it, he did (at the cost of three men's lives) set a "farthest north" record of 86° 34′ that stood until Robert Peary's second Arctic expedition of 1905. He then (after a few years of attending to his naval and royal duties) organized the first fully fledged climbing expedition to the Ugandan Ruwenzori, those fabled "Mountains of the Moon" that Henry Morton Stanley had sighted from the shores of Lake Victoria in 1889 and pronounced to be the ultimate source of the Nile. The Englishmen Douglas Freshfield and Arnold Mumm had made a pioneering reconnaissance of the Ruwenzori in 1905, but the duke's expedition of the following year was the first to ascend its principal peaks and to establish that the range formed a watershed independent of Lake Victoria and was thus not the true source of the Nile. Though largely disregarded or even forgotten today, when

Luigi Amedeo, Duke of the Abruzzi
(1873–1923), a "right royal
mountaineer." From Charles
Morris, ed., *Finding the North Pole*
(Philadelphia: Standard, 1909).
Courtesy of the Rochester
Public Library.

the geographical mysteries of the "dark continent" no longer hold the Western imagination in thrall as they once did, this African odyssey of 1906 was widely celebrated at the time and confirmed the Duke of the Abruzzi's place at the very fore of mountain explorers.[52]

He had yet to test himself against the Himalaya, however, had yet to establish just how high he could climb, and it was with this simple object in mind that he led his life's last big expedition, to K2 in 1909. He had not forgotten his pledge to avenge Mummery's death on Nanga Parbat, but for one intent on the world's altitude record—recently set at 24,000 feet by two Norwegians on Kabru—Nanga Parbat was a risky proposition that offered nothing in the way of nearby alternatives. The advantage of K2, in the duke's mind, was that besides being politically accessible, it was thickly surrounded by several other peaks that exceeded Kabru in height. Should his attempt on the world's penultimate peak fail, the duke might still set the altitude record on one of its neighbors. Not that height above sea level was his only concern: like most early Himalayan expeditions, excepting Graham's and Mummery's, the duke's came publicly packaged with all kinds of romantic and scientific justifications. But privately it was really about claiming K2 for Italy and the House of Savoy.[53]

That the entire team should be Italian was, therefore, for the duke an absolute given.

From Courmayeur in the Val d'Aosta came four professional guides: Joseph and Laurent Petigax, father and son (who had been with the Workmans on the Chogo Lungma and with the duke in the Ruwenzori), and the Brocherel brothers, Alexis and Henri (who had twice been with the Englishman Tom Longstaff in Garhwal-Kumaon). Supplementing the guides were three Italian "porters": Emilio Brocherel, Albert Savoie, and Ernest Bareux. Federic Negrotto, the duke's aide-de-camp and a ship's lieutenant in the Italian Navy, came along as expedition cartographer, Filippo De Filippi, the duke's old friend and shipmate, as expedition doctor and chronicler. Both of these men were reputable Alpine climbers in their own right and De Filippi, for one, had been with the duke in Alaska. But the most notable addition to the party was De Filippi's cousin, Vittorio Sella, who besides being a highly accomplished mountaineer was then and remains now the greatest of all mountain photographers.

Fifty years old at the time of the K2 expedition, Sella had been born and raised in the textile town of Biella in the Italian Piedmont, just northeast of the royal seat of Turin. His father, Giuseppe Venanzio Sella, was a textile master and amateur photographer who had published the first Italian-language treatise on photography in 1856. His uncle, Quentino Sella, statesman and diplomat, was a renowned climber and founder of the Italian Alpine Club. Vittorio was thus in a sense "predestined to devote his life to the depiction of vertiginous landscapes," as a recent admirer has said. But he also worked hard at it from the time of his youthful apprenticeship to the chemical side of his father's textile business. Sella was not, it should be said, the first notable Alpine photographer: by the time he started carrying his bulky Dallmeyer camera into the hills, Aimé Civiale, Louis and Auguste Bisson, and Sella's own mentor Vittoria Besso had been producing beautiful mountain images for twenty years. But Sella was the best climber among them, and beginning in 1879, when he shot his first Alpine panorama from the summit of Monte Mars, he began to combine this physical talent with the new technology of dry collodion and gelatin bromide plates to produce images of unrivalled clarity and artistry. "From 1880," he later recalled, "I made up my mind to combine photography with Alpinism, and I took no interest at all in the lower parts of the mountains, and confined myself to photographic work on the summits, and to those higher regions of the Alps, which were little known and had not been photographed."[54]

In June 1882, three months after recording the first winter traverse of the Matterhorn, Sella returned to that famed summit and shot a 360-degree panorama that struck contemporary viewers with the force of vicarious revelation. On the strength of this and other early images, he secured the high-profile services of Spooner's of London, photographic agents, and the eager patronage of such famed mountaineers as Edward Whymper and John Tyndall. By the mid-1880s he was the photographic illustrator of choice for any book on the Alps, not just because he could faithfully reproduce the details of the landscape but because he combined the requirements of verisimilitude with a unique artistic vision. He could always, as the mountain writer Ronald Clark put it, "see the essentials of a mountain scene and then so utilize the effects of sun, shadow, and atmosphere that

Vittorio Sella (1859–1943), self-portrait, 1889.
© 2005—Fondazione Sella, Biella, Italy.
Courtesy, Fondazione Sella, Biella, Italy.

those essentials were composed within the bounds of the ground glass plate as though on a painter's canvas." His Alpine excursions established Sella's reputation, but his two expeditions to the Caucasus in 1889 and 1890, and his famous panorama from the summit of Elbruz especially, confirmed and enlarged it and proved that his was a vision that transcended a particular range or place. "Those who have never seen a great mountain view," wrote one English reviewer of the Elbruz panorama, "may look on this presentment and form some actual idea of the reality: those who have held that there is nothing to be seen or learnt on great peaks may look at it—and repent."[55]

In 1890, "in consideration of his recent journey in the Caucasus and the advance made in our knowledge of the physical characteristics and the topography of the chain by means of his series of panoramic photographs," the Royal Geographical Society awarded Sella its annual Murchison Grant. Two years later he visited England for the first time and met Freshfield, Mummery, and other renowned members of the Alpine Club who had begun to collect his work. His first American exhibitions opened that same year at the Appalachian Mountain Club in Boston, the National Geographical Society in Washington, and the American Museum of Natural History in New York. In 1893 a traveling exhibition organized by Charles Fay of the Appalachian Mountain Club stopped at seventy-five cities across the United States, including Bridgeport, Connecticut, where over 20,000 people paid to see it. In 1896 one of the great works of mountaineering history, Freshfield's *Exploration of the Caucasus,* prominently featured Sella's photographs and added to his popularity and stature.[56]

The Duke of the Abruzzi was well aware of all this: he and Sella were compatriots after all, not just of Italy but of the Piedmont. They had many friends and climbing acquaintances in common. When it came time to find a photographer for his Alaskan venture, then, none but Sella would do. But it was Douglas Freshfield and not the duke who first took Sella to the Himalaya. The occasion was Freshfield's 1899 circuit of the Kangchenjunga massif, and it marked the full flowering of Sella's genius. His new Ross and Co. camera was a notable advance on the Dallmeyer in that it produced twenty-by-twenty-five-centimeter film negatives along with smaller twenty-four-by-eighteen-centimeter glass plate negatives, and with it Sella shot several photographs—the famous crest of Siniolchu, for instance, or the moody portrait of Jannu from Chunjerma—that in all the years since have never been matched. For as Ansel Adams once observed, there is no faked grandeur in them; "rather there is understatement, caution, and truthful purpose." Sella was the greatest of mountain photographers, Adams believed, because he captured "not only the facts and forms of far-off splendors of the world, but the essence of experience which finds a spiritual response in the inner recesses of our mind and heart."[57]

In 1906, a veteran now of the Caucasus, Alaska, and Sikkim, Sella joined the Duke of the Abruzzi in Africa and captured on film and glass the mysterious allure of the Ruwenzori. He did not, at first, want to go to K2 in 1909, however. He was, after all, now fifty years old and no longer the climber he had once been. He was, moreover, at the height of his reputation; his photographs were selling at prices once reserved for oil paintings and he no longer felt free to leave his shop for six months at a time. And finally, Sella had grown weary of his expeditionary companions, none of whom—not even the duke, who looked on photography as a simple tool of documentation—fully shared or appreciated his aesthetic interests. Returning from the Ruwenzori in 1906, Sella had written privately of his "daily disappointment about the sentiments and the moral quality of almost all of my companions, in whom you would not find a speck of poetry or of interest for the really beautiful things, should you look for it with a microscope."[58] How the duke overcame Sella's reluctance in 1909 we do not know: an appeal to patriotism, perhaps, to mountains, or to friendship. But much to the benefit of posterity (for his masterful images of the Karakoram remain likewise unrivalled), Sella and his assistant, Erminio Botta, were both on board the P & O steamer *Oceana* when on March 26 the duke set sail from the port of Marseilles for Bombay.

Also on board with the duke and company were some 13,000 pounds of stores and equipment: everything from clothing and climbing gear to food and medicine, cameras, photogrammetric survey supplies, meteorological instruments, and more, all in seemingly

Jannu at sunset from Chunjerma Pass, 1899. Photograph by Vittorio Sella.
© 2005—Fondazione Sella, Biella, Italy. Courtesy, Fondazione Sella, Biella, Italy.

limitless profusion. Still, the duke had come a long way since the time he insisted on lugging ten iron bedsteads up Alaska's Malaspina Glacier; on the Baltoro he would sleep on
the ground, or on air mattresses, anyway. His was nonetheless a princely procession, and it
famously set the Himalayan standard for expeditionary encumbrance. Fortunately, it also
set the Himalayan standard for both administrative efficiency and personal camaraderie.
Like most early Himalayan ventures, this one ultimately met with hardship, failure, and
disappointment. But to the end it preserved clarity and harmony of purpose. Though it
built on Conway's example, the duke's was, as the English climber Bill Tilman once said,
"the original Himalayan expedition in the grand style," and in this respect despite its
failure it set a lasting precedent that even today, though seldom acknowledged, is seldom
altogether ignored.[59]

From Bombay, where he embarked on Good Friday, April 9, the duke proceeded via
Rawalpindi to Srinagar, where he enjoyed the lavish hospitality of Francis Younghusband,
then British resident at the Court of Kashmir. The duke's unassailable royalty appeased
whatever misgivings Younghusband might otherwise have had about a foreign expedition
in Kashmir, and he helpfully negotiated with the maharajah's government a free customs
pass for all the duke's stores, thus saving him both time and expense. The maharajah himself
met the duke at Gunderbal, one day out of Srinagar, and lent his own royal blessing. The

expedition then proceeded up the Sind Valley and over the Zoji La (11,578ft), the lowest point in the Great Himalayan axis between the Indus Valley and the Vale of Kashmir and from time immemorial the trade route between Chinese Turkestan, Tibet, and India. At Dras, the first substantial village on the far side of the Zoji La, the duke met up with A. C. Baines, his British liaison and transport officer. Baines had recruited some 300 Ladakhi and Balti porters and some sixty transport ponies, and thus fortified the expedition wound its stately way up the Indus Valley to Skardu, where it met a right royal welcome featuring dancers, native orchestras, the inevitable polo match, and all manner of local dignitaries.

May 13 saw the caravan at Askole, the settlement just below the Baltoro where Eckenstein and Conway had acrimoniously parted company in 1892. From here Sella climbed to 13,000 feet and shot his panorama of the Mango Gusor range and the upper Braldu Valley. A week later, from a high snowy ridge above Urdukas—the once-pristine, now-polluted promontory where the duke pitched his main Base Camp—he shot his famous "Panorama B" of the lower Baltoro Valley. As reproduced in De Filippi's eventual expedition volume, these remarkable panoramas, just two among many, for the first time made it possible for armchair mountaineers to picture in their mind's eye the physical scale of the Himalaya. Conway had illustrated his expedition account with delicate pen and ink sketches, the Workmans theirs with Fanny's inadequate Kodak snapshots. Sella's work was of an altogether different visual order. With it, photography disclosed its full potential and began to displace lengthy descriptive narrative as the conventional way of marking individual and collective achievement in the mountains.[60]

On May 23, leaving Baines in charge of the expedition's main base at Urdukas, the duke departed in stages for Concordia from where, a day later, he first saw K2, "the indisputable sovereign of the region, gigantic and solitary, hidden from human sight by innumerable ranges, jealously defended by a vast throng of vassal peaks, protected from invasion by miles and miles of glacier."[61] The resemblance to the Matterhorn as seen from Valtournanche was, De Filippi thought, obvious, and many climbers have noted it since, though it reflects in this first instance a fanciful effort to reduce the mountain to an alpine scale and claim it imaginatively for Italy. The duke had no illusions, however, of a quick alpine ascent: on a small stretch of glacial moraine below the dip in the Southwest Ridge that he named the Negrotto Pass after his aide-de-camp, he put in a heavy encampment complete with tents and stone wall shelters. From Urdukas back on the Baltoro, Baines kept the supply line of fresh eggs and meat, water, fuel, mail, and even newspapers moving while the duke lay siege to K2 in what became the approved Himalayan fashion.

Not that he dallied. On May 26, while De Filippi and others saw to the fortification of the camp, the duke entered the western tributary glacier that he named the Savoia (in honor of his house) and noted the broad rounded col at its head (henceforth, the Savoia Saddle) that might, he thought, afford access to K2's Northwest Ridge. In the meantime, Alexis and Emilio Brocherel went up the Godwin-Austen for a look at the Northeast Ridge, which they dismissed out of hand, together with the whole eastern side of the mountain, as "extremely steep, covered with ice and exposed to avalanches of séracs." This left, for the moment, the indistinct Southeast Spur that met the summit ridge just below the shoulder at about 25,300 feet (7,500 meters). For two days the duke's Italian guides ferried tents, ropes, pitons, stoves, sleeping bags, and food to the foot of this spur. The way thus prepared for him, the duke began his ascent on May 30 and reached a sheltered nook at the base of a rocky tooth large enough for two Whymper tents: Camp IV (18,245ft). Here he waited for three days while his four guides tried to force a passage higher through steep snowy couloirs and rotten, ice-encrusted rock. Finally, at a hard-won 20,500 feet, they gave up, not because they had met with any insurmountable obstacle but because, they told the duke, "it was obviously hopeless to attempt so formidable an ascent when the difficulties from the outset were such as to render the task only just feasible for unloaded guides, while there could be no question of transport of camp material, even when reduced to the barest necessities."[62] The duke conceded the point (without once having left his comfortable perch), and ordered a retreat from the spur that now, in honor of this modest but pioneering effort, bears his name.

Thus rebuffed on the south, the duke now resumed his explorations of the western Savoia Glacier in hopes of gaining the favorably tilted Northwest Ridge. On June 7, after twelve hours of laborious step-cutting, he and three guides reached the 21,870-foot Savoia Saddle only to discover that a succession of impossible pinnacles and towers barred further progress up the ridge while a broad overhanging cornice blocked even a look at the North Face. "And that was all," De Filippi tersely observed. "As a reward of his labours the Duke thus saw utterly annihilated the hopes with which he had begun the ascent." But it was not a dead loss, this sojourn on the Savoia. From an icy hummock at the head of the glacier Sella had shot his timeless portrait of the great western wall of K2 as well as the western panorama, "Panorama E," which according to Jim Curran helped inspire the American attempt on the Northwest Ridge in 1975.[63]

All that remained for the duke was to explore the upper basin of the Godwin-Austen and the eastern slopes of K2. Nothing he saw led him to question the Brocherels' initial judgment that the Northeast Ridge was impossible. He therefore settled for a thorough reconnaissance of the basin and a token effort from "Windy Gap" on Skyang Kangri, Crowley's "Staircase Peak." Bad weather and the unspecified illness of one of his guides (Alexis Brocherel) stymied this effort at roughly 22,000 feet, but not before the duke (no slouch with a camera himself, it turned out) had captured the famous photograph of the eastern face of K2 that would ultimately serve as frontispiece to De Filippi's expedition account. Sella, meanwhile, had climbed a depression in the circle of mountains around the amphitheater of Broad Peak (Sella Pass) and from there shot his "Panorama F" southeastward toward the utterly unknown mountains of the eastern Karakoram. Little though he knew it, just five days earlier Tom Longstaff (along with Arthur Neve and A. M. Slingsby) had crossed the Saltoro Pass onto the Siachen Glacier, seen the group of mountains that Sella was about to photograph, and named the greatest of them Teram Kangri (24,487ft/

7,464m), or "ice peak of Teram." By the time De Filippi's book appeared, Longstaff had seen Sella's photograph and confirmed the identification: a fortuitous instance of Anglo-Italian topographical collaboration.[64]

By the end of June, the Duke of the Abruzzi had concluded that K2 was and would forever remain unassailable: a confident verdict that discouraged further attempts on the mountain for almost thirty years. But he had not surrendered his hope of a height record and so set out in July to climb Chogolisa, Conway's "Bride Peak" (25,157ft/7,668m), a beautifully proportioned snow-clad mass of a mountain eighteen miles south of K2 on the upper Baltoro. A staging attack on the Chogolisa Saddle (20,784ft) that the duke expected to take two days instead took a discouraging eight, and Sella, having safely seen his patron thus far and captured his "Panorama P" of the upper Baltoro, now retired to the main base at Urdukas, pausing en route to take his famous portrait of the great monolith of Muztagh Tower (page 330). De Filippi, Negrotto, Alexis Brocherel and Laurent Petigax were all now for various reasons hors de combat, so it was the duke alone with two of his guides (Joseph Petigax and Henri Brocherel) and one Italian porter (Emilio Brocherel) who attempted the remaining 4,326 feet on Chogolisa from July 10. To this point in the expedition the duke had not enjoyed four consecutive days of good weather, nor would he now, but oddly enough it was neither wind, cold, nor blizzard that did him in—it was fog. On July 18 he had climbed to within 510 feet of the summit and 700 feet higher than anyone else had ever been when a blinding mist descended and stopped him in his tracks. For two hours he waited, hoping for a fugitive wind to brush the mist away, but it never came, and at 3:30 in the afternoon, knowing he had to be back on the saddle by nightfall, he turned around and descended, little consoled by having set a height record (24,600ft/7,498m) that would stand for thirteen years.

And so ended what Francis Younghusband would later describe as "the most perfectly organized expedition that had then come out to the Himalaya."[65] In its main objective—the climbing of K2—it had failed—indeed, failed as completely as Eckenstein and Crowley's expedition had done. But in setting a particular example of how Himalayan mountaineering might at its best be conducted it had demonstrably succeeded. No one died or was even seriously hurt in the duke's party. No egos clashed, no friendships died, no porters struck or mutinied. The duke's primary mountaineering mission comported perfectly well with his secondary scientific mission; indeed, in this case the two seem genuinely to have complemented one another. Whether Negrotto's meticulously gathered meteorological data ever proved of any particular importance or use is doubtful. But his 1:100,000-scale photogrammetric map marked a great advance on those of his predecessors and proved the foundation of subsequent exploration and mountaineering in the region. The duke's long sojourn on the Chogolisa Saddle forever exploded the Workmans' quaint notion that no

Camp below the West Face of K2, 1909. Photograph by Vittorio Sella.
© 2005—Fondazione Sella, Biella, Italy. Courtesy, Fondazione Sella, Biella, Italy.

one could sleep at heights exceeding 20,000 feet, just as his near success on the mountain itself effectively proved human ability to adapt to 25,000 feet. The simple fact of his royal presence, as ably narrated by Filippo De Filippi, established a presumptive Italian claim to the mountain that time ultimately honored. The duke himself never returned to the Himalaya, but he left the name of Abruzzi on one of its greatest mountainsides. And by having the foresight to invite Vittorio Sella along, he ensured his expedition's greatest legacy: a collection of breathtaking photographs that has forever imprinted on the world's mind the solemn grandeur of the Karakoram in that slower, quieter time.

Toward Everest, 1893–1914

Ever since the Great Trigonometrical Survey had fixed its height (a little low) at 29,002 feet in 1856, the mountain then still known as Himalaya Peak XV had attracted interest as a topographical curiosity, as probably, though not yet definitively, the highest mountain in the world. No European had as yet been any nearer to it than Phalut, a small village near Sandakphu on the Singalila Ridge in Sikkim, but Everest—or Gaurisankar, as it briefly came to be known, thanks to Hermann Schlagintweit's mistaking it for a quite different mountain thirty-six miles to the west—quickly captured the European imagination. No sooner had the Alpine Club been founded in 1857 than members began to speculate on the problem of altitude and the possibility of one day climbing to the highest earthly height. In 1876 an eccentric American Alpinist named Meta Breevort seems quite seriously to have made up her mind to try when suddenly she died in Oxford of rheumatic fever. What she would have found had she persisted, of course, was that any thought of climbing Everest was moot as long as both Tibet and Nepal remained jealously closed to foreigners. The early Himalayan expeditions of William Graham and Martin Conway naturally stimulated further discussion of Everest, however, and in 1893 a young Charles Bruce, fresh off the Conway expedition, actually proposed to Francis Younghusband, then political agent in Chitral, that the two of them make a clandestine dash across Tibet and climb the mountain from the north. Remarkably, Mortimer Durand, then foreign secretary to the government of India, raised no objection to this mad scheme, but not surprisingly nothing came of it, and for the moment these two like-minded adventurers returned to their routine posts.[66]

Three years after the discouraging death of Mummery on Nanga Parbat, the idea of climbing Everest received fresh impetus from the arrival of George Nathaniel Curzon in India as viceroy. An experienced trans-Himalayan traveler in his own right, one who had won the gold medal of the Royal Geographical Society for his exploration of the source of the Oxus, Curzon was also an unabashed imperialist, a true believer in Britain's civilizing mission and a determined adherent of the "forward school" of frontier diplomacy. When he learned of Douglas Freshfield's plan to cross surreptitiously into Tibet and Nepal for the purposes of a circuit of Kangchenjunga, far from objecting he encouraged further trespass all the way to the ramparts of Everest. "I have always regarded it as rather a reproach that having the tallest, and in all probability, the second or third tallest mountains in the world on the borders of British Protected or Feudatory territory, we have for the last 20 years equipped no scientific expedition and done practically nothing to explore them," he wrote to Freshfield in July 1899. "I should like to see a thoroughly competent party sent out to ascend or attempt the ascent of Kangchenjunga or Mount Everest." Thus emboldened, Freshfield sounded out both the Royal Geographical Society and the Royal Society in London but found both too absorbed in Antarctic exploration to spare any thoughts for Everest. Curzon's efforts to secure permission for an approach to Everest through Nepal proved similarly fruitless, and there the idea languished, though Freshfield and Curzon evidently met to discuss it further when the former came out to India later in the year.[67]

The frontier, meanwhile, remained for Curzon a paramount imperial concern. In 1901, having weathered the worst of a plague and famine that beset his early tenure in India, he detached the whole troubled area west of the Indus from the Punjab and created a new North-West Frontier Province answerable directly to Calcutta. To the north, in the Hindu-Kush, he pushed the British sphere of influence up to Chinese Sinkiang, thus effectively doubling the size of Kashmir and preempting the threat of any Russian incursion through the Karakoram. Tibet remained, to his mind anyway, dangerously unsettled, a likely focus of Russian intrigue, and in 1903, following the elaborate coronation durbar in Delhi that marked the ceremonial apogee of the Raj, he summoned Francis Younghusband from his residency at Indore and put him at the head of a military mission to Lhasa. The British government later disavowed the treaty that Younghusband imposed on the Dalai Lama at the point of a bayonet, and Younghusband himself was effectively reprimanded for the ill-judged massacre of 700 Tibetans at Chumi Shengo in April 1904. But what was done was done: for good or ill, Tibet had entered reluctantly into a client relationship with Great Britain that would eventually decide the course and context of the early Everest expeditions.[68]

Before withdrawing from Lhasa in September 1904, Younghusband detailed a small survey party under Captain Cecil Rawling up the Brahmaputra to the trading town of Gartok in western Tibet. Rawling's route took him through the fortress town of Lhatse Dzong (La-tzu) and over the Kara La (17,900ft), from where he and his chief surveyor, Captain C. H. D. Ryder, obtained a clear view of the Mahalangur Himal from a distance of fifty miles. "Towering up thousands of feet, a glittering pinnacle of snow, rose Everest," Rawling wrote,

> a giant amongst pigmies, and remarkable not only on account of its height, but for its perfect form. No other peaks lie near or threaten its supremacy. From its foot a rolling mass of hills stretch away in all directions, to the north dropping to the Dingri Plain, 15,000 feet below. To the east and west, but nowhere in its immediate vicinity, rise other great mountains of rock and snow, each beautiful in itself, but in no other way comparing with the famous peak in solemn grandeur. It is difficult to give an idea of its

stupendous height, its dazzling whiteness and overpowering size, for there is nothing in
the world to compare it with. Its northern face had the appearance of a sheer precipice,
but the distance was too great to decide upon this with certainty.[69]

If Everest was to be climbed, Rawling later concluded, it had to be by the relatively
gentle Northeast Ridge. But Curzon still held out hopes for the unseen southern side of the
mountain. In April 1905, after a four-year interval, he again urged Freshfield to organize
a joint Alpine Club/Royal Geographical Society expedition through Nepal. "It has always
seemed to me a reproach that with the second highest mountain in the world for the most
part in British territory and with the highest in a neighbouring and friendly state, we, the
mountaineers and pioneers par excellence of the universe, make no sustained and scientific
attempt to climb to the top of either of them," he wrote in near paraphrase of himself, and
to prove he was in earnest this time he offered to put £3,000 of his government's money
toward the expedition's expenses. Freshfield took the proposal to the Alpine Club, where
it received polite endorsement in the form of £100, but the Royal Geographical Society
remained essentially uninterested. "The main current of feeling here," wrote society president George Goldie to Curzon, "is that while the ascent of Mount Everest would be a very
sporting venture and might also yield answers to some interesting questions, it would have
to be treated as part of some wider (it could not well be loftier) geographical work."[70]

In August 1905, having lost his long struggle with Lord Kitchener for control of
the Indian Army, Curzon resigned his viceroyalty and returned to England. His successor,
Lord Minto, was a member of the Alpine Club and equally well disposed toward the ascent
of Everest, but when in December Balfour's Conservative government fell over tariff reform
and the austere John Morley succeeded St. John Brodrick at the India Office, the political
prospects for an expedition darkened. As befit the biographer and self-anointed torchbearer
of Gladstone, Morley was a "Little Englander" who deplored frontier adventurism of any
kind. In James Bryce, the new Irish secretary and also member of the Alpine Club, would-be
Himalayan mountaineers had a cabinet member more sympathetic to their hopes, and in
1906, when Charles Bruce proposed to lead a limited expedition to Everest in commemoration of the fiftieth anniversary of the founding of the Alpine Club, Freshfield appealed
to him directly. "I think you will agree it will be a sad exhibition of nervousness if such an
opportunity of exploring the highest mountains in our sphere of influence in the world,
is lost," he wrote. "The men and the money are not to be found everyday. I know well
that mountaineering has been discredited in India by Crowley and the Workmans. But it
will be hard if the right men are refused facilities which have been allowed to the wrong
ones. . . . If an English party do not go soon I have good reason to believe application will
be made on behalf of the Duke of the Abruzzi." In the end, however, even this appeal to
national ambition would not move Morley, who believed the proposed expedition violated
the spirit of the recently concluded Anglo-Russian Convention. In February he vetoed it
on "considerations of high Imperial policy."[71]

Thus denied all access to Everest, Bruce went instead in 1907 to British Garhwal with a strong party that included Arnold Mumm (a twenty-year Alpine veteran who in 1905 had joined Douglas Freshfield in an early expedition to East Africa's Ruwenzori range), Mumm's inseparable Swiss guide, Moritz Inderbinnen, the Brocherel brothers, Alexis and Henri, of Courmayeur, nine of Bruce's Gurkhas, and Tom Longstaff, who two years earlier had explored the eastern approaches to Nanda Devi and with the Brocherels attempted the remote peak of Gurla Mandhata (25,242ft/7,694m) on the Indian border of western Nepal. Bruce's objective—or rather, their common objective, for "we were that rare combination an integrated party without a 'leader,'" Longstaff said—was Trisul, the great trident of Lord Shiva that stands watch over the outer sanctuary of the goddess, Nanda Devi.[72]

From the district capital of Almora they moved north through the subtropical valleys of Kumaon into Garhwal and over the Kuari Pass (12,140ft) to Tapoban, the last sizable village before the Rishi Ganga and the Nanda Devi basin. They reached the cypress glade of Surain Thota, their base for Trisul, on May 8, too early to attempt the climb, so at Bruce's suggestion they killed time exploring the glacial valleys beneath Dunagiri and Changabang, two conspicuous giants of the northern sanctuary wall. On June 2, from "the fairy meadow of Dibrugheta," they crossed the Rishi torrent and pitched an Advanced Base Camp (Juniper Camp) at 13,100 feet in the Trisuli Nala. Bruce by this time had been hobbled by a bad knee, and Mumm (who for all his Alpine experience had turned out to be overrefined for the rough work of Himalayan exploration) had developed severe diarrhea, and so on June 12 it was left to Longstaff, the Brocherels, and the redoubtable Karbir (the best of Bruce's Gurkhas) to rush the summit from a camp on the glacier at 17,400 feet. Trisul, it turned out, was not a technically demanding mountain, but it was high, the highest mountain yet climbed (again discounting Graham's alleged ascent of Kabru in 1883), and its safe and successful ascent in 1907 not only vindicated Longstaff's faith in "rush tactics," it also tremendously encouraged those who would aim even higher.[73]

Ultimately of greater significance to the Everest story than Longstaff's ascent of Trisul, however, was the attempt a few months later of two little-known Norwegians, Carl Wilhelm Rubenson and Monrad-Aas (whose first name eludes us), on Kabru, the great southern satellite of Kangchenjunga on the Singalila Ridge in Sikkim. For not only did these two Scandinavian interlopers get within 100 feet of a higher and much more demanding mountain; they were also the first to discover and publicize the remarkable mountaineering abilities of the Sherpas, or "easterners," those distinctive and now-famous ethnic Tibetans whose forebears had crossed the Nangpa La into the Khumbu Valley of eastern Nepal from the mid-sixteenth century. Needless to say, Rubenson and Monrad-Aas did not find them there, in Nepal. Sherpas had been migrating to the Bengali hill town of Darjeeling for seasonal work since the mid-nineteenth century; by 1901, the Darjeeling district census counted 3,450 of them living year-round in and around the shantytown of Toong Soong Busti, just off the broad town square of Chowrasta. Like their distant cousins the Bhotias (literally, people of Bhot, or Tibet), the Sherpas initially worked as porters, rickshaw-wallahs,

or general day laborers in the rapidly growing tourist and government station. How precisely
Rubenson and Monrad-Aas happened on them they did not say, but on their return from
Kabru they singled them out from among their many types of native porter for particular
praise. "The natives whom we found most plucky were Nepalese Tibetans, the so-called
Sherpahs," Rubenson wrote with a deft English touch. "If they are properly taught the
use of ice axe and rope I believe that they will prove of more use out here than European
guides, as they are guides and coolies in one, and don't require any special attention. My
opinion is that if they get attached to you they will do anything."[74]

Here in passing amid an otherwise obscure report on a failed attempt on Kabru
is the first suggestion of what would prove the decisive conceptual breakthrough in the
organizational history of Himalayan mountaineering. But having said that much, Rubenson
said no more, and his prophecy went largely unnoticed. Charles Bruce was evidently aware
of the Sherpas by 1910, but attached as he was to his Gurkhas he was surprisingly slow to
recognize their unique qualities.[75] The man responsible for the lasting "discovery" of the
Sherpas, then, was no Norwegian, nor even (despite what some say) an Englishman, but a
Scotsman, an unassuming chemist whose remarkable (and remarkably unsung) climbing
career in the years before and after the First World War is inseparably bound up with the
history of Everest and of high-altitude physiology.

Born in Aberdeen in 1868, Alexander Mitchell Kellas was the second of the nine
children of James Fowler Kellas, secretary and superintendent of the Mercantile Marine
Company, and his wife, Mary Boyd. After grammar school he studied chemistry at Aberdeen University, Heriot-Watt College in Edinburgh, and then University College London,
where he was for a time a research assistant to Sir William Ramsay, the discoverer of argon
and the first British recipient (1904) of the Nobel Prize for Chemistry. He took his doctorate
in chemistry at Heidelberg University in 1897, and three years later was appointed lecturer
in chemistry at London's Middlesex Hospital Medical School, a post he held until incipient
mental illness forced his retirement in 1919. He never married. After chemistry, his one
passion in life was mountaineering, which he discovered in the Grampians of Highland
Scotland while a student at Aberdeen. By the time he went to Heidelberg he knew all the
mountains of Scotland and Wales intimately and had climbed extensively in Switzerland
also. Though not a particularly daring or innovative climber, more a hill walker than a
mountaineer, he was absolutely tireless. And because of his particular scientific background,
he was the first to think systematically and seriously about the effects of high altitude and
diminished atmospheric pressure on human physiology. He wrote very little, however, drew
little attention to himself, and thus has fallen into ill-deserved obscurity.[76]

Kellas first went out to India in 1907 at the relatively advanced age of thirty-nine.
With three local porters and two ponies in support, he spent two weeks trekking in the
Pir Panjal in Kashmir before heading east for Sikkim and the Zemu Glacier. Accompanied
by two unnamed Swiss guides, he tried three times to climb Simvu (22,348ft/6,812m), an
eastern satellite of Kangchenjunga, and twice to reach Nepal Gap, the conspicuous low

Alexander Kellas (1868–1921), 1921.
Reprinted by permission of the
Royal Geographical Society.

point on Kangchenjunga's north ridge between Gimmigela (then "the Twins") and Nepal Peak (22,670ft/6,910m). All of these efforts failed on account of fresh snow, bad weather, or (in the case of Nepal Gap) open and impassable crevasses. But overall the trip was "interesting enough as an introductory tour," and the repeated failure on Simvu especially, Kellas later said, "made me determined to return and try climbing with Nepalese coolies [i.e., Sherpas], who seemed to me more at home under the diminished pressure than my European companions."[77]

Two years later, in August 1909, Kellas returned to Sikkim and, accompanied this time only by native porters (of whom several were Sherpas) and Crowley's late nemesis, Rigo de Righi (whose experience on Kangchenjunga had evidently improved neither his personal disposition nor his adaptability to altitude), attempted the outlying peak of Pauhunri (23,375ft/7,125m) in the extreme northeast. Driven back by a storm at 21,700 feet, he then moved west into Lhonak, crossed the Jonsong La onto the Jonsong Glacier and with one unnamed Sherpa climbed Langpo Peak (22,814ft/6,954m) at the termination of Kangchenunga's great north ridge: an ascent "similar as regards difficulty," he later noted, "to that of the Zermatt Breithorn from the Leichenbratter hut."[78] On September 22 he reached 22,000 feet on the west ridge of Jonsong Peak, evidently alone. He then moved east of the Kangchenjunga massif, tried for a third time unsuccessfully to reach Nepal Gap, and made a second attempt on Pauhunri before retiring in October to Darjeeling. This, Kellas's first mountaineering expedition (as he saw it), stood fair comparison with any other to date, but true to form, he wrote nothing about it beyond a few itinerary notes ten years after the fact. The Workmans would have made a huge illustrated book of it, but next to them Kellas was a shy and self-effacing man who explored the Himalaya purely for exploration's sake.

Of Kellas's eventual eight seasons in the Himalaya, the most ambitious came in 1911, when he returned to Sikkim and made no fewer than ten first ascents above 20,000 feet, notably Sentinel Peak (21,292ft/6,490m), Chomoyummo (22,404ft/6,829m), and Pauhunri. Not content merely to climb, moreover, Kellas *traversed* these peaks, that is, he ascended one side and descended the other, a dangerous trick that even today's mountaineers seldom attempt. With him on most of these climbs were two Sherpas, Sonam and Tuny (or, sometimes, "Tuny's brother"), and by the end of the season Kellas was convinced of their qualities as "first rate climbers [who] could be used for serious climbing of the big peaks like Kangchenjunga, after proper training." He had also confirmed to his own satisfaction that what the world still knew as "mountain sickness" but he preferred to call "mountain lassitude" resulted from the body's diminished formation of oxyhemoglobin during respiration and that its effects could be countered by slow but steady acclimatization. In this respect, he queried Longstaff's recommendation of "rush tactics" and urged would-be Himalayan summiters to "camp high and start as early as you safely can." Technically, he advised nothing beyond careful adherence to "the ordinary mountaineering rules regarding use of ropes, etc." His originality lay rather in his ability to live and travel lightly off the land in perfect partnership with the Sherpas. Though a member of the Alpine Club, he generally avoided "society," in the colonial sense of the word, and he positively abhorred publicity.

> He who first met the Highland's swelling blue
> Will love each peak that shows a kindred hue
> Hail in each crag a friend's familiar face
> and clasp the mountain in his mind's embrace,

Byron had written a year or two before his death in 1824, and it was in this solitary and romantic spirit that Kellas, chemist though he was, embraced what he called "the most philosophical sport in the world."[79]

In 1912 Kellas returned to Sikkim for a fourth time with two Sherpas—Nema and the improbably named Anderkyow—and finding Kangchenjunga in deplorable condition settled instead for Kangchengyao (22,601ft/6,889m), a lesser outlier on the main Himalayan axis. Increasingly now his thoughts were turning to Everest and the "Chomokankar or Chomo Langmo group" (as he called it, in deference to native nomenclature) to the west. In 1911 he had been frustrated by his failure even to catch a glimpse of the Everest massif and so dispatched one of his Sherpas to photograph the eastern approaches: an interesting reversion to the clandestine tactics of the Indian Survey. He knew of course of the political prohibitions on travel in Tibet and Nepal, but he did not much respect them, and at some unknown time he evidently laid plans for a Sherpa-supported furtive approach by way of Kharta and the Kama Valley. "It was a most elaborately detailed plan; thought out to the last ounce of food and water," Kellas's friend John Baptiste Noel later recalled. Unbeknownst to Kellas, Noel himself, then a handsome young lieutenant in the East Yorkshire Regiment, had in 1913 disguised himself as an Indian Muslim and gotten within forty miles—nearest yet—of Everest from the east before being apprehended and turned back to Darjeeling by a company of Tibetan soldiers. Back in London, Noel and Kellas eventually compared notes on the northern and eastern approaches and resolved to attempt a furtive reconnaissance of Everest together as soon as mutual circumstances permitted.[80]

Meanwhile, all efforts to gain access to Everest by official means had met with continued frustration. In the winter of 1908, at the British Residency in Kathmandu, Charles Bruce raised the subject directly with the Rana prime minister, Maharajah Chandra Shamsher, who initially seemed well disposed and in fact himself proposed, according to Bruce, a joint Anglo-Nepalese expedition via Hanuman Nagar and the Dudh Kosi. But Chandra's writ was not law in the Nepalese Durbar, and on this point it soon ran up against what Longstaff described as insuperable political and religious prejudices. The resident advised against pressing the case. "It is of course extremely dull and tiresome here and it perhaps would be interesting to go to places hitherto unvisited by white men," he wrote to the Foreign Office from Kathmandu. "But I see no good to be got out of [an expedition to Everest] for the Government, and the personal satisfaction is not to be considered in a matter of this sort." Curzon of course could not have disagreed more; he thought it "the duty of the Englishman if possible to win the tops before anyone else," and in June 1909 he appealed unavailingly on Bruce's behalf to Morley, who despite lending an interested ear ultimately refused once again to intervene.[81]

Two and a half years later an era closed in the history of modern exploration when first Roald Amundsen and then Robert Falcon Scott reached the South Pole. Robert Peary had already claimed to have reached the geographic North Pole in 1909 (as indeed had another American, Frederick Cook), but it was Amundsen's undisputed conquest of the South Pole and, even more, the poignant defeat and death in retreat of Robert Scott that seized the public imagination and indirectly sealed Mount Everest's fate. For one thing, with the capture of the poles the exploratory impulse in all its forms—national, individual, and institutional—needed another virgin prize, and this it found in the Himalaya, henceforth analogously styled "the third pole." Furthermore, the enormous publicity surrounding "the race to the pole" together with the extravagant national commemoration of Scott's martyrdom suggested an entire rhetoric in which to couch Himalayan aspiration, a high rhetoric of struggle and honor and fellowship and sacrifice that no one had as yet fully deployed.

In this respect, of course, the tragedy of Scott merely anticipated the greater tragedy of his entire generation. In 1913, with the interest and support this time of the Royal Geographical Society, Cecil Rawling (late of the Younghusband mission to Lhasa) outlined plans for an Everest reconnaissance the following year that the India Office surprisingly did not reject out of hand. But nor had it yet approved them when, on June 28, 1914, a young Bosnian nationalist named Gavrilo Princip assassinated the Archduke Franz Ferdinand, heir to the Austro-Hungarian throne, in Sarajevo. Five weeks later, all Europe was at war, Rawling was in France, Bruce was in Egypt, Noel had left his Indian regiment for the King's Own Yorkshire light infantry, and no one, no one anywhere, was thinking about Mount Everest. The First World War scuttled all plans for Himalayan exploration and then, after four long harrowing years, shaped the military style and spirit in which it would resume.

CHAPTER THREE

"Because It Is There"
George Mallory and the Fight for Everest
1921–1924

Armistice Day—November 11, 1918—found First Lieutenant George Herbert Leigh Mallory comfortably behind the lines with the 515th Siege Battery between Arras and the Channel coast. All the fighting of late had been farther south, and Mallory had suffered only the routine tedium of life in a quiet sector of the western front. Still, he had been on the Somme in 1916, had lost friends in plenty, had seen and endured the Great War at its worst, and he had every reason to feel surprise at finding himself a survivor. "The prevalent feeling I make out, and in part my own, is simply the elation that comes after a hard game or race of supreme importance, won after a struggle in which everyone has expended himself to the last ounce," he wrote to his wife, Ruth, then home caring for their two small children at Westbrook in the Wey Valley. Like many of the Great War generation, Mallory had grown up with what he called "a disgust for the appearances of civilisation so intense that it was an ever-present spiritual discomfort, a sort of malaise that made us positively unhappy." But now, on November 11, life presented itself as a gift very much worth having. "What a wonderful life we will have together! What a lovely thing we *must* make of such a gift!" he wrote Ruth, as he eagerly awaited his demobilization and restoration to the quiet routines of husband, father, and teacher.[1]

In London, meanwhile, along the stately corridors of the Royal Geographical Society's imposing new home at Lowther Lodge, Kensington, news of the Armistice quickly revived interest in Cecil Rawling's long-deferred plans for Mount Everest. Unfortunately, Rawling himself was now dead, killed in the Ypres Salient in October 1917. John Noel, Tom Longstaff (who spent the last years of the war as assistant commandant of Gilgit Scouts), and Alexander Kellas had survived, but many experienced officers of the Indian Survey—still in those days the likeliest recruits to any Himalayan expedition—had been killed, along with many promising young British Alpinists (including Mallory's sometime partner Siegfried Herford). Charles Bruce, absent Rawling the logical leader of an Everest expedition, had been seriously wounded at Gallipoli, and Geoffrey Winthrop Young,

Mallory's mentor and arguably the greatest British climber of his time, had lost a leg while serving with an ambulance unit on the Isonzo front in Italy. In short, the war had severely depleted the ranks of potential Everest climbers. Far from discouraging the idea, however, the death and maiming of so many men gave the ascent of Everest a kind of memorial urgency. No mere geographer's or climber's whim, Everest became, after the war, a national imperative, a supremely elevated point of redemption for a sacrificed generation.

Hardly was the ink dry on the Armistice, then, before Sir Thomas Holdich, president of the Royal Geographical Society, wrote to Edwin Montagu, Lloyd George's secretary of state for India, seeking authority for an exploration of the Everest region under the combined sponsorship of the Royal Geographical Society and the Alpine Club. Montagu forwarded the request to the viceroy, Lord Chelmsford (with whom he had just initiated a policy of federal self-government for India), noting only that "a task of such magnitude and geographical importance, if it is to be undertaken at all, should be entrusted to qualified British explorers acting under the highest geographical auspices of the British Empire." Thus far Chelmsford agreed, but he worried that any such expedition might interfere with his plans to install wireless surveillance stations at Gyantse and Lhasa. Having lost the Russian bogeyman to revolution and civil war, the government of India had contrived to find a new one in expansionist Japan and once again forbade the expedition on grounds of imperial policy. "However much one may sympathise with the desire to conquer Mt. Everest," one India Office mandarin noted in April 1919, "the results of such a conquest would be largely academic and ought not to weigh against a means of minimizing Japanese influence in Tibet."[2]

Sensing here a less than absolute refusal, supporters of the expedition kept the pressure on throughout the immediate postwar period. At a highly publicized Royal Geographical Society lecture in March 1919, John Noel for the first time described his illicit approach to Everest in 1913 and made a passionate case for an ascent from the north in memory of Rawling. "Now that the poles have been reached," he argued, in what became a conventional justification, "the next and equally important task is the exploration and mapping of Mount Everest." Three months later, Sir Francis Younghusband, the great soldier-explorer who had led the armed mission to Lhasa in 1904, acceded to the presidency of the "Jog" (as he called it), determined to make "this Everest venture" the main feature of his tenure. "If I am asked what is the use of climbing this highest mountain," Younghusband proclaimed in his inaugural address, to the chagrin of the scientifically minded, "I reply, No use at all: no more use than kicking a football about, or dancing, or playing the piano, or writing a poem, or painting a picture." The climb would simply "elevate the human spirit" (so to speak) and reassure men that they were "getting the upper hand on the earth [and] acquiring a true mastery of their surroundings."[3]

Public response to the idea of climbing Everest at this embryonic stage was mixed. The newspapers, sensing a story, were keen, though *Punch* lampooned the "Himalayans at Play" and the London *Daily News,* long ahead of its time, wished that "some corner of the globe would be preserved for ever inviolate." Among Britons generally, Everest had not as yet the mystery and allure of the poles, but it was sufficiently vast, forbidding, cold, and remote to be of some interest, especially in its unconquered state, and Younghusband felt confident of success in his appeal to national ambition. The government remained wary, but in the summer of 1920 the India Office agreed to allow Lieutenant Colonel Charles Howard-Bury, an Anglo-Irish landowner of suitably aristocratic pedigree, to proceed to India at his own expense to confer with the viceroy and other highly placed officials including Charles Bell, the British agent in Sikkim and the government of India's unofficial representative to the Dalai Lama in Lhasa. Bell himself disapproved of the proposed expedition as likely to offend the religious and political sensibilities of the Tibetans. "[They] will not believe that the explorations are carried out only in the interests of geographical knowledge and science," he told the viceroy. "They will suspect that there is something behind what we tell them." But he agreed to make the case to the Dalai Lama in quiet conjunction with a long-standing but as yet unfulfilled British promise to supply Tibet with weapons. "I explained that the ascent was expected to have scientific results that would benefit humanity, and that a good many people in Britain wanted Britons to be the first to climb the highest mountain in the world," Bell later recalled, in tones that suggest his own lingering skepticism and perhaps his surprise when His Holiness offered no objection. Once assured of Tibetan consent, the viceroy offered his own in turn, and the expedition was on. The news reached London on December 20, 1920.[4]

A few months earlier the Royal Geographical Society's Everest Expedition Committee had resolved "that the principal object of the expedition should be the ascent of Mount Everest, to which all preliminary reconnaissance and survey should be directed." But now, with official sanction actually in hand, disagreement arose over what precisely the expedition was about. The evangelical Younghusband saw it as something of a secular pilgrimage intended to dispel "the ridiculous idea of the littleness of man." He wanted the mountain climbed for its own sake. But in the society at large, as Younghusband later recalled, "there still lingered the notion that climbing Mount Everest was sensational but not 'scientific.' If it were a matter of making a *map* of the region, then the project should be encouraged. If it were a question merely of climbing the mountain, then it should be left to mountaineers and not absorb the attention of a scientific body like the Royal Geographical Society." Within the Alpine Club, needless to say, feeling unanimously favored the climb, and ultimately the climbing imperative prevailed. A joint Royal Geographical Society and Alpine Club committee convened for the first time on January 12, 1921 and formally gave "the ascent of Mount Everest" priority over the geological, meteorological, and botanical goals of the expedition.[5] Science still had its well-placed champions, however, both on the joint committee and on the expedition itself, and in looking to explain the successive failures of these early Everest efforts, one can reasonably begin with some residual uncertainty, even conflict of purpose.

No such conflict found its way into the newspapers, though. "Mount Everest to

Be Scaled," read an early headline in the *Morning Post,* and but for a handful of dramatic variations on "scaled"—assaulted, assailed, defied, challenged—all the other dailies followed this simplified line. The climbing party had not even been named yet; the summit remained a remote vision; but already in January 1921 virtually all the clichés that we have used ever since to evoke the "assault on Everest" had been assembled in the public mind. Consider this passage from (somewhat improbably) the *Lady's Pictorial* of January 22, 1921:

> There are still worlds to conquer and adventure to be made that will demand endurance and courage. Some folk think we have reached the limit in exploration. Not so. There is Mount Everest yet to be scaled. Never has the foot of man trodden its snowy heights, the highest in the world. Who first faces and triumphs over the intense cold, avalanches, terrific winds, blinding snowstorms, loneliness, and unknown other perils of this mountain of mystery and magic will be forever famous. Already volunteers are forthcoming. What an adventure! What a thrilling story to tell! But, alas! What certain sacrifice of life must be made in the effort.[6]

One might expect the traumatic and disillusioning experience of the western front to have forever discredited such innocent and archaic sentiment as this in favor of irony, cynicism, and world-weariness. But what do we have here, if not the spirit of August 1914 revived and deployed in another context? Volunteers, adventure, conquest, sacrifice: for the *Lady's Pictorial,* as for the British press generally, the impending attempt on Everest elided easily with the war and seemed to afford a few lucky survivors one more chance to die gracefully for their country.

But who were the lucky few to be? From the outset, Younghusband had conceived of the expedition in large-scale, military terms, and the logical choice of leader, in his mind as well as everyone else's, was Charles Bruce, the big and boisterous brigadier general who had been with both Conway in the Karakoram and Mummery on Nanga Parbat and had a unique reputation as a popular, fatherlike leader of native regiments. "Bruce's knowledge of the Gurkhas and their dialects makes him the one man who could get natives to work at over 20,000 feet," Douglas Freshfield had assured Lord Curzon as early as 1906, and now the British public seized on him as "The Man to Conquer Everest." As it happened, though, Bruce had just accepted command of the Glamorganshire Territorials and was unavailable. In his place the Everest Committee settled on Howard-Bury, who had already been of such diplomatic service to the expedition. Howard-Bury was no mountaineer, at least not "in the Alpine Club sense of the word," as Younghusband put it, but he was an unassailably pukka sahib with considerable Himalayan experience and a private fortune to boot.[7] At a time when the ethic of the gentleman-amateur still obtained in British sporting and scientific circles, Howard-Bury's willingness to undertake the leadership of the expedition at his own expense naturally appealed to the committee, though it complicated the leader's relations with some of the expedition's younger members, who expected compensation for their services.

To accompany Howard-Bury, the committee chose a party that reflected the joint, not to say divided spirit of the undertaking. There were two surveyors, Henry Morshead, a veteran explorer who had reached 23,420 feet on Kamet in 1920, and Oliver Wheeler, an authority on the new method of photogrammetric surveying and, as a Canadian, the Everest Committee's one colonial concession; one geologist, A. M. Heron, whose energetic shoveling was soon to arouse the religious suspicions of the Tibetans; one doctor-*cum*-naturalist, Alexander Wollaston, a veteran of the Ruwenzori who won Howard-Bury's respect by paying his own way; and four climbers led by Harold Raeburn, a tough and obstinate Scotsman who had made the first solo traverse of the Meije in the Dauphiné Alps and reached 21,000 feet on Kangchenjunga. Kellas, as a leading authority on high-altitude physiology and one of the most experienced Himalayan climbers living, was from the beginning an inescapable choice. But he was old and in ill health, exhausted, so it was later said, by a relentless series of climbs in the Garhwal and Sikkim Himalaya the previous year. Neither he nor Raeburn, who at fifty-six was also old by climbing standards, was expected to go very high on Everest. "For the higher climbing that might be necessary," Younghusband recalled, "one name was immediately mentioned by the Alpine Club members, and that name was Mallory."[8]

Mallory of Everest

With the possible exception of the peculiarly assonant "Hillary," no name is so indelibly associated with the world's highest mountain as that of George Mallory. He is "Mallory of Everest," as the title of one of many biographies has it. Everest is "Mallory's mountain," Sir Edmund Hillary once generously said, and few of the thousand-some odd people who have followed Hillary and Tenzing to the top since 1953 would disagree. So strong is the claim that in retrospect the choice of Mallory in 1921 seems inevitable, the necessary prelude to one man's date with destiny. In fact it was surprising in several respects. Mallory had no Himalayan experience whatsoever, and his Alpine record, while perfectly respectable, was hardly remarkable. A competent rather than a brilliant or innovative climber, he had yet to fulfill his mountaineering potential.[9] Moreover, he had a rebellious, countercultural disposition that ill suited the high-Tory style of the expedition. Howard-Bury disliked him, as did Arthur Hinks, the brilliant and formidable secretary of the Royal Geographical Society who was to dominate the proceedings of the Everest Committee for the next twenty years. But Mallory had an undeniable air about him that inspired the Alpine Club's confidence, and whatever his limitations or abilities as a climber, certainly he came to grips with Everest as no other human ever has. He was the central, tragic protagonist of what Younghusband called "the epic of Everest" and the first (and still most compelling) celebrity of Himalayan mountaineering.

An obscure thirty-five-year-old schoolmaster when his Tibetan odyssey began, George Herbert Leigh Mallory was in many respects a typical child of the late-Victorian middle class. He was born in June 1886 at Mobberley, a prosperous, leafy village fifteen miles south of Manchester, in Cheshire. His father, Rev. Herbert Leigh Mallory, was "a thoroughly conventional parson who expected things to go on pretty much in the usual way," as Mallory's son-in-law and first biographer David Robertson put it. His mother, Annie Jebb, on the other hand, while in most respects the epitome of domestic respectability, combined chaotic forgetfulness with a decidedly unconventional spirit of adventure: two qualities she imparted in equal and fateful measure to her eldest son. "We were rather exceptionally unruly children," George's sister Avie once recalled of the four of them, but George especially "had the knack of making things exciting and often rather dangerous."[10] He was forever fording swollen streams, braving incoming tides, dodging approaching trains, and so on. And he climbed everything that it was at all possible to climb: trees, walls, cliffs, downspouts, and (on one suspiciously legendary occasion) the prominent square stone tower of St. Wilfrid's, his father's parish church.

In September 1900, already a veteran of two different boarding establishments, George won a mathematics scholarship to Winchester, after Eton the most renowned and competitive of English public schools. Here he attracted the attention of R. L. G. Irving, a youthful and energetic college tutor—later a tireless contributor to mountaineering literature—who happened then to be on the prowl for an Alpine climbing partner. George had never seen a mountain, much less climbed one, but he was tall, lithe, graceful, and willing, and for Irving that—added to a demonstrated knack for climbing drainpipes—was recommendation enough. Accompanied by Mallory's friend and schoolmate Harry Gibson, the two men went to Switzerland in August 1904 and indulged in a most unconventional (and thus controversial) orgy of guideless ascents, beginning with the Vélan, graduating to the Grand Combin and the Dufourspitze, and culminating in a harrowing, storm-tossed traverse of Mont Blanc (15,774ft/4,808m) from the Dôme Hut to the Grand Mulets. George loved it all, but it was this climactic traverse of Mont Blanc, "carried through after long imprisonment by storms on a few biscuits and scrapings of honey," that hooked him on climbing forever. "From that day," Irving later recalled, "it was certain that he had found in snow mountains the perfect medium for the expression of his physical and spiritual being."[11]

In 1905, having failed the Woolwich entrance examination the previous year and thus ruined his chances of a military career—something he did not really want anyway—Mallory went up to Magdalene College, Cambridge, on a history scholarship. History had been an afterthought, a desperate, eleventh-hour substitute for mathematics, and despite the close, even loving encouragement of his tutor, Arthur Benson—the first of his many Cambridge conquests—Mallory never really took to it. He did not do especially well on either part of the History Tripos. But he read widely and creatively, developed a talent for writing, conversation, and debate, and for the Members' Prize Essay made a good start on what would ultimately become a perfectly reputable book on James Boswell.[12] Moreover, simply to be at Cambridge in these heady years of Edwardian innovation amounted to a considerable education. The nation generally was in a restive mood, as the Liberal landslide of 1906 was shortly to prove. But at Cambridge things were downright subversive, as a whole generation of undergraduates shook off Victorian constraints and embraced causes ranging from women's suffrage to free love.

Mallory's introduction to this charged atmosphere came in February 1907 when he was admitted to the Trumpington Street salon of Charles Sayle, librarian, bibliophile, and one of the quintessential figures of Cambridge in the years before the First World War, when, as Benson later said, it was a place "of books, music, and beautiful young men." Through Sayle, Mallory met Jacques Raverat, then studying mathematics at Emmanuel but soon to become a painter on the outer orbit of the Bloomsbury Group, Charles Darwin, the grandson of the great biologist and a correspondingly free thinker, Geoffrey Keynes, aspiring surgeon and the younger brother of the economist, and Rupert Brooke, the promising young poet whose good looks, sensual energy, and magnetic charm made him the stuff of legend even before he died a martyr's death on Scyros in 1915. Together these and many others constituted what Cottie Sanders (a climber and novelist better known to the literary world by her pseudonym of Ann Bridge and to the social world by her married name of Mary O'Malley) called the Cambridge School of Friendship. "They held personal relationships as so important that they held only a few other things as being of any importance whatever," Sanders later recalled. "Conventional inessentials simply had no meaning for them. They were extraordinarily attached to one another; they stuck closer than brothers; there was, literally, nothing they wouldn't do for one another. They enjoyed each other furiously; delightedly, they examined and explored every means of knowing people better and liking them more, from the simplest pleasures of food and exercise taken together to the final closeness of the common acceptance of some sorrow or some truth."[13]

The affinity with Bloomsbury here is striking, and given the proximity of family and college connections, Mallory inevitably came to the attention of this slightly older, intellectually more formidable Cambridge coterie. "Mon dieu!—George Mallory!" Lytton Strachey famously exclaimed on first meeting this paragon. "When that's been written, what more need be said? My hand trembles, my heart palpitates, my whole being swoons away at the words—oh heavens! heavens!"[14] But it was James Strachey, the future translator of Freud, and not his older brother Lytton who evidently initiated Mallory into the pleasures of "the higher sodomy," as Bloomsbury called it. The precise nature of "l'affaire George" is unclear and ultimately uninteresting. What is interesting and of some significance to the history of Himalayan mountaineering is that George Mallory emerged onto Everest from a point of cultural and political rebellion. He was a Fabian socialist who read H. G. Wells, grew his hair long, dressed peculiarly (black flannel shirts and colored ties), canvassed for women's suffrage, slept with men, and posed for a series of sensual portraits by Duncan Grant. None of this made it into the funeral orations of 1924, but perhaps it should have, for to some extent it determined the kind of climber Mallory was and the approach he would ultimately take to "his" mountain.

There was, in fact, a close association between mountain climbing, understood not simply as a recreational activity but a higher art form, and the Cambridge School of Friendship. Charles Sayle, the Trumpington Street *salonnier,* was a founding member of the Climbers' Club, a group devoted to mountaineering at home in the rocky wilds of north Wales and Cumbria. At his encouragement, Mallory, Geoffrey Keynes, and Hugh Wilson (another member of "Sayle's menagerie" and a lively antiphilistine) climbed in Wales together over the long vacations in 1907 and 1908 and put up a number of classic routes, among them the famously impossible Slab Climb on Lliwedd that, according to legend, Mallory improvised in failing light in order to retrieve a pipe he had absentmindedly left behind on a ledge. Rupert Brooke was more hiker than climber, and Bloomsbury was generally too cerebral, not to say effete, for the mountains. On being shown the Black Cuillin on Skye, Lytton Strachey pronounced them, in a shrill falsetto, "*simply absurd.*" But Geoffrey Keynes's brother Maynard climbed occasionally in the Alps, Duncan Grant at least once in Wales. And their friends Adrian, Vanessa, and Virginia Stephen (later Woolf), whose homes in Fitzroy and Brunswick squares were the formative epicenters of the Bloomsbury Group, were of course the children of Sir Leslie Stephen, onetime president of the Alpine Club and the author of *The Playground of Europe,* the original mountaineering classic. "It would have been difficult, in fact," David Robertson observes, "to move for long in any Cambridge intellectual circle without encountering someone who climbed or had a climber's blood in him."[15]

And so it happened that in February 1909, Maynard Keynes (an incurable matchmaker) introduced Mallory to Geoffrey Winthrop Young, formerly of Marlborough and Trinity, Keynes's onetime teacher at Eton, and now, at age thirty-three, Great Britain's foremost Alpine mountaineer. The introduction might have gone badly: the preceding December Young had been one of fourteen members of the Alpine Club to deprecate publicly R. L. G. Irving's guideless escapades with Mallory and other students in the Alps. But of course on meeting Mallory, Young too was smitten, moved privately to ecstasies on the "six feet of deer-like power concordant with the perfect oval of the face, the classic profile and long, oval, violet eyes" and the "gravely beautiful tenor voice." He at once invited Mallory to join his famous Easter climbing party at Pen-y-Pass, on the Pass of Llanberis, the rugged heart of Snowdonia. Here the company included several legends of British climbing, from J. M. A. Thomson, who had invented and named the Avalanche Route on Lliwedd in 1907, to Oscar Eckenstein, two-time veteran of the Karakoram. But Mallory was unintimidated. "He swung up rock with a long thigh, a lifted knee, and a ripple of irresistible movement," Young later recalled. "A perfect physique and a pursuing mind came together as it were in a singleness of power, as he rushed into motion."[16]

The following summer, having passed muster at Pen-y-Pass, Mallory joined Young and Donald Robertson for an Alpine season marked, Young later wrote, by "some hairbreadth happenings which are incidental to alpine inexperience." For all his catlike agility and balance, Mallory, it turned out, was dangerously forgetful of details, as when, on one famous occasion, he set off on a perilous descending pitch without tying in to the rope. He

George Mallory (right) and Siegfried Herford at Pen-y-Pass, 1913. Photograph by Geoffrey Winthrop Young. Reprinted by permission of the Alpine Club Library.

survived his share of falls, though, and by the end of the year had come to think of climbing not as a diversion or recreation but as a calling, an essential part of his psychological and spiritual being. It would not pay the bills, though (not yet, anyway), and on coming down from Cambridge in 1909, Mallory faced the persistent question of what to do with his life. Two years earlier he had thought briefly of following his father into holy orders. But now, though he retained a surprisingly conventional Christian faith, he found he could not abide the company of parsons. "They're excessively good, most of them, much better than I can ever hope to be," he told his tutor, Arthur Benson; "but their sense of goodness seems sometimes to displace their reason."[17] As for schoolmasters, they were largely priggish fools, but Mallory had a Victorian faith in the civilizing force of education, and in September 1910, after a long continental interlude spent climbing and learning French, he accepted a probationary appointment at Charterhouse, a reasonably well-known public school in rural Surrey.

Looking back on these days from the distance of 1924—the year in which Mallory died—Virginia Woolf famously remarked that "on or about December 1910 human character changed."[18] She was thinking specifically of the arrival of Samuel Butler and Bernard Shaw on the literary scene and of the great postimpressionist exhibition that had opened at the Grafton Galleries the preceding November and marked the definitive arrival of modernist art in England. But she knew perfectly well that December 1910 had also seen the climax of a constitutional crisis over the authority of the House of Lords and the second general election of that year. In fact the whole period from the death of King Edward VII in May 1910 to the outbreak of war in August 1914, while Mallory settled uncomfortably into the humdrum life of a schoolmaster, was one of the most tumultuous in British history, as trades unionists, Irish nationalists, Ulster Loyalists, and militant feminists separately but simultaneously trained their rebellious energies on Westminster and threatened to pitch the country into anarchy and civil war. Mallory tried to acknowledge all this in his teaching, tried, that is, to introduce modern art, thought, and politics into an arid curriculum still dominated by Latin and Greek, but with limited success. According to Robert Graves he was wasted at Charterhouse, where "the boys generally despised him as neither a disciplinarian nor interested in cricket or football." Eventually "the falseness of his position told on his temper," Graves recalled; "yet he always managed to find four or five boys who were, like him, out of their element, befriending and making life tolerable for them."[19]

Mallory's intimacy with the Bloomsbury Group deepened in the years after Cambridge. Lytton Strachey, Maynard Keynes, and Duncan Grant all visited him at Charterhouse and competed and connived for his affections. Geoffrey Young remained a confused cross between climbing partner, mentor, and lover. By way of a close friendship with Cottie Sanders, however, Mallory came to a belated appreciation of women, and in 1914 the heterosexual side of his nature asserted itself permanently when he met and fell in love with Ruth Turner, the middle daughter of Thackeray Turner, a well-known architect and onetime associate of the great designer-craftsman-poet-rebel William Morris. She was not well read and took little interest in politics. But Ruth Turner shared Mallory's love of the outdoors. She had a flair for language, an artistic sensibility, a generous, sympathetic, uninhibited nature, and a Botticellian beauty to match Mallory's own. "Seldom were two people more perfectly adapted to the purpose of modifying, rounding off, and completing each other," David Pye recalled, and even Mallory's masculine suitors had to rejoice in the match. "It is *big,* just *big,* that nature," wrote Geoffrey Young on meeting Ruth. "I could *shout.*"[20] Both he and Duncan Grant were in attendance—Young as best man—when George and Ruth were married by George's father on July 29, 1914.

Four days later the German Army crossed the Belgian frontier and England was at war. Some of Mallory's closest friends—Rupert Brooke, Robert Graves, Geoffrey Young, Geoffrey Keynes—were among those millions who immediately answered the call to serve, and Mallory felt similarly compelled, not by some unquestioning patriotism but by the millennial spirit of the great adventure. "I feel almost as if a tide of centuries has swept over us in the last fortnight," he wrote to a friend in mid-August. "We are basking in the sun and watching the dawn of tremendous hopes." Unfortunately, Mallory's was one of those "reserved" occupations deemed essential for home service, and he was quite powerless to join up until his headmaster could replace him in the classroom. Meanwhile, he tried to appease his guilty conscience by giving lectures on the war and composing a pamphlet—*War*

Work for Boys and Girls—in which he exhorted children to eschew jingoism in favor of self-discipline, spiritual growth, and clear thought. He and Ruth were blissfully happy. They went climbing together in the Lake District and Wales; they moved into a new house in Godalming in March 1915; in September they had their first child, Frances Clare. But as the war dragged on, and friends and students continued to die, Mallory's impatience to be a part of it grew. "There's something indecent, when so many friends have been enduring so many horrors, in just going on at one's job, quite happy and prosperous," he wrote Arthur Benson on the day he learned of Rupert Brooke's death.[21] Finally, just before England's epochal resort to conscription in January 1916, Mallory's headmaster consented to his replacement at Charterhouse, and he accepted a commission in the Royal Garrison Artillery. After a crash course in gunnery at Weymouth, he crossed to Le Havre on May 4, 1916 and reported to the Fortieth Siege Battery, just north of Armentières.

At the front he immediately felt the "irreconcilable wrongness" of war. "When I have looked upon the good green and blossom of spring in this beautiful country and seen beautiful buildings, war has seemed more than ever inconceivable and monstrous," he told Ruth. Even so, after a few weeks of desultory shelling and foraging for food behind the lines, he felt eager for some real action, and in June he found it when his battery moved south into Picardy to join in the Somme offensive. He experienced the unprecedented horrors of July 1, 1916 from the relative safety of the artillery lines. "It is a battle of which we see as it were only the rim of a seething cauldron," he wrote.[22] But in the months to come, as the British Fourth Army obstinately persisted in its futile assaults on the impregnable German lines, Mallory narrowly escaped death on several occasions while manning forward observation posts or laying telephone wire to the trenches. It reminded him of climbing: the same sense of knife-edge danger, the same complete trust in one's companions. "It is curious how often I am taken back to the Alps, partly through an association in the code of conduct," he told Ruth. His nerves, he found to his relief, were "unaffected by the horrible." But "'Oh! The pity of it!' I very often exclaim when I see the dead lying out, and anger when I see corpses quite inexcusably not buried."[23]

On September 26, three months into the Somme offensive, the British finally took Thiepval, their objective on the first day. No breakthrough followed, however, and in the autumn rains the offensive sputtered to an inconclusive close. After a well-earned Christmas leave and a frustrating spell at brigade headquarters three miles behind the lines, Mallory returned to his battery in March 1917. These were quieter days on the western front; his routine duties allowed him ample time to read—H. G. Wells, Henry James, George Eliot, and Shakespeare—to write almost daily to Ruth, and to reflect on life after the war. In May an old climbing injury to his ankle forced him home for surgery and a long convalescence at Westbrook. The news that Geoffrey Young had lost a leg at Monte San Gabriele cast a pall over the birth of Mallory's second daughter, Beridge, in September and probably inspired the writing of the best of his climbing essays, a spiritual account of his 1911 ascent of Mont Blanc by the eastern buttress of Mont Maudit. "Have we vanquished an enemy?"

Mallory famously asks himself. "None but ourselves. Have we gained a success? That word means nothing here. Have we won a kingdom? No . . . and yes. We have achieved an ultimate satisfaction . . . fulfilled a destiny. . . . To struggle and to understand—never this last without the other; such is the ultimate law."[24]

In January 1918, reports of Robert Graves's death the preceding year having fortunately been exaggerated, Mallory served as best man at Graves's ill-fated marriage to Nancy Nicholson. To his intense frustration, he spent the following spring and summer "frittering away days and weeks in England as one can only do in the Army." By the time he got back to France in September 1918, the German offensives had expired, the Americans were in the line, and the war was almost over. "I should have liked to return home, if not a hero, at least a man of arms more tried than I have been," he confessed to his father; "my share has been too small; my instinct now is to want more fighting." News of the Armistice naturally moved him to relief and "untroubled joy." But the war on the whole had let him down and left him with a vague sense of unappeased longing.[25]

Unlike the shell-shocked Robert Graves, who came back unable to sleep, to use a telephone, to travel by train, or to see more than two people in a day, Mallory resumed the routines of life without outward difficulty. But he found teaching ever more a drag on his spirits and yearned for some larger way to make his mark. What he would most have liked was to be a writer—a novelist, perhaps, or a notable historian. But the sad truth, as Maynard Keynes once observed to Geoffrey Young, was that Mallory lacked brilliance; despite the company he kept, he was not an intellectual. He did have some interesting ideas about educational reform, and during the war he had attempted to commit some of them to paper. After the war he, Geoffrey Young, and David Pye talked briefly about opening a school of their own that would break down the distinction between work and play, lessons and leisure, and teach arts and crafts, farming, and the obligations of citizenship to pupils of all social classes. But nothing came of it. Young, meanwhile, despite the loss of a leg, had resumed his climbing parties at Pen-y-Pass. George and Ruth joined him there at Easter 1919, and George alone in 1920, when Ruth was pregnant with their third child, John. In the summer of 1919 Mallory returned for the first time in seven years to the Alps, where Young found that his climbing style had decidedly matured. "His early idea of 'leadership,'" Young wrote, "was to go 'over the top' at the first rush. He lacked the detachment of an officer."[26] Now, it seemed, the war and marriage had aged him: he climbed more carefully, more mindfully, more deliberately.

In June 1920, his idea of opening a "school of the future" having foundered, Mallory wrote to Gilbert Murray, Regius Professor of Greek at Oxford University and secretary of the League of Nations Union, to ask if the union had any use for his services. "Perhaps the most important thing about me which I ought to tell you is that I think and feel passionately about international politics," he wrote, and every indication is that this was true. Like most on the English left, Mallory had been appalled by the vindictive spirit of the Treaty of Versailles. His friend Maynard Keynes's book *The Economic Consequences of the Peace* (1919) had persuaded him that the reparations clauses, if enforced, threatened the survival of German democracy and thereby the peace of Europe. He was eager now to get involved in some form of work that promoted international reconciliation and social reform. Ireland too was much on his mind, as in the aftermath of war it fell into turmoil, terror, and civil war. In December 1920 he went to Ireland, to see the terror firsthand and—who knows?—perhaps deliberately to put himself in the way of danger, which he certainly did. His feelings were mixed: there had been terrible atrocity and wrongdoing on both the Republican and Unionist sides, he found. "But national aspirations, a passionate idealism, are to be found only on one side," he wrote. "It is to this fact that Irishmen appeal when they exclaim, 'If only people in England knew! If only they would come and see!'" Mallory went and saw, but to what purpose we will never know, for he came home to a letter from Percy Farrar, former president, now secretary, of the Alpine Club and a Pen-y-Pass acquaintance, inviting him to join a British expedition to Mount Everest. "Party would leave early April and get back in October. Any aspirations?"[27]

1921: The Reconnaissance

Any aspirations? George Mallory in 1921 positively exuded aspiration, but whether he wanted to go off and climb Everest was at first unclear. He had already endured one prolonged separation from his wife and did not welcome the thought of another. He had a house, a job, and three small children to care for. And he frankly recoiled from the quasi-official, flag-waving spirit of the expedition, wondering, as he put it to his sister Avie, whether it might not turn out to be "a merely fantastic performance." But Geoffrey Young—who had almost certainly proposed him to the Everest Committee in the first place—persuaded him that however distasteful the expedition, Everest itself represented the opportunity of a lifetime, that "the label of Everest" would attach to him and ease his way in all that he undertook as a teacher and writer. Ruth especially accepted the practical wisdom of this, and once assured of her support, Mallory relented. On February 9 he met with Farrar, Harold Raeburn, and Francis Younghusband in London and "without visible emotion" formally accepted the committee's invitation to join the expedition. "It seems rather a momentous step altogether, with a new job to find when I come back," he wrote to Young the next day, "but it will not be a bad thing to give up the settled ease of this present life. Frankly I want a more eminent platform than the one in my classroom—at least in the sense of appealing to minds more capable of response."[28]

The addition of Mallory to the climbing party immediately aroused the suspicions of Arthur Hinks, the hidebound secretary of the Royal Geographical Society, for whom the expedition was primarily about filling in blanks on the map. In mid-February, in his capacity as honorary secretary to the Everest Committee, Hinks wrote to Mallory to assure him that territorial reconnaissance and not mountain climbing was the order of the day, whatever his friends at the Alpine Club might think, and to insist that he put himself under the complete authority of Colonel Howard-Bury, the botanically inclined expedition leader. In reply Mallory conveyed his understanding that while reconnaissance was the first object of the expedition, the summit was the second and the only one with which he, as a member of Raeburn's climbing party, was concerned.[29]

Another row soon followed over the vexed business of publicity. To cover its expenses, the Everest Committee had entered into exclusive contracts with *The Times* and the *Philadelphia Ledger* (for publication of expedition telegrams), with the *Graphic* (for publication of expedition photographs), and with Edward Arnold (for publication of the official expedition volume). These arrangements, the modest beginnings of commercial mountaineering, were already too much for Hinks, who combined a gentlemanly distaste for money with a pathological dread of publicity: he would have preferred a secret expedition by private subscription. But they gave him the excuse he needed to impose, in effect, a ban of silence. In early March he required everyone involved to sign a statement binding themselves "not to hold any communication with the press or with any press agency or publisher, or to deliver any public lecture, or to allow any information or photograph to be published either before, during or after the expedition without the sanction of the Mount Everest Committee." For Mallory, who unlike the others had no independent income, who had, in fact, quit his job and staked his fortune on the climb, this was a near deal-breaker, and he pleaded for a less indefinite, time-limited injunction. Impossible: Himalayan mountaineering as Arthur Hinks understood it made no concessions to individual interest or ambition. The committee would pay his passage to India and advance him £50 toward boots and equipment. Beyond that, Mallory would have to "be content to rely on being treated with every consideration."[30]

Of more immediate concern to Mallory was the state of the climbing party. Both Raeburn and Kellas had Himalayan experience (which Mallory, again, did not), but at fifty-six and fifty-three respectively, they were old by the standards of the time and unlikely, Mallory thought, to be of much use on the mountain. George Finch, an Australian-born climber with an unrivalled Alpine record, was only thirty-three, but he had contracted malaria during the war and did not look at all well. "I have moments of complete pessimism as to our chances of getting up—or of getting back with toes on our feet," Mallory wrote to Young in early March. He himself passed his medical exam convincingly on March 17. Finch, to his own dismay, did not, ostensibly because he was underweight and anemic but really (or so Finch believed) because he was an uncouth colonial with long hair and a dubious family history. Whatever the cause, Finch's dismissal left the climbing party woefully deficient in strength, and when the committee proposed to replace him with Bill Ling, another middle-aged Scotsman, Mallory's patience expired. "The substitution of Ling for Finch," he wrote to Hinks, "will in all probability very materially weaken the advance party." The challenge of Everest lay not in its technical difficulty but in its height and colossal scale, he explained, and for that "we want men who can last." No doubt Ling would be of use lower down, but for the top "we ought to have another man who should be chosen not so much for his expert skill but simply for his powers of endurance." Hinks was unmoved. "The fact that you have been in close touch with Farrar all along has no doubt made you imbibe his view which is hardly that of anybody else, that the first object of the expedition is to get to the top of Mount Everest this year," he wrote to Mallory in declining to augment the climbing party. Fortunately, from Mallory's point of view, Ling declined the committee's invitation, and by going over Hinks's head to Younghusband, Mallory secured a place for his friend and fellow Irving protégé Guy Bullock, "a tough sort of fellow who never lost his head and would stand any amount of knocking about."[31]

Chomolungma—Mount Everest—the 29,035-foot eminence of the earth, stands at roughly 87° east and 28° north on the remote northeastern border of Nepal and Tibet. Today, those wishing to climb it typically fly to Kathmandu, the capital of Nepal, take a light plane or helicopter to Lukla in the Khumbu Valley, and then walk for a few days to the southern Base Camp on the Khumbu Glacier beneath the beautiful satellite mountains of Pumori and Nuptse. In 1921, however, air travel was in its infancy, the Kingdom of Nepal was strictly forbidden territory, and the southern approach to Everest was quite unknown. Simply to get to the mountain required a five-week sea voyage to Calcutta, the second city of the empire at the head of the Bay of Bengal, an eighteen-hour train journey to the remote hill station of Darjeeling, and a six-week trek first northeast through the tropical forests of Sikkim and then west across the arid wastes of the Tibetan plateau. The position of the mountain had been fixed from a distance in 1849, its height established in 1852. But except for Rawlings's survey party of 1904 and John Noel, who had surreptitiously approached from the east in 1913, no Englishmen had been anywhere near it or had any precise idea of how to reach it. Everything immediately north of the mountain was still, in 1921, unexplored and unsurveyed. This first expedition thus faced an obvious, difficult, and historically unique challenge. If they wanted to climb the mountain, first they had to find the base of it.

Accompanied by thirty-five cases of expedition luggage, Mallory left England on the *SS Sardinia* on April 8, 1921. Of his fellow Everesters—as they now took to calling themselves—three (Morshead, Wheeler, and Heron) were already in India. Kellas had gone off on a preliminary climbing expedition in Tibet. Raeburn, the climbing leader, had left England in March and Howard-Bury, Wollaston, and Bullock had sailed from Marseilles. Thus left to bring up the rear alone, Mallory had ample time on board ship to doubt the wisdom of having quit his job for this. "The Lord knows what I shall find to do hereafter or where it will be done," he wrote to Robert Graves. "I can't think I have sufficient talent to make a life-work of writing, though plenty of themes suggest themselves as wanting to be written about." His fellow first-class passengers appalled him: one could not possibly have gathered forty-three people with less intellectual life about them, he told Ruth.[32] So he kept to himself, read huge chunks of *Martin Chuzzlewit,* ran around the deck to keep fit, and admired the Mediterranean landscape slipping lazily by outside his porthole. By way of Gibraltar, Suez, and Colombo, he arrived in Calcutta on May 10, arranged for the transport of the expedition luggage, and made his way north to Darjeeling, where in the stupendous shadows of Kangchenjunga, the world's third-highest mountain, the rest of the party had already assembled. The governor of Bengal, Lord Ronaldshay, honored the occasion with a formal dinner at Government House on May 11; Morshead and his surveyors left for Tibet on May 13; the *chhoti barsat,* the little monsoon, annual precursor of worse things to come, blew ominously into Sikkim on May 15; and then, quite suddenly, they were off: 5 Englishmen, 2 Scots, 1 Canadian, 17 Sherpas, 21 Bhotias, 2 Lepchas, and about 100 government-of-India-issue mules.

The mules made it as far as Sedonchen, a mere five days out of Darjeeling. Sleek, fat beasts accustomed to army service on the plains, they were wholly unsuited, it turned out, to the steep, wet trails of the Sikkimese jungle, and those that did not die had to be abandoned in favor of what local ponies and yaks the expedition could scrounge. The men fared better, though the relentless heat and rain ruffled the English temperament and complicated the inevitable questions of personal compatibility. "Kellas I love already," Mallory wrote to Ruth. "He is beyond description Scotch and uncouth in his speech—altogether uncouth." Howard-Bury, on the other hand, was the English landlord to a fault: superior, intolerant, and opinionated. "For the sake of peace, I am being very careful not to broach certain subjects of conversation," Mallory said. And Raeburn, besides being overly "touchy about his position as leader of the Alpine party," was "dreadfully dictatorial about matters of fact," and worse, "often wrong."[33] From the outset Mallory foresaw trouble on the mountain. But for now he settled contentedly into the trek and tried to admire the lush, botanical profusion of the semitropical landscape.

Nine days out of Darjeeling, the expedition crossed the Jelep La, the 14,390-foot pass into the Chumbi Valley of Tibet. "Goodbye beautiful wooded Sikkim," wrote Mallory, "& welcome—God knows what!" The air turned suddenly dry, the sky blue, the scenery refreshingly alpine and European in aspect. In two scant days, however, the flowers and trees of the Chumbi Valley, "where everything seemed near and friendly," gave way to the gravel and dust of the Tibetan plateau, "where everything seemed unfriendly and far." The great enemy now was the wind: "a dry, dusty, unceasing wind, with all the unpleasantness of an east wind at home." The mountains, finally, were beguilingly close at hand, but "it is no use pretending that mountains are always beautiful," Mallory told Ruth. Chomolhari, a legendary peak rising abruptly out of the Tuna plain to the staggering height of 24,000 feet (7,315 meters), "was certainly a very tremendous sight, astounding and magnificent," he conceded; "but in broad daylight, however much one may be interested by its prodigious cliffs, one is not charmed—one remains cold and rather horrified."[34]

At the remote Tibetan village of Dochen, just beyond the shallow turquoise waters of the Bam-tso, the expedition finally left the high road to Lhasa and bore west over the 16,500-foot Dug La for Everest and the unknown. For some days now, in addition to suffering the inevitable effects of altitude—headache, nausea, fatigue—the party had all been afflicted in varying degrees with the equally inevitable dysentery. And one of them, Kellas,

Camp at Shekar Dzong, as photographed in 1924. Reprinted by
permission of the Royal Geographical Society.

who had left Darjeeling already in a weakened, vulnerable state, was mortally ill. From
Phari onward, too weak to walk, too weak even to ride on a yak, he had to be carried in a
sort of makeshift litter suspended from the shoulders of four porters. "Can you imagine
anything less like a mountaineering party?" Mallory asked David Pye. At Tatsang on June 4,
Kellas seemed to rally and insisted cheerfully that everyone march on ahead of him, but
the next day's stage, which included the crossing of a difficult 17,200-foot pass, proved too
much for him, and he died alone in agonies of intestinal distress ten miles short of Kampa
Dzong. Howard-Bury was appalled and disinclined now to take chances with anyone else.
On June 7, having seen Kellas into the ground on a stony, windswept hillside overlooking the three great Sikkimese peaks of Chomoyummo, Pauhunri, and Kangchengyao, he
sent the obviously ailing Raeburn packing back to Darjeeling and put Mallory in charge
of a climbing party suddenly reduced to two men, neither of whom had any Himalayan
experience. The chances of an ascent were infinitely slim, but "don't be hopeless about the
expedition," Mallory urged Ruth; "we may yet do very well."[35]

On June 6, 1921, the very day, as fate would have it, of Kellas's burial, Mallory
finally experienced "the strange elation of seeing Everest for the first time." Quitting camp
early in the perfect morning, he clambered 1,000 feet up the barren slopes behind the
rugged fortress of Kampa Dzong—"itself a singularly impressive and dramatic spectacle"—
turned, and there away to the west it was: "a prodigious white fang excrescent from the
jaw of the world." A slight haze obscured as yet the upper ramparts, but "this circumstance

added a touch of mystery and grandeur," Mallory recalled; he left Kampa Dzong fully satisfied that the highest of mountains would not disappoint. For seven frustrating days following, Everest hid behind the lower, intervening ranges, leaving Mallory and Bullock continually to wonder where it had gone. Each morning they impatiently pushed ahead of the main party, hoping to recover the lost vision, and each day they were disappointed, until, on June 13, they came to a broad, sandy plain where the Bhong Chu, flowing from the west, bends southward into Arun Valley. Mallory quivered with expectation. "It was not only that no European had ever been here before us," he later told Ruth, "but we were penetrating a secret: we were looking behind the great barrier running north and south which had been as a screen in front of us ever since we turned our eyes westwards from Kampa Dzong." Leaving their ponies to graze at the river bottom, the two men scrambled up to a rocky crest overlooking the gorge. To the southeast, Kangchenjunga was clear and eminent, strong and monumental, "like the leonine face of some splendid musician with a glory of white hair." But to the southwest . . . nothing but dark clouds. "We gazed at them intently through field glasses as though by some miracle we might pierce the veil," Mallory wrote; and presently the miracle happened:

> We caught the gleam of snow behind the grey mists. A whole group of mountains began to appear in gigantic fragments. Mountain shapes are often fantastic seen through a mist; these were like the wildest creation of a dream. A preposterous triangular lump rose out of the depths; its edge came leaping up at an angle of about 70° and ended nowhere. To the left a black serrated crest was hanging in the sky incredibly. Gradually, very gradually, we saw the great mountain sides and glaciers and arêtes, now one fragment and now another through the floating rifts, until far higher in the sky than imagination had dared to suggest, the white summit of Everest appeared. And in this series of partial glimpses we had seen a whole; we were able to piece together the fragments, to interpret the dream. However much might remain to be understood, the centre had a clear meaning, as one mountain shape, the shape of Everest.[36]

Here, from a distance of fifty-seven miles, above the village of Shiling, was a genuinely notable sighting of Everest, notable not only because it was for Mallory "beyond other adventures unforgettable" but because, as he said, "the vision of Everest inhabiting our minds after this day had no small influence upon our deductions when we came to close quarters with the mountain."[37] He and Bullock were looking at Everest from the northeast. Toward them, a long arête, the Northeast Ridge, came down from the summit to a broken black shoulder that they at once judged an insuperable obstacle. To the right of the shoulder, however, forming the skyline to the north, what Mallory rightly deduced to be a subsidiary ridge looked reasonably passable and seemed to be joined by a col to a sharp peak to the north (Changtse). From the direction of this col a valley came down to the east and evidently drained into the Arun. So there it was: in one first, fleeting vision from a distance of nearly sixty miles, Mallory had dimly discerned a route—eastern valley to northern col to northern ridge to northeastern ridge to summit—that was to dominate Western comprehension of the mountain for the next three decades.

The 1921 Everest reconnaissance began in earnest on June 19, when the expedition reached Tingri, a sizable village of some 300 houses set on a hillock in a broad salt plain forty miles north by northwest of Everest. Here Howard-Bury set up a Base Camp in strictest military fashion and dispatched his various parties on their appointed tasks: Wheeler and Morshead to photograph and survey the northern and western approaches, Heron to collect rocks, Wollaston to tend the sick and gather in dead birds and beetles, Mallory and Bullock to reconnoiter the mountain. For his part, Howard-Bury had already sized up Everest and pronounced it unclimbable. Once having set up darkroom, sickbay, and mess tent to his satisfaction, he set off to join Wheeler and Heron in the neighboring Kyetrak Valley, leaving Mallory and Bullock to their own (he thought) incompetent and uncompanionable devices. So it was that on June 25, accompanied by their cook, their sirdar, and sixteen Bhotia porters, Mallory and Bullock discovered the Dzakar Chu near the village of Chobuk, turned south up the Rong Chu, stumbled on the fabled Rongbuk Monastery, and were the first Westerners to behold the stupendous North Face of Everest. Viewed from the south, Everest is a shy and retiring mountain, lurking almost inconspicuously behind the satellite peaks of Nuptse and Lhotse. But here, from the north, as Mallory put it, "there is no complication for the eye. The highest of the world's great mountains, it seems, has to make but a single gesture of magnificence to be lord of all, vast in unchallenged and isolated supremacy. To the discerning eye other mountains are visible, giants between 23,000 and 26,000 feet high. Not one of the slenderer heads even reaches their chief's shoulder; beside Everest they escape notice—such is the pre-eminence of the greatest."[38]

So much for wonder and astonishment: now for the hard work of prolonged reconnaissance in a mountain environment that Mallory found bafflingly unfamiliar. In all his Alpine experience, for instance, glaciers had served as highways to the mountain, sometimes treacherous but usually accommodating routes of easy access. In the eastern Himalaya, however, as Mallory to his frustration now discovered, glaciers are a bewildering maze of boulders, melt channels, and towering fifty-foot ice pinnacles called *penitentes*. No course seemed to lead anywhere in this "fairy world of spires," and he and Bullock soon found that the only way to get on was to struggle along the glacial moraines to the side. Here, heat and distance took their toll, as well as altitude, of course. At 16,000 to 18,000 feet above sea level, the Rongbuk Glacier is considerably higher than the summit of Mont Blanc, and Mallory confessed to a level of exhaustion that he had never reached in the Alps: it was, he wrote, "a new sensation to find it an almost impossible exertion to drag oneself up a matter of 150 feet." Up ahead, however, Everest continually beckoned, and despite his physical lassitude, Mallory was in high spirits. "My darling, this is a thrilling business altogether," he wrote Ruth after his first day on the glacier. "I can't tell you how it possesses me, and what a prospect it is. And the beauty of it all!"[39]

Beautiful; but was it climbable? The nearer Mallory and Bullock approached, the

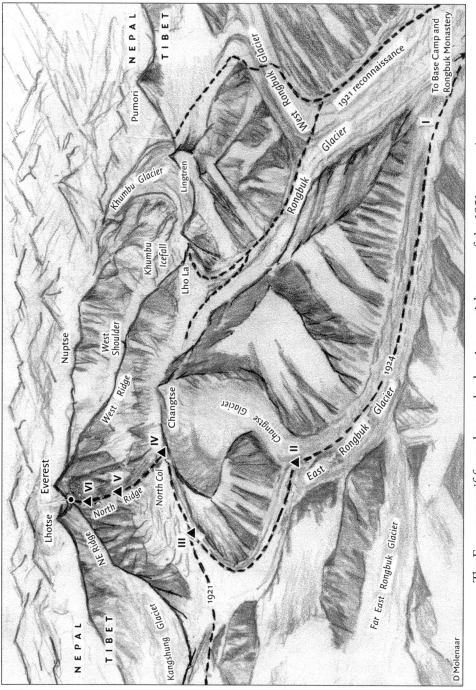
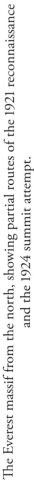

The Everest massif from the north, showing partial routes of the 1921 reconnaissance and the 1924 summit attempt.

D Molenaar

more discouraging the prospect seemed. Up ahead, the Rongbuk Glacier ran itself ("like the Charge of the Light Brigade") up against the 10,000-foot precipice of the North Face. "From the mountaineer's point of view so far as we have seen it no more appalling sight could be imagined," Mallory told Ruth; "it has no easy halfway house, nothing to help one." This left (of what he could see) the two great arêtes, or ridges, running down from the summit like the limbs of a giant, "simple, severe, and superb." Of the two, he much preferred the relatively gentle Northeast Ridge, which, he now confirmed, could certainly be reached by way of "a sort of rock rib" (the North Ridge) running down to the broad col between Everest and Changste. Unfortunately, the col itself—the Chang La, they called it, or North Col—proved inaccessible, at least from this side, and for the moment Mallory turned his attention to the forbidding Northwest Ridge (today more often known as the West Ridge). On July 7, following a successful surveillance climb of the 22,500-foot (6,858-meter) peak later known as Ri-Ring, he and Bullock pushed into the tributary West Rongbuk Glacier, hoping to find that it rounded the Everest massif to the south. Hitherto fine, the weather now turned foul, and Mallory's spirits drooped. "I sometimes think of this expedition as a fraud from beginning to end, invented by the wild enthusiasm of one man, Younghusband; puffed up by the would-be wisdom of certain pundits in the A.C.; and imposed upon the youthful ardour of your humble servant," he wrote to Rupert Thompson, a friend from the Pen-y-Pass days. "The prospect of ascent in any direction is almost nil, and our present job is to rub our noses against the impossible in such a way as to persuade mankind that some noble heroism has failed once again."[40]

On July 12 (the very day that Mallory wrote this prophetic letter) the weather cleared, and he and Bullock pushed on into the West Rongbuk, only to find that far from rounding the mountain, it skirted a forbidding frontier range, the impregnable western extension, as it were, of Everest's Northwest Ridge. After several inconclusive forays, the two men climbed to a low point in the ridge between Lingtren (22,072ft/6,714m) and Pumori (23,493ft/7,161m) and looked over into yet another enclosed glacial valley that they called the Western Cwm, thus forever conferring an unlikely bit of Welsh nomenclature on what would ultimately prove, after 1950, the high road to Everest. For now, Mallory wanted no part of it. Completely inaccessible from where he stood, the glacier below was in any case terribly steep and broken and unlikely (he thought) to yield the promising gap he could now make out between Everest and the great neighbor that Howard-Bury had christened Lhotse (South Peak). Everything suggested to him that the great arête rising off of what was probably a high southern col—though he could only deduce the existence of this—would be the easiest line up Everest (as indeed it was to prove), but even had it not been politically out of bounds, he simply saw no practical way to get to it.

This left the North Col, "the col of our desires," as Mallory now took to calling it. Was it somehow accessible from the east? On the very first day of their reconnaissance, Mallory and Bullock had crossed a stream coming into the Rongbuk Valley from the east and deduced the existence of an eastern tributary glacier. The stream seemed too small to be

The Rongbuk Glacier and the North Face of Everest from Ri-Ring, 1921.
Photograph by George Mallory. Reprinted by permission of the
Royal Geographical Society.

of much significance, however, and they had left it unexplored, preferring to push on to the
south and west. Thwarted in the west, Mallory now thought to return to this stream to see
where it would lead him when word came in from Howard-Bury that all his (Mallory's)
photographs had failed for the simple and inexcusable reason that he had been inserting
all the film plates backward. To his great frustration, Mallory now had as far as possible to
repair this hideous error and spend several precious days retracing his photographic footsteps. Howard-Bury, meanwhile, had moved his base from Tingri to the eastern village of
Kharta, where Mallory hurriedly joined him at the end of July. Thus for all his good work
in the Rongbuk Valley, he had missed what later proved the essential topographical detail:
the East Rongbuk Glacier.

Nestled in the Arun Valley at the relatively moderate elevation of 12,300 feet,
Kharta, Howard-Bury's base for the eastern reconnaissance, seemed positively tropical after
the stony wastes of the Rongbuk. "I have been half the time in ecstasy," Mallory wrote to
Ruth of his recuperative days here. "To see things grow again as though they liked growing,
enjoying rain and sun—that has been the real joy." But nothing, not even profusions of
butterflies and wildflowers, could keep him long from the task at hand, and on August 2 he
and Bullock set off again for the col of their desires. Misled by a guide who assured them
that Chomolungma lay to the south, they stumbled unwittingly into the luxuriant Kama

Chomolunzo and Makalu, 1921. Photograph by George Mallory.
Reprinted by permission of the Royal Geographical Society.

Valley and the greatest mountain amphitheater in the world: Everest, Lhotse, Pethangste, Chomolunzo, Makalu: "I'm altogether beaten for words," Mallory wrote. "The whole range of peaks from Makalu to Everest far exceeds any mountain scenery that ever I saw before." Unfortunately, the Kama Valley, for all its alpine splendors, led not to the North Col but to the formidable eastern (now Kangshung) face. Leaving this challenge to "other men, less wise," Mallory and Bullock retreated to Kharta, impressed but discouraged and, in Mallory's case, feverish.[41]

One last hope remained: the Kharta Valley itself, running parallel to the Kama just one ridge line to the north. On August 13, with Mallory momentarily hors de combat, Bullock followed this valley onto the Kharta Glacier only to find that it ended in a high pass one range shy of Everest. From this (and remembering that paltry stream), Bullock now deduced the existence of an eastern glacier that turned and flowed north, back into the Rongbuk Valley. "Into the Rongbuk Valley!" Mallory exclaimed. Refusing as yet to concede so hateful and (to him) discreditable a possibility, Mallory rallied his strength, and on August 18 set out to climb the 22,000-foot Lhakpa La, Bullock's high pass at the head of the Kharta Glacier. It was an appallingly difficult climb, the hardest push, Mallory told Winthrop Young, that he had ever made on a mountain, and by the time it ended in midafternoon, the whole ridge from Everest to Changtse was draped in cloud. But there, sure enough, not 800 feet below, was the suspected glacier, leading across an easy cirque to the foot of the North Col. A way to the mountain had been found, and Mallory allowed himself a moment's well-earned pride. "As we came down the long weary way my thoughts were full of this prospect and this success," he told Ruth. "I don't know when I have allowed myself so much enjoyment from a personal achievement. I fairly puffed out my chest with pride and the consciousness of something done well; of a supreme effort made and happily rewarded and of a big task accomplished."[42] At the same time, however, if only inwardly, he rebuked himself for having overlooked what Oliver Wheeler, completing his northern survey, now confirmed: the stream issuing out of that small defile in the Rongbuk Valley did in fact lead on to the East Rongbuk Glacier and the North Col. A way to the mountain had been found, yes; but a much easier way, the way followed by all northern expeditions ever since, had been missed.

With the climb of the Lhakpa La and the belated discovery of the East Rongbuk, the 1921 Everest reconnaissance was essentially complete, and the expedition might have retired with dignity. But Mallory was determined to have a go at the mountain, at least as far as the Northeast Shoulder and perhaps even to the "supreme object" beyond. On the last day of August, he and Bullock moved up with several porters to a 17,300-foot camp in the Kharta Valley to await the expected break in the monsoon. Three weeks later they were still there, pinned down by weather and nearing the end of their physical and emotional tethers. Relations with Howard-Bury, never easy, now broke down altogether over some alleged misuse of stores. "He has economy on the brain," Mallory wrote; "I can't bear his meanness."[43]

Happily, Howard-Bury largely kept his distance from this advance base, but on September 6 the long-lost Raeburn unaccountably showed up, "looking extraordinarily old & grizzled. When he is not being a bore I feel moved to pity though that's not often," Mallory confided to Winthrop Young. "He takes no part luckily." Bullock remained reasonably steadfast. But by now he and Mallory had simply been in one another's company too long and had "drifted into that common superficial attitude between two people who live alone together—competitive and slightly quarrelsome, each looking out to see that he doesn't get done down in some small way by the other." September 9 brought letters from home and news of the truce in Ireland, which made him feel more like praying than anything he could remember, Mallory said. "I shan't be sorry to get back to civilization & know again what's going on in the world," he told Winthrop Young; "it's a poor world perhaps but it remains of interest even here—if only as a contrast to Tibet, which is a hateful country inhabited by hateful people." Even the mountains had paled for him. Makalu was "indescribably impressive," he conceded, but on the whole they were "disappointing & infinitely less beautiful than the Alps."[44]

It was, in short, a disheartened and fatigued little band that set out on history's first attempt on Everest when the weather finally cleared on September 22. Four months had passed since they had left Darjeeling, and while today's maxim of Himalayan climbing—

The 1921 Mount Everest reconnaissance expedition. Standing (left to right):
Alexander Wollaston, Charles Howard-Bury, A. M. Heron, and Harold Raeburn.
Sitting: George Mallory, Oliver Wheeler, Guy Bullock, and Henry Morshead.
Reprinted by permission of the Royal Geographical Society.

get in, get up, get out—may be reckless in the opposite extreme, the 1921 expedition had
unquestionably been at high altitude too long, well past the fleeting point of effective acclimatization. Add to this the challenge of the route and the astonishingly inadequate (by
today's standards) clothing and equipment—Bullock was climbing in woolen sweaters and
lugging a suitcase around—and the only wonder is that they managed as well as they did.
Six Europeans—Mallory, Bullock, Morshead, Howard-Bury, Wollaston, and Wheeler—and
ten Sherpas made "Windy Gap" (the Lhakpa La) in the bitter late-afternoon cold. The next
morning three—Mallory, Bullock, and Wheeler—stumbled down the snow slopes to the
East Rongbuk Glacier and pitched camp at the elusive eastern foot of the North Col. Here
they had hoped for respite from the unrelenting wind, but night came "with no gentle
intentions," Mallory said. Fierce squalls descended from the towering cliffs above and threatened to tear the poor Mummery tents off their moorings. Somehow Mallory slept, woke,
rallied his charges, and at 7:00 A.M. on September 24 led them gingerly onto the slopes of
Everest. It was a slow, methodical, step-cutting grind through a jumble of avalanche debris.
"Nothing very remarkable remains in my mind about the ascent to the North Col," Mallory
later told Younghusband, "except perhaps Wheeler's black beard coming up behind me."[45]
Only one steep pitch around the corner of a *bergschrund* caused any particular anxiety, and
by noon they were there, on the cherished Chang La, at 23,000 feet.

Mallory quickly took stock. Up above, unbroken spindrift obscured his view of the Northeast Ridge, but the rock rib leading to it looked reassuringly easy. "If ever we had doubted whether the arête were accessible, it was impossible to doubt any longer." He felt sorely tempted to go on. But the wind was fierce, devilish, cyclonic—the kind of wind, Mallory later said, in which no one could have lived more than an hour—and though he himself felt strong and capable of at least another 2,000 feet, Bullock was spent and Wheeler already frostbitten. Keep it safe, "keep it 'right,'" Geoffrey Young had counseled him in July; "let no desire for result spoil the effort by overstretching the safe limits within which it must move." Who can say whether these words came back to Mallory now, as he looked longingly across the great North Face of Everest? But this time, this first time, he heeded them. After 200 faltering yards in the teeth of the maelstrom, he turned his little band around and retreated down the col. "It is a disappointment, there is no getting over it, that the end should seem so much tamer than I hoped," he wrote to Ruth from the safety of Kharta. "As it is, we have established the way to the summit for anyone who cares to try the highest adventure. . . . Now homewards with all speed."[46]

1922: The Assault

Back in London, both the Alpine Club and the Royal Geographical Society presented the 1921 Everest reconnaissance to the public as an unqualified success. "A Way Up Found," *The Times* reported in mid-October, and most other newspapers, despite their resentment at *The Times*'s exclusive rights to Howard-Bury's dispatches, obligingly took this triumphal and patriotic line.[47] Privately, though, Hinks was disappointed. No height record had been set, and thanks to Mallory's incompetence with the camera, the photographic survey remained muddled and incomplete. No sooner had the party left India than Hinks began to organize a return expedition for the following spring.

Mallory initially wanted no part of it. "I'm tired of travelling and travellers, far countries and uncouth people, trains and ships and shimmering mausoleums, foreign ports, dark-skinned faces, and a garish sun," he told David Pye. "What I want to see is faces I know, and my own sweet home; afterwards, the solemn facades in Pall Mall, and perhaps Bloomsbury in a fog; and then an English river, cattle grazing in western meadows." Since leaving Bombay he had been writing a report on the reconnaissance for the Alpine Club and working himself into a rage at the thought of "that wonderful Everest Committee and all the solemn divergences of opinion that must have passed between their nodding heads, the scrutiny of photographs and discussion of letters, with grave doubts coughed up in phlegmy throats as to whether the party are really 'on the right track,' and all the anxious wisdom devoted to spoon-feeding the Glaxo-loving public." He wouldn't go back to the mountain next year, he told his sister Avie, "for all the gold in Arabia."[48] But as time and the miles passed, his reluctance diminished. Everest was gratifyingly in the news; Mallory arrived home to find himself a modest celebrity. And he had, after all, found a plausible route to the summit.

The thought of other climbers achieving immortality on the strength of his reconnaissance must ultimately have been unbearable. Days after his return to England in late November, Mallory met with Hinks and agreed to join the second attempt in the spring.

Three months of frantic activity followed. For all his aversion to publicity, Hinks appreciated its fund-raising value and was not above a bit of "American hustle" (as Howard-Bury disapprovingly put it). On December 20 he staged a set-piece occasion at the Queen's Hall, London, featuring Mallory, Raeburn, and Wollaston. With Edward Arnold and Co. he arranged for the publication on rewarding terms of the first of many "official" expedition volumes, *Mount Everest: The Reconnaissance,* and timed its appearance to coincide with the 1922 climb. Despite his generally dim view of Mallory's competence and character, Hinks recognized his worth as the public face of the expedition and in January dispatched him on a whirlwind lecture tour covering thirty cities in under ten weeks. "The public interest is immense," Mallory reported back to Younghusband from Manchester. "A crowd was turned away from the Free Trade Hall . . . which held about 3,000, and it was a splendid audience to talk to, quick/responsive & sensible & yet quite willing to listen when I spoke of the beauty of what we saw."[49]

After publicity there was the sensitive business of the new expedition personnel. At Hinks's insistence, the Everest Committee shelved Howard-Bury in favor of Charles Bruce, the more obvious and now available choice. Bruce in turn insisted that the new party be not only, as he liked to say, BAT (British All Through), but that it be a convinced *climbing* party in terms of age, strength, and ability. Of the veterans of the 1921 expedition, only Mallory and Morshead, the surveyor, returned in 1922. The newcomers included E. L. Strutt, a thirty-year Alpine veteran and future president of the Alpine Club; Tom Longstaff, whose 1907 ascent of Trisul still ranked as history's highest; Edward Norton, grandson of the golden age Alpinist Alfred Wills and a distant relation of Mallory; Howard Somervell, a Lakeland climber, artist, and doctor who was to replace Bullock as Mallory's tent-mate and friend; A. W. Wakefield, another Lakelander and famous fell-runner; John Noel, the expedition photographer whose illicit approach in 1913 had started the Everest business in the first place; Colin Crawford, the transport officer; and that same George Finch of unrivalled ability but questionable pedigree who had mysteriously been deemed medically unfit in 1921. As expected, the addition of Finch proved the most decisive and divisive, for not only was he an uncouth colonial who allegedly bathed and cleaned his teeth but once a year—"Six months' course as a lama novice in a monastery would enable one to occupy a Whymper tent with him," said Bruce—worse still, he was a fervent pro-ponent of such peculiar innovations as quilted eiderdown clothing and compressed bottled oxygen.[50]

Oxygen, to be sure, had appeared in the Himalaya as early as 1907, when A. L. Mumm took some cylinders along on the Alpine Club's Jubilee expedition to the Garhwal. They had not worked well, however, and the whole business was treated as a joke until Kellas began his sophisticated studies of high-altitude physiology on Kamet in 1920. Kellas had in fact brought a primitive breathing apparatus along to Everest in 1921, but no one else on the expedition knew how to use it, and when he died it had simply been abandoned. Ultimately it was not Kellas's research but that of the Oxford pathologist George Dreyer (who had worked on the problem of altitude with the Royal Air Force during the war) that persuaded the Everest Committee to try bottled oxygen in earnest in 1922. Dreyer's experiments (on Finch, among others) in an early decompression chamber seemed to prove the benefits of supplemental oxygen, and with his assistance the Air Ministry designed for the committee an apparatus consisting of four steel cylinders, two breathing masks, various tubes and regulator valves, and a Bergans carrying frame. Fully loaded, the thing weighed thirty-three pounds and, in theory, could keep a climber wherever he went at the simulated altitude of 15,000 feet for up to seven hours.[51]

Mallory was horrified. "When I think of mountaineering with four cylinders of oxygen on one's back and a mask over one's face, well, it loses its charm," he told David Pye. No one needed to persuade him of the debilitating effects of altitude; he recalled his own breathless stupor on the North Col perfectly well. But he ardently believed in gradual acclimatization and his own deep-breathing technique as the only sporting remedies. When, at Oxford on January 31, Sir Walter Raleigh told him that the physiologists all agreed on the need for oxygen on Everest, Mallory answered that the physiologists could go "explode themselves in their diabolical chamber, but we would do what we could to explode their damnable heresy." Hinks, for once, was sympathetic. Far better, he raged in print, "to discover how high a man can climb without oxygen than to get to a specified point, even the highest summit in the world, in conditions so artificial that they can never become 'legitimate' mountaineering." For his part, Finch argued that bottled oxygen was no more artificial or illegitimate an aid than food, tents, or warm clothing. He could accept the reasoning of those—and Mallory was among these too—who argued that the weight of the apparatus and the effort involved in carrying it would offset the benefits it provided; this, he said, could only be determined on the mountain. But to condemn it "on the ground that its employment was unsporting and, therefore, un-British" was hypocritical and inconsistent with the adoption of "other scientific measures which render mountaineering less exacting to the human frame."[52] The higher stakes here are obvious. Behind this vexed issue of supplemental oxygen lay the age-old quarrel between gentlemen and players, between the amateur/aristocratic ethic of sport for sport's sake and the professional/bourgeois ethic of success. Finch was a divisive figure not just because he championed new methods; he portended the modern age.

The 1922 Everest expedition left England in early March, hoping to reach the Rongbuk Glacier by early May and thus avoid the torment of the summer monsoon. Mallory sailed on the *Caledonia* with Somervell, Wakefield, Noel, Strutt, and Finch. In contrast to 1921, they were, Mallory wrote, "a happy, smiling party with plenty of easy conversation." In Somervell especially Mallory discovered a kindred liberal and literary spirit: the two took to reading Shakespeare aloud in their cabins. On first acquaintance in London, Strutt had seemed "a dry, stiff soldier." But now he turned out to be an entertaining chatterbox, and on learning that Curzon had once tried to have him court-martialed as a traitor, Mallory concluded that he had to be a good man. Finch was abrasive and fanatical, but eventually Mallory had to concede that the oxygen classes he had imposed on the team were "extremely interesting," as were Noel's demonstrations of his newfangled motion picture equipment. The afternoons saw deck tennis or deck cricket among the six, the evenings those moments of "seasoned silence," as Mallory called them, when he would sit alone in the ocean breeze and read Maynard Keynes on the revision of the Treaty of Versailles or Virginia Woolf's second novel, *Night and Day*.[53]

From Bombay, where they docked with their two tons of luggage—including the famous tins of quail in aspic for which they were subsequently ridiculed—the six made their way by railroad stages to Calcutta and Darjeeling, where they joined Bruce and the main body of the expedition, now swollen beyond precedent to 13 Europeans, a Tibetan interpreter, 5 Gurkhas, 40 Sherpas, an innumerable assortment of cooks, orderlies, and porters, and some 300 pack animals. Here was mountaineering on an exorbitant scale, and the 1922 files of the Everest Committee archives are full of cables from Bruce demanding more money and Hinks's outraged replies. From Darjeeling the expedition simply followed the previous year's route, north through the Chumbi Valley and west across the Tibetan plateau to the White Glass Fort of Shekar Dzong. Mallory was surprised "to experience a friendly feeling towards this bleak country on seeing it again," but not all joined him in this. "A usual and by now a welcome sound in each new place," he told Ruth, "is Strutt's voice, cursing Tibet—this march for being more dreary and repulsive even than the one before, and this village for being more filthy than any other." Everest, on the other hand, was more wonderful even than Mallory had remembered, "and all the party were delighted by it," he said, "which of course appealed to my proprietary feelings."[54]

At Shekar Dzong the expedition left the 1921 trail and struck due south over the Pang La for Everest. On April 30 they reached the Rongbuk Monastery, where the dignified and charismatic head lama, Dzatrul Rinpoche, emerged from his seclusion to ask through an interpreter where in heaven's name they were going and why. "I was fortunately inspired to say that we regarded the whole Expedition, and especially our attempt to reach the summit of Everest as a pilgrimage," Bruce later wrote in terms that Younghusband would certainly have approved. But the lama recalled the whole exchange quite differently. "I was told," he noted in his journal, "'This mountain is the highest in the world. If we can ascend it and reach the summit, the British Government will give us big pay and a title.'"[55] Whatever was said—and there are likely elements of truth in both versions—the visual evidence of Noel's expedition film, *Climbing Mount Everest* (1922), suggests a perfectly amiable encounter, complete with ceremonial exchange of gifts and various entertainments. Once assured that the sahibs meant no harm to the local wildlife, the lama blessed the expedition, urged firmness and caution on them, and sent them on their way. They made Base Camp at the foot of the Rongbuk Glacier precisely on schedule on May 1.

From here, Bruce's plan called for advance by stages, laying and stocking through repeated marches a series of six ascending camps or depots roughly five miles apart on the glacier and 2,000 vertical feet apart on the mountain. Longstaff called it the "polar method" in ominous deference to Robert Scott, and the name has stuck. But the true inspiration for this cumbersome business seems to have been the British Army's incremental experience of the western front. "In this Polar method of advance," wrote John Noel, "there is an essential psychological principle to be maintained. Each advance, each depot built, must be considered as ground won from the mountain. It must be consolidated and held, and no man must ever abandon an inch of ground won, or turn his back to the mountain once he has started the attack. A retreat has a disastrous moral effect. If the band of men are checked by unforeseen emergencies or bad weather, they must hold their ground and advance again as soon as opportunity permits. The battle is half lost once an assaulting party turns its back to the mountain. They must keep going forward until they win through."[56] Despite the Tibetan context, one could hardly ask for a clearer articulation of the Great War mentality; in laying siege to Everest in this way, the 1922 expedition established a military model for Himalayan mountaineering that lasted half a century. And this despite its patent failure in 1922.

Things began well enough. By May 9 a party of four led by Strutt had successfully reconnoitered the East Rongbuk (which Mallory and Bullock had overlooked in 1921) and loosely established the first three intermediate camps: Camp I (17,800ft) near the snout of the glacier, Camp II (19,800ft) in a lateral hollow beneath a fabulous ice cliff, and Camp III (21,000ft) on a terminal moraine under the shelter of Changtse, an hour's march from the foot of the North Col. Mallory and Somervell moved "up the line"—the inevitable trench metaphor—on May 10 and with the Sherpa Dasno forced a passage up the North Col, where they found the wind less ferocious than the year before. Their hope was to establish Camp IV the next day, but thanks to the unexpected defection of many porters, the all-important supply line had broken down, and instead they spent three precious days at Camp III reading poetry and discussing politics while the weather turned for the worse. "I forget the details of George Mallory's views on most of the many subjects we discussed," Somervell later recalled, "but in general he took always the big and liberal view. He was really concerned with social evils. He hated anything that savoured of hypocrisy or humbug, but cherished all that is really good and sound."[57]

Finally, on May 16, Strutt, Norton, Morshead, and Crawford arrived with a convoy of porters and Camp IV was secured on the 23,000-foot North Col with six Mummery tents and over 500 pounds of food and assorted supplies. At this point, the original plan called for Mallory and Somervell to make a first attempt on the summit without oxygen, Finch and Norton a second attempt with. But Bruce was losing confidence in the heavy and unreliable oxygen equipment, and with Finch laid low with dysentery and the weather deteriorating, he decided to augment the first oxygenless attempt with Norton and Morshead. Finch was incensed and Mallory dismayed. From his point of view, twice as many men meant twice as much equipment and twice the chance of some debilitating setback. "We shan't get to the top; if we reach the shoulder at 27,400, it will be better than anyone here expects," he wrote to Ruth from Camp III. Up on the col, though, the weather was clear, the prospects "extraordinarily promising," and at 7:00 A.M. on May 20, history's first "assault on Everest" began when Mallory, Somervell, Norton, Morshead, and four unnamed porters set out from Camp IV hoping to establish Camp V on the North Ridge at 26,000 feet.[58]

They climbed quickly at first. The helpful stones underfoot soon gave way to hard snow, however, and having no crampons they were reduced to the arduous and time-consuming business of cutting steps. The sky was clear, but "the sun had no real warmth," Mallory recalled, and their silk shirts, woolen sweaters, scarves, and cotton overcoats little discouraged the frigid Himalayan wind. At midday, already spent and frostbitten, the four Englishmen dismissed their porters and made camp after a fashion in the miserable lee of the ridge at 25,000 feet. The night brought seven inches of fresh snow, the morning plunging temperatures. After a few faltering steps on the steep ledges, Morshead declined to continue, leaving the other three to soldier on as best they could. "The details of our climbing during the next few hours are not such as merit exact description," Mallory later wrote. It was a tedious and breathless business of stepping up from ledge to snow-covered ledge at the miserable rate of 400 vertical feet an hour. By noon they knew they were not going to make the Northeast Shoulder, let alone the summit, and at 2:30 P.M. they turned around, little consoled at having reached the record height of 26,985 feet. Near catastrophe struck, as so often, on the descent, when the badly frostbitten Morshead (safely retrieved from Camp V) lost his footing and dragged Norton and Somervell off the mountain with him. Mallory, in the lead, saw nothing, but "hearing something wrong behind" instinctively drove in his ax, belayed, and was "in plenty of time when the strain came."[59] Saved but shaken, the party proceeded with painstaking caution into the gathering dark, finally reaching the safety of Camp IV on the North Col by candle-lantern light.

Now it was Finch's turn, Finch's chance to prove the worth of "English air," as the Sherpas called it. On May 25, while Mallory and company stumbled like walking wounded into Base Camp, he, Geoffrey Bruce (a Gurkha captain who happened to be the general's nephew), and Tejbir Bura (a Nepalese officer attached to Bruce), left the col for Camp V and the summit. "I shan't feel in the least jealous of any success they may have," Mallory wrote disingenuously to Ruth. "The whole venture of getting up with oxygen is so different from ours that the two hardly enter into competition." But of course it was a competition, as Finch well knew, and he was determined, for starters, to place Camp V higher than Mallory had done, which he did (just) at 25,500 feet. The night brought a violent storm that continued into the morning, but rather than retreat, the three men chose to wait it out. They passed the time with hot tea, oxygen, and cigarettes (which Finch thought improved respiration at high altitudes). On the 27th the weather cleared, and they set off early in hopeful spirits. Tejbir collapsed almost at once under the fifty-pound weight of his cylinders, and when even an appeal to the honor of his regiment would not rouse him, Finch and

Geoffrey Bruce and George Finch return to the
North Col from their summit attempt in 1922.
Reprinted by permission of the
Royal Geographical Society.

Bruce carried on without him. They climbed steadily and well, certainly proving to Finch's satisfaction the benefits of the oxygen. "Never for a moment did I think we would fail," he later recalled; "progress was steady, the summit was there before us; a little longer, and we should be on the top. And then—suddenly, unexpectedly, the vision was gone."[60] Bruce's breathing apparatus had failed, and by the time Finch repaired it, the fight had gone out of them. They turned back at 27,300 feet: 315 feet higher than Mallory had managed and a mile farther on, but still just shy of the crest of the Northeast Ridge.

The question now was whether to try again. Tom Longstaff, the expedition doctor, strongly advised against it. Of the experienced climbers, only Somervell, he said, was fit to continue; the rest were all suffering from various degrees of frostbite or heart strain (or both) and ought immediately to retire. Bruce too had misgivings, what with the monsoon coming on and "the flower of the men's condition" gone. But he was under considerable pressure from Younghusband and Hinks to stay on and accomplish something more notable than a height record, and when Wakefield gave him a second, less gloomy medical report, he reluctantly authorized a third attempt by Finch, Mallory, and Somervell. "The finger is far from well, and I risk getting a worse frostbite by going up again," Mallory told Ruth, "but the game is worth a finger, and I shall take every conceivable care of both fingers & toes. Once bit twice shy!"[61]

With Wakefield and Crawford in support (and none too happy at having to return to the mountain so soon), the three appointed climbers left Base Camp under thickening clouds on June 3. Finch made it no farther than Camp I before succumbing to exhaustion and leaving Mallory in charge. The next two days brought heavy snow and ought, in retrospect, to have discouraged any further thought of proceeding. But the mountain had Mallory under its Siren spell. On June 7 he led a party of seventeen men on four separate ropes up the freshly snow-shrouded slopes of the North Col. He was of course aware of the danger of avalanche and tested the stability of the snow as he went. "Every test gave a satisfactory result," he later recalled, and he had dismissed any thought of an avalanche from his mind when, at 1:50 P.M., some 600 feet below the safety of the col, he "heard a noise not unlike an explosion of untamped gunpowder" and felt himself being swept away.[62] Needless to say, all was panic and confusion for some time, but when the snow settled the awful truth was clear: an avalanche had broken free from the lee of the col above and swept seven Sherpas —Lhakpa, Nurbu, Pasang, Pema, Sange, Dorje, and Remba—over a cliff to their deaths.

From the melancholy refuge of Base Camp, Mallory at once wrote to Younghusband, accepting responsibility for the accident but insisting that it did not reflect any spirit of recklessness or any carelessness of life on his part. The tragic irony, in fact, is that Mallory had more regard for Sherpa well-being than the other climbers on the expedition, yet only he had lost any of them. The relatives of the dead men and the Rongbuk lama were quick to forgive: these were matters of fate and destiny, not human error. But Mallory could not let himself off so philosophically. "The consequences of my mistake are so terrible," he wrote to Ruth; "it seems impossible to believe that it has happened for ever and that I can do nothing to make good. There is no obligation I have so much wanted to honour as that of taking care of those men." One thought finally put his mind somewhat to rest, and by the time he came to write his account for the expedition volume, he was able to express it in ways that intimated a modern, postcolonial comprehension of the Sherpa people. "The work of carrying up our camps on Mount Everest is beyond the range of a simple contract measured in terms of money," he wrote; "the porters had come to have a share in our enterprise, and these men died in an act of voluntary service freely rendered and faithfully performed."[63]

1924: The Repulse

Despite what Bruce privately called the "rather humiliating" and "quite unnecessary" ending to the 1922 expedition, the Mount Everest Committee immediately applied to the Tibetan government for permission to return in 1923.[64] In fact Younghusband wanted to go out and set up a Base Camp in advance of the climbing party as early as the autumn of 1922. But Bruce wanted time to recruit new climbers, improve on his equipment, and generally absorb the hard lessons of the last year. At his suggestion (and with Lhasa's approval), the committee decided to defer the next effort to 1924. This allowed a full year for advance publicity and preparation, and it meant that the summit attempt would coincide more or less precisely in time with the opening of the much-anticipated British Empire Exhibition at Wembley. From its vaguely understood place on the outermost fringes of India, Everest was about to occupy the symbolic center of British colonial consciousness. Two failed attempts had added to its public allure and made it seem a worthy object of national ambition, a worthy geocolonial successor to the elusive (and now lost to the Norwegians) South Pole. Mallory himself was only partly responsible for and dimly aware of all this. But by 1924 he was clearly inseparable from the mountain in the public mind and, as "Mallory of Everest," ready to take his place alongside "Scott of the Antarctic" in the annals of British martyrdom.

Meanwhile, back from India, out of a job, and in urgent need of money, he took on a strenuous schedule of lecture engagements for the Mount Everest Committee. From mid-October to mid-December, he toured the British Isles as far afield as Aberdeen and Dublin, speaking to schools, geographical societies, climbing clubs, and the like in exchange for 30 percent of the ticket proceeds. Then, in January, he left for a three-month fund-raising tour of the United States. After a promising start in Washington and Philadelphia—where 3,000 people turned out to hear him—this largely flopped. His New York appearance filled only half of the Broadhurst Theater and, worse still, attracted no press attention beyond a brief *New York Times* report (calculated to appeal to anti-Prohibitionists) on how he had drunk a shot of brandy at 27,000 feet. "Mallory is a fine fellow and gives a good lecture," wrote Lee Keedick, the American agent, to Gerald Christy, his British counterpart, "but the American public don't seem to be interested in the subject." When the Chicago Geographical Society refused to put on a public lecture and offered only $100 for a speech to their members, Keedick advised Mallory to leave off. "It is just one of those curious examples of a thing not being marketable for anything near its real value." Hinks attributed the lack of interest to politics: "So far as I can judge the great American public is getting to hate us more and more, which does not worry me very much except when it is a matter of business," he told Mallory.[65] Against Keedick's advice, Mallory pushed on to Montreal, Toronto, Toledo, Chicago, Buffalo, Rochester, and Boston, but interest never revived, and in the end the tour earned him a negligible £250.

That is, £250 and a kind of rhetorical immortality, thanks to an unnamed reporter in Philadelphia who asked him (as hundreds had done before) why he wanted to climb Everest and quoted his imperishable reply: "Because it is there." Whether this was a flippant dismissal, a throwaway remark by a tired and naturally impatient man, as Mallory's friends tended to believe, or whether it was an inspired bit of spontaneous profundity, as his biographers imagine, is hard to say: Mallory was readily capable of both. Whatever he meant by it, over time the phrase took and would be endlessly borrowed, most famously, perhaps, by John F. Kennedy in justifying the American exploration of space. In truth, Mallory's motives for climbing Everest were several: thrill, adventure, fame, fitness, fortune. He even allowed, in the same Philadelphia interview, for some benefit to geological and botanical science. But he then reverted to his original thought and said that the mountain's mere existence as the highest in the world was an irresistible challenge. None of this suggests flippancy, and in fact in a manuscript prepared for his Broadhurst Theater lecture, Mallory had closely anticipated the essence, if not the precise form, of the famous phrase: "I suppose we go to Mount Everest," he said, "because—in a word—we can't help it. Or, to state the matter rather differently, because we are mountaineers."[66]

Shortly after his return to England in April, Mallory accepted the unexpected offer of an extramural lectureship at Cambridge, thus complicating the question of whether he would return to Everest. Bruce, who besides returning as expedition leader had now assumed both the presidency of the Alpine Club and the chairmanship of the Mount Everest Committee, very much wanted him, but for six months Mallory refused to commit, pending further discussion with his family and formal leave from Cambridge. The committee meanwhile proceeded with other selections, including (among newcomers) Bentley Beetham, a Lakeland schoolmaster and climbing partner of Somervell, and Noel Odell, a Cambridge climber-geologist. Finch was dropped: besides being a generally abrasive and ungentlemanly character—"an absolute swine," is how Bruce ungenerously put it—he had lately incurred Hinks's wrath by withholding his own photographs from the committee and, worse, lecturing on his own initiative and pocketing all the proceeds. In his place the committee initially chose R. B. Graham, yet another Lakelander with a reputation for great staying power. But Graham, a Quaker, had been a conscientious objector during the Great War, and when (to Mallory's great dismay) his selection proved politically controversial, he reluctantly yielded his place to John de Vere Hazard, an odd customer whose only recommendation seemed to be that he had been with Henry Morshead on the Somme. Norton would return as deputy leader, Noel as "photographic historian." The final place went to a wholly unknown undergraduate oarsman at Oxford, Andrew Comyn Irvine.

Born at Birkenhead in April 1902 and raised in Park Road South, not half a mile from Herbert Mallory's rectory, Sandy Irvine was at twenty-one by far the youngest addition to any of these early Everest expeditions. He had no climbing record to speak of but was a highly accomplished sportsman who had accompanied Odell and Longstaff on a Merton College sledging expedition to Spitsbergen in 1922. Odell especially had been impressed by Irvine's strength, endurance, and temperament and on returning to England recommended him to Bruce as a promising Everester. Some on the Everest Committee objected to his youth and inexperience, but when it turned out that to his physical prowess Irvine added mechanical and practical ingenuity—qualities that Mallory notably lacked—Bruce took him on as an experiment. "Irvine represents our attempt to get one superman, though lack of experience is against him," Mallory told Geoffrey Young.[67] Thinking that strength and stamina counted for more on Everest than technical ability, Mallory on balance supported Irvine's nomination and from the outset saw in this youthful, fair-haired paragon an appealing climbing partner.

The question of Mallory's own involvement in the new campaign remained open until late October, when at Hinks's forceful request the Cambridge Syndicate granted him six months' leave at half pay. It was "an awful tug" to contemplate leaving Ruth and the children again, but "I have to look at it from the point of view of loyalty to the expedition and of carrying through a task begun," Mallory stoically told his father. Ruth, for her part, regretted the lost income and this time had strong premonitions of danger (or so her daughter Clare later claimed), but she agreed that it would be "rather grim" to see anyone other than George claiming the summit, and at the end of the month she gave her reluctant consent. On November 6 the committee's doctors pronounced Mallory "fit in every respect" and he was in. "I hate leaving anxieties behind," he told his father, "but it means a lot that we now know pretty well all about the risks and how to manage for the best."[68]

Hinks, meanwhile, had turned his attention from personnel to finances. As of November 1923 the Mount Everest Committee showed a surplus balance of £2,474, thanks largely to Mallory's and Finch's lecturing efforts. The cost of the new expedition, however, was likely to exceed that by a factor of five—the second expedition had cost £12,538—and if it failed—if, that is, no one reached the summit—the return on lectures the third time around would no doubt be negligible. In addition, then, to the standard publicity contracts with *The Times* (for expedition dispatches) and Edward Arnold (for the expedition volume), the Everest Committee for the first time sought out corporate sponsorship, accepting money in exchange for product endorsements. Norman Collie was joking (and alluding to a celebrated Pears' Soap advertisement featuring Admiral Dewey) when he suggested that the committee approach Sunlight Soap with an offer to plant their logo alongside the Union Jack on the summit. Yet Hinks was, in fact, despite himself, starting to think along these lines. The days of the full-blown commercial climbing industry were still far off; Hinks was not selling places on the team. But the 1924 Everest expedition nevertheless marks a distinct shift from the traditional idea of exploration in search of resources to the modern idea of exploration as itself a resource, as a marketable product available for investment.[69]

If anyone appreciated the commercial value of Mount Everest in 1924, however, it was not Hinks nor Bruce nor Mallory, however, but John Noel, the expedition photographer, whose skill with a camera was matched only by his flair for promotion. In 1922 he had already hit on the profitable idea of dispatching portions of his film in progress to Europe for immediate distribution through Pathé Pictorial News—the distant progenitor, if you will, of today's simultaneous Internet transmissions. The completed travel film, *Climbing Mount Everest,* opened in theaters in December 1922 and despite its lack of human drama and heavy reliance on static landscape shots—"the Everest expedition was a picnic in Connemara surprised by a snow-storm," said George Bernard Shaw on seeing the film—it did well enough to encourage Noel in the thought of a bolder, full-length epic feature. On being named to the new expedition in 1923, he at once formed his own film production company, Explorer Films, Ltd., and offered the Everest Committee £8,000 for exclusive photographic rights. He invested in all the latest technology, including a state-of-the-art, battery powered, 35mm Newman camera with a twenty-inch Hobson telephoto lens ("resembling a baby Lewis gun") and Eastman Kodak Panchromatic film. His hope, as he explained it to Bruce, was "to make a film that can compete in the cinematograph trade with the usual productions," and before even leaving England he advertised it accordingly as the romantic story of "man's passionate struggle to conquer the dreadful virgin of the snows." Mount Everest, the *Weekly Dispatch* promised, "will be characterised as an inhuman 'vampire'—a whitened Jezebel of the Himalayas—who contemptuously flings blinding storms and deadly avalanches upon her too daring suitors." In the end she would yield, of course; Noel's advance publicity assumed a triumphant ending. He knew the difficult odds the expedition faced, however, and quietly planned to make a second, more conventional travel film "dealing with the life of the people in Tibet, Sikkim and Bhutan" to be released in the event of mountaineering failure. As a further hedge against his bets, he decided early on to bring back with him, if possible, a small group of Sherpa porters or Tibetan lamas to act as "live prologue" to the film—a concept with some precedent, it seems, in the movie trade but one that was nevertheless soon to land both Noel and the Everest Committee in considerable controversy.[70]

Accompanied this time by Beetham, Hazard, and Irvine, Mallory sailed from Liverpool on the *SS California* on February 29, 1924. "This is going to be more like war than mountaineering. I don't expect to come back," he had recently said to Geoffrey Keynes, and the evidence of a hurried visit to Robert Scott's widow, Kathleen (who had subsequently married Geoffrey Young's brother Hilton), speaks further to some sort of personal foreboding. To Ruth, though, he wrote hopefully of life after Everest and the good prospects of the expedition. Between Hindustani lessons, oxygen drills, potato-sack races with Irvine, and the freshly cut pages of André Maurois's life of Shelley, the voyage spun out pleasantly enough, and it was, Mallory said, a good, fit, and "amazingly nice" party that converged once again on the Mount Everest Hotel in Darjeeling in the third week of March. Bruce soon had the formidable organization of men and materiel well in hand. The oxygen sets had arrived from Calcutta variously broken and mangled, but Irvine—"a great dab at things mechanical"—had salvaged them, and Mallory (influenced, perhaps, by the personal improvement of Irvine upon Finch) had already resigned himself to their use above 26,000 feet when the caravan moved out for Kalimpong on March 26.[71]

In Cambridge it had snowed, and Ruth and the children were making snowmen in the garden, but in Sikkim the weather was unusually mild, and Mallory felt full of "valley-ease and warmth and languor and the delights of the lotus-eater." Below Pedong, he, Odell, and Irvine raced down 2,000 feet to the Rongpo Chu and bathed "properly," that is to say, nakedly, in a well-placed diving pool. Beetham had already been stricken with dysentery, and two days out of Phari, Mallory too came down with "a slight colitis

George Mallory and Andrew Irvine aboard the
California en route for Everest, 1924. Reprinted
by permission of the Salkeld Collection.

or something of the kind" that had Somervell suspecting appendicitis. The real medical
anxiety, though, was Bruce, who since Yatung had been feeling feverish and "a little bit
seedy." On April 6 at Phari, the general celebrated his fifty-eighth birthday with a bottle
of 140-year-old rum and talked in his bluff way about soldiering on. But two days later he
succumbed entirely to a recurrence of an old malarial infection. Mindful of poor Kellas's
fate in this particular corner of a foreign field, Hingston, the expedition doctor, ordered
him back to Darjeeling. "We've lost a force, and we shall miss him in the mess," Mallory
wrote, but Norton made a splendid substitute. "He knows the whole *bandobast* from A to
Z, and his eyes are everywhere; is personally acceptable to everyone and makes us all feel
happy, is always full of interest, easy and yet dignified, or rather never losing dignity, and
a tremendous adventurer."[72]

Better still, Norton at once named Mallory deputy leader in charge of climbing
and asked him to devise the expedition's plan of ascent. Eager to oblige, Mallory with-

drew to his tent and there by sudden inspiration—a "brain-wave," he called it—arrived at a wholly original plan that called for not one but three camps above the North Col and two pairs of climbers, one with oxygen and one without, making simultaneous attempts on the summit from the two highest camps.[73] The chief merits of this variation on classic siege tactics, in Mallory's view, lay in the mutual support afforded the two summit teams, the effective compromise on the still-divisive oxygen question, the margin of error and reserve strength allowed, and, above all, the respectful division of the upper mountain into humanly manageable parts. Norton approved the plan at once and left to Mallory the thornier business of naming the summit teams. The two obvious choices were Somervell and himself, both oxygen skeptics. But Mallory's strictures on this subject had weakened as his resolve to be done with Everest strengthened. Somervell, he decided, would lead the gas-free attempt from Camp VII, accompanied by Norton or Hazard. He himself would lead the gas attempt from Camp VI, accompanied by Irvine.

Mallory's fateful choice of Sandy Irvine over the immeasurably more experienced Noel Odell as his climbing partner surprised Norton at the time, and it has led some since to wonder whether some kind of romantic attraction had come into play. Mallory certainly liked Irvine, and saw in him a reflection of his younger, eager self. Moreover, he had a deeply aesthetic sensibility that could influence his personal judgments. Asked to account for the choice of Irvine, the Bloomsbury artist Duncan Grant said that "it would have been characteristic of Mallory (with his own superb proportions) to choose, of two equal objects, the more beautiful." But this was the fight for Everest, not an Alpine holiday lark, and Mallory surely made his choice on two simpler, more practical grounds. First, Irvine knew the oxygen sets inside out: in light of Mallory's own mechanical inaptitude, this was especially compelling. Second, he was incomparably strong, and strength, in Mallory's mind, counted for more on Everest than any amount of experience. The choice then, though difficult, was clear, and having made it, Mallory brimmed with confidence. "We're going to sail to the top this time, and God with us," he wrote Tom Longstaff, "—or stamp to the top with our teeth in the wind."[74]

The 1924 Everest expedition reached Base Camp at the foot of the Rongbuk Glacier on April 29, intending to put four men on the summit on May 17, well in advance of the expected break of the monsoon. From the beginning, pitiless weather and rigid adherence to a far too cumbersome expedition design played havoc with these hopes. Simply to establish the first three camps on the East Rongbuk was, as Mallory conceded, an overly compli-cated business involving carefully orchestrated, interlocking relays of over 200 Tibetan and Sherpa porters and untold tons of gear. Given perfect conditions, it might just have worked. But from May 4 snow began to fall, temperatures plunged to minus twenty-two degrees Fahrenheit, ill-clad and demoralized porters abandoned their loads, and (as Noel recalled) "the whole transportation system crumpled." By May 11 the expedition was in total disarray, hopelessly strewn about the glacier, and Norton ordered a general retreat to Base Camp. "It has been a very trying time with everything against us," George told Ruth, and who could possibly deny it?[75] Even so, reading the relevant chapter in the official expedition volume, with its constant reference to loads, relays, dumps, depots, supply lines, and columns of porters, one cannot help but conclude that quite apart from the weather, the expedition had simply collapsed under its own weight.

Back in London, the great British Empire Exhibition had opened at Wembley on April 23, just as the Everest expedition neared Base Camp. As with all such exhibitions, pride of place went to India, the jewel in the crown and the raison d'être of empire for the past century. Built at a cost of £180,000, the India Pavilion—the last and greatest one of its kind—covered three acres and claimed to put all of India on display, from native arts, crafts, and customs to the infinite blessings conferred by British rule. But the star attraction, prominently placed at the center of "Bengal Court" (and thus aggressively appropriated for the Raj) was a full relief model of Everest, five feet, six inches high and twenty-five feet around. Built by Sifton Praed and Co. on a scale of two feet to the mile, the model was the property of the government of India: the Mount Everest Committee had declined to contribute toward its cost. The committee had provided the necessary maps and photographs, however, and once the model went on display, Hinks took a strong proprietary interest in it, endlessly fiddling and fussing over its topographical details. Displayed in conjunction with *Climbing Mount Everest,* Noel's film of the 1922 expedition (then playing in the exhibition cinema hall) and accompanied by maps, photographs, picture postcards, and the like, the model gave visitors as complete a vicarious experience of Everest as the visual technology of the time allowed. Little stick pins marked the mountain's most celebrated features insofar as they were known—the south side of the mountain remained wholly unexplored—and tracked the progress of the climbers telegram by telegram. Just how many people saw the exhibit we cannot say: attendance records for the India Pavilion do not exist. But A. W. Vincent, the controller of the India Section of the exhibition, assured Hinks of "its receiving a very great deal of attention," particularly from "conducted parties" and schoolchildren, and other such fragmentary evidence suggests a great success.[76] Certainly the exhibit brought the Himalaya home as nothing else had done before and, by way of its placement in Bengal Court, located Everest at the symbolic center of the British colonial imagination.

Little of this, had he even known it, would have been of much comfort to Norton as he marshaled his scattered forces at Base Camp for a second attempt on the mountain. His great, almost irrational obsession now was the monsoon, and the need to get up and down again before it broke. On May 12, in consultation with Mallory, he drew up a new schedule setting a target summit date of May 29—Ascension Day, at it happened. There followed five days of enforced inactivity during which, Noel remembered, Mallory "seemed ill at ease, always scheming and planning." To Ruth George admitted disappointment in his comrades: Somervell seemed "a bit below his form of two years ago," Norton "not particularly strong." Irvine had "much more of the winning spirit" and had been "wonderfully hard-working and brilliantly skillful about the oxygen." But he himself,

George assured Ruth, was "the strongest of the lot, the most likely to get to the top, with or without gas."[77]

On May 17, after a full week's rest and an inspirational visit to the Rongbuk lama, the expedition again moved up the line. Camps I, II, and III were restored and reoccupied, and on May 20 Mallory and Norton finally forced a route up the 1,000-foot ice slopes of the Chang La. The next day Somervell, Irvine, and Hazard established Camp IV, leaving Hazard and twelve porters in possession: a good start, but there the effort stalled, once again beset by cold and storm. On May 23, after riding out the storm for a day, Hazard lost his nerve and evacuated the col, inexcusably leaving four porters stranded and forcing "the old gang" of Mallory, Norton, and Somervell to expend their few remaining energies in a desperate (and successful) rescue on May 24. Next day the storms continued, and the party again withdrew to the relative security of Camp I, where, on the evening of May 26, Norton summoned a final council of war. The expedition was in a pitiable state: sick, spent, and discouraged. Of the fifty-five high-altitude porters, only fifteen were fit to continue and Norton contemplated withdrawal from the mountain. But May 27 broke "cloudlessly fine," and the climbers instead settled on a last, desperate plan. Scrapping the oxygen altogether in order to save weight, they would dash up from the col by way of Camps V and VI in two groups of two: Mallory and Geoffrey Bruce (now "the only plumb fit man") to be followed by Norton and Somervell. "It is fifty to one against us," George wrote in a final letter to Ruth, "but we'll have a whack yet and do ourselves proud. Great love to you."[78]

May 28 continued fine, hot even, and "the firebrands," as Norton called them, "wanted to be up and away." But Norton insisted on another day's rest and recuperation. The fifteen stalwart Sherpas, now appreciatively nicknamed the Tigers, assembled at Camp II, where the famous "old firm" of Irvine and Odell fashioned a rudimentary ladder out of rope and tent pegs for the difficult Chimney Pitch below the col. Back at Camp I, Mallory wrote a few last letters, read a few last poems, lingered listlessly in his sleeping bag, and endlessly turned the coming effort over in his mind. Six days from here to the summit, he reckoned, and the first four went precisely as planned. June 1 saw him, Geoffrey Bruce, and four Sherpa porters safely ensconced in the lee of the North Ridge at 25,200 feet. The next morning, however, despite the promising weather, three of the four Sherpas refused to budge, done in, they insisted, by their labors of the preceding day. "Show's crashed," Mallory tersely wrote in a note sent down with the Sherpas to Norton, "—wind took the heart of our porters yesterday and none will face going higher."[79] After lingering behind to improve Camp V and put in a third tent placement, he and Bruce retreated to the col, their best opportunity lost.

The chance now fell to Norton and Somervell, and they made the most of it. Setting out from the North Col at 6:00 A.M. on June 2, they reached Camp V without incident by early afternoon. Next morning their Sherpas too were immovable, but Norton appealed relentlessly to their sense of obligation and honor—"If you put us up a camp at 27,000 feet and we reach the top, your names shall appear in letters of gold in the book that will be written to describe the achievement," he later remembered saying—and finally three of them, Norbu Yishay, Lhakpa Chedi, and Semchumbi, agreed to carry on.[80] The weather continued fine and the wind had dropped, but it was nevertheless a breathless plod over loose scree and the notorious sloping slabs of the North Face. By early afternoon, Semchumbi was done in and Norton called a halt, gratefully dismissed the three Sherpas, and pitched Camp VI in a narrow, north-facing cleft in the ridge at 26,800 feet.

Mallory's plan, from this point, had always been to make directly for the Northeast Ridge and follow its gentle line to the summit. But Norton did not like the look of the two conspicuous protuberances, or "steps" in the ridge, and next morning, June 4, he and Somervell set off diagonally across the North Face, hoping to reach the summit by way of the great couloir or gully that falls from the summit pyramid. An hour out of camp they reached the lower edge of the distinctive band of yellow limestone that encircles the upper ramparts of Mount Everest. This afforded easy going for a while, and miraculously the weather still held. The altitude took its inevitable toll, though, and soon their pace was wretched: eight to ten respirations per step and ten to twelve steps between rests. By noon Somervell was finished: physically drained and wracked by a suffocating pain in his throat. Norton left him sitting under a rock and, at Somervell's own urging, carried on without him, skirting the top edge of the Yellow Band into the Great "Norton" Couloir. Here "the going became a great deal worse," Norton recalled.[81] The downward-sloping ledges narrowed to a few scant inches concealed in powdery snow. Earlier in the day Norton had removed his goggles to be more sure of his footing, and now he was seeing double as he felt his way, tile by ever-steepening tile, across the couloir. He was tantalizingly close, 200 feet from the base of the summit pyramid. But this was no place for an unroped climber, and time had run out besides. At 1:00 P.M. he turned around, 900 feet shy of the summit and, at 28,126 feet, higher on earth than anyone else would climb (and live to tell about it) until 1952.

Mallory, meanwhile, grievously disappointed at the anticlimactic ending of his and Bruce's effort, had come down resolved on yet one more try, with oxygen this time, and with Irvine. It was not so much a matter of bulldog tenacity, or sheer determination to conquer, Younghusband later wrote, as "the imagination of the artist who cannot leave his work until it is completely, neatly, and perfectly finished."[82] He found Irvine agreeable, even eager, and on June 4, the same day as Norton's near miss, the two of them climbed up the col with oxygen in the encouragingly record time of two and a half hours. Norton, staggering half dead and blind into Camp IV that night, thought it a forlorn hope and once again queried the choice of Irvine when the obviously fit and well-acclimatized Odell lay ready to hand. But Mallory would not be swayed, and in the end Norton deferred to his judgment and wished him well. June 5 was given to the usual preparations, and at 8:40 the following morning they were off: Mallory, Irvine, and eight Sherpa porters.

A famous photograph by Noel Odell captures the moment of departure. Slightly hunkered against the wind, Irvine stands waiting, his oxygen-cylindered back to the camera,

Noel Odell's photograph of Mallory (left) and Irvine (right) as they prepare to leave Camp IV on the North Col for their fateful summit attempt. Reprinted by permission of the Royal Geographical Society.

his hands stuffed into his pockets, his ice ax at the ready to his left. Facing the camera next to him, just off balance, Mallory looks down at his face mask in one hand while reaching for his ice ax with the other, poised to depart. Both men are wearing cotton Shackleton jackets, breeches, and cashmere puttees. Irvine wears his trademark wide-brimmed floppy hat, Mallory his air force helmet, goggles, and woolen scarf. Immediately behind them are the battered tents of Camp IV and the lightly trampled snowfields of the North Col. Hindsight plays tricks, of course, but there is an undeniable air of finality to the scene, of ominous expectation. Moments after the shutter fell, "the party moved off in silence," Odell wrote, and was soon lost to view.[83]

At 5:00 that evening, four of Mallory's Sherpas returned to the col and confirmed that he and Irvine had reached Camp V in good time. "There is no wind here and things look hopeful," Mallory had scribbled in a note to Odell. The next day, June 7, Odell and Sherpa Nema moved up to Camp V, where Sherpa Lakpa met them with two more notes from Mallory, one for Odell apologizing for the derelict state of Camp V—he and Irvine had evidently left in a confused muddle that morning—and one for Noel, the cameraman, alerting him to the likely time of their final approach to the summit pyramid on the morrow. All Sherpas now withdrew with thanks to Camp III: the mountain was left to Hazard at Camp IV, Odell at Camp V, and Mallory and Irvine at Camp VI. The next morning, June 8, 1924, Odell set off alone to Camp VI with a few emergency provisions and Mallory's compass, which he—Mallory—forgetful to the end, had characteristically left behind at Camp V. The day was not unduly cold, and, oddly intent on a little high-altitude geologizing, Odell took a circuitous route outward over the North Face. The upper mountain had been shrouded in mist and cloud all morning. But at 12:50 P.M., just as Odell had climbed a little crag as a test of his condition, the sky cleared and the entire summit ridge came into view. His eyes, Odell later said, became fixed on a tiny black spot silhouetted against the snow beneath a rock step in the ridge. It moved, and then another black spot moved up to join it. "The first then approached the great rock step and shortly emerged at the top; the second did likewise. Then the whole fascinating vision vanished, enveloped in cloud once more."[84]

CHAPTER FOUR

"A Random Harvest of Delight"
1929–1933

News of her husband's disappearance and death reached Ruth Mallory in Cambridge on June 19, eleven days after the fact. By then the 1924 expedition had withdrawn from the mountain, leaving a memorial cairn to Mallory, Irvine, Kellas, and the seven lost Sherpas of 1922 behind. "We were a sad little party," Norton later recalled; "from the first we accepted the loss of our comrades in that rational spirit which all of our generation had learnt in the Great War, and there was never any tendency to a morbid harping on the irrevocable." But the tragedy was "very near," he said, the sense of loss "acute and personal." From the comfortable distance of London, Hinks somehow turned tragedy to triumph. "COMMITTEE WARMLY CONGRATULATES WHOLE PARTY HEROIC ACHIEVEMENTS," he pompously cabled to Norton over the name of Norman Collie (then acting president of the Everest Committee). "ALL DEEPLY MOVED BY GLORIOUS DEATH LOST CLIMBERS NEAR SUMMIT." Douglas Freshfield immediately queried the choice of words. "'Warmest congratulations,'" he wrote to Hinks, was "a queer way to mark so great a tragedy." But he conceded the difficulty of the job, remembering how he himself had labored to compose such a telegram in Robert Scott's case, and his own suggested alternative—"Committee received with feelings profound sorrow and pride news death Mallory & Irvine in heroic assault on summit"—put an equally triumphal if somewhat more mournful gloss on the tragedy. There was no stopping it: from the moment *The Times* released the news to the public on June 21, the high rhetoric of empire and war took over. Mallory and Irvine were "the glorious dead" and Everest "the finest cenotaph in the world."[1]

Among Mallory's acquaintance, meanwhile, and among an enthralled public too, the endlessly compelling but hopelessly speculative discussion of whether he and Irvine had reached the summit at once began, essentially never to end. Noel Odell, the man in the best literal position to judge, for now at least thought it probable that they had and then lost their way on the descent and died of exposure. Norton, however (partly out of concern for the two families), insisted they had died quickly in "an ordinary mountaineering accident." The summit, he allowed, remained a hypothetical possibility—they may, after all, have fallen on the descent—but on balance he believed that Mallory would have been "the last man to press on" beyond the point of safe return and had therefore probably not reached the top. At best it remained "a case of 'not proven.'" To Ruth the circumstances of her husband's death were entirely inconsequential. "It is his life that I loved and love," she told Geoffrey Young, and in writing to George Trevelyan, another old friend from the Pen-y-Pass days, Young echoed her sentiment: "In weighing the balance, I attach no glamour or importance to the circumstance of his death; it was as accidental a consequence as his choice of life, and of his temperament, as my losing my leg. It was his life was important." In writing to Younghusband, however, Young attached great significance to the circumstances of Mallory's death and felt compelled to counter Norton's skepticism:

> From nearly twenty years experience with him as a mountaineer, I am prepared to say that, while Mallory was aware of risks, especially of those of Everest, and a most careful mountaineer, when a crisis came in action he invariably threw in all of his forces and *acted:* his was not a temperament that was capable of detached judgments or nice balances once opposition had provoked his initiative. I accordingly maintain that far from being "the last man to press on, etc.," he was, on the contrary, of all the great mountaineers I have known, the *most* likely to have decided for advance at all hazards and to have postponed the difficulties of darkness, descent, etc.—to the moment when he had to meet them. He had taken immense risks in his climbing life—many of them with a single companion inferior to Irvine—and he had always just pulled off success by his great powers. He might well think, that with such a goal in view, he might trust to be able to do so once again.[2]

And so the issue was joined, between the rational skeptics and the romantic faithful who hold to this day, with Young, that "the peak was first climbed [in 1924] because Mallory was Mallory." The king meanwhile paid public tribute to "these two gallant explorers" and extended his sympathies to the families. Memorial services followed at Magdalene College, Charterhouse, and finally St. Paul's Cathedral, where on October 17 the bishop of Chester took as his text the Latin version of Psalm 84:5—*Ascensiones in corde suo disposuit*—and in concluding adapted the lament of King David: "Delightful and very pleasant were George Mallory and Andrew Irvine; in life, in death, they were not parted." That same evening, a joint public meeting of the Alpine Club and the Royal Geographical Society at the Albert Hall received the final report of the expedition and resolved to keep up the good fight.[3]

Far from discouraging the idea of climbing Everest, the loss of two Englishmen at or near the summit gave it added memorial urgency and in the public mind strengthened the presumptive British claim to the mountain. On November 5 the Mount Everest Committee formally applied to the Tibetan government for permission to return in 1926, and Arthur Hinks wrote privately to Colonel Frederick Marshman Bailey, Sir Charles Bell's successor as political officer in Sikkim, asking him to use his influence with Lhasa in the committee's favor and against both Finch (who, according to Hinks, had "a private scheme for getting out next year and stealing a march on the Committee") and the rival Swiss and German expeditions now said to be in the making.⁴ Like Bell before him, Bailey, though a creditable explorer and adventurer himself, had little use for the Everest expeditions, regarding them as noisy intrusions on a delicate frontier. But Everest chroniclers attribute too much responsibility to him for the political debacle that followed. The curtain came down on Everest in 1925 because the Tibetan government had had quite enough of the antics of Captain John Noel.

It was Noel, recall, whose illicit foray into Tibet in 1913 had begun the Everest business in the first place, and though the Tibetans had ultimately consented to it, they never much liked it, always fearing a recurrence of Younghusband's violent "diplomatic mission" to Lhasa in 1904. In the wake of the 1921 reconnaissance, they had strongly objected to Heron's demon-disturbing shovel and to Morshead's independent surveying beyond the authorized vicinity of Everest. The 1922 expedition passed without incident, thanks to Bruce's close attentiveness to these sensitive matters, but in 1924 the Tibetans again objected to various territorial transgressions and then more seriously to Noel's film, *The Epic of Everest,* which as originally released in India included an unflattering scene of a local man eating lice. "The Tibetans say that this is not typical and will give the world the wrong impression," Bailey wrote urgently to Hinks, at whose insistence Noel agreed to cut the scene before the film opened in London. But Noel kept an equally objectionable scene showing an old man killing fleas with his teeth and, worse still from Lhasa's point of view, he insisted on retaining the "live prologue" featuring six holy lamas whom he had illegally spirited away from a monastery in Gyantse. The Mount Everest Committee, suddenly conscious of a grave offense to Tibetan political and religious sensibilities, tried desperately to distance itself from Noel's theatrical antics, but they could not disown him completely; he had, after all, largely underwritten the 1924 expedition. In April 1925 Lhasa demanded the return of the "dancing lamas" and indefinitely forbade any further expeditions to Everest.⁵

With Tibet and Nepal both closed to foreign travelers and Chomolungma thus off limits, the attention of the climbing world turned in the late 1920s to those parts of the Himalaya accessible from British India. Not that this lessened the challenge or the allure. Kangchenjunga may be a mere forty-five miles from Darjeeling, but it is still the third-highest mountain in the world and unquestionably the iciest. Nanda Devi in Kumaon may be only seventy-five miles from Almora and rise no higher than 25,645 feet—roughly the height of Mallory's Camp V on Everest—but it is strongly defended by a surrounding ring of precipitous ridges and for all anyone knew unassailable. And so it went, from the western, trans-Himalayan ranges of the Karakoram (K2, Broad Peak, the Gasherbrums) through the Punjab Himal (Nanga Parbat and the Nun Kun massif) and Garhwal-Kumaon (Kamet and Nanda Devi) to Sikkim (Kangchenjunga) and Assam (Chomolhari). To retreat to British India in 1925 was to discover an endless and astonishing variety of climbing possibilities.

And here, unlike in Tibet, no one country, group, or committee had any exclusive claim. With the exception of the northern face of Nanga Parbat (closed for political reasons), the mountains were more or less open to all who could muster the will and wherewithal to go. So go they did, in ever-increasing numbers, on expeditions ranging from the massive, state-sponsored, quasi-military assault on some 8,000-meter giant to the small, private, quiet exploration of some hidden valley or lesser mountain. Recalling his own invitation to accompany Frank Smythe to Kamet in 1931, Eric Shipton (later of Everest fame) wrote that Himalayan mountaineering was then "in a state analogous to the early years of the golden age in the Alps, when the simple mountain explorer, with no special ability, was still free to pick the plums in a random harvest of delight."[6]

The clearest institutional expression of the advent of this golden age of Himalayan mountaineering was the founding of the Himalayan Club in 1927–28. The idea of a club along the lines of the venerable Alpine Club in London had been around since 1866, when the intrepid William Henry Johnson of the Indian Survey proposed it to the Asiatic Society of Bengal. Nearly twenty years later, Douglas Freshfield urged in the *Alpine Journal* "the formation at Calcutta or Simla of an Himalayan Club, prepared to publish 'Narratives of Science and Adventure' concerning the mountains," and the idea was much in the minds of those who worked and traveled in Kashmir in the years before the First World War. But the war intervened, and afterward the idea simply languished until Sir Geoffrey Corbett, an accomplished trekker and longtime member of the Alpine Club, was posted to India as secretary for commerce and industry in 1926. From his bungalow in Simla, the Indian summer capital, Corbett enjoyed expansive views of the snows of the Punjab Himal. His daily ritual included a walk from the ridge to the summit of Jakhu Hill, and it was here, legend has it, "on the path behind Jakko," that he conjured his vision of an "Alpine Club of India" in October 1927.[7]

In Calcutta, meanwhile, a small group of Himalayan enthusiasts led by William Allsup and H. W. Tobin had already (by ten days or so) established a "Mountain Club of India," but this was to prove short-lived and Corbett did not know of it when he broached his idea to Major Kenneth Mason of the Indian Survey. Unlike Corbett, Mason was quite the old Himalayan hand. Between 1910 and 1913 he had worked on the survey of Kashmir, linking the Indian to the Russian triangulations in the region north of Hunza. Recalled to England on the outbreak of war in 1914, he served on the western front (1914–15) and in Mesopotamia (1916–18), where he earned the Military Cross for his part in the relief of Kut al-Amara. After the war he returned to an India that had changed, he thought, much for the worse. "The cost of everything had risen, political agitation and restlessness were upsetting loyalties, and, coupled with retrenchment, were hampering science and scientific departments," he later groused. Yet despite these hindrances, in 1925 Mason led a pioneer- ing survey of the Shaksgam Valley in the northern Karakoram, then still a "blank on the map," and thus won the Founder's Gold Medal of the Royal Geographical Society. By his own admission, he was not a particularly skillful mountaineer—though he had climbed with Ernest Neve in Kashmir before the war and had one modest first ascent (Kolahoi) to his credit—but he knew the Himalaya intimately and, more important, perhaps, he occupied a sufficiently prominent place in the edifice of the Raj to attract the exclusive sort of membership he and Corbett had in mind. Together they addressed a circular letter to about 100 mountaineers of note and experience, including Conway, Collie, Freshfield, Younghusband, Bruce, Norton, and every surviving member of the Everest expeditions. The response (rhetorical and financial) surpassed their expectations, and the Himalayan Club—so named so as not to intimidate nonclimbers—came formally into existence in the New Delhi offices of Sir William Birdwood, commander in chief of the Indian Army, on February 17, 1928.[8]

The principal object of the Himalayan Club, as defined in the Memorandum of Association, was "to encourage and assist Himalayan travel and exploration, and to extend knowledge of the Himalaya and adjoining mountain ranges through science, art, literature, and sport."[9] It was not, in other words, exclusively a climbing club. It aimed to promote and encourage interest in the mountains among geologists, botanists, artists, writers, explorers, and sportsmen of all sorts. It was, however (apart from a handful of mountain rajas), exclusively European: that the people of India might share in this love of the mountains of India had not as yet occurred to the colonial mind, and even if it had, simple prejudice would have worked to discourage it. Membership in the Himalayan Club was strictly by invitation and limited to those who had "done things" in the mountains, plus the obligatory decorative gang of viceroys, governors, generals, and such. On paper the club had all kinds of luminary officers, but Corbett and Mason were the moving spirits behind its early work. First, they appointed "local secretaries" in the hill stations of Srinagar, Chamba, Simla, Almora, and Darjeeling to assist and advise members in all matters relating to mountain travel, including food, transport, equipment, and the recruitment of porters. For those needing more distant, preliminary sorts of help, they placed "local correspondents" as far afield as Delhi, Lahore, and London. As club editor, Mason undertook the collection and publication of maps, route books, and district guides based on the authoritative data of the Indian Survey and gathered them together in the club library at Simla.

Finally, in 1929, Mason launched the *Himalayan Journal,* the Indian equivalent of the *Alpine Journal* and thereafter the more or less definitive record of Himalayan achievement. Already by then the club had attracted considerable notice in Europe and served as first point of contact for those contemplating an attempt on the highest heights. No sooner had the first issue of its journal appeared, in fact, than Mason received a letter from Willi Rickmer Rickmers, a well-known German climber and of late the leader of a German-Soviet expedition to the Pamirs, asking for help on behalf of a group of young Bavarians who, having climbed extensively in the Alps and the Caucasus, now hoped to come out to India. "They want to test themselves against something difficult," Rickmers said, "some mountain that will call out everything they've got in them of courage, perseverance, and endurance."[10] Everest, needless to say, was out of the question politically as well as off limits sentimentally. But contrary to common legend, the British laid no exclusive claim to the Himalaya as such, and despite recent national enmities, Mason assured Rickmers of the club's full support both in England and ultimately in India.

Paul Bauer and the Munich School

And so the Germans came at last to the Himalaya. Their leader in 1929 was Paul Bauer, a thirty-three-year-old notary who over the past few years had come to the fore of the so-called Munich School of mountaineering. On a purely technical level, this signified an unrestrained commitment to innovation, to climbing hitherto unimaginable routes by whatever means or methods available. It may have been an Englishman, Oscar Eckenstein, who designed the ten-point crampon in 1908, thus largely freeing climbers from the laborious business of cutting steps in the ice, but it was the Germans who proved willing to use it, along with the piton and the carabiner, those conjoined miracles of simple technology that made possible the placing of points of belay on an otherwise sheer face or pitch. In 1922 one German, Fritz Rigele, successfully adapted the piton for use on ice—voilà, the ice peg—and another, Willo Welzenbach, finally discarded the long ice ax in favor of a short-handled pick with which he found he could claw his way up frozen slopes he could not climb otherwise. Together these several new tools made possible the kind of direct assault on a mountain face or wall for which the Munich School was best known. Not for them the tired and well-worn mountain ridges: a new chapter in the history of mountaineering opened in August 1925, when two Bavarians, Willo Welzenbach and Eugen Allwein, climbed straight up the North Face of the Dent d'Hérens in under sixteen hours.

But there was always more to what English purists derided as "the dangle and whack school" than technical innovation and audacity. In fact "school" is not the right word to describe what was really a climbing fraternity founded on the common experience of national defeat and marked, as Bauer said, by a "stern, warlike, disciplined spirit which was our heritage from the Great War." Bauer's own case may be taken as instructive. Born in the featureless borderland of the Rhineland Palatinate in 1896, he spent an unremarkable childhood dreaming of Alpine adventure and glorying in the imperial pretensions of the Kaiser. In August 1914, fresh from a cycling tour through the Dolomites, he went willingly to war, fully convinced of its necessity and confident of its outcome. Captured in 1918, he spent the last weeks of the war in an English prison and then returned disoriented and disheartened to a Germany that had grown terribly strange to him, a Germany, he later wrote, in which "love of Fatherland, heroism and self-sacrifice were looked down upon and denigrated." Precisely when he made his way to Munich to study law is unclear, but already by 1919 he would have found there a vibrant center of radical reaction, the city of Hitler, the very forcing ground of National Socialism. An enthusiastic member of the Freikorps (volunteer paramilitary formations of demobilized soldiers unreconciled to defeat and violently hostile to socialism), Bauer may well have participated in the brutal suppres-

Paul Bauer (1896–1990), leader of the 1929 and
1931 German Kangchenjunga expeditions.
Reprinted by permission of the German
Alpine Club.

sion of the Munich Räterepublik (Councils Republic) in May 1919. He seems not to have joined the Nazi Party until after the seizure of power in 1933, but he nevertheless prided himself on being an "old soldier," as the saying went, an early convert to the cause. Already by 1923, the year of the abortive Beer Hall Putsch, Adolf Hitler was for him, he later said, *der Mann, den wir nicht antasten ließen,* the man we would not see impugned.[11]

The real focus of Bauer's corporatist longings in the wake of the war, however, was neither the Nazi Party nor one of the many other reactionary political factions that then plagued Germany, but the Akademischer Alpenverein München, the student climbing club of Munich University. Founded in 1892, the Akademischer Alpenverein was by now a well-established institution, a recognized complement, in fact, to the older (and now merged) German and Austrian Alpine Clubs (Deutschen und Österreichischen Alpenvereins). But given its placement in the university, it remained a force for youthful innovation, the genius loci of the Munich School. Here Bauer found both a talented corps of technical ice climbers and a close, consoling fellowship of men endowed, he said, with "special spiritual gifts."

From Munich the mountains beckon continually on the southern horizon, and Sunday after Sunday, summer and winter, from the time of the hyperinflation of 1922–23 to the Great Depression, Bauer and friends fled the sound and fury of the city for the restorative silences of nature. Always avoiding the mountain huts and well-worn mountain paths, they deliberately sought out the most difficult and direct routes the Bavarian Alps had to offer, and when these no longer satisfied, they ventured farther afield to Italy, Switzerland, and France. "It was imperative for us to escape at last from the crushing narrowness into which Germany had been forced by the war," Bauer later recalled. In 1928, while three other Munichers—Eugen Allwein, Erwin Schneider, and Karl Wien—accompanied Rickmer Rickmers on his joint German-Soviet expedition to Peak Lenin in the Pamirs, Bauer led his own party of four into the Caucasus and attempted Dykh-tau, at 17,077 feet (5,205 meters) the second-highest mountain in Europe. A storm turned him back 100 feet shy of the summit (first reached by Mummery in 1888), but on the whole the expedition met expectations and encouraged Bauer in still greater ambitions. "It is now quite obvious to me," he wrote to his friends on his return to Germany, "that in 1929 we must go to the Himalayas."[12]

Once having resolved on the Himalaya and secured the blessing of the several governments involved—the British needed only to be reassured that Everest was not on the program—Bauer set about organizing an expedition that perfectly reflected his stern, Germanic spirit. Having made a close study of the Everest expeditions, he concluded that they suffered from material extravagance, conflict of purpose, and hopeless heterogeneity of personnel. In the first place, then, he demanded "spartanlike simplicity." Everything, down to the level of boot studs and coffee beans, was minutely counted, measured, weighed, and discarded if it did not meet the test of strictest necessity. The main idea here was to keep the number of porters to a minimum and bring a kind of alpine mobility into the Himalaya. Beyond this practical consideration, though, lay a philosophical insistence on self-denial and even suffering as essential parts of the mountaineering experience. Far more than his English counterparts, Bauer thought of the mountain camp as an existential extension of the trench. Climbing, for him, was, like war, "an opportunity to test those qualities which had become superfluous in every day life, but which to us were still the highest qualities in the world: unshakeable courage, comradeship, and self sacrifice." Moreover, the war and the vengeful settlement that followed—"the Carthaginian Peace," as Keynes famously called it—had reduced Germany to a state of primitive austerity, and Bauer thought it fitting that a German expedition adopt a corresponding ethos. Relying mainly on small contributions from members of the Akademischer Alpenverein for funds, he disdained to invoke the sponsorship of a "sensation-loving press" or to indulge the company of "a few wealthy patrons" who might have helped pay the way. Critics charged him with failing to represent Germany with adequate dignity, but Bauer was unmoved. "Our enemies had robbed us," he later wrote, "and we had no need to conceal the fact."[13]

Nor had Bauer any need to conceal his "mountaineering ideals" under the cloak of scientific research. In his mind the purpose of the expedition was pure and simple: to climb a great Himalayan peak and by so doing restore the tarnished honor of the fatherland. He had no interest in personal ambitions, height records, or "sensational effects." The group, *die Mannschaft*, was everything, and in composing it Bauer relied exclusively on long personal acquaintance and the brotherhood of the Akademischer Alpenverein. Ultimately they were nine: Bauer himself, Eugen Allwein (veteran of Peak Lenin in the Pamirs), Ernst Beigel (who had been with Bauer in the Caucasus), Peter Aufschnaiter (later, with Heinrich Harrer, of *Seven Years in Tibet* fame), Julius Brenner, Wilhelm Fendt, Karl von Kraus, Alexander Thoenes, and Joachim Leupold (who had recently achieved the first longitudinal winter traverse of Mont Blanc). Each was a highly accomplished Alpinist with first ascents to his credit, but there were purposefully no "big shots" (*Kanonen*) among them, for the first principle of Bauer's expedition was "unconditional, military obedience" (*militarischen Gehorsam*), and he would brook no challenge whatsoever to his authority. The British Everest expeditions had already been too manly and military for the likes of George Mallory, but the Germans set a whole new standard here. Their main motive, Younghusband later remarked, was to prove that Germans were men. "They did love mountains," Younghusband said. "But they loved their country more. And it was to show the world that Germany still produced men that they set forth to pit themselves against some of the monarchs of the Himalayas."[14]

Against just which monarch of the Himalaya the Germans would pit themselves in 1929 was as yet unclear when they sailed from Genoa for Calcutta at the end of June. Plan A called for an attempt on Kangchenjunga via Darjeeling and the Zemu Glacier, but this depended on the government of India's doubtful willingness to allow the expedition to enter the autonomous Kingdom of Sikkim. Alternatively, plan B called for Kamet in the British Garhwal and plan C for Nanga Parbat, the great western anchor of the Himalayan chain that within a few years was to become the Germans' *Schicksalsberg*, their mountain of destiny. Failing all three, Bauer would content himself with a photographic survey of some portion of the foothills, but of course it never came to that. From the moment he first paid a respectful call on the British consul general in Munich, Bauer had played his diplomatic cards with care and tact, and in mid-July, as his ship approached the tropical way station of Colombo, he got word of Delhi's consent to a temporary encroachment on Sikkim. Plan A, then: Kangchenjunga.

The Five Treasures of the Snows

Kangchenjunga—or, locally, "Kangchendzonga"—the "five treasures of the snows," is the most easterly of the Himalayan giants, standing at 88° 9' on the border of Sikkim and Nepal. At 28,169 feet (8,586m), it is the third-highest mountain in the world, but in 1929, when the Germans set out to climb it, this had not been definitively established, and Kangchenjunga was generally assumed to share pride of second place with K2, the king of the Karakoram. Of all the 8,000-meter peaks, Kangchenjunga is the most accessible and easily approached by way of Darjeeling and the Singalila Ridge. But it is also, ironically, among the most difficult to climb, for by virtue of its relatively exposed position twelve miles south of the main Himalayan axis it catches the full force of the annual southwest monsoon and accumulates the greatest annual snowfall of any mountain in Asia. An incomparably beautiful and beguiling mountain, it is also incomparably dangerous: an appalling maze of knife-edged ridges and ice-armored precipices. "There is no doubt," wrote Sir John Hunt, the leader of the first indisputably successful Everest expedition, "that those who first climb Kangchenjunga will achieve the greatest feat of mountaineering, for it is a mountain which combines in its defences not only severe handicaps of wind, weather, and very high altitude, but technical climbing problems and objective dangers of an order even higher than we found on Everest."[15]

A mountain so high and yet so within reach exerts an irresistible appeal, and as we have seen, Kangchenjunga had long been the object of Western attention when the Germans arrived on the scene in 1929. Sir Joseph Hooker, the English naturalist better known for his Antarctic exploits, explored its vicinity as early as 1848 and even attempted the neighboring peaks of Kangchengyao (22,601ft/6,889m) and Pauhunri (23,375ft/7,125m) before landing himself in a Sikkimese prison for trespass. Eight years later, Hermann Schlagintweit, the eldest of three well-known Bavarian explorer-brothers, followed the Singalila Ridge east out of Darjeeling as far as the village of Phalut, from where he sketched both Kangchenjunga and the Everest-Makalu group in the near northwest. William Woodman Graham's disputed ascent of Kabru came in 1883, Douglas Freshfield's historic circumnavigation of the Kangchenjunga massif (to which we owe Vittorio Sella's immortal series of mountain photographs) in 1899, and Aleister Crowley's misguided and lamentable attempt on the mountain itself in 1905. The incomparable Kellas climbed extensively in the region between 1907 and 1912, and Harold Raeburn (Everest 1921) and C. G. Crawford (Everest 1922 and 1933) surreptitiously reconnoitered the Yalung Glacier in 1920, but no one again attempted "Kanch" (as climbers invariably know it), until May 1929, when one E. F. Farmer of New Rochelle, New York, decided to have a go alone.

Not surprisingly, given the inevitable outcome, little is known of either Farmer or his quixotic solo effort, one of several such that tragically punctuate the history of Himalayan mountaineering. He simply showed up in Darjeeling one day, recruited four porters (including Lobsang Sherpa, who had been on Everest in 1924), and set off into the mountains, telling no one of his intentions. After wandering in Sikkim for a while, he furtively crossed the Kang La into Nepal, skirted the village of Tseram to escape detection, and made his way up the Yalung Glacier to the southwestern foot of Kangchenjunga. From here, on May 26, he started up the Talung Saddle, the low point in the ridge between Kangchenjunga and its nearest neighbor to the south. His ill-equipped porters wisely desisted at noon, but Farmer (who alone among them had crampons), against Lobsang's advice, carried on alone, ostensibly for "photographic purposes." Up and up he went, hour after hour, through the drifting mists. At 5:00 P.M. Lobsang spotted him near the entrance to the Talung Cwm and

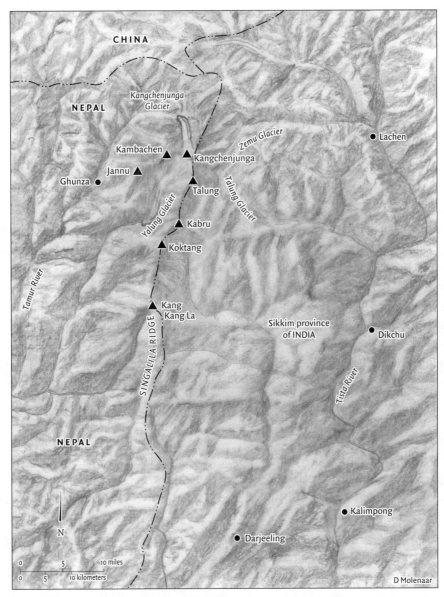

Darjeeling and the Kangchenjunga massif.

urgently waved to him to descend, but by nightfall he had not, and the porters reluctantly withdrew to their camp on the glacier. The next morning they climbed to a nearby vantage point and saw him once more, impossibly high and clearly in extremis, moving jerkily with arms outstretched. And that was that: they never saw him again. Old Himalayan hands at once derided Farmer as an incompetent fool, an innocent American who had not the least idea of what he was getting into. Little did they expect that one day others would in effect attempt what Farmer did—the unassisted, lightly equipped, solo ascent of a Himalayan giant—and succeed. Farmer was a misguided innocent, no doubt. But he was also in some (admittedly foolhardy) respects a climbing visionary.[16]

One month after Farmer's disappearance, Paul Bauer and his party arrived in Calcutta, where Kenneth Mason (who had faced Bauer across 100 yards of no-man's-land in 1915, it now turned out) eased their way through the thicket of colonial authorities, supplied them with invaluable Ordnance Survey maps, and sent them on their way to Darjeeling, the inevitable starting point for any attempt on Kangchenjunga. Since Mallory's day and the founding of the Himalayan Club, Darjeeling had become an organized center of the registration and recruitment of Sherpas. At the request of H. W. Tobin, the club's local secretary, fifteen Sherpa veterans of Everest had already assembled in town; had he wished to do so, Bauer might simply have chosen a recognized sirdar from among them and left all further recruitment of porters to him. But his experience as a platoon and company commander had taught him that order and discipline depended on the close, fatherly touch, and he was determined to dispense with native intermediaries whenever possible. Over the next three days Bauer himself, assisted by Allwein and Kraus, the expedition doctors, chose 86 porters out of the aspiring crowd—Bruce had needed over 200—and solemnly handed each one a cash advance of fifteen rupees. It remained only to convince their skeptical English friends that they were adequately equipped, that truly they had no need of the tables and chairs that had gone with Mallory to Everest. Blitzkrieg and not siege was the style of assault these hardened veterans of the western front had in mind, and by August 14, 1929, less than three weeks after landing in Calcutta, they were already camped on the upper Zemu Glacier at the northeastern foot of Kangchenjunga.

What followed was, in the words of the *Alpine Journal*, "a feat without parallel, perhaps, in all the annals of mountaineering."[17] Having reconnoitered the terrific 3,000-foot precipice leading to the lowest point in the North Ridge between Kangchenjunga and the Twins and judged it impossible, having dismissed out of hand the great Southeast Ridge joining Kangchenjunga to Simvu, Bauer quickly settled on a steep subsidiary northeastern spur that rose menacingly off the Zemu Glacier to a point on the North Ridge just 1,500 feet shy of the summit. Even to attain the base of the spur took a delicate maneuver through a 700-foot icefall; to attain its crest took a harrowing climb of a 2,800-foot wall; and here, at roughly 19,000 feet, the Germans' troubles were just beginning. Above them reared 6,500 feet of icy pinnacles and corniced ridge the likes of which had never been attempted. Day after day, for the better part of a month, the lead climbers hacked, clawed, and carved their way in painstaking increments along the spur, while followers stocked the camps and made safe the route. Where they could neither surmount nor circumvent the great ice towers in their way, the leaders tunneled through them—a wholly original and uniquely German method of advance. At the higher camps, in lieu of tents, they dug ice caves large enough to hold six men—an astonishing physical feat at these altitudes, and one seldom attempted since.

October 3 finally found six Germans (Bauer, Beigel, Allwein, Aufschnaiter, Kraus,

The Zemu Glacier and Kangchenjunga, 1929, with the Northeast ("Bauer")
Spur prominent middle right. Reprinted by permission of the German Alpine Club.

and Thoenes) and four Sherpas (Chettan, Lewa, Ila Kitar, and Pasang Anju) dug in comfortably at 22,288 feet and confident of winning the North Ridge and the summit beyond.
Then, as so often at the moment of highest hopes, the weather deteriorated. Not that it
had been fine up to now: for weeks the Germans had been contending with an unusually
prolonged autumn monsoon. But now a violent blizzard struck the ridge, pinned them
down for three days, and finally forced them into a memorable death-defying retreat. Bauer's
"reconnaissance in force" (as he had termed it) thus ended in a rout, but not before he had
infinitely raised the technical standard of Himalayan mountaineering and restored to his
own satisfaction the tarnished honor of his countrymen.[18]

The following year, much to Bauer's annoyance, the initiative on Kangchenjunga
passed to Günter Oskar Dyhrenfurth, a German-born, Swiss-naturalized geologist. Forty-
four years old at the time of this, his first Himalayan effort, Dyhrenfurth had extensive
Alpine experience and had commanded a corps of mountain guides on the Italian frontier
during the First World War. But he was nevertheless an average climber and an autocratic
leader who assembled around himself a "makeshift international party" rich in talent but

poor in common spirit or purpose. In addition to Dyhrenfurth's wife, Hettie (better known at the time as a lawn tennis player than a mountaineer), the party included the Swiss cartographer and second-in-command Marcel Kurz (then considered the greatest living authority on winter mountaineering), the Austrian Erwin Schneider (a veteran of the 1929 German-Soviet Pamir expedition), the Germans Herman Hoerlin (Schneider's highly accomplished Alpine partner) and Ulrich Wieland (an up-and-coming member of the Munich School) and, most notably, perhaps, the Englishman Frank Smythe, who besides being one of the leading mountaineers of his day—renowned in particular for his skill on snow and ice—was also arguably the first man other than a porter or guide to make a professional living out of climbing mountains.[19]

Born in 1900 into what one biographer describes as "a fairly well-to-do Kentish rentier family," Francis Sydney Smythe was by all accounts a frail, sickly, slightly built child who from an early age seems to have found in mountains a psychic refuge from the daily humiliations of the classroom and playing field. Indifferently educated at Berkhamsted School (where his fellow pupils included, oddly enough, his great climbing contemporary H. W. Tilman) and then Faraday House Engineering College, he halfheartedly pursued a career in electrical engineering that took him by turns to Yorkshire (where he learned the rudiments of rock climbing alongside Howard Somervell on Almscliff Crag), South America (where he evidently resisted the appeal of the Andes), and Switzerland (where he spent every spare moment deepening his acquaintance with the Alps). Invalided out of the Royal Air Force in 1926, he worked briefly for the Eastman Kodak Company—a fact of some significance, surely, to his eventual success as a mountain photographer—before giving himself over exclusively to climbing. By nature a loner, a social misfit, even, Smythe climbed without guides (still unconventional in those days) and without regular partners, though he did team up with fellow Briton T. Graham Brown for two celebrated first ascents of the Brenva Face (the Sentinelle Rouge and the Route Major) of Mont Blanc in 1927 and 1928. A sound rather than brilliant mountaineer, "he owed his outstanding success to his remarkable endurance," Eric Shipton once recalled. "In adverse conditions he seemed to have a fakir-like ability to shut himself in a mental cocoon, where he was impervious to fatigue or boredom, discomfort or psychological stress, and thus emerged with his resources quite unstrained."[20]

Smythe was also an indefatigable writer—indeed, the most prolific and popular mountaineering writer since Whymper—and like Whymper before him, he often stood accused by the stuffy traditionalists of the Alpine Club of climbing less for love of mountains than for love of the gain they brought him. This was unfair: a prominent critic of sensational achievement for its own sake, Smythe valued mountain travel above mere peak-bagging and he had a genuinely romantic disposition. But he did draw unconventional levels of attention to his adventures by way of every medium at his disposal—books, newspapers, photographs, the radio—and his books, to the mingled disdain and envy of others, were unusually successful. The 1930 International Himalaya Expedition (as Dyhrenfurth styled

The climber as celebrity: Frank Smythe,
signed photograph, July 1934. Reprinted by
permission of the Royal Geographical Society.

it) achieved first ascents of four separate 7,000-meter peaks. In retrospect, however, it is notable mainly for having inspired *The Kangchenjunga Adventure,* Smythe's second book of an eventual twenty-six, and the best-selling contribution to Himalayan literature before Maurice Herzog's *Annapurna* (1950).

And this despite being the story of a failure, and a rather ignominious failure at that. Unlike Bauer, who had set an altogether new standard in advance preparation and planning, Dyhrenfurth simply showed up in Darjeeling one day, having told no one of his coming and with no clear sense of where he was going. The Zemu Glacier afforded the nearest practical line of approach to the mountain, but Dyhrenfurth did not want to follow in Bauer's footsteps, and when permission to enter the Kingdom of Nepal unexpectedly arrived, he decided on a northwestern approach by way of the Kangchenjunga Glacier. This involved a grueling three-week march over a series of high passes that almost broke the bloated expedition—the largest to date, Smythe thought—at the outset. It being April, the weather remained cold and unsettled, the passes snowbound. A discerning leader would have proceeded slowly. But Dyhrenfurth was a leader of "the old teutonic school type who believed that the will was everything," as Smythe's biographer puts it, and instead he subjected his hastily assembled army of over 400 inexperienced and ill-provisioned porters to a punishing schedule of forced double marches.[21]

Eight days in at Dzongri, just beneath the 16,454-foot Kang La on the border of Sikkim and Nepal, fifty Lepcha porters—some of them already frostbitten and snow-blind—rebelled and dropped their loads; many others simply melted away or adopted a stance of passive resistance. H. W. Tobin, the chief transport officer and representative of the Himalayan Club, strove mightily to bolster morale and improvise a system of porterage relays, but he himself had been injured in a fall and soon withdrew to Darjeeling in disgust. By May 3, the day on which Phuri, one of the expedition sirdars, died on the Kang La, the caravan was hopelessly strung out along the route and reduced mainly to looting and foraging for food. Had the Nepalese government not intervened and sent fresh porters and emergency provisions, the whole expedition would have been called off. That the lead party ever reached Base Camp at all was later reckoned a miracle.[22]

And here, of course, their troubles were only beginning. Dyhrenfurth's hope, based on a few passing remarks in Freshfield's *Round Kangchenjunga*, was that the eastern tributary of the Kangchenjunga Glacier might somehow lead on to the low point in the North Ridge between the summit and the Twins, Kangchenjunga's nearest neighbors to the north. It led instead to sheer ice cliffs that Smythe and Wieland immediately judged impossible. To their right, the great Northwest Face rose 11,000 feet in serried terraces directly to the summit: an inconceivable alternative. But Dyhrenfurth judged that a leftward traverse of the lower terrace might yet yield the North Ridge, and thence the summit, and rather than beat a sensible retreat without setting foot on the mountain, he ordered what was in effect the first frontal assault on a Himalayan wall. For eight consecutive days, while Dyhrenfurth nursed a sore throat at Base Camp, first Smythe and Wieland, and then Schneider and Hoerlin hacked their way step by vertical step up a 900-foot ice cliff before the inevitable avalanche routed the whole party, obliterated their route, and tragically killed Chettan Sherpa, a two-time veteran of Everest and "in his time one of the most famous of the Tigers."[23]

At a Camp I conference on May 10, the day after the avalanche, Smythe, by now the expedition's self-appointed Jeremiah, suggested retiring from Kangchenjunga altogether. But Dyhrenfurth had not done with the mountain yet, and undaunted by either Chettan's death or the continuing chaos at the rear—much of the expedition's food and equipment had still not reached Base Camp—he ordered a desperate attempt on the Northwest Ridge above the western tributary glacier. One wonders what he was thinking, for here the difficulties are as great as or greater than those of Bauer's Northeast Spur and they culminate not in the main summit of Kangchenjunga but the outlying peak of Kangbachen (25,928ft/7,903m). Not that the party ever got that far. Schneider and Wieland's lead pitch on the ridge was, Smythe later said, "probably the finest piece of rock climbing ever done at such an altitude," but it led nowhere, and with the spring monsoon now impending, Dyhrenfurth finally conceded defeat. As a consolation prize, Smythe and Schneider (despite being weighed down by the eight-pound climbing boots that Dyhrenfurth had unwisely imposed on the expedition) bagged Ramthang Peak (21,981ft/6,700m), and the entire party withdrew on skis—then a Himalayan novelty—to Base Camp at Pangperma. From here, rather than retrace their footsteps to Darjeeling, they rounded Kangchenjunga to the north, crossed the Jonsong La, and as a final consolation climbed Jonsong Peak, a technically undemanding mountain but still, at 24,550 feet (7,483 meters), the highest conquered to date.[24]

From the outset of the International Himalaya Expedition, Paul Bauer had quietly resented what he regarded as a thoughtless intrusion on his and the Akademischer Alpenverein's sacred turf. In a report of May 6, 1930, to the Executive Committee of the German and Austrian Alpine Club, he dissociated himself as fully as possible from Dyhrenfurth, whose only contribution to German mountaineering, he said, was English-style fundraising.[25] The self-promotion, the lack of preparation, the absence of teamwork, and the conspicuous failure of leadership all reflected poorly on Germany, Bauer said, and it was, therefore, with a redoubled sense of national purpose that he returned to Kangchenjunga in 1931 with five veterans of 1929—Allwein, Aufschnaiter, Brenner, Fendt, and Leupold—and four younger newcomers: Hans Hartmann, Hans Pircher, Hermann Schaller, and Karl Wien.

Trouble arose this time in Darjeeling, when the Sherpas essentially went on strike, demanding the exclusion of any Bhotia (Tibetan-born) porters from the expedition. According to Bauer, the Sherpas had felt ill used and underpaid (relative to the Bhotias) by Dyhrenfurth in 1930 and were in fact bringing a legal case for repayment against H. W. Tobin, the local secretary of the Himalayan Club and paymaster to the 1930 expedition. No other source corroborates this, but certainly by 1931 the Sherpas had become fiercely protective of their name and reputation as high-altitude porters and were increasingly determined to keep a closed shop.[26] A day and a half's pleading and persuasion (by Bauer and Bahadur Laden La, head of the Darjeeling police) brought them around on this occasion, and mid-July found the expedition once again camped at the foot of the Northeast Spur of Kangchenjunga.

From here everything went wrong, proving once again that in the Himalaya, simple misfortune can overwhelm even the best-laid plans. One porter, Babu Lal, and the sirdar Lobsang (a veteran of Everest 1924), died of a mysterious tropical fever. Leupold and Fendt were soon too ill to be of use, Allwein developed a crippling sciatica, and Bauer himself, the hardiest of the lot, strained his heart through overexertion. Meanwhile, temperatures soared and turned the solidly frozen spur of 1929 into a treacherous vertical maze of mush and falling rock. After two and a half weeks of floundering around and dodging avalanches, the expedition finally gained Camp VIII on the ridge, only to be repaid with tragedy when, on August 9, Hermann Schaller and the Sherpa Pasang fell 1,750 feet to their deaths on the Zemu Glacier below.[27]

For Bauer personally, the resumption of the climb despite the tragedy was a foregone conclusion. But the porters were now reluctant to the point of refusal, and no sooner had Bauer somehow prevailed on them to continue than word came through of a run on the banks back home, the embargo on payments, and the threatened collapse of German credit. "It was then that the ranks wavered," Bauer recalled. "Under these circumstances could we stay there? Ought we to, in fact—should we not save every penny for Germany? Is not our place at home, to stand by our families, to save our very existence from catastrophe?" In the end, of course, such thoughts of home and (implicitly) the unjust burden of reparations only heightened Bauer's resolve to stick to his post. "If everything else should totter, we would stand fast," he decided, and on August 16, following a respectful pause in honor of Schaller and Pasang, the climb indeed resumed. Another month's toil brought Hartmann and Wien to the 25,500-foot crest of the Northeast Spur, a scant mile from the mountain's summit. Between them and the summit ridge, however, stood an unexpected 400-foot slope: steep, freshly snow covered, and obviously ripe for avalanche. Bauer was bold, but he was not suicidal, and on September 19 he ordered a general retreat and an end to an expedition that "for skill, endurance, cold blooded courage and especially for *judgement*," the *Alpine Journal* said, "will stand as the classical model for all time."[28]

Kamet Conquered

The Englishman Frank Smythe had returned from Kangchenjunga in 1930 convinced of the need to think smaller when it came to Himalayan mountaineering. He was not so far ahead of his time as to imagine the very small, alpine-style climbs of the 1970s; the greater Himalayan peaks, he believed, would never yield to anything but prolonged "siege tactics." But nor evidently would they yield to such grossly bloated efforts as Dyhrenfurth's in 1930, and it was with some compact medium in mind that Smythe set out for the Himalaya again in 1931. His object was Kamet, the 25,447-foot climax of the Zanskar Range in British Garhwal that the Bavarian brothers Adolf and Robert Schlagintweit thought they had climbed to 22,239 feet in 1855. Tom Longstaff, Charles Bruce, and A. L. Mumm had made a preliminary reconnaissance of the eastern and western approaches to Kamet in the wake of their success on Trisul in 1907, and between them Charles F. Meade and Captain A. M. Slingsby of the Fifty-sixth Frontier Force Rifles had made no fewer than four attempts on the mountain itself between 1911 and 1913. On the last of these, Meade and his Alpine guide, Pierre Blanc, reached the broad 23,420-foot northeastern col between Kamet and Abi Gamin ("Meade's Col") before succumbing to altitude-induced lassitude. After the war, the ubiquitous Kellas returned to Garhwal with Henry Morshead and climbed above Meade's Col to within 1,800 feet of the summit. But he had no Sherpa support on this occasion, and the attempt faltered when his local porters rebelled and refused to pitch camp for him in the intense cold. Soon thereafter, the British obsession with Everest began, and Kamet was left undisturbed for a decade.[29]

Smythe's attraction to this hitherto most-visited of Himalayan peaks was simple: it was, in his view, the highest unclimbed and politically accessible mountain that afforded a reasonable chance of success. And success on Kamet, he hoped, would result in the formation of a nucleus of mountaineers young enough to resume the attack on Everest should the opportunity again arise. Time permitting, Smythe also intended a traverse of the Badrinath Range and some dutiful exploration of the Gangotri and Alaknanda rivers, the two parent tributaries of the Ganges. But Kamet itself was undoubtedly uppermost in his mind when he sailed from Portsmouth for Bombay in April 1931.

From Mombasa, Kenya, meanwhile, at Smythe's invitation, a young coffee planter named Eric Earle Shipton had also sailed for Bombay and the Kamet expedition. Just twenty-three years old at the time of this, his first Himalayan adventure, Shipton was a true child of empire. Born in Ceylon—today's Sri Lanka—in 1907, the son of a tea planter who died before he was three, he never had a settled home but traveled ceaselessly with his bereaved mother throughout India and the colonial East. From the age of ten, he endured the inevitable (for one of his class) succession of English boarding schools without obvious damage, but he was an abnormally shy, slow-learning, and thus frequently beaten child who of necessity lived reclusively, "dreaming of exotic far-off places." A chance reading of Edward Whymper's *Travels amongst the Great Andes of the Equator* focused his dreams on mountains, and from the age of seventeen he climbed extensively in the Alps while on family holidays. He never went to university, "something that would dog him for the rest of his life," his biographer notes, "and always give him a sense of inferiority in the presence of the university men who filled the ranks of the top British climbers at the time."[30] Instead, in the time-honored fashion of those with limited prospects at home, Shipton returned to his colonial roots and emigrated in 1928 to Kenya.

Kenya between the wars was "a paradise for energetic people intent on living free from the constraints of formal society. Game abounded in expansive veld and savannah, land for farming was cheap, and the climate pleasant." Mountains abounded too, of course, and as luck would have it, Shipton's first posting as an apprentice planter was at Nyeri in the Aberdarre highlands, twenty miles from the foot of Mount Kenya. "Arriving on an East African farm with an ice-axe, climbing boots and several hundred feet of rope seemed for some reason rather ridiculous," Shipton later recalled, but in fact the colony harbored a few kindred spirits, among them Percy Wyn-Harris, a notable alumnus of the Cambridge University Mountaineering Club and now the assistant district commissioner in nearby Kakamega.[31] Wyn-Harris had already failed once on Mount Kenya. Now he proposed a joint attempt with Shipton, and on New Year's Day, 1929, accompanied only by an old school friend of Shipton named Gustav Sommerfelt, the two men set out from Nairobi in a rented truck for Chogoria, a remote village at the eastern foot of the mountain.

At Chogoria, the trio hastily recruited a band of fifteen Meru porters and plunged into the tropical forest with no precise idea of where they were going. They emerged at the head of a gorge in full view of the mountain, paid off their porters, and carried on alone to the Northeast Face of Batian (17,058ft/5,199m), the greater of Mount Kenya's famed twin peaks, first climbed by Halford Mackinder in 1899. Rebuffed here by a granite cliff

400 feet below the summit, they rounded the mountain to the south, traversed the slightly lesser but still virgin peak of Nelion (17,022ft/5,188m), and climbed Batian by way of the Gate of Mists (as Mackinder had called it), the distinctive gap between the two snow peaks. Satisfied, they retraced their steps, walked to Chogoria, and hitchhiked back to Nairobi in the truck of a Dutch missionary. Early though it was, this climb of Mount Kenya has all the important features of the Shipton style. At age twenty-one, he had already arrived at that distinctive cross between aimless, leisurely wandering and spontaneous, alpine-style climbing that was to be both his signal contribution to Himalayan mountaineering and also, eventually, his undoing.

In April 1929 Shipton moved from Nyeri to Turbo in the Uasin Gishu region bordering Uganda. Here he came to the attention of Harold William Tilman, a distinguished, twice-wounded veteran of the western front (where he had served under Edward Norton) who in 1919, on resigning his commission, had drawn a farm in Sotik, sixty miles south of Turbo, in a lottery for ex-servicemen. By his own admission, Tilman had no climbing experience to speak of—most of his spare time had been given rather more conventionally to big game hunting—but he had been intrigued by accounts of Shipton's exploits in the *East African Standard* and now wrote to propose a climb of Kilimanjaro (19,340ft/5,895m), the highest mountain in Africa, though an otherwise undemanding one. The two men met in Nairobi and from there embarked on what one fellow climber described as "one of the most fruitful partnerships and entrancing sagas in the history of mountain exploration."[32]

Wise, taciturn, phlegmatic, and melancholic to the point of misanthropy, Tilman turned out to be the perfect complement to Shipton's youthful impetuosity, and between them they worked out a philosophy of exploration—travel cheap and light, move fast, and live off the land—that would endear them to a later generation of countercultural climbers. Kilimanjaro was a mere prologue. The two men sealed their partnership six months later with a first traverse of Mount Kenya that Shipton always remembered as one of the most enjoyable and difficult climbs he had ever undertaken: "a perfect and wholly satisfying episode, shared with an ideal companion." Now the Ruwenzori beckoned, the famed "Mountains of the Moon" that straddle the border of Uganda and today's Democratic Republic of the Congo (and that first Freshfield and Mumm and then the Duke of the Abruzzi had explored in the opening decade of the century), but these would have to wait a while. In 1931 Tilman briefly turned gold digger at Kakamega, and Shipton, "too dazzled by the glitter of the Himalaya to be much tempted by the lure of gold," he said, accepted Smythe's invitation to Kamet.[33]

From Bombay, the traditional "Gateway of India," where he met up with Smythe and helped attend to expedition arrangements, Shipton made his way by rail across the Great Thar Desert to Delhi and beyond. Initially he was not impressed: "India is a vile place—hundreds upon hundreds of miles of hot, dusty ugliness," he wrote to his friend Madge Anderson from Delhi. But once in the pine and deodar forests of the Himalayan foothills, he was of course captivated for life. From Kathgodam, then as now the lone rail-head for Garhwal and Kumaon, he and Smythe traveled by bus to Ranikhet, a highland cantonment built by the British in the years following the 1857 mutiny. Here they met the other English members of the party (Wing Commander E. B. Beauman of the Royal Air Force, Captain E. St J. Birnie of the Indian Army, R. L. Holdsworth, teacher and sportsman, and Raymond Greene, the expedition doctor and, incidentally, brother of the novelist Graham) and the ten Sherpas that the ever-ready Himalayan Club had dispatched from Darjeeling (Achung, Nima Tendrup, Nima Dorje, Nima, Ondi, Pasang, Ang Nerbu, Nerbu, Dorje, and, as sirdar, that same Lewa who had been with Smythe and Dhyrenfurth on Kangchenjunga). At six Europeans, ten Sherpas, and sixty locally recruited porters, the Kamet expedition was restrained by the Himalayan standards of the day, but to Shipton, unaccustomed as he was to the sahib treatment, it seemed downright extravagant. "I doubt if de Saussure ever traveled in greater comfort," he later recalled. "The Sherpas saw to all our needs, acting as valets to look after our personal belongings, rousing us in the mornings with mugs of tea, pitching and striking our camps and even removing our boots. We had a cook, and meals were served in a mess-tent. We ate a certain amount of local produce, but for the most part we were provisioned from a large stock of tinned delicacies. Apart from Bill Birnie [the transport officer] we had nothing to do but saunter along the well-made paths through the lovely foothills of Garhwal, enjoying the woods of oak and pine and the flower-starred valleys of that most alpine of Himalayan districts."[34]

Of course they still had a mountain to climb, but here too, in Shipton's judgment, Kamet proved "a gentle and wholly delightful initiation." Ten leisurely marches brought the party over the 12,800-foot Kauri pass and into the Dhauli Valley, another seven to their Base Camp at the broken junction of the East Kamet and Raikana glaciers. From here they had only to follow a fairly well-worn route to Meade's Col (23,420ft), the low point in the ridge between Kamet and Abi Gamin, and then make a long day's dash for the summit. From the outset Smythe had talked portentously about employing "siege tactics," but in the end he hardly needed to. The weather held good, the party held strong, the one technical challenge of the route—a 1,000-foot rock wall between Camps III and IV—turned out to be (in Shipton's telling, anyway) "not unduly exacting," and on June 21, 1931, just a fortnight after pitching Base Camp, Smythe, Shipton, Holdsworth, and Lewa reached the 25,447-foot summit, the highest claimed to date (though men had been much higher on Everest). Smythe was in hypoxic raptures, but "my mind was too dull to feel any elation," Shipton later recalled. "The grandeur of the scene did not make a slight impression on me. I only remember a long muddle of driving myself to do things."[35] The cold and the hour did not allow for proud lingering in any case. Having lit the inevitable pipe and planted the inevitable Union Jack, the four men beat a quick retreat to Camp V on the col, where Bill Birnie met them with the inevitable cup of tea.

Two days later Raymond Greene, Bill Birnie, and (most notably, perhaps), the local Bhotia Kesar Singh repeated the ascent and Smythe was satisfied. The party withdrew from the mountain having to some extent restored a national morale shattered by a succession of failures on Everest. Shipton, for all that he thought the summit "a foregone conclusion," did not altogether disdain this effect; once returned to the less rarefied atmosphere of Base Camp, he joined in the general celebration of a job well done. But far more enjoyable and memorable for him than "the conquest of Kamet" was the month that followed, as the expedition (less the badly frostbitten Lewa, who paid for the honor of being first on the summit with the outer joints of several toes), finding itself with a month to spare, set off westward for the holy Hindu shrine of Badrinath and thence northward for the hitherto unexplored Tibetan frontier. Shipton was in heaven, crossing unnamed passes and climbing unnamed peaks with aimless and unscheduled abandon. Here indeed was for him the Himalayan golden age, the "random harvest of delight" of which he later spoke, and the tragedy of his life was that it was soon to lead him to the "grim and joyless business" of Everest.[36]

The Naked Mountain

On July 5, 1931, while Paul Bauer and company made their way up the Zemu Glacier to the foot of Kangchenjunga and Frank Smythe and company withdrew victorious from Kamet, two well-known lions of the Munich School, Willo Welzenbach and Willy Merkl, made a death-defying first ascent of the North Face of the Grands Charmoz, an ice-clad granite wall rising 3,600 feet above the Mer de Glace in the Chamonix Valley. Less than a month later two relatively unknown brothers, Franz and Toni Schmid, also of Munich, scaled the iconic Matterhorn Nordwand from bottom to top in under thirty hours. Between them, these two dramatic and controversial ascents, achieved with full benefit of what traditionalists derided as "artificial aids"—the piton and carabiner—caused a public sensation and touched off that race for the big north walls that notoriously characterized (some would say disfigured) Alpine climbing in the 1930s. The nationalist element was not new: witness the Italian Jean-Antoine Carrel's patriotic determination to beat Whymper, an Englishman, to the top of the Matterhorn in 1865. But it unquestionably reached new extremes in the 1930s, as swarms of (especially) young German men, the self-styled *Bergkameraden* ("mountain warriors"), imbued with the exalted ethos of National Socialism and egged on by revisionist patriots at home, aspired to ever-greater, more daring, even suicidal feats in the name of the risen fatherland. The frenzy culminated in the grisly struggle for the Eigerwand that killed eight climbers between 1935 and 1938. "This is not alpinism. This is war," commented the great French guide Armand Charlet, and the English too looked on amazed and appalled as the Germans everywhere sacrificed prudence and traditional "mountaineering ethics" to national prestige.[37] The Himalaya did not, as yet, allow for the kind of full frontal assault in which the Munich School specialized. But if any one mountain entered irrevocably into German nationalist consciousness in these tormented years, it was neither the Grands Charmoz nor the Matterhorn nor even the Eiger, but Nanga Parbat, the naked mountain. Here, at the western extremity of the Great

Himalaya, towering above the upper reaches of the Indus River in Kashmir, the Germans found their *Schicksalsberg,* their mountain of destiny.

In the thirty-seven years since Mummery and the Gurkhas Raghobir and Goman Singh had vanished from the Diamir Face, few Europeans had so much as approached Nanga Parbat. No less an authority than Charles Bruce (who had been to the mountain with Mummery) had pronounced it impossible, and though only eighty miles north of Srinagar and the Vale of Kashmir, it bordered on the perennially troubled districts of Gilgit and Baltistan and (as the Germans were to discover) fell only tenuously within the British sphere of influence. In 1913 the inexhaustible Kellas came as near as the adjacent Ganalo Ridge and decided Nanga Parbat might be climbed from the north after all, but first war and then the struggle for Everest intervened, and "Diamir" (as Kashmiris prefer to call it, the "King of Mountains") was left in regal isolation.[38] Paul Bauer briefly considered it as an alternative to Kangchenjunga in 1929, but the father of the German obsession with Nanga Parbat was not Bauer (despite his own later assertions to the contrary) but his Munich compatriot and sometime partner Willo Welzenbach, of Grands Charmoz fame. Obliged by illness to withdraw from Rickmer Rickmers's 1928 expedition to Peak Lenin in the Pamirs and mysteriously "unavailable" for Bauer's attempts on Kangchenjunga, Welzenbach decided in 1929 to mount his own Himalayan expedition. Influenced by his reading of Mummery's letters and Norman Collie's *Climbing on the Himalaya* (one of the few reliable sources of information on the Mummery expedition), he settled on Nanga Parbat as the one available 8,000-meter peak that offered a reasonable chance of success.

Over the course of a year, Welzenbach prepared for Nanga Parbat with unrivalled thoroughness. He corresponded extensively with Charles Bruce, Kenneth Mason (then superintendent of the Indian Survey), Ernest Neve (honorary secretary of the Himalayan Club in Srinagar), and H. J. Todd (the political agent in Gilgit). Early in 1930 he presented a meticulous expedition plan to the central committee of the German and Austrian Alpine Club and received its backing. He secured leave from his work for the city of Munich and had just received permission from the British consulate general to enter Kashmir when the German Foreign Office blocked his expedition in favor of G. O. Dyhrenfurth's to Kangchenjunga. Annoyed, Welzenbach pushed his plans back a year, to 1931, only then to be thwarted by Paul Bauer, who intended to return to Kangchenjunga in 1931 and objected to Welzenbach's Nanga Parbat venture "on the grounds that it would divide German forces" and risk alienating the British, whose favor he, Bauer, had carefully cultivated.[39] A bitter dispute followed that did indeed divide German climbers, and somewhat irrevocably, much to the detriment of the subsequent efforts on both mountains. When Welzenbach refused to yield, the Foreign Office again intervened and gave Bauer's expedition priority. Disdaining a place on it—he thought Kangchenjunga an impossible waste of time—Welzenbach at last secured government approval for 1932, but by then the Weimar Republic was in its death throes, Germany beset by political and economic crisis, and the Munich City Council decided it could not dispense with its civil engineer. Heartbroken, Welzenbach

Willy Merkl (1900–34), 1932, leader of the 1932
and 1934 German efforts on Nanga Parbat.
Reprinted by permission of
the German Alpine Club.

yielded the Nanga Parbat expedition to his friend and partner of the Grands Charmoz, Willy Merkl, on the unspoken understanding that he invite no one who had accompanied Bauer to Kangchenjunga.

Thus constrained, Merkl set about assembling a team of eight that included, most notably, Fritz Bechtold, another Bavarian who had climbed with Merkl in the Caucasus and the Alps, Peter Aschenbrenner, an Austrian guide whose status as a "professional" raised a few indignant eyebrows, Fritz Wiessner, a Dresden-born chemist who had climbed extensively in the Dolomites and Pennine Alps before emigrating to the United States in 1929, and Rand Herron, an American friend of Wiessner who brought to the team not only considerable climbing ability but a ready and available fortune. A second American, Elizabeth Knowlton, came along as expedition scribe (though she was a good climber too and one of the first women to reach 20,000 feet in the Himalaya).[40] In simple mountaineering terms, it was a strong and experienced team, but no one involved had been to the Himalaya, or even to India, and from the beginning this inexperience showed. Not only did Merkl neglect to involve the now-indispensable Himalayan Club in the logistical arrangements of the expedition, he seems to have left Munich without first securing the permission of the British to approach Nanga Parbat through the often-disturbed and thus closed district of Chilas. For a few anxious days in Srinagar, it looked as though the expedition would have to attempt the mountain from the south, an appalling, impossible proposition: the southern face of Nanga Parbat is the highest mountain wall in the world, rising 15,000 sheer feet above the Rupal Valley. The authorities then relented and allowed the northern approach, but only on the strict condition that the expedition avoid all inhabited villages in the Chilas valleys. Besides greatly complicating the line of march and thus slowing down the approach, this condition made it difficult to live off the land as planned and often forced the expedition back on its own fairly meager provisions.

And then there was the business of the porters. To save money, and perhaps simply to demonstrate a measure of strategic independence, Merkl decided not to recruit any Sherpa or Bhotia porters in distant Darjeeling, but to rely on a combination of Kashmiri, Balti, and Hunza hill men from the valleys around Nanga Parbat. These were strong types all, well accustomed, like the Sherpas, to life and labor at high altitudes. But they were far less accustomed or accommodated to life among Europeans and had developed nothing like the Sherpa guild mentality. They were, in truth, impressed labor, and their sullen reluctance and independence of purpose undermined the prospects of Merkl's expedition from the outset. In *The Naked Mountain,* her firsthand expedition account, Elizabeth Knowlton speaks contemptuously of the "native Bolshevism" with which the sahibs had continually to contend, and some have tried to put a nationalist gloss on this and render the expedition's labor difficulties in explicitly anticolonial terms.[41] True, Gandhi had marched to the sea and made salt in 1930, and much of India, including parts of the Northwest Frontier Province and neighboring Kashmir, had now answered his call to nonviolent noncooperation. The writing was indeed on the wall for the British Empire. But this was not Merkl's problem. The "general strikes" to which he and Knowlton refer were not Gandhian protests but abject refusals on the part of inexperienced, underpaid, and underfed tribesmen to risk either their lives or the wrath of the gods for a purpose they did not comprehend.

The German American Himalaya Expedition (so called in deference to Herron and Knowlton) departed Srinagar, the capital of Kashmir, on May 23, too early in the season for a safe crossing of the 13,800-foot Burzil Pass over the main Himalayan range, but taking a page out of Dyhrenfurth's book Merkl forced it anyway, thus squandering the goodwill of his forty Kashmiri porters at the outset. Eight days in at Astor, the last authorized village on the Gilgit Road, every man jack of them quit except Ramana, the famous "Nanga Parbat cook" who was to become a familiar fixture of these expeditions. Enter Lieutenant R. N. D. Frier of the Gilgit Scouts, on loan from the British to serve as a much-needed transport officer but also to keep a watchful eye on these Germans and enforce the agreed restrictions on their travel. Through the Nahim Tesseldar, the local ruler in Astor on British sufferance, Frier conscripted 160 porters from the nearby settlements, and the expedition proceeded haltingly in awkward relays over the eastern subsidiary ridges of the Nanga

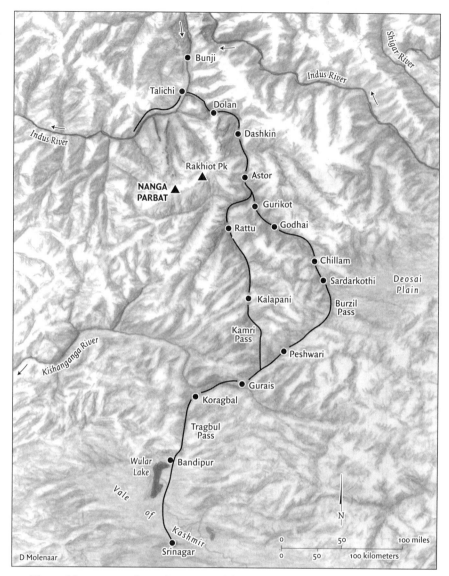

The trekking route from Srinagar to the Indus River and Nanga Parbat,
1932 and 1934.

Parbat massif. A hoped-for approach up the Buldar Glacier proved an icy dead end under
the ramparts of Chongra Peak (22,388ft/6,824m), and less the Astori porters (whom Merkl
had prematurely dismissed as "the weakest and least willing of the coolies"), the expedition
proceeded over one more ridge into the northern Rakhiot Valley.[42]

Here, on the far-flung Kashmiri frontier of the British Raj, midway between
Nanga Parbat and the upper Indus River, the Germans uncannily found themselves at
home. Thus Willy Merkl:

After a short way along the path, the Fairy Meadow [*Märchenwiese*] opened out before us. It lies there in sublime charm among the light green of the pasture, covered with the stars of the edelweiss and embraced by the trunks of ancient timber forests. Just like a corner of undestroyed paradise, the fabulous meadow appeared to us above the glacier and beneath the towering, ice-clad northern flank of Nanga Parbat. Astonishing! Here at 3,000 meters, high above the glaciers, stood an ancient timber forest with mighty fir trees and glowing birches. As we gazed at it, we felt deeply the kinship with the mountains of our homeland [*Heimat*], only here the feelings and impressions of the Alps were magnified in the unimaginable massiveness of the Himalaya, homeland for the Indo-Germanic peoples, who were born in these mountains and fell under their power. Here we raised our second Rakhiot camp, and to the strains of "Dear Homeland, We Greet You" cut into our first Bavarian smoked ham [*Geselchte*], a memorable occasion that even the unrestrained picking of the edelweiss by our Saxon comrade Felix Simon could not diminish.[43]

Never mind that no one had died yet, or that a single German had yet to set a foot on the mountain, or that five more expeditions were to follow before a climber finally reached the summit. Here in the Fairy Meadow in 1932, Nanga Parbat had already cast her spell and caught these heartsick Germans in a death embrace.

By mid-June, Peter Aschenbrenner and Herbert Kunigk (the twenty-four-year-old Bavarian baby of the party) had reconnoitered the upper valley and concluded that it was passable, that it offered a reasonable line of approach to the summit. Superficially, the situation recalled that which confronted the British on Everest: a climb from a northern glacier to a northeastern ridge and thence westward above the north face to the summit. But whereas the East Rongbuk Glacier rises gently for 4,600 feet to the base of Everest's North Col, the Rakhiot Glacier begins lower, rises higher, and is everywhere broken by crevasses and icefalls. The climb from the glacier to the ridge is twice as high as the North Col climb, three times as dangerous, and four times as long in point of time.[44] Given its relatively protected position south of the Karakoram, Nanga Parbat is often spared the cyclonic winds that scour Everest's north face, but as a result it is, like Kangchenjunga, a snow- and ice-clad mountain, everywhere draped with hanging glaciers and prone to avalanche. From where the Germans stood in their Fairy Meadow, the challenge would be to follow the glacier south to a big moraine under the Buldar Peak, thread a steep route eastward through icefalls to a high plateau below the Northeast Ridge, somehow surmount or circumvent the subsidiary Rakhiot Peak, and then follow the ridge first west to a high col between the Northeast and Southeast peaks (the "silver saddle") and then north across a broad plateau to the out-of-sight summit. It was a long, roundabout, and labyrinthine route full of objective dangers, but it was a route nevertheless, and rather than risk a desperate reconnaissance of Mummery's Diamir Face, Merkl committed to it and dispatched Herron and Kunigk to find a site nearer the snow line for a permanent base.

Meanwhile, at Fairy Meadow, the pastoral idyll broke on June 19 when Wiessner discovered that eight loads of irreplaceable high-altitude clothing and equipment intended for the Hunza porters had been stolen, probably by the dismissed Astoris in the Buldar Valley. This was a crushing blow that reduced the corps of mountain porters to nine—the most that Merkl could even meagerly equip—and severely delayed the placing of successive camps. Not that the Hunza porters were working out well anyway. Much to the Europeans' annoyance and bewilderment, they simply refused to eat either tinned food or rice, insisting on their familiar chapatis, round wheaten flat breads that could be prepared only over open wood fires below the snow line. When Wiessner (through Ramana the cook, who had a smattering of English) sternly explained that for now it was rice or nothing, the Hunzas packed their gear and left, leaving the expedition momentarily high and dry. Two days later, rather than risk the wrath of the mir of Hunza, their tribal overlord who had detailed them to the expedition in the first place, they returned, but they would not yield on the matter of food, and to the end the expedition faced the unusual logistical challenge of continually provisioning its porters from below.

Somehow in the face of these difficulties (all of them the fruit of Himalayan inexperience), the expedition made its way gingerly up the mountain over the course of the month of July. A close call with an avalanche at Camp I provoked yet another general strike, and Frier prevailed on the Hunzas to continue only by raising their wages to five rupees per day, five times the miserable one rupee originally agreed. Even at that "princely wage" (as Knowlton describes it), they remained reluctant and increasingly inclined to all manner of debilitating illnesses.[45] At Camps II and III on the terraces of the icefall, Merkl experimented with Bauer's caves, but found them more trouble than they were worth and reverted to wind-swept tents. Camp IV at 20,000 feet on edge of the plateau below Rakhiot Peak became from July 9 a sort of advance base from which the expedition mounted its inconclusive assault on the Rakhiot Ridge. On July 16 Aschenbrenner and Kunigk climbed Rakhiot Peak and judged it impassable for porters. The route thenceforth skirted the base of the peak to the west and crossed a wide, steep, snow-filled ice trough that the Germans called the "Mulde" and the Americans the "amphitheater." From here it was less a matter of climbing than swimming one's way through waist- or even chest-deep snow, freshly fallen and frighteningly unstable. Herron and Bechtold established Camp VI at 22,000 feet in the lee of a bergschrund in the amphitheater on July 26, and three days later, Merkl, Bechtold, and Wiessner finally broke through to the ridge and could see the summit of Nanga Parbat, a discouraging two miles and 3,600 vertical feet away.

And there, at 23,000 feet on the Rakhiot Ridge, the 1932 attempt expired. The worst of the climbing lay behind them (or so they overconfidently hoped), but the hitherto remarkably stable weather now deteriorated and forced a retreat to Camp IV, where a dwindling band of demoralized climbers languished for an inconceivable three weeks, stymied by storms, refractory porters, food shortages, and their own unshakeable lassitude. Bechtold, Simon, and the frostbitten Aschenbrenner gave up in disgust and left for home on August 13. Wiessner, Herron, and Merkl stayed manfully behind, and after a week's

Fritz Wiessner (1900–88) relaxes
at Base Camp, Nanga Parbat, 1932.
Reprinted by permission of
the German Alpine Club.

recuperation at Base Camp made one last halfhearted and unsupported effort that barely made it back to Camp IV. On September 2 Elizabeth Knowlton was sitting by a Base Camp fire finishing her dinner when through the thickening dusk she heard the unmistakable voice of Fritz Wiessner calling out bitterly to the Jemadar: "Nanga Parbat 'finish'! Nanga Parbat 'finish.' . . . "[46]

But the struggle for Nanga Parbat was just beginning.

Return to Everest

Even before quitting Camp IV for the last time in 1932, Merkl had begun to talk of "next year," of a second attempt on Nanga Parbat in 1933, but by then "the situation in Germany" (as Elizabeth Knowlton evasively put it) had reached the point of culminating crisis.[47] Soon after the expedition's return (less Rand Herron who, having survived Nanga Parbat, ironically fell to his death from a pyramid at Giza on the way home), Adolf Hitler became chancellor of Germany and domestic revolution overwhelmed even the best-laid plans. What the Nazis called *Gleichschaltung*—literally, "putting into the same gear"—meant primarily and most urgently the purging of the civil service, the abolition of the Weimar party system, the dissolution of the state governments and parliaments, and the co-optation of the trade union movement. But from there it extended to the wholesale reconstruction of German civic, associational, and even recreational life. Unimpressive physical specimen though he was, Hitler had long taken a strong interest in sports, or rather "physical exercises" (*Leibesübungen*), as the Nazis preferred to say. According to *Mein Kampf,* the raising of "totally sound bodies" was the "first concern" of National Socialist education, and as early as April 1933, Hitler himself appointed SA Grüppenführer Hans von Tschammer und Osten Reich sports commissioner (later Reichssportsführer) and charged him with the Gleichschaltung of all organized forms of physical exercise, including, as it happened, mountaineering.

Given its existential and militaristic overtones, mountaineering in fact occupied a fairly prominent place in the National Socialist weltanschauung. Both of Hitler's two original Nazi cabinet members, Hermann Göring and Wilhelm Frick, were members of the German and Austrian Alpenverein and Frick, in his capacity as minister of the Interior, took a direct interest in its reorganization along National Socialist lines. In June 1933 he and Tschammer und Osten met together with three representatives of the Alpenverein (Rehlen, von Klebelsburg, and von Sydow) and assured them the club would neither be dissolved nor deprived of its international status provided it accept the creation of a distinct German Chapters Group and come into line with National Socialist doctrine on the Jewish question and the Führerprinzip. A month later, on the direct recommendation of Eugen Allwein (a two-time veteran of Kangchenjunga), Tschammer und Osten summoned Paul Bauer to Berlin and put him in charge of the hiking, mountaineering, and camping section (Fachsäule XI) of the new German Reich League for Physical Exercises. In this capacity, and deriving his charge "directly from the highest authority of our state," Bauer presided over the creation of the Reich League of German Mountaineers (Reichsverband der Deutschen Bergsteiger), a Nazi state organization whose purpose, as Bauer explained it to the mountaineering section of the Alpenverein, was "to lead German mountaineers to a consciousness of their high calling, to guide the rising generation that they may learn to be fearless and ready for action, possessed by the light of lofty ambition, and calmly and unswervingly prepared for any struggle." There was nothing particularly new about any of this, Bauer insisted to those traditionalists who found such exalted language repellent. The Alpenverein had always tied its activities closely to the state and worked "for the good of the people as a whole." But now for the first time "the breakthrough of the heroic worldview for which our Führer Adolf Hitler has fought throws our mountaineering activities into the proper light before the eyes of the public," he declared at a general meeting of the club. More clearly and consciously than ever before, the Alpenverein through the Reich League would now be serving "the state, the people, and the future."[48]

It was in this heady and violent atmosphere of national renewal, and with the explicit sponsorship of the Nazi state, that Merkl undertook to lead the second German attempt on Nanga Parbat in 1934. No longer the concern just of a small and nationally mixed group of mountain climbers, Nanga Parbat had become, as one contemporary put it, "the cause of the entire German people," and Merkl would approach it accordingly, conscious now of returning the swastika to the Indo-Aryan land from whence it came.[49]

In London, meanwhile, one unsurprising effect of this aggressive German appropriation of the Himalaya was to revive national designs on Everest, Great Britain's mountain of destiny. The long-moribund Mount Everest Committee had been reconstituted under the chairmanship of Admiral Sir William Goodenough (president of the Royal Geographical Society) in March 1931 in hopes of soon securing permission to reenter Tibet. "The Committee feel that the fact that two bodies of our countrymen lie still at the top [of Everest] or very near it, may give this country a priority in any attempt that may be made to reach the summit and they are anxious that this may be recorded," Goodenough wrote to the secretary of state for India, William Wedgwood Benn. Replying for Benn, J. C. Walton of the India Office was not encouraging. Tibetan attitudes had not changed in the past five years, India generally was in an agitated state, and "under present conditions" the secretary respectfully declined to intercede with Lhasa on the Everest Committee's behalf. The committee then briefly scouted the idea of an approach to the mountain through Nepal until General Bruce pointed out that the Dyhrenfurth debacle of 1930 had left the Nepalese more hostile to foreign incursion than ever before. Early in 1932, Frank Smythe, fresh from success on Kamet, approached the India Office privately about the possibility of mounting his own small-scale expedition to Everest, but this too Benn discountenanced, and all bets were off when suddenly in July 1932 the political office in Sikkim reported an unexpected change of heart in Lhasa. The recent renewal of territorial hostilities along the Sino-Tibetan frontier had evidently persuaded the Dalai Lama of the potential usefulness of well-armed friends and moved him to give "reluctant permission" to an Everest expedition to enter Tibet in 1933 provided that all its members were British.[50]

Thus authorized to proceed, the committee put its mind at once to the pressing question of leadership. "We must have a leader who has it in him right down to the nails of his toes," wrote Francis Youngsband to Goodenough. "Mallory had it in him *while he was on the mountain,* but he hadn't it in him as the big idea; at the back of his mind he thought it rather a bit of sensationalism. We must have men who can realize that it is a big thing of the whole human spirit." Norton was such a man, Younghusband thought; so too was Geoffrey Bruce, but both declined leadership of the new expedition, pleading prior commitments. The obvious alternative in several respects was Frank Smythe, who at thirty-two was in his climbing prime and of proven Himalayan ability. But Smythe was simply not a gentleman in the eyes of the Mount Everest Committee. The product of a second-rate public school, he had not attended university and had no military service record to speak of. Since his success on Kamet, he had taken to offering the committee unsolicited advice on how to climb Everest, he had a reputation for being arrogant and uncompanionable and, worst of all, he earned his living by writing books about climbing. In short, "the stench of professionalism" clung to Smythe, and though reconciled to including him on the team, the committee turned for leadership to Hugh Ruttledge, a Cheltenham- and Cambridge-educated India hand who, between 1925 and 1929, while serving as deputy commissioner of Almora, had explored extensively in Garhwal and Kumaon and north along the Tibetan frontier. Ruttledge spoke Urdu fluently and had an intimate feel for the Himalaya. "He had a sure and friendly touch when dealing with the Dzongpens, the mule-teers, and the sherpa and other porters, as well as a natural authority, tempered by a real liking for those who lived in wild places," the climber Jack Longland later recalled. But he was distinctly middle-aged and no mountaineer; from the outset of the 1933 expedition, his selection as leader exposed a divide between the old India hands and the "thrusting young Alpinists" who had come of age between the wars and had little use for the stodgy old British Empire.[51]

From Kamet came the core of the expedition: Frank Smythe, Eric Shipton, Bill Birnie, and Raymond Greene. To these known quantities Ruttledge added George Wood-Johnson (who had been on Kangchenjunga with Smythe), Percy Wyn-Harris (who had climbed Mount Kenya with Shipton), Hugh Boustead (a soldier-adventurer who had climbed in Sikkim and was now commandant of the Sudan Camel Corps), Jack Longland (one of the bold new breed of home-grown rock climbers and president of the Cambridge University Mountaineering Club), Lawrence Wager (Longland's partner), and Tom Brock-lebank ("the inevitable rowing blue"). Altogether it was one of the strongest and ablest teams ever to attempt Mount Everest, but ego abounded, not always happily. Socially, nothing distinguished it from the teams of the 1920s; all of these men came from the same upper-middle class that had served up the membership of the Alpine Club since its founding in 1857.[52] For money too the expedition relied on the traditional combination of private patronage and modest company sponsorship: £100 from His Majesty the King plus "'Ovaltine' for Everest!" Having been burned by John Noel's antics in 1924, the committee naturally vetoed any suggestion of an expedition film in 1933. And it broke with tradition by selling its newspaper rights to the *Daily Telegraph* rather than *The Times* for the unprecedented sum of £3,500.

The nine years since the death of Mallory had seen few significant advances in mountaineering gear, few that the English would consider adopting, anyway. The one con-cession to the march of progress was a wireless, the unsolicited gift of one D. S. Richards, honorary secretary of the Joint Committee of the Incorporated Radio Society of Great Britain and the Wireless League, who actually accompanied the expedition to Tibet and with the assistance of four officers and NCOs of the Royal Corps of Signals kept Base Camp in radio contact with Darjeeling and Camp III. All were highly amused, but in fact on its first trial in the Himalaya the radio proved its worth, making it possible for Ruttledge to receive daily weather forecasts from the Alipore Observatory in Calcutta and exchange reports with the Everest Committee in London within the space of twenty-four hours.[53]

From Darjeeling, where it gathered clamorously in late February, the expedition moved off in easy fifteen-mile stages along the customary route: north through the Chumbi Valley and then west across the Tibetan plateau. At 16 Englishmen, 170 assorted Sherpas, Bhotias, and Gurkhas, and over 350 pack animals, the bandobast was as large as any assembled to date. Each sahib had his own pony, his own personal Sherpa, and his own spacious Whymper tent in which to enjoy his postprandial brandy and cigar. Shipton was alternately amused and horrified. "The sight of our monstrous army invading the peaceful Tibetan valleys, the canvas town that sprang up at each halting place and the bustle and racket that accompanied our arrival and departure gave me a feeling of being chained to a juggernaut," he later wrote, "and I longed to return to these lovely places free and unshackled by the trappings of our civilisation." Just one week out of Darjeeling, Shipton and the other young bucks (Longland, Wyn-Harris, and Wager) could not resist a side jaunt up an unnamed 17,000-foot mountain just north of the Natu La: to them "a satisfying and nearly perfect episode."[54] But Ruttledge disapproved of it as wasteful of energy and forbade any further such private excursions. Trouble arose briefly at Shekar Dzong, where Ruttledge discovered some stores had been pilfered and the local Dzongpen obliged him with some random flogging in an apparent effort to extract confessions. Otherwise, the expedition lumbered amicably along, reaching Base Camp in the Rongbuk Valley on April 17, twelve days earlier than any of its predecessors and supremely confident of success.

Two weeks earlier, the history of Everest had intersected sensationally with the history of aviation when two Westland PV3s piloted by Lieutenant David McIntyre and Sir Douglas Douglas-Hamilton (the Marquis of Clydesdale) overflew the 29,035-foot summit for the first time. The idea of such a stunt had long been around. In fact the Mount Everest Committee had briefly discussed the possibility of aerial reconnaissance with Sir Alan Cobham, Great Britain's leading aviator, in 1924, and though nothing came of it—partly, no doubt, because of Arthur Hinks's strong aversion to public spectacle—Cobham did fly over some lesser peaks the following year. In 1927 the ever-imaginative John Noel actually proposed landing a man on Everest from above, but he was in disgrace over the dancing lama affair, and nothing more came of the aeronautical idea until 1932, when the publicity surrounding the forthcoming Ruttledge expedition awakened the interest of Major L. V. Stewart Blacker, a decorated veteran of the Royal Flying Corps turned private arms manufacturer. Promising a perfect photographic survey of the hitherto unexplored southern approaches to the mountain, Blacker secured the backing of the Royal Geographical Society, which in turn smoothed his way with the Air Ministry, the India Office, and (through the India Office) the government of Nepal. All he needed now was money, and this he got in plenty from Dame Fanny Lucy Houston, an eccentric adventuress, anti-Bolshevik, and nudist with a passionate attachment to the British Empire.[55] Blacker and his committee justified what henceforth became known as "the Houston-Mount Everest Expedition" in all kinds of worthy scientific ways. For Lady Houston herself, however, it was all about overawing truculent natives and strengthening the moral claims of the empire. Geoffrey

Dawson of *The Times,* meanwhile, saw a chance to get his own back at the expense of the Mount Everest Committee and gave the Houston expedition full headline treatment while ignoring the Ruttledge expedition altogether.

After months of planning and days of hanging about waiting for good weather, the two PV3 biplanes, specially fitted with IS3 Pegasus engines (the brand-new pride of the Bristol Aeroplane Company), set off from their base near Purnea in Bihar, about 160 miles southeast of Everest, on the morning of April 3. In and of itself, the altitude was not the challenge; by 1933 planes had already flown over 40,000 feet above sea level. The challenge was to capture the topography in a complete series of "survey strip" photographs while somehow negotiating the powerful downdrafts that naturally develop in the lee of the great mountains. Newspaper accounts made much of hair's-breadth clearances of knife-edged ridges and the like, but in truth the flights were fairly routine but for the failure of one cameraman's oxygen supply and Clydesdale's daring passage through Everest's famous ice plume. For posterity's sake, both planes cleared the summit by 100 feet from the southeast at 10:05 A.M. The aerial survey was largely a bust, thanks to the dusty haze that typically cloaks the Himalaya at lower altitudes. But the survey was never what this publicity stunt was really about, and its failure did not stop Blacker from proclaiming a great success. "Days must pass before we can appreciate what we have seen in those few sublime crowded minutes looking down on the world's last penetralia," he boasted grandly in *The Times.* "Overriding the winds, man's act had torn the veil from another of Nature's secrets. The uttermost peak is no longer inviolate."[56]

Down on the Rongbuk Glacier, needless to say, no one estimated the significance of the flights in such ultimate terms. Ever the gentleman, Ruttledge later congratulated the fliers on "the brilliant success of their brave exploit" and thanked them for sending him an aerial photograph of the Northeast Ridge. But the climbers generally were contemptuous of the Houston expedition and no doubt secretly delighted when *The Times* displayed as Everest a full-page photograph of nearby Makalu. So much for the highly vaunted benefits of aerial reconnaissance.[57]

Meanwhile, the work of trudging up Everest from below went on. Influenced by his understanding of previous failures, Ruttledge had insisted on a slow, painstaking approach up the glacier for the sake of both gradual acclimatization and preservation of his climbers' energies. The unfortunate effect he had not counted on was the lethargic stupor that inactivity induces at high altitude. Shipton especially chafed at the time spent in sleeping bags waiting for supplies to be carried here and there, waiting for the weather to clear, waiting for red blood corpuscles to multiply. "I sometimes thought that bedsores were a more serious hazard than frostbite or strained hearts," he later quipped.[58] Camp III at the foot of the North Col was fully occupied by May 2, but the weather deteriorated thereafter, the face of the col had changed for the worse since 1924, and ten more boring and precious days were to pass before Shipton and Smythe managed to secure a route to Camp IV on a humpbacked ice shelf 200 feet below the col itself.

A Houston-Westland PV3 approaches the summit of Mount Everest from the south, April 3, 1933. Reprinted by permission of the Royal Geographical Society.

"Shipton and Smythe are a magnificent pair. I believe they'll get to the top," Ruttledge reported to Bruce back in London on May 19. But one day later his confidence plummeted when despite perfect weather and good conditions, the party charged with establishing Camp V (Wyn-Harris, Birnie, and Boustead) unaccountably dropped its loads at 24,000 feet, 1,000 feet short of the ordered target of 25,000 or higher. An almighty row followed at Camp IV, with Wyn-Harris grumbling about "the fucking soldiery" (namely Birnie, on whose command, evidently, the party had turned around) and Ruttledge seething over "the most disgraceful day in the annals of Everest." Fortunately, the weather remained fine and two days later the same party, augmented by Raymond Greene, made good the damage and placed Camp V at 25,700 feet. But two fine days had been lost, and though frayed nerves led him to blow the incident all out of proportion, Ruttledge proved weirdly prophetic when in the midst of the row he said: "It may be we lost not two days but twenty years."[59]

On May 29, after four days of storm, Wager, Wyn-Harris, Longland, and nine Sherpas, including Ang Tharkay and Rinzing Bhotia (both of whom later received the coveted Tiger's Badge of the Himalayan Club), placed Camp VI on a tiny sloping ledge in the lee of the Northeast Ridge at 27,400 feet, 600 feet higher than Mallory's Camp VI in 1924. From here, after little sleep and a meager breakfast, Wager and Wyn-Harris set

A Sherpa bears the burden on Everest, 1933.
Photograph by Frank Smythe. Reprinted by
permission of the Royal Geographical Society.

out for the summit, still dramatically underestimating the distance they had to cover. Like
Mallory before him, Wyn-Harris was a "ridge man." He believed, that is, that the way to
the summit lay along the ridge crest and not across the great north face. So it was not,
perhaps, altogether miraculous that a little before 7:00 A.M., about 250 yards east of the
first step and 60 feet below the ridge, he stumbled on a Willisch of Täsch ice ax that he
assumed to have been Mallory's but that turned out to have been Sandy Irvine's. What this
astounding discovery revealed about Mallory and Irvine's fate he did not, for now, pause to
consider. Leaving the ax for the moment where it lay, he and Wager continued their traverse
toward the ridge and successfully skirted the first and second steps, only to be brought

up short, as Norton had been before them, by the treacherous snow-covered slabs of the Great Couloir. At 12:30 P.M., having climbed to within roughly 900 feet of the summit, they turned back, retrieved Irvine's ax, climbed up to the ridge to have a first human look down on the colossal Kangshung Face, and retreated to the safety of Camp VI.

Shipton and Smythe made their forlorn bid the following day. Shipton had diarrhea, had not slept in days, and felt "as weak as a kitten." Moreover, in his two pairs of woolen pants, five pairs of socks, and seven Shetland wool sweaters, he felt "about as suitably equipped for delicate rock climbing as a fully rigged deep-sea diver for dancing the tango," he later recalled. He gave out in two hours. Smythe carried on alone across the Great Couloir more or less to the point Wyn-Harris and Wager had reached, and there accepted the inevitable. A harrowing, separate descent followed, with Shipton nearly falling to his death between Camps VI and V, and Smythe lingering dangerously a day behind in a state of listless confusion. "We reached Base Camp, a set of crocks, what with frostbite, strained hearts, etc.," Shipton wrote to Madge Anderson. But Ruttledge was not ready to concede defeat. After a week's recuperation at Base Camp, he reoccupied Camp III in hopes of another attempt. But by now the monsoon had definitively broken, and when the Mount Everest Committee back in London vetoed his suggestion of a smaller postmonsoon attempt—"MONEY NOT AVAILABLE FOR AUTUMN STOP"—the expedition withdrew to Darjeeling, little cheered by a routine congratulatory telegram from the king.[60]

On the long road home, the dispirited members of the 1933 expedition put a brave face on things and attributed their misfortunes to the weather. "Under the conditions prevailing in 1933, Everest is impossible by any route," is how Smythe put it publicly. But privately he and others knew that in mid-May, at least, conditions had been relatively favorable and a real opportunity lost, and not surprisingly back in England recriminations began to fly. They began quietly, with the younger men muttering to each other about superannuated climbers and overcautious, outdated methods. Then, when Lhasa unexpectedly granted permission for yet another expedition, and the hoary old Mount Everest Committee solemnly gathered at Kensington Gore once again, things turned downright noisy. Ostensibly at issue was the leadership; a young faction led by Wager, Longland, Brocklebank, and (reservedly) Greene wanted to dump the mild-mannered and indecisive Ruttledge in favor of Colin Crawford. "They are the products of their time," Ruttledge wrote privately to Sydney Spencer in extenuation of the behavior of his critics, "and, as you know, the young man of today is primarily critical. It is in his blood to criticise anyone of the war or pre-war period. I don't believe there is an atom of personal ill-will in all this. But unfortunately, since we came home there has been a lot of wild talking, & that always breeds trouble. We need not disguise from ourselves, now, that the party was not very well assorted. I realised that very soon; and I laid down for myself a definite policy and stuck to it. By the time we reached the mountain I knew we had 5 members who would never 'fit in.' But I had to make what use I could of them. Inevitably, the competent members were overworked, and I think there is some sub-conscious resentment over this."[61]

What Ruttledge did not fully appreciate was that the generational resentment against him was largely symptomatic of a deeper frustration with the Alpine Club, the Royal Geographical Society, the Mount Everest Committee, and the whole cozy orchestration of Everest affairs. Years later, when passions had cooled considerably, Jack Longland, one of the anti-Ruttledge conspirators, recalled the whole episode as but one in "the recurring struggle between the young active climbers who climb the big mountains, and the older men who run a club such as the Alpine Club and, in the main, decide the policy of the enterprises with which it is associated." Even so, he continued, "it is difficult to over-emphasise the frustration felt by young climbers in the mid-nineteen thirties, believing, as they did, that the conduct of both the Club and of Everest affairs was largely in the hands of people who had not been near a serious climb for years." As it happened, even as the 1933 expedition had been floundering about pointlessly on Everest, Marco Pallis had led a small expedition to the Gangotri region of Kumaon that had culminated in Charles Warren and Colin Kirkus's pioneering alpine ascent of Bhagirathi III. The young Turks (mindful also, no doubt, of the aggressive German tactics in these years) wanted to bring some of this lean alpine audacity to the business of climbing Everest. Smythe was only partially with them (or rather, as Longland less sympathetically put it, "Frank pretended to be on our side, but he wasn't"). He agreed that Ruttledge's expedition had been bloated with deadweight and that the next one should include only "absolutely first class Alpine mountaineers who are capable of tackling great Alpine climbs." But fundamentally he remained a believer in siege methods, and he supported Ruttledge in the leadership knowing that he would never be leader himself and that when it came to it, Ruttledge would rely largely on him: he would lead by proxy.[62]

As for Eric Shipton, he washed his hands and rid his mind of the "grim and joyless business" of Everest by lingering behind with Wager in Tibet and satisfying his urge for fast, unburdened exploration. With some misgiving, he had evidently decided to abandon farming altogether and pursue a "nebulous career as Himalayan traveller," and it was with that appealingly aimless purpose in mind that he then cast his gaze widely over the Abode of Snow until it lighted on the sanctuary of the goddess, Nanda Devi.[63]

CHAPTER FIVE

"Himalayan Hey-Day"
1934–1939

The Sanctuary

A legend in Kumaon tells of a beautiful princess who long ages ago spurned the amorous advances of a Rohilla raja and thus brought war and ruin to her father's kingdom. In fear for her life and virtue, the princess fled a battle at Ranikhet to the icy summit of a stupendous mountain revered as the birthplace of Parvati, the consort of Lord Shiva, and surrounded on all sides by an impenetrable wall of precipitous peaks and ridges. Here she remained, inviolable and eternal, until she became one with the mountain itself, the blessed goddess, Nanda Devi. At 25,642 feet (7,816 meters), she is the queen of the Garhwal Himalaya, the highest and holiest of Indian mountains, and without question the loveliest. All mountains are feminine, of course, in both Eastern and Western eyes; "conquest" is seldom a purely military trope. But given the particular (and somewhat paradoxical) details of her mythology—the virgin princess, the mother goddess, the voluptuous consort of Shiva, the god of fertility—and the unique features of her topography, no mountain is quite so alluring as Nanda Devi. She is the supreme temptress who, as Hugh Ruttledge put it, imposes on her votaries a formidable admissions test, the Rishi Gorge, and even then defends her virtue with every beguiling resource at her disposal. If Everest was about war in the Western imagination, Nanda Devi was more often about love.[1]

Nanda Devi stands on the Indo-Tibetan frontier midway between Everest and Nanga Parbat in what was under the British the Kumaon Division of the United Provinces of Agra and Oudh and is now the Indian state of Uttarakhand. Adjoining her just to the east is a subsidiary twin, Nanda Devi East, who moors the goddess to her sanctuary wall. From Nanda Devi East the wall rears away northwest to Changabang and Dunagiri and southwest to Maiktoli and Trisul before curving in again on itself and forming the near-perfect ring of "the outer sanctuary." From Changabang and Maiktoli, two internal ridges converge on the upper Rishi Gorge to form "the inner sanctuary," the virgin's second and still more impregnable citadel. Altogether the inner sanctuary wall measures seventy miles in circumference and features no fewer than nineteen peaks of over 21,000 feet. Its rim averages 20,000 feet in height and is nowhere lower than 18,000 feet except where it is narrowly cleaved at its western extremity by the torrential chasm of the Rishi Gorge (once the earthly home of the seven great *rishis,* or sages of Hindu mythology). Enclosed within are 240 square miles of glacier and alpine pasture, a wild mountain paradise out of which, from a base elevation of 13,000 feet, the goddess rises "Like some vast sculpture made / By powers not conceived by man."[2]

Before 1934 only three explorers had grappled with Nanda Devi, and none had forced her inner sanctuary. The first, William Woodman Graham, negotiated the lower gorge as far as the Rhamani tributary in 1883. He had hoped to attempt Nanda Devi but, finding the upper gorge "a trench worn to the most impassable smoothness," contented himself with lesser summits on the northern sanctuary wall. Then in 1905, while exploring the Pachu and Lawan valleys to the east of Nanda Devi, the incomparable Longstaff reached the low point on the wall ever since known as Longstaff's Col (19,390ft) and was the first Westerner—and so far as anyone knows the first person—to see the inner sanctuary. Two years later, as we have seen, Longstaff returned to Garhwal with Charles Bruce and Arnold Mumm for his celebrated ascent of Trisul—then the highest mountain yet climbed—but once again skirted the sanctuary. Hugh Ruttledge reconnoitered Nanda Devi on two occasions while serving as deputy commissioner of Almora district between 1925 and 1929—once from the northeast by way of the Timphu Glacier and once from the southwest by way of the Nandakini Valley—but on neither occasion did he manage to cross the sanctuary wall. (In retrospect, the most significant innovation of these expeditions was the employment of Sherpas outside the Everest region; by now they were regarded as essential adjuncts of any Himalayan campaign.) Then, in 1932, three years after his retirement, Ruttledge returned to Nanda Devi and, accompanied by Emile Rey of Courmayeur and six Darjeeling Sherpas, reconnoitered the face of the Sunderhunga Col (18,500ft) just east of Maiktoli on the southern sanctuary wall only to find it an impassable mass of seracs and overhanging arêtes. "And so vanished the last hope of a straightforward approach to Nanda Devi," Ruttledge wrote; and the goddess kept her secret still when he returned to England to assume command of the 1933 Everest expedition.[3]

Though he had been to Garhwal himself with Smythe in 1931 and even seen the entrance to the Rishi Gorge, Eric Shipton first became interested in the problem of the Nanda Devi Sanctuary listening to Ruttledge talk about it on Everest. Here seemed a unique challenge after his own wanderer's heart, and once back in England he sought out Tom Longstaff, the great doyen among mountain explorers and the greatest living authority on Nanda Devi. Longstaff encouraged the idea and urged Shipton to concentrate his efforts on the gorge, but he was skeptical about Shipton's remarkably lean budget, which called for a total expenditure of £150. This Shipton had hoped to raise by interesting some newspapers in the project, but Nanda Devi proved too obscure an ambition for them, and against his

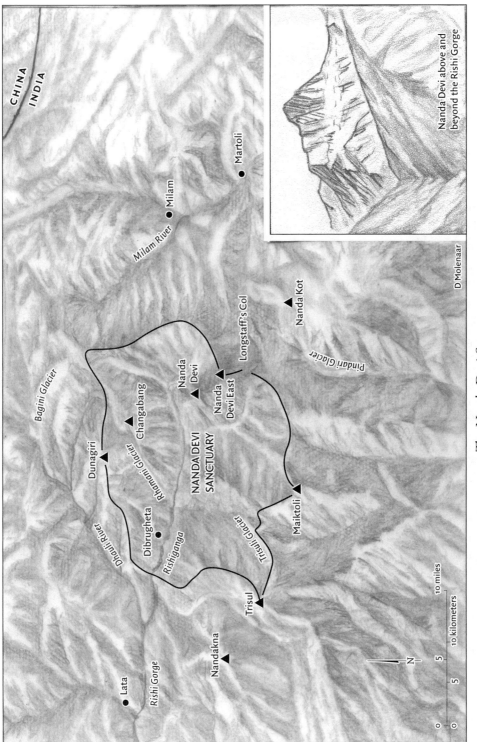

The Nanda Devi Sanctuary.

Within the map:

CHINA

INDIA

Milam

Milam River

Martoli

Bagini Glacier

Lata

Rishi Gorge

Nandakna

Dunagiri

Changabang

Nanda Devi

Nanda Devi East

Longstaff's Col

Nanda Kot

Pindari Glacier

NANDA DEVI SANCTUARY

Dhauli River

Dibrugheta

Rhamani Glacier

Rishiganga

Trisuli Glacier

Maiktoli

Trisul

N

0   5   10 miles

0   5   10 kilometers

Nanda Devi above and beyond the Rishi Gorge

D Molenaar

finer inclination, Shipton yielded to the mercenary strategy of lecturing about Everest.
Through Karma Paul, the Tibetan interpreter to the Everest expeditions, he recruited
three Sherpa porters, Ang Tharkay, Pasang Bhotia, and (when the veteran Rinzing proved
unavailable) a newcomer, Kusang Namgir.

    There remained only the critical matter of finding one like-minded companion:
"the greatest asset a mountaineer or traveler can have when embarking upon a difficult
undertaking," Shipton said, "more valuable by far than any amount of money, equipment
or fine weather." He thought first of Noel Humphreys, a veteran explorer of the Ruwenzori
and "a keen exponent of the art of travelling light," but Humphreys was committed to an
Arctic expedition, and Shipton had almost reconciled himself to the exclusive company
of the Sherpas when he unexpectedly received a letter from Bill Tilman who, after an
unsuccessful spell as a prospector in Kenya, had bought himself a bicycle and ridden it
right across the breadth of Africa to Douala in the French Cameroons, where he boarded
a steamer for England. He was now personally and professionally at loose ends and wrote
to propose a fortnight's climbing in the Lake District. Shipton counterproposed seven
months' climbing in India. Tilman accepted at once and the famous partnership was sealed.
After thinking better of the notion of riding to India by bicycle, the two men set sail from
Liverpool on April 6, 1934.[4]

    The rest is a more than twice-told tale. From Calcutta, where with some comic
misadventure they met up with Ang Tharkay, Pasang, and Kusang (whose metropolitan
experience, up to now, extended no farther than Darjeeling), Shipton and Tilman made
their way to Ranikhet, where they engaged twelve local Dotials to help carry their food and
gear as far as Josimath in the Dhauli Valley, some ten miles below the Rishi Ganga. They had
brought some food with them, including ten tins of pemmican (an imperishable compound
of shredded meat, dried fruit, and suet) and several ten-pound cheddar cheeses. But for
the most part their plan was to live off the land and share the local diet of lentils, chapatis,
and *tsampa* (roasted barley meal). For gear they had two small Meade tents, down sleeping
bags, primus stoves, ropes, cameras, survey instruments, and lanterns. Today it all sounds
ample, but at the time such a kit gave Tilman and Shipton a wide reputation for Spartan
simplicity, to which they added an unconventional element of Athenian democracy. Sahibs
though they were, they (for the first time among British climbers) shared with their Sherpas
the same fire, the same food, the same tent, the same burden of load carrying. "We soon
came to regard them as fellow mountaineers rather than servants," Shipton later claimed,
"and they felt with us the excitement of anticipation and the joy of success." Between the
sahibs themselves, however, this wilderness intimacy could only extend so far. When, after
seven months of continuous companionship, Shipton casually suggested that Tilman call
him Eric, Tilman demurred, "became acutely embarrassed, hung his head and muttered,
'It sounds so damned silly.'"[5]

    Tilman in fact could be "astringent company," Shipton recalled. Reclusive and
ascetic by nature, he had "little use for small talk and none for abstract discussion." But he

Eric Shipton (left) and Bill Tilman outbound
from Liverpool, 1934. Reprinted by
permission of the Alpine Club Library.

had "an effervescent humour" that won the hearts of the Sherpas, who affectionately called
him Balu Sahib (Mr. Bear) because of his ill-kempt, shaggy appearance.[6] Tilman did not
write a book about the Nanda Devi reconnaissance; this he left to Shipton, whose idea it
was. But his books about his later climbs are notable for their unusually close attention
to and full human evocation of individual Sherpas. Even Shipton appears as a shadowy
figure next to the fully realized Tenzing or Pasang Kikuli. But none who knew them both
doubts the strength of Tilman's attachment to the younger Englishman. Though usually
content to defer to Shipton's more experienced mountaineering judgment, Tilman had
the definite air of the older and wiser man and looked on Shipton with something like
suppressed fatherly regard.

Twelve "blissful saunters" from Ranikhet brought the party to the village of Surai
Thota in the upper Dhauli Valley. Here they turned south and, following in Graham's footsteps, entered the middle Rishi Gorge by way of the snowbound Durashi Pass and Dibrugheta, a hanging valley well known to local shepherds and to Tilman oddly reminiscent
of the Lake District. On May 28 they reached the junction with the Rhamani Nala (the
farthest point reached by Graham and Longstaff), dismissed their Dotial porters, pitched

a Base Camp, and began their attempt on the upper Rishi Gorge. The obstacles were innumerable, the dangers indescribable, the route tortuous and imperceptible: it took nine long days to cover four short miles and "until the last moment," Shipton said, "the issue remained in doubt." But finally, on June 6, they found "the last frail link along the precipices of the southern side" and entered the inner sanctuary with enough food to last them three weeks. The goddess had yielded her secret at last.[7]

It was paradise, of course; what else could it have been? Towering peaks, spreading glaciers, mile after mile of blooming alpine meadow, grazing herds of wild bharal, and soaring over it all "the peerless spire of Nanda Devi," ever changing in form and color as they moved.[8] Secretly, between themselves, Shipton and Tilman had not ruled out the thought of an attempt on the goddess. But now, seeing what would be involved and considering the state of their provisions, they did so at once, and after one short foray onto the lower buttresses just to establish their claim, they gave their precious time over to a painstaking instrument survey of the northern basin. Not that they neglected to climb. In the course of their survey they summited an unnamed 21,000-foot peak, attempted a 23,000-footer, and reached three different cols on the eastern and northern rims.

When the monsoon arrived toward the end of June, they retreated down the Rishi Ganga to Josimath, rested, and carried on up the Pilgrim Road to the holy town of Badrinath. From here they undertook a vigorous two-month reconnaissance of the Badrinath Range, which to them was of considerably more than topographical interest. For this range forms the watershed between the three main sources of the Ganges—the Alaknanda, Bhagirathi, and Mandakini rivers—and is therefore traditionally revered as the home of the gods. First they ventured up the Bhagat Kharak Glacier, forced a series of unexplored passes north to the Arwa Valley, and then crossed the watershed to the Gangotri Glacier and Gaumukh, the Cow's Mouth, the very birthplace of Mother Ganga. Then, in August, they attempted a southern crossing of the watershed by way of the Santopanth Glacier, which proved infinitely more difficult than they had expected. For a week they lived on tree fungus and bamboo shoots while trying to hack their way out of a trackless forest ravine. Eventually, they found their way to the pilgrim town of Kedarnath, and were thus, as Shipton boasted, "the first outside the pages of Hindu mythology to effect a direct connection between the three main sources of the sacred River Ganges."[9]

In September, the monsoon having ended, Shipton, Tilman, and the three Sherpas returned to Nanda Devi to complete their survey of the sanctuary and if possible at least find a line of approach up the mountain itself. Their main ambition now, though, was to force their way out of the sanctuary by the eastern or southern wall and thus complete its traverse. Longstaff's Col—the eastern point from which their hero Tom Longstaff had looked down into the sanctuary in 1905—proved a nonstarter; they could not reach it. This left the 18,000-foot southern depression that Ruttledge had reconnoitered from outside in 1932: the Sunderdhunga Col. Setting out to find it on September 10, Shipton became distracted by the prominent ice peak then known to the Survey of India as East Trisul but

The 1934 Nanda Devi party (left to right): Ang Tharkay, Eric Shipton,
Pasang Bhotia, Bill Tilman, and Kusang Namgir. Reprinted by
permission of the Royal Geographical Society.

now known as Maiktoli. Leaving Tilman (who not for the first time on this expedition was
suffering the effects of altitude) in the care of Pasang, he climbed it with Kusang and Ang
Tharkay on September 12, an ascent not repeated until 1961. Two days later he and Tilman
both climbed to 21,000 feet on Nanda Devi's Southeast Ridge and satisfied themselves that
it could be done. That was enough: on September 16 they escaped the sanctuary by way
of the Sunderdhunga Col and thus completed a trip—the word they much preferred to
"expedition"—that set new standards in the annals of Himalayan exploration.

The Wrath of Nanga Parbat

Pausing to assess the chances of an ascent of the South Ridge in *Nanda Devi,* his pathbreaking account of the 1934 reconnaissance, Eric Shipton specifically recommended against
those "prolonged siege tactics which are so much the fashion in the Himalayas nowadays."
The inherent danger in this method of incremental advance through heavily stocked camps,
as he saw it, was that it put too many men too high on the mountain. "In high mountains,
mobility is the keynote of efficiency and safety," he wrote, "and it is for this reason that I
find it hard to believe that a large, heavily organised expedition will ever achieve success on
Everest."[10] He eventually proved wrong in this, of course. But at the time he was writing,
homebound from Nanda Devi in 1934, the argument seemed much in his favor, for even
as he and Tilman were scampering lightly about the Badrinath watershed, unbeknown to
them a German siege of Nanga Parbat had gone disastrously wrong. Sixteen men—five

Germans and eleven Sherpas—had been overtaken by storm in the upper camps, and before it was over nine of them had died. It was the worst climbing disaster since an entire party of eleven had perished in a storm on Mont Blanc in 1870, and its consequences were far-reaching. Besides provoking political upheaval in the German climbing establishment, it fatefully strengthened the hold of Nanga Parbat on the German imagination and (much to Shipton's dismay) confirmed a stridently nationalist understanding of Himalayan mountaineering.

Willy Merkl had left Kashmir in 1932 eager to return in 1933, but the advent of the Nazi dictatorship put everything into a state of confused suspension. Ruttledge had all the Sherpas booked for Everest in any case, and given his experience with the Hunza alternative in 1932, Merkl hardly wanted to force the issue. Paul Bauer, meanwhile, had had plans of his own for Kangchenjunga in 1933, but he was now heavily involved in the work of Gleichschaltung, of bringing German mountaineering into line with the new political dispensation. He would not return to the Himalaya until 1936. Bauer's boss, Reichssportsführer Tschammer und Osten, badly wanted a Himalayan boast for his boss, Adolf Hitler, and was prepared to encourage whatever acceptable proposal came along, but the direct involvement of the Nazi state in the 1934 Nanga Parbat expedition has been exaggerated.[11] As it happened, in fact, Merkl pulled something of an end run around the Nazi state. Through his friend and professional colleague Heinz Baumeister, he appealed for money directly to the Sports Association of the German State Railroad, a Weimar organization not (as yet) under Tschammer und Osten's control. Supplemental grants from the German and Austrian Alpenverein and the German Scientific Aid Association (Notgemeinschaft der deutschen Wissenschaft) certainly made this the most lavishly funded and best-equipped German expedition to date, and the Reich Sports Ministry certainly appropriated it as a national undertaking, but it began as a quasi-independent venture, as Bauer would be quick to point out in the aftermath of the disaster.

Of the veterans of 1932, only Fritz Bechtold and Peter Aschenbrenner, the Austrian guide, returned in 1934. The most notable addition was Willo Welzenbach, the very father of the Nanga Parbat idea whose professional commitments had forced him to cede it to Merkl in 1932. "Insist upon being climbing leader. Do not go otherwise," Welzenbach's mother urged him—wisely, as it turned out. At the time, though, Welzenbach's eagerness to climb Nanga Parbat overrode such cautionary scruples, and with some misgivings he accepted the subordinate position of deputy leader. Other newcomers included Alfred Drexel (Merkl's colleague on the Bavarian Railroad and Welzenbach's partner on four north wall ascents in the Bernese Alps), Erwin Schneider and Uli Wieland (both veterans of Dyhrenfurth's Kangchenjunga expedition), Peter Müllritter (the expedition photographer), Willy Bernard (the expedition doctor), and a three-man scientific team of Richard Finsterwalder, Walter Raechl, and Peter Misch.

Late trouble arose over Misch, the geologist, when it turned out that his father (a Göttingen philosopher who happened to be Wilhelm Dilthey's son-in-law) had been born a Jew. Strictly speaking, this should have barred him from the expedition, which as far as Tschammer und Osten was concerned fell under the provisions of the Law for the Restoration of the Professional Civil Service, the first (April 1933) formulation of the so-called Aryan Paragraph, which aimed to exclude Jews from all aspects of public life. But Finsterwalder, the chief scientist and cartographer, appealed the case all the way to Hitler's deputy Rudolf Hess, arguing that "an otherwise healthy law had here been applied to a guiltless man," and one way or another Misch was along when (disregarding superstition) the expedition sailed from Venice aboard the Lloyd Triestino liner *Conte Verde* on Friday, April 13, 1934.[12]

Also sailing on the *Conte Verde* that day were the members of G. O. Dyhrenfurth's international expedition to Gasherbrum I (Hidden Peak), a 26,469-foot giant of the Karakoram just 100 miles northeast of Nanga Parbat across the Indus Valley. The mountains were getting crowded, and though Bechtold later dismissed newspaper talk of the "bitter rivalry" between the two expeditions—pointing to friendly shipboard games of quoits as evidence—the voyage did bring into uncomfortable juxtaposition two starkly opposed political styles. Though born in Germany, Dyhrenfurth had adopted Swiss citizenship and twice now had deliberately favored the "international" approach to mountaineering. As a democrat (and the husband of a Jew), he deplored the current state of affairs in Germany, and after the Anschluss would resign his thirty-four-year membership in the German Alpine Club as "a matter of honor."[13] He was every bit as wedded to the large-expedition concept as Merkl, and as Smythe had discovered on Kangchenjunga, he could be just as dictatorial. But he attached no national significance to what he was doing and would have been appalled at the Nazi flag flying weirdly alongside the Union Jack in Bechtold's cabin. Politics aside, the summer of 1934 would for the first time see two large expeditions simultaneously attempting two different eight-thousanders well within sight of one another. Even during their friendly games of quoits, the climbers must have sensed that a race was on.

The 1934 Nanga Parbat expedition reached the fondly remembered Fairy Meadow to find it still under the "dirty, repulsive remnants of winter snow." Merkl had learned from past mistakes and recruited thirty-five Sherpa and Bhotia porters in Darjeeling, but initially at least the relatively deplorable state of the Rakhiot Glacier defeated this logistical advantage. The snow line fell considerably lower on the mountain than it had in 1932, complicating the business of route finding and forcing Merkl to establish an intermediate Base Camp at 10,800 feet. Here the scientists departed for their circumnavigation of the Nanga Parbat massif, a momentous first that was to culminate in the making of an extraordinarily meticulous topographical map that is still in use today. The main party, meanwhile, had to excavate Base Camp from beneath seven feet of snow: a laborious task at 13,000 feet that consumed several precious fair days. Already by June 1, as he, Aschenbrenner, Drexel, and Schneider struggled in adverse conditions to establish the lower camps, Welzenbach felt growing disquiet at what he perceived as Merkl's misdeployment of the expedition's workforce. In particular, Merkl had sent several of the Sherpas off with the scientists, leaving the climbing party to depend on the less reliable Baltis. More generally, to Welzenbach's

A Sherpa at Camp II on Nanga Parbat, 1934. Chongra Peak behind.
Reprinted by permission of the German Alpine Club.

mind, he seemed caught up in "organisational dilemmas" to the point of forgetting what
the expedition was all about: climbing Nanga Parbat.[14]

Despite these difficulties, and despite consistently conflicting instructions from
below, the advance party had just reached Camp IV on the highest glacial plateau below the
northern precipices of Rakhiot Peak and was poised for the assault on the mountain proper
when tragedy struck on June 8. Alfred Drexel died suddenly of what Willy Bernard, the
expedition doctor, diagnosed as pneumonia but was almost certainly high-altitude pulmonary edema, a hypoxia-induced swelling of the lung tissues. Both a personal and practical
blow to the expedition, the death of Drexel also broke its unified front and forced hitherto
suppressed hostilities to the surface. First, Schneider openly objected to Merkl's insistence
on filming Drexel's burial, which he thought commercially motivated and irreverent. This
in turn led Merkl (who had, bear in mind, promised Tschammer und Osten and the Nazi
authorities an uplifting and nationally glorifying film of the expedition) to threaten to

banish Schneider from the mountain. "Merkl is increasingly trying to act like a dictator who tolerates no comments," Welzenbach wrote home. "He really seems to believe that a stern and uncompromising attitude serves to establish his authority and to suppress the inferiority complex which he obviously feels as an upstart." In losing Drexel, Welzenbach feared, the expedition had lost "an effective mainstay in the battle against Willy's delusions of grandeur and persecution mania." Merkl's old friend Fritz Bechtold, meanwhile, was assuming more and more backstage influence over him and putting the expedition to his own official narrative purposes—something to bear in mind, Welzenbach's biographer cautions, when reading Bechtold's memorial account. "I am assuming a cautious attitude for the time being," Welzenbach assured his parents, "but I fear that we will have a row sooner or later."[15]

Drexel was buried in a Nazi flag on a rounded moraine above Base Camp on June 11. Ten perfectly clear days later, the climb had still not resumed and, as it turned out, the best chance for the summit had been lost. The official explanation for these days of idleness was a shortage of tsampa—the indispensable high-altitude food of the Sherpas—but Welzenbach suspected that Merkl simply felt a lack of urgency and liked playing "the role of pasha" at Base Camp. He also (Merkl, that is) wanted to put as many men as possible on the summit together for the greater glory of Germany; so while a small assault party might have proceeded with the food on hand on June 12 or 13, as Welzenbach in fact urged, instead everyone waited. "The expedition is too large and cumbersome," Welzenbach confided to his parents. "In it there are several camp-followers who are only a burden on the advance because they require porters, food and tents. These men are no use to the expedition but all the same want to go to the summit. You can't hope to take a party of ten to twelve up an 8000 meter peak. The result is that nobody gets to the top. But all preaching is of no avail here. Willy always knows best."[16]

On June 22 the prized tsampa arrived and the expedition lumbered forward. The advance base of Camp IV was reoccupied on June 25, seventeen long days after it had been evacuated. In consideration of time lost and of the impending monsoon, Merkl grudgingly accepted Welzenbach's judgment that hauling full depots slowly up the mountain now made no sense and that the attack had to be forced through to the summit. Accordingly, during the first week of July, the entire climbing contingent of six sahibs and sixteen porters made their way through Camp V (21,950ft) over the shoulder of the Rakhiot Peak—which, in true German style, Welzenbach, Schneider, and Aschenbrenner had fixed with ice pegs and ropes—to Camp VI (22,818ft) in the first trough of the long corniced ridge between Rakhiot Peak and the Silver Saddle. Three porters (Ang Tenjing, Palten, and Nima) fell ill and retreated down the mountain unaccompanied on July 5. Everyone else proceeded over a fifty-foot black rock outcrop the climbers called the Moor's Head (*Mohrenkopf*) and across the ridge to a billowy snow crest below the southeast peak they called the Whipped Cream Roll (*Shaumrolle*). Here, at Camp VII (23,570ft), the stage was set for perfect disaster. Nineteen men (Merkl, Welzenbach, Bechtold, Wieland, Schneider, Aschenbrenner, Tundu,

A much too crowded Camp VI on the Rakhiot Ridge.
The Moor's Head and Silver Saddle beyond. Reprinted by
permission of the German Alpine Club.

Nurbu, Pasang, Nima Dorje, Pinzo Norbu, Nima Tashi, Da Thundu, Kitar, Pasang Kikuli, Nima Norbu, Dakshi, Ang Tsering, and Gaylay) were high on the mountain, effectively cut off from support below and still separated from the summit by a far greater lateral distance than they knew. Merkl had yielded to Welzenbach on the point of mobility and speed, but he had clung to his grandiose notion of a group pilgrimage. As was easy to see in retrospect, the combination of the two—small kit, large numbers—was fraught with hazard and left the expedition hopelessly at the mercy of the weather.

Tragedy unfolded from July 6. That morning Tundu and Nurbu reported ill and Bechtold "volunteered" to escort them down the mountain, thus probably saving his and their lives. Meanwhile, Welzenbach led off upward, shortly to be overtaken by the two Austrians, Schneider and Aschenbrenner, who were in much the best form and left to themselves

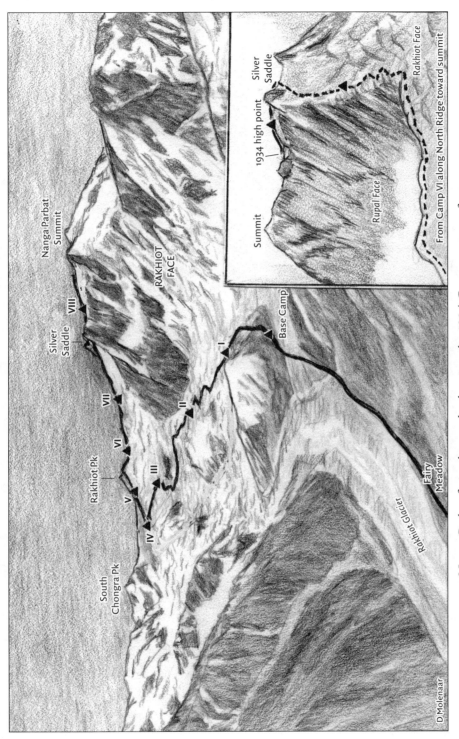

Nanga Parbat from the north, showing the 1934 German route of ascent.

Summit

1934 high point

Silver
Saddle

Rupal Face

Rakhiot Face

From Camp VI along North Ridge toward summit

Nanga Parbat
Summit

Silver
Saddle

VIII

VII

Rakhiot Pk

VI

V

III

IV

RAKHIOT
FACE

South
Chongra Pk

I

Base Camp

II

Rakhiot Glacier

Fairy
Meadow

D.Molenaar

would probably have made the summit this day. Instead, not wanting to break away entirely, they waited for two hours on the Silver Saddle before conferring with Welzenbach and proceeding on to their high point just shy of the north summit or "forepeak" of Nanga Parbat (26,000ft). Here again they waited until, shortly after 2:00 P.M., they saw Merkl and Wieland emerge on to the Silver Saddle with the main body of Sherpas and set about making camp. In frustration and bewilderment, Schneider returned to the Silver Saddle to urge Merkl to move the camp higher toward the forepeak, but Merkl refused, insisting that the Sherpas were done in for the day. That night the storm struck. Unwilling to give up this close to the prize, Merkl decided to ride it out for a day—July 7—thus giving rise to later (unfair) speculation that he relished peril for its own sake and, like all Germans, had a reckless disregard for the elements. By the morning of July 8, however, he knew he was beaten and ordered a retreat that, as his half brother Karl Herrligkoffer would later write, "for sheer protracted agony has no parallel in mountaineering history."[17]

The plan (as devised by Welzenbach and Wieland) called for the two strongest climbers, Schneider and Aschenbrenner, to lead down the mountain with Pasang, Nima Dorje, and Pinzo Norbu. Merkl, Welzenbach, and Wieland would follow close behind with the remaining eight Sherpas. All moved off in good order, leaving some tents and sleeping bags behind in hopes of an early return, but the storm continued unabated, and with visibility down to a dozen yards, the two groups quickly became separated. On reaching the easy ground above Camp VII, Aschenbrenner and Schneider unroped (in order to save the Sherpas exhausting detours, they later claimed) and carried on independently all the way to Camp IV, where they assured an astonished and worried Bechtold that the others would arrive at any moment.[18] In fact, the others were unimaginably far behind, strung out along the Rakhiot Ridge in various states of desperation. Once unroped, Pasang, Nima Dorje, and Pinzo Norbu had made it no farther than Camp VII, where they spent a harrowing night with no food or drink and one sleeping bag between them. Merkl, Welzenbach, Wieland, and their eight Sherpas (Nima Tashi, Da Thundu, Kitar, Pasang Kikuli, Nima Norbu, Dakshi, Ang Tsering, and Gaylay), meanwhile, had fared even worse, and collapsed in a bivouac between Camps VIII and VII, with three sleeping bags between them. There Nima Norbu died sometime during the night of July 8–9.

The next morning, July 9, Ang Tsering, Gaylay, and Dakshi stayed at the bivouac, too ill, they said, to continue. Welzenbach, Merkl, Wieland, and the four other Sherpas left without them for Camp VII, where they could expect neither food, bedding, nor fuel. Wieland died 100 feet from the camp tent. Merkl and Welzenbach, now utterly spent and insensible, sent Kitar, Pasang Kikuli, Nima Tashi, and Da Thundu on to Camp VI in hopes of their finding help, but the four lost their way and spent the night in a snow cave. Meanwhile, the three abandoned Sherpas, Pasang, Nima Dorje, and Pinzo Norbu, had left Camp VII for Camp VI but they too failed to find it in the swirling snow and sheltered in an ice cave on the ridge. The next morning these seven Sherpas converged on the difficult traverse of the Rakhiot Peak. Nima Dorje and Nima Tashi died in the fixed ropes above

Camp V, Pinzo Norbu just six feet short of the tent. The four severely frostbitten survivors staggered into the safety of Camp IV in the late afternoon, July 10.

Up above, five men were still clinging to their lives: Ang Tsering, Gaylay, and Dakshi at the high bivouac between Camps VIII and VII, Merkl and Welzenbach at Camp VII. None of them moved at all on July 10. Dakshi died sometime that night, and in the morning, July 11, Ang Tsering and Gaylay moved down to Camp VII, where they found Merkl and Welzenbach alive but in extremis, Merkl in a hypoxic stupor and Welzenbach "writhing with pain on the snow." On July 12 Ang Tsering tried to persuade the Germans to move down, but Merkl favored waiting, confidently insisting in his deluded state that rescue would come from below. In fact, all rescue attempts had long since foundered in the bottomless snow beneath the Rakhiot Peak. Willo Welzenbach died at Camp VII sometime that night, July 12–13. In the morning, July 13, Merkl, Gaylay, and Ang Tsering struggled down to the saddle in the Rakhiot Ridge, where Merkl collapsed. Ang Tsering courageously carried on alone in hopes of yet finding help—a gesture that was to win him the Medal of Honor of the German Red Cross. Gaylay "stood by his master," as the fond paternal version has it, and died by his side at the foot of the Moor's Head on the 15th or 16th of July, some eight or nine inconceivable days into the ghastly retreat.[19]

"The conquest of the peak is expected for the glory of Germany," Reichssportsführer Tschammer und Osten had told Merkl before the expedition's departure, and now, in the aftermath of the disaster, with ten men dead, 200,000 Reich marks spent, and the peak definitively unclimbed, there was bound to be an angry reckoning. Initially, of course, everyone in the mountaineering community joined in the general public chorus of praise for both the glorious dead and the brave survivors. But when Erwin Schneider began to talk about leading a return expedition to Nanga Parbat under the renewed auspices of the Reichsbahn and the German and Austrian Alpenverein, Paul Bauer (who had his own plans for Kangchenjunga that year) immediately initiated a backstage campaign against him. First, he announced in November 1934 that as of October last the Reichssportsführer had commissioned him to be the "special overseer of all undertakings and appearances of German mountaineers overseas." Nothing less than the international reputation of Germany was at stake, and in order to secure this reputation, Bauer said, the Reichssportsführer would no longer promote or permit any expeditions that had not been sanctioned by the mountaineering section of the Reich Sports Ministry (i.e., himself).[20]

When Schneider, evidently unimpressed by this pompous pronouncement, proceeded with his plans for Nanga Parbat anyway, Bauer raised the temperature and denounced both the Austrians, Schneider and Aschenbrenner, directly to Tschammer und Osten:

> Today it is impossible for mountaineers, who esteem comradeship, to understand how Schneider and Aschenbrenner could leave their porters behind in a snowstorm, thus condemning them to a certain death. The explanations I have heard are pure excuses. The firm rule in blinding weather is that the team must stay together and that those in the lead are to wait for those following behind. Those who, like Schneider and

Aschenbrenner, continue on without regard for stragglers, cannot be regarded as good mountain comrades. It is very dangerous when people of such questionable conduct carry on as heroes; the bad example they set on Nanga Parbat could corrupt the younger generation of mountaineers. I could not bear responsibility for that.[21]

A week later Bauer widened his denunciation even to the glorious dead. In a long, passionate letter to Tschammer und Osten, he reiterated his original misgivings about the 1932 and 1934 expeditions and distanced himself both philosophically and politically from Welzenbach, his erstwhile comrade in the Akademischer Alpenverein München:

> Welzenbach was the man for whom success was everything, whereas for me the manner and the style of mountaineering counted for more. He strove for records, felt himself to be a mountaineering star, and systematically promoted himself. I on the other hand represented a completely different view that prevailed in the AAVM [Akademischer Alpenverein München] against the Welzenbach style. In addition, I should say that I have for a long time felt myself to be an old soldier, and in the AAVM consistently pursued a national and National Socialist course. For us, Adolf Hitler was already, in 1923, a man we would not see impugned. Welzenbach, on the other hand, belonged to the Bavarian Peoples' Party and stood with a few of his kind in opposition, which for characteristic reasons they never owned up to, for they would have found no support in the AAVM. Nevertheless, they were just as dogged and confident in their views as we were.

And Merkl was no better. He and Welzenbach both "surrounded themselves with rich people" instead of a "tightly knit team." Like their friends Schneider and Hoerlin (who had been with Schneider on Kangchenjunga in 1930), they failed to understand that mountaineering was "a national matter." In 1930, 1931, and 1932 they had based their plans on the participation of "wealthy foreign mountaineers," and Schneider and Hoerlin had even accompanied "the sprig of a Jew Dyhrenfurth" (*dem Judenstämmling Dyhrenfurth*) to the Himalaya, "where they had not even had the courage to hoist the German flag but hoisted instead the Swabian and Tyrolean flags!!"[22]

In extenuation of such ugly sentiments, we might consider the fraught political circumstances of the time and the possibility that Bauer was simply saying what Tschammer und Osten wanted to hear. Still, an objective reading of the archival record of the "Bauer-Schneider Controversy" (*Streit Bauer-Schneider*) strongly suggests that Bauer was the man on a mission, and it was only at his insistence that the Reichssportsführer convened in March a "Court of Honor" (*das Ehrengericht*) to pass judgment on Schneider and Aschenbrenner's conduct. The stakes were high; at issue was the future course and leadership of German Himalayan mountaineering, and Schneider was not friendless. Behind him stood the Reichsbahn, the Austrian climbing community, and the combined forces of the German and Austrian Alpenverein. In February, in fact, the executive committee of the Alpenverein, fully awake to the wider implications of the controversy—fully aware, that is, that they too were under attack—commissioned its own inquiry into Schneider's conduct, acquitted him of any wrongdoing, and in view of his obviously supreme fitness recommended him for the leadership of the next Nanga Parbat expedition. Behind Bauer, though, ranged the greater forces and resources of the Nazi state, and on March 11, 1935, after an elaborate hearing that Bauer had carefully choreographed in advance, Reichssports-führer Tschammer und Osten, without formally accusing Schneider and Aschenbrenner of anything, nevertheless found them to be "without honor" and effectively disqualified them from any future Himalayan expeditions. In other respects, the ruling essentially gave teeth to Bauer's November proclamation and established that "any prospective expe-dition, regardless of the source of its funding, must in every case get the approval of the Reichssportsführer before being announced or discussed in public."[23] On paper at least, the Alpine Club had been outmaneuvered and Paul Bauer confirmed in his place as dictator of German mountaineering.

But still the Alpenverein stubbornly refused to submit. On April 3, 1935, Her-man Hoerlin placed the club's objection to the Court of Honor's ruling directly before Tschammer und Osten, arguing that in the critical moment of unroping, Schneider and Aschenbrenner had every confidence that the Sherpas would be safe and therefore had done nothing wrong; it was a question of conscious intention. And three months later, Philip Borchers, who had led a strong team that included Schneider to Peru's Cordillera Real in 1932, respectfully informed Bauer that the Alpenverein was proceeding with plans for a Nanga Parbat expedition in 1936. Bauer for the moment remained calm, told Borchers that he and Bechtold had plans for the mountain of their own, and invited the Alpenverein to participate in some vague, subordinate capacity. The executive committee (*Hauptausschuss*) of the Alpenverein stalled for a month and then essentially turned the tables on Bauer, respectfully inviting *him* to join *them* on the understanding that Borchers would lead the expedition and that half of its members would be selected by the Alpenverein.[24]

It all seems petty, this squabbling over control of the next expedition, until one recalls that Nanga Parbat was no ordinary mountain. It was an *Achttausender,* an eight-thousander, one of a prized few in the world. More, it was *der Schicksalsberg der Deutschen,* the German mountain of destiny, and now recognized and reserved as such by the British Foreign Office. Unimaginably huge prestige would attach to those who climbed it, prestige and power within the German sports organizations. Essentially at issue here was the political independence and autonomy of the Alpenverein. In this obscure bureaucratic struggle over control of a mountain climb lay an instance of institutional resistance to Nazism.

At any rate, sometime in the summer of 1935 Bauer despaired altogether of the Alpen-verein and conceived of yet another mountaineering institution, the German Himalayan Foundation (Deutsche Himalaja-Stiftung). Sadly, none of the originating documents of the foundation survived the Second World War, but from the evidence of what came before and after, we can discern roughly what Bauer had in mind. First he needed some sort of neutral buffer, an institutional firewall between his office, the mountaineering section of the Reich

Sports Ministry, and the Alpenverein. He needed a new, unencumbered, uncontroversial organization focused exclusively on Himalayan priorities. Second, he needed something to improve his standing in the eyes of the British, still of course the ultimate authority in all matters Himalayan. The British liked and admired Paul Bauer, who unlike Merkl had always taken great care to make the proper obeisances before them, but they were distinctly put off by his new guise as a Nazi functionary. By cloaking his state office with an independent foundation, where the Himalaya at least was concerned, Bauer eased British misgivings and made certain that Nanga Parbat would remain a German preserve. Finally though, and most important, the Himalayan Foundation was about money. The 1934 expedition had left massive debts, and the heirs of the survivors were now claiming that such funds as remained were "apportionable commercial profits" owed to them, though in fact, as Bauer pointed out, they derived originally from the voluntary contributions of (mostly) German railwaymen. "These bickerings," Bauer later explained, "led to the creation of the Deutsche Himalaja-Stiftung as a legal institution to which were made over all equipment, instruments, negatives, pictures, and copyrights of the two Kangchenjunga expeditions (1929, 1931), and the two Nanga Parbat expeditions (1932, 1934)."[25] In other words, the foundation abolished all private claims on expeditions past and future and brought all fund-raising, marketing, and publicity under Bauer's indirect control.

Headquartered by design not in Berlin but in Bauer's old stomping ground of Munich, the Himalayan Foundation was officially announced on May 15, 1936, and registered with the Bavarian government eleven days later. By then, the British government had already authorized a French attempt under Henri de Ségogne on Gasherbrum I ("Hidden Peak") in the Karakoram and was unwilling to allow another expedition up the sensitive Gilgit Road. Bauer therefore put Nanga Parbat off until 1937 and in the summer of 1936 took the small party of Karl Wien, Adolf Göttner, and Günther Hepp—the chosen core of the Nanga Parbat team—to the Kangchenjunga massif on a training expedition. After unsuccessful attempts on the eastern Twin (22,982ft/7,005m) and Tent Peak (24,163ft/7,365m), the four friends (supported by six Sherpas) climbed Siniolchu (22,594ft/6,887m)—"the most beautiful mountain the world," Freshfield had said—and Simvu North (21,610ft/6,587m) before crossing the northern watershed into Lhonak. It was a notable expedition in its own right and amply vindicated Bauer's preference for the small tight circle of friends. But it was mere preliminary nevertheless. As Wien later put it, homage to the dead demanded that the Germans return to Nanga Parbat—and return they would, with still more tragic consequence.[26]

Everest: Reconnaissance and Repulse

Shipton and Tilman had left the Nanda Devi sanctuary in September 1934 fully intending to return the following summer; having reconnoitered the mountain, they now, of course, wanted to climb it. But "it soon became apparent," Shipton later wrote, "that Mount Everest was the most immediate barrier to the enchanting plans that had begun to crowd upon my imagination." Quite unexpectedly, the Tibetan government in March 1935 issued a two-year passport to the Everest Committee, effective more or less immediately. The leadership spat that this provoked among Everest veterans—and between the climbers and what Longland called the "self-perpetuating oligarchy" of the Everest Committee—had ended in a compromise whereby Shipton would lead a light reconnaissance in 1935 and Ruttledge a full-blown assault in 1936. Shipton had qualms and Tilman was positively reluctant: "I think the idea of traveling with a large party oppressed him," Shipton wrote. In the end, though, neither could resist the thought of wandering freely for months among the peaks and valleys of the Everest massif or the opportunity of proving to the world the advantages of traveling light. They signed on and invited three upstart alumni of the Cambridge University Mountaineering Club to join them: Charles Warren (a pediatrician whose alpine ascent of Bhagirathi III with Colin Kirkus in 1933 had so impressed the young Turks), Edwin Kempson (a housemaster of Marlborough College and a twelve-year Alpine veteran), and Edmund Wigram (a strong but relatively inexperienced student at St. Thomas' School of Medicine). From New Zealand came Dan Bryant, whose amiable disposition inspired Shipton, fifteen years later, to invite another Kiwi to Everest. Finally, at the insistence of the Mount Everest Committee, came Michael Spender, brother of the poet Stephen and a brilliant surveyor but "a man whose overbearing conceit had made him most unpopular on each of his several expeditions." He and Shipton nevertheless became great friends.[27]

Shipton's six-point charge from the Everest Committee was to study monsoon snow conditions on the North Face of the mountain; to scout out alternate routes from the west by way of either the Northwest Ridge or the mysterious Western Cwm; to report on the present state of the North Col for the benefit of the 1936 team; to test his men as candidates for 1936; to try out new designs of tents and other equipment; and generally to correct and complete the northern survey, which, thanks to the "all-absorbing problem of reaching the summit," had been left to languish since Howard-Bury's reconnaissance of 1921.[28] He had a budget of £1,400: the mere balance from 1933 and hardly a king's ransom, but by living frugally off the land Shipton thought he could make it last. With the help of Dr. S. S. Zilva of the Lister Institute of Preventive Medicine, he worked out a stringent daily diet consisting of pemmican, cheese, flour, lentils, dried vegetables, and nuts supplemented by local mutton and eggs. It was a far cry from the Fortnum and Mason approach of previous expeditions, and Shipton later had to concede its monotony. But it kept the expedition members fit, lightened their loads, and brought them home under budget: a triumph in principle.

Arriving in Darjeeling two days ahead of the main party, Tilman and Bryant—without, it seems, once speaking to one another—saw to the by now routine business of recruiting Sherpa porters. From Nanda Devi came three old friends: Ang Tharkay, Pasang Bhotia, and Kusang Namgir. From Kamet came Kusang Sitar, from Nanga Parbat the interpreter Jigmey Ishering, and from Kanch and Everest the veterans Ang Tenzing, Rinzing

Eric Shipton (seated far right) recruiting Sherpas and distributing boots
in Darjeeling. The young Tenzing Norgay stands fourth from left.
Reprinted by permission of the Royal Geographical Society.

Bhotia, and Tsering Tharkay. Altogether Tilman engaged what he thought was a sufficient
and experienced crew of fourteen, but looking them over Shipton decided he wanted two
more and chose out of a late assembly of twenty hopefuls Ang Tsering (not to be confused
with the Ang Tsering who had survived Nanga Parbat in 1934 and was still convalescent
in Darjeeling) and a smiling newcomer of nineteen known then as Tenzing Bhotia but
known to history as Tenzing Norgay.

   Though he later styled himself a Sherpa, and indeed became, in the eyes of the
world, the most famous Sherpa of them all, Tenzing was not in fact native to the Solu
Khumbu region of Nepal. He was born, probably in 1914, in the village of Tshechu, east of
Everest in the Kharta region of Tibet: thus Tenzing Bhotia, *Bhotia* meaning, literally, people
of Bhot, the Sanskrit transliteration of Bod, or, Tibet. His father, Mingma, was a yak herder,
and but for a brief and unpropitious spell in a monastery, Tenzing spent his childhood
wandering with the animals from his father's house at Dangsar on the Kharta Chu to the
various seasonal grazing grounds in the surrounding valleys. Charles Howard-Bury brought
his 1921 reconnaissance to these valleys, and legend has it that as a small boy Tenzing met
George Mallory either near Dangsar or below the Langma La, the pass into the Kama Valley
that Mallory crossed on August 3, 1921 en route to the Kangshung Glacier and the eastern
face of Everest. To say, as some have done, that this chance encounter inspired in Tenzing

the ambition to climb Everest one day is altogether too fanciful. But as his biographer Ed Douglas says, it may have suggested to him the possibility of working as a porter for the *chilina-nga*, the "pale foreigners." Dorjee Lhatoo, who married Tenzing's niece and became a renowned climbing Sherpa himself, told Douglas that Tenzing "remembered expeditions coming to the Kharta Valley when he was small [and] talked about how he would look up to these Sherpas and Bhotias who seemed to have a very good life, wealthy, with fancy clothes and heavy boots."[29]

At some point in the early to mid-1920s Tenzing's father lost his herd to a mysterious disease and the family, like generations of Tibetans before them, migrated for work over the 18,753-foot Nangpa La into Khumbu. Here they would have been treated as socially inferior outsiders, "Khambas," the Sherpas called them, immigrants who arrived with nothing but "a basket and a stick." Tenzing's own recollection of these painful years is deliberately vague, but Douglas speculates that Mingma may have "mortgaged" his teenage son to a prominent Khumbu family as a day laborer or shepherd. Socially this was a dead end; Tenzing's chances of complete assimilation into established Sherpa society were not good; and not surprisingly he quickly contemplated escape to "the outside world." The catalyst was love. At some point in 1931 or 1932, Tenzing met and fell in love with Dawa Phuti, the daughter of a prosperous Sherpa trader at Thame on the Bhote Kosi, the village that Tenzing later claimed as his native home. As a mere Khamba, Tenzing had no hope of marrying a Sherpani, and in fact Dawa Phuti's father had already arranged her marriage to someone else when the two lovers took matters into their own hands and fled with one blanket and no money for Darjeeling, or Dorje Ling, as Tibetans called it, the "place of thunderbolts."[30]

Darjeeling in the early 1930s was at a crossroads in its history. On the one hand it was still the "Queen of the Hills," the summer seat of the governor of Bengal where a ruling clique of civilian and military officials mixed with a sprinkling of Calcutta merchants and maintained the timeless social rituals of the Raj. Trevor Braham, later an honorary secretary of the Himalayan Club and longtime editor of the *Himalayan Journal,* remembered Darjeeling as a mix of Surrey and Tibet: "It possessed the uncrowded atmosphere of an English country town, with summer homes built in Tudor, Georgian or Victorian style in a setting of neatly trimmed lawns and flower beds." On the other hand, it had in the past ten years become the noisy center of mountain tourism, a place where large floating populations of Sherpas, Bhotias, Tibetans, and Bengalis competed for jobs as rickshaw pullers and porters. "They were slow to integrate with the local population," Braham recalled, "and they used to live exclusively in their own ethnic groups on the outskirts of the town, in villages like Bhutia Busti and Toong Soong Busti. Many of the older men trained by Kellas, Bruce and Ruttledge had established their reputation as high-altitude porters, a tradition which was being handed down to a younger generation."[31]

Initially avoiding the Sherpa and Bhotia shantytowns below the ridge, Tenzing found work tending cows at Alubari, a small hamlet above Darjeeling in the direction of

Tiger Hill, already in his day a popular tourist destination that offered a distant glimpse of the Everest-Makalu massif. But his idea still was to join that second generation of high-altitude porters, and in February 1933 he made his way eagerly to the Planters' Club in hopes of landing work with Ruttledge's Everest expedition. But he had no *chit,* no lovingly preserved letter of reference from a previous employer, nor any official certificate from the Himalayan Club. Worse still, at a lean five feet eight inches, with closely cropped hair and Nepali clothes, he did not look like a Sherpa. The sahibs dismissed him from the verandah at a glance, and he wandered back miserably to his cows at Alubari, wondering if he would ever get a job.[32]

In January 1934 a devastating earthquake struck the border country of Bihar and Nepal, destroying buildings and killing people from Kathmandu to Darjeeling. Tenzing returned to Khumbu to check on his parents and help them rebuild their house. He then lingered, tending crops and yaks, and once crossing Nangpa La to fetch salt in Tibet, before returning in the fall to Darjeeling, where "all the talk" was of the late disaster on Nanga Parbat, of the death of six Sherpas and the valor of Gaylay, who had stood by and died with his sahib. "Even though I had not yet been on a mountain, such a story made me, too, proud to be a Sherpa," Tenzing later recalled.[33] Scorning the cows of Alubari, he moved into the shantytown of Toong Soong Busti, where as luck would have it his landlord was Ang Tharkay, the veteran Sherpa who had been with Bauer on Kangchenjunga in 1931, Ruttledge on Everest in 1933 and, most recently, Shipton and Tilman in Garhwal in 1934. Ang Tharkay was of course a given when the Shipton reconnaissance arrived in town looking for porters in 1935, and it may have been at his urging that Shipton took a chance on an inexperienced sprig of nineteen with nothing but a winning smile to recommend him.

The 1935 reconnaissance left Darjeeling by way of Kalimpong and the Teesta Valley in late May. Trouble arose at Gangtok when the status-conscious Sherpas refused to carry any loads. "Since in principle carrying loads wasn't something Sherpas did before base camp, we protested, deciding unanimously to strike and go home," Ang Tharkay later recalled.[34] Shipton brokered a face-saving compromise whereby the Sherpas carried for one more day, and the party moved more or less amicably along for Lachen and the Kongra La. From here, Shipton kept well south of the well-worn road to Everest and skirted the Tibetan frontier to the village of Sar, where he paused for two weeks to explore the Nyönno Ri, a lesser but beautiful massif rising to 21,859 feet (6,663 meters) above the Arun Gorge, north of the main Himalayan range. The weather was perfect, and though Shipton thus managed a splendid little bit of original exploration and filled in one more blank on the Himalayan map, critics subsequently wondered whether he ought not to have made straight for Everest and seized a rare opportunity. By lingering for two weeks in the Nyönno Ri, he instead began to acquire a reputation for waywardness that the Everest Committee would one day deem unsuited to its single-minded purpose.

From Sar the party proceeded westward on June 26, just as the monsoon rains began to fall. They reached Rongbuk on July 4 to find Dzatrul Rinpoche alive and well and ready as always to offer his blessing and advice. Scorning the old Base Camp and the whole elaborate business of ferrying supplies up the glacier, they reached Camp III below the North Col "without much incident or effort," Shipton said, and with enough food to last them three weeks: a clear vindication, thus far, of the simple approach. They had just left Camp III to inspect the lower slopes of the col when, on the morning of July 9, Charles Warren was startled to come upon "a perfectly good pair of boots and a tent." Thinking he had found a dump left in 1933, he went nearer and "got a bit of a shock" at finding a dead body lying huddled in the snow. "At once the thought flashed through my mind—Wilson!" Warren later recalled. "I shouted back to Eric—'I say, it's this fellow Wilson!'"[35]

"This fellow Wilson" was Captain Maurice Wilson, M.C., a briefly celebrated Yorkshireman who in the summer of 1932 had decided that his mission in life was to climb Mount Everest alone. Then thirty-four years old, he had been born in Bradford in 1898, the third son of a weaver's overseer in a local woolen mill. Just sixteen when the war broke out, he enlisted two years later as a private in the Fifth Battalion of the West Yorkshire Regiment (the Prince of Wales' Own). Raised to corporal and eventually nominated for a commission, he served with distinction in Flanders, winning the Military Cross for conspicuous gallantry and devotion to duty in the face of the enemy at Meteren, the fourth battle of Ypres. Demobilized in July 1919, he returned to Bradford "a restless, unsettled and vaguely unhappy man," a case study in postwar neurasthenia. Unable to adjust to civilian life, he emigrated, first to the United States, then to New Zealand, where he pursued a "bewildering kaleidoscope" of jobs, ranging from quack medicine to farming. En route back to England in 1932, he happened to befriend a group of Indian Yogis who introduced him to their philosophy of self-discipline and denial. How much of it stuck with him is unclear, but three months later, when his health suddenly deteriorated, Wilson went not to a doctor but to an unnamed mystic in Mayfair who prescribed faith and fasting. Somehow Wilson emerged with a theory that (as Shipton described it) "if a man were to go without food for three weeks he would reach a stage of semi-consciousness on the borderland of life and death, when his physical mind would establish direct communication with his soul." He would emerge from this stage, Wilson believed, purged of all bodily and spiritual ills and with redoubled physical strength.[36]

At the same time that he was working all this out, Wilson happened on some old newspaper accounts of the 1924 Everest expedition. The Houston aerial expedition, meanwhile, was much in the current news, and somehow out of this elaborate mix of suggestions, Wilson arrived at his life's purpose. He would buy an airplane, fly it to India, crash it on the lower slopes of Everest, and prove his theory of man's infinite capacity by climbing the mountain alone.

Instead he died, of course, but not before giving the skeptics a thing or two to think about. With no previous flying experience, and in the face of considerable official obstruction, he managed to fly his Gipsy Moth *Ever Wrest* to Purnea in Bihar solo in two weeks: "a minor epic in the history of aviation," his memoirist says. Here all his efforts to obtain permission to fly over Nepal failed, but rather than abandon his idiosyncratic crusade, Wilson sold *Ever Wrest* and proceeded to Darjeeling, recruited three Sherpas (Tewang Bhotia, Tsering Tharkay, and Rinzing Bhotia, all of whom had been with Ruttledge the year before), and slipped surreptitiously into Tibet disguised as a Buddhist monk. When he reached Rongbuk he assured Rinpoche Lama that he was a returning member of the 1933 expedition and thus secured some supplies that Ruttledge had left stashed there. After one failed attempt, and against all odds for one of no mountaineering experience, he reached the traditional Camp III at the foot of the North Col on May 14, one week short of a year after taking off from Stag Lane Airfield, Edgeware. Here, good to his word, he left his Sherpas behind and carried on alone, evidently expecting to find intact the steps that Ruttledge's team had cut on the mountain in 1933. Instead he found a bare windswept ice cliff utterly beyond his modest competence. For two weeks he tried heroically to claw his way up the mountain, once getting as far as the forty-foot ice wall below the col itself, before succumbing to exhaustion and cold. The final entry in his diary read, "Off again. Gorgeous day."[37]

Even Shipton had to concede that Wilson had taken the minimalist approach a bit far, though as he sat on a rock listening to Kempson read aloud from the diary, he could not suppress some admiration for the man's conviction. "It was not mountaineering, yet it was magnificent," Smythe later wrote, and it must have been with some such sentiment in mind that Shipton and his friends consigned Wilson's pathetic remains to a crevasse on the East Rongbuk Glacier. The next day they began their own attempt on the North Col, which initially fared little better. The slopes were in good condition but the climbers were not, having perhaps overindulged in the toffees and chocolates they recovered from a 1933 depot. Halfway up a hard snow began to fall and the Sherpas, evidently spooked by the discovery of Wilson's body, refused to go any farther. A "heart to heart" (i.e., a dressing-down) in Camp III that evening soon set matters right, and two days later—a record six days after leaving Rongbuk—Shipton, Kempson, Warren, and nine Sherpas occupied Camp IV at the foot of the Northeast Ridge with enough food to last fifteen days. The plan now was to take a light camp up to 26,000 feet, investigate the snow conditions on the upper mountain, and perhaps—though Shipton's charge from the Everest Committee specifically forbade it—even attempt the summit. But the weather had now definitively turned against them. After four days of hanging about and one brief foray onto the Northeast Ridge for form's sake, the whole party retreated gingerly down a newly avalanched slope to the glacier on July 16, leaving some tents and stores against the possibility of a late-summer return.[38]

There followed what Shipton many years later described as "a veritable orgy of mountain climbing." En route to Camp II, the entire party climbed Khartaphu (23,710ft/ 7,227m), an easily accessible peak above the Lhakpa La and overlooking the Kharta Glacier. Shipton then sent Spender, Kempson, and Warren off to climb Kharta Changri (23,270ft/ 7,093m), still farther to the east, while he, Tilman, and Wigram climbed P 7071, Mallory's old "Kellas Rock Peak" (23,198ft/7,071m) and several unnamed peaks above the confluence of the East and Far East Rongbuk glaciers. From Base Camp, Shipton and Bryant then headed up the West Rongbuk and climbed Lingtren (22,027ft/6,714m), from where they looked down longingly into the mysterious Western Cwm and imagined the joy of exploring it. Tilman and Wigram, meanwhile, went up the main Rongbuk to investigate the Lho La and the West Ridge, which they at once pronounced "utterly impracticable in its lower section." All this was, as Unsworth says, "a reappraisal in depth" of Mallory's work in 1921, and in practical terms added nothing to his conclusions. But the peak-bagging was impressive, and it was not over. After a failed attempt on Changtse (24,868ft/7,580m), the impressive North Peak of Everest on August 16, the party reassembled at Rongbuk and commenced a high sweep eastward, ultimately ending up in the Dodang Nyima range of north Sikkim. By the time they returned to Darjeeling in late September, they had climbed twenty-six peaks of over 20,000 feet, as many as had been climbed, Longstaff noted, "since the days of Adam."[39]

As far as the problem of Everest went, however, Shipton's reconnaissance had ironically done nothing but confirm existing (and quite mistaken) notions: that the mountain could be climbed only in the brief interval between the end of winter and the onset of the monsoon; that the West Ridge (or Northwest Arête, as they knew it then) would never be an accessible route; that the only feasible northern route was the Norton/Somervell traverse of 1924. In retrospect, as far as Everest was concerned, Shipton's greatest accomplishment in 1935 was the accidental discovery of Tenzing, who throughout the expedition had demonstrated all the superlative qualities that would eventually mark him out as a climber and sirdar. At the time, of course, Shipton had hoped to convince the "Establishment" (as he called it) of the virtues of a light, mobile party, but though these had obviously made for an unprecedented haul of lesser peaks, they had evidently counted for nothing on Everest itself, and much to his disappointment, Ruttledge set about organizing the 1936 assault on strictly conventional lines. Shipton thought of resigning his place and later wished he had: "Having tasted the joys of simplicity and freedom in two long seasons of unrestricted travel, I felt so out of sympathy with the enterprise that I certainly should have had the strength of mind, the integrity, to refrain from joining it," he wrote. But as Jack Longland once said, "for Shipton Everest came rolling around like some boring old clock, and it was difficult for him to refuse."[40]

As one of the mutineers who refused to support Ruttledge in the leadership, Longland himself was "excused" from the 1936 expedition, as of course was Colin Crawford, Ruttledge's rival. Of other notable hopefuls, Noel Odell was dropped for being too old, Tilman and Bryant for their tendency to altitude sickness, and a young officer named John Hunt for inadequate lung capacity: it seems he failed to blow a column of mercury high enough to satisfy the medical examiners. Eventually the team consisted of veterans Shipton, Wyn-Harris, Kempson, Warren, Wigram, and Smythe (who, more than Ruttledge, really ran the show) and newcomers Jim Gavin (who had climbed with Smythe in the Alps) and Peter Oliver (who had made a notable second ascent of Trisul in 1933). One of sixteen porters in 1935, Tenzing was one of sixty in 1936, and when even this number proved insufficient to Ruttledge's needs, John Morris, the transport officer, dispatched Ang Tharkay and Ang Tsering to Khumbu to round up 100 or so more. Larger and more elaborate than any to date, the vast caravan rumbled in two parts across the Tibetan plateau in March and early April. Ruttledge had already singled out Shipton and Smythe as his likely summit team, and the two men shadowed the caravan, climbing hills beside the trail "so as to evolve a perfect harmony of movement."[41] Everest, as it came into view, appeared in perfect condition, and the expedition was in high hopes when it reached the Rongbuk Monastery (where Tenzing took the opportunity to visit his cousin Trulshik Rinpoche, now a twelve-year-old Rongbuk lama). But in Ceylon the monsoon had already broken a full month ahead of schedule. The first snow fell on Everest on May 10, just as Smythe, Shipton, and Warren had gained the North Col, and once it began, it never let up. The 1936 expedition ended before it ever really got started.

Not that they did not make a game effort. On May 13 Rinzing Bhotia led a party of four sahibs and three Sherpas onto the col, the first lead climb by a Sherpa in the history of Everest. Harris and Kempson followed the next day with forty-six more porters and two light valve radio sets intended for use in the higher camps: another first. For once, it seemed, climbers and porters were in equally fine fettle, but the mountain, cruelly, was not. Two feet of fresh snow draped even the normally exposed crest of the North Ridge, and up above on the North Face, the line of Norton's 1924 traverse was utterly indiscernible. Smythe waited it out for three days, hoping against hope for a change in conditions that never came. The combination of fresh snow and warm temperatures made the entire mountain an avalanche trap, and on May 18, haunted, no doubt, by indirect memories of 1922, Ruttledge ordered a general withdrawal to Camp I. In effect, that was that. Smythe and Shipton led two futile attempts to reach the col on June 4 and 5, the second of these ending in an admonitory avalanche. Shipton took his frustration out on Changtse, the mountain that had defeated him in 1935 and defeated him again now. Smythe meanwhile proposed a mad dash at Everest by way of the main Rongbuk Glacier and the western approach to the North Col that Mallory had ruled out in 1921. On inspection, it did not look half bad, but Ruttledge wisely forbade an attempt on it, and the expedition withdrew in frustration bordering on despair. There were no lessons to be learned, really; the failure of the 1936 expedition was no one's fault. Nevertheless, it was the fourth downright failure, the sixth if one counts the two reconnaissances of 1921 and 1935, and it went down badly with the Alpine Club, the Mount Everest Committee, and the public generally, which was beginning to weary of the packaged rhetoric of "siege," "assault," and "repulse." George Ingle Finch may have been a maverick outsider with old scores to settle with the Everest Committee, but in October 1936 he unquestionably spoke for many when he publicly described "the present position" as one in which "we are beginning to make ourselves look very ridiculous."[42]

The Ascent of Nanda Devi

Back in Darjeeling after what he called the most boring expedition of his life, Shipton happened to meet Major Gordon Osmaston, a distinguished soldier and geographer who was now directing the Indian Survey's triangulation of the Great Himalaya, which had been suspended in 1924 for want of funds. Having completed a primary series of the Gangotri region of Garhwal (the Bhagirathi and Kedarnath groups), Osmaston now wanted to take on the Nanda Devi basin and, not surprisingly, asked Shipton to guide him up the Rishi Gorge and assist in the selection of surveying stations. Delighted at the opportunity to shake the snows of Everest off his feet, Shipton agreed at once, gathered a few porters together (including Tenzing and Ang Tharkay), and set off again for the sanctuary of the goddess. One day out of Josimath, while camped at Lata, near the mouth of the Rishi Gorge, he and Osmaston unexpectedly met the "bearded and tattered figure" of Peter Lloyd rushing down the steep path toward them. Lloyd, they knew, had been with a mixed Anglo-American party attempting Nanda Devi that summer, and he brought them astonishing news: the goddess had yielded at last. Noel Odell and Bill Tilman, two climbers deemed unfit for Everest, had reached her summit on August 29. This was undoubtedly, Shipton thought, "the finest mountaineering achievement which has yet been performed in the Himalaya," and he immediately confessed his wish that he had been part of it and not wasted his time on "that ridiculous Everest business." The Nanda Devi expedition, he felt, was "a model of what such an expedition should be" in that it consisted exclusively of mountaineers un-burdened by a vast bulk of stores and superfluous personnel. Beyond vindicating Tilman and Odell personally, the ascent vindicated the Shipton and Tilman style of mountaineer-ing, and Shipton understandably took vicarious pride in it. "By Jove, it will shake the old fools at home," he wrote, "and will do far more good towards getting the right spirit in the Himalayas than anything else could have done."[43]

Though Shipton does not say so, surely what most shook "the old fools at home"—by whom he meant the worthies of the Everest Committee—was that the inspiration for the ascent of Nanda Devi came not from Great Britain at all but from the United States, from Massachusetts, from the other Cambridge—to be precise, from Harvard. Founded in 1924, the Harvard Mountaineering Club had for some years, under the influence of Bradford Washburn, been the main force behind the resurgence of climbing in Alaska, which had languished in the aftermath of the first ascent of Denali (Mount McKinley) in 1913. None of its members had as yet been to the Himalaya, but in 1932 two of them, Terris Moore and Arthur Emmons (both of whom had climbed with Washburn in Alaska), had led an epic first ascent of Minya Konka (now Gongga Shan), a remote giant in Szechwan China then vaguely rumored to be higher than Everest. It turned out to be over 4,000 feet lower, but at 24,789 feet (7,556 meters) it was nevertheless a worthy adversary, far higher than anything Alaska had to offer. Just to find it tested these relatively inexperienced climbers to the utmost. They were "up to their necks in something they had never gotten into before at all," Washburn later said in appreciation, and indeed Emmons paid for Minya Konka with the better part of both of his feet. Even so, conducted as it was without benefit of porters—something that distinguished it from every Himalayan expedition of the era—the ascent was a notable piece of exploratory mountaineering and dramatically announced the arrival of American climbers in Asia.[44]

After Minya Konka, Terris Moore put mountaineering behind him and took up flying. But Emmons, despite his gruesome experience with gangrenous frostbite, remained keen and on his return to the United States broached the idea of a Himalayan climb to two younger compatriots in the Harvard Mountaineering Club, Adams Carter (who had climbed Alaska's Mount Crillon with Washburn in 1934) and William Farnsworth "Farnie" Loomis (a New England rock climber). They in turn spoke to Charlie Houston, another Harvard man, who had been with Washburn and Carter on Crillon and in 1934 had joined in a first ascent of Mount Foraker (17,400ft/5,300m), after Denali the second-highest peak of the Alaska Range. Finding him receptive but too distracted by the cares of medical school to take a leading organizational role, Loomis and Emmons became "the spear-carriers" and set to work on what they hoped would be a lightweight attempt on Kangchenjunga.[45]

It was brash, to say the least—four American college students without a lick of Himalayan experience proposing to attack the Bauer Spur on the third-highest mountain in the world—and early on it occurred to Loomis that they ought to include some battle-hardened Brits. As it happened, Graham Brown, Smythe's old partner turned nemesis, had been with Houston on Foraker in 1934 and despite the age difference—Houston was then twenty-one, Brown fifty-two—the two had become good friends. In 1935 Emmons and Houston had waylaid Brown at a hotel in Italy and with high-spirited shenanigans made him an honorary member of the Harvard Mountaineering Club.[46] Brown now accepted their invitation to Kangchenjunga and agreed to approach Shipton and Tilman on their behalf. Shipton, alas, was committed to Everest, but Tilman agreed to come along, as did Noel Odell of Everest fame, and Peter Lloyd, a rising star of the Cambridge University Mountaineering Club who, like John Hunt, had been left off of the Everest expedition for not scoring well on the required Royal Air Force medical evaluation.

Loomis, meanwhile, had gone to England to purchase equipment and to consult with various political and climbing authorities, several of whom, as Houston recalls, tactfully intimated that Kangchenjunga was "a bit much for a group of neophytes" and suggested the party go to Nanda Devi instead. This was fine with the Americans. To them both mountains were new, of course, but there was nevertheless more "freshness and originality" about Nanda Devi, not to mention more chance of success. Tilman, on the other hand, preferred Kangchenjunga, which would to him have been new ground, and he still held out hope for it when he sailed in advance of the main party to gather porters and arrange transport in March 1936. But in the end the choice was moot. No sooner had Tilman tied up at Calcutta than the oracle at the India Office spoke and informed him, with regret but without explanation, that the British-American Himalayan Expedition (as the Americans had restyled their original Harvard Kangchenjunga Expedition) would not be permitted to enter Sikkim. This left Nanda Devi, the second string to their bow, and after an "all too brief but peaceful fortnight on the glaciers south of Kangchenjunga," Tilman and the two good Sherpas he had managed to scrounge from the leavings of the Everest expedition, Pasang Kikuli and Pasang Phuta, made their way to Ranikhet, the familiar staging town of Garhwal, at the end of May.[47]

Loomis, meanwhile, had disembarked in Bombay intending to make for Darjeeling. Tilman just caught him by telegram at the American consulate, summoned him instead to Ranikhet, and together the two made their way over Kauri Pass to Josimath, the famous pilgrim village above the confluence of the Alaknanda and Dhauli rivers. Here Tilman recruited fourteen Bhotia porters from the village of Mana (three of them veterans of his 1934 reconnaissance) and organized a preliminary provisioning expedition up the Rishi Ganga. Much to his relief, he found the route up the gorge in much the same condition as in 1934: treacherous but passable. Tilman himself barely escaped death when a rockfall knocked him off a narrow ledge above a stretch of smooth sloping ground that he and Shipton had dubbed "The Slabs." Unroped, he fell twenty feet headfirst onto the slabs, rolled for a bit, "and then luckily came to rest before completing the 1,400 odd feet into the river."[48] A sprained shoulder, a bruised thigh, a cracked rib, and some flayed skin made up the total damage, and in his expedition memoir Tilman typically makes light of it. But it had been a near thing, and the next day he gratefully rested and recovered his nerve while Loomis and the Bhotias completed the traverse of the gorge. June 25 saw the whole reconnaissance party safely back at Ranikhet, having successfully stashed 900 pounds of food just inside the Nanda Devi Sanctuary.

In their absence, the supply of food and equipment at the Ranikhet Forest Bungalow had grown to alarming proportions, and taking advantage of the quiet interval before the others arrived, Tilman and Houston (and from June 28 Arthur Emmons) set to work "scrapping and bagging," as Tilman called it, ruthlessly weeding out inessentials and packing what remained into manageable sixty-pound loads. By prior arrangement, four additional Sherpas—Nuri, Da Namgyal, Nima Tsering, and Kitar Dorje—arrived from Darjeeling on July 3, closely followed by all remaining sahibs except for Adams Carter, who for some obscure reason had gone to Shanghai. Houston's father, Oscar (who had organized and led the first ascent of Alaska's Mount Foraker), had come with him in hopes of accompanying the expedition into the sanctuary, but Tilman and Odell doubted his fitness for the rigors of the Rishi Gorge and eventually insisted he remain behind—a harsh judgment that Houston's father accepted without argument though never fully forgave.[49] From the village of Doti in Nepal came thirty-seven professional porters, but Tilman engaged no sirdars, cooks, herdsmen, translators, or "other idlers." He was determined to keep things as lean as the climbing demands of the gorge and mountain allowed. All well and good for Odell, as a scientist, to lend some seriousness to their otherwise "frivolous proceedings," but if

Tilman had had his way, Odell's cumbersome glacial drill along with Houston's medicinal oxygen cylinders would never have left the bungalow at Ranikhet.[50]

Still missing Carter, who wired that he would catch up on the trail, the bandobast left Ranikhet on July 10 for the 175-mile walk to Nanda Devi. By now the monsoon had definitively broken; for three weeks the rain was continuous. But the Americans' spirits would not be dampened. The jaded Englishmen were naturally less exuberant. Tilman smoked much and said little, unless to complain of the Logan tents the Americans had insisted on bringing that somehow managed to stay more dry outside than in, he said. But Noel Odell confessed to some ecstasies at being back in the mountains—it had been twelve years since he watched George Mallory disappear into the mists of Everest—and for the most part these two groups of climbers separated by a common language (as Shaw would have put it) settled into one happy company. Accustomed as they were to fending for themselves on the trail, the Americans initially resisted the solicitous attentions of the Sherpas Tilman had assigned individually to each of them. Before long, however, "they acquiesced not unwillingly in the ways of the country," Tilman said, "and were as ready as the rest of us to shout 'koi hai' [anyone there?] on the slightest pretext."[51]

Ten days brought the party to Josimath, where as before Tilman recruited ten additional Bhotia porters from Mana, near Badrinath. This immediately made for trouble with the Dotials, who had evidently envisioned a closed shop, and for a day or two Tilman lived "in constant dread that some triviality would blow up the smouldering fires." Now sixty-one men strong (thirty-seven Dotials, ten Bhotias, six Sherpas, and eight Sahibs), the bandobast proceeded up the Dhauli Valley to Lata, their last link to the outside world, and into the Rishi Gorge by way of the Durashi Pass and the Dibrugheta alp, "an emerald gem in a somber setting of dark green pines."[52] From here the route required a forging of the Rhamani River just above its junction with the Rishi and beneath the fortress peak of Rishi Kot (20,459ft/6,236m). But not surprisingly, given the season, the water was high, so high and fast, in fact, that the Dotials refused the crossing altogether, dropped their thirty-seven loads, and went home. This was a serious setback that threatened an end to the venture altogether, but Tilman half welcomed the opportunity for more scrapping—first to go was the American rice, which in his view had all the taste and nutrition of a boiled shirt—and the proud Bhotias were positively delighted to be rid of their barefooted rivals. Everyone pitched in, Bhotias, Sherpas, and sahibs alike, and in double and treble relays ferried forty days' worth of provisions along the walls of the upper gorge and into the sanctuary.

Finally, on August 4, the expedition established a lower Base Camp at 15,000 feet on a high moraine shelf above Nanda Devi's Southeast Glacier. The preparatory drudgery was over, and to mark the occasion Loomis after supper produced a flask of apricot brandy that, though small, nevertheless soon had the Americans in their cups and happily regaling these taciturn Brits with terrifying tall tales of Alaska. "The already long glaciers of that frozen land increased in length," Tilman recalled of these stories, "the trees which seemingly burgeon on these glaciers grew branches of ice, the thermometer dropped to depths unrecorded by science, the grizzlies were as large as elephants and many times as dangerous, and the mosquitoes were not a whit behind the grizzlies in size or fierceness, but of course many times more numerous. And amid all these manifold horrors our intrepid travelers climbed mountains, living the while on toasted marshmallows and desiccated eggs, inhabiting tents similar to ours, and packing loads which to think of made our backs ache. To echo and amend Dr Johnson, 'Claret for boys, port for men, but Apricot Brandy for heroes.'"[53]

The next morning Adams Carter showed up, having repeatedly lost his way en route, and the party was at full strength as it began to climb the mountain. From Moraine Camp, as Tilman called it, the route ran up several miles of toilsome glacier to the foot of the Southeast (or "Coxcomb") Ridge that he and Shipton had reconnoitered in 1934. Above a 3,000-foot rock pedestal—the head, that is, of the glacial cirque connecting Nanda Devi and Nanda Devi East—the ridge ran straight to the summit like a flying buttress and seemed to demand little in the way of technical climbing until the last few thousand feet. But it was narrow and steep and (thanks to the foreshortening) much longer than the climbers knew: about three miles. Camp I was placed at 19,200 feet on a rock ledge hardly large enough for the three tents. Here, Nuri, Da Namgyal, Pasang Phuta, and Kitar sickened and lost heart, leaving the climbers with just two Sherpas—Nima and Pasang Kikuli—in support. This was inconvenient, but downright tragic was the loss of the tea, which somehow went over the edge to the glacier below on August 9. "The Brits said they were going home; they said you couldn't have an expedition without tea," Houston recalled many years later.[54] But somehow the Americans persuaded them to make do with cocoa and kindred drinks, and after days of recurrent storm, the climb resumed through Camp II under an overhang at 20,000 feet to Camp III on the snowy shoulder of the ridge at 21,000 feet. Here, the two remaining Sherpas, Nima and Pasang succumbed to dysentery and snow blindness respectively and descended, leaving the sahibs to face the wrath of the goddess alone.

Up to now, though everyone had naturally deferred to Tilman as the one who knew the ground, the Nanda Devi expedition had had no official leader; most unusually, it had proceeded haphazardly by rough democratic consensus. But with the final effort at hand, someone had to take formal charge and choose the summit teams, and on August 21, snowbound at Camp III, the entire party elected Tilman leader by secret paper ballot.[55] The next morning Tilman named Odell and Houston the first summit team. Graham Brown did not take this well and fell into a paranoid funk that Houston later attributed to altitude sickness. Two days of blizzard followed and tempers inevitably flared, but by frequently shuffling tent assignments, Tilman kept personal grievances from festering and developing into open hostility. Finally, on August 24, Odell, Lloyd, Loomis, Houston, and Tilman carried on to Camp IV at 21,800 feet. Above this, the face steepened sharply and the party resorted to the laborious business of step-cutting. At the base of a difficult rock gully they rested a little, "but it was no place for a long sojourn without prehensile trousers," Tilman wrote. "There was not enough snow to afford a step, much less a seat, and the angle of the rock was such that mere friction was of no avail—boots, hands, and ice-axe were all needed to prevent the beginning of a long slither which would only end on the glacier 6000 ft. below."[56] Above the gully the grind of cutting resumed as far as the foot of a rock tower on the ridge. Lloyd, the rock climber, now took charge, and led the party up a difficult chimney to the top of the tower in under an hour. By now it was 4:00, and leaving Houston and Odell to fend for themselves, Tilman, Lloyd, and Loomis retreated to Camp IV to await the final issue.

All the next day, August 26, a dense mist enshrouded the upper mountain. Tilman, Lloyd, and Loomis spent the day helping Graham Brown and Carter ferry supplies from Camp III to Camp IV and looking anxiously above for evidence of Houston and Odell. They saw none, but the following morning while sitting down to breakfast at Camp IV, they were "startled to hear Odell's familiar yodel, rather like the braying of an ass." Sensing an SOS, Tilman sent the strong-lunged Carter outside to open communications. This proved impossible, but within a few minutes Carter returned to the tent and reported hearing one clear and alarming phrase: "Charlie—is—killed." Tilman and Lloyd set out at once with bandages and spare clothing, followed later by Graham Brown and Carter with splints and hypodermic syringe. In six hard anxious hours Tilman and Lloyd reached the high bivouac at 23,500 feet, where they were first relieved and then annoyed at finding Houston very much alive, not "killed" but "ill," poisoned, it seemed, by a bad tin of bully beef he had shared with Odell the previous evening. At Houston's suggestion, Tilman took his place in the summit team and remained with Odell at the high bivouac while Lloyd, Graham Brown, and Carter saw the stricken patient safely down to Camp IV.[57]

On August 28, drawing from Houston and Odell's experience two days earlier, when they had missed the summit by a scant 300 feet, Tilman and Odell moved the bivouac higher, to 24,000 feet. "Our evening there will long be memorable," Odell later wrote, "for one of the most magnificent sunset scenes it had been our privilege to witness at high altitudes: dark masses of threatening cloud lay amongst the distant peaks, in strong contrast to vivid scarlet, gold, and greenish tints of the western sky." They feared for the weather of the morrow. But the cold night broke to a promising morning, and setting out at 6:15 A.M.—late by today's standards, early by theirs—these two veteran climbers who had been rejected as unfit for Everest made their way alternately through vilely soft snow and over broken rock and rotten cornice to the easy summit slopes. A choice between the last bit of ridge and an adjacent snow corridor presented itself at the last, and Tilman had just paused to consider this when an avalanche in the corridor settled the issue. They made for the ridge and at 3:00 found themselves on the culminating point of British India. "It gave us a curious feeling of exaltation to know that we were above every peak within hundreds of miles on either hand," Tilman later wrote in the fine English tradition of ironic understatement. "I believe we so far forgot ourselves as to shake hands on it." But with the joy in victory, he added, "came a feeling of sadness that the mountain had succumbed, that the proud head of the goddess was bowed."[58]

Far below—though Tilman could not know this—the Pindar River was in flood. Even as he and Odell had approached the summit, forty people had drowned in the village of Tharali. And as they descended, Kitar Dorje died at Base Camp of unspecified intestinal ailments. The goddess had avenged the violation of her sanctuary "blindly but terribly," Tilman later wrote, and his main feeling, as he retreated over Longstaff's Col in the company of the recovered Charlie Houston, was one of remorse.[59]

Successes and Failures

Insofar as the summit is the ultimate measure of mountaineering success, rather than the discovery of the route, say, or the simple height above sea level gained, then the ascent of Nanda Devi—which at 25,642 feet is not much higher than the traditional Camp V on Everest—was the greatest success of Himalayan mountaineering before 1950. (No less an authority than Tom Longstaff wrote to Charlie Houston expressing his "profound admiration for the team that without any flummery pulled off the finest climb yet done in the Himalaya.") But it was not the exclusive success that it sometimes seems. In fact, while the German and British mountaineering establishments continued to focus their heavy, high-stakes efforts on Nanga Parbat and Everest, a number of lesser but still quite reckonable peaks had begun to fall almost unnoticed to expeditions conceived on the Shipton/Tilman scale. Kamet, Bhagirathi III, Siniolchu, and Simvu North all succumbed to small parties of friends between 1930 and 1936. William Graham claimed to have climbed Kabru, the southern neighbor of Kangchenjunga "with no great difficulty" in 1883, but in 1935 the Englishman C. R. Cooke really did climb it, in winter no less, and alone (though with the help until summit day of G. Schoberth and six Sherpas, including the incomparable Ang Tharkay, Ang Tsering II, and Tilman's Pasang Phuta). Two years later Cooke returned to Sikkim with John Hunt, later of Everest fame, and from Nepal Gap at the head of the Zemu Glacier, Hunt climbed the southwestern summit of Nepal Peak. Cooke then moved south to reconnoiter Kangchenjunga from the Twins Glacier and with Pasang Kikuli and Dawa Thondup climbed to within 1,000 feet of the North Col, suggesting at least a future alternative to Bauer's Northeast Spur.[60]

Back in Garhwal, meanwhile, the Western monopoly on Himalayan climbing had finally been broken in October 1936 when a small Japanese team led by Yaichi Hotta and sponsored by the Rikkyo University Mountaineering Club (and including the Olympic skier Sakuta Takebushi) made the first successful ascent of Nanda Kot, a superbly proportioned mountain just outside the Nanda Devi Sanctuary and first attempted by Longstaff in 1905. A year later Frank Smythe, no less keen than Shipton now for a break from large and elaborately organized expeditions, returned to Central Garhwal and with Sherpa Wangdi Nurbu climbed Deoban (22,489ft/6,855m), Nilgiri Parbat (21,239ft/6,474m)—"the finest snow and ice-peak I have ever climbed," Smythe wrote—and (with Peter Oliver) Mana Peak (23,857ft/7,272m), after Kamet and Abi Gamin the third mountain of the range.

An attempt on Nilkanth (21,640ft/6,596m) failed—no shame here; though relatively low, Nilkanth is a difficult mountain that would not be climbed for decades—as did a too-ambitious attempt on Dunagiri, proud defender of Nanda Devi's northwestern sanctuary wall, but before they called it a day and gave themselves over to plant collecting in the Bhyundar Valley, Smythe and company had had a Himalayan holiday worthy of Shipton and Tilman and notable for having inspired *The Valley of Flowers,* arguably Smythe's finest contribution to mountaineering and travel literature.[61]

In 1938 an Austro-German party under Rudolf Schwarzgruber took advantage of Osmaston's new survey maps of the Gangotri region and in the space of five weeks climbed Bhagirathi II (21,364ft/6,512m), Chandra Parbat (22,073ft/6,728m), Mandani Parbat (20,317ft/6,193m), Swachand (22,050ft/6,721m), and Sri Kailas (22,742ft/6,932m). A year later, picking up where Smythe had left off, André Roch led a small Swiss expedition to Garhwal and with six inexperienced Sherpas climbed Dunagiri by the well-reconnoitered Southwest Ridge. He then turned to the lesser but difficult-of-access Kosa group south of Kamet and climbed Rataban (20,229ft/6,166m) and Ghori Parbat (22,007ft/6,708m). A first attempt on the more formidable Chaukhamba (23,418ft/7,138m) ended in the deaths of Sherpa Gombu and a local Dotial porter, Ajitia; otherwise, this was a successful expedition that notably announced the arrival of the Swiss on the Himalayan scene. A tragedy on Tirsuli (23,208ft/7,074m) marred the first Polish Himalayan expedition in 1939, but not before Jakub Bujak and Januscz Klarner, both of the Polish Mountaineering Club, had claimed the greatest remaining prize in Garhwal, Nanda Devi East, on July 2.[62]

In sum, of the roughly 600 Himalayan mountains that exceed 6,000 meters (19,685 feet) in height, some 75 had been climbed by the time of the Second World War. Of the more select company of 7,000-meter (22,965-foot) peaks, 22 had been climbed, beginning with Trisul in 1907. The highest summit yet reached was Nanda Devi's (25,642 feet), roughly the thirtieth highest in the Himalaya, the highest point Norton's 28,126 feet on the North Face of Everest. All in all, given the rudimentary (not to say primitive) equipment, the imperfect (not to say misleading) maps, the absence of effective supplemental oxygen, and the infinite difficulties of access and approach, it amounted to an impressive collective achievement, one that Shipton justifiably remembered in terms of a "Himalayan Hey-Day."[63] Yet not one of the most select company of 8,000-meter (26,246-foot) peaks had fallen, and the public perception, riveted as it was for the most part on the mighty trinity of Everest, Kangchenjunga, and Nanga Parbat, was one of continuing futility, frustration, and failure. One obvious recourse was to look elsewhere to break the 8,000-meter mark, but of the remaining eleven mountains that reach this fetishized height, six were politically off limits in Nepal and one (Shishapangma) was virtually unknown. This left the great giants of the Karakoram: Broad Peak, Gasherbrum I, Gasherbrum II, and of course K2, the second-highest mountain in the world.

An Italian expedition led by Aimone di Savoia-Aosta, the Duke of Spoleto (nephew of the Duke of the Abruzzi), and including a young geologist named Ardito Desio, reconnoitered the upper Baltoro in 1929 and thus (in their own minds, anyway) strengthened Italy's informal claim to K2. But the first actual climbing party to visit the Karakoram between the wars was G. O. Dyhrenfurth's "International Himalaya Expedition 1934." Like his earlier international expedition to Kangchenjunga, this was a large and makeshift affair that even included professional actors for the making of a feature film. Dyhrenfurth had failed to recruit any Sherpas, however, and like Merkl before him he found the local Baltis frequently inclined to strike. Somehow he managed a fairly thorough reconnaissance of Gasherbrum I, Conway's old "Hidden Peak," and on July 6 two of the team, Hans Ertl and André Roch, climbed to 20,350 feet (6,200 meters) on the Southeast Buttress (the "IHE Spur") before being caught in the same storm that routed the Germans on Nanga Parbat some 120 miles to the southwest. By the time the storm cleared, the expedition had neither the time nor the resources to resume the attempt on Gasherbrum and quickly settled instead for notable first ascents of Sia Kangri (24,350ft/7,422m) and the southeastern summit of Baltoro Kangri, Baltoro Kangri V (23,867ft/7,275m). Also notable was Hettie Dyhrenfurth's ascent (with her husband and Ertl Höcht) of Sia Kangri C, formerly Queen Mary Peak IV (23,861ft/7,273m), the westernmost summit of the Sia Group, which set an altitude record for women that stood until the mid-1950s.[64]

Two years later, in 1936, while Ruttledge was on Everest for the second time and Bauer and friends were in Sikkim training for Nanga Parbat, Henri de Ségogne led the first French Himalayan expedition to the Karakoram and resumed the fight for Gasherbrum I. Sponsored by the French Alpine Club and organized on a grand national scale, the expedition boasted several of the leading Alpinists of the day, including Pierre Allain (who just the previous year had made a celebrated first ascent of the North Face of the Petit Dru) and Jean Leininger (Allain's partner on the Walker Spur of the Grandes Jorasses). But none of them had Himalayan experience, and Ségogne wisely compromised national pride to the point of including Captain Norman R. Streatfeild, M.C., of the Bengal Mountain Artillery, as transport and liaison officer. He made no concessions to economy. At 11 Europeans, 35 Sherpas—most of them newcomers passed over by Ruttledge—eighty tons of stores and equipment, and some 670 local porters, the expedition was one of the largest to date; even Dyhrenfurth later faulted it for "serious over-elaboration." Even so, it made good preliminary progress over the Zoji La and up the Indus Valley to Skardu, the inevitable staging town for the central Karakoram. Here the bandobast crossed the Indus in the antiquated ferry that legend assigned to Alexander and proceeded 100 miles up the Braldu Valley to the Baltoro Glacier and Base Camp at 16,500 feet. Eschewing Dyhrenfurth's "IHE Spur" as too long and indirect, the French attacked the steeper, rockier "south spur" to a point just shy of the prominent subsidiary shoulder they called Hidden Sud (23,194ft/7,069m). From here the Southeast Ridge rose to the main summit at the reasonably moderate rate of one foot in three over a mile. Technically, their difficulties were behind them, and the French were fully confident of success when—what else?—the monsoon set in three weeks earlier than expected and routed them in a matter of days. All in all, it had been a splendid national debut, but the honor of the first eight-thousander was still there for the taking when the Germans returned to their *Schicksalsberg* in 1937.[65]

The leader this time was Karl Wien, who had been with Rickmer Rickmers in the Pamirs in 1928 and with Bauer in Sikkim in 1931 and 1936. Why Bauer himself did not lead he never explicitly said: either he was too distracted by his administrative duties in Berlin or, more likely, he felt the need to mollify the traditionalists of the Alpenverein who resented his aggressive appropriation of Nanga Parbat on behalf of the Nazi state. Fritz Bechtold, oddly, did not go out either, but he and Bauer were very much the rear command and Wien the field captain of a team that included Himalayan veterans Adolf Göttner (Sikkim 1936), Günther Hepp (Sikkim 1936), Peter Müllritter (Nanga Parbat 1934), and Hans Hartmann (Kangchenjunga 1931) and newcomers Uli Luft, Pert Fankhauser, and Martin Pfeffer, friends and Alpine partners of the others for many years. Twelve select Sherpas met the expedition in Srinagar and accompanied it up the now-familiar trail to Astor and the Rakhiot Glacier. The route up the mountain was familiar too, and all went precisely according to plan up to June 11, when seven Germans, nine Sherpas, four Baltis, and one Englishman (the transport officer D. M. B. Smart) occupied Camp IV in a shallow declivity at 20,280 feet on the snow plateau beneath the Rakhiot Peak. Over the next three days heavy snow frustrated efforts to reach Camp V. The four Baltis faltered, and on the morning of June 14, Smart accompanied them down to Base Camp, where he found Uli Luft preparing to ascend with provisions and five fresh porters. What happened next at Camp IV we will never fully know. Luft arrived there at midday on June 18 to find it obliterated beneath an avalanche of terrible proportions. Sixteen men lay deeply entombed in thousands of cubic feet of snow and ice.[66]

Two days later, June 20, a Sunday, Paul Bauer happened to be at the office of the Himalaja-Stiftung in Munich when the black news arrived by way of Gilgit, Simla, and London. Unwilling to accept that all his friends were dead but Uli Luft, he flew at once to Karachi with Bechtold and Karl von Kraus (Kangchenjunga 1929) and boarded a train for Lahore, the capital of the British Punjab. Here the three met Emil Kuhn, a survivor of Nanga Parbat 1934, and proceeded by plane to Gilgit, courtesy of the Royal Air Force, and thence by foot to the Fairy Meadow and Base Camp. "I'm so glad you've come," was all that a still-dazed Uli Luft could say as Bauer rallied the few surviving Sherpas for what he still dimly hoped was a search-and-rescue mission.[67] Bad weather and unstable ice hampered their progress through the lower camps, no one but Luft was adequately acclimatized, and Bauer had malaria besides. But the thought of the dead kept him going, and on July 20, precisely one month after getting the dreadful news, he emerged above the final icefall onto the snow plateau below Camp IV.

Only then did he appreciate the scale of the disaster. From the Rakhiot Peak south toward Chongra Peak, a massive cornice had broken away, taking much of the lower snow slopes with it. The avalanche field covered fifteen acres at a depth of ten to thirteen feet, and in this whole solid mass of frozen debris there was not the slightest evidence of a camp. The expedition had simply been snuffed out like a candle by the mountain it had come to climb. Here and there across the field, Luft, Kraus, and the surviving Sherpas had dug a few deep trenches, turning the plateau into a ghastly frozen mockery of the western front. They were on the point of giving up, five days of random digging having turned up nothing, when Luft stumbled on an ice ax, then two cigarette ends, then an empty can: the camp was near, and the next few days witnessed a grim excavation. At sirdar Nursang's request, the Germans left the bodies of the Sherpas undisturbed, but they retrieved those of Pfeffer, Hartmann, Hepp, Wien, and Fankhauser, buried them again with solemn ceremony, and withdrew mournfully from the pitiless mountain. Müllritter and Göttner they never found.

The loss of these sixteen men at (their wristwatches and diaries revealed) 12:10 A.M. on June 15, 1937 remains to this day the single greatest disaster in the history of Himalayan mountaineering. But it was no one's fault, and unlike the 1934 disaster, it provoked no controversy, inquiry, or recrimination at home. If anything, 1937 stilled all controversy and the German (indeed the world) mountaineering community stood solidly and cooperatively behind Bauer as he set out to avenge his (now) eleven dead countrymen in 1938. The British immediately granted a permit, the Alpenverein made no trouble, Tschammer und Osten extended full state support, and every indication is that Hitler himself now took a vengeful interest in Nanga Parbat. The problem was the climbers: they were mostly dead. But Bauer had Bechtold and Luft, the willing survivors, at his disposal, and with their help he quickly assembled a young but talented team of Alpinists including Mathias Rebitsch, Rolf von Chlingensperg, Stefan Zuck, and Ludwig Schmaderer (another Municher who with Ernst Grob and H. Paidar had attempted the East Summit of the Twins in 1937). Nursang agreed to return as sirdar, and though most of his Sherpa compatriots were either committed to Tilman on Everest or understandably reluctant to accompany any Germans to Nanga Parbat, ten newcomers ultimately signed on.[68]

Out of Rawalpindi, the 1938 expedition had an entirely new road through the Kaghan Valley across the Babusar Pass at its disposal, greatly simplifying the line of approach. And Bauer had inventively arranged for parachute drops of the expedition's supplies at three strategic locations on the mountain itself in hopes of accelerating the siege. As it turned out, these parachute drops were hit-or-miss affairs that usually resulted in "an unholy, portentous muddle." Few Himalayan expeditions have resorted to them since. But everything else "went without a hitch," Bauer recalled, and June 1 saw the fourth German expedition to Nanga Parbat safely installed at Base Camp.[69]

Thereafter, suffice it predictably to say, the weather conspired against them. Mid- to late June, in the Germans' previous experience, had always been fine on Nanga Parbat; Bauer's schedule was premised on that simple fact. In 1938 the whole of June was perversely foul, and the climb stalled from the start. Camp IV was not pitched until June 25, ten days behind schedule, and then only to be abandoned until mid-July. Finally, on July 22, after repeated failures on the Rakhiot Peak, Bauer led the small party of Luft, Bechtold,

The dangerously exposed tents of Camp IV (lower right) beneath the Rakhiot Peak as seen from the slopes of Chongra Peak in 1934. In 1937 the heavily crevassed snow slopes above gave way and buried the sixteen men at Camp IV in an instant. Reprinted by permission of the German Alpine Club.

Zuck, and four Sherpas up on to the Rakhiot Ridge where, just by the prominent Moor's Head, they were startled to come upon the perfectly preserved bodies of Willy Merkl and Gaylay. "This unexpected encounter with the dead made a deep impression on us all, in spite of the austerity of purpose with which we had armed ourselves for the assault on Nanga Parbat," Bauer later recalled.[70] To his dismay, the Sherpas were especially spooked, or otherwise reluctant to continue, anyway. After two faltering advances toward the Silver Saddle without them, Bauer packed it in. He was of course acutely mindful of the perils of this particular ridge in poor weather, and when the crisis came he defied the reputation of his countrymen and chose prudence and caution over daring. As far as the summit goes, the 1938 expedition fared no better than the previous three, but to Bauer's credit, it was the first German attempt on Nanga Parbat from which everyone returned alive.

And the last serious attempt, as it turned out, before the Second World War. Before quitting the mountain altogether in 1938, Bauer had sent Luft and Zuck over to have a look at the western Diamir Face that Mummery had attempted in 1895. Merkl's Rakhiot route, he had evidently concluded, was simply too long and exposed. It was time to try something more direct, and in 1939, encouraged by Luft and Zuck's photographs, he sent the small team of Peter Aufschnaiter, Lutz Chicken, Heinrich Harrer, and Hans Lobenhoffer back to Nanga Parbat for a full Diamir reconnaissance. After a tentative and frightening foray to 18,050 feet on Mummery's "second rib," a direct line to the summit, the four men climbed to about 20,000 feet on the middle rib of the North Peak before retreating in the face of technical difficulties and continual rockfalls. Their plan then was to return in force to the Diamir Face in 1940, but by the time they got back to Karachi in late August, war was imminent and they could not get home. Interned at Dehra Dun on the outbreak of war, Aufschnaiter and Harrer later escaped to Tibet, where they remained in the service of the Dalai Lama until the Chinese invasion of 1950.[71]

Everest 1938

On Everest, meanwhile, far on the other end of the Great Himalaya, the weather in the summer of 1938 had been no better than on Nanga Parbat, and Bill Tilman's lightweight expedition, the seventh and last of the prewar Everest expeditions, had failed no less definitively than the previous two, though considerably more cheaply and, happily, without loss of life. Offering his own account of the expedition, Tilman almost apologized for having "no hardships to bemoan, no disasters to recount, and no tragedies to regret," for his would be, he worried, one of the duller chapters in the Everest saga, except perhaps insofar as he had broken away from the "traditional grand scale upon which all previous expeditions had been organized."[72] To that extent, at least, his story had novelty, he hoped, and it required at the outset a word or two of explanation of how so peculiar an Everest expedition ever came to be.

To begin with, the striking success of a relatively small party on Nanda Devi in

1936, juxtaposed as it was to the simultaneous and highly publicized failure of a large party on Everest, had finally set the tide of climbing opinion running Shipton and Tilman's way. The hard facts of the Depression, meanwhile, the daily evidence of poverty and hunger at home, had many questioning the need to spend lavish sums of public money on what was, at the end of the day, a pointless, even private ambition. True, in the immediate aftermath of the 1936 failure, Sir Percy Cox, the secretary of the Everest Committee, windily reaffirmed that "the conquest of Mount Everest has become in a sense a national enterprise upon which all hearts have been set." But outside the confines of Kensington Gore, few looked on Everest this way anymore. The strident nationalism of German mountaineering had, if anything, encouraged a countertendency in Great Britain, a reversion to Mallory's somewhat flippant "because-it-is-there" style of justification. Three days after the publication of Cox's statement, Charles Meade, after Tom Longstaff the grand old man of Himalayan mountaineering, wrote to *The Times* urging an attempt on Everest along the lines of Shipton's 1935 reconnaissance. The editor of the *Mountaineering Journal,* E. A. M. Wedderburn, applauded Meade's letter, saying it summarized the view of most mountaineers throughout the country. And in September Frank Smythe wrote privately to Percy Cox, aligning himself explicitly for the first time with Shipton and urging that Everest be put in the hands of "a small party of friends accustomed to climbing together, as in the Alps."[73]

This was altogether too revolutionary for Cox: what had a "party of friends" to do with a national enterprise? But his Everest Committee was bankrupt in any case and in no position to resist when Tom Longstaff unexpectedly stepped in and offered to finance a small expedition to Everest on three conditions: that there be no advance publicity, that selected climbers pay their own way as far as possible, and that either Shipton or Tilman be named leader. In February 1937 the committee met quietly with Shipton, Tilman, Smythe, and Charles Warren to discuss this extraordinary proposal; in March they grudgingly accepted it and named Tilman the expedition leader.

With the attempt itself still a year away, Shipton and Tilman seized the day and gave the summer of 1937 over to a joyous exploration (with Michael Spender and John Auden) of the Shaksgam and northern Karakoram. This was a true "blank on the map," as the title of Shipton's expedition memoir has it, and even for two men who prided themselves on being able to "organise a Himalayan expedition in half an hour on the back of an envelope," it proved a worthy challenge and timely rehearsal for the Everest expedition to come. That same summer, on the far-off Tibetan border of Bhutan, Freddie Spencer Chapman (late private secretary to the political officer in Sikkim) set a new lightweight standard when he climbed Chomolhari (23,999ft/7,315m) in five days with two friends, three Sherpas, and £39. Here, out of nowhere, was a true inspiration—the Eighth Wonder of the World, said Charles Bruce—and Shipton and Tilman, when they heard of it, resolved all the more to show what such speed and parsimony could do on Everest. They recognized, of course, the considerable difference between 24,000 and 29,000 feet, and they knew that height alone was no adequate measure of difficulty. Tilman never intended to climb Everest as he had climbed Nanda Devi: he conceded the need for at least two more camps and many more porters. "But if the provision of two more camps entails more equipment and more porters," he argued, "it need not entail a small army with its transport officers, doctors, wireless officers, and an army's disregard for superfluity." Objectionable enough on practical grounds, the bloated expeditions of the past, Tilman argued, had a corrupting, demoralizing, and unbalancing effect on the economic life of the country and villages through which they passed, and were therefore morally objectionable as well. On his expedition, the tendency to take two of everything, "just to be on the safe side," would, he said, "be firmly suppressed."[74]

What emerged in the end was something of a compromise between Nanda Devi 1936 and Everest 1936 that pleased everyone and no one. The party numbered seven: Tilman, Shipton, and Smythe, of course—the core of the climbing team—plus Noel Odell (now forty-six years old), Peter Oliver (in place of Jack Longland, whose employer refused him leave of absence), Peter Lloyd (from Nanda Devi, the one newcomer to Everest), and Charles Warren (whose credentials as a climber overcame Tilman's initial unwillingness to take a doctor). As for equipment, "the sole innovation . . . was that we took only essentials and not too much of those," Tilman said. No radios, no skis, no plane tables, no glacial drills. Tilman of course was all for jettisoning the oxygen sets too; to his way of thinking, an oxygen cylinder on the back of a mountain climber made about as much sense as a diesel engine on a sailboat. But he finally agreed to take four—two open circuit and two closed—if only to silence the oxygen lobby and as hedge against frostbite or pneumonia. On food he would not be moved: two pounds per man per day, chosen on the strictest principles of simplicity and value for weight. In the end this meant a steady diet of badly cooked porridge and pemmican, and Noel Odell, for one, came back from Everest in 1938 full of complaints about the meager rationing. Tilman took this in his stride. "If a man expects to have a choice of three or four kinds of marmalade for breakfast it is a disagreeable surprise to find none at all," he conceded. "The supply of candles may have been short, but we were never reduced to eating them."[75]

Of the climb itself in 1938, suffice it almost to say (as Shipton did) "L'homme propose, Dieu dispose." From Darjeeling, where he recruited twelve crack Sherpas, including sirdar Ang Tharkay and, once again, Tenzing Bhotia (who had most recently accompanied Jack Gibson and John Martyn of the Doon School in Dehra Dun on a first ascent of Bandarpunch [20,721ft/6,316m] in the Garhwal), Tilman proceeded first to Kalimpong and Gangtok, where the expedition gathered in early March, and thence by way of Tangu and the Sebu La to Kampa Dzong, Shekar Dzong, and Rongbuk. Finding themselves well ahead of schedule—an encouraging benefit of traveling light—they dallied their way up the East Rongbuk Glacier and pitched Camp III at the foot of the North Col on April 26. The mountain above was in perfect condition, a mighty black obelisk. But the temperature was low, too low for a safe attempt, and with several of his party suffering from the usual Himalayan afflictions—sore throat, racking cough, headache, dysentery—Tilman

The incomparable sirdar Ang Tharkay (left) and a young brother,
Mount Everest, 1938. Reprinted by permission of the
Royal Geographical Society.

decided to retreat eastward over the Lhakpa La into the Kharta Valley for a period of rest
and recuperation—"to fatten up for the kill," Shipton said. By the time everyone returned
to Rongbuk on May 14, the summer snows had begun, the wind had dropped to nothing,
the black obelisk of ten days before "looked like a sugar cake," and the eastern slope of
the North Col was a death trap. Tilman sent Shipton and Smythe off to reconnoiter the
western approach from the main Rongbuk Glacier that Smythe had briefly considered in
1936. He, Oliver, Odell, and Warren, meanwhile, reached Camp IV by the usual eastern
route on May 28, and the next day Tenzing and Tilman (despite the latter's "manifold
infirmities") gamely climbed up the North Ridge to 24,500 feet. But col and mountain
were in equally vile condition. At 1:00 Tilman called a halt, retreated to Camp IV, and on
the next day withdrew the expedition from the East Rongbuk altogether.[76]

Prospects from the other side looked little better. The western slope of the North
Col "was a bloody place," Shipton wrote: "long, continuously exposed and very steep."
He saw at once why Mallory had rejected it as a route.[77] But now they had no alternative,
and on June 5 Shipton, Smythe, Lloyd, Tilman, and some twelve to fifteen porters risked
this virgin slope and survived it to occupy Camp IV on the col. The next day Smythe
and Lloyd led off for Camp V, Smythe without oxygen and Lloyd with—the first use
of supplemental oxygen on Everest since 1924. Several disheartened porters abandoned
their loads en route, but the indefatigable Tenzing and Pasang Bhotia made return trips as
needed, and by the end of the day Camp V was pitched on a commodious snow platform

at 25,800 feet. From here, after a day's rest, Smythe and Shipton (from the beginning the designated summit pair) moved up with Tenzing and Pasang to Camp VI on a scree slope below the Yellow Band at 27,200 feet. Neither men nor mountain were in any shape for a summit bid, but on June 9 Shipton and Smythe gave it the old college try in waist-deep snow before accepting defeat far short of the First Step. Tilman and Lloyd followed two days later, hoping at least to gain the summit ridge, but they had not even reached the Yellow Band before Tilman's hands and Lloyd's feet had gone distressingly numb. They returned to Camp IV to find Pasang Bhotia in dire straits, unable to speak and paralyzed down his right side. Here, if any more were needed, was an urgent reason to give up. The last climbing expedition to Everest before the war ended in an arduous litter carry of the unfortunate Pasang down the treacherous eastern slopes of the North Col.

Triumph and Tragedy on K2

Tilman had hoped to invite Charlie Houston along to Everest in 1938, but the Everest Committee would not countenance an American, and as it turned out Houston had other plans anyway, though not initially of his own making. For some time now, ever since admiring "the wild and distant sea of peaks that is the Karakoram" from the flanks of Nanga Parbat in 1932, the German-born American Fritz Wiessner had yearned to lead an expedition to K2, which despite its glamorous status as the world's second peak had not been properly attempted since the Duke of the Abruzzi expedition of 1909. His subsequent study of Vittorio Sella's unsurpassed photographs of K2 (taken on the Abruzzi expedition) strengthened Wiessner's ambition, and in 1936 he and Dick Burdsall (of Minya Konka fame) laid a formal proposal before J. Ellis Fisher, then president of the American Alpine Club. Fisher in turn enlisted the aid of Edward Groth, the American consul in Calcutta, who after much delay secured permission for a small party accompanied by a British liaison officer to enter the Kashmiri province of Baltistan and attempt K2 in the summer of 1938. This was short notice, too short for Wiessner, who over the years had, according to two friends, "developed a habit of letting others make a first try at anything he had in mind."[78] Suddenly pleading professional obligations, Wiessner yielded his permit to Houston for purposes of reconnaissance and requested a second for purposes of assault in 1939.

Still just twenty-five years old, a third-year medical student at Columbia University's College of Physicians and Surgeons, Houston set about organizing the First American Kara-koram Expedition along the light, mobile lines he had learned firsthand from Washburn in Alaska and then Tilman on Nanda Devi. Six being in his mind the optimum number of climbers, he invited, first, his good friend Bob Bates, a fellow alumnus of the Harvard University Mountaineering Club who had been with him on Mount Crillon and with Washburn on a first ascent of Mount Lucania in the St. Elias Range, and then of course Dick Burdsall, the forty-two-year-old engineer who had been a "perennial agitator" for a Himalyan expedition ever since coming down from Minya Konka in 1932. From the rival

Yale University Mountaineering Club came Bill House, a twenty-five-year-old forester who had been Wiessner's partner on a celebrated first ascent of Mount Waddington in British Columbia in 1936. Farnie Loomis, to Houston's dismay, could not get away; in his place he interestingly nominated one Paul Petzoldt, a rancher and mountain guide from far-off Jackson Hole, Wyoming. The worthies of the Alpine Club in New York frankly doubted whether "this Wyoming packer and guide" would fit in socially with the others and comport himself as required in the company of their British and Indian hosts. But for Houston, Loomis's recommendation together with Petzoldt's unassailable record (which included a one-day double traverse of the Swiss Matterhorn) trumped such Ivy League objections. The Wyoming packer came along, and with the addition of Captain Norman Streatfeild, the British liaison officer late of Gasherbrum I, Houston's "small party of friends" was complete.[79]

On April 14, 1938, leaving poor Houston behind to take his third-year medical exams, House, Bates, Burdsall, and Petzoldt sailed aboard the *S.S. Europa* for London, where they spent a few days collecting clothing and equipment ordered on the advice of David Robertson, an American friend in Cambridge who was soon to marry George Mallory's second daughter, Beridge. Then across the channel to Paris where, on idly looking over the expedition supply crates, Paul Petzoldt discovered that Houston (who of course shared the eastern climbing establishment's disdain for ironmongery) had packed little in the way of climbing hardware. "My God! We hardly had a piton or a carabiner," Petzoldt later incredulously recalled. "And hell, you could look at K2. That's rock! And there's places on it, if you fell you'd go down 10,000 feet before you would land."[80] Repairing at once to a Parisian climbing shop, Petzoldt bought fifty pairs of the dreaded German innovations and quietly stashed them out of sight among the rest of the expedition's gear. From Paris the four then proceeded to Marseilles, boarded a P & O steamer for Alexandria and Bombay, and caught the Frontier Mail for Rawalpindi, where they met Streatfeild and the six Sherpas whom Bill Tilman had recruited on their behalf in Darjeeling: Pintso Sherpa, Pemba Kitar, Tse Tendrup, Ang Pemba, Sonam, and the Tiger Pasang Kikuli, a veteran now of Kangchenjunga, Everest, Nanga Parbat (where, like Ang Tsering, he won the Medal of Honor of the German Red Cross) and, most recently, Nanda Devi.

Houston, meanwhile, had survived his exams and sailed on the *Queen Mary* for London, where he met with Tom Longstaff, E. L. Strutt, and other notable Himalayan veterans. At the Alpine Club he learned to his surprise that Graham Brown, his erstwhile Nanda Devi partner, had just gone out with James Waller, J. B. Harrison, R. A. Hodgkin, and Jimmy Roberts of the First Gurkha Rifles (later famous as the founder of the commercial trekking industry in Nepal) to attempt Masherbrum (25,659ft/7,821m), a lesser giant of the Karakoram not twenty-five miles southwest of K2, just across the Baltoro Glacier. These days climbers are well accustomed to encountering several other expeditions—not just in the same region but on the same mountain or even mountain ridge as themselves. But in 1938 such encounters were unprecedented, and not surprisingly "some friendly rivalry"

The 1938 American Alpine Club Karakoram expedition. Standing from
second left: Bill House, Charlie Houston, Norman Streatfeild,
Paul Petzoldt, Bob Bates, and Dick Burdsall. Seated (not in order):
Pintso Sherpa, Pemba Kitar, Tse Tendrup, Ang Pemba, Sonam,
and Pasang Kikuli. Courtesy of the Henry S. Hall Jr.
American Alpine Club Library.

(as Roberts later put it) set in between the two teams, though they never actually met.[81]
For now Houston took the news of unwanted company in his stride and proceeded by
air—another portent of things to come—to Amsterdam and Karachi. He caught up with
his team in Rawalpindi on May 9, just a day after they had arrived.

From 'Pindi (as the British affectionately called this last northern outpost of the
Punjab), the reunited party proceeded to Srinagar, where the British resident wished them
well and saw them off on their month-long, 350-mile march to K2. The trail followed the
Sind Valley east over the Zoji La (11,000ft) into Baltistan and then north along the Dras and
the Indus. This was well-known country by now, but these young Americans felt themselves
at the end of the earth, or rather in Kipling's "mysterious land beyond the passes," and they
reveled in every unexpected and evocative sight. Four days out, near the village of Dras,
they came upon the initials "H.H.G-A." and the date "1861-2-3" carved into the marble
cliffs above the river and knew they were in the footsteps of Godwin-Austen, the original
explorer of the central Karakoram and the Baltoro approach to K2. After lush Kashmir, the
landscape of Baltistan seemed barren, dry, and dusty. But each evening brought the tired
trekkers to an irrigated village oasis where they were welcomed as curiosities and friends

and treated to all manner of local entertainments, from polo in its ancient, original form to clamorous mountain songs and dances. "This march-in was a wonderful time to shakedown, get to know each other, to dream, to plan, to hope together," Houston recalled years later. "Here, where the Great Game was even then being played, we were already 'inspired by a single hope and bound by a single purpose.'"[82]

Twelve days brought Houston and Company to Skardu, the provincial capital of Baltistan and a busy trading center where they bought some equipment cast off by the French two years before and hired fifty-five Balti porters to see them to Askole, the last village on the trail, eight days of hard scrambling away. On May 26 they crossed the Indus on Alexander's proverbial barge and proceeded up the Shigar Valley to the village of Yuno, where their Balti porters, in what Houston called "a surprisingly modern spirit," sat down and refused to continue unless paid the exorbitant sum of four and a half rupees each for the twenty-five-mile carry to Askole. Houston appealed to Streatfeild, who thought that "for the sake of future expeditions" the agreed rate of two and a half rupees had to be honored, and for two tense days the game hung in the balance until the *chuprassi* (a sort of captain of police) of Skardu arrived "carrying an impressive paper, and an even more impressive club."[83] Houston had no more labor problems, but at Askole the expedition halted again when Petzoldt went down with an alarmingly high fever and severe pains in his bones. Leaving Houston to minister to the cowboy as best he could, Bates led the rest of the party on past the Biafo Glacier (where their only American predecessors in the Karakoram, William Hunter and Fanny Bullock Workman, had climbed and surveyed at the turn of the century) and up the Braldu toward Paiju and the mighty Baltoro. Houston and a revived Petzoldt caught them at Urdukas, two days up the Baltoro, and together everyone carried on past Masherbrum and Muztagh Tower to Concordia and Base Camp at the confluence of the Savoia and Godwin-Austen glaciers.

Now for the promised work of reconnaissance. K2, as Filippo De Filippi had noticed in 1909, is essentially a quadrangular pyramid supported at the corners by four main buttress ridges: the Northwest, the Southwest, the Southeast, and the Northeast. Of these, the most appealing at first glance was the Northwest, which (like Mallory's North Ridge on Everest) rises off of a high col, the Savoia Pass, 3,000 feet above the cirque of the Savoia Glacier. Abruzzi's party had reached this pass with tremendous effort, and though they had not liked the look of the uniformly steep ridge above, Sella's photographs showed the strata to be sloping upward and thus possibly amenable to climbing. Accordingly, on June 14 the Americans skirted the foot of the Angel, the outlying anchor of K2's forbidding Southwest Ridge, and headed up the Savoia Glacier in high hopes of pulling off a surprise ascent. As it turned out, they failed repeatedly even to reach the Savoia Pass, the slopes of which they found to consist of impossibly steep and dangerously crevassed green ice. On June 21, therefore, they moved their base three miles up the Godwin-Austen Glacier to the foot of the Southeast or "Abruzzi" Ridge (as they named it, in honor of the duke who had climbed it to some 20,000 feet in 1909). From here, Bates, Burdsall, and Houston

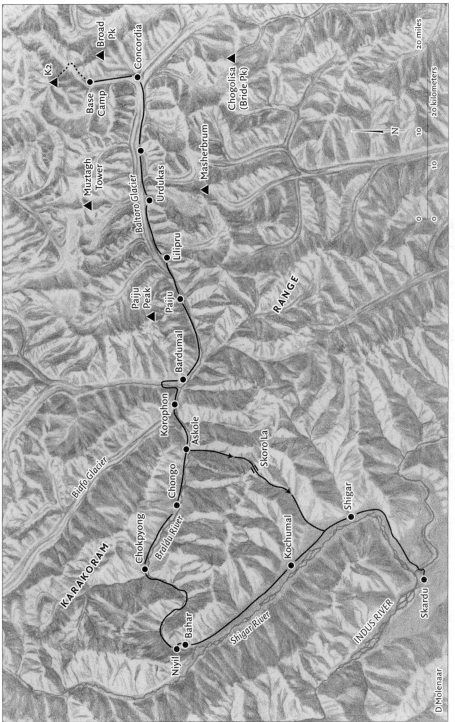

The trekking route from Skardu to K2 and back, 1938.

reconnoitered the Northeast Ridge while House and Petzoldt climbed a rocky spur across the glacier to have a better look at the Abruzzi.

No one liked what he saw. Below an appealing shoulder at 25,164 feet, the Northeast Ridge was long, steep, knife-edged, and dangerously corniced; Houston provisionally ruled it out. As for the Abruzzi, it was less a ridge, really, than a confused cluster of steep, parallel rock ribs and couloirs that converged on a massive snow and ice plateau at 25,000 feet. Above the plateau, the route looked passable, leaving aside the problem of altitude. Below, however, it looked forbidding, and before committing to it Houston decided to have a firsthand look. On June 19 he and House (a late substitute for Petzoldt, who had once again gone down with a fever) climbed the Abruzzi Ridge to about 19,000 feet, and though they were delighted to come upon a few wooden relics of 1909—fragments of the duke's supply crates—they returned otherwise discouraged. What had looked from below like "good honest ledges" turned out to be loose rock frozen into hanging ice and snow.[84] This would do only as a last resort, Houston decided, and in some desperation he sent Bates and House up the Savoia Glacier for another look at Northwest Ridge while he and Streatfeild made a token climb to 20,000 on the Northeast.

"The expedition spirits were now at a very low ebb," House later wrote. "From one side of the mountain to the other we had been unable to find a route. Two weeks had been spent apparently to no other purpose than to convince us that no way we had seen was possible." Houston himself still held out slender hopes for the Northeast Ridge, but Petzoldt and House favored the Abruzzi, and at a somber "council of war" on June 28 Houston democratically deferred to their judgment: the Abruzzi it would be. From an advanced base at the foot of the ridge, Petzoldt and House found a first campsite on the mountain at 19,300 feet on July 2. Leaving Burdsall and Streatfeild behind to manage camp affairs and conduct the obligatory scientific studies, Bates and Houston joined them there on July 3, and the game was on. For twenty-five days these four young friends leapfrogged their way up the mountain in what Houston later called "half siege-, half alpine style." The higher they climbed, the tougher the going got, and even Houston had to admit that Petzoldt's hardware frequently came in handy, though he still deplored it on principle and teasingly regretted turning the mountain into a cog railway. Above Camp III (20,700ft) a vertical pinnacle (later christened Petzoldt's Gendarme) obstructed them until Petzoldt surmounted it by way of an overhanging crack. A more serious obstacle was a 150-foot red rock buttress above Camp IV (21,500ft) that House finally bested by way of his famous eponymous chimney on July 16. The next day a storm struck the ridge, and the four men contemplated retreat as they lay huddled in their sleeping bags at Camp V (22,000ft). But July 18 dawned fine, and Houston and Petzoldt proceeded on to Camp VI (23,300ft) and beyond to have a look at the famous Black Pyramid that caps the Abruzzi Ridge. "This was to be the crux of the climb," Houston later wrote, "for, ever since our first examination of it, we felt that the last thousand feet leading onto the great snow shoulder was by far the most difficult and inaccessible stretch of all." And difficult it turned out to be, but on July

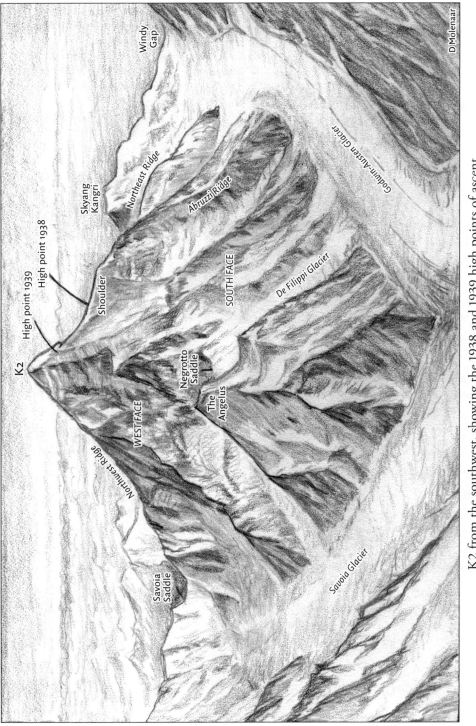

K2 from the southwest, showing the 1938 and 1939 high points of ascent.

Windy Gap

Northeast Ridge

Skyang Kangri

Shoulder

High point 1938

High point 1939

K2

WEST FACE

Northwest Ridge

Savoia Saddle

Negrotto Saddle

The Angelus

Abruzzi Ridge

SOUTH FACE

De Filippi Glacier

Godwin-Austen Glacier

Savoia Glacier

D.Molenaar

19, thanks in part to Petzoldt's detested pitons, it yielded, and the Ivy League doctor and the Wyoming rancher shook hands and shared "a restful cigarette" on the gentle, 25,000-foot snowfields of K2's Southeast Shoulder.[85]

What to do now? With the conquest of the Abruzzi Ridge, the promised reconnaissance was successfully concluded: the way for Wiessner to take to the summit next year was clear. But needless to say, having come this far, Houston and company wanted to pull off the great feat themselves, and after dinner at Camp VI that night came another council of war, "by far the most serious and decisive of the many we had had," Houston wrote. Bates reckoned they had about ten days' supply of food and fuel with them at Camp VI, not enough for a strong assault on the summit, still almost 5,000 feet and probably two campsites away. Supplies abounded below, and they might have descended, rested, and returned fully stocked for the assault. But the season was getting on, and if the monsoon broke while they were on the mountain . . . well . . . "Remember Nanga Parbat" was the simple mantra in every climber's mind in these years. Petzoldt favored daring, Houston caution, and after lengthy debate the four men took a vote that ended in reluctant compromise. "With sore hearts," Houston recalled, "we agreed to establish two men in Camp VII as near the 25,354-foot point as possible, with the understanding that they were to go as high as possible for the summit in one day, and return to Camp VI the next day, in order to begin the retreat to the Base Camp."[86]

On July 20, then, as agreed, all four climbers plus Pasang Kikuli (the one remaining Sherpa at this point) struggled over the Black Pyramid to the forty-five-degree snow slope of the shoulder. Bates, House, and Pasang then descended, leaving Houston and Petzoldt to struggle on to a small campsite (Camp VII) 3,550 feet below the summit. Supper was tea and pemmican, and it was on turning to light the stove for the tea that Petzoldt discovered they had neglected to pack any matches: an astonishing, probably altitude-induced oversight that threatened their very survival. After a moment's panic, Houston scrounged nine scruffy and fragile matches from his pocket, two of which failed before the stove flickered into life. Three more failed in the morning, and the whole enterprise was hanging by the thread of three matches when Houston and Petzoldt set out from Camp VII on July 21. Above the shoulder, the severity of the snow slopes lessened and Petzoldt, the fresher of the two, made good progress toward the final summit cone. But Houston's progress was, by his own admission, "ludicrously slow. Every inch I gained in altitude was an effort. My legs were so weak I was forced to rest every five or six steps, and soon fatigue made me forget all danger from above."[87] Finally, at the base of the summit cone, roughly 26,000 feet, he could go no farther. Petzoldt carried on a short way up the gully that led to the summit, far enough to satisfy himself that it was possible, and regretfully turned around. Retrieving Houston from his hypoxic reveries, he forced a rueful whoop of victory, and together the two men descended safely to Camp VII in a deepening twilight.

Houston was content. "Our mandate from the American Alpine Club was to find a feasible route," he later wrote. "We never expected to summit. We never expected to get as high as we did." But Paul Petzoldt, having gotten so high, would have liked to go just a bit higher, and for the rest of his life he regretted the decision to retreat in the face of thick clouds and an allegedly ominous ring around the sun. "Jesus Christ," he later said. "We weren't turned back by bad weather. We made up our mind not to climb the mountain. If we'd have brought up a little bit more food and planned to get to the summit, we could have come back as conquerors of K2." True, but they also might not have come back at all. Back in May, Edward Groth, the American consul in Calcutta, had (with the example of Nanga Parbat in mind) urged Houston to temper any summit ambitions with "the wisdom of assuming no risks which might hold disastrous consequences." The prospect of future American expeditions depended on the safe return of this one, Groth had argued, and while such political considerations were no doubt far from Houston's mind at 26,000 feet, the underlying logic was not. "Bound by the standards and practice of that time, facing bad weather, and very tired from five hard weeks of exploration and load-carrying, we were right to turn back," he later wrote. "Others, years later, pushed the envelope further; some did great and heroic deeds, others died, needlessly, victims to ambition and to the mind-numbing effects of great altitude. We lived to climb again, for many years. In true mountaineering, the summit is not everything. It is only part."[88]

Now it was Fritz Wiessner's turn. Houston's mixed success on K2 was precisely what this rather different sort of mountaineer had been counting on, and as soon as he heard of it in New York he set about organizing the return expedition that would, he felt certain, achieve the first ascent of an 8,000-meter peak. All he needed was a first-class team. But this, sadly, he was not to have: a simple, preliminary fact that accounts as much as anything for the tragedy that followed. It was late 1938. The United States had relapsed into acute depression the year before. People were strapped for cash and, with war looming ominously on the horizon, disinclined to invest what they had in recreational ventures abroad. Yet Wiessner might still have gathered a competent team had he not been the person he was: talented, well educated, and sophisticated, yes, but also domineering, autocratic, and willful to the point of obstinacy. "Fritz had been reared in the school of absolute obedience to authority that characterizes much of the Teutonic ethos," write two who knew him well. "He may have been ideally suited to command a German venture, but his background did not lend itself to directing Americans, whose informal and democratic practices, even on expeditions with a formal commander, require decisions to be based on mutual discussion and debate."[89] Just how far Wiessner's Teutonic style contributed to his difficulty in raising a team for 1939 is hard to say: no one turned him down explicitly on these grounds. But turn him down they did, one by one—Bill House, Sterling Hendricks, Alfred Lindley, Bestor Robinson, Roger Whitney, and who knows how many other well-known climbers— until Wiessner was left with a decidedly lackluster crew that should probably never have gone to K2 in the first place.

It consisted of Chappell Cranmer, scion of a prominent Colorado family and an undergraduate at Dartmouth College who had climbed with Wiessner in the Canadian

Rockies in 1938 and shown moderate promise; George Sheldon, Dartmouth classmate and friend of Cranmer who had all of two seasons' experience in the Tetons; Tony Cromwell, an independently wealthy, middle-aged New Yorker who boasted the longest but not most distinguished list of ascents of any member of the American Alpine Club and who joined Wiessner only on the understanding that he would not climb high; Jack Durrance, another, slightly older Dartmouth student who had worked as a mountain guide in Wyoming and led a first ascent of the North Face of the Grand Teton; and finally, Dudley Francis Wolfe, a large, clumsy, myopic, and middle-aged sportsman whose only qualification for K2 (discounting some heavily guided experience as a skier and mountaineer) was his fortune. In sum, it was probably the weakest team ever to attempt an 8,000-meter peak before the days of commercial expeditions, but it had an undeniable force and talent in its leader, and had things gone a little bit differently at one or two critical moments, it just might have claimed the second greatest Himalayan prize.

From different directions the climbers converged in April on Srinagar, where they met their obligatory transport officer, one Lieutenant George "Joe" Trench, and their nine Darjeeling Sherpas, five of whom had been with Houston on K2 the year before: sirdar Pasang Kikuli (now unrivalled among Sherpas), Phinsoo Sherpa, Pemba Kitar, Sonam Sherpa, and Tse Tendrup. Of the four others, two (Pasang Dawa Lama and Dawa Thondup) were highly experienced Tigers and two (Pasang Kitar and Tsering Norbu) were newcomers. All told, the Sherpa team was as strong as the climbing team was weak and gave the expedition a fighting chance. Trench, on the other hand, was a disappointment: a lazy, intolerant, and inept substitute for the incomparable Streatfeild, who had recently been recalled to active duty in Europe. Trench spoke no local languages, and at the suggestion of Kenneth Hadow (local secretary of the Himalyan Club and, by coincidence, grandnephew of the Douglas Hadow who died on the first ascent of the Matterhorn in 1865), Wiessner took along Chandra Pandit, a teacher at a local mission school and an enthusiastic member of the recently founded Kashmir Climbing Club, as interpreter and native confidant. Finally, there was the cook, Noor. Eighteen strong in all (six American climbers, a British transport officer, nine Sherpas, a Kashmiri Pandit, and a cook), the expedition left Srinagar on May 2, followed Houston's trail to the Baltoro, and pitched Base Camp at the foot of the Abruzzi Ridge on May 31.

The next day, June 1, while Wiessner and Cromwell went off to rule out the Northeast Ridge, things started to go wrong. Chappell Cranmer emerged from his tent feeling unwell, and by the end of the day he was mortally ill, coughing up huge quantities of frothy mush from his lungs, vomiting and defecating uncontrollably, and babbling nonsense about baseball games at Dartmouth.[90] Wiessner had not thought to bring a doctor along, but Jack Durrance at least aspired to medical school, and though he did not know high-altitude pulmonary edema when he saw it—few did as yet—his diagnosis of pneumonia was not too far mistaken, his resort to ammonium chloride and phenobarbitol not too misguided. The crisis passed, Cranmer slowly recovered and remained with the expedition at Base Camp until mid-July. But he was obviously out of it as far as the mountain was concerned, and with Tony Cromwell having already decided not to climb higher than Camp IV, Wiessner's team was reduced at a stroke to four.

Even so, climbing began as planned on June 5 and proceeded more or less on schedule until June 21, when a furious storm struck and pinned everyone down at Camps II and IV for eight long days. "We would lie in our sleeping bags swathed in several sets of woollen underwear, wind suits, gloves and hats," George Sheldon recalled. "At any moment we expected to be blown into nearby Tibet. We had nothing to read except the labels on food cans [and] the eternal banging and cracking of the tent made us virtually psychopathic cases." Even Wiessner, who had endured several such storms on Nanga Parbat, was rattled; the others, fair-weather climbers for the most part up to now, were shattered and worse still, in Sheldon's case, frostbitten. When the storm finally abated on June 29, Sheldon retreated from Camp IV, never to return. "The storm left its mark on us," he later wrote, with his own experience mostly in mind. "Days of inactivity in the rarefied altitude had drained us of that elusive spirit which gives a man the power to carry on when the body is through."[91]

Wiessner aside, the surprising exception to this general state of demoralization was Dudley Wolfe. He was not quick, he was not competent, he was not helpful; but he was proving to be stubborn and steady. During the storm he attached himself to Wiessner with acolyte devotion, and until his final dying days he never let go. On July 1, while Durrance, Sheldon, and Cromwell lingered at Camp II, still reeling from the effects of the storm and unsure of what to do with themselves, Wolfe followed Wiessner's lead through House's Chimney to Camp V, there to await supplies from below while Wiessner and Pasang Ki-kuli pressed on to Camp VI above. But the expected supplies did not arrive. Already, by July 1 and 2, communication between the upper and lower mountain had broken down, and a peculiar dynamic set in whereby Wiessner, accompanied but otherwise unassisted by Wolfe, carried on up the mountain regardless of the condition of the other climbers or the state of his line of supply. "We move only as puppets, it is definitely a one man's trip," Durrance commented in his diary on July 2.[92] He had not seen Wiessner for ten days and would not see him for seven more, an odd circumstance that speaks immediately to the expedition's dangerous state of malfunction.

Finally, on July 9, Wiessner "came forth from the hanging fogs of K2," having established Camp VI below the Black Pyramid at 23,400 feet, and was visibly annoyed at finding Durrance and Cromwell hanging about doing nothing at Camp II. To Durrance he looked worn and thin, the inevitable result of two weeks at high altitude, but his arrival nevertheless had a bracing effect on the party and July 11 saw a general progress of sahibs and Sherpas to Camp IV. It was a long, hard, rock-volleyed haul, and it did Cromwell in; after a day's rest, he descended to Base Camp, never to return. Durrance meanwhile, climbed with Wiessner to Camp V, where they rejoined Dudley Wolfe, the "K2 hermit," and hauled him up to Camp VI under the Black Pyramid. Here Durrance assumed that Wolfe would stop.

"It is unfair to take a man along and use valuable time hauling him about just because he was able to finance the undertaking," he commented in his diary, "and also dangerous if conditions hit him just right when he is dependent on his own resources." But Wiessner, for reasons of his own—loyalty, friendship, financial obligation—had settled on Wolfe as his summit partner and would not order him down as long as he wanted to continue. For Durrance this was the final, discouraging humiliation. "Sleepless nights combined with emotional upset that I had [not] been selected to make summit dash with Fritz, long stay at Camp II (weeks) and two day haul from II to VI with heavy pack . . . consumed all my reserves and more," he later wrote.[93] On July 13, en route to Camp VII, he succumbed to altitude sickness and retreated to Camp VI, hoping to ascend again the next day. Instead, after a miserably breathless and sleepless night, he descended to Camp II, taking Dawa and the frostbitten Pasang Kikuli with him.

Durrance's descent completed the final isolation of the summit team from the rest of the disheartened expedition. True, Wiessner and Wolfe had Pasang Kitar, Tse Tendrup, and the inestimable Pasang Lama with them. And they had Tsering Norbu and Phinsoo in wavering support at Camp VI. But with the limited exception of Durrance (who had at least halted his descent at Camp II), their compatriots had turned their backs on them when the two men set out for Camp VIII and the summit on July 14. In fact, down at Base Camp, deputy leader Tony Cromwell was already packing up to leave the mountain, and on July 17 he inexplicably sent a note up to Durrance at Camp II asking him to clear all tents and sleeping bags from Camps II, III, and IV. Perplexed and feeling a little put upon, Durrance nevertheless complied, thus contributing his own part to the unfolding tragedy above.[94] As for Sheldon and Cranmer, they left Base Camp altogether on July 18, hoping to be back at Dartmouth in time for the start of the fall semester and sparing not a thought, it seems, for their fearless leader and his hapless companion above.

Having parted company with Durrance on July 13, Wolfe and Wiessner carried on with Pasang Lama, Tse Tendrup, and Pasang Kitar to Camps VII and VIII, where Wiessner dismissed the latter two Sherpas with orders to remain in support at VII and carry supplies forward to VIII. A light storm then blew in and prevented further progress until July 17, when Wiessner, Wolfe, and Pasang Lama left Camp VIII at 25,300 feet for the intended Camp IX at the base of the final summit cone. Not 300 yards out of camp, however, Wolfe was stopped by a difficult bergschrund on the shoulder and Wiessner ordered him back to Camp VIII, either to follow up later with others or to remain in close support. Exhausted by the effort of crossing the bergschrund themselves, Wiessner and Lama bivouacked under a sheltering boulder at 25,800 feet and the next day, July 18, pitched Camp IX (26,050ft) on the large flat area at the foot of the Southeast Ridge of the summit pyramid that Petzoldt had identified a year earlier as the likeliest site. "Our position on the mountain was extremely favorable," Wiessner later wrote. "We had built up a series of fully stocked camps up the mountain; tents with sleeping bags and provisions for many weeks stood ready at Camps II, IV, VI, and VII. Added to that Wolfe stood at Camp VIII with further supplies (if indeed, he was not already on the way up to us), and here at Camp IX we had provisions for 6 days and gasoline for a longer period than that."[95]

In fact, though Wiessner did not know it, their position on the mountain was extremely *unfavorable*. Back at Camp VII, Tendrup and Kitar had lost heart in the storm of July 15–16 and when the weather cleared, rather than carry supplies forward to Camp VIII as ordered, they descended to Camp IV. Tsering and Phinsoo had stood by their post at Camp VI, but they were not moving supplies forward either, and Camps VII and VIII were far from fully stocked. Wolfe, meanwhile, had not budged from Camp VIII, and under bewildering orders from Cromwell and Durrance, Pasang Kikuli and Dawa Thondup were busily clearing Camps II and IV. The logistics are complex and confusing: the essential point is that even as Wiessner and Pasang Lama set out on their summit bid—the first on an 8,000-meter mountain to include a Darjeeling Sherpa—the elaborate support structure that Wiessner imagined stretching down the mountain was indeed imaginary.

The weather, though, was favorable, and after a quiet night and a good breakfast, the two men left Camp IX for the summit at the surprisingly late hour of 9:00 A.M. on July 19. For nine hours they moved steadily upward through some of the most difficult rock pitches in the Himalaya. "Although we could speak only a few words of each other's language, it seemed to me as if I were climbing with an old and completely dependable friend," Wiessner later wrote, and Pasang Lama also later testified to the ease and strength of this unexpected partnership. But it was not enough; there simply wasn't time. Come 6:00 P.M. they were at 27,450 feet, still 800 feet and probably three or four hours from the summit. Wiessner wanted to continue into the dark, but Pasang Lama, understandably and responsibly, refused. "No, Sahib," he said, "tomorrow," and refused to pay out the rope. For once on this expedition, Wiessner submitted to the will of another and turned around, regretful but still confident of the summit, even after Pasang Lama managed to lose their crampons while freeing them from a tangle in the rope on the descent. Tired and expectant, the two reached the safety of Camp IX at around 2:30 A.M. on July 20.[96]

The day broke fair and warm, and as no one had come up from Camp VIII with additional supplies—a mildly disquieting surprise—Wiessner discarded his earlier plan to move the tent 800 to 1,000 feet higher and instead gave the whole day over to rest and recovery. Down below, meanwhile, Pasang Kikuli had been surprised to come upon Tendrup and Kitar (the defectors from Camp VII) at Camp IV, and having thoroughly dressed them down, he sent them back up the mountain to await developments. On July 20, while Wiessner lay naked on his sleeping bag in an open tent at Camp IX, Tendrup (so he later said) climbed to within 500 feet of Camp VIII, as high as he dared toward a threatening cornice, and called out three times. He had neither seen nor heard anything of Wiessner or Wolfe Sahib for six days now, and from the state of the snow slopes around the tent (where unbeknown to him Dudley Wolfe lay soundly sleeping), he concluded that they and Pasang Lama must have been swept away in an avalanche. Reporting as much to Tsering and Kitar at Camp VII (and, bear in mind, having just a few days earlier watched Pasang Kikuli strip the tents at Camp IV), he took what to him seemed the obvious and responsible course: he gathered up the mattresses, sleeping bags, and food, and headed down the mountain, camp by camp, salvaging as much as he and his companions could carry. By July 23 they were at Base Camp, having stripped the upper mountain of everything but the tents.

Feeling restored by their day in the sun (and having no idea, of course, what was transpiring below), Wiessner and Pasang Lama set out again for the summit on July 21 and again fell short, owing in part to the loss of the crampons and the time-consuming need to cut steps in the snow. The next day, out of food and still more puzzled by the absence of relief from below, they descended to Camp VIII, where they were astonished to find Wolfe alone, without matches and reduced to melting water in a fold of his tent. "Those bastards," Wolfe shouted, "they never came up here." Only four days of rations remained at Camp VIII—not enough to resume the climb—and in growing bewilderment Wiessner and Pasang Lama roped up the hapless Wolfe and continued down. About 500 feet above Camp VII, Wolfe tripped on the rope and fell, taking Wiessner and Pasang Lama with him. Sixty feet from oblivion over the Godwin-Austen Glacier, Wiessner stopped the fall with the pick of his ax, and battered and bruised the three staggered at dusk into Camp VII, only to find it completely cleared. "A distressing sight," Wiessner wrote in his diary, especially as Wolfe had lost his sleeping bag in the fall and he, Wiessner, had left his at Camp IX in expectation of a quick return.[97] It was too late in the day to descend to Camp VI, and the three men spent a miserable night shivering under a single narrow sleeping bag and cursing their teammates below.

In the morning, July 23, Wolfe did not feel up to continuing and Wiessner, who had not relinquished thoughts of the summit and still intended a quick return to Camp IX, made the fateful and later highly controversial decision to leave him at Camp VII while he and Pasang Lama descended to Camp VI for fresh men and supplies. More disappointment: two tents laid down, a duffle bag with food, but no stove, no sleeping bags, no mattresses— worst of all no people. Desperate now, the two men staggered on through Camps V, IV, and III to Camp II, where they spent a second night in the cold with only a collapsed tent as cover. "To describe in words the horrible feelings and thoughts I had during the day, would be futile indeed," Wiessner wrote in his diary. "Is there any possibility of an excuse for such a condition? Does one sacrifice a great goal and human beings in such a way?" Finally, on July 24, they staggered into Base Camp, where they met Tony Cromwell and three Sherpas returning from a search for their dead bodies up the Godwin-Austen Glacier. "Thank God you're alive," Cromwell said with a relieved smile, but Wiessner would have none of thankfulness. To the extent that his ravaged voice and lungs allowed, he burst into an angry and subsequently damaging tirade, accusing his deputy of everything from negligence to reckless abandonment to attempted murder. There would be lawsuits galore, Wiessner icily promised, and Cromwell would pay.[98]

Meanwhile, the helpless Wolfe was stranded at Camp VII, a circumstance that seemed not overly to concern Wiessner, who in his deluded and mentally deteriorated state was still contemplating a renewed attempt on the summit, but that greatly concerned Durrance, who honestly doubted his own or anyone else's fitness to go and get him. Still, they had to try, and on July 25, the same day that the disgraced Cromwell and the disgraced Tendrup left Base Camp for Askole with the main porter caravan, Durrance, Phinsoo, Pasang Kitar, and Dawa Thondup headed back up the mountain on a rescue mission. They reached Camp IV in good time the next day, but there Dawa Thondup sickened and collapsed, and when Pasang Kitar flatly refused to carry on with Phinsoo alone, Durrance had no choice but to accompany Dawa back down to Base Camp in hopes of finding willing substitutes. Wiessner was out of the question, but Pasang Kikuli and Tsering Norbu heroically came forward and climbed the 7,000 feet from Base Camp to Camp VI in a single day, an unprecedented achievement that unknowingly anticipated the alpine-style ascents of later years. The next day, July 29, leaving Tsering Norbu in support at Camp VI, Kikuli, Kitar, and Phinsoo climbed on to Camp VII, where they found Dudley Wolfe lying in his feces: listless and insensible. As he refused to accompany them, the three Sherpas had no choice but to make him tea and retreat to Camp VI, promising to return the next day. This a storm prevented, however, and it was not until July 31—by which time Wolfe had been above 21,500 feet an inconceivable forty days—that Pasang Kikuli, Pasang Kitar, and Phinsoo Sherpa climbed up once again to bring him down. Neither they nor Dudley Wolfe were ever seen again.[99]

"It is difficult to record in temperate language the folly of this enterprise," wrote Kenneth Mason, the old India hand, of Wiessner's K2 expedition in 1955, and even now, fifty years later, the mention of Wiessner's name in mountaineering circles will provoke a strong reaction.[100] The tragedy was not quite on the scale of Nanga Parbat 1934, but it had the same elements of human and natural drama, of mystery and perilous misadventure. These were, moreover, the first deaths on an American Himalayan expedition, and that the leader was, despite his recent naturalized citizenship, so obviously German at a time when Hitler was leading the world into ruin ensured that there would be a bitter reckoning.

It started at Bandipur, north of Srinagar, where Tony Cromwell, obviously still smarting from Wiessner's Base Camp tirade, met Wiessner and Durrance on their return from the mountain, read the draft of their innocuous expedition report, and pronounced it a scandalous cover-up. Wiessner had murdered Wolfe and the three Sherpas pure and simple, he said, and on his return to Srinagar he wrote as much to Joel Ellis Fisher, recently president and now treasurer of the American Alpine Club. It was of course a preposterous and vindictive charge, but it got the attention of both Colonel D. M. Fraser, the British resident in Kashmir, and Edward Groth, the American consul, who at Fraser's request met with Wiessner and Durrance in Srinagar on September 4, the day after Great Britain's declaration of war on Germany. After seven hours of conversation, Groth concluded that the expedition's misfortunes arose not from any particular error on the mountain but from a fundamental clash of national temperaments. "Confidentially," he wrote in a private memorandum to the secretary of state in Washington,

> I believe that one of the primary factors precipitating the dissension which finally arose
> was the inescapable fact that, although on paper and by law, Wiessner is an American
> citizen, he is still in many respects largely German in his outlook and actions. . . . With
> his German background, also owing to the fact that he possesses a large share of Ger-
> man bluntness (a national characteristic which was apparently unknown to all but one
> of his colleagues and fellow-expedition-members) it is not remarkable that there should
> have been a clash of temperaments. Wiessner is undoubtedly an excellent climber and a
> good leader, but, like every German, he is very forceful in giving commands and totally
> unaware that the abrupt, blunt manner in which the order may have been given might
> have wounded the feelings of his associates, who in this instance, being Americans,
> naturally had a different attitude and outlook in matters of this sort.[101]

For their part, the Americans made too little effort to analyze or understand Wiessner's temperament, Groth continued, nor had they sufficient experience of situations in which there
must and will be a leader. Their attitude seemed to be that as they had borne a share of the expedition's expenses, they should have a corresponding share in its running, a logical expectation in ordinary situations, but a naive and dangerous one on an 8,000-meter mountain.

Back in New York, the American Alpine Club appointed a formal committee of
inquiry into the tragedy under the chairmanship of Walter Wood. Its four other members—
Joel Ellis Fisher, Bill House, Terris Moore, and Bestor Robinson—were all well-acquainted
with Wiessner, even considered him a friend. After close study of the paper trail and extended meetings with the surviving climbers, they dispassionately attributed the tragedy
to "indefinite understanding as to movements of summit and support parties." They also
faulted the expedition's "human administration," however, and Wiessner, taking this as a
personal rebuke, registered a formal protest with Walter Wood and appealed to others to
write an alternative report focusing on Jack Durrance's role in the evacuation of the camps.
Eventually he was heard; over the years, as anti-Germanic passions cooled, blame for the
tragedy came to rest largely and unfairly with Durrance (who had cleared the lower camps
only on orders from Cromwell). At the time, however, the attention of the world was obviously and imperatively elsewhere. When the Council of the American Alpine Club met
to discuss the Wood report on May 18, 1940, the Wehrmacht was approaching Paris, the
British Expeditionary Force was falling back on Dunkirk, Winston Churchill had moved
into 10 Downing Street and in his first speech as prime minister, five days earlier, promised
his people nothing but "blood, toil, tears, and sweat." Suddenly the question of who was
responsible for the death of poor Dudley Wolfe seemed trivial in the extreme. After a brief,
perfunctory discussion of K2, Joel Fisher suggested the council send a message of support
and sympathy to the Alpine Club in London conveying its "deep feeling at this time of
stress." The suggestion carried unanimously, the meeting dispersed, and mountaineers
everywhere turned their minds to the greater hazards of war.[102]

CHAPTER SIX

The Golden Age Postponed
1940–1950

The May 1939 issue of the British *Alpine Journal* reported a number of recent mountaineering triumphs, or near triumphs, in the Himalaya. For those readers not distracted that spring by more ominous events elsewhere, the effect must have been heartening. Indeed, lacking access to any other source of news, a reader of the leading European and American climbing journals might reasonably have concluded that the great nations of the world coexisted in a spirit of cooperative harmony. The exploration and ascent of the great peaks in the Himalaya was an international enterprise in which climbers from the European continent, the British Empire, Japan, and the United States followed one another's exploits with keen and, for the most part, generous interest.

Along with Bill Tilman's account of the 1938 British Everest expedition, the *Alpine Journal* carried a report from Charlie Houston on the American expedition to K2 and one from Fritz Bechtold on the German expedition to Nanga Parbat.[1] True, none of those expeditions had reached the summits of the mountains they attempted—and indeed, in the two decades following the Great War, no one had succeeded in climbing any of the fourteen Himalayan peaks with altitudes above 8,000 meters, stretching from Nanga Parbat in the west to Kangchenjunga in the east. Nonetheless, mountaineers, along with the growing corps of experienced Sherpas, had learned much of value about the challenges of high-altitude climbing in the Himalaya.

The highest summit yet attained was Nanda Devi in the Indian Garhwal, scaled by Tilman and Noel Odell in 1936. But the 25,642-foot summit of Nanda Devi was by no means the highest elevation reached by climbers in the Himalaya. British climbers on Everest, starting with Edward Norton in 1924, had several times breached the 28,000-foot mark, an elevation higher than the summits of eleven of the fourteen highest peaks. There was thus every reason in that peacetime spring of 1939 for optimism. It seemed likely that a successful first ascent would be achieved on one or another of the great 8,000-meter peaks in the near future, perhaps before the year was out.

So many parties set off to climb in the Himalaya in the spring and summer of 1939 (among them two British, two German, one American, one Swiss, and one Polish) that porters were hard to come by in Darjeeling.[2] The Germans were en route to a reconnaissance of the Diamir Face of Nanga Parbat, with another full-scale expedition planned for 1940. An American expedition led by Fritz Wiessner was heading to K2 in 1939 to make yet another attempt on the Abruzzi Ridge; if that party failed, Charlie Houston and his friends were eager for a rematch with the mountain the following year, as were Italian mountaineers. The British planned to send an expedition to Everest in 1940, and again in 1941 and 1942 if necessary. And a group of New Zealand mountaineers hoped to climb Kangchenjunga in 1940. It was starting to be said within climbing circles that this was the "Golden Age of Himalayan Mountaineering."[3]

As things turned out, the golden age would have to be put off. With the exception of the Swiss, all of the nations that sent major climbing expeditions to the Himalaya in the 1930s—Britain, Germany, Italy, France, Poland, Japan, the United States—were about to be swept up in the Second World War. The bright hopes of the 1939 climbing season came to nothing, leaving climbers a sense of futility. In early September Fritz Wiessner wrote from Srinagar to Dudley Wolfe's former wife, Alice, to reflect on the disaster that had left Wolfe dead at Camp VII on K2. "I have never been so hard hit in my life," Wiessner confessed, "first to lose the summit which seemed in my hands, then the terrible realization of Dudley's and the Sherpas' deaths, and now a war."[4] No one would have the chance to return to K2 or any of the other 8,000-meter peaks for many years to come. As E. L. Strutt, veteran of the 1922 Everest expedition, noted sadly in the *Alpine Journal*'s spring issue for 1941, "Since September 1939, mountaineering . . . has become but a subject of reminiscence."[5]

High Conquest or World Conquest?

The United States was not yet at war when Strutt's lament appeared. Fierce debates between isolationists and interventionists divided Americans. But few American Alpine Club members could be counted among the opponents of aid to Britain. "In America at peace," Charlie Houston wrote to the *Alpine Journal* in 1941, "are many whose hearts are with their friends abroad."[6]

Among the Americans whose sympathies were decidedly in the pro-Britain, anti-Axis camp was a New York writer named James Ramsey Ullman. In the waning months of American neutrality in 1941, Ullman published *High Conquest: The Story of Mountaineering*. His book was the first attempt at a comprehensive history of the subject by an American author and the work that made his reputation as a popular writer.[7] Looking back at the Himalayan expeditions of the 1930s, Ullman saw the present world conflict foreshadowed on the slopes of Nanga Parbat, littered as it was with the dead of unsuccessful German efforts. "The Germans were engaged in all-or-nothing assaults," Ullman wrote. "They were after victory, and nothing else mattered. And while feeling sorrow for the brave individuals who lost their lives, one cannot but feel that collectively they met the fate that they deserved. Blind, mindless force is no more the key to the conquest of a great mountain than to the conquest of the world."[8]

Given the year in which it appeared, Ullman's indictment was understandably bitter. It was also not completely fair. German mountaineers were certainly daring in technique and willing to take risks deemed inappropriate by their Anglo-American counterparts. And some of them *were* Nazis. But their Himalayan expeditions were hardly the suicidal "all-or-nothing" affairs Ullman described. The expeditions to Nanga Parbat in 1932, 1934, 1937, and 1938 differed little in strategy or tactics from those undertaken by the British on Everest or the Americans on K2: the avalanche of 1937 that took sixteen lives had not been brought on by Nazi ideology but by ill luck and a badly chosen camp location. The 1938 German expedition had returned from the mountain unscathed if unsuccessful. And it was not as though expeditions launched by Western democracies were immune to mountaineering tragedy: the British had lost quite a few of their own climbers, as well as Sherpas, on Everest and other mountains—including Nanga Parbat. Wartime thinking, however, drew stark dichotomies, and it became a commonplace in American and British mountaineering circles to equate German cragsmanship with Nazi aggression.

In the closing months of the Second World War, British geographer Kenneth Mason wrote to his friend Harry Tyndale, editor of the *Alpine Journal,* offering his own thoughts about the links between mountaineering and war. With Allied armies encircling Berlin from east and west, Mason wondered about the wartime fate of his "old Hun pals" Peter Aufschnaiter, Richard Finsterwalder, and Paul Bauer. Mason had first met Aufschnaiter in India in 1929, when the young German climber had been a member of Paul Bauer's expedition to Kangchenjunga. They renewed their acquaintance in the fall of 1938 during the Munich Crisis, when Aufschnaiter had visited Mason in Oxford while preparing for the next year's reconnaissance of Nanga Parbat. Mason heard, to his relief, that Aufschnaiter was "interned in India" by British authorities at the start of the war, and thus likely to sit it out in safety.[9]

He was not as optimistic about Finsterwalder, the cartographer on the 1934 Nanga Parbat expedition. Mason feared that Finsterwalder was "probably buried under the ruins of his job in Hanover," where he taught at the university. And then there was Bauer, whom Mason had helped with the arrangements for the Kangchenjunga expedition in 1929; on that occasion, the two men learned that they had faced each other as enemies in 1915 at a distance of 100 yards in the trenches of the western front in France. Bauer, Mason recalled, was a man "desperately envious of everything in the British way of life, but couldn't see how to achieve any of it in Germany." Bauer's most recent trip to the Himalaya had been on the 1938 Nanga Parbat expedition. All Mason knew about Bauer's subsequent fate was that he "was in uniform by the end of 1939."[10]

Concern for German acquaintances did not diminish Mason's satisfaction with the impending Nazi defeat. "How closely the German mentality as seen during the last

3 or 4 years follows its pattern on the Grandes Jorasses or the North face of the Eiger; or even more so perhaps that of the failures on Nanga Parbat!" he wrote. "It seems as though the Avalanche has now gained control and that Germany is doomed. Who will be of the Relief Party? There isn't one!"[11]

Mason's "Hun pal" Peter Aufschnaiter had indeed been arrested by British authorities in August 1939, as he and other German climbers were preparing to leave India. What Mason did not know but would learn after the war was that Aufschnaiter and fellow climber Heinrich Harrer had escaped from the British internment camp at Dehra Dun in April 1944 and were slowly making their way even then toward the Tibetan capital of Lhasa, as famously described in Harrer's postwar account *Seven Years in Tibet*. As for the others, Richard Finsterwalder survived the bombing of Hanover and would help rebuild its university after the war. And Paul Bauer served throughout the war as a Wehrmacht officer, fighting on the eastern front in 1942–43 before being reassigned to training troops in mountain warfare.[12]

British climbers too were swept up in the war. Many were already in uniform as officers in the Indian Army when war broke out. Among the first to die in the conflict was Major Norman Streatfeild of the Bengal Mountain Artillery, who had served as liaison officer to the French Hidden Peak expedition and the first American K2 expedition. In 1940 he was stationed in Belgium with the British Expeditionary Force. During the "phony war" that preceded the German Blitzkrieg, he entertained his troops by showing films of his Himalayan climbs. After he was killed in action at Dunkirk, Charlie Houston wrote his obituary for the *Alpine Journal*.[13]

A survivor of the Somme in the Great War, Bill Tilman remained on the reserve list of officers in the 1930s. When war broke out, he put aside his uncompleted manuscript for a book about the 1938 British Everest expedition, rejoined the British Army, and sailed for France with a field artillery regiment. He too was at Dunkirk, though he made it safely back to England. For the next five years he survived one remarkable and dangerous assignment after another. In 1941 he fought in the battle of El Alamein. As if duty as a regular army officer were not strenuous enough for a man well advanced into middle age, he then transferred to Special Operations. In August 1943 he parachuted behind enemy lines in Albania to serve as a liaison officer with local partisans. (It was his first parachute jump; he thought practice would be a waste of time.) A year later he parachuted into northern Italy, where he linked up with Italian resistance fighters in the mountains, taking a brief excursion from duty in late January 1945 to climb Monte Serva. In the closing days of the war in Italy Major Tilman and his partisans helped liberate the city of Belluno.[14]

Frank Smythe also bade farewell to civilian life in 1939, but not to the mountains. Smythe was given command of the newly established Commando Mountain and Snow Warfare Centre at Braemar in the Scottish Cairngorms. His was a "most unwarlike character," in the judgment of the chief instructor at the school, Indian Army major John Hunt, but effective nonetheless in inspiring common soldiers with his own deep love of mountaineering.[15]

Like many other men in uniform, Smythe dreamed of more congenial pursuits when peace returned. In December 1943, while on training exercises in Alberta, Canada, he wrote to the editors of the *Alpine Journal* and the *American Alpine Journal* proposing that, once the war was over, a climbing party "not above in eight in number" be assembled for "a joint Anglo-American Expedition to Mt. Everest." An international effort on Everest would be of great symbolic importance for the climbing community and the world: "I am all against parochialism and international rivalry in mountaineering. The Germans introduced it both to the Alps and Himalayas and I hope post-war days will see this spirit dead. What could be a better or more worthy fulfillment of our joint ideals in this war than that an American and a British mountaineer should stand together on the highest point of Earth?"[16]

December 1941 brought the United States into the war. Charlie Houston was already in uniform when the bombs fell on Pearl Harbor, assigned to duty at the U.S. Naval Air Station at Pensacola, Florida. The American military did not always successfully match the man with the job, but in this case his posting as a naval flight surgeon could not have been better designed. Houston conducted research on the effects of oxygen deprivation, a condition posing a deadly threat not only to Himalayan mountaineers but also to pilots and aircrews who might experience a sudden loss of their oxygen supply while in flight. By the end of the war Houston's unit had trained 55,000 pilots and other crewmen to recognize the symptoms of the onset of hypoxia.[17]

Houston's dedication to the war effort could not stave off longings for the mountains. As he wrote to K2 expedition mate Bob Bates in October 1942: "Sometimes when the low clouds are grey and stormy, and the rising or setting sun picks out a snowy white thunder head high above and makes it look like a great Himalaya from Darjeeling or Kashmir, well, when that happens I just about burst into tears. You all just don't know how GODDAM flat it is down here."[18]

Houston had briefly considered another military posting, one that would have at least gotten him out of lowlands, if not back to the Himalaya. Since the start of the war leaders of the American Alpine Club and the National Ski Patrol had advocated the creation of an elite unit specially trained for combat on mountainous terrain or in winter conditions. While climbing in the Swiss Alps in 1939, Bob Bates and Adams Carter had seen Swiss Mountain Troops on maneuvers and had been impressed by their prowess. When war broke out soon afterward they concluded that American troops might soon be engaged in similarly demanding terrains in defense of the North American continent (Alaska in particular) and, if necessary, in Europe. The humiliation that Finnish ski troops inflicted on their Russian opponents in the "winter war" of 1939–40 provided further evidence of the potential for an elite unit of soldiers trained in winter and mountain warfare techniques. The Germans were known to have at least a dozen specially trained mountain divisions. Carter and Bates lobbied both U.S. secretary of war Henry Stimson (an enthusiastic climber and honorary member of both the British and American Alpine clubs), and U.S. army chief of staff George C. Marshall on the need for mountain troops. William Cameron Forbes, a prominent Massachusetts investment banker and former U.S. diplomat, wrote to General Marshall on Carter's behalf in early December 1940, and Marshall responded, "With the world situation as it is at present, there is a possibility that a trained mountain unit might fit in with the details of one or more of our plans."[19]

Shortly before Pearl Harbor the army established the Eighty-seventh Mountain Infantry Battalion, the core of the unit that eventually became the Tenth Mountain Division. Recruits, drawn heavily from college ski teams, the Forest Service, and similar backgrounds, many of them recruited through civilian outdoors groups, trained at the newly established Camp Hale in the Colorado Rockies. Houston wrote to Bob Bates in September 1942 to say he was "severely tempted" to give up his research in Florida and join the mountain troops, but finally decided he was best suited to the work he was already doing. Paul Petzoldt, Houston's K2 climbing partner, signed up with the mountain troops and trained the new unit's medics in mountain rescue techniques. At the end of 1944 the division shipped out for the Italian front; in heavy fighting in the winter and spring in the North Apennine Mountains and the Po Valley, nearly a quarter of the men who served in the unit were killed or wounded.[20]

Veterans of American expeditions to the Himalaya played important roles in equipping the mountain troops. Starting in 1941 Bob Bates, Bill House, and Terris Moore served as civilian advisers to the War Department to oversee development of cold-weather clothing and equipment. (After Pearl Harbor Bates enlisted in the army and served in the Quartermaster Corps, ending the war with the rank of lieutenant colonel; in 1942 he traveled with Bradford Washburn to test cold-weather gear on Mount McKinley; in 1944 he was sent to Italy to instruct troops in cold-weather survival.) The innovations designed for the army's mountain troops would have long-range implications for mountaineers. Fritz Wiessner suggested that a German-developed synthetic fiber known as Perlon be used to produce a new kind of climbing rope for mountain troops, more flexible and stronger than the old hemp ropes. Bates tested one of the new ropes in 1942 by tying off one end on his desk and rappelling out the window of his Washington office building, to the consternation of the secretaries on lower floors who saw him bouncing down the side of the building past their windows.[21]

For combat soldiers as for mountaineers, good footwear was essential. In 1939 Italian climber Vitale Bramani devised a cleated rubber sole for climbing boots that he called Vibram. The new soles gripped better on slippery surfaces and did not conduct the cold to the climber's feet the way the traditional nailed boots did. Adams Carter and Bob Bates, having seen climbers wearing boots with the new soles in Switzerland in 1939, recommended that the army adopt them. Carter tracked down a pair belonging to a New Hampshire climber, and by 1943 knockoff copies were issued to the mountain troops (although when the Tenth Mountain Division reached Italy, in a typical wartime snafu, the boots and other specially developed cold-weather gear remained behind in the United

Terris Moore, Bob Bates, and Einar Nilsson on Mount McKinley in 1942, testing cold-weather gear for the military. Courtesy of the Henry S. Hall Jr. American Alpine Club Library.

States). The army also developed its own ice axes, pitons and piton hammers, mountain tents, and sleeping bags, some of which would be purchased as surplus by mountaineers after the war.[22]

Wartime Himalaya

The Second World War was fought in many places and on many terrains, some familiar, like the mountains and plains of northern Italy, others previously unknown, like the jungles of Guadalcanal. In 1939 the Himalaya was a region that many in the West had heard of but relatively few had ever seen. That would change during the war, as tens of thousands of American and British military personnel were sent to fight the Japanese in the China-Burma-India (CBI) theater. Airmen ferrying supplies from India to Chiang Kai-shek's beleaguered forces in China became intimately familiar with the Himalayan mountains, a daunting landscape even for those flying high above them. Nearly 1,000 planes would be lost during the war flying over "the Hump."[23]

Some Allied airmen found the mountains not just a dangerous obstacle but an object of fascination. In the summer of 1942 Colonel Robert L. Scott of the U.S. Army Air Corps' "Flying Tigers" took an unauthorized joyride in his Republic P43A pursuit plane over Tibet and Nepal, photographing the Potala Palace in Lhasa and then flying over Nepal from Kangchenjunga to Everest. His exploit was celebrated in the American papers, and he wrote about it himself in his best-selling 1944 memoir, *God Is My Co-pilot*. His superiors were less enthusiastic; two weeks after Scott's Himalayan tour they banned such flights. Scott described his feeling toward Everest as one of "reverence," though he chose an odd way to show it. "I tried to salute by firing the two fifty-caliber guns into the glacier," he reported, but found they were frozen and inoperable. (And he may not have been flying over Everest at all; *God Is My Co-pilot* reproduced an aerial photograph he had taken of an impressive-looking Himalayan mountain, labeled as Everest; in reality it was Makalu.)[24]

Three years later a Royal Air Force (RAF) de Havilland Mosquito fighter-bomber, piloted by New Zealander C. G. Andrews and British airman C. Fenwick, flew over Mount Everest, swooping down to within thirty feet of the summit taking photographs. Unlike Scott's well-publicized flight, the exploit was kept quiet, probably out of concern with offending Nepalese and Tibetan authorities. In 1947 another RAF pilot would repeat the exploit.[25]

The war ended at last and the soldiers came home. For climbers of a certain age, like Tilman, Smythe, and Houston, the war had represented a great detour in their lives: in Houston's phrase a "GODDAM flat" interlude. For the postwar generation of Himalayan climbers, the years between 1939 and 1945 often had a different impact, enlarging their vision of the paths they could pursue in life. Were it not for the war, a gangly New Zealand youth named Edmund Percival Hillary might have grown up to inherit his father's beekeeping business in Auckland, and with it a lifetime of hard work and obscurity, enlivened by reading the occasional mountain expedition book (a genre for which he had early on developed a fondness). Instead, Hillary enlisted in the Royal New Zealand Air Force (RNZAF) in 1944 and trained as a navigator for Catalina flying boats. While in training he found time to climb his first "decent mountain," New Zealand's 9,465-foot Mount Tapuaenuku, soloing it while on a three-day pass. Following training he was dispatched to Fiji. There he passed his off-duty hours shooting crocodiles and reading tales of mountaineering adventure. One of the books he found in the RNZAF library was James Ramsey Ullman's *High Conquest,* which "without too many qualms" he carried off when reassigned to the Solomons. At the end of the war, age twenty-six, he found himself at a "loose end," willing to do his part in his family's beekeeping business but missing the "taste of freedom." When the chance came to climb with an old air force buddy and soon afterward with Harry Ayres, New Zealand's best-known guide, he knew that what he really wanted to do for the rest of his life was spend as much of it as possible in the mountains.[26]

Hillary had big mountains close at home to explore, but British mountaineers were less fortunate. "My survey of the war shattered world in the autumn of 1945," Bill Tilman would write a few years later, "was directed naturally to the Himalaya, to the ways and means of getting there, and to the chances of finding like-minded survivors with the same extravagant ideas." In England he felt trapped, as though he were "a bird in a cage, beating my head vainly against the bars of shipping offices which had no ships, stores which had no equipment, and export and currency regulations which would not yield." He had to content himself with completing the manuscript of his long-set-aside book about the 1938 Everest expedition and composing an article for the newly revived *Himalayan Journal* entitled "The Problem of Everest." Once again picking up the banner of the small, lightweight expedition, he declared it would be "a retrograde step if we ever revert to the grandiose standards of earlier expeditions" to the mountain.[27]

Tilman's old climbing partner Eric Shipton returned to England on leave from consular service abroad a few months later. He met a receptive audience when he urged the Alpine Club to renew the Everest campaign at the earliest possible opportunity. Geoffrey Winthrop Young told Shipton that the club would be delighted if he would accept the leadership of the next expedition, with a tentative departure date the spring of 1947. Soon afterward the Alpine Club and the Royal Geographical Society revived the prewar Everest Committee, now renamed the Himalayan Committee. Shipton envisaged a small-scale expedition of six climbers equipped with the latest wartime improvements in gear, including the new nylon climbing ropes. Unfortunately, someone leaked the news of the proposed expedition to the London *News Chronicle* before the Himalayan Committee had the opportunity to approach the authorities in Lhasa for permission, leading to a minor diplomatic flap. Lord Wavell, newly appointed viceroy of India, preoccupied with famine in Bengal, mutinies in the Royal Indian Navy, negotiations over Indian independence, and similar pressing issues, had little time for furthering what must have seemed to him the petty ambitions of British mountaineers. He informed the Alpine Club that for the foreseeable future there would be no expeditions to Tibet.[28]

The only climbers with easy access to the Himalaya in the first year of peace were those fortunate enough to have found themselves stationed in military outposts or otherwise employed in the region. Wilfred Noyce, assigned as a climbing instructor at the Aircrew Mountain Centre in Kashmir in 1944, was one of them. Along with Ang Tharkay, perhaps the best known of the Sherpas to have accompanied the prewar British expeditions, he made a second ascent of Pauhunri in eastern Sikkim via its North Face in the fall of 1945. The following year J. O. M. (Jimmy) Roberts and George Latimer, on leave from their Gurkha Battalion, undertook a reconnaissance of unclimbed Saser Kangri (25,170ft/7,672m) in the eastern Karakoram. Jack Gibson, a schoolmaster at the Doon School in Dehra Dun, organized a small expedition in 1946 to attempt Bandarpunch (20,721ft/6,316m) in the Garhwal. They reached 18,000 feet and turned back. The Doon School expedition was chiefly notable as the first such after the war in which Tenzing Norgay found employment.[29]

Americans were also eager to return to the Himalaya. The American Alpine Club had responded enthusiastically in 1943 to Frank Smythe's proposal for a joint British-American expedition to Everest, but a follow-up invitation had yet to arrive from London. The country's leading Himalayan mountaineer, Charlie Houston, was still in uniform in 1946. He was conducting a new round of experiments at the U.S. Naval School of Aviation Medicine in Pensacola on the effects of hypoxia. His own plans for peacetime were suggested by the title he gave his research project: "Operation Everest."[30]

The Climbing World of the Late 1940s

For Americans, the chief mountaineering excitement in 1945 was literary rather than expeditionary. James Ramsey Ullman followed up the success of his climbing history, *High Conquest*, with a climbing novel. Published in the last days of the war, *The White Tower* was hailed by book reviewer Orville Prescott in the *New York Times* as "a rousing spectacular adventure story." It told a somewhat improbable tale, freighted with symbolic import, of the wartime attempt to climb a Swiss mountain by a downed American pilot and a German officer on leave from his unit. Knowledgeable mountaineers in both America and Europe scoffed at its technical errors, but such quibbles did not bother the general reading public. A Book of the Month Club selection, *The White Tower* went on to sell over half a million copies.[31]

The book's success prompted *Life* magazine, arbiter of postwar American middle-class tastes, to run its first-ever cover story on mountain climbing in December 1945, including a six-page photo spread entitled "The 'White Tower's' Author Shows How to Master a Strenuous Sport." Ullman and several companions decked out in the latest in high-altitude gear demonstrated for *Life*'s photographer an array of traverse and belay techniques that would not have seemed out of place on the Eigerwand, although they were in fact staged on the gentler slopes of New Hampshire's Mount Washington.[32]

Ullman had been accepted as a member of the American Alpine Club in 1941

James Ramsey Ullman began climbing as a
Princeton undergraduate. James Ramsey Ullman
Papers, Manuscripts Division, Department of
Rare Books and Special Collections, Princeton
University Library. Reprinted by permission
of Princeton University Library.

largely on the strength of the publication of *High Conquest,* and in 1946 the club's journal
praised his most recent literary achievement: "Mr. Ullman has done an outstanding service
for mountain climbing in presenting the subject in a way which has aroused great interest
in mountaineering among the American public . . . on the subway and suburban trains,
war workers and shop girls are engrossed in reading it."[33]

Not everyone in the American mountaineering community was happy with Ullman's
role in bringing their sport to the attention of war workers and shopgirls. Some were deeply
attached to the traditional exclusivity of mountain climbing—exclusive in its command of
esoteric skills, but equally exclusive in the social world upon which it drew for recruits. Most
of the American Alpine Club's membership was concentrated in the northeastern United
States: white, Protestant, well educated, affluent, and well known to one another. Well into

the 1960s, the number of attendees at the club's annual membership meeting, usually held in New York City, ran to a figure of 50 percent or higher of the total club membership.[34]

Both skill and breeding made Robert Underhill part of the American mountaineering aristocracy: a former Harvard philosophy professor, mentor of the Harvard Mountaineering Club, a stalwart of the New England–based Appalachian Mountain Club (AMC) and the American Alpine Club, which he had joined in 1928, Underhill possessed a distinguished record of first ascents on rock faces in the United States from New England to Yosemite, and had introduced the latest and most sophisticated European rope-management and belaying techniques to his American climbing colleagues in the 1930s. In the summer of 1946 Underhill had been out for a weekend hiking trip with his wife, Miriam, in New Hampshire's White Mountains, where the AMC maintained a system of huts, when he encountered a crass interloper. As he wrote afterward to AAC president Henry S. Hall:

> Have you the pleasure of a personal acquaintance with Mr. James Ramsey Ullman? Neither have I but Miriam and I have just spent a night at the Lakes of the Clouds hut where he was present with his two boys. Unless I miss my guess, he is a lowgrade New York Jew—at any rate, his boys are beautifully Jewish and he is incontestably lowgrade. He says "thoid" for "third," sucks his soup, bends down over the table and dribbles oatmeal back into his bowl, and wipes his mouth with the back of his hand. . . . The New York Chapter of the A.M.C. would never let such a mutt through their censors; can the A.A.C. be less choosey? (I here overlook the man's other fine qualifications, of course: namely that he has a non-existent climbing record and has written a lousy book.)[35]

"Low grade" is a subjective category that varies with the eyes of the beholder. Ullman, who was half Jewish on his father's side (his mother, Kate Ramsey, was of Scotch-Irish descent), was a 1925 graduate of Phillips Andover Academy and a 1929 graduate of Princeton University, institutions that in that time and place laid considerable stress on both table manners and diction. If Ullman lacked the social standing to belong to the American Alpine Club, then the organization was destined to remain—as some clearly intended—the preserve of a self-selected elite.[36]

Mountaineering was definitely not a sport for ordinary folk, at least in the United States. The American Alpine Club counted a total of 302 active members in 1945, 9 of them honorary. The British Alpine Club was slightly larger, with 586 members, 20 of whom were honorary.[37]

On the European continent, however, it was a different story. Although the various national alpine clubs had fallen into organizational disarray during the war, with the arrival of peace they swiftly reorganized and soon dwarfed their Anglo-American counterparts. By 1950 the French Alpine Club (Club alpin français) counted 31,000 members; the Italian Alpine Club (Club alpino italiano), had over 80,000.[38] Mountaineering was a mass participation sport in western Europe, and the exploits of top mountaineers were followed by the general public with an interest second only to soccer.

And it was in the European Alps, not the Himalaya, where the cutting edge in international mountaineering could be found in those first years after the war. European climbers returned to the great north faces of the Alps, where high standards were established by such Swiss climbers as René Dittert and Raymond Lambert, Italians like Walter Bonatti, and the new generation of Chamonix guides, Lionel Terray, Louis Lachenal, and Gaston Rébuffat, among others. At the start of the 1950s, as travel and currency restrictions eased, young British climbers like Tom Bourdillon were finally able to return to the Alps, where they came to embrace such long-despised continental techniques as the extensive use of pitons and runners for protection from falls and for use in artificial (aided) climbing, making possible bolder ascents of harder routes.[39]

The year 1947 proved important to Himalayan climbing. It was the year that saw the return of the first significant European expeditions to the region. It also was the year of a remarkable, if doomed, solo attempt on Everest. Earl Denman, a Canadian-born resident of South Africa, showed up in Darjeeling looking for Sherpas to aid him in a quest to slip into Tibet and attempt Everest from the north. Denman believed the mountain could be climbed solo and without the use of artificial oxygen. He was also strongly opposed to nationalism in mountaineering, and by climbing it on his own may have hoped to remove Everest as a symbol of national competition.[40]

The Sherpas he met in Darjeeling were understandably skeptical. They remembered all too well the fate of Maurice Wilson on his quixotic solo attempt on Everest thirteen years earlier. They also knew that with the end of the war the British and perhaps other Europeans would soon be renewing their attempt to climb Everest, and assuming responsibility for leading another deluded Western climber to his probable death on the side of the mountain would not enhance their credentials for future employment. Yet in the end Denman managed to persuade two of the most experienced Sherpas, Tenzing Norgay and Ang Dawa, to accompany him. Tenzing thought Denman had no chance at all of success, but he also decided that he was both fitter and saner than Maurice Wilson. And besides, for Tenzing, "the pull of Everest was stronger for me than any force on earth."[41] The eccentric Denman offered him the chance to go there when no one else was able to do so.

Denman, disguised as a Tibetan, and the two Sherpas made their way surreptitiously across the border and by early April reached the Rongbuk Monastery. On April 10 they left the monastery and four days later camped at the foot of the North Col. By now the scale and challenge of Everest was beginning to sink in. The skies turned black and a furious wind blew down on them from the mountainside. It was bitterly cold. They ventured a short way up the side of the mountain, then gave up and headed back, to Denman's despair but to the relief of Tenzing and Ang Dawa. "I had been critical of large expeditions," Denman would write later, "but now the scales were turned. No expedition, large or small, could have battled on in the face of the prevailing conditions. But a large expedition would have had a chain of camps, or at least a base camp, to retreat to, there to wait and to try again when conditions had improved. . . . We were a spent force." Tenzing had been right: Denman was no Maurice Wilson. "He was a brave man," Tenzing would say judiciously, "a determined, almost fanatic man with a fixed idea. But he was not crazy."[42]

Tenzing had no sooner returned to Darjeeling from Everest than he found employment on another expedition, this one of a more traditional character. The quasi-official and well-financed Swiss Foundation for Alpine Research (Fondation suisse per l'exploration alpine) had decided to send a party of climbers to the Garhwal Himalaya. The expedition was led by Himalayan veteran André Roch, back in the region for the first time since 1939. It was also notable for including a woman, Annalies Lohner, as a full member of the climbing party, which might not have happened except that the climb happened to be her idea in the first place.[43]

The Swiss kept their aims modest on this first postwar expedition, limiting themselves to peaks in the range of 20,000 feet. And in this they were very successful, making a total of six first ascents, an achievement that won them a photo spread in *Life* magazine. Roch, Tenzing, René Dittert, Alfred Sutter, and Alexandre Graven made a first ascent of Kedernath (22,769ft/6,940m) on July 11, followed on August 1 by the first ascent of Satopanth (23,211ft/7,075m) via its North Ridge by Roch, Dittert, Sutter, and Graven.[44]

This proved an important expedition for Tenzing. When Wangdi Norbu, sirdar of the expedition, was injured, Roch promoted Tenzing to the position, an important step up in his career. It was also the first expedition on which he reached the summit of a Himalayan peak. Tenzing developed strong and lasting ties to the Swiss climbers. He came to prefer their company to that of other Europeans with whom he climbed. The Swiss were mountain people like the Sherpas, and unlike the British and French had no history of colonial rule in Asia. An easy, joking informality prevailed between Sherpas and sahibs. Indeed, that common term of address for Europeans seemed inappropriate when applied to the Swiss. Afterward Tenzing would say that he thought of the Swiss climbers "not as sahibs or employers, but as friends."[45]

The Swiss Foundation for Alpine Research sponsored a second expedition that year, bound for the Karakoram. This expedition was more of an international affair; its two Swiss climbers, Hans Gyr and Robert Kappeler, invited Bill Tilman and Canadian climber Campbell Secord to join them in a reconnaissance of Rakaposhi (25,550ft/7,788m). Both Gyr and Kappeler were making their first trip to the Himalaya and welcomed the experience that Tilman and Secord brought to their effort (Tilman was, of course, Tilman, and Secord had been on the first serious reconnaissance of Rakaposhi in 1938). Their attempts on Rakaposhi's Southwest Spur and Northwest Ridge fell short of the summit, though Tilman still enjoyed the liberating feeling of no longer being a caged bird.[46]

After Rakaposhi, Tilman bade farewell to the rest of the party and crossed the Mintaka Pass into China's northwestern Xinjiang province. There he rendezvoused with Eric Shipton, who was serving his second tour of duty as British consul in Kashgar. The two old climbing friends set out on August 11 on one of their trademark lightweight attempts, this time on the West Ridge of Muztagh Ata (24,756ft/7,546m). They were accompanied on the mountain by Gyalgen, a Sherpa veteran of Everest who was serving as Shipton's servant in Kashgar. Their summit bid came on August 13, but they were defeated by the wind and bitter cold. They returned to their camp without incident, but Shipton, wearing nailed boots, suffered painfully frostbitten toes. Tilman, with a pair of the new Vibram-soled expedition boots, escaped with a milder case.[47]

The End of Empire

As Britain's two most famous climbers hobbled off Muztagh Ata on August 14 and 15, a historical era in South Asia was coming to an end. The British Raj was no more, and in its place two new states, India and Pakistan, officially came into existence. Even before the formalities of partition and independence, bloody rioting broke out between Hindus and Muslims in the soon-to-be-separate nations, forcing as many as 10 million to flee their homes and leaving hundreds of thousands dead. The Swiss climbers Gyr and Kappeler, whom Tilman had left with the expedition's Sherpas in what became part of Pakistan, had to disguise their porters as sahibs to smuggle them safely out of Muslim-controlled territory.[48]

War once again rendered the mountains of South Asia inaccessible. The state of Kashmir, nestled between India's and Pakistan's northern borders, once optimistically billed as "the Switzerland of the east," was ruled by a Hindu maharajah and was home to sizable Hindu and Buddhist communities in Jammu and Ladakh. But the vast mountain territories were overwhelmingly Muslim, as was the densely populated Vale of Kashmir. Pakistanis had assumed the state would fall to them. Instead, after months of uncertainty and provocative incursions by Pathan irregulars, the maharajah ceded Kashmir to India. The result was war between India and Pakistan, with fighting in the streets of towns like Skardu, traditional stepping-off place for expeditions to the Baltoro region. In 1948 the United Nations brokered a ceasefire along a "line of control" that left Srinagar and the Vale of Kashmir in India, with Skardu, Gilgit, and the great peaks of the Karakoram in Pakistan. But neither side recognized the line of control as an international boundary. This would not be the last war in the twentieth century fought for control of Kashmir.[49]

Gloom spread among Western mountaineers who, since the end of the Second World War, had eagerly looked forward to their return to the Himalaya. As Lieutenant Colonel H. W. [Harry] Tobin, who took over as the *Himalayan Journal* editor from Wilfrid Noyce in 1947, despaired editorially: "The swift evolution as independent states of India and Pakistan brings in its train the early repatriation of nearly all active [British] members of the Himalayan Club. And the hitherto simple access to the great mountains of India's northern borderlands will be enjoyed only by those who will work in the new states. Consequently, unless, or until, mountaineering is taken up seriously by Hindu, Muslim, Sikh, and others, the very *raison d'etre* of the Club will be no more."[50]

Tobin proved too pessimistic. Western mountaineers possessed at least one asset much valued by the newly independent governments in the region, and that was foreign capital. Once the fighting subsided along the newly drawn borders, mountaineers would return to both countries, and the Himalayan Club would survive as well, although it would lose the role it had played as labor contractor for foreign expeditions. Tobin himself would remain editor of the *Himalayan Journal* until his death in 1957; in 1960 the journal would come under Indian editorship for the first time.[51]

Other conflicts in the region would have profound consequences for the future of Himalayan climbing. In 1947 a twelve-year-old boy in Tibet had his horoscope cast. He was Tenzin Gyatso, Tibet's fourteenth Dalai Lama, and his horoscope predicted a foreign threat endangering Tibet in the near future. As Tibet closed its borders to outsiders, the Tibetan army, 8,500 men strong, prepared itself for war. Meanwhile, Mao Zedong's Communists completed their conquest of power in China and almost immediately began threatening Tibet. The Dalai Lama's precautions proved effective in preventing any new mountaineering expeditions from entering the country but could not repel the 80,000 Chinese People's Liberation Army troops who crossed the border in October 1950. In the aftermath of the invasion, the Dalai Lama fled to safety near the India-Sikkim border (along with two European companions, Peter Aufschnaiter and Heinrich Harrer). He would return to Lhasa in August 1951, after having been promised that Tibet could continue to enjoy local autonomy and religious freedom under Chinese Communist rule. But these proved empty promises, and in 1959, when a national uprising against the Chinese occupation was crushed, the Dalai Lama fled again, this time into permanent exile.[52]

Tibet no longer provided access to the Himalaya for Western mountaineers. Mallory and Irvine's route on the north side of Everest was out of bounds, save to mountaineers from Communist nations. Also lost was any possibility for Western mountaineers to approach seven other 8,000-meter peaks from the Tibetan side: Lhotse, Makalu, Cho Oyu, K2, Gasherbrum I and II, and Broad Peak. One additional 8,000-meter peak, Shishapangma, lay entirely within Tibet's borders. Shipton and Tilman's foray to Muztagh Ata turned out to be the last time Western mountaineers would climb in China for the next three decades.[53]

Nepal's Opening to the World

But at just that moment, new possibilities for Western mountaineers opened up in Nepal. The formerly forbidden kingdom was, as Bill Tilman noted at the start of the 1950s, "the largest inhabited country still unexplored by Europeans." Nepal stretches 525 miles long on a roughly east-west axis, with Sikkim to the east and India to the west. It is 90 to 150 miles wide, with India to the south and Tibet to the north. Although not all of the country is mountainous, the northern third of Nepal rises dramatically in elevation and accounts for roughly one-third of the Himalaya. Tilman excitedly catalogued the possibilities opening up to mountaineers in the region: "There can be no country so rich in mountains as Nepal.

. . . Apart from Everest and Kanchengunga and their two 27,000 ft. satellites, there are six peaks over 26,000 ft., fourteen over 25,000 ft., and a host of what might be called slightly stunted giants of 20,000 ft. and upwards, which cannot be enumerated because they are not all shown on existing maps."[54]

Western mountaineers knew little more about the Nepalese Himalaya than the approximate height of its foremost peaks. In the 1920s a British-trained detachment of the Indian Survey had been permitted by the government of Nepal to enter the country (although without its British officers). The quarter-inch map they produced of the country would prove faulty in many details, particularly in the mountainous regions.[55] Nepalese mountains that straddled borders, like Everest and Kangchenjunga, had been at least partially explored. But mountains wholly contained within Nepal's borders, like Annapurna and Dhaulagiri, had never been approached by mountaineers.

As of 1945 only a few hundred Westerners had visited Nepal. Fewer still had been permitted to stay. The only Europeans living in the country at the end of the war were the British ambassador and a small embassy staff, and they were confined in their movements to Kathmandu, Nepal's capital city.

Nepal was not only unwelcoming, it was virtually inaccessible by modern transport. The most common entry route, apart from that taken by the Sherpas who traveled by foot across mountain passes from Tibet or Sikkim, was at the Indian border railhead at Raxaul. From there, rail passengers transferred to the narrow gauge Nepal State Railway. This little toylike train took four hours to cover the twenty-five or so miles across the southern Nepalese plain to Amlekanj, where passengers transferred to car or bus for a twenty-four-mile trip that led upward through the Shivalik mountain range and descended on the far side to the village of Bimpedi. Near Bimpedi was an electrically powered ropeway, where baggage could be deposited for conveyance to Kathmandu. The ropeway could not handle bulky or exceptionally heavy items, which had to be carried by porters. Nor could it carry passengers, who continued on foot over two mountainous passes before descending into the valley of Kathmandu.[56]

On arrival in Kathmandu, visitors found a city with no hotels, a rudimentary electrical system, and a single telephone line that linked it to India. Kathmandu's streets, paved with broken red brick and gravel, were crowded with people, cows, dogs, and chickens. In the late 1940s, for the first time, a few cars and buses appeared as well; these were carried by porters, disassembled, over the southern mountain range into the city, where they were reassembled. Western visitors to the city felt like they had stepped into the pages of an exotic fairy tale and routinely invoked comparisons with Shangri-la.[57]

The first plane ever to land in Nepal arrived in April 1949; regular air service from India commenced in the summer of 1950. The Kathmandu airport consisted of a grassy pasture, equipped with windsock, and planes were scheduled to arrive once a week, monsoon permitting. It tended to be a bumpy flight. "There's talk of a tourist industry," a *New York Times* correspondent reported in 1951, but the prospect seemed far-fetched.[58]

Nepal was a country of roughly 7 million inhabitants in the late 1940s, few of whom would actually claim the description "Nepalese." They were far more likely to identify themselves as members of an ethnic community, such as Gurungs, Tamungs, Gurkhas, or Sherpas. Officially a monarchy ruled by King Tribhuvan Bir Bikram Shah Dev, the powerful Rana family exercised the real authority over Nepal's affairs. For over a century the Ranas possessed hereditary title to the office of prime minister and the titles of maharaja and supreme commander in chief and marshal of Nepal. Nepal may have seemed to Westerners a fairy-tale kingdom, but the Ranas were not benevolent rulers. Taxes went directly into their pockets, building them large palaces in Kathmandu and healthy bank accounts abroad.[59]

Although the Ranas had succeeded in keeping Nepal off limits to visits from foreigners, and radios and foreign newspapers were banned, it proved impossible to shut out disruptive ideas from abroad. A Nepali Congress Party was founded in exile in 1946 in India and agitated for political reforms. Western influences filtered back through the scores of Sherpas who met foreign mountaineers on expeditions, and the thousands of Gurkha soldiers who served abroad in the British Army in the two world wars (Gurkhas are a particular ethnic group living in central Nepal, but "Gurkha" soldiers were actually drawn from many parts of Nepal and many ethnic groups, including Sherpas). Contacts with Americans began when agents from the United States Office of Strategic Services (OSS) recruited Nepalese living in India during the Second World War to serve as saboteurs in the war against Japan.[60]

None of this made the Ranas happy. Western democratic ideas were not welcome; but even less welcome was the prospect of a Chinese-sponsored Communist revolution or invasion. The Ranas cautiously—very cautiously—began to open Nepal to Western visitors, hoping to gain powerful anti-Communist allies while containing contacts with the West for their own ends. With India and Pakistan gaining independence, Great Britain's star was clearly setting in South Asia. Nepal's first gesture of a new openness to Western contact was made to the United States. The American chargé d'affaires in New Delhi, George R. Merrell, traveled to Kathmandu in 1946 to discuss the establishment of formal diplomatic relations between the United States and Nepal, initiated on a limited basis the following year.[61]

Chargé d'affaires Merrell was convinced that the Himalaya was a region of vital strategic importance to the United States in the emerging cold war with the Soviet Union and allied Communist nations; in a cable to Washington in January 1947 he argued that "in an age of rocket warfare," Tibet might provide a valuable launching pad for American missiles. He may have harbored similar thoughts regarding Nepal; in any case, he worked diligently to broaden contacts between the two countries on both the official and informal levels. It was at Merrell's suggestion that an ornithologist named S. Dillon Ripley, associate curator of the Peabody Museum of Natural History at Yale University, asked the Nepalese government in 1946 for permission to lead an expedition to observe and catalogue the country's birds. Ripley led two such trips, the first in the spring of 1947 to Kathmandu and the surrounding valley, the second in November 1948, which took him further afield, to the western Karnali river valley and to the hills east of the Arun River around Mangalbare. He brought back hundreds of specimens of birds, and the articles he wrote for *National Geographic* gave many Americans their initial view of the splendors of Nepal's countryside.[62]

At first the Nepalese government drew a sharp line between Western scientists, who were welcomed, and Western mountaineers, who were not. An Indian scientific party explored the upper Kosi Valley in 1948; the following year a Swiss geologist, Dr. Arnold Heim of Zurich, was allowed to fly from India into Nepalese airspace and photograph Annapurna and Dhaulagiri. When the British Himalayan Committee applied for permission to approach Everest from the south, however, they were turned down, as were the Swiss when they sought permission for an overland reconnaissance of Dhaulagiri. But in 1949 the authorities relented a little, allowing British and Swiss mountaineers the chance to visit the country, so long as scientists accompanied them.[63]

The British party consisted of Bill Tilman and Peter Lloyd (who had climbed with Tilman on Nanda Devi in 1936 and Everest in 1938) along with botanist Oleg Polunin and geologist J. S. Scott. Their destination was north central Nepal. Four Sherpas, including Tenzing Norgay, whom Tilman knew from the 1938 Everest expedition, accompanied the party. This would be Tenzing's first trip back to Nepal since running away to Darjeeling in 1934; it would also be the first time he had seen the Nepalese mountains west of Everest. Setting out from Kathmandu in May and not returning until September, the expedition headed north toward the Tibetan border, exploring the glacial systems of the Langtang, Ganesh, and Jugal Himals. "Sometimes we would be in deep jungles, sometimes high in the mountains," Tenzing would tell James Ramsey Ullman, "working our way across great glaciers and snowy passes, and in both places, most of the time, we were breaking routes that no men had ever used before." Although Tilman and Lloyd made a first ascent of Paldor (19,343ft/5,896m) via its Northeast Ridge, Tilman was frustrated by the requirement that the expedition be primarily devoted to scientific inquiry: "Singleness of purpose is a sound principle," he concluded.[64]

Meanwhile, a Swiss expedition under the leadership of René Dittert headed for northeastern Nepal. They established Base Camp at the foot of Kangchenjunga Glacier and reconnoitered mountains along the Nepalese-Sikkim border, including the Ramthang Glacier approach to the western side of Kangbachen (25,928ft/7,903m). They also racked up the first ascent of Pyramid Peak (23,294ft/7,100m). Dittert and another member of the party, Dr. Edouard Wyss-Dunant, discussed the possibility of organizing a Swiss attempt on Mount Everest, if and when the Nepalese relented on their opposition to mountaineering expeditions tackling the big peaks.[65]

The Return to 8,000 Meters

While these small British and Swiss parties were in the field in 1949, the Federation française de la montagne, the French mountain climbing association, applied to the Nepalese government for permission to conduct a full-scale mountaineering expedition within Nepal's borders. Its application came at just the moment when Nepalese authorities were finally ready to let Western mountaineers have a crack at one of their 8,000-meter peaks. To the delight of the French, and the consternation of climbers from other Western nations who felt they had a better claim, the Nepalese government decreed that in the spring of 1950 the French would be allowed to attempt either Dhaulagiri I (26,795ft/8,167m), the sixth-highest peak in the world, or Annapurna I (26,493ft/8,091m), the tenth-highest.

The summits of the two mountains lie twenty-one miles apart, on opposite sides of the gorge cut by the Kali Gandaki River, Dhaulagiri to the west, Annapurna to the east. Both mountains are part of massifs, or mountain groups, including many impressive subordinate peaks. (The Dhaulagiri massif includes one summit over 26,000 feet, and three more over 25,000, while the Annapurna massif includes two summits over 26,000 feet, and three more over 24,000.)

The French climbing establishment, headed by the noted Alpinist Lucien Devies, assembled a team of France's strongest mountaineers for the expedition.[66] Devies chose Maurice Herzog, an engineer from Lyon and general secretary of the Groupe de haute montagne, as expedition leader. The rest of the climbing team was younger than Herzog. Three leading Chamonix guides, Louis Lachenal, Lionel Terray, and Gaston Rébuffat, were selected, along with two others who, like Herzog, were considered "amateur" climbers (that is, not professional guides): Jean Couzy, an aeronautical engineer, and Marcel Schatz, a physicist. Jacques Oudot was chosen as expedition doctor, and Francis de Noyelle, a diplomat attached to the French embassy in New Delhi, as liaison officer. Marcel Ichac, the celebrated mountain cinematographer, would also join the expedition, the only member with previous experience in the Himalaya.

During the Second World War, Frank Smythe had expressed the hope that in the postwar era "parochialism and international rivalry" could be set aside in mountaineering. Shipton, Tilman, Houston, and others shared that ideal. But the French climbing establishment and the French government (which provided one-third of the expedition's funding) did not. As Lionel Terray would note, the expedition's fund-raisers "were able to convince bankers and industrialists of the worthiness of our cause and of the prestige that would accrue to France if we succeeded."[67] The outlook of the organizers of this first large postwar expedition to the Himalaya would find many imitators in the decade to follow.

But for some expedition members, unlike their sponsors, the notion of climbing for national glory was troublesome. This was not because they lacked patriotism: after the fall of France in 1940, Terray, Lachenal, and Rébuffat had all joined the newly established and quasi-military youth organization Jeunesse et montagne, whose recruits, under the command of French army officers, were trained in skiing and mountaineering. These skills were put to deadly use in the last years of the war; Terray and Rébuffat joined the resistance, fighting the Germans in the Alps. For young men coming from this background, the nationalist trappings of the 1950 expedition might seem consistent with their wartime commitments. Herzog, who also fought with the resistance, happily embraced the idea of climbing for national prestige, and his writings are laced with martial imagery. But Terray, for one, was suspicious of those who would exploit patriotic rhetoric for less worthy or appropriate ends. Though willing to risk his life in the liberation of his country in 1944–45, he had no desire to reenlist in the French Army for France's new war in Indochina. "Recruiting officers appeared on the scene, extolling the charms of the Mysterious East; but, for all its promise of adventure, not many of us were tempted by the idea of a colonial war, in which the word patriotism took on a more equivocal note."[68]

On March 28, 1950, two days before the scheduled departure of the expedition, Lucien Devies oversaw the administration of an oath to the assembled mountaineers in the Paris office of the Club alpin français. As a condition for joining the expedition, each of the climbers had to repeat the words, "I swear upon my honor to obey the leader in everything regarding the Expedition in which he may command me." This ritual had also been required in 1936 of the members of the French Hidden Peak expedition. But a lot had happened in the intervening years of war and occupation to sour the younger mountaineers on such rituals, as well as on the idea of unquestioning obedience to leaders. Although he and the others dutifully repeated the oath, Rébuffat scribbled a note afterward describing the experience as "Depersonalization . . . A certain Nazification."[69]

Eight of the nine members of the expedition flew on an Air France DC-4 to New Delhi, with stops in Cairo and Karachi en route (direct flights from Europe to India were not yet possible). Francis de Noyelle would join them in India. They carried with them three and a half tons of supplies, including such innovations as nylon ropes and outerwear, down jackets, and rubber-soled leather boots with felt lining. They were able to cut down on the amount of food they needed to bring because they planned to buy fresh food from villages located near Dhaulagiri and Annapurna. They also held down on weight by their decision to climb without the aid of bottled oxygen.

From Delhi they made a short connecting flight to Lucknow, where Ang Tharkay, sirdar for the expedition's Sherpas, joined them, along with Sherpa Angawa. Then they traveled by train to Nautanwa, on the Indian-Nepalese border, where six more Sherpas were waiting to join them. The climbers and their equipment were transferred to trucks that carried them to Butwal, a village situated at the southern fringe of Nepal's mountainous region. From then on they proceeded by foot, except for Lachenal and Terray, who served as an advance guard and rode ahead on horseback. One hundred and fifty porters carried their supplies. Their destination was the Kali Gandaki Valley of north central Nepal, an ancient trade and pilgrimage route to Tibet.[70]

The Frenchmen were eager to see the mountains they hoped to climb, and on

April 17 they got their first look at Dhaulagiri, whose name means "the white mountain." "An immense ice pyramid, glittering in the sun like a crystal, rose up 23,000 feet above us," Herzog would write. "The south face, shining blue through the mountain mists, was unbelievably lofty, out of this world. We were speechless in the face of the tremendous mountain whose name was so familiar to us, but the reality so moved us that we couldn't utter a word. Then slowly the reasons for our being here conquered our awe and our aesthetic pleasure, and we began to examine the gigantic outline from a practical point of view." And from a practical point of view, what they saw was not encouraging. "'Just look at the east arête on the right!' 'Yes, it's impossible,'" Herzog wrote later, re-creating the party's reaction to this first distant glimpse of Dhaulagiri. Seeing the mountain, he concluded, "was cold water on our hopes."[71]

Of the other mountain they were authorized to climb, Annapurna, the "Mother Goddess of Harvests," there was as yet no sign. To the east of the Kali Gandaki rose a range of mountains cresting at 15,000 feet called the Nilgiris, which blocked any possible view of Annapurna. It also blocked their access to the mountain. There was one break in the otherwise impenetrable façade of the Nilgiris, a deep gorge toward its southern flank out of which poured the waters of the Miristi Khola River. The maps the French party carried, based on the 1920s Indian Survey of Nepal, suggested that the valley carved by the river swung north to a high pass called the Tillicho, which might provide access to the North Face of Annapurna. None of the local people they questioned, however, knew anything about such a pass, or what one could expect to find by following the gorge of the Miristi Khola.[72]

The twisting path through the valley of the Kali Gandaki led steadily higher. On April 21 the French party reached Tukucha at 8,500 feet. This was a market town of several hundred inhabitants, located midway between Dhaulagiri and Annapurna. There they set up an initial Base Camp. The residents of Tukucha stared with wonder at their European visitors; the French stared back. Life in Tukucha and surrounding villages was disconcertingly primitive to Herzog's eyes: "The women wore very becoming colored aprons," Herzog noted, "and their typically Mongolian faces were adorned with pats of cow-dung applied to both cheeks." In contrast, Lionel Terray felt drawn to the Nepalese and their way of life. Terray had been horrified by the extent of poverty visible in Delhi, where he felt as if "a whole nation had just emerged from Buchenwald and Auschwitz, covered in nothing but vermin and foul rags." There was material deprivation in central Nepal as well, but it seemed to lack the desperate quality of the Indian variety. The intensely cultivated terraces above the river gorge provided food sufficient for a simple and decent life. The Nepalese countryside had a "biblical charm," Terray felt. Here was a landscape where, "for once, man has not destroyed the harmony of nature so much as completed and embellished it."[73]

The climbers set to work on route finding. Herzog dispatched Jean Couzy to climb a 13,000-foot peak in the Nilgiris range above Tukucha to get a look at Dhaulagiri's eastern face. Mountaineering instinct and tradition told them to seek a ridge they could follow to the summit; ridge routes tended to be more direct and offered less danger from avalanche and rockfall. But from where he stood, Couzy judged the Southeast Ridge of Dhaulagiri "absolutely frightful," fraught with "great technical difficulties."[74]

Although Couzy's report, as Herzog noted, "didn't do much to encourage optimism," Dhaulagiri still seemed like a more promising mountain for the expedition to attempt than the yet-to-be-seen Annapurna. On April 24 parties set out from Tukucha to explore Dhaulagiri's eastern and northern approaches. Lachenal and Rébuffat made an initial foray to the eastern glacier, and other small groups returned repeatedly over the next two weeks, searching for a route up the Southeast or the Northeast ridges, or the East or South faces—all in vain.

In the meantime, Herzog, Terray, and Ichac had ventured north of Dhaulagiri and failed to catch a glimpse of the mountain, let alone find a route to its base. Instead, they stumbled upon an unmapped valley headed by limestone cliffs, which they named Hidden Valley. Terray and Oudot returned a few days later and climbed a 17,500-foot saddle above the valley (later known as the French Pass or the French Col), which gave them a view of Dhaulagiri. The problems presented by the North Face of the mountain and its connecting ridges seemed insurmountable. "It's absolutely unclimbable, that Dhaulagiri" Terray exclaimed to Herzog. "It's fiendishly difficult!"[75]

While they were in the midst of exploring the mountain, a Buddhist monk visited the French camp at Tukucha, and Ichac asked him if the expedition would be able to climb Dhaulagiri. After a dramatic pause he replied, "Dhaulagiri is not propitious to you. It would be best to give it up and turn your thoughts to the other side." What other side? Ichac wanted to know. "Towards Muktinath," the monk replied, a village that lay to the north of Annapurna.[76]

Finding their way to the "other side" would not be easy. Herzog had already dispatched Couzy, Oudot, and Schatz to get a look the Miristi Khola, the breach in the wall of the mountains on Annapurna's western flank. They had been intrigued by the amount of water pouring out of the gorge into the Kali Gandaki, more than they would have expected if the Miristi Khola simply drained the glaciers of the Nilgiris. Scaling the South Ridge of the Nilgiris, they were rewarded with a distant view of Annapurna. But it was still not clear if they could get there from where they stood. The Miristi Khola gorge, several thousand feet below them, looked as though it might have its origin in the waters that melted from Annapurna's glaciers. It also looked impassable. And there was no sight of the fabled Tilicho Pass.

Since the Miristi Khola seemed so unpromising an approach, Herzog, acting in accordance with the monk's advice, set off on May 8 with Rébuffat and Ichac to explore the possibility of finding a northern approach to Annapurna. Here they found an east and a west pass below Tilicho (24,405ft/7,134m), a mountain due north of Annapurna. They also found that to the south of the Tilicho passes lay yet another intervening wall of high mountains blocking their view of an access to Annapurna. They named it the Great Barrier. "But where the devil *is* Annapurna?" Ichac blurted out in frustration.[77]

Another week had passed and they were running out of time. The Indian Meteorological Service predicted the arrival of the monsoon by the end of the first week of June.
That left them only three weeks in which to find and climb their mountain. On May 14
the expedition held what Herzog called a "council of war" at their Tukucha Base Camp.
Until this point they had been acting as explorers rather than mountaineers. Their efforts
had done much to correct the shortcomings of the existing maps but little to get them to
the summit of a mountain. Now they would have to commit themselves to a route and
follow it through, wherever it would lead. They knew much more about Dhaulagiri than
they did about Annapurna, but what they knew was not encouraging. So they would
gamble on the unknown, returning to the Miristi Khola, and see if they could push their
way up the gorge to Annapurna.

An advance guard of Terray, Lachenal, and Schatz, accompanied by four Sherpas,
set off that very afternoon. Terray, in his enthusiasm for finally setting out to climb a
mountain, belted out a French Army song and twirled his ice ax over his head like a drum
major's baton. They scaled the Nilgiris and followed a high traverse eastward above the
path of the Miristi Khola. A couloir led them 2,000 down to the river, which they crossed
and then followed on its southern side. The river itself bent increasingly in a northeastern
direction, which meant that, as the monk implied, their route to the mountain would be
from the north—but on the southern side of the Great Barrier. Finally the river led to the
glacial moraine below the Northwest Spur of Annapurna. They had reached the mountain.
Now they had to climb it.[78]

From Base Camp on the North Annapurna Glacier, Terray and Lachenal, and
later Terray and Herzog, spent five days trying to push a route up the Northwest Spur. In
a virtuoso display of high-altitude technical climbing, they reached a point on the ridge at
over 19,000 feet on May 22, but there they ran into a dead end. They were five days closer
to the onset of the monsoon, and no closer to the summit of Annapurna.

Fortunately, acting on a hunch and on their own initiative, Lachenal and Rébuffat
had in the meantime found a route around and to the east of the Northwest Spur.[79] This
placed them directly below Annapurna's North Face. Faces were supposed to offer the more
difficult routes to the summit, in the Himalayas as in the Alps, but ridges had not served
the expedition well, and the North Face was the only alternative they had left in the time
remaining to them.

On May 23 the climbers established Camp I on the north glacier at 16,750 feet.
The snowfields above offered a relatively gentle slope and posed few technical difficulties,
although menaced by avalanches and falling ice.[80] A pattern of regular afternoon snowfall,
leaving a foot or more of new snow, made breaking trail a difficult and exhausting task. Still,
after so many delays and false starts, their progress was now nothing short of spectacular.
By May 28, with Terray setting a ferocious pace, they had established Camp IV at 23,500
feet, just below a formidable curving ice cliff they named the Sickle. Once they surmounted
that obstacle, they would be on the upper glacier that led directly to the summit.

Annapurna North Face, 1978: "The Sickle" can be seen above the dark patch of rock in the upper-right-hand side of this photograph, taken by Arlene Blum. Courtesy of Arlene Blum.

Progress came at a cost. Of all the climbers, Terray and Herzog had acclimatized the best and expected to make the summit bid as a team. But when Couzy and Lachenal had been too exhausted to complete an essential carry of supplies to Camp IV, Terray stepped in. With Rébuffat and a Sherpa team he made the carry to Camp IV on May 30. In doing so he wore himself out. Lachenal, having had a rest day, found his own strength coming back. So Lachenal took Terray's place on the summit team.

Herzog and Lachenal set out from Camp II on May 31 for the final push to the summit. On the way up they encountered and said farewell to Terray and Rébuffat, who were descending to Camp II for a rest. Herzog told them, "When we come down it'll mean the top's been reached. It's all or nothing."[81]

Accompanied by Sherpas Ang Tharkay and Sarki, they reached Camp IV on June 1, setting up a tent slightly higher in a more protected site, Camp IVA. And on June 2 they picked their way up a gully that allowed them to surmount the Sickle to establish Camp V, their assault camp, at 24,280 feet. Herzog offered Ang Tharkay the chance to accompany them on the summit bid the next morning. The Sherpa richly deserved the honor: he had gone to Kangchenjunga in 1931, to Nanda Devi in 1934, and to Everest in 1933, 1935, and 1938. "You are the Sirdar, and the most experienced of all the Sherpas," Herzog told him. "I should be very glad if you will come with us." There was a pause, and Ang Tharkay replied, "Thank you, very much, Bara Sahib, but my feet are beginning to freeze."[82]

As Ang Tharkay and Sarki headed down the gully to Camp IV, Herzog and Lachenal settled in for the night. They drank tea but ate nothing, and got no sleep. The wind howled unceasingly, and the rear of the tent collapsed from accumulated spindrift snow. When they woke at dawn on June 3, it was bitterly cold but no longer snowing. It seemed easier to forgo the morning ritual of lighting the stove and melting snow to make tea. They were robbing their bodies of food and liquid due to the apathy caused by high altitude, for which they would later pay a price.

By 6:00 A.M. they were heading up the glacier that stretched above the Sickle toward the summit. Lachenal's feet began to trouble him. Several times he had to stop to take off his boots and massage feeling back into his stockinged feet. The felt-lined leather boots they had brought to the mountain were proving inadequate. "I don't want to be like Lambert," Lachenal told Herzog, referring to the famous Swiss guide Raymond Lambert, who suffered severely frostbitten feet following an emergency bivouac on Mont Blanc in 1938. Sometime later, as Herzog would record, Lachenal asked him, "If I go back, what will you do?" Herzog pondered the question:

> A whole sequence of pictures flashed through my head; the days of marching in sweltering heat, the hard pitches we had overcome, the tremendous efforts we had all made to lay siege to the mountain, the daily heroism of all my friends in establishing the camps. Now we were nearing our goal. In an hour or two, perhaps, victory would be ours. Must we give up? Impossible! My whole being revolted against the idea. I had

made up my mind, irrevocably. Today we were consecrating an ideal, and no sacrifice was too great. I heard my voice clearly: "I should go on by myself."

I would go alone. If he wished to go down it was not for me to stop him. He must make his own choice freely.

"Then I'll follow you."[83]

It would be many years before Lachenal's feelings about the exchange would be revealed. His posthumously published expedition diary, part of a memoir entitled *Carnets du vertige,* had been stripped of certain lines that Herzog and Lucien Devies found embarrassing or inappropriate for public consumption. "For me," Lachenal wrote in one of the censored passages: "This climb was only a climb like others, higher than in the Alps but no more important. If I was going to lose my feet, I didn't give a damn about Annapurna. I didn't owe my feet to the Youth of France. Thus I wanted to go down. I posed the question to Maurice to find out what he would do in that case. He told me he would keep going. I didn't need to judge his reasons; alpinism is too personal a business. But I guessed that if he continued alone, he would not return. It was for him and for him alone that I did not turn around." Lachenal's own decision to continue to the summit was not, in his words "a matter of national glory." It was instead *une affaire de cordée.* Mountaineering ethics, the mystique of two men bound together by a rope (although in reality they climbed ropeless that day), meant that Lachenal felt he had no choice but to continue on with his partner, come what may. Herzog, on the other hand, suffered no doubts as he plodded up the hill, increasingly swept along on a cloud of euphoria: "This diaphanous landscape, this quintessence of purity —these were not the mountains I knew: they were the mountains of my dreams."[84]

Above the glacier they came to a final couloir leading to the summit. The snow was hard and they kicked steps with their cramponed boots, leaning on their ice axes to recover their breath. "A slight detour to the left, a few more steps," Herzog wrote of the final moments of their ascent, "the summit ridge gradually came nearer—a few rocks to avoid. We dragged ourselves up. Could we possibly be there?"[85]

They were. At 2:00 P.M. on the afternoon of June 3, 1950 Maurice Herzog and Louis Lachenal stood atop Annapurna. Not only were Herzog and Lachenal the first to climb an 8,000-meter summit, they had done so on a first attempt, on a mountain never before even reconnoitered. Herzog knew he had secured his own place in mountaineering history as he ran through a mental list of his predecessors in the Himalaya: Mummery, Mallory and Irvine, Bauer, Welzenbach, Tilman, Shipton. "Never had I felt happiness like this," Herzog would remember, "so intense and yet so pure." His exaltation was understandable, but also a danger sign. More was at work than the satisfaction of achieving a historic goal. Both men, but especially Herzog, were oxygen deprived, dehydrated, and exhausted. They had taken the pep pills prescribed by Dr. Oudot, and these too may have contributed to Herzog's blithe enjoyment of the ritual of summit photos. Lachenal impatiently photographed Herzog displaying the tricolor and then (to Lachenal's increasing

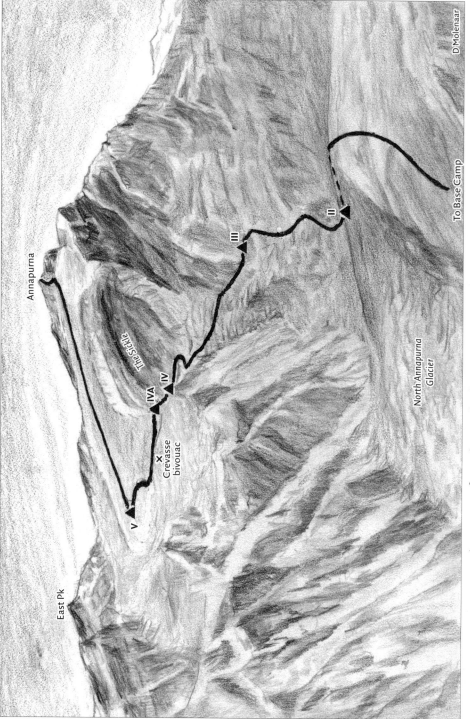

Annapurna from the north, showing the 1950 French route of ascent.

irritation) a banner from his employer. When Herzog loaded another roll of film in the camera, Lachenal finally snapped, "Are you mad? We haven't a minute to lose: we must go down at once."[86] And taking his own advice, he left the summit.

Herzog followed a moment later. Soon after he stopped and took off his pack (he later would not remember why). He had removed his gloves to undo the pack's bindings and laid them on the ground beside it. It was a small gesture that would have large consequences, for as Herzog watched in horror, his gloves slid out of his reach and down the slope, lost forever. In his deteriorating state, it never occurred to him that he was carrying a spare pair of socks in his pack that he might have used to cover his hands.

From that moment on, and for the next two days, almost everything that could go wrong did. If the ascent was a diaphanous dream, the descent proved a nightmare. As night fell Herzog stumbled in to Camp V, which now consisted of two tents instead of the one they had left that morning: Rébuffat and Terray had climbed to the site and put up a tent in the meantime in the hope of making their own summit bid the following day. Hearing Herzog's footsteps in the snow, Terray bounded from the tent and greeted Herzog, happily seizing his hands in greeting, "only to find to my horror," he would later write, "that I was shaking an icicle." And where was Lachenal? Herzog didn't know but assured Rébuffat and Terray that he should be along any moment. But of course Lachenal had been ahead of Herzog on the descent, so that made no sense except to a man starved of oxygen. Terray and Rébuffat were heating water and caring for Herzog in the tent when they heard a faint cry for help. Peering out, Terray spotted his old climbing partner lying on the slope 300 feet below the campsite. He glissaded down to rescue Lachenal, who had lost his footing, along with his ice ax and one of his crampons. Lachenal begged his friend not to take him back up the slope to Camp V but rather to continue with him down to Camp II, where he hoped Dr. Oudot could save his frozen feet. In the gathering dark and a mounting snowstorm, without rope or crampons, it would have been suicide to attempt the descent. Finally Terray persuaded him to come up to the shelter of Camp V. Back in the tent, Terray removed Lachenal's frozen boots, having to cut through the leather to peel them away: "My heart sank at the sight of the feet inside, white and utterly insensible," Terray recalled. "Annapurna, the first eight-thousander, was climbed, but was it worth such a price?"[87]

The price exacted by Annapurna on the climbers only increased the next day. The weather did not improve. They had to find their way around and down below the Sickle to the safety of Camp IV, but a full day's effort left them lost and shelterless. In their condition, and in such weather, an open bivouac would have killed all four of them. Finally, at their most desperate moment, Lachenal stumbled into a hidden crevasse, which fortunately proved to be snow filled and with a cavity large enough to shelter all four men for another night. They had no food or water and only one sleeping bag, which Terray had had the foresight to bring along. "One feels pretty small in the bottom of a crevasse 23,000 feet up in the Himalaya," Rébuffat recalled of that night. And at first light the next morning, June 5, an avalanche poured in on them, burying the boots that they had taken off the night before to be able to massage their feet. It took a long desperate search to find all four pairs. And when they emerged into the sunlight they found that both Terray and Rébuffat had gone snow-blind overnight, having taken off their goggles while they searched for a route down the mountain the previous day. Somehow, miraculously, two men with frozen feet leading two blind men edged their way down the mountain, calling out to their friends below—and were saved. Marcel Schatz, waiting anxiously at Camp IVA, heard them calling, climbed up to meet them, and brought them down the mountain to safety. "We returned to earth in a fearful mix-up of pain and joy, heroism and cowardice, grandeur and meanness," Terray later wrote enigmatically.[88]

More pain was to come, especially for Herzog and Lachenal. Dr. Oudot did what he could to save their frostbitten extremities but eventually wound up amputating all of Lachenal's toes and all of Herzog's toes and fingers. It would take them nearly a month and a half to return to France, prolonged for an extra week when, to the dismay of his teammates, Herzog decided to travel to Kathmandu to be honored there by the maharajah. Finally, on July 17, they arrived at Orly airport in Paris, greeted by an ecstatic crowd as national heroes. Whatever meanness and cowardice Terray had seen on Annapurna would be forgotten; what was remembered and celebrated was the heroism and grandeur.[89]

"Victoire sur l'Himalaya," proclaimed *Paris Match* in its cover story of August 19, 1950, followed by the magazine's exclusive account of the expedition. The issue sold a record number of copies. The cover photo, endlessly reproduced in years to come, showed Herzog with his ice ax and tricolor atop Annapurna. "Pour la premiere fois," the photo caption proclaimed, "un drapeau flotte sur un sommet de plus de 8.000 metres et c'est le drapeau français brandi par Herzog au sommet de l'Annapurna."[90]

Had Herzog and his comrades been German, had the mountain they climbed been Nanga Parbat, and had the year been 1937, their do-or-die assault on the summit might have been regarded (at least by non-Germans) as a Nazi perversion of true mountaineering. Instead, when the president of the French Republic, Vincent Auriol, awarded Herzog and Lachenal the Legion of Honor in a ceremony in the Elysée Palace on October 25, he compared the ascent of Annapurna to the battle waged by the French Resistance against the Nazis. "Messieurs," he proclaimed: "You've shown the world a magnificent example of French solidarity. We know what France did during the Occupation, and how brave the French were in the Resistance. Most of you, I think almost all of you, were *résistants,* and now you have shown what the French are capable of in peacetime."[91]

Herzog took such praise as his due. If the others were disturbed, they kept their doubts to themselves. But late in life Rébuffat wrote some notes on the Annapurna expedition, including a comment on the reception they received when they returned to France: "Oh, if only Herzog had lost his flags, instead of his gloves, how happy I would have been!"[92]

For nearly a year following his return, Herzog recuperated in the American Hospital at Neuilly. There he dictated the manuscript for what would become the most successful expedition book of all times, entitled simply in its English edition *Annapurna*. Following its initial publication in 1951, it would be translated into dozens of languages, and go on to sell over 11 million copies. Before 1950 there had been mountaineers whose Himalayan exploits had won acclaim within their own nations: Shipton in England, Merkl in Germany, the Duke of the Abruzzi in Italy. There had also been a single internationally known Himalayan mountaineer, George Mallory, whose fame was posthumous and based largely on the mystery surrounding his disappearance on Everest in 1924. With the publication of *Annapurna,* Maurice Herzog became the first living international climbing celebrity whose name was known to the general public as well as to mountaineering enthusiasts.

As an author, Herzog was not a great prose stylist like Bill Tilman (for one thing, he was utterly lacking any sense of irony). But he certainly knew how to end a book. The last line in *Annapurna* became perhaps the most famous catchphrase in mountaineering history since Mallory's "Because it is there." "There are," Herzog wrote, "other Annapurnas in the lives of men."[93]

Annapurna could be read as both a story of heroic triumph over the natural world and an equally or even greater spiritual transcendence over suffering. In his review for the *New York Herald Tribune,* James Ramsey Ullman described the book as "a gallant and moving story, in some ways a terrible story," which he predicted would become "one of the classics of climbing literature." Herzog's description of the ascent of Annapurna was conventionally inspirational, but what really stayed with readers was the account of the descent and the sufferings that his and Lachenal's triumph exacted. No one who read the account of the mortification and amputation of Herzog's fingers and toes would soon forget it. *Time* magazine's anonymous reviewer wrote dismissively of the first half of the book as "a boy camper's letter to a chum" but found the story of the retreat from the summit a "harrowing ordeal-by-nature calculated to shiver the spirit of the toughest armchair explorer."[94]

The first 8,000-meter mountain had fallen. But, Everest, the greatest prize in mountaineering, remained to be claimed. Unless mountaineers from the Soviet Union or China got there first from the Tibetan side, the summit of Everest could be reached only one way—from Nepal. And if and when that happened, there would be no doubt that the golden age of Himalayan mountaineering had indeed arrived.

CHAPTER SEVEN

"Don't Be a Chicken-Hearted Fellow"
Everest
1950–1953

In his 1943 memoir *Upon That Mountain,* Eric Shipton reflected on the disappointments experienced by the British expeditions to Everest in the 1930s. He drew an analogy between the difficulties that his generation of climbers encountered on Everest and those an earlier generation faced in climbing the Matterhorn. In the mid-nineteenth century, the "Golden Age of Alpine Climbing," the Matterhorn had defied repeated attempts by the best Alpinists of the era to reach its summit. Finally, in 1865, Edward Whymper led a party to the top. In a few years the mountain would come to be regarded almost, if not quite, as the proverbial "easy day for a lady." Why, then, had it taken so long to climb initially?

"It was certainly not that these men were incompetent," Shipton argued. Rather, he thought the "reason must be sought in that peculiar, intangible difficulty presented by the first ascent of any peak." Those difficulties were multiplied in the Himalaya where, unlike the Alps, climbers could not retreat from a failed attempt on a mountain to spend the night in a comfortable inn and return refreshed the next day to try again. "No, it is not remarkable that Everest did not yield to the first few attempts," Shipton concluded; "indeed, it would have been very surprising, and not a little sad if it had, for that is not the way of great mountains. . . . It is possible, even probable, that in time men will look back with wonder at our feeble efforts, unable to account for our repeated failure, while they themselves are grappling with far more formidable problems. If we are still alive we shall no doubt mumble fiercely in our grey beards in a desperate effort to justify our weakness. But if we are wise we shall reflect with deep gratitude that we seized our mountaineering heritage, and will take pleasure in watching younger men enjoy theirs."[1] As it turned out, Shipton and his gray-bearded generation had further contributions to make in preparing the way to the summit of Mount Everest. In the end, however, it would be left to a younger generation to carry off the prize.

Everest's Southern Exposure

Bill Tilman was the first veteran of the 1930s Everest expeditions to have the opportunity to approach the mountain from the south. And, serendipitously, he would do so in the company of his old climbing companion from Nanda Devi, Charlie Houston. Tilman spent the late spring and summer of 1950 in the glacial systems around Manaslu, Himalchuli, and north of the Annapurna massif. He was accompanied by George Lowndes, a veteran officer of the Garhwal Rifles who served as expedition botanist, Gurkha officer Major Jimmy Roberts, Dr. Charles Evans, J. H. Emlyn Jones, and New Zealander Bill Packard, along with four Sherpas and a small military escort. The expedition enjoyed the support of the Himalayan Committee in London, which viewed it, as Tilman put it, as a step towards "building up a nucleus of experienced Himalayan climbers such as had existed between the wars."[2]

Tilman and his comrades knew that a French expedition had preceded them to central Nepal, to try either Dhaulagiri or Annapurna. Although the British were not equipped for and lacked permission from the Nepalese government to attempt an 8,000-meter peak, they hoped to make at least one respectable climb. They concentrated their efforts on another peak on the Annapurna massif, Annapurna IV (24,688ft/7,525m). Their timing, however, was not good, as they set up Base Camp on the day the monsoon began. They made three summit attempts on Annapurna IV, getting within 750 vertical feet of the top, but were defeated by the weather, altitude sickness, and some mild cases of frostbite.[3]

Meanwhile that spring, another party was making preparations to visit Nepal. Oscar Houston, a New York lawyer, enlisted the aid of Loy Henderson, American ambassador to India and minister to Nepal, to secure permission from the Nepalese government for a visit to the region bordering the south side of Mount Everest. Oscar Houston was sixty-seven years old and, while spry for his age, not the obvious candidate to lead the first-ever reconnaissance of the Nepalese side of Mount Everest. But he would be accompanied by his son Charlie, on Charlie's first trip back to the region since the 1938 K2 expedition. And for a climber of Charlie Houston's experience, the trip his father was planning to Everest was more holiday jaunt than serious expedition. Permission came in April for Houston's party to set off the following October.[4]

The other two members of the party were Betsy Cowles, a family friend and (unusually for a woman of the era) a member and officer of the American Alpine Club, and Anderson Bakewell, another family friend, who was studying to be a Jesuit priest at St. Mary's College in Kurseong, India.[5] This small and informal group would undertake a journey that would have been the envy of many of the great expeditions of the prewar era. They would make their way to the southern flank of Mount Everest through the Solu Khumbu region, home to Nepal's Sherpa population, an area never before visited by Westerners.

Houston-Tilman Everest reconnaissance party, 1950: from left, Anderson
Bakewell, Oscar Houston, Betsy Cowles, Bill Tilman, and Charlie Houston.
Cowles Photograph Collection. Courtesy of the Henry S. Hall Jr.
American Alpine Club Library.

Oscar Houston, along with his wife and Betsy Cowles, went to Kathmandu in early
October for some preexpeditionary sightseeing as the personal guests of the maharajah.
Charlie Houston was still in New York and would join them later in India. At a reception
at the British embassy, the senior Houston had a chance encounter with Bill Tilman, whom
he had not seen since 1936. On that occasion, Oscar accompanied Charlie, Tilman, and
several other climbers as far as the Rishi Gorge, the entrance to the Nanda Devi Sanctuary where, at Tilman's instigation, it was gently suggested to Oscar that he was too old to
proceed further. On impulse, or perhaps to show that there were no hard feelings left over
from Nanda Devi, Houston invited Tilman to join their party to Everest.

Tilman had reservations (an unrepentant misogynist, or so he liked to claim, he had
never before gone on an expedition with a woman). But the chance to get a close-up view
of Everest's southern exposure was too good to pass up. Tibet no longer offered access to
Everest. And, sight unseen, climbers knew that the southern, Nepalese side of Everest could
offer some decided advantages over the traditional northern route. The approach marches
through Nepal were shorter and, if the monsoon were avoided, more pleasant than the
route across the barren Tibetan plateau. Unlike the northern exposure, in shadow most of
the day, Everest's southern exposure would mean a better chance of climbing in sunshine,

mitigating to an extent the extreme cold of high altitude. And unlike on the Tibetan side of the mountain, where the rock strata near the summit sloped downward, climbers on the Nepalese side of the mountain would encounter upward sloping sedimentary strata at higher elevations, offering them more secure footing. None of that would matter if there weren't a suitable route on the south side, and that is what Tilman wanted to find out. He was also attracted by the prospect of "seeing Sherpas, as it were, in their natural state," in their home villages of the Khumbu region.[6]

Oscar and Charlie Houston, Tilman, Cowles, and Bakewell rendezvoused in Jogbani, the Indian railhead on the Nepalese border, on October 29 (setting off from Jogbani, rather than Kathmandu, they avoided the difficulties and expense then involved in transporting expedition supplies to the Nepalese capital). They were joined by six Sherpas from Darjeeling, including Tilman's old friend Gyalgen, with whom he and Shipton had attempted Muztagh Ata a few years before. They traveled north from the border by truck and car to Dharan, where the road ended. From there, accompanied by eighteen porters recruited in Nepal, they proceeded by foot over the hills to the village of Dankhuta, perched on a ridge between the Tamur and Arun valleys. The visitors greatly admired Dankhuta, which Tilman would praise as "a spotlessly clean little town." Among the local sites of interest they noted was an English-language school where someone had written on a wall, "Gather courage, don't be a chicken-hearted fellow." Those words of encouragement for times of adversity became the expedition's whimsical motto.[7]

From Dankhuta they descended into the Arun Valley. Charlie Houston, whom Tilman described admiringly as "a man who does nothing by halves," came equipped with fishing equipment for two, and he and Tilman tried their luck in the Arun River.[8] They turned westward, crossing three mountain passes, including the 11,800-foot Salpa La. This brought them at last into the valley of the Dudh Kosi, or Milk River, whose silt-filled waters drain from Mount Everest and other high peaks.

It was a three-day hike along the river to the Sherpa town of Namche Bazar perched at 11,000 feet on a ridge between the Dudh Kosi and the Bhote Kosi rivers. Arriving on November 14, they found a community of about thirty whitewashed houses. The Westerners were delighted with the friendly reception they received and impressed by the general air of prosperity the village displayed, the product of trade with Tibet as well as remittances from Darjeeling Sherpas employed on expeditions. Tilman noted the windows that dotted the two-story houses: "To find glass in a Himalayan private house, fourteen days' march from civilization, is a little remarkable."[9]

From Namche, Houston and Tilman went on ahead up the Dudh Kosi Valley on November 15 with four porters to make better time, while the others followed at a more leisurely pace. On a hilltop located a mile beyond the confluence of the Dudh Kosi and Imja Khola rivers, they came upon Tengboche Monastery. Sitting at a height of 12,300 feet, the monastery had been constructed in 1923 and rebuilt after an earthquake ten years later. "[S]ince none of [the lamas] had seen a white man before," Houston would write, "they

Namche Bazar, 1950. Cowles Photograph Collection.
Courtesy of the Henry S. Hall Jr. American Alpine Club Library.

were astounded by the two ragged travelers who dropped into their midst." Tengboche was a quarter the size of the Rongbuk Monastery on the north side of Everest, which had been a familiar stopping place for the prewar British expeditions. Tilman found Tengboche "incomparably more beautiful and less austere" in its setting than its Tibetan counterpart. They still had not seen the mountain above Tengboche, which was swathed in clouds. But the next morning the clouds parted. "Bathed in the first light of morning," Houston later wrote reverently, Everest's "ridges of steep and broken rock stood out boldly, accentuating the purity of the white snow which in places lay almost vertical."[10]

From Tengboche, Houston and Tilman proceeded alone to the foot of the mountain, while their companions remained behind enjoying the hospitality of the lamas. They hiked to the little village of Pangboche, and then on to Everest. They made camp at 16,500 feet, just below the Khumbu Glacier, which flows from Everest's south flank. Along the way they were entranced by views of Makalu, Chamlang, and Ama Dablam.

Head lama of Tengboche Monastery, 1950. Cowles Photograph Collection.
Courtesy of the Henry S. Hall Jr. American Alpine Club Library.

As Tilman knew from his own experience, the climbing on Everest's northern lower
flank was relatively easy; the serious difficulties started higher on the mountain, above the
North Col. From the south, in contrast, as Tilman and Houston immediately noted, the
approach itself was fraught with difficulty and danger. As the Khumbu Glacier descends
from the mountain's side, it is forced through a narrow chute between Everest and Nuptse.
Tilman and Houston were appalled at the prospect of expeditions having to thread a route
upward through the resulting mass of jumbled ice towers, blocks, debris, and crevasses to
the enclosed valley of the Western Cwm, which lies 2,000 feet above. Standing at the foot
of the Khumbu Icefall, Houston concluded that while it probably "could be forced," it certainly did not offer mountaineers "a very attractive route of access" to the mountain.[11]

Houston and Tilman were on a tight schedule. They were due back in Jogbani on
December 6, which left them only two full days for their reconnaissance. Before they departed they wanted to get a look at what lay beyond the icefall. And so on November 18, their

Kala Patar: Houston and Tilman climbed the dark slopes
of Kala Patar, behind which rises Pumori. Photograph
by John A. Woodworth, 1978. Photo courtesy of
the Appalachian Mountain Club Archives.

last day beside Everest, the two men started up Kala Patar (18,192ft/5,643m), a scree-covered subsidiary peak of Pumori.[12] Tilman, who had spent the last few months tramping around the Annapurna region and had reached a height of over 22,000 feet on Annapurna IV, was well acclimatized, but Houston, who only three weeks earlier had left New York, was at a disadvantage. As a result, they were forced to halt about 300 feet below Kala Patar's summit.

From that vantage point, Tilman photographed the southern view of Everest's summit. They could see a steep ridge dropping from the summit, which they surmised must end up on the South Col. They could not see the col itself because it was blocked from view by a shoulder of Nuptse, as was the lower face of Lhotse. The ridgeline leading to the summit did not seem like a promising route.

Their limited view led them to misread the mountain. The ridge visible to them from Kala Patar was not linked to the South Col at all. It was Everest's Southwest Ridge, which connects to a buttress (later named the South Pillar) that falls steeply and directly to the Western Cwm. What they could not see from where they stood was that further to the east lies another ridge, Everest's Southeast Ridge, the ridge that actually connects to the South Col, and one that is, at least relatively, less forbidding. Had they climbed the additional 300 feet to the summit of Kala Patar, they would have found a broader vista opening up to them, in which their mistake would have been apparent.[13]

Betsy Cowles sent an informal expedition newsletter home to a circle of friends, keeping track of events as they unfolded. Her entry for November 23 reported that "there is *not* a good practicable climbing route up Everest from the south. . . . The north route, hitherto used by the British climbers, is much simpler and easier, despite its disadvantages of weather and position. Charlie and Bill went to over 19,000 feet and worked hard for four days. They looked weary and thin but of good cheer about everything."[14]

Cowles didn't get all the details right (Houston and Tilman reached a high point of under 18,000 feet), but her summary of their opinion of the likelihood of climbing the mountain from the south was accurate. On the journey out the two climbers drafted a statement that they passed on to a *New York Times* reporter in New Delhi: "Our conclusions about the south face were that it presented much greater climbing difficulties than the north side. The southern face is precipitous and broken by long and intricate ridges that would be technically difficult and dangerous. The south face may well be impossible and we could see no practicable climbing route."[15]

The report they brought back from Everest may have been pessimistic, but, as Betsy Cowles noted in her newsletter, the party remained in good cheer: "As I write, the Sherpas are cutting up like kids after school. . . . Such laughter and gaiety! They are the dearest, most frolicsome people. (I intend to be as Sherpish as possible in the future.) Charley, at my elbow, is singing: 'Hi Diddly Dee/A Sherpa's life for me.'"[16]

Whether or not Everest could be climbed from the south, the Solu Khumbu, with its whitewashed houses and friendly inhabitants, and Tengboche Monastery, with its spectacular view of the "purity of the white snow" on Everest's flanks, seemed like paradise compared to the rest of Asia in 1950. While Houston and Tilman were engaged in their reconnaissance, China had invaded Tibet. In Korea, United Nations forces north of the 38th parallel were being battered by Chinese assaults in what many believed was the opening battle of a third world war. There were also dramatic events unfolding in Nepal. Like most experiments in which authoritarian regimes tinker with minor reform, the Rana family's attempt to encourage, control, and channel Western contacts for their own purposes proved a failure. King Tribhuvan allied himself with the Nepali Congress Party, which was in turn backed by India. In November 1950 he and his family sought asylum in the Indian embassy in Kathmandu and then went into exile in India. As the Houston party prepared to leave the country, the nation's political future seemed uncertain. (A popular revolt and international pressure led to King Tribhuvan's return to power as a constitutional monarch in February 1951 and the curbing of the power of the Ranas.)[17]

Houston's report for the *American Alpine Journal* reflected both his admiration for the tranquility of the Solu Khumbu and his anxiety about world politics: "It was hard to return from this happy primitive land to a world in which our first news was of the U.N. reverses in Korea and of political unrest along many borders. It seemed at least debatable that we were returning to civilization."[18]

Further Reconnaissance

The following spring in London, a young surgeon by the name of Michael Ward, then performing his national service in the Royal Army Medical Corps, followed Houston and Tilman's advice (and example)—gathering courage, even in the face of their gloomy report from Everest. Twenty-six years old in 1951, Ward had been fascinated by the mountain ever since reading Frank Smythe's *Camp Six* as a boy. In his off-duty hours that spring, he methodically searched the archives of the Royal Geographical Society for clues to the lay of Everest's southern flanks. He found Mallory's 1921 photo taken from the col between Pumori and Lingtren, photos from the 1933 Houston-Westland flight, a 1935 photo by New Zealander Dan Bryant, again taken from Pumori Col, and Bill Tilman's photo taken from Kala Patar. And, in an unmarked envelope, he stumbled upon photos taken by RAF pilots who overflew the mountain in 1945 and 1947. Unlike Houston and Tilman's visual line of sight from Kala Patar the previous year, the RAF photographs clearly showed Everest's Southeast Ridge, broad and snow covered, leading down toward the South Col (which was not, however, visible in the photo). Ward wondered if this Southeast Ridge–South Col connection might prove the key to the summit. He proposed to the Himalayan Committee that it sponsor an expedition to Nepal to take a closer look.[19]

Compared to the energy displayed by the Swiss Foundation for Alpine Research or the French mountaineering establishment, the Himalayan Committee seemed inert. Since 1945 the committee had sporadically entertained the idea of reviving the assault on Everest but had not managed to get a single British climber anywhere near the mountain. Nor was it inclined to display much sympathy when enthusiastic young people like Ward came round with their own ideas about the next big step in Himalayan climbing. Ward described the committee's reception to his proposal for an Everest reconnaissance as "distinctly cool and skeptical."[20]

To speak on his behalf Ward recruited some influential figures with Himalayan experience, Campbell Secord and W. H. (Bill) Murray. In May they managed to convince the Himalayan Committee to go so far as to ask the Nepalese government for permission to send a reconnaissance to Everest that fall. The committee's endorsement of the proposal was grudging, and Ward believed they secretly hoped it would be turned down. The Nepalese authorities, however, were proving increasingly open to such proposals and surprised everyone by approving the plan six weeks later. Ward and his friends began hasty preparations for an August departure.[21]

Other climbers signed on for the expedition, including Tom Bourdillion, fresh from a season of hard climbing in the Alps, and Alfred Tissieres, a Swiss biochemist working at Cambridge University, who was a friend of Secord. Although Bill Murray was at first slated to be expedition leader, there was a sudden change of plans in mid-June when Eric Shipton returned from China. By chance he bumped into Secord. As Shipton recalled their encounter, Secord said to him: "'Oh you're back are you? What are you going to do now?' I told him that I had no plans, to which he replied, 'Well, you'd better lead this expedition.' I said, 'What expedition?'"[22]

It did not take Secord long to convince Shipton to sign on. Murray graciously stepped aside as leader, for he understood that the doubters on the Himalayan Committee would feel reassured if the expedition came under the direction of an old Everest hand like Shipton. Shipton was also able to secure funding from that traditional source of media largesse for mountaineers, *The Times*. Influenced by Tilman's pessimistic assessment of the previous year, Shipton harbored personal doubts about the likelihood of actually discovering a southern route to Everest's summit. But he was not about to turn down the chance to see a part of the world he had long dreamed of visiting: "I had heard so much about it from the Sherpas; indeed during our journeys together in other parts of the Himalaya and Central Asia, whenever we came upon a particularly attractive spot, they invariably said, 'This is just like Sola Khumbu,' and the comparison always led to a long, nostalgic discourse about their homeland. . . . it had become, to me at least, a kind of Mecca, an ultimate goal in Himalayan exploration."[23]

Tissieres and Secord withdrew from the expedition before its departure for personal reasons, and Shipton, preferring to keep the party small, also turned down several requests from climbers who wished to join (among them the Swiss climber René Dittert). Just before departing England, however, he received a cable from the New Zealand Alpine Club, notifying him that a party of four young New Zealanders was climbing in India's Garhwal region and asking if some of them might be allowed to join the Everest reconnaissance. Shipton was initially inclined to say no. But en route to Delhi he changed his mind, in an impulsive decision that would have a lasting impact on the history of Himalayan mountaineering. A couple of extra climbers with recent Himalayan experience might prove useful.[24]

When the New Zealand climbers—Earle Riddiford, George Lowe, Ed Cotter, and Edmund Hillary—returned from their Garhwal expedition to their hotel in the hill town of Ranikhet, there was a cable waiting for them from Shipton: "Invite any two of you to join my party if you can get own permission enter Nepal, bringing own food and supplies."[25] After a debate as to whom should have the privilege of going, Riddiford and Hillary hurried to catch up with the British climbers.

Shipton's party, along with twelve Sherpas led by Ang Tharkay, set off from Jogbani on the Nepalese border on August 27. They followed the route to the Solu Khumbu
taken by the Houston-Tilman expedition the previous year. Hillary and Riddiford arrived
in Jogbani five days later and headed up the monsoon-soaked and leech-infested Arun
Valley in pursuit of Shipton, finally catching up in Dingla, west of the Arun River, on
September 8. For Hillary, who had read Shipton's book about Nanda Devi as a teenager,
it was a thrilling encounter with the man he regarded as "the ideal in mountain climbing."
Although the expedition was moving through territory new to all of them, there were
plenty of reminders of bygone expeditions. Shipton was greeted by many Sherpas who
knew him from the prewar days on Everest. And when the expedition reached Tengboche
Monastery on September 25, he noticed that the signal gong used to summon the monks
to meals and prayer was a decades-old British oxygen cylinder, retrieved by a Sherpa from
the East Rongbuk Glacier.[26]

Just as Hillary was delighted to meet Shipton, the older climber was glad to have
Hillary along, admiring the younger man's drive and enthusiasm. He chose Hillary as his
partner on September 30 when, seeking to get a good look at Everest's South Face, he
climbed the ridge linking Pumori and adjoining Kala Patar. Whereas Houston and Tilman the previous year had gone no higher than 18,000 feet, Shipton and Hillary topped
the ridge at 20,000 feet. The extra 2,000 feet made a big difference. After catching their
breath, they looked over at Everest. For Shipton, what first drew his attention was the view
into Tibet and Everest's North Face: "[W]ith our powerful binoculars we could follow
every step of the route by which all attempts to climb the mountain had been made. How
strange it seemed to be looking at all those well-remembered features from this new angle,
and after so long an interval of time and varied experience; the little platform at 25,700
feet where we had spent so many uncomfortable nights, Norton's Camp 6 at the head of
the north-east spur, the Yellow Band and the grim overhanging cliffs of the Black Band,
the Second Step and the Great Couloir. They were all deep in powder snow as when I had
last seen them in 1938."[27]

For Hillary, a first-time visitor, it was the future rather than the past that drew
his attention:

> Almost casually I looked towards the Western Cwm, although I didn't expect to see
> much of it from here. To my astonishment the whole valley lay revealed to our eyes. A
> long, narrow, snowy trough swept from the top of the ice-fall and climbed steeply up
> the face of Lhotse to the head of the Cwm. And even as the same thought was sim-
> mering in my own mind, Shipton said, "There's a route there!" And I could hear the
> note of disbelief in his voice. For from the floor of the Cwm it looked possible to climb
> the Lhotse glacier—steep and crevassed though it appeared—and from there a long
> steep traverse led to a saddle at 26,000 feet—the South Col. Certainly it looked a dif-
> ficult route, but a route it was. In excited voices we discussed our find. We had neither
> the equipment nor the men to take advantage of our discovery, but at least we could

Edmund Hillary on the 20,000-foot ridge of Pumori
looking across the Khumbu Glacier to Nuptse, 1951.
Reprinted by permission of the
Royal Geographical Society.

try to find a route up the ice-fall and then return next year and attack the mountain
in force.[28]

While Shipton and Hillary were admiring the view from Pumori's flank, Riddiford,
Ward, Bourdillion, and Sherpa Pasang were exploring the route through the lower Khumbu
Icefall. Shipton and Hillary joined Bourdillion and Riddiford on October 2 at the foot of
the icefall (Ward, feeling unwell at high altitude, returned to Base Camp with Murray). A
day and a half of heavy snow kept them pinned in camp. But October 4 dawned sunny, if
cold, and the two Englishmen and two New Zealanders, accompanied by Pasang and two
other Sherpas, tackled the icefall again. They fought their way upward through snow that
often reached their hips, penetrating the maze of ice towers and crevasses to within forty
feet of the Western Cwm. They might have gone further, but Shipton decided the snow
conditions were too threatening (an avalanche of a snow slope swept Riddiford to the edge

of a deep crevasse). Shipton wanted to do some exploring in the region anyway and hoped
that a few weeks away would give the icefall time to solidify.

Shipton and Hillary again paired up and spent the next two weeks exploring the
unmapped Imja and Hongu glacier systems south of Everest. From a high pass they gazed
out onto the Barun Glacier, which stretches to the foot of 27,790-foot Makalu. The valleys
below Makalu had never been visited by Europeans, and indeed had only been seen by a
few Nepalese herdsmen. "It was all new country, completely unexplored," Hillary would
recall, "and I quickly caught Shipton's fervour for such untravelled places." He vowed some
day to return and explore the ground that led up to the base of Makalu.[29]

On October 19 Shipton and Hillary returned to Base Camp and two days later
proceeded on to the icefall; the others had yet to return. They discovered that the icefall
had indeed changed in the interval they were away, but not for the better. In one stretch
so many huge ice blocks had collapsed since their last visit that they took to calling it the
"Atom Bomb" area. One of the lessons of the 1951 reconnaissance was that there was never
a "good" or "better" time to climb the icefall; one set of hidden crevasses and ready-to-
topple ice towers would just be replaced by another. A few days later the other climbers
joined Hillary and Shipton in the icefall, and on October 28 they stood at the threshold
of the Western Cwm.[30]

At the threshold, but not over it. A vast crevasse, 100 feet deep and stretching between 100 and 300 feet across, blocked their entrance. Such obstacles could be surmounted,
with time and commitment, but Shipton decided they had done enough for one expedition. Besides, leaving now would give him more time for exploring unknown territory on
the way back from the mountain.

Shipton's caution had nothing to do with a lack of courage, a virtue he had displayed on scores of difficult precipices. Instead, it reflected the ingrained values of prewar
British mountaineering, a code that set strict limits on acceptable levels of risk taking.
The reconnaissance party had taken great chances in finding a route through the icefall;
prudence now dictated retreat. Shipton was worried about the Sherpas, who would have
to bear heavy loads on repeated journeys up through the icefall. And he worried too about
the climbing party, for to abandon moderation was to invite retribution. Just what was
moderate or prudent on the side of a mountain like Everest was, of course, a matter of
subjective judgment, however self-evident the boundaries may have seemed to Shipton's
generation of mountaineers. It would be left to the next generation to push those limits.
"Looking back on it, with greater experience," Michael Ward would write some years later,
"there is no doubt that we should have continued. Subsequently I have made decisions to
continue in much more dangerous circumstances—decisions which reflect both a change
in my attitude towards mountaineering as well as a better understanding of conditions
in the Himalayas. In modern mountaineering objective dangers are now accepted much
more readily than in the past."[31]

Even before they had reached the top of the icefall, Shipton had reported success to London in finding "a practicable route from the West Cwm to the summit of Mount Everest." Shipton's expedition book, published the following year, included an illustration marking out the most likely route up the mountain, a dotted line that wound through the Khumbu Icefall to the Western Cwm, climbing leftward up Lhotse Face to the South Col, and then continuing up the Southeast Ridge to the summit.[32] Shipton and his comrades planned to return to Everest in 1952 to follow that line to its terminus, and in doing so bring the story of three decades of gallant British attempts on the mountain to a satisfying conclusion.

They were not to get that chance, however, at least not in 1952. The Himalayan Committee dawdled with its application to Nepal for a permit for a full-scale expedition on Everest. It did not seem to occur to the committee's members that in light of recent changes in the political circumstances of South Asia, neither Nepal nor other European countries would necessarily continue to respect the convention that had made Everest a "British mountain" in the 1920s and 1930s. In May 1951 the Swiss filed application for permission to go to Everest the following year, and the Nepalese government gave it to them.[33]

Although Shipton was disappointed, he had no deep stake in the notion of Everest as a British preserve. Soon after he traveled to Zurich and generously advised the Swiss climbers on the best route for their attempt. Back in London there were last-minute efforts by the Himalayan Committee to salvage some sort of British role in this decisive moment in the epic of Everest. Perhaps, it suggested, Shipton could serve as a coleader on the 1952 expedition, and perhaps British climbers could join the climbing party. The Swiss did not flatly reject these proposals, for they respected Shipton and may have felt they could benefit from British help in the Khumbu Icefall. Negotiations dragged on through December but in the end came to nothing. Another proposed compromise, allowing the Swiss to make the premonsoon attempt in the spring, followed by a postmonsoon attempt in the autumn by the British, was vetoed by the Nepalese government. The Swiss, and only the Swiss, would be allowed to attempt Everest in 1952.[34]

Cho Oyu Reconnaissance

As consolation, the Nepalese awarded the British permission to launch their own Everest expedition in 1953.[35] They also gave permission for the British to attempt another mountain of their choosing in 1952, so the year would not be spent idly. The veterans of the 1951 reconnaissance decided to tackle the world's eighth-highest mountain, Cho Oyu (26,905ft/8,201m), which lies seventeen miles to the northwest of Everest. Like Everest, Cho Oyu sat astride the Nepalese-Tibetan border. The area was well known to the Sherpas, who frequently crossed the 18,754-foot Nangpa La, which lies just to the mountain's west and was the main trade route between the Solu Khumbu and Tibet. It had been approached but never reconnoitered by the 1921 Everest expedition. In the 1951 Everest reconnaissance, Murray and Bourdillon scouted Cho Oyu for possible routes, crossing the Nangpa

La onto the Kyetrak Glacier (later known as the Gyabrag Glacier) in Tibet and taking a close-up look at the north side. Shipton and Ward had also identified a possible route on the south side.

As the first full-scale British expedition since before the war, Cho Oyu would be a good shakedown for the 1953 Everest expedition, a chance to test both men and equipment. And if the mountain could be climbed, so much the better. The Himalayan Committee put Shipton in command. He would be joined again by Hillary, Riddiford, and Bourdillion. Newcomers on the expedition included Campbell Secord, Charles Evans, Alfred Gregory, Roy Colledge, and New Zealander George Lowe. Another addition was Dr. Lewis Griffith Cresswell Evans Pugh, who had helped train ski troops during the Second World War at the British Army's mountain warfare school in Lebanon and after the war joined a British naval expedition to the Arctic, where he studied physiological reactions to extreme environments. Drawing on his wartime research on high-altitude physiology, Pugh planned to conduct a three-week series of tests on Cho Oyu on the climbers and their oxygen equipment. His larger goal was to solve the problem of the last 1,000 feet on Everest, enabling climbers to break through the barrier of 28,000 feet, which had stopped all the prewar expeditions, by figuring out how to improve the delivery of oxygen by artificial means at high altitude.[36]

The expedition established Base Camp on April 29 at 18,500 feet in the Bhote Kosi Valley to the southwest of Cho Oyu. The party made an initial attempt on the mountain via the Southwest Ridge. When this proved unproductive, Hillary, Lowe, and several Sherpas made a quick crossing of the Nangpa La to get another look at the northwest approach. They spotted a route they thought would work. Although Hillary acknowledged the possibility of being caught "like rats in a trap" if Chinese soldiers from the garrison at Tingri spotted them, he argued for boldness. But Shipton remained reluctant to run the risk of a full-scale attempt from the Tibetan side of the mountain.[37]

He finally agreed to allow Hillary, Bourdillion, Gregory, Secord, and Lowe to return to the northern side of the mountain to see how far they could get in a quick foray. But he would not allow them to establish any interim camps to stockpile supplies on the Tibetan side. If they wished to reach the summit, they would have to climb with what they and their Sherpas could carry on their backs in an alpine-style thrust. "The length of our communications and the limits of our mobility would make a powerful attempt impossible," Hillary wrote of the decision, "and I think that we were already doomed to failure." From their high camp at 21,500 feet they did what they could, but in the end were halted at 22,400 feet by a difficult ice cliff. Lacking the supplies for the siege tactics necessary to tackle the obstacle, they returned to Base Camp on the Nepalese side on May 12. Although members of the expedition accounted for eleven first ascents on peaks ranging between 21,000 and 23,000 feet, upon leaving Cho Oyu, Hillary felt "almost a sense of shame that we'd allowed ourselves to admit defeat so readily."[38] It was not a good portent for the forthcoming British expedition to Everest.

Swiss Attempt on Everest

Whether there would be any British expedition to Everest in 1953 was a question now in the hands of their Swiss rivals. Dr. Edouard Wyss-Dynant and René Dittert had first discussed the possibility of a Swiss expedition to Everest at the conclusion of their 1949 foray to Nepal. Now they were on their way, with Wyss-Dynant as expedition leader and Dittert as climbing leader.[39] Nine climbers, three scientists, and fourteen Sherpas made up the expedition, cosponsored by the Swiss Foundation for Alpine Research, the City and Canton of Geneva, and L'Androsace, the Geneva mountaineering club. André Roch was the most experienced Himalayan climber on the expedition, at least among the Swiss. But no one could match the experience of Tenzing Norgay, serving as sirdar on his fifth trip to the mountain.

Tenzing knew several of the Swiss climbers from previous expeditions. One of those new to him was Raymond Lambert. A Geneva guide, Lambert had survived being trapped in a crevasse high on Mont Blanc for five days in 1938. As a result of the ordeal, he had lost the tips of four fingers and all of his toes to frostbite, which is why Lambert's name had come to mind to Louis Lachenal on Annapurna two years before as a cautionary example. Lambert's injuries did not, however, stop him from continuing to guide and climb at the highest levels in specially designed shortened climbing boots. Lambert appealed to the Sherpas. His lack of self-pity regarding his maimed feet had something to do with it. The Sherpas also admired his combination of mountaineering professionalism and personal openness. Tenzing was particularly taken with him and would later describe Lambert as "the closest and dearest of my friends."[40]

The Swiss expedition set out from Kathmandu on March 29. The path the Swiss took to Everest that spring, traveling east until they hit the Dudh Kosi River then following it north through the villages of Lukla, Ghat, and Namche Bazar and finally bending north-east to Tengboche and on to Everest (and, as Tenzing would add, "always up and down, up and down"), would become the standard mountaineering, and later trekking, route.[41]

On April 20 the expedition established their Base Camp below the Khumbu Glacier by a small lake known as Gorak Shep. They would soon shift it higher, to a site directly on the glacier at 17,225 feet. They began the attack on the icefall on April 25. It had held up the British for nearly a month in 1951. The Swiss, enjoying the advantage of Shipton's advice and precedent, secured a passage to its top in just four days. Like Shipton's party, the Swiss found their path to the Western Cwm blocked by a giant crevasse, but unlike Shipton they were prepared to tackle it. Swiss climber Jean-Jacques Asper climbed down sixty feet to a snow bridge in the crevasse and gingerly made his way across it to the other side. He then climbed up the far side and secured the ropes he carried. The climbers soon had an elaborate rope bridge set up, which permitted laden porters to cross. Every step they took up the mountain from that point on would make mountaineering history. "With the Khumbu conquered," Dittert wrote, "we were certain, not of getting to the top, but of climbing high."[42]

Raymond Lambert and Tenzing Norgay on Everest, 1952.
Courtesy of the Swiss Foundation for Alpine Research.

To climb high, the Swiss would have to lay siege to the mountain. Dittert, a native son of the only mountaineering nation that had fought no wars in the twentieth century, was a reluctant convert to the language of martial conquest that had traditionally been employed on Everest expeditions:

> Headquarters! Operations!—and I, who had always smiled at this military language when I found it in stories of the Himalaya, was using it too! Whether I wished it or not, the concept of a campaign was forced upon me more strongly every day. . . . my previous Himalayan experience had made me a convinced adept of light expeditions. Like Tilman and Shipton, I thought it necessary to sacrifice weight for speed, but here one was dimly aware from the start that the problem was different. One would not dream of pushing an assault party forward recklessly, carrying eight or ten days' provisions, taking with them a few Sherpas and transporting their camping equipment a little higher every day. The distances are too great, the defences too powerful. It is necessary to occupy the conquered terrain, that each camp established shall be sufficiently provided with equipment and food to become in some degree another base camp. . . . To put a party of four men in fighting condition above 26,000 feet requires three hundred men at the start in Katmandu. More or less the proportions of war.[43]

Now that the route was open to the Western Cwm, the siege could begin in earnest. Sherpas ferried supplies through the icefall and over the rope bridge, while the Swiss climbers pushed ahead, establishing Camps III, IV, and V in the Western Cwm, the highest just below Lhotse Face at 22,639 feet, established May 11.

The first two weeks of May had been mild by Everest standards; indeed, the climbers were bothered by the midday heat trapped in the cwm by the surrounding mountain walls. The walls also seemed to shut out all noise, except the occasional sound of an avalanche roaring down one or another of the mountain faces; the Swiss called it the Valley of Silence. By mid-May they were ready to begin their push up to the South Col, which lay nearly 3,500 vertical feet above Camp V. As they gazed up at the South Col from below, the Swiss decided to ignore Shipton's advice, which had been to angle their way up Lhotse Face in a long traverse to the col. Instead, they would attempt a more direct route, straight up the face, alongside a black rocky buttress that began at about 24,000 feet and ran up to a high point looking down on the col. They named it l'Eperon des genevois, or Geneva Spur.[44]

On May 15 Dittert, Roch, Lambert, and Tenzing began the ascent to the South Col. They made good progress on their first day, reaching the foot of the spur and working their way up its right side. However, they soon discovered the principal disadvantage of their route, which was that it offered no place suitable for an intermediate camp. It would be a long haul from Camp V to the South Col.

For the next week they worked to secure the route, fixing ropes beside the spur and beginning to ferry supplies up to a small supply dump they established at 24,600 feet. On May 21 the weather turned bad, with gale force winds and a foot of new snow, a reminder that time was running out before the onset of the monsoon.

From this point on, two things became increasingly clear: that the ascent was not going according to plan and that the progress the Swiss continued to make up the mountain was largely dependent upon Tenzing's efforts. On May 25 Lambert, René Aubert, Leon Flory, Tenzing, and six other Sherpas set off from Camp V, hoping to reach the col before nightfall. But three of the Sherpas dropped out en route from either altitude sickness or incipient frostbite. After ten hours of climbing, the remaining climbers were still hundreds of feet below the col and approaching exhaustion. The sun had dropped behind Pumori and darkness was fast approaching. Finding a small hollow in the snow slope, they hacked out platforms for an emergency bivouac at 25,600 feet and spent a sleepless night, the three Swiss climbers huddled together in one two-man tent, the four Sherpas in another. In the darkness Tenzing brought tea, biscuits, and cheese to the sahibs, and the next morning brought them cups of hot chocolate. "Fine day, Sahibs!" Tenzing announced cheerfully.[45] He was the only one of the four Sherpas who showed any interest in going higher. Two of the Sherpas agreed to ferry gear up to the bivouac site that they had been forced to leave further down the slope when the other Sherpas had turned back the day before. The third remained idle, sick and miserable in his sleeping bag.

Tenzing, Aubert, Flory, and Lambert pushed on alone up the Geneva Spur. When they reached its top, they were actually looking down on the South Col from an elevation 200 feet higher. The Swiss climbers climbed down to the col, where the wind forced them to move about on all fours, "clinging to the earth like insects," as Lambert would later write, as they struggled to erect the tents of Camp VI. It took them two hours. Tenzing, meanwhile, had climbed back down to the bivouac site, where he shamed the reluctant Sherpas into continuing on up to the South Col. He made three separate trips down to the bivouac site that day to bring up more supplies.[46]

Although they were still a long way from the summit, reaching the South Col was in itself a major achievement—at 25,854 feet, Camp VI was just 600 or so feet lower than the height of Annapurna's summit. Unlike the summit of an 8,000-meter peak, where climbers could linger for no more than a few minutes, the Swiss and Sherpa climbers could live for several days on the South Col's barren, windswept mountainscape. "I have been in many wild and lonely places in my life," Tenzing would say, "but never anywhere like the South Col."[47]

As before, when the expedition first stepped out on the Western Cwm, the climbers were making mountaineering history with every step they took. Looking up at the summit ridge leading to the top of Everest from an angle never before beheld by human observers, they could not see their ultimate goal. The true summit of Everest was blocked by a small subsidiary dome, the South Summit, at what Lambert would estimate from below was 28,200 feet (actually 28,710 feet). Clouds filled the lands below them, with only the peaks of Kangchenjunga and Makalu rising above them in the distance. They were short of gear, and the three Sherpas whom Tenzing had coerced up to the col were feeling the effects of altitude and refused to carry any higher.

Increasingly anxious about the impending arrival of the monsoon, the Swiss climbers decided to push on up the Southeast Ridge on May 27. While the three other Sherpas headed down to the relative comforts of Camp V, Tenzing packed a tent in his rucksack and set out with Lambert, Flory, and Aubert. The original plan was to climb as high as they could that day in a reconnaissance, pitch the tent as a high camp, and return to the col for the night. But as they were climbing, Lambert and Tenzing each independently decided it would be foolish to return to the South Col when they were so near the summit. When they reached a height that Lambert estimated at 27,560 feet a little after 4:00 P.M., they came to a small rocky platform with room enough for their one tent. Tenzing pointed to the site and said to Lambert, "Sahib, we ought to stay here tonight."[48] Lambert readily agreed. When Flory and Aubert joined them a few minutes later, Lambert told them of the new plan. There was room for only two in the tent, so Flory and Aubert wished the others good luck and headed back to the South Col.

Lambert and Tenzing were now ensconced at Camp VII. It was a meager camp from which to attempt the conquest of the world's highest mountain. The Swiss had learned to use the language of siege warfare in their assault on the mountain: as René Dittert would say, the challenge of Everest was to "put a party of four men in fighting condition above 26,000 feet."[49] But now they were down to two men, and those two lacked what they required to be in anything like fighting condition the next day. They had a tent but no sleeping bag, no stove, little food, and not enough bottled oxygen. They melted a little water over a candle flame and huddled together for warmth.

After a long, sleepless night, Lambert and Tenzing set off the next morning at

6:00 A.M., May 28, in a chilly mist, carrying enough oxygen to last for six hours. Their oxygen equipment proved faulty. In the intense cold the valves stiffened, and the climbers found they could draw oxygen into their lungs only when they were at rest, not when they were laboring to climb. "We felt our legs grow even heavier and become like lead," Lambert would write, "while our brains also solidified and lost their faculties. From time to time the fog enveloped us and we were afraid of being caught by the storm. At moments we could see Lhotse, but it was sinking more and more into cloud."[50]

Five and a half hours of hard climbing gained them 650 feet—which, if Lambert's estimates were correct, would put them at 28,210 feet, a new altitude record. In fact, they were probably about 300 feet lower than their estimate, having overestimated the height of their high camp. They were high on the mountain, but they had not surpassed the record set by Norton back in 1924, who had reached 28,126 feet without oxygen. They could go on until their oxygen ran out, which would not be long, and then perhaps continue without it. But, given the hour and their physical condition and the unknowns that lay ahead of them, the risk was too great. "If I had ignored that imperious, unmistakable signal which drew me towards the valleys as the shepherd's horn draws the strayed flock in the mountains," Lambert would write, "we should have disappeared, just as Mallory and Irvine disappeared for ever one evening in the year 1924; for they also must have heard that warning, though they did not wish to listen to it."[51] Lambert and Tenzing looked at each other, came to a wordless agreement to live another day, and turned back.

A second assault party led by Dittert moved up to the South Col the following day, but bad weather and physical deterioration sapped the climbers' spirits. On June 1 they abandoned their camp and headed down the mountain. On the way out Dittert was asked if he regretted not getting to the summit. And although it sounds a little too magnanimous to be true (even for so virtuous a people as the Swiss), Dittert said he had no regrets: "I think we have done some good work. On Everest one expedition climbs on the shoulders of the other. We climbed upon the shoulders of Shipton. He climbed on those of Houston. Those who come after will climb on ours. It's only right."[52]

Postmonsoon Attempt

Gabrielle Chevalley led the fall expedition, departing from Kathmandu on September 10. This was the first postmonsoon expedition that set out with the goal of actually climbing Everest. Lambert was back, along with Tenzing. In addition to serving as sirdar, Tenzing was also a full member of the climbing team, the first Sherpa to be awarded that distinction. Four other Swiss climbers and the Swiss American filmmaker Norman Dyhrenfurth (son of Swiss geologist Gunther Dyhrenfurth) were on the expedition. Learning from their mistakes in the spring, they brought along improved oxygen equipment. And after an initial attempt to return to the South Col via the Geneva Spur, they switched their efforts to the route Shipton had recommended, up the Lhotse Face.

But ill luck and tragedy dogged their efforts. On October 31, before they abandoned the Geneva Spur route, Sherpa Mingma Dorje was fatally injured when he was caught in falling debris from a collapsing serac on the northern edge of the Lhotse Face. His was the fourteenth death recorded on the mountain and the first on the south side. Tenzing dug his grave. Three other Sherpas were injured in a 600-foot fall off the Lhotse Face later that same day. It was November 19 before they finally reached the South Col, and winter weather with its sixty-mile-an-hour winds soon put an end to the expedition. "Had we persisted," Lambert wrote in the official expedition account, "there would now be four or five dead men at the Col."[53]

In London the news of the Swiss defeat was received with quiet satisfaction: the British would get their turn at Everest after all. As the Swiss climbers prepared to go home, Lambert asked Tenzing if he would return to Everest the following year with the British expedition. He had already been contacted over the summer by Eric Shipton, who was eager to recruit him as sirdar for the expedition, an invitation that was renewed by Charles Wylie in the fall. Ill and exhausted by two attempts on the mountain, Tenzing said he would prefer to wait until the Swiss again attempted Everest. Lambert thought he should reconsider. "Take the chance," he urged. "It doesn't matter who it is with." Lambert gave him the red scarf he had around his neck and then hugged him good-bye. Tenzing wept at their parting.[54]

While the Swiss were making their second attempt on the south side of Everest, another expedition may have been having far greater difficulties on the north side of the mountain. In the fall of 1951 rumors reached the West of Soviet plans to launch a secret assault on the old North Col route of Everest the following year. Although both Soviet and Chinese officials later denied its existence, it is possible that a large Soviet mountaineering expedition departed Moscow for Everest in mid-October 1952. Soviet climbers were rumored to have established a high camp at 26,800 feet when the expedition leader, Dr. Pawel Datschnolian, and five other climbers disappeared. Rumors of the disaster were carried to the West by Tibetans climbing over the Nangpa La. No trace of the Russian climbers has ever been found.[55]

The British Choose a Leader

While other expeditions to Everest foundered, the British began serious preparations for their own attempt. The stakes of failure were higher than for any of the prewar British expeditions. In those days the failure of any single expedition did not preclude the eventual possibility of a British first ascent, since no one else could snatch the prize away in the meantime. That was no longer the case. The Swiss had almost succeeded in the spring of 1952, and if the British did not climb Everest in 1953 it would be the French who had the next chance at it in 1954—and to see the mountain go to those traditional rivals, who already claimed the honor of having climbed the first 8,000-meter peak, would be even more humiliating than losing out to the Swiss.

When the British expedition to Cho Oyu ended, Shipton stayed in Nepal to do what he liked best, wander through still more unexplored territory. Some of his wanderings were in Hillary's company. Hillary noted that once Shipton had shed "the cares of a large expedition," he was "a new man and reveled in the type of expedition in which he excelled." Most of the other members of the party returned home before Shipton, to England and New Zealand. And some went home bearing a grudge. Soon after his return to London, Campbell Secord wrote to the Himalayan Committee to complain of Shipton's failures as a leader on Cho Oyu, his criticisms endorsed by Griffith Pugh, Alf Gregory, and Earle Riddiford. Secord found a sympathetic hearing among some members of the committee, who were dismayed by the contrast between the Swiss near triumph on Everest and what seemed a halfhearted British effort on Cho Oyu. Shipton, it was said, "lacked drive," and what was needed was "new blood."[56]

Those dissatisfied with Shipton began considering alternate leaders. The candidate who aroused the most enthusiasm was Colonel John Hunt, a veteran of the Indian Army then stationed with British occupation forces in Germany. Born in India, an Alpine Club member since 1935, Hunt was a veteran climber with experience in the Karakoram as well as the Alps. (He had reached an altitude of 24,500 feet on Saltoro Kangri in 1935.) He had been provisionally selected for the 1936 Everest expedition, only to be rejected after a cardiograph at his medical exam turned up a false report of a heart murmur. During the war he had been an instructor at the Commando Mountain and Snow Warfare school in Braemar before gaining a combat command in Italy.[57]

Among Hunt's other qualifications, he spoke Urdu, which would be understandable in Nepal, where people spoke a related language. He was also known as a master of logistics and was currently involved in planning for British Army maneuvers in Germany. Finally, he was friendly with some members of the Himalayan Committee. Basil Goodfellow, honorary secretary of the committee, had met Hunt in the Alps in the summer of 1951, and they had spent several pleasant weeks climbing together. Goodfellow took it upon himself to write to Hunt in early July, telling him, "Most people feel a new leader is required and your name stands out."[58] The "most people" was a telling phrase; the Himalayan Committee as a whole had not yet agreed on the need for a new leader, let alone that it should be Hunt. Shipton still had influential supporters within the group, including Sir Laurence Kirwan, secretary of the Royal Geographical Society.

Shipton returned to England unaware that his position as leader of the coming expedition was in jeopardy. A meeting with the Himalayan Committee on July 28 at the Alpine Club headquarters, a week after his return, did nothing to enlighten him. Two of his more determined opponents on the committee, Basil Goodfellow and Colonel Harry Tobin, editor of the *Himalayan Journal,* were absent, and no one present, including Himalayan Committee president Claude Elliott, took on the unpleasant task of sharing their doubts with Shipton. They had a perfect opening to do so: Shipton himself expressed concerns about his own qualifications, reiterating his own well-known preference for small, lightweight expeditions, which the 1953 venture clearly would not be. But the committee reassured him that he was still its choice as leader. He proposed taking along Dr. Charles Evans as a coleader, and came away with the impression that the committee approved of his choice.[59]

There was, of course, nothing new about leadership struggles on Everest expeditions. Young Turks were always seeking to overthrow the incompetent relics who had led previous expeditions. What was different this time was the degree to which the relic in question was kept in the dark about the nature and source of the challenge to his leadership. Although no one at the July 28 meeting was prepared to discomfort a revered figure like Shipton with anything like a direct criticism, theirs was a tactfulness that bordered on bad faith.[60]

In July Basil Goodfellow had offered John Hunt the position of organizing secretary on the expedition. The role of organizing secretary was to provide administrative support for the expedition leader. Hunt would have been very happy to take on the position, but he was even more enthusiastic when Claude Elliott wrote to him shortly afterward with the offer of deputy leadership of the expedition. Shipton was not consulted on either offer, although he would not have objected to Hunt as organizing secretary. But he still assumed that, as he had discussed with the Himalayan Committee on July 28, Charles Evans would serve as his deputy on the expedition. And so, on August 22, when Hunt and Shipton met at the Royal Geographical Society, Shipton was taken aback by Hunt's assumption that the two of them would be running the expedition jointly. It was, Hunt would write, "a sadly disillusioning encounter" and "like 1936 all over again," referring to the year he had been rejected from an earlier Everest expedition, led by Hugh Ruttledge. Hunt returned to duty in Germany convinced his last chance to play a role in the conquest of Everest had been lost.[61]

But it was Shipton, not Hunt, who would lose out in the end. The final blow fell at the September 11 meeting of the Himalayan Committee. This time it was Shipton's allies, Laurence Kirwan of the Royal Geographical Society and geologist Lawrence Wager (veteran of the 1933 Everest expedition), who were absent. Shipton was asked to leave the room while the committee deliberated his fate. When he was allowed to return, an hour later, he was presented with an ultimatum; he could continue to play a role in 1953 only if he accepted the position of "Co-Leader" with John Hunt. Once the expedition reached Everest Base Camp, Shipton would have to surrender even that diminished authority: Hunt would function as sole leader of the expedition when the actual climbing began. Shipton was told that "the Himalayan committee felt it was necessary to recognize that the Everest expedition was of national importance" and thus deserved "a man of dynamic personality, drive and enthusiasm" in its leadership.[62]

Clearly the committee no longer believed that Shipton possessed such personal qualifications; his role on the expedition would be purely ceremonial. "Then, for the first time," Shipton would later write, "it dawned on me that there must have been a great deal of backroom diplomacy since the last meeting, of which I had been totally unaware."[63] Without waiting for Shipton's reply, the committee sent a telegram that same day to Hunt, asking him to assume leadership.

Shipton wrote to Himalayan Committee president Claude Elliott two days later to announce his "reluctant but firm conclusion" that he would "not join the expedition" under such circumstances. Were he to accompany the expedition in the role of titular leader, as proposed by the Himalayan Committee, the result would only be "an embarrassment to the [real] leader, a possible source of friction in the party, of conflicting loyalties and divided council."[64]

Shipton was humiliated by the position he had been placed in by the Himalayan Committee. He was also left jobless, at age forty-six, and some bad years followed for him of marginal employment and marital problems, until he reemerged as an explorer of Patagonia in the late 1950s. In his public statements about the expedition, Shipton hid his bitterness, passing off his resignation as the product of a "friendly difference of opinion." The following spring he wrote an article about the Everest expedition for the American magazine *Colliers* in which he made light of the differences that led to his replacement: "The present expedition of 12 climbers is one of the largest ever to make the Everest try. I prefer smaller parties, which is one reason I did not go along (we mountaineers have strong opinions on our hobby)."[65]

When news of Shipton's ouster broke, there was an uproar in the mountaineering community. Tom Bourdillon, who had agreed with Shipton on the need for caution on Cho Oyu, was so angry that he wrote to the Himalayan Committee to resign from the 1953 expedition; Shipton, however, persuaded him to reconsider. Hillary was also upset, writing to Harry Ayres that "Everest never will sound quite the same without Shipton." Others, however, while regretting Shipton's all-too-public humiliation, understood the committee's reasoning in bringing on a new leader. As Bill Murray wrote confidentially to his sister Margaret: "[W]hile [Shipton] excels at running small expeditions which set out without plans . . . and seize chances as they come, he is no leader for a big party employing siege tactics. This is no discredit to Shipton. He is unrivalled as a Himalayan mountaineer and his is a truer mountaineering than laying siege to one big peak. . . . But I have no doubt that Hunt is the better leader for Everest."[66]

John Hunt's Expedition

Hunt arrived back in London on October 8 and with characteristic energy soon had expeditionary headquarters up and running in two rooms in the Royal Geographical Society, overlooking Kensington Gardens. Among the many matters competing for his attention personnel questions were the most important—and awkward. Hunt was being pressed to accept more climbers from New Zealand (Shipton had already extended invitations to Hillary, Lowe, and famed New Zealand guide Harry Ayres), and the Himalayan Committee had, somewhat halfheartedly, told the American Alpine Club the previous spring that there might be room for one or two Americans on the expedition as well. Hunt would have none of it; he would take Hillary and Lowe, since they had already taken part in earlier expeditions, but no newcomers from New Zealand like Ayres, and no Americans whatsoever. "The reason for this," Basil Goodfellow wrote to New Zealander Earle Riddiford, who had asked that more New Zealanders be included, "is that Hunt feels (and we agree with him) that it is of the most vital importance . . . to have the party as far as possible welded into one unit before they leave Britain. This welding implies not only that the party should know each other and should have had a chance to climb with each other, even if only in the U.K., or in Switzerland in winter, but also that the special clothing and oxygen equipment which is virtually being tailormade must be fitted to each man, and tested by him in the field. Clearly to have even two members from New Zealand joining the party for the first time in the field jeopardizes the efficiency of these arrangements. To increase the number beyond two would be quite unjustifiable."[67]

With Shipton's departure, the last remaining personal connection among the British climbers going to Everest in 1953 with the prewar Everest expeditions was severed. The final party would consist of John Hunt; the two New Zealanders, Hillary and Lowe; a number of other veterans of the 1951 and 1952 Shipton expeditions, including Charles Evans, Tom Bourdillion, and Alfred Gregory; plus Michael Ward as expedition medical officer and Griffith Pugh as physiologist. Newcomers included George Band, a geology student at Cambridge University and, at twenty-two, the youngest member of the expedition; Michael Westmacott, a statistician at Rothamsted Experimental Station and president of the Oxford University Mountaineering Club; Wilfrid Noyce, a veteran of many Himalayan expeditions and master of Charterhouse School; and Charles Wylie, along with Hunt the other serving military officer on the expedition—a major in the Tenth Gurkha Rifles on leave to serve as organizing secretary for the expedition. Tom Stobart, a veteran outdoor filmmaker, would be cameraman for the expedition film. James Morris, a correspondent from *The Times,* would join the expedition in Nepal as reporter. (It was a mark of the importance already attached to the upcoming attempt that *The Times* decided to send its own reporter; on all previous British expeditions to Everest, the expedition leader had had the responsibility of sending off dispatches to the newspaper.)[68] And, after the Swiss returned from their postmonsoon expedition, the British were able to secure Tenzing Norgay's agreement to join the expedition as sirdar.

The 1953 British Everest expedition was not planned on the back of an envelope, as per the famous Shipton-Tilman formula. It was a meticulously planned and lavish operation. *The Times* provided £10,000 funding in exchange for exclusive coverage from the mountainside. The newspaper expected to get a good return on its investment; thanks to the French success on Annapurna, the popularity of Herzog's book about the expedition, and the Swiss near success on Everest in 1952, public interest in the upcoming Everest expedition was greater than at any time since the 1920s. The actual cost of sending the

John Hunt and Geoffrey Winthrop Young, 1953.
Reprinted by permission of the Alpine Club Library.

British party to Everest would run to double the amount provided by *The Times*. Public donations, plus direct and indirect government subsidies, made up the difference.[69]

Starting in October 1952, as Wilfrid Noyce would recall, and continuing until the expedition boarded ship for Bombay in mid-February, "we received almost daily sheafs of instructions, programmmes, schedules, allocations, emanating from John Hunt and Charles Wylie."[70] Hunt had studied the Swiss failure on the mountain in the spring of 1952 closely and was determined to avoid the mistake of getting high on the mountain without sufficient logistical support for the summit teams. The French had brought three and half tons of equipment with them on their 1950 expedition to Annapurna; the Swiss brought more than four tons to Everest in the spring of 1952; the British would bring thirteen tons with them in 1953. Hunt's greatest achievement on the Everest expedition was in figuring out how to order, pack, and deliver (on the appropriate day and to the appropriate elevation on the mountainside) that mass of material. During the fall of 1952 he drew up provisional plans for where each climber and supply item would be on the mountainside on "X-Day," the start of the assault, "X+1," and so on, until the summit would be reached. Afterward, Hunt would devote two separate chapters in his expedition account to planning and equipment, titled with brisk efficiency "Preparations: One" and "Preparations: Two."

One of the ways in which a Hunt expedition differed from a Shipton expedition was the attention paid to food. In the 1930s, under Shipton and Tilman, the diet of the

Everest expeditions had relied heavily on local food supplies, especially bulky foods like rice, potatoes, and tsampa. Shipton had followed the same dietary strategy on the expeditions he led to Nepal in 1951 and 1952. Tom Bourdillion, who had lost thirty-five pounds on the 1951 reconnaissance, suggested that in planning for the 1953 expedition "the most important point about food is that there should be some." Hunt saw to it that the climbers were well supplied with a diet that, although drawn from military rations, included canned meats and fish, bacon, eggs, butter, cheese, fruit, coffee, and even fruitcake. (Hunt himself would report gaining five pounds in the first few weeks on the mountain.)[71]

The climbers would be equipped with the latest in high-altitude clothing, including cotton-nylon windproof outer garments that could be worn over down jackets and pants. Herzog's *Annapurna* account of postexpeditionary surgery was fresh in the minds of the climbers, so special attention was paid to footwear. Each climber was issued two pairs of boots: a lighter pair for lower on the mountain and a heavier pair with nearly an inch of kapok insulation and specially designed insulating soles for use higher on the mountain. Also reflecting the influence of Herzog's experience, climbers were issued lightweight silk gloves to be worn under heavier outer gloves; the outer layers could be shed to perform intricate tasks like tinkering with oxygen sets or strapping on crampons, while the silk gloves still provided a measure of protection against frostbite.[72]

The most intense preparations were those involving oxygen. In the 1920s and 1930s the British had never quite made up their minds about bottled oxygen; some of the highest forays on the north side of Everest were done without it. This time, Hunt decreed, all high-altitude climbing, by British climbers and Sherpas alike, would be with use of bottled oxygen, which would also be used for sleeping at high altitude. Based on the study conducted on the 1952 Cho Oyu expedition, Griffith Pugh recommended that when climbers were climbing high on the mountain they should be using oxygen at a rate of four liters a minute, double the rate used on the prewar expeditions. This meant that the expedition would need to haul in a prodigious supply of bottled oxygen, 173,000 liters all told (compared to the 25,000 liters the Swiss had brought along in the spring of 1952).[73]

The expedition would carry two different types of bottled oxygen systems: twelve open-circuit sets and eight closed-circuit sets. With the older open-circuit set, climbers breathed a mixture of bottled oxygen and the surrounding air. Each breath of oxygen from the tank diminished the remaining supply, since the climber expelled his breath into the atmosphere. With the newer closed-circuit system, the climber breathed pure oxygen, unmixed with air from outside the system. Instead of simply expelling his breath into the atmosphere, he breathed into a tube that carried the expelled breath to a soda-lime canister that cleansed it of CO_2, and thus allowed some of the oxygen to be recirculated and reused. The advantages of the closed-circuit system were that the climber breathed 100 percent oxygen, effecting a physiological altitude of sea level or even lower and enabling a longer use of a canister of oxygen than with the open-circuit system. The disadvantages of the closed-circuit system were greater weight, complexity, a tendency for valves to freeze shut, the discomfort of a tight mask, and the theoretical concern that sudden failure of the system could have far more drastic consequences to the climber—being suddenly transported from sea level to 28,000–29,000 feet—than the open-circuit transition from perhaps 20,000 feet or so to the same ambient altitude. The Swiss had used a closed-circuit system in the spring of 1952, abandoning it for a more reliable open-circuit system in the fall. Tom Bourdillon, however, remained a strong proponent of the closed-circuit system, and Hunt was willing to submit both systems to the ultimate test on Everest.[74]

Finally, all the preparations were made, and it was time to depart. This was the ninth British expedition to leave for Everest, the seventh to set off with the intention of climbing to the summit. Most of the British contingent of the expedition left England on February 12, 1953, traveling by sea, because Hunt thought that a long voyage would give expedition members the opportunity to become acquainted. In Kathmandu the British party was joined by the two New Zealanders and by a contingent of twenty Sherpas, led by sirdar Tenzing Norgay. More Sherpas would be recruited en route to the mountain, bringing the total to thirty-six.

Tenzing was a source of great interest to the British and New Zealand climbers. His contributions to the Swiss expeditions were well known and led Hunt to invite him to join as a full member of the climbing party. Wilfrid Noyce recalled his first impression of Tenzing: "There was his now famous shy smile, showing whitest teeth, as he shook hands with the sahibs. . . . He looked much larger than the other Sherpas, and his dress of military-style shorts and puttees, topped by a green beret, gave him a more commanding appearance."[75]

There had been some trouble in the fall in recruiting Sherpas for the expedition, a product of ill feeling left over a pay dispute dating back to the 1951 Everest reconnaissance. The Himalayan Club, which had traditionally overseen the labor market for Sherpa porters and climbers, found its power to set rates of pay eroding. As C. E. J. Crawford reported from India in October 1952 to Harry Tobin in London: "Ever since the war with the growing popularity of the Himalayas there has been a steady 'spoiling of the market'; the Swiss I think have been the worst 'offenders' and they really take no notice of the Club's recommended rates. . . . This, of course, is what is very much behind the dissatisfaction I have been writing about. It is rather similar to the effect of the Americans on the servant problem here during the war."[76]

The "servant problem" resurfaced in Kathmandu. Both the climbers and the Sherpas were staying at the British embassy, since there were as yet no real hotels in Kathmandu. However, while the climbers stayed in the embassy, the Sherpas were consigned to the garage, a former stable offering little in the way of comfort, including toilets. The Sherpas made their dissatisfaction known by urinating in the street outside the embassy. The decision to lodge the Sherpas in the garage had been made by the embassy staff, not the expedition leaders, but Hunt made matters worse by reprimanding the Sherpas for relieving themselves in public. The whole episode was symptomatic of deeper issues, as far as Tenzing was concerned. The "English in general are more reserved and formal" than other

Europeans, Tenzing would tell James Ramsey Ullman, "and especially is this so . . . with people not of their own race." Tenzing attributed this trait to the fact that "they have so long been rulers in the East." Tenzing had made good English friends over the years and admired them as brave and fair: "But always, too, there is a line between them and the outsider, between sahib and employee, and to such Easterners, as we Sherpas, who have experienced the world of no-line, this can be a difficulty and a problem."[77]

The expedition departed Kathmandu in two waves, on March 10 and 11. A total of 350 porters carried supplies for the expedition (a month later there would be a second delivery to Everest by the porters). Seventeen days of hiking brought them to Tengboche, where a preliminary Base Camp was established. After sorting equipment, the climbers and Sherpas set out in small parties for three weeks of acclimatizing exploration and climbs.[78]

Hillary led a small advance group up the Khumbu Glacier to reconnoiter the Khumbu Icefall, while the rest of the group came up later. They set up Camp I below the icefall on April 12. In the icefall they found flags from the last year's Swiss expedition that had been used to mark their path—now, just a few months later, completely useless because the ice had shifted so much. The climbers used an aluminum ladder brought from England to bridge the worst of the crevasses, later replaced with logs cut from forests near Tengboche. By April 16 they were able to put in Camp II midway up the icefall. The following day Hillary, George Lowe, and George Band reached its top edge. As usual, there was a large crevasse to cross before the climbers could reach the Western Cwm, but experience had taught them to come prepared. The crevasse was spanned with three sections of the aluminum ladder bolted together, avoiding the necessity for the complicated rope bridge the Swiss had made use of the previous year.[79]

Once the expedition was moving up the Western Cwm, John Hunt proved good on his promise to lead "from the front," doing his share and more of finding routes, breaking trail, and carrying supplies.[80] Camp III went in above the icefall on April 22 at 19,400 feet, followed by the establishment of Camp IV at 21,200 feet on May 1, at the site of the old Swiss camp halfway up the Western Cwm. Camp IV would serve the expedition at Advance Base Camp with a large buildup of supplies necessary for the final stages deposited there. Camp V would go in a few days later at 22,000 feet just below Lhotse Face.

Hunt wrote to his wife, Joy, on April 28 to report that "we seem to be up to schedule and able to stick to the long-determined programme." By the beginning of May the expedition was poised to begin its ascent of Lhotse's glacier, with a long upward traverse to the top of the Geneva Spur, the route that Shipton had recommended in 1951 and that the Swiss had followed on their postmonsoon expedition in 1952. With Bourdillion and Evans, Hunt made a reconnaissance of the Lhotse Face on May 2. At forty-two, Hunt was a decade older than the average age of the party and often looked drawn and tired after a day's climbing. But he was always ready the next day to carry the burden of leadership. Shipton still had admirers among the climbers, but Hunt's efficiency and stamina, as well as his personal decency, won over the doubters. Some of the climbers, including Hillary, had feared that Hunt, coming from a military background, would try to run the expedition in authoritarian fashion, but soon discovered they were mistaken. "John's instant charm was a formidable weapon in his armory," Hillary noted. "Like many leaders he was a lonely and withdrawn figure at times, but he could produce at will a warm and powerful personality." The 1953 Everest expedition was remarkable for many things, not least of which was the lack of disharmony among the climbers. "What a very happy party you've got going," Tom Bourdillion remarked to Hunt on the march in to Everest, an especially meaningful comment coming from the climber who had been the most upset by Shipton's downfall the previous year.[81] Even the Sherpas came to admire Hunt, despite his early missteps in expeditionary labor relations.

News from the mountain was slow to reach the outside world. The expedition carried walkie-talkies among its supplies, but those were good only for communicating between camps on the mountain (and then only sporadically). Correspondent James Morris sent out regular bulletins about the expedition's progress, but it took a runner six or seven days to carry them all the way back to Kathmandu, where they could be cabled by an assistant to London, finally appearing in *The Times* seven or eight days after Morris had written them. (Morris also secretly prepared and sent back to London obituaries of all the climbers, "just in case.") Even with the delay, mountaineers around the world knew as April turned to May that critical days were soon approaching on Everest. Seventy-year-old Charles Howard-Bury, leader of the first British reconnaissance of Everest back in 1921, stopped by Alpine Club headquarters soon after Hunt's party left and expressed two wishes to T. S. Blakeney, the club's assistant secretary: one, that "whoever reached the summit would find that Mallory got there first," and two, that "the ascent would coincide with the date of the Coronation" of Queen Elizabeth II, scheduled for June 2.[82]

As the climbers made their way up the Western Cwm, it was apparent to just about everyone, and certainly to John Hunt, that Tenzing, on his seventh expedition to Everest, and Hillary, on his second, were the strongest climbers. They first climbed together on April 26 and more and more often shared a rope on the day's climbing. They were not friends, exactly; Tenzing would never speak of Hillary in the glowing terms he reserved for Raymond Lambert and a few other European sahibs. But they climbed well together and shared a mutual respect.

The two made an incongruous pair, with Hillary, six feet three inches tall, towering over Tenzing, five feet eight inches tall. To careful observers, however, there were some similarities. Michael Ward said of Tenzing that he moved with "a natural grace and ease . . . characteristic of those who spend their lives traveling in the mountainous country. It seemed as if he were on oiled wheels." And Wilfrid Noyce said of Hillary, "His angular figure seemed somehow made for going uphill; fashioned into the slope as he took long easy strides up it."[83] They were as similar in their ambition as in their style. It had long been noted among European mountaineers that Tenzing was an anomaly among Sherpas in his passionate desire to get to the top of big mountains, especially Everest. And while

Hillary presented himself to the world as a simple rural beekeeper (which wasn't entirely untrue), he was highly competitive whenever he set foot on a mountain. On more than one occasion in the early days of the expedition, he pushed himself ahead of the rest at breakneck speed, for no other reason than to prove just how fit he was feeling.

On May 7, at a meeting at Base Camp, Hunt laid out his strategy for the summit assault. Once the expedition was installed on top of the South Col, two separate two-man parties would move into position for summit bids, a day apart. The first team would consist of Tom Bourdillion and Charles Evans. Using closed-circuit oxygen sets, they would climb directly from the South Col to the South Summit, or all the way to the top if they could. Meanwhile, two other climbers, in a supporting role, would make a carry up to about 28,000 feet on the Southeast Ridge to establish an assault camp. Then the second team, consisting of Hillary and Tenzing using open-circuit oxygen sets, would occupy the high camp and make their own summit bid the following day.[84]

The strategy Hunt outlined on May 7 later proved a source of controversy. Since Bourdillion and Evans were in the first assault team, it might seem reasonable to conclude that Hunt's goal was to give British mountaineers a first crack at the mountain. (Tenzing, for one, thought so and was upset that he had not been included in the first assault team.) But there is good reason to think otherwise. Before he had left England, Hunt had been told by Edward Norton, leader of the 1924 expedition, to "put your assault camp on, or very close under the Southern Summit." This reflected British practice in the 1920s and 1930s, when they pushed their high camps on the north side successively higher, whenever conditions permitted. It also reflected the Swiss strategy in 1952. Hunt said in his expedition book that Norton's suggestion was advice he would "remember particularly."[85]

Why, then, would Hunt have Bourdillion and Evans set off on their summit bid from the South Col, at 26,000 feet, instead of from the soon-to-be-established assault camp at 28,000 feet? The second team of Hillary and Tenzing would need only to ascend a little over 1,000 feet to gain the summit; the first team of Bourdillion and Evans would have to climb over 3,000 feet. The ostensible reason was that the closed-circuit oxygen system employed by the first team, although heavier, was more efficient than the open-circuit oxygen system carried by the second team. The closed-circuit system would provide Bourdillion and Evans with a richer oxygen content, which would allow them to climb faster than Hillary and Tenzing, thus eliminating the need to set off from a high camp between the South Col and the summit. However, the closed-circuit system was also notoriously prone to malfunctioning at high altitude.[86]

Hunt faced a dilemma in choosing summit parties. He had to weigh both national considerations and personal abilities in his choice. As Hillary understood, it would never have done for Hunt to pair the two New Zealanders together, though that is what they would have preferred; if Hillary and Lowe had summited, it would have been hard to portray the conquest of Everest as anything but a triumph of New Zealand *climbers,* rather than the triumph of a British *expedition.* The Hillary-Tenzing pairing did not present the same

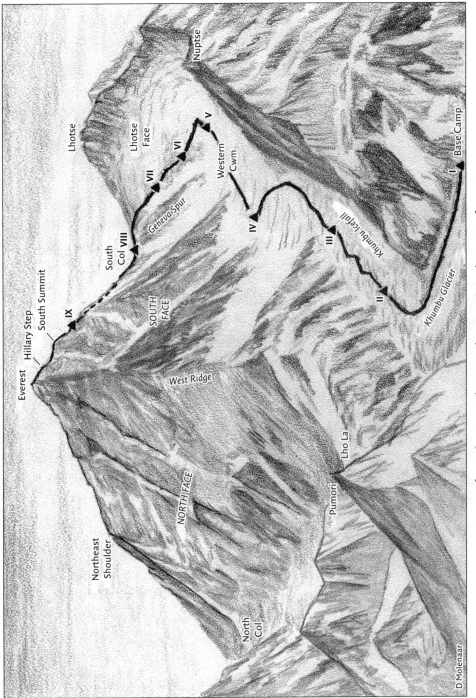

Everest from the west, showing the 1953 British route of ascent.

D. Molenaar

problem: because they shared no common national background, Tenzing, in effect, diluted Hillary's "New Zealandness," making him instead a representative of the "British Commonwealth" as well as his own homeland. By leading off with Bourdillion and Evans as the first summit pair, Hunt satisfied the requirements of British national prestige, for two British climbers would have first shot at the top. If they made it, all to the good. But if they failed (as Hunt may well have expected), then they would have cleared the way for the two strongest climbers on the expedition, Hillary and Tenzing.[87]

At the meeting on May 7 Hunt assigned Lowe, Westmacott, and Band to push the traverse up the Lhotse Face to the South Col, establishing Camps VI and VII en route; Noyce and Wylie would be in charge of leading the Sherpa parties ferrying supplies up to the South Col; and Gregory and Hunt himself would do the carry up the Southeast Ridge to establish a high camp at 28,000 feet. But for the first time on the expedition there were unexpected delays. Lowe, Westmacott, and Band all suffered from varying degrees of altitude sickness as they led the way across the Lhotse traverse, and they had bad weather to contend with on top of that. Hunt had hoped to make it up Lhotse Face in less than a week, but one week dragged on to two without their reaching the South Col. On May 20 Hunt wrote to his wife expressing frustration at the lack of progress: "The party preparing the route up the Face has unaccountably failed to finish its job—our wireless communications have broken down and we can only watch events from here [at Advanced Base Camp]. They spent all yesterday in Camp; today—as 2 days ago—they started out, only to return. It is tantalizing and desperately disappointing."[88]

The breakthrough came the next day, May 21, when Wilfrid Noyce and Sherpa Annullu finally reached the South Col. That same day Tenzing and Hillary set out from Advanced Base Camp to lend a hand in getting the flagging Sherpa parties up to the South Col, even though as members of one of the two summit parties they were supposed to be hoarding their energies for the actual summit bid. As Hunt reported to his wife: "Wilf [Noyce], one of those leading the Sherpas, had made a wonderful change in the stalemate on Lhotse Face, by going up to the South Col with one Sherpa; but it was by no means sure the rest would go up the next day (22nd). There were 14 of them up at Camp VII, and on those loads the assault depended. Only Ed and Tenzing could tip the balance, and I sent them up from Adv[ance] Base, knowing well the risk of prejudicing their effort in the second assault. But first things first, and it worked."[89]

The final stages of Hunt's plan were ready to be put in motion. Bourdillion and Evans arrived on the South Col on May 25 in preparation for their summit bid the following day. Hunt and Sherpa Da Namgyal joined them, for they would carry supplies high on the Southeast Ridge for Hillary and Tenzing's assault camp.

The next morning, May 26, Hunt and Da Namgyal were the first to head up the ridge. Bourdillion and Evans had hoped to get an early start, but it took them an hour's effort to get the frozen valves of one of the oxygen sets functioning. They finally set off at 7:30 A.M. They soon passed Hunt and Da Namgyal on the slope and climbed steadily up the ridge. They passed the site of the Swiss assault camp and the high mark of Lambert and Tenzing's climb the previous May.

Five and a half hours after setting out, Bourdillion and Evans stood on top of the South Summit of Mount Everest. They had reached a height of 28,720 feet, higher than anyone else had ever climbed on Everest, and higher than the summit of any of the other 8,000-meter peaks. They had breached a psychological as well as a physical barrier. Norton, Smythe, Harris, Wager, Lambert, and Tenzing had all halted at about 1,000 vertical feet below the summit—Bourdillion and Evans were within 300 feet of it. But ahead of them stretched a heavily corniced knife-edge ridge that looked anything but inviting. Bourdillion and Evans believed that they still faced as much as three or four hours climbing to the summit, and then many more hours to get back down to the South Col. By that time their oxygen supply would have long since been used up, and no one yet knew if it was possible to survive for long at such heights without it. In addition, Evans's oxygen set was malfunctioning. Bourdillion was tempted to go on alone, but that was something else that no one had ever done before on an 8,000-meter peak, so in the end he decided to turn back with Evans.[90]

While Bourdillion and Evans were making their summit bid, Hunt and Da Namgyal followed them up the Southeast Ridge with supplies for the high camp. They hoped to reach a snow shoulder below the South Summit at what they thought was about 28,000 feet (the feature would later be dubbed "The Balcony," and actually sits on the ridge at about 27,690 feet), but were unable to make it that far. Instead, they dropped their loads at 27,350 feet and retreated to the South Col.

While the other teams were climbing the Southeast Ridge, Hillary and Tenzing, along with Gregory, Lowe, and three Sherpas, climbed from Camp VII up to the South Col. When Hunt and Da Namgyal, exhausted, stumbled down at midday to the col, Hillary and Tenzing helped them back to the tents. Earlier in the day, when Bourdillion and Evans had been seen to reach South Summit, the Sherpas on the South Col cheered, convinced that this was the day Everest would be climbed. Tenzing and Hillary kept their thoughts to themselves, but when they saw Bourdillion and Evans arrive back at the South Col at about 4:30, exhausted and grim faced, they were both moved at the two men's suffering and secretly relieved at their failure.[91]

Bourdillion and Evans gave Hillary and Tenzing a firsthand account of what to expect on the climb to the South Summit and their impression of what lay beyond their own high point. Precisely what they had to say on those topics is not clear. As John Hunt remembered the conversation, Bourdillion and Evans described the last stretch of ridge to the summit as "formidable"; as Hillary remembered it, they said the ridge "wasn't climbable"; as Tenzing remembered it, Evans simply said, "[I]f the weather's good you'll make it. You won't have to come back again next year."[92]

The next day, May 27, was supposed to be the day Hillary and Tenzing moved up the ridge to their assault camp, but gale-strength winds sweeping down on to the col forced a delay. While Bourdillion, Evans, Hunt, and Da Namgyal retreated to Advance Base Camp in the Western Cwm, Hillary tinkered with the oxygen apparatus, and both he and Tenzing ate and drank as much as they could. The next day the weather was more promising, and the summit team, supported by Lowe, Gregory, and Sherpa Ang Nyima, set off to establish the assault camp, heavily laden with supplies.[93]

At 2:30 that afternoon they found a spot below a rock bluff at what they estimated to be 27,900 feet where the angle of the slope decreased to about thirty degrees, and decided to place Camp IX there. (They were actually at about 27,640 feet.)[94] Lowe, Gregory, and Ang Nyima dumped their loads and said farewell. Hillary and Tenzing prepared a platform on the sloping ground for their tent. After two hours of prying out loose stones, the best they could do was create two adjacent shelves as a base, the lower nearly a foot below the higher. They pitched their tent and took stock of their supplies. Although Hillary found they had less oxygen on hand than he had hoped, Bourdillion and Evans had told him that they had abandoned two partially filled bottles about 500 feet below the South Summit, which Hillary and Tenzing could use on their downward climb. If carefully rationed, it might be just enough.

When Hillary and Tenzing settled down for the night, all of John Hunt's careful planning paid off. In May 1952 Lambert and Tenzing had had little to eat and virtually nothing to drink the night before their summit bid; Hillary and Tenzing dined in their high camp on sardines, biscuits, chicken noodle soup, fresh dates, canned apricots, and hot lemon drink. And while Lambert and Tenzing had sat up the night before their summit bid, sleepless and shivering, Hillary and Tenzing settled into their sleeping bags, breathing oxygen to help them sleep. (They didn't have quite enough oxygen to use continuously through the night; instead they slept with oxygen from about 9:00 to 11:00 P.M., awoke and made themselves hot lemon drinks from 11:00 P.M. to 1:00 A.M., and then slept again with oxygen for another short stretch.)

At about 3:30 A.M. on May 29, Hillary and Tenzing began to stir. They breakfasted on hot lemon drink, coffee, biscuits, and sardines. Hillary found that his boots had frozen overnight, so he warmed them over the stove and kneaded them until they were flexible enough to fit his feet in. "I'm afraid I may get frostbitten, like Lambert," he told Tenzing, in what was perhaps an unconscious echo of Lachenal's comment to Herzog on their summit day on Annapurna three years earlier.[95] As the sun rose, they could see Tengboche Monastery 15,000 feet below them. It had been two and a half years since Tilman and Houston, standing in front of Tengboche, had gazed up at the place where they now had their camp. It had been less than a year and a half since Hillary and the British reconnaissance expedition had stood at the foot of the Western Cwm after finding a route through the Khumbu Icefall. It had been a year and a day since Tenzing and Raymond Lambert had made their own summit bid.

It was bitterly cold outside their tent, but the skies were clear and there was little wind. At 6:30 A.M., with Tenzing in the lead, the two climbers set off. The slope was steep and the snow was deep, with only a light crust covering it, through which their boots sank.

After a while, as his feet warmed, Hillary took over the lead. He gave himself a pep talk: "Ed, my boy, this is Everest—you've got to push it a bit harder!" At one point, after sliding back a few paces in the treacherously shifting snow, Hillary asked Tenzing if he thought they should continue. Tenzing replied unemotionally, "Just as you wish."[96]

They reached the South Summit at 9:00 A.M., four hours earlier than Bourdillion and Evans had gotten there three days before. They stopped to drink from their water bottles, discard a used oxygen bottle, and plot their course up the summit ridge. Hillary calculated they should have just enough oxygen to make the summit and then to return far enough to retrieve Bourdillion and Evans's discarded oxygen bottles, which had been cached a little below the South Summit, each bottle about a third full. To make sure they didn't run out before then, they adjusted the valves on their equipment to reduce their oxygen flow to three liters a minute, a liter below the consumption rate that Griffith Pugh had recommended.

Stepping off from the South Summit, they were for the first time that day on un-trodden territory. With Tenzing belaying him, Hillary cut steps up the slope. The snow was harder than below the South Summit, and Hillary was heartened. But he had to pick his steps carefully. If he strayed too far to the left he risked a fall of 8,000 feet to the Western Cwm, while if he strayed too far to the right, with its overhanging cornice, he risked a 10,000-foot drop to the Kangshung Glacier. Still, Hillary would recall, it was "exhilarating work—the summit ridge of Everest, the crisp snow and the smooth easy blows of the ice-axe all combined to make me feel a greater sense of power than I had ever felt at great altitudes before."[97]

An hour after leaving the South Summit, Hillary and Tenzing came to a high rock step. They were not surprised, for it was one of the features of the ridge visible in the RAF aerial photographs that Michael Ward had found in the Royal Geographical Society archives. How they would get up it was still a question. It was steep and smooth, forty feet high in Hillary's estimate, fifteen feet in Tenzing's (both of them underestimated the actual height; it was later measured and found to be fifty-seven feet). Merely an interesting rock climb in Wales, at nearly 29,000 feet the step posed a formidable obstacle. After looking it over for a minute, Hillary found the solution: "I noticed a long vertical crack between the rock and the ice of the cornices on the right. This crack was about 40 feet high and large enough to take the human body. I crawled into it and started jamming and forcing my way up it; my crampons on the ice behind me and my face towards the rock." If the ice behind him had given way, only Tenzing's belay from below would have kept him from falling off the mountain down 10,000 feet to the Kangshung Glacier. He levered his way up the crack to the top, which turned out to be just as far as the rope that held him from below would reach. He pulled himself up and lay on top of the rock, "panting furiously." After resting a moment, he belayed Tenzing to the top of the rock formation that thereafter would be known as the Hillary Step.[98]

After both men had caught their breath, they turned their faces to the summit. It was closing in on 11:30 A.M., May 29, 1953. Hillary was in the lead: "I had been cutting steps continually for two hours, and Tenzing, too, was moving very slowly. As I chipped steps around still another corner, I wondered rather dully just how long we could keep it up. Our original zest had now quite gone and it was turning more into a grim struggle. I then realized that the ridge ahead, instead of still monotonously rising, now dropped sharply away, and far below I could see the North Col and the Rongbuk glacier. I looked upwards to see a narrow snow ridge running up to a snowy summit. A few more whacks of the ice-axe in the firm snow and we stood on top."[99]

Hillary was the first to step on the summit of Everest; Tenzing followed a moment later. Hillary reached his hand out to shake Tenzing's; Tenzing embraced Hillary. Both climbers thought of their predecessors on the mountain. Hillary looked down toward Tibet, over the North Col and East Rongbuk Glacier, thinking of Mallory and Irvine; there was no visible evidence on the summit that they had reached it before disappearing in 1924. Tenzing thought of his own personal history with the mountain and the men with whom he had climbed. He was wearing a woolen balaclava that Earl Denman had given him in 1948 and the red scarf that Raymond Lambert had given him in 1952.[100]

Hillary dug his Kodak Retina camera out of his pack and took one of the most famous color photographs of the twentieth century, showing Tenzing holding his ice ax above his head with the flags of the United Nations, Britain, Nepal, and India unfurled to the wind. He also took shots looking out from the summit in each direction at the surrounding peaks. For all his ambition, Hillary's actions on the summit bespoke an essential modesty. It is otherwise difficult to account for the fact that no photograph exists of Edmund Hillary atop Mount Everest.[101]

There was time for a few more summit rituals. Tenzing left biscuits, sweets, and a colored pencil given him by his daughter in a hole he dug in the snow; Hillary added a crucifix John Hunt had given him two days before on the South Col. They also left behind the flags from Tenzing's ice ax. For a few moments they took off their oxygen masks and breathed the thin air, which contained but a third of the air pressure at sea level. A less exalted but reassuringly human detail would be left out of the official accounts; after having consumed several cups of tea in the morning to ward off dehydration, Hillary felt the need to relieve a full bladder and took the opportunity to urinate while he was standing on one of the few flat spots available to him that day.[102]

At 11:45 they began their descent. By 12:45 they were back at the South Summit. The soft snow below the South Summit gave them their worst moments, and they picked their way carefully, fearing an avalanche that would sweep them over the edge and down to the Kangshung Glacier. They retrieved Evans's and Bourdillion's oxygen bottles as planned. When they reached Camp IX at about 2:00 P.M., they paused long enough to make themselves a hot drink. They also packed up the sleeping bags and air mattresses, knowing that there were no extras waiting for them down at the South Col. After that, feeling tired but moving with skill and determination, they made their way back to the South Col and Camp VIII. As they approached from above, they could see little black dots on the col moving upward toward them.

Tenzing Norgay on the summit of Everest, 1953.
Photograph by Edmund Hillary. Reprinted by
permission of the Royal Geographical Society.

George Lowe was the first to reach them, bearing a thermos of hot tomato soup
and a fresh bottle of oxygen. Hillary confirmed their victory by telling his old climbing
partner, "Well, we knocked the bastard off." It's probably not how Mallory would have
put it, but for Hillary the phrase conveyed a wary adversarial affection for the mountain.
"Thought you must have," Lowe replied casually, pouring a cup of soup for the tired
climbers.[103]

They spent the night at the South Col camp talking over the climb with Lowe
and Wilfred Noyce, then trying to get some sleep. The next morning, May 30, they set off
down the mountain. Charles Wylie was there to congratulate them at Camp VII, but the
celebration really began when they reached Camp IV on the Western Cwm. Hunt and
others had kept an uneasy vigil there for the past two days, scanning the slopes for any
evidence of the outcome of Hillary and Tenzing's summit bid. The two had last been seen
from below at about 9:00 A.M., above the South Summit, but what had happened after that

no one below the South Col would know on May 29 or the following morning. Up on the South Col on the afternoon of summit day, Wilf Noyce had carried out the agreed-upon signal for a successful climb, arranging two sleeping bags on the edge of the col in a cross, but mist had prevented Hunt from seeing the message.

Down below on the Western Cwm, the rest of the expedition waited anxiously through the evening of May 29 and the next morning. Late in the morning they spotted five climbers—Hillary, Tenzing, Lowe, Noyce, and Pasang Phutar—making their way down the Lhotse Face. James Morris would not need to wire an obituary to *The Times*. But there was still no way to know if Hillary and Tenzing had reached the summit. Finally, shortly after 2:00 p.m., the little party was spotted about 500 yards away, wearily trudging toward Camp IV, Hillary and Tenzing roped together. Tom Stobart had already headed up the glacier to film their return; the rest of the expedition followed in his tracks, still in suspense. And then their hearts lifted as they saw George Lowe triumphantly wave his ice ax and point to the summit. "[F]rom that moment on," Tenzing would recall, "there has never been such excitement in the history of the Himalayas." Hunt, abandoning any trace of British military reserve, laughed and wept and embraced the climbers. As he wrote to his wife: "Everyone crowded round, everyone was equally mad, the Sherpa team were grasping these two splendid, lucky people by the hand, grinning broadly. Such a scene as I've imagined, but never believed could come true—Everest was climbed yesterday by Ed and Tenzing, at 11:30 a.m. We'd made it, exactly according to plan."[104]

Hillary and Tenzing told and retold the story of the climb. They ate and drank and raised a toast to Eric Shipton. James Morris scribbled a coded dispatch, sending it by runner to Namche Bazar where, by prearrangement, an Indian Army radio transmitter forwarded it to the British ambassador in Kathmandu. The embassy cabled the message to *The Times*, where it was decoded and forwarded to Buckingham Palace and the British Foreign Office. The next day, June 2, as crowds gathered in the streets of London to witness the coronation ceremony of Queen Elizabeth II, *The Times* hit the streets with its exclusive coverage of Hillary and Tenzing's triumph. To the editors of *The Times*, the British expedition's ascent of Everest signaled the beginning of a new Elizabethan age: "Seldom since Francis Drake brought the Golden Hind to anchor in Plymouth Sound has a British explorer offered to his Sovereign such a tribute of glory as Colonel John Hunt and his men are able to lay at the feet of Queen Elizabeth for her Coronation Day."[105]

By June 2 the Everest climbers had descended to Base Camp. There they were able to tune in a BBC broadcast and learned that the news of their triumph had reached Britain and the rest of the world. "Somehow hearing it officially over the radio from half the world away made the climb sound far more important and real," Hillary remembered. Eric Shipton was among those in London for the coronation who learned the news of the climbing of Everest that day. He wrote to Geoffrey Winthrop Young a few days later to share his elation: "Tremendous news about Everest. Coming when it did it's a perfect climax to the long story. I'm delighted that it was Hillary who got there. He is a grand person and

Edmund Hillary and Tenzing Norgay back at Camp IV after their ascent of
Everest. Photograph by Alfred Gregory. Reprinted by permission of
the Royal Geographical Society.

one of the few I know with character strong enough to withstand the public acclamation
which will be coming his way!"[106]

Edmund Hillary—soon to be Sir Edmund Hillary, KBE—and Tenzing Norgay
were about to find out what it meant to have become two of the most famous people in the
world. Their lives would be irrevocably changed by what happened on Everest on May 29,
1953. And the world of Himalayan climbing would be changed as well. Thanks to Hillary
and Tenzing, and to Herzog before them, there was now a mass audience of nonclimbers
that avidly followed the exploits of Himalayan expeditions. One of those enthusiasts, Alfred
B. Fitt of Grosse Pointe, Michigan, wrote to James Ramsey Ullman on the very day that
the news arrived in the United States of Everest's ascent:

> Some months ago my wife and I read "Annapurna." That started us on a binge of read-
> ing about high climbers, and one of the books we ran across was yours about the Mt.
> Everest expeditions. We got to know the North Col, the first and second steps, the

slabs below the ridge; we agonized and theorized over Mallory and Irvine and the ice axe found in 1933 (neither of us think they made it to the top), and in general we got about as excited about the world's highest mountain as it is possible for people who will never see the Himalayas. . . . Now tonight, buried in all the Coronation hoop-de-do we are told that Mt. Everest has at last been conquered. A new Zealander named Hillary (Hillery?) and a "native climber"—presumably a Sherpa . . . have gotten to the top. My first reaction was depression. Somewhere in your book, or perhaps in Younghusband's or Frank Smyth[e]'s, there is a discussion of the usefulness of an unclimbed Mt. Everest. Now the mightiest mountain has succumbed; puny man has stood on the top of the world. What next?[107]

CHAPTER EIGHT

The Golden Age of Himalayan Climbing 1953–1960

What next, indeed? The American reader who had asked James Ramsey Ullman that question the day the news broke of the first ascent of Everest would get his answer before the summer of 1953 was over, as yet another 8,000-meter peak saw its first ascent.[1] Two more would be climbed in 1954, another two in 1955, three in 1956, and one each in 1957, 1958, and 1960. In the same seven years there were repeat ascents of several already-climbed 8,000-meter peaks, plus first ascents of smaller but challenging Himalayan mountains. Expeditions from France, Great Britain, Germany, Italy, Austria, Japan, the United States, Switzerland, and the People's Republic of China shared the collective glory of these ascents. The men who reached the summits enjoyed national and sometimes international renown. It was, at last, truly the golden age of Himalayan climbing—both as a sport and as a popular spectacle.

The string of first ascents did not necessarily make it a happy age for Himalayan climbers. Although some expeditions proved congenial as well as triumphant affairs, many others were torn by conflicts—between overbearing leaders and restive climbers, between rival climbers, or between the competing goals of climbing for national glory and climbing for personal fulfillment. But the public image of expeditionary mountaineering as a noble endeavor—a "High Adventure," as Sir Edmund Hillary titled his account of climbing Everest—survived the decade unscathed.

Everest Aftermath

John Hunt managed to write *The Ascent of Everest,* the official account of the British Everest expedition, in just thirty days in the summer of 1953. Rushed into print for September publication, the book became an international bestseller. If *The Ascent of Everest* was not quite the lyric triumph of Herzog's *Annapurna,* Hunt's book was nonetheless a workman-like piece of prose, detailed and carefully organized (much like the expedition he had led).

And it opened with a masterful restatement of the core values of expeditionary culture that Hunt had inherited from the preceding six decades of British ventures to the Himalaya: "This is the story of how, on 29th May, 1953, two men, both endowed with outstanding stamina and skill, inspired by an unflinching resolve, reached the top of Everest and came back unscathed to rejoin their comrades."[2]

Uplifting words, and true enough. But some less-than-inspirational events taking place in the aftermath of May 29 would have complicated Hunt's narrative had he chosen to include them. Three weeks after weeping tears of joy at the sight of Hillary and Tenzing returning from the summit, Hunt sent a letter to the Himalayan Committee in London, informing it of "astonishing developments" on their return to Kathmandu: "Very briefly, Tenzing appears to have been 'got at' by local politicians—we are pretty certain that the Communist Party was behind it—whose motives were twofold (a) to make use of the Everest success in order to enhance Nepalese nationalism, particularly at the expense of India (b) to discredit the British Expedition as a whole and to stir up trouble with Europeans and Orientals. . . . The particular points which, in the National and Communist interest, the Politicians wished to secure were his Nepalese nationality and a statement to the effect that he had reached the summit first." And if Communists and Nationalists were not bad enough, there was also the problem of Ang Lhamu, Tenzing's wife, who had traveled from the family home in Darjeeling to greet her husband on his return from Everest. "[She] is a formidable woman," Hunt complained to the Himalayan Committee, "whose dominating interest is money." Tenzing had announced he would not be traveling to England with the rest of the expedition to join in the victory celebrations, a decision Hunt blamed on Ang Lhamu's mercenary instincts: "When it became clear that Tenzing would not be receiving a large cash reward from the people of England, the visit was off."[3]

The troubles began even before they reached Kathmandu. Tenzing was approached on the trail by reporters eager to obtain an exclusive interview. Unlike the British and New Zealand climbers, who were bound by the expedition's contractual publishing agreement with *The Times*, Tenzing was free to sell his story to the highest bidder. He agreed to talk with a wire service correspondent, resulting in a story then picked up in London by the *Daily Express*, *The Times*'s leading rival. Despite Hunt's disapproval, Tenzing was unapologetic about this arrangement: "For the first time in my life I was in a position to make a considerable sum of money, and I could not see why it was not right and proper for me to do so."[4]

As Hunt had intimated to the Himalayan Committee, others sought to exploit Tenzing's celebrity for political ends. Stirred by the triumph of Indian independence the previous decade and by the overthrow of the Rana family just two years earlier, Nepalese nationalists found the Sherpa conqueror of Everest a convenient rallying symbol for their cause. When the Everest expedition reached Dhaulagat, a village on the outskirts of Kathmandu, Tenzing would recall: "[A] crowd of Nepali came out to meet me and almost tore me away from the rest of the expedition. I have been often asked since if they were Communists, and this I do not honestly know. But I do know that they were nationalists, with very strong ideas, and what they were interested in was not Everest at all, or how Everest was really climbed—but only politics. They wanted me to say that I was a Nepali, not an Indian. And also, that I got to the top ahead of Hillary."[5]

Born as he was in Tibet, raised in the Solu Khumbu, and living for the last two decades in India, questions of national identity had little meaning for Tenzing. Nevertheless, confused by the uproar, he signed a statement that someone thrust into his hands declaring that he, and not Hillary, had been the first to step atop Everest—a statement that, being illiterate, he could not even read.

Honors showered down upon the climbers unequally, depending on who was handing them out. While Hunt and Hillary had been knighted by the new Queen Elizabeth, Tenzing had received only the less prestigious George Medal. When the mountaineers reached Kathmandu, on the other hand, they found the streets festooned with banners that depicted a heroic Tenzing hauling an exhausted-looking Hillary to the top of the mountain. Hillary took it in good humor, but Hunt was not amused.[6]

No previous foreign expeditions to Everest or other Himalayan mountains had ever been upstaged by any of the Sherpas they employed. But with the climbing of Everest the rules had changed, leaving the British as well as the Sherpas uncertain and fumbling in their responses.

John Hunt was an intelligent man of liberal instincts who recognized that the age of empire was over in South Asia. But he still had no way of thinking about Tenzing's assertion of an independent perspective on the meaning of the Everest ascent except to subsume it under the heading of Communist subversion. Sensing none of Tenzing's confusion, Hunt made matters worse when he attempted to set the record straight at a press conference in Kathmandu. According to the summary of his remarks that appeared in English newspapers, Hunt declared himself "surprised to read newspaper reports that Tensing [sic] had reached the summit first and then dragged Mr. Edmund Hillary up. He emphasized that Tensing's role was second throughout the final assault when Mr. Hillary was seen to be leading, cutting footholds in the ice face, with Tensing below."[7]

What Tenzing found most galling was Hunt's statement that he was "a good climber within the limits of his experience." Tenzing was not alone in objecting to Hunt's patronizing tone, for the slight to the Sherpa climber reverberated loudly in a region that had only recently thrown off colonial rule. "Leader's Views Resented/Tensing Voices Protest," the *Times of India* reported on June 23: "Tensing said he could not believe that Sir John Hunt could have insinuated that 'I have no experience. Is there any living man who has been on Everest seven times in a total of eleven expeditions?' he asked."[8]

In the end, Hillary, Hunt, and Tenzing—and, behind the scenes, the Indian and British governments—realized that the postexpedition bickering was in no one's interest. The British Foreign Office helped persuade Tenzing to accompany the rest of the expedition to England by quietly arranging to pick up the tab for his wife and his two teenaged daughters' traveling expenses. And Hillary and Tenzing, the two men who had been bound together by a climbing rope not so many days before, released a carefully worded statement describing how they reached Everest's summit "almost together."[9]

And so it was that after weeks of conflict, John Hunt stood before the cheering crowd that had gathered at the London airport on July 3 to greet the returning heroes who had conquered Everest, a broad smile on his face and Hillary and Tenzing standing at his side. At the press conference that followed, faced with the inevitable question of who had reached the summit first, Hunt replied with the answer he should have given in Kathmandu: "This couldn't matter less. You get to the top of a difficult mountain only as a result of climbing with companions as a team on a rope." *The Times* noted in its report on the press conference that "Tensing was in Colonel Hunt's keeping, and their arms were often locked together in comradeship as they faced the battery of cameras."[10]

Public adulation in Britain cancelled out the memory of the ill will so evident in Kathmandu. Thrust into a strange new world of pomp and ceremony, Tenzing maintained a dignified bearing and came to be viewed by the British public as nature's gentleman. At a dinner party in London honoring the climbers, *Times* correspondent James Morris was not at all surprised to hear one of the distinguished guests remark how good it was to see that "Mr. Tenzing knew a decent claret when he had one."[11]

After a fortnight in Britain Tenzing headed home with his family to India. A few weeks later John Hunt wrote to him, sending along an advance copy of *The Ascent of Everest* and assuring him of his personal regard: "I hope that you will find that your own big part in the Expedition has received the credit that it deserved. Let us always remember that we were a *united team* and let nothing come between us to spoil the comradeship which we all built up together."[12]

But Tenzing had not, in fact, forgotten the slights he had experienced at the start and close of the Everest expedition. Settling in Darjeeling, he helped establish a Sherpa Climbers Buddhist Association to register and hire out Sherpas for Himalayan expeditions. Recruitment and regulation of climbing porters had traditionally been the prerogative of the British-run Himalayan Club, and the grandees of the British climbing establishment were not happy with Tenzing's organization, which they felt encouraged demands for higher wages by Sherpas. That was not an example of the kind of team spirit John Hunt had had in mind. Tenzing took on additional responsibilities the following year as director of field training for the newly organized Himalayan Mountaineering Institute (HMI) in Darjeeling. Founded at the initiative of Indian prime minister Nehru and modeled on the Swiss Foundation for Alpine Research, the HMI trained young Indian mountaineers with the goal of creating "a thousand Tenzings."[13]

The other expedition veterans kept up a frenzied schedule of travel, ceremonies, and lectures lasting well into 1954, including visits to France, the Soviet Union, and the United States; their lecture fees, along with sales of John Hunt's book and showings of the expedition film, *The Conquest of Everest,* would turn a tidy profit for the Himalayan

Committee. After taking time off in August to wed Louise Mary Rose, daughter of the president of the New Zealand Alpine Club, Hillary rejoined Hunt and the others on the lecture circuit.[14]

At the start of 1954 Sir Edmund and Lady Hillary, along with George Lowe and Charles Evans, embarked on a six-week tour of the United States, including numerous public lectures and slide shows, television appearances, and a White House reception hosted by President Dwight Eisenhower, all in all a far cry from the indifferent reception Mallory had received on his post-Everest tour of the United States in 1923. Upon arrival in New York City in January, Hillary visited the Empire State Building and showed his wife the sights from the roof observatory. According to the caption accompanying the United Press news photo, Hillary told reporters "he wanted to visit the world's tallest building to see how the lift works."[15]

It is difficult to imagine Mallory making a similar joke. The ascent of Everest would have been a sensation, regardless of who pulled it off, but Hillary's antipodean good humor and lack of pretense charmed the American press and public. Meanwhile, the absent Tenzing was nearly forgotten. As one Washington State newspaper noted of Hillary: "The quality of this modest man is evidenced by the quick instinct to share full credit with the native guide with whom he embraced when they reached the summit together last May 29." For Americans, it took the publication in 1955 of Tenzing's autobiography, *Tiger of the Snows,* written in collaboration with James Ramsey Ullman, to restore him to his rightful place in the story.[16]

Hermann Buhl Climbs Nanga Parbat

Following the news of Hillary's and Tenzing's ascent of Everest, the *New York Times* carried a feature story from its South Asian correspondent headlined, "Six Other Asian Peaks Are Targets of Expeditions This Year." Two of the most significant expeditions were taking place in Pakistan: a German-Austrian expedition had already headed south from Gilgit to attempt Nanga Parbat, while an American expedition was getting ready to head northeast from Skardu to attempt K2.[17] It would be some time before the news from Everest caught up with the members of these expeditions as they made their ways to and up their respective mountains.

Hermann Buhl, for one, learned of the ascent only on June 16, when he was camped at 20,180 feet on the northeastern Rakhiot Face of Nanga Parbat. Buhl toasted the British success with a can of Munich beer he had hauled up the mountainside. Two and a half weeks later he would have his own moment of triumph standing atop the world's ninth-highest mountain. Just as remarkably, he would be standing there alone—the only occasion on which a single climber would make the first ascent of an 8,000-meter peak.[18]

Buhl, a climber from Innsbruck, Austria, established a reputation as one of Europe's leading mountaineers in the early 1950s by completing a number of daring Alpine climbs, including an unprecedented winter ascent of the Eiger North Face. The Nanga Parbat expedition was his first trip to the Himalaya. Like everyone else on the expedition, he was only too aware of Nanga Parbat's deadly reputation. The mountain had claimed the lives of thirty-one climbers between 1895 and 1950, more than any other Himalayan peak. As Buhl would write, Nanga Parbat had established itself as "a symbol to conjure with in the world of mountaineers and for millions elsewhere, too. That peak of many names—sometimes called the Fateful Peak, or the Mountain of Terror; that cloud-piercing giant which had already devoured thirty-one victims; that pitiless domain demanding its holocaust and giving nothing in return, luring men into its thrall, never to set them free again."[19]

The organizer and leader of what was known as the Willy Merkl Memorial Expedition (Willy-Merkl-Gedächtnisexpedition), Dr. Karl Maria Herrligkoffer of Munich, had a personal score to settle with Nanga Parbat. Merkl, buried on the Rakhiot Ridge at 22,800 feet, had been his elder half brother. Although Herrligkoffer's deputy and climbing leader, Peter Aschenbrenner, had been on the 1932 and 1934 expeditions to Nanga Parbat, Herrligkoffer himself was a Himalayan novice. His family tie to Merkl was the only credential Herrligkoffer could claim when he set out to organize the first postwar German attempt in the Himalaya. Veteran German mountaineers like Paul Bauer were skeptical about his qualifications and annoyed by his impudence; Herrligkoffer, Bauer wrote, was "a man unknown in mountaineering circles and without experience of the subject."[20] The German Alpine Club, which had sponsored the Merkl expeditions, would have nothing to do with Herrligkoffer's project.

He did, however, win the endorsement of the Austrian Alpine Club as well as the Munich branch of the German Alpine Club. And he managed to persuade some top German and Austrian climbers to join his ten-member team, including Buhl and Buhl's frequent Alpine climbing partner and fellow Austrian, Kuno Rainer, along with Fritz Aumann, Albert Bitterling, Hans Ertl, Walter Frauenberger, Otto Kempter, and Hermann Köllensperger. One personal quality Herrligkoffer had going for him, as even Paul Bauer conceded, was a "tenacity of purpose." He was determined to send his climbers up the exact same route on the Rakhiot Face that had killed his half brother. "German climbers must achieve Merkl's objective," he declared on the eve of the expedition.[21]

Unlike the 1930s German expeditions, no Sherpas accompanied the climbers on this trip to Nanga Parbat. Newly independent Pakistan and India were enemies. And though the Sherpas were not native to India, the facts that they were non-Muslims and were hired for expeditions in Darjeeling made them unwelcome to Pakistani authorities.[22] Herrligkoffer's climbers would have to rely on the support of porters from Pakistan's Hunza Valley, who were inexperienced and reluctant to carry high on the mountain.

The expedition established Base Camp on May 25 at 13,000 feet and made steady progress in the days that followed. Camp I went in at 14,600 feet at the foot of the Rakhiot Icefall on May 26, Camp II at 17,400 feet above the icefall on May 31, Camp III at 20,180 feet on the upper Rakhiot Glacier on June 10, and Camp IV at 22,000 feet at the base of

Karl Herrligkoffer on Nanga Parbat, 1953. Reprinted by permission of the
German Alpine Club.

Rakhiot Peak's ice wall on June 12. Then the weather worsened, and a week of heavy snows
kept the climbers pinned in their tents at Camp III. It was there, on the fifth day of the
storm, that Buhl learned the news of the ascent of Everest.

Conditions failed to improve much over the next two weeks, but Hermann Buhl
and Otto Kempter continued to prepare the route for porters carrying loads to higher
camps. "At times we got the impression that mountaineering in the Himalaya consisted
of nothing but breaking trails and superhuman exertions," Buhl later recalled.[23] From
Camp IV they could see their route spread out before them all the way to the summit: the
Silver Saddle at 24,540 feet, the summit plateau that stretched above it, climbing to the
Subsidiary Summit (or Fore Peak) at 25,953 feet, which could be climbed or circumvented
to reach the deep notch known as the Bazhin Gap that linked Nanga Parbat's secondary
summit to the main summit massif, and then above that a rocky ridge leading to the
Shoulder at 26,478 feet, and beyond that the summit itself. Buhl was climbing strongly
and clearly destined for inclusion in the first summit team, although his regular partner,
Kuno Rainer, was felled by an attack of phlebitis. Instead the newly formed team of Buhl
and Kempter would make the first summit attempt.

That is, if Herrligkoffer permitted them to do so. For the first but not the last time,
Herrligkoffer was in a contest of wills with his lead climber. As much as he wanted to fulfill his
brother's destiny by conquering the Killer Mountain, Herrlifkoffer also wanted everyone on
the expedition to understand that he was in control from his headquarters at Base Camp. In
Herrligkoffer's expeditionary philosophy the greatest sin was "the zeal of individuals." There
was no point in climbing a mountain, he thought, if all that resulted was fame and glory

for an independent-minded climber. "If I had to choose between the two," he would write, "I would always go for the collaborative expedition that didn't reach the summit."[24]

Buhl had a different climbing philosophy. Herrligkoffer had been advised by radio of the imminent arrival of the monsoon, and from Base Camp the conditions higher up on the mountain looked extremely poor. On June 30 he radioed an order to Camp III, where four climbers and four Hunza porters were in place for the push to the summit, for everyone to retreat to the safety of Base Camp. But Herrligkoffer's climbers chose to rely on their own judgment. Up at Camp III, where Buhl, Kempter, Frauenberger, and Ertl sat, the weather seemed to be improving, not deteriorating. "We were well acclimatized," Buhl would write of their defiance, "and saw no need for a descent to Base Camp in search of recovery. We intended to make the best use of the good weather. Camp III was as good a convalescent home as we could wish for."[25] Herrligkoffer threatened to cut off any further support for their effort, but Buhl and his comrades were equally adamant. On July 1 they headed up, not down, the mountain. At Camp IV they received another order to return to Base Camp, which again they defied.

The following day the four climbers established Camp V at 22,640 feet on the ridge leading up to the Silver Saddle, just above the rocky feature called the Moor's Head. This would be their high camp. It left them with 4,000 vertical feet still to climb to the summit, more than twice the distance climbed by Hillary and Tenzing from the British Camp IX to the summit of Everest a month earlier. The original plan had been to put in at least one more camp higher up, perhaps in the Bazhin Gap, the dip in the ridge just 1,000 or so feet below the summit. But there was no time for that now. Buhl and Kempter would make their summit bid the next day. Frauenberger and Ertl would have liked to have stayed at Camp V to make their own summit bid, but there was room for only two. "They sportingly stood down," Buhl acknowledged gratefully, "being the older men, leaving the great chance to us youngsters. . . . It was most comforting to know that two comrades on whom we could rely to the last gasp would be protecting our rear."[26]

At 2:00 A.M. on July 3, Buhl was ready to start but Kempter, feeling the effects of altitude, was not. Displaying that zeal of individualism that Herrligkoffer found so disagreeable, Buhl headed up the mountain alone, with Kempter following about three quarters of an hour later. Like Herzog and Lachenal on Annapurna, Buhl and Kempter climbed without oxygen. By 7:00 A.M. Buhl had reached the Silver Saddle. Kempter, climbing in Buhl's footsteps, reached it an hour later, but at that point decided he had had enough.

Buhl watched Kempter turn back. A little over a month before, standing on the South Summit of Everest, Tom Bourdillion had considered going on alone to climb the 300 feet to Everest's true summit without his partner Charles Evans—but then decided the prudent thing would be to turn back. Buhl still faced over 2,000 feet of vertical gain before he could reach the summit of Nanga Parbat, but he did not hesitate for an instant to continue on alone. The two men were born in the same year, but they were climbing in different eras.

Hermann Buhl on Nanga Parbat, 1953. Reprinted by permission of
the German Alpine Club.

To lighten his load Buhl shed his rucksack on the summit plateau above the Silver
Saddle. He stowed a few items of gear in his pockets including, fortunately, an extra pair
of gloves. He skirted the edge of the Subsidiary Summit and at 2:00 reached the Bazhin
Gap, higher up than anyone had climbed on the mountain before. From there the summit
rose 1,000 vertical feet above him. He swallowed two stimulant tablets for an energy boost.
He surmounted the Shoulder, the hump on the ridge below the main summit. From the
Bazhin Gap, Buhl had hoped to reach the summit in one hour, but the ridge proved difficult, and the hours stretched on and on as he found himself taking five breaths for each
step forward. Near the top of the ridge he found his path blocked by a gigantic gendarme
(a climbing term for a rock pinnacle atop a ridgeline) and, in an unprecedented feat of
solo technical climbing at that attitude, did a hanging traverse around it on the Diamir
(western) Face, regaining the ridgeline on its far side.

Finally, at 7:00 P.M., seventeen hours after setting out, crawling on hands and
knees, he reached the summit. "Nothing went up any further, anywhere," Buhl would
recall. "There was a small snow plateau, a couple of mounds, and everything fell away on
all sides from it." In gathering darkness, he built a small cairn. He took some photographs
of the surrounding mountains and of a pennant from his Innsbruck climbing club that he
tied to his ice ax. Before he began his descent, he tied the Pakistani flag to his ice ax and
jammed it into the mountain top, leaving it as evidence of his climb. (German newspapers
would report that Buhl had raised the German flag atop the mountain, but he had not, in
fact, brought one with him.)[27]

Buhl slowly retraced his steps down the mountainside, using ski poles for balance and regretting his decision to leave his ice ax behind. He hoped to get as far as the Bazhin Gap before it became completely dark, and then cross the summit plateau in the moonlight to reach the safety of Camp V. But that was not to be. A broken crampon strap slowed him, and at 9:00 P.M. he was still picking his way carefully down the summit ridge. Finding it too dark to continue, he halted by a rock slab at around 26,000 feet. With nothing to shelter him, he stood upright by the rock for the next seven hours. Fortunately, there was no wind near Nanga Parbat's summit that night. Despite the precariousness of his situation, Buhl felt "amazingly relaxed; everything seemed so normal."[28]

At 4:00 A.M. it grew light enough to renew his descent. He made it back to the plateau above the Silver Saddle, where he found his rucksack. He had eaten nothing since the previous afternoon, but now was too dehydrated to swallow any of the food in his pack. All he was able to get down was more stimulant pills along with the antifrostbite drug Padutin. Exhausted and hypoxic, he began to converse with an imaginary companion. Buhl had lost a glove, his companion pointed out helpfully, and needed to do something about it. Fortunately, he found the pair he had earlier tucked in a pocket, thus avoiding Maurice Herzog's fate on Annapurna.[29]

Down he went, through the Bazhin Gap, around the Subsidiary Summit, across the summit plateau to the Silver Saddle, and onward toward the Moor's Head. Finally, at 7:00 P.M. on July 4, forty-one hours after setting out for the summit, exhausted and frostbitten, Hermann Buhl reached his waiting comrades Walter Frauenberger and Hans Ertl at Camp V.[30] Three days later he was back in Base Camp.

At Camp V Buhl was a hero to his teammates. But not so when he reached Base Camp. There was no John Hunt waiting there with tears in his eyes to embrace him. Instead, as Buhl would recall, he received "the coolest of receptions" from Dr. Herrligkoffer.[31] Herrligkoffer had not forgiven Buhl's defiance, which seemed to rob him of the satisfaction he might otherwise have felt in fulfilling Willy Merkl's legacy on Nanga Parbat. In the months that followed Herrligkoffer repeatedly downplayed Buhl's importance to the expedition's success. Angered, Buhl broke the expedition contract by publishing his own version of the climb, *Nanga Parbat Pilgrimage,* and giving public lectures without Herrligkoffer's permission.

The dispute between leader and climber led to a round of nasty legal proceedings that divided the German and Austrian mountaineering communities. Buhl alienated the Austrian Alpine Club by refusing to pay his share of expedition expenses from his publishing and lecturing profits. But it was Herrligkoffer's reputation that suffered the worst beating: reviewers mocked the closing words of his expedition account, "Of the nine members of the team, six have remained my friends," hardly as inspiring an ending as, say, Herzog's "There are other Annapurnas in the lives of men."[32]

Hermann Buhl never doubted he was right in following his instincts on Nanga Parbat. As he wrote in his own account of the expedition: "You cannot climb a great mountain, least of all a 26,000 foot peak like Nanga Parbat, without personal risk. The leaders of the 1953 Expedition would not face this truth. . . . The summit party shouldered the risk involved. They were entitled to do so, for they were in a position to interpret the conditions and the weather correctly. There was nothing wild or rash about our decision; it was governed by deliberate judgment. . . . I myself took the risk on my final ascent of the Summit; and I was entitled to do so and to say so."[33]

The Americans Return to K2

The British triumph on Everest had been marred by postexpeditionary conflicts between John Hunt and Tenzing Norgay, the German/Austrian triumph on Nanga Parbat by disputes both on and off the mountain between Herrligkoffer and Buhl. The third attempt to climb an 8,000-meter peak in 1953, the American expedition to K2, would stand out as a happy exception to the other expeditions—or would have, had it not been for a change in the weather.

To reach the summit of K2 from Base Camp on the Godwin-Austen Glacier involved more than 11,000 feet of vertical gain, about the same as on Everest from the south side. But as prewar expeditions had already discovered, K2 posed technical problems for mountaineers far more difficult than those found on Everest's South Col route. K2's southeastern or Abruzzi Ridge, which would in time become the "standard" route up the mountain, was about twenty degrees steeper overall than the route that Hillary and Tenzing had climbed on Everest. And K2 was 8° latitude farther north than Everest, which made for colder temperatures and more vicious storms, even without the dangers that the arrival of the monsoon posed to climbers on Everest.[34]

Charlie Houston had always intended to return to K2. The expedition he led in 1938 had solved the single most challenging technical problem along the way, known as House's Chimney, after Bill House who led the pitch. Fritz Wiessner had nearly climbed the mountain the following year, though his expedition had ended tragically in the deaths of one of the climbers and three of the Sherpas. Houston was determined to prove not only that the mountain could be climbed but that it could be done with the due attention to safety that he felt Wiessner had neglected. But the war put his plans on hold indefinitely.

Even before his military discharge in 1946, Houston began planning for a new K2 expedition, along with 1938 veterans Bob Bates and Bill House. A new armed conflict, this time between Pakistan and India, caused more delay. As soon as an uneasy truce settled over the region in the early 1950s, Houston, Bates, and House resumed their efforts. Planning included prolonged and high-level negotiations with the State Department and the Pakistani government, and Houston half expected the effort to come to nothing; he wrote to American Alpine Club president Henry Hall in July 1950, as the Korean War began, "[I]t seems rather ostrich like to plan a trip in 1951 to India etc when the world is apparently ready to destroy itself any minute."[35]

It was not until February 1952 that official permission arrived from Pakistan, too late to launch an expedition that year. But Houston was determined to go in 1953, writing to Hall, "[W]e will try to let nothing short of a world war stop us."[36]

When House dropped out of the expedition due to personal considerations, Houston and Bates were left as the only veterans of the earlier effort (although House continued to handle the expedition's financial affairs). They put out word that they were looking for recruits and eventually interviewed forty candidates before deciding on the five they would invite to join them: George Bell, Bob Craig, Art Gilkey, Dee Molenaar, and Pete Schoening. All of the new recruits were younger than Houston and Bates, and although they were strong climbers, none had previous Himalayan experience. Apart from climbing credentials, Houston and Bates were looking for people who could get along: their team, they would write in the official expedition account, would not have any place "for the brilliant climber who thinks only in terms of personal success" (the comment likely intended as a reference to Fritz Wiessner). There would be one other experienced high-altitude climber along, Captain Tony Streather of the British First Gloucestershire Regiment. Although his official title on the expedition was transport officer, Streather would function on the mountain as one of the climbing team.[37]

The resulting party of eight climbers was smaller than the Everest and Nanga Parbat expeditions that year, though larger than either the 1938 or 1939 American K2 expeditions. Houston would have preferred a smaller group but knew he needed more climbers since Sherpas could no longer be used on expeditions in the Karakoram as high-altitude porters. Although Houston had become an expert during the war on the use of supplementary oxygen to offset the effects of high altitude, he preferred to do without its aid, reducing the weight of supplies that had to be lugged up the side of the mountain.

The expedition left the United States on May 25. The Americans hopscotched their way by plane across the globe in three days, from London to Frankfurt to Beirut to Karachi to Rawalpindi. In the prewar years expeditions for K2 had departed from Srinagar, a 240-mile, two-week approach march across the Zoji La and north along the Dras and Indus rivers just to reach Skardu, leaving an additional 100 or so miles to trek to K2. The Srinagar to Skardu route was no longer possible, since Srinagar was located in Indian-controlled Kashmir. But there was now a better and quicker alternative, which was to fly directly from Rawalpindi to Skardu's newly opened airport, a one and a half hour flight by DC3. En route they flew past Nanga Parbat, though too far up and away from the mountain to pick out the climbers who at that moment were forging a route up the Rakhiot Glacier.[38]

They departed from Skardu on June 5 on the approach march to K2. They had been joined in Rawalpindi by their Pakistani liaison officer, army doctor Mohammad Ata-Ullah. As he got to know the Americans better, Colonel Ata-Ullah noticed that they did not behave like the sahibs he had read about in mountaineering literature. The Americans "were all for equality," he would later write, and showed it by their willingness to "pitch their own tents, fetch their own water, wash their own dishes. . . . They were tough guys; they would look after themselves." As for the expedition leader, Ata-Ullah observed that Houston "was determined never to be anything more than the first among equals."[39]

News of the British triumph on Everest reached the Americans after they arrived in Pakistan. Houston wrote to his father on June 9 from their campsite on the Braldu River: "I think we are secretly a little disappointed to have the British make Everest before we could make our peak—but none of us have voiced this feeling, and for myself I don't think it matters at all. The prime thing being for us to get our climb done well and safely and the top if possible. We have high hopes and a good party."[40]

Ten days later, on June 19, they established Base Camp at 16,250 feet on Godwin-Austen Glacier below K2. This was familiar ground even after an absence of fifteen years: old bits of rope and pitons jogged Houston and Bates's memories and helped them in finding the route followed by the earlier expeditions. For the next two weeks they found the climbing "relatively easy," as Houston would recall, "the weather mostly fair, and the altitude barely noticeable."[41] Camp I went in at the old campsite at 17,700 feet just below the Abruzzi Ridge. Camp II, established on July 1 at 19,300 feet, was also at the old campsite. There they found supplies left from the 1939 expedition, including a large Logan tent that they set up for the use of the Hunza porters. Camp III, the highest point on the mountain to which the Hunzas would carry, went in a week later, at 20,700 feet; remembering the rockfall that threatened the old camp in 1938, Houston had it moved to a more protected site. Camp IV, at 21,500 feet, was again at the same site used by the 1938 and 1939 expeditions, and they recovered more supplies there, including three sleeping bags that they dried out and kept as spares.

Camp IV lay directly below House's Chimney. This time Houston led the way up the 150-foot smooth and vertical crack in the wall, reaching the top with "considerable exhilaration."[42] Having surpassed that obstacle, the climbers were able to put in Camp V at the old site at 22,000 feet, 300 feet above the chimney. They hauled supplies up the chimney with a pulley system.

Storms in mid-July slowed their progress, but by the third week of July the climbers were again pushing the route up the mountain. Houston wrote a letter from Camp IV on July 18 to be sent back to expedition friends and supporters in the United States. After giving an account of the climb to date, he concluded: "I have purposely left mention of our surroundings until last, because nothing I can say will show you the immensity, the starkness, the wildness of this country. As we go higher and higher—more ranges open up—those to the east being unmapped, unnamed, unexplored, those higher ones to the West being better known, but no less tremendous. All of us appreciate to the utmost the great privilege of being in this marvelous and unique area."[43] If all went well, Houston predicted they would be ready for their summit bid between August 1 and 3.

On July 21 they reached the site of Camp VI at 23,300 feet, a site used by both the 1938 and 1939 expeditions. The veterans of the 1930s expedition felt apprehensive as they approached it, because it was from this camp that Pasang Kikuli, Pasang Kitar, and Phinsoo had set out to rescue Dudley Wolfe on the last day of July in 1939 and never returned. They were moved by the relics they found of the earlier expedition, including torn tents, sleeping bags, and a bundle of tea wrapped in a blue handkerchief, "sad reminders" of the Sherpas' courage and devotion, Houston later wrote.[44]

The Abruzzi Ridge merged into the Black Pyramid, 1,000 feet of "relentless steepness" and dangerous exposure that they nonetheless surmounted in a single day of inspired climbing, placing Camp VII, at 24,500 feet, on a six-by-four-foot platform carved into the slope (the more spacious site of the 1938 and 1939 Camp VII had in the meantime "slid off" the mountain).[45] On July 31 Pete Schoening and Art Gilkey led the way to what they intended to be their next-to-last campsite, Camp VIII at 25,300 feet, about 500 feet above the highest rocks of the Black Pyramid, still below the shoulder of the Abruzzi Ridge. They were joined at Camp VIII by the other six climbers over the next two days.

As they assembled at their high camp, they were healthy, acclimatized, well equipped, and optimistic. "We were within striking distance of the goal," Houston would write. "The summit might still be ours." All they needed were two consecutive days of good weather—one to put in Camp IX at about 27,000 feet, and one the following day to get a pair of climbers to the summit. With three days of consecutive good weather they might even get two parties to the top. By secret ballot the climbers chose Craig and Bell to be the first summit team, Gilkey and Schoening the second. One thing they had neglected to bring with them was the American flag. It was still back at Base Camp. Instead, in the early stages of the climb, they had carried a red umbrella with them, with the words "American K2 Expedition 1953" taped on the outer surface, planning to employ it as a prop for their summit photos—though in fact it made it only as far as Camp III.[46]

It turned out they would not have three days, or two days, or even one more day of good weather. They were in communication with Ata-Ullah in Base Camp by walkie-talkie, and on July 31 he relayed the news that they could expect a day or so of bad weather. The next two days were unsettled, with periods of sunshine mixed with high wind, cloud, and snow. The climbers remained optimistic; when Houston saw the sun peep through the clouds on August 1 he felt he was getting a message from it saying, "Go on, the storm is over. The sky will soon be blue . . . " But the sun had lied, for on August 3 the storm grew worse. "Cloudy, blowing, stormy. Awoke with splitting headache and nausea," Dee Molenaar recorded in his diary. Still, their optimism remained unchecked, as evident from the same entry in Molenaar's diary: "Latest plan: six to [Camp] IX tomorrow, leaving two there for summit try next day."[47]

Later generations of Himalayan climbers would see the onset of a storm such as the one they were experiencing as a signal to retreat to a lower camp to avoid the physical deterioration that sets in at high altitude. But with plenty of supplies, it seemed to make more sense to stay put. As Dee Molenaar would recall, "[W]e thought that by [staying] up that we were saving our acclimatization, and so we were actually getting weaker and

K2 from the south, as viewed from the north shoulder of Broad Peak,
showing the 1953 American route of ascent.

not thinking as clearly as we should."[48] On the night of August 4 the tent that Bell and Houston shared was wrecked by the storm, and they had to crowd in with the others. And still the storm continued.

On August 7 the weather improved slightly and they moved outside their tents. But instead of experiencing relief at their new mobility, they suddenly discovered that one of their members was in mortal danger. Art Gilkey, who until then had been regarded by the others as among the strongest of the party (hence his selection for the second summit team), took a single step outside his tent and collapsed unconscious in the snow. His left leg had been bothering him for the past five days from what he thought was a "charley horse." When they brought him back into a tent and Houston examined him, he realized Gilkey was suffering from thrombophlebitis, a clotting in the veins of his left leg. This represented a potentially lethal condition if a blood clot broke off and wound up migrating to his lungs.

Some of the others cherished the hope that Gilkey's condition might improve on its own, and with a break in the weather they might still reach the summit. But as far as Houston was concerned, there was no longer any question of climbing K2. And worse— although he kept the thought to himself—he believed Gilkey was already doomed. His condition would not improve at high altitude, and there was simply no way they could evacuate an incapacitated man down the Black Pyramid or House's Chimney, to reach the safety of Base Camp 9,000 feet below. Still, they decided they would have to try. The climbers packed some gear. Gilkey would have to be lowered and dragged down the slope, wrapped in his sleeping bag and the remains of the wrecked tent. They planned to descend nearly 2,000 feet on the first day of their retreat from Camp VIII. There was nothing at Camp VII but a tiny ledge, with a one-man bivouac tent that they had previously cached there in case of emergency. But if they could make it to Camp VI, they would find ample supplies and shelter waiting for them.

They started down around 10:00 A.M. on August 7, but the attempt quickly had to be abandoned. Below Camp VIII the slopes were covered with two feet of powder snow lying on ice, ideal avalanche conditions. The next day they stayed in camp, hoping for a break in the weather that would allow them to descend by another route that lay along a rock rib to the east of the avalanche slope. In the meantime, as a last act of defiance to the mountain, Schoening and Craig set off up the slope above Camp VIII and climbed another 499 feet before turning back in dense cloud.

On August 9 the storm picked up fury. Gilkey talked about getting better in a day or so, and perhaps resuming the climb. But Houston listened to Gilkey's cough and knew that blood clots were already settling in his lungs. They were all suffering from dehydration, because they were unable to melt enough snow to provide adequate drinking water. Houston began to wonder if any of the party would make it off the mountain alive.

On August 10 they decided to go down regardless of the weather, in a last desperate attempt to save Gilkey's life. They would try a new route, down an ice gully that lay alongside a rock rib to the west of the avalanche slope and that they hoped would connect them back to the main route just past Camp VII. After packing their personal gear and a light-weight tent, they set off at around 9:00 A.M. Sedated with morphine but conscious and uncomplaining, Gilkey was again wrapped in sleeping bag and tent and alternately towed and lowered down the mountainside by his comrades. In the storm it would have been difficult for the climbers to descend on their own, let alone carry out a mountain rescue. But they had no choice. "Each of us realized that he was beginning the most dangerous day's work of his lifetime," Bates would recall.[49] It took them six hours to make a few hundred feet down the steep slope below their camp. They had survived one brush with an avalanche that nearly carried away Craig and Gilkey. By midafternoon it was clear they would have no chance of reaching Camp VI that day; instead they would need to traverse to their left across an icy slope to the tiny platform that was Camp VII. Bob Craig worked his way over to it alone and began clearing a larger space for their tents.

At around 3:00 P.M. the climbers were arrayed across the slope to the west of Camp VII, with Gilkey belayed from above by Schoening. Another rope ran from Gilkey to Molenaar, who was standing nearest to Craig. They had just succeeded in lowering Gilkey over the edge of a rock cliff when George Bell, stumping along on frostbitten feet, lost his footing. "Goddamn, there goes Bell!" Molenaar, who was looking up the slope, yelled in warning. But it was not just Bell, for he was roped to Tony Streather who was below him on the slope, and as he slid he pulled Streather off his feet. Streather had been standing down the slope from a rope that linked Gilkey to Houston and Bates. The two ropes became entangled, pulling Houston and Bates down. *"This is it!"* Bates remembered thinking as the magnitude of their disaster sunk in. "We had done our best, but our best wasn't good enough."[50]

Four men slid downward, helplessly heading for the precipice below. And then the tumbling men snagged the rope linking Molenaar and Gilkey. Molenaar started to slide. Gilkey did not, because he was tied in to Schoening above him by another rope. If Schoening had fallen that would have been the end, as all seven men would have hurtled into space, tumbling thousands of feet to their deaths on the Godwin-Austen Glacier. Bob Craig would have watched them die from the site of Camp VII. If he had managed to descend from 24,500 feet alone, someone would have been alive to tell the tale; if not, the fate of the 1953 American K2 expedition might have entered mountaineering lore as one of those enduring puzzles to be endlessly debated in the climbing journals, like the disappearance of Mallory and Irvine.[51]

But at that moment of impending doom, Schoening held fast and saved them all. To keep Gilkey on belay as they had lowered him over the rock cliff, Schoening had jammed his ice ax into the snow behind a small boulder, wrapping the rope once around the ax and then around his waist. When he saw the others fall, he instantly put all his weight onto the ax. The nylon rope stretched and tightened on him—but it held, and Schoening held.[52]

The American K2 expedition may have been on belay, but it was not yet out of

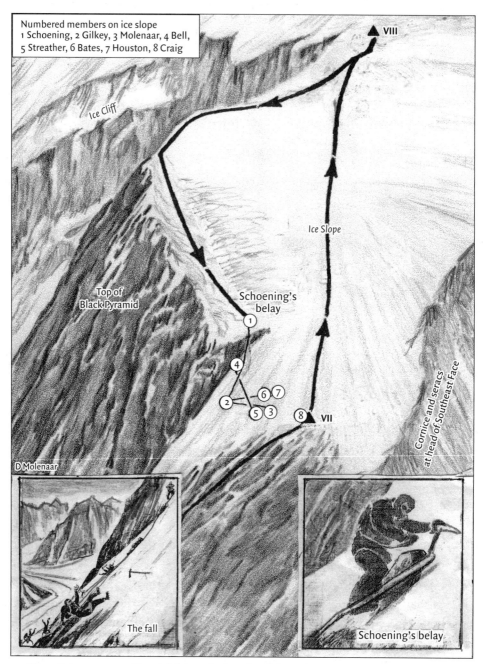

Numbered members on ice slope
1 Schoening, 2 Gilkey, 3 Molenaar, 4 Bell,
5 Streather, 6 Bates, 7 Houston, 8 Craig

Ice Cliff

VIII

Ice Slope

Top of
Black Pyramid

Schoening's
belay

Cornice and seracs
at head of Southeast Face

VII

D Molenaar

The fall

Schoening's belay

Expedition veteran Dee Molenaar's sketch of the Schoening belay on K2, 1953.

danger. Streather, displaying the characteristic British gift for understatement, would later say of the moment he stopped sliding down the mountain to certain death that it "really was an extremely tense situation." Craig made his way over to Gilkey and anchored him to the slope with two ice axes, allowing Schoening to release his belay. Of the others, Bell's hands as well as his feet were now frozen (he had lost his mittens in the fall), Molenaar was suffering from a cracked rib and a gashed leg, and most of the rest were shaken up and bruised. Houston was the most seriously injured, unconscious and suffering from concussion when Bates climbed down to where he lay on a ledge above a sheer drop. Houston was unresponsive to Bates's efforts to get him back up the slope and out of danger until Bates reminded him of his wife and eight-year-old daughter. "Charlie," he told him, "if you ever want to see Dorcas and Penny again, climb up there *right now!*" Houston climbed up.[53]

The climbers clearly could go no farther that day. They would have to work their way over to Camp VII and set up the two tents they were carrying to get shelter for the night if they were to survive, and they could not do it with Gilkey in tow. For the moment they left him anchored to the slope, about 150 feet west of the campsite. Craig explained to Gilkey that there had been an accident and that they were leaving him for a short time but would return. Gilkey said he understood. "Yes, I'll be fine," he told Craig, "I'm OK."[54]

They got their tents up. In the distance they heard a few indistinct shouts from Gilkey but could do nothing for him for the moment. Then there was silence. When the tents were finally up, Bates, Craig, and Streather returned to check on their injured teammate. But to their befuddlement and then horror, they saw that the gully was empty. There were no ice axes, no ropes, and no Art Gilkey. Gilkey was twenty-seven years old when he disappeared; he had completed his doctoral thesis in geology at Columbia University on the day he departed for K2. In the years that followed the others would wonder whether he had been swept away by an avalanche or had somehow caused his own death in an act of self-sacrifice that allowed the rest of them to live.[55]

It took the survivors five more days to fight their way off the mountain. On the night of August 10 Houston seemed in the worst shape, disoriented and hallucinating. On August 11 they made it only as far as Camp VI. Molenaar recorded their painful progress in his diary: "Foggy, windy, but we must move down. Charlie, Pete, and Craig, on first rope, move down ahead in a steep gully. Charlie still whoozy but makes it OK to VI. Our fixed ropes placed enroute up were encased in ice and covered by new snow, so it was ticklish climbing down, especially on the 'shingles/slabs' of the 'black pyramid.' Enroute down, we passed a tangle of ropes and torn sleeping bag that had held Art, with track of blood speckling snow below, indicating he had died quickly. Poor Art. We all passed by this wreckage silently, and I had no desire to photograph it."[56] At Camp VI they were able to contact Ata-Ullah at Base Camp by walkie-talkie and advise him of their situation. As they worked their way down the mountain Houston's concussion improved, but Bell's frostbitten feet became even more painful.

On August 13 they descended House's Chimney. Houston was determined to see the rest of the party safely beyond the obstacle before he descended, so he went last, belaying the others and lowering their rucksacks to them. By the time he was ready to join them it had grown dark. The chimney had more than one rope dangling down its length from the top, including rotting remnants left from the 1930s expeditions, and in the darkness Houston feared he might choose the wrong one. But he made it down to rejoin his comrades. The next day they were met at Camp II by their six Hunza porters, who wept when they saw them staggering down the mountain. Finally, on August 15, the battered climbers reached Base Camp. Ata-Ullah and the Hunzas built a ten-foot-high cairn as a memorial for Gilkey on a rocky point near the confluence of the Savoia and Godwin-Austen glaciers. The surviving climbers decorated it with flowers, flags, and Gilkey's ice ax, and Bates read Psalm 23, "Yea, though I walk through the valley of death, I will fear no evil."[57]

The K2 expedition became legend among mountaineers, its members honored for the gallantry of their conduct under extreme conditions. As Nick Clinch, a rising American climber, would write a few years later, the "finest moment in the history of American mountaineering was the Homeric retreat of Dr. Houston's party of K2 in 1953." Charlie Houston summed up the highest ideals of expeditionary culture when he wrote of his K2 comrades, "We entered the mountains as strangers, but we left as brothers."[58]

The Italians Climb K2

When Charlie Houston reached Rawalpindi at the end of August 1953, he told reporters he hoped to return to K2 the following year. But the Americans would have to get in line, for there was another Westerner in Rawalpindi eager to talk to Houston. He was geographer and geologist Ardito Desio, there to make preparations for an Italian expedition to K2 the following year. Desio's involvement with the mountain predated Houston's, which he had first seen as a member of the Duke of Spoleto's 1929 expedition. Before heading home to the United States, Houston generously shared his knowledge of the mountain with his Italian rival, the two of them poring over photos of the route up the Abruzzi Ridge. Shortly afterward Desio set off with the famed Italian Alpinist Ricardo Cassin on a reconnaissance of the lower reaches of the mountain.[59]

Desio's expedition would bear little resemblance to the 1953 American effort, save for the route it intended to climb on the mountain. It was a quasi-official national enterprise with powerful sponsors, including the Italian Alpine Club, the Italian Olympic Committee, and the Italian National Council for Research (a scientific body). The Italian press and public raptly followed preparations for the expedition. As Walter Bonatti, one of the climbing stars Desio recruited, would recall, "a real fever of enthusiasm for the enterprise spread throughout Italy, which for reasons of national pride had become a matter of interest to the entire nation."[60]

Desio was convinced that the American failure was the product of too few men and resources. His climbers would use oxygen in their summit attempt. And unlike Houston,

Desio had no intention of being first among equals. "The expedition will of necessity be organized along military lines," Desio wrote in a planning document in December 1953, "in a sense that will be familiar to all who have spent some part of their lives—especially under wartime conditions—in our Alpine regiments." Desio, the commander, would stay back at Base Camp, issuing inspirational communiqués to the climbers on the front line. "The honor of Italian mountaineering is at stake," he reminded them in one message. "Remember if you succeed in scaling the peak the entire world will hail you as champions of your race" ran another.[61]

The eleven climbers he recruited for his alpine regiment were required to pledge to obey Desio. Long before the expedition left Italy, it was clear that Desio would brook no dissent, or even potential challenge, to his authority. Ricardo Cassin was passed over in the team selection process, supposedly for medical reasons; some suspected his exclusion had less to do with his health than with his prestige as a climber. "If Cassin had come," Lino Lacedelli commented many years later, "all the newspaper would have focused on him rather than Desio."[62]

In addition to the climbers, the expedition included four scientists, a doctor, a filmmaker, and ten high-altitude Hunza porters. Five hundred additional porters—four times the number hired by the Americans—would be required to carry over thirteen tons of supplies, including 230 oxygen cylinders, to Base Camp. All of this, naturally, was quite expensive. The American expedition had cost $30,000. Desio raised 100 million lira to pay for his expedition (in 2008, the equivalent sum in dollars would be in the vicinity of $2,100,000).[63]

At the end of April 1954 the expedition set off from Skardu in three groups. Delayed en route by storms and porter unrest, all the mountaineers and gear were finally deposited at Base Camp on May 28. In a final reconnaissance, Desio flew around K2 in a DC3, in the first aerial circumnavigation of the mountain.

The Italians had set out relatively early for K2, and in the beginning stages of their climb were several weeks ahead of the American advance up the mountainside. Their progress was not without cost. On June 21 Mario Puchoz, a thirty-six-year-old climbing guide from Courmayeur, died at Camp II, apparently of pulmonary edema. The sixth climber to die on the mountain, he was carried down to be buried next to Art Gilkey's memorial cairn. In July the weather turned against them, and it was not until July 28 that they were able to establish Camp VIII at 25,400 feet, placing them at the same point on the mountain as the American's highest camp a year earlier. Sickness and altitude were wearing down the lead climbers, who were spending far too much time near the 8,000-meter level. There were also logistical problems, since few of those 230 oxygen canisters had actually made it up the mountain to the high camps. Desio began to consider the possibility of withdrawing the expedition from the mountain and renewing the assault in the fall with fresh climbers from Italy.

He would not have to do so. At Camp VIII on July 29 Walter Bonatti, Lino

Lacedelli, and Achille Compagnoni worked out a plan to place Lacedelli and Compagnoni, and possibly others, in position to make a summit bid in two days' time. Bonatti and Pino Gallotti would descend to a site near Camp VII, where oxygen equipment had been cached, and bring it back up to the assault camp that Lacedelli and Compagnoni would establish the same day. This new Camp IX, they agreed, was to be located on a snow shoulder beside a snow channel known as the Bottleneck at 25,900 feet. The four climbers set out on July 30, Lacedelli and Compagnoni heading up, Bonatti and Gallotti heading down. Near Camp VII and the supply dump, Bonatti and Gallotti met up with Erich Abram and two Hunza porters, Mahdi and Isakhan (unlike the Americans the previous year, the Italians had persuaded some of their Hunzas to accompany them high up the mountain). The five laden climbers then returned to Camp VIII, where Gallotti and Isakhan reached their physical limit and remained.

Mahdi was climbing well beyond his capabilities and would rather have stayed at Camp VIII with the others. But Bonatti persuaded him to continue with the promise that he could be part of the summit team if he completed the carry to the new Camp IX. This was not Bonatti's finest moment, for he had no intention of taking the Hunza porter with him to the summit. Mahdi had no experience using oxygen equipment and was not equipped with high-altitude boots. There would, in any case, only be two oxygen sets available for the summit team no matter how many climbers were prepared to go on from Camp IX.[64]

At 3:30 P.M. Bonatti, Abram, and Mahdi set off from Camp VIII bearing the oxygen canisters and other equipment. At 4:30 the three climbers scaled an ice wall and were rewarded with a clear view of the summit. But looking up the mountain they could not see the tent marking the location of Camp IX at what they thought was the agreed-upon location. Bonatti called out "Lino! Achille! Where are you? Where have you put the tent?" They called back, unseen from some distance ahead, "Follow the tracks!"[65] The three climbers kept following the footprints of the lead team, but by 6:30 they still had not found them. Abram was losing sensation in his feet and decided to turn back to Camp VIII. Now there was only Bonatti and Mahdi left: if there were to be a summit ascent the next day, it was up to them to deliver the oxygen sets to Lacedelli and Compagnoni. And it was getting dark.

Lacedelli and Compagnoni had pitched their two-man tent, but not at the site they had agreed upon the day before with Bonatti. At Compagnoni's insistence, they had climbed higher and further to the left than originally planned, establishing Camp IX at about 26,575 feet. It would be many years before the true reason for this choice of camp-site would be revealed. On the fiftieth anniversary of the climb, Lacedelli, asked by an interviewer "Why do you think Compagnoni wanted to traverse to the left?" replied: "I believe he didn't want Bonatti to reach us. When I saw Bonatti come towards us I asked Compagnoni why he didn't want him to reach us and he said that it was just the two of us who had to make the final climb to the summit. To me it didn't matter if it was the two of us or another pair. If there had been four of us it would have been even better. . . . But Compagnoni said that was not possible as there were only two oxygen [sets]. I suggested we take turns to use the oxygen, I even said that I was willing to climb without oxygen, but there was no changing his mind."[66]

In the gathering darkness Bonatti called out to Lacedelli and Compagnoni with increasing desperation. Finally, on a steep section of the Abruzzi Ridge, he gave up and dug out a small platform for an emergency bivouac. Mahdi was panicking and could go no farther in safety, either up or down. Suddenly they heard a call and saw a light shining down at them from a point no more than 100 yards away, across a couloir and further up the slope to their left. Lacedelli shouted to Bonatti that he and Mahdi should leave the oxygen sets where they were and retreat. Bonatti knew that in their present condition this was impossible. He wanted Lacedelli and Compagnoni to come down and lead them to the shelter of the tent, but his shouts got no further response. Bonatti and Mahdi could do nothing but huddle together against the cold. They were at about the same height as Hermann Buhl's unplanned bivouac the previous year on Nanga Parbat, but the weather that night on K2 was far worse than that Buhl had experienced. Both men suffered greatly. Bonatti beat his freezing limbs with his ice ax to restore sensation. But it was Mahdi, in his inferior shoes, who paid the greatest penalty: he would lose half of each foot to frostbite and never climb again. At dawn Mahdi rose and clambered down the slopes on his frozen feet, and Bonatti followed soon afterward.

Meanwhile, Compagnoni and Lacedelli prepared for their summit attempt. At first light they left their tent. They were astonished, according to Lacedelli, to see Bonatti on the slopes below, believing that he and Mahdi had descended to safety the night before. They climbed down the 100 yards or so to Bonatti and Mahdi's bivouac site to retrieve the oxygen sets, then turned around and headed back.

Compagnoni and Lacedelli plodded slowly upward, passing the high points achieved by the previous expeditions to the mountain. Their oxygen may or may not have run out several hours before they reached the summit (the amount of oxygen in their canisters was another of the enduring controversies of the expedition). With or without oxygen, they climbed past the point of complete exhaustion, suffering from cold, dehydration, and hallucinations. Both were convinced at one point that Mario Puchoz, their dead comrade, had joined them on the ascent.

Once they reached 27,500 feet on the summit pyramid, Wiessner and Pasang Dawa Lama's highpoint in 1939, they passed on to untrodden terrain. They climbed over broken rock until at last, just before 6:00 P.M., the slope turned to a flat surface and they knew they had reached the summit. They pulled out the Italian and Pakistani flags for summit photographs and shot a few seconds of movie film (a first on the summit of an 8,000-meter peak). Compagnoni was showing distinct signs of hypoxia. He told Lacedelli that he would prefer to spend the night on the mountaintop and come down the following day. Lacedelli responded by threatening to hit him with his ice ax if he didn't descend immediately. They set off in darkness down the mountain, stumbling and falling repeatedly but somehow making it safely back to Camp VIII around 11:00 p.m., where Bonatti, Abram, Gallotti, Mahdi, and Isakhan awaited them. Compagnoni's hands were frozen, and he would lose several fingers.[67]

Compagnoni and Lacedelli, with Bonatti's indispensable assistance, had climbed the second-highest mountain in the world. They brought to a successful conclusion a four-decade-long quest by Italian mountaineers to claim the summit of K2. But unlike the Americans who had failed to climb the mountain the previous year, the Italians did not leave K2 as brothers. In an ever-escalating and decades-long series of charges and countercharges, the climbers would accuse each other of recklessness, of sabotage, even of attempted murder. Walter Bonatti wrote many years later that the "whole story of this mountain's conquest is miserable and sordid."[68]

For the moment, in the immediate aftermath of the expedition, the disputes were overlooked in the wave of patriotic celebration in Italy inspired by the news from K2. The triumphant climbers were decorated by the Italian government; a commemorative postage stamp was issued in their honor; they were received in the Vatican by Pope Pius XII; and a documentary film, *Italia K2,* played to packed houses. The newspaper *Corriere della sera* called the news of the ascent "[t]he best news for the Italians for many years."[69]

Charlie Houston wrote a letter to the *New York Times* offering his congratulations to the Italian climbers and also expressing the hope that with the highest and second-highest mountains in the world now climbed, "more climbers will make expeditions for the love of climbing, rather than for pride of conquest." For their part, the Italians invited Houston in the fall to the celebration in the Palazzia Venetia in Genoa, where Ardito Desio was awarded the Columbus International Medal before a wildly enthusiastic audience. To his surprise, Houston was called to the podium, where Lacedelli presented him with his red umbrella, which the Italians had recovered at the site of the American Camp III on K2.[70]

When he returned from Italy Houston sent out a letter to veterans of the American expedition, describing the ceremonies in Genoa. While he had found the Italian climbers, including Desio, "completely unassuming," he nonetheless got "quite sick of the 'Gloria Italia'" that resounded in the speeches that evening: "The nationalistic feeling is extremely strong and to me a little sickening. However, there is no question about the fact that the climb gave Italy a great shot in the arm at a very necessary time. It is perfectly astonishing the enthusiasm for mountaineering in Italy." In conversation with the Italians, Houston got the impression that "in their eyes our expedition was distinctly amateurish." Nor could the Italians "understand our interest in running a small expedition in a casual, and perhaps an off-hand way." There were many things to be admired about the Italian effort, Houston concluded, "but make no mistakes about it, it was not a happy party. They may have reached the summit, but they certainly lacked some of the things which made our party so outstanding."[71]

The Austrians Climb Cho Oyu

While the Italians tackled K-2 with eleven climbers, an Austrian expedition only three members strong was attempting the first ascent of Cho Oyu (26,905ft/8,201m), the world's sixth-highest mountain. Two years earlier Cho Oyu had turned back an expedition of Britain's finest Himalayan climbers, equipped with oxygen, most of whom would be on Everest in 1953. In 1954 the Austrians would be successful, climbing without oxygen. In ascending Cho Oyu with such a small and lightly equipped party, the Austrians anticipated by several decades later trends in Himalayan climbing.

The Austrian team was led by Herbert Tichy, a journalist, geologist, and climber with considerable Himalayan experience, and included Helmut Heuberger and Sepp Jöchler.[72] They were accompanied by seven Sherpas. The Sherpa sirdar was Pasang Dawa Lama, veteran of some of the most difficult and desperate climbs in the Himalayas in the 1930s, including the 1939 attempt on K2.

Tichy's leadership style had more in common with Houston's than with that of Desio or Herrligkoffer. "I was supposed to be the expedition's leader," he would write, "but we were not disciplined on military lines, and when a decision had to be made we sat down and discussed the matter."[73] Tichy's democratic impulses extended to the Sherpas. In a move unusual for expeditions of the era, he provided them with the same clothing and gear as the European climbers. And Tichy's respect for Pasang's experience and abilities proved to be of critical importance in the eventual success of the expedition.

The expedition set off from Kathmandu at the beginning of September and reached Cho Oyu three weeks later. They would follow the British route, which meant crossing over the Nangpa La into Tibet. Tichy did not share Shipton's fears of encountering Chinese border guards, figuring they were too high on the mountain to be noticed or bothered, so his Base Camp, unlike Shipton's, was in Tibet. Camp I went in at 19,000 feet at the foot of the West Buttress, followed by Camp II at 20,350 feet, and Camp III at 22,500 feet, just below the ice wall that had stopped the 1952 British expedition. And then, as Tichy wrote, something unexpected happened: "We had no sooner reached Camp III, or rather the site for it, and thrown down our loads, and ourselves panting beside them on the snow, than Pasang proceeded to get out ice-pitons and snap-hooks [carabiners]. It was two or three o'clock in the afternoon, just the right time for putting up our tent, making tea and getting ready for an evening's rest. But Pasang wouldn't hear of it. . . . he fixed his eyes on the ice-fall as though it had personally insulted him."[74]

Given the difficulties that Shipton's party had encountered with the icefall in 1951, Tichy's preference for calling it a day was understandable. However, he and Sherpa Adjiba obediently followed Pasang through the deep snow up to the base of the wall, where they roped up behind him. Pasang led the pitch and an hour later stood triumphantly atop the icefall that Shipton's party had estimated would take two weeks to surmount. "Perhaps we had been fortunate immediately to find the only possible flaw," Tichy wrote, or "perhaps the ice had altered since Shipton's attempt."[75] One thing that had certainly altered in this instance was the willingness of a Western climber to be guided in mountaineering decisions by a Sherpa.

Two days later they had established Camp IV above the ice wall at 23,000 feet. But on October 6 they were hit by a blizzard. When Tichy's hands became badly frostbitten trying to hold down a windblown tent, the climbers were forced to retreat to Camp I to recuperate.

Back at Camp I they had another surprise, encountering members of a rival European expedition with designs on the same mountain. This French-Swiss party, led by Raymond Lambert, had abandoned an attempt to climb Gaurishankar (23,405ft/7,134m) and was looking for another potential first ascent. Claude Kogan and Denis Bertholet, the advance guard of the expedition, had a proposition for Tichy: they should join forces to tackle Cho Oyu together. Although such things had happened in the Alps, never before had two expeditions competed to climb the same mountain in the Himalaya at the same time, and to Kogan and Bertholet (and Lambert, for whom they spoke) it seemed they were offering a fair compromise.

The Austrians, for their part, were understandably unenthusiastic, since they, not Lambert, had been given a permit to climb Cho Oyu. Not only that, but part of what Tichy was hoping to prove was that a small group of climbers could tackle and climb an 8,000-meter peak. Finally, he got the newcomers to agree to allow the Austrians to make one last try on their own. While they headed back up to Camp III, Lambert's expedition began putting up their own fixed ropes to prepare for a later attempt.[76]

While the agreement with Lambert's party was being hashed out, one important member of Tichy's expedition was out of contact. Pasang had earlier hiked back to Namche Bazar to acquire additional supplies. Returning with his purchases, Pasang had reached the village of Marlung, thirty miles from Cho Oyu, when he learned about the interloping Lambert expedition. Outraged, he made an epic push to join the Austrians at their high camp, traveling thirty miles and gaining nearly 10,000 feet of elevation in just two days. Even more remarkably, when he rejoined his companions at Camp III on October 18, he was strong enough to continue with them that same day up to Camp IV.[77]

The next day, October 19, was to be their summit day. Tichy's hands were still painfully swollen, and he intended to go no higher than Camp IV, while Sepp Jöchler and Pasang carried on. Jöchler was a climber of sterling abilities (he had climbed the North Face of the Eiger with Hermann Buhl in 1952), and no one was more highly motivated than Pasang to reach the summit of Cho Oyu. They could surely continue on their own, without any further aid from their expedition leader. Still, Tichy was not content. That night he debated with himself whether to do the sensible thing and remain in Camp IV or risk everything to accompany his friends: "I hated my helplessness. If I wrapped my hands up really warmly and if the summit wasn't too difficult, perhaps I could go too? But two hours of storm and my hands would be irretrievably dead. Dared I take the risk?" Finally he made his decision and crept into Jöchler and Pasang's tent to tell them he would join them in the morning. "'Good,' said Sepp, 'I hoped you would.' Pasang nodded. 'That is good.'"[78]

As the summit party began their preparations to depart in the early morning hours of October 19, Tichy had to have the others help pull his frozen boots onto his feet. He gripped his ice ax with his right hand, knowing that as the warmth of the sleeping bag wore off, his hand would tighten into a clawlike grip upon it. At first light they set off. They would have to gain close to 4,000 feet of elevation to reach the summit, more than the British on Everest and the Italians on K2 had to climb on their summit days, and roughly what Hermann Buhl had climbed on Nanga Parbat. When they reached the shoulder of the Northwest Ridge (thereafter known as Tichy Ridge), Pasang gave Tichy hot coffee from a thermos and placed rice in his mouth for him to swallow. Despite the misery of his hands and the feeling that his toes were beginning to freeze, Tichy experienced "an indescribable impersonal happiness," a closeness to God "and the essentials of the universe." He had, he thought, "broken through a metaphysical boundary and reached a new world." Climbing the mountain reminded Tichy of a line from "The Marriage of Heaven and Hell" by the poet William Blake: "If the doors of perception were cleansed everything would appear to men as it is, infinite."[79]

Tichy was not alone in suffering from the cold. Jöchler, who had frozen his feet on the Eiger, was also in a bad way as they made their way up the slope. Tichy considered ordering him to return to safety but decided that each man on the climb knew his own limits and should thus make his own decisions. Finally the summit came in view, and with it a magnificent vista of Mount Everest to the east. At 3:00 P.M. they stepped onto the top of Cho Oyu. Pasang stuck his ice ax on the summit, with the flags of Austria, Nepal, and India attached. Tichy was surprised to find that although "normally no lover of flags," the sight of "these symbols of my fatherland and the two countries that I think of and love so much" in this setting brought unashamed tears to his eyes.[80]

Tears also flowed down and froze upon Pasang Dawa Lama's face. In 1939 Pasang had forced Fritz Wiessner to turn back when they were a short distance from the summit of K2. Darkness had been approaching, and he may have saved both their lives in doing so, although Wiessner believed he could have summited safely had he been alone. But climbing standards for Sherpas had changed as much as they had for sahibs in the intervening years. Tenzing's success on Everest had brought new aspirations to the Sherpas. On Cho Oyu's summit that October afternoon, Tichy heard Pasang whisper over and over the single word, "peak."[81]

The British Climb Kangchenjunga

With the ascent of Everest in 1953 followed by that of K2 in 1954, Kangchenjunga (28,168ft/8,596m) had now gained the status of the world's highest unclimbed peak. The mountain had first been attempted by Aleister Crowley's expedition in 1905 (which ended in the death of a climber and three porters) and had withstood three more unsuccessful expeditions in three years between 1929 and 1931. In 1955 the Mount Everest Foundation funded the attempt on Kangchenjunga in what turned out to be the last great nationally organized British expedition.

The team assembled for the attempt included eight climbers and an expedition doctor along with twenty-eight Sherpas led by Dawa Tenzing, who had been deputy sirdar on the British Everest climb and who was the brother of Ang Tharkay. Other familiar faces from Everest included expedition leader Charles Evans and George Band. Additional climbers with Himalayan experience included Tony Streather and Norman Hardie. Among the newcomers was the youngest of the party, twenty-four-year-old Joe Brown.

Age was not the only distinction setting Brown apart. Scottish climber Tom Patey became famous in British climbing circles in the 1950s and 1960s for composing ballads and ditties mocking the mountaineering establishment's pretensions. In one of his most famous, he took on the Alpine Club's recruitment strategy for Himalayan expeditions:

> Our climbing leaders are no fools
> They went to the very best Public Schools
> You'll never go wrong with Everest Men
> So we select them again and again
> Again and again and again and again.

Joe Brown broke the mold, for not only had he not been on Everest, he had definitely not gone to the very best public schools (or indeed, after the age of fourteen when he dropped out to become a plumber's apprentice, any kind of school). Following a Dickensian childhood in a Manchester suburb (fatherless, six siblings, and a mother who took in washing to support the family), Brown had discovered rock climbing on the grit stone surfaces of the local quarries, where he used an old clothesline for his belays.[82] As his skill increased he moved on to climb in Wales and then to the Alps.

Brown would soon become one of the best-known representatives of a new generation of British "hard men" from working-class backgrounds who took up rock climbing and mountaineering in the years after the war. Few joined the Alpine Club, at least in their younger days. Instead they nurtured their talents in local or regional climbing clubs. With another Manchester plumber, Don Whillans, and other local climbers, Brown formed the Rock and Ice Club, a climbing club that, like its Glasgow counterpart Creagh Dhu, became legendary for pub brawls as well as for notable first ascents of forbidding rock faces. In the Alps Brown and Whillans propelled themselves to the front rank of British climbers in 1954 by making the third ascent of the West Face of the Dru (climbing it in record time) and putting up a new route on the West Face of the Blaitière. After news of their ascent of the Dru became known, Chamonix guides stopped them in the street to shake their hands.[83]

None of which put any money in Brown's pockets. When he was invited by Charles Evans to join the Kangchenjunga expedition he was pleased, but also embarrassed. Evans told him that all his expenses, including travel and equipment, would be paid for, and also, as Brown would recall, "that £20 pocket money would be ample. I couldn't tell him that I hadn't got £20."[84]

The 1955 expedition would focus its efforts on the Yalung or Southwest face. A 1954 reconnaissance expedition led by John Kempe had identified two possible routes up the lower portion of the Southwest Face, one via a rib dubbed Kempe's Rock Buttress, the other known as Pache's grave, for it passed by the burial site of Alexis Pache, who had died in an avalanche in 1905.[85]

As they gathered in Darjeeling, the expedition members could already see their goal in the distance. "Rosy at dawn, brilliant and remote in sunshine, cold and repellent in shadow," George Band wrote in the expedition report for the *Alpine Journal,* Kangchenjunga "seems to float above the haze and darkness of the valleys between, its great mass filling the north-western horizon."[86]

They left Darjeeling on March 14 in a truck convoy that carried them to the foot of the Singalila Ridge on the Nepalese border, where the road ended. From there they continued on foot. Although most of the prewar expeditions had climbed from the Sikkimese side of the mountain, Sikkim had closed its borders to Westerners after the Second World War. So, by necessity, the British would make their attempt from Nepal. The climbers promised the Sikkimese they would not desecrate the summit by standing upon it; that sacred spot would remain inviolate.

They hiked through forests ablaze with rhododendrons and primula to the foot of the Yalung Glacier and continued to the Southwest Face of the mountain, where they established Base Camp on April 12. The Kempe's Rock Buttress route involved tackling an icefall that George Band decided made "the Khumbu Icefall look like a children's playground."[87] Abandoning their initial plan, they moved Base Camp left along the face to a site near Pache's grave and from there followed a steep snow gully up the mountain that allowed them to bypass the icefall. By April 26 they had established Camp I at 19,700 feet, two-thirds of the way up the face's Western Rock Buttress. Camp II went in at 20,400 feet and Camp III at 21,800 feet. On May 13 they reached the Great Shelf, an ice terrace stretching across the Southwest Face at about 24,000 feet, which George Band called "the equivalent of the South Col on Everest."[88] There they placed Camp V.

Evans selected two summit parties, the first consisting of Band and Brown, the second of Streather and Hardie. Band and Brown's summit bid was delayed when the climbers were trapped for three days at Camp IV by a raging blizzard. On May 22 the skies cleared, and from their advanced camp on the mountainside the climbers could see all the way to Everest. On May 24 the two lead climbers, supported by Evans, Neil Mather, and Dawa Tenzing, established Camp VI at 26,900 feet, halfway up the Gangway, a long, steep snowfield that led to the West Ridge of the mountain. The others left Band and Brown

Kangchenjunga from the southwest, showing the 1955 British route of ascent.

at their high camp and made their way down the mountain. The lead climbers slept with oxygen that night, keeping their boots on in their sleeping bags to ensure that they would not freeze. Waking to good weather, Band and Brown set out at 8:15 on May 25.

Their route at first was straight up the Gangway. They did not want to follow the Gangway all the way to where it joined the West Ridge, due to the rough broken character of the ridge at the junction. Instead, they planned to traverse upward across the snow

George Band and Joe Brown, Kangchenjunga, 1955.
Reprinted by permission of the Royal Geographical Society.

patches and broken rock of the Southwest Face. They turned off the Gangway too soon, however, and wasted an hour and a half venturing out onto an unpromising stretch of the face. They had to retrace their steps and then continue farther up the Gangway until they found a more promising line to traverse. Five hours of climbing finally brought them to the West Ridge, still 400 feet short of the summit pyramid. Their oxygen was running low, and the ridge ran straight into a formidable rock wall. As Band noted, "the wall was broken by several vertical cracks about twenty feet high, with a slight overhang to finish. Joe was keen to try one." Band was dubious but impressed as Brown cranked up his oxygen flow and efficiently climbed the crack to the top. "George, we're there!" he shouted, and Band followed on the rope.[89]

Surmounting that obstacle, they found themselves a mere five vertical feet from the summit. It would have been an easy walk up, but they halted where they were and, as agreed, left the summit untouched. It was 2:45 P.M. In the distance they could see Everest, Lhotse, and Makalu silhouetted against the horizon. "One expects to be overwhelmed by a terrific feeling of triumph at the top of a mountain, especially one as big as Kangchenjunga," Brown would write of their achievement. Instead, "we felt only relief at not having to step up yet again and also a great feeling of peace and tranquility. After spending so long on a mountain one tends to lose sight of the fact that there is a top and that the point of the expedition is to get there."[90]

Fifteen minutes later they began their descent. Their oxygen ran out shortly afterward. They reached Camp VI at 7:00 P.M. to be greeted by Hardie and Streather, who had climbed up that day to prepare for their own summit attempt. The four men spent a cramped night together in Camp VI's one two-man tent, Brown suffering from snow blindness and Band from frostbitten fingertips. The next day Hardie and Streather followed their teammates' footsteps most of the way up. Just short of the summit, however, they took a variant route that allowed them to circumvent the rock wall that Brown had ascended, instead following a snow slope that led to the mountain's South Ridge. They arrived at the high point just short of the summit at 12:15 P.M. and then descended safely.[91]

The ascent of Kangchenjunga was celebrated by the *American Alpine Journal* as "a model of great mountaineering."[92] Outside the international climbing community the expedition attracted only a fraction of the attention of the Everest climb two years earlier, even in Britain. There were no knighthoods awarded to the men who summited, even though Band and Brown were actually the first British subjects to climb an 8,000-meter peak. Hillary and Tenzing on Everest were a tough act to follow. And what's more, the climbers themselves seemed to have made a conscious decision to downplay the nationalist trappings of their endeavor; Charles Evans's official report neglected to mention whether either of the summit parties had unfurled British flags at the mountain's top.

Makalu, Manaslu, Lhotse, Gasherbrum II

The French, like the British, enjoyed their second ascent of an 8,000-meter peak in 1955, when Lionel Terray and Jean Couzy reached the summit of Makalu (27,765ft/8,463m), the world's fifth-highest mountain, on May 15 via its North Face and East Ridge. Expedition leader Jean Franco, Guido Magnone, and Sherpa sirdar Gyalzen Norbu summited May 16. The following day the rest of the French party climbed to the top of Makalu, the first time an eight-thousander had seen an entire expedition team reach the summit. All in all, the climb went so smoothly, with near-perfect weather and snow conditions, that the climbers sounded a little disappointed afterward that it had not proven more demanding. Franco described Makalu's summit, where three summit ridges came together, as "a perfect pyramid of snow so sharp that one could cover it with a hand, one finger towards Tibet, another toward Nepal, a third towards Everest."[93]

Three more expeditions set out to climb 8,000-meter peaks in 1956, two in Nepal and one in Pakistan. The first in the field was a twelve-member Japanese Alpine Club expedition, led by the venerable Japanese Alpinist Yuko Maki, that set out to climb the world's eighth-highest mountain, Manaslu (26,781ft/8,163m). Japanese mountaineers had limited experience in the Himalaya in prewar years, the most notable effort a 1936 attempt on Nanda Kot. In the years after World War II, as they recovered from the humiliation of defeat and rebuilt their country from the ruins left by American bombing raids, the Japanese were heartened by international sporting victories won by their athletes, like the gold medal won by wrestler Shohachi Ishii in the 1952 Helsinki Olympic games. They were eager to win distinction in the Himalaya as well, concentrating their efforts on Manaslu, located forty miles to the east of Annapurna.

The 1956 Japanese success had been prepared by previous expeditions. In 1952 Kinji Imanishi led five climbers from the Japanese Alpine Club on a reconnaissance of Annapurna IV and Manaslu. Three more Japanese expeditions to Manaslu came in the next three years, to scout and then attempt the mountain. Success came with the Yuko Maki expedition: Toshio Imanishi and Sherpa sirdar Gyalzen Norbu left their assault camp at 8:00 A.M. on May 9 and reached the summit via the North Side at 12:30 P.M. Gyalzen Norbu, who had climbed Makalu with the French the previous year, became the first man to reach the summit of two eight-thousanders (although not by a first ascent the first time). The initial summit party was followed two days later by another successful ascent by Kiichiro Kato and Minoru Higeta. The attempt upon Manaslu was covered extensively in the Japanese press, and the triumphant mountaineers were hailed on their return as conquering heroes (like the Italians who climbed K2, they got their own postage stamp). Inspired by this success, mountain climbing became a major sport in Japan, centered in university climbing clubs. Although Japanese mountaineers would make their mark on many of the world's mountain ranges, their greatest interest remained fixed on the Himalaya.[94]

In 1956 the Swiss returned to the Everest massif. Four years earlier they had come within a few hundred vertical feet of claiming a first ascent of Mount Everest. They had twin goals in mind for the 1956 expedition: to make the second ascent of Everest and, more important, to make a first ascent of its neighbor Lhotse (27,939ft/8,516m), the world's fourth-highest mountain. Led by Albert Eggler of Berne and well equipped by the Swiss Foundation for Alpine Research, the Swiss climbers followed the familiar route up the Khumbu Icefall, the Western Cwm, and Lhotse Face to the South Col. From there they used a cable hoist to lift supplies for their summit bids. They also had the advantage of being equipped with front-point crampons, which reduced the need for step-cutting on steep and icy slopes. Though previously employed in Alpine climbing, this was the first time twelve-point crampons were used on a Himalayan expedition. On May 18 Fritz Luchsinger and Ernst Reiss reached the summit of Lhotse via a couloir on the mountain's western face. The summit came to such a sharp point that there was no room for Luchsinger and Reiss to sit or put down their rucksacks; they cut a little platform slightly below the summit, pulled themselves up to it, and held on and peered over the other side.[95]

The expedition then shifted its attention to Everest. Two separate teams, one consisting of Ernst Schmied and Jürg Marmet, the other of Adolf Reist and Hans Rudolf von Gunten, reached Everest's summit on two successive days, May 23 and 24, the mountain's second and third ascents. This was the first expedition to climb two separate eight-thousanders.[96]

The third major Himalayan effort that season was launched by Austrians in the Karakoram. An eight-man team led by Fritz Moravec set out to climb Gasherbrum II (26,360ft/8,035m), the thirteenth-highest mountain in the world. The expedition members lost much of their equipment when an avalanche engulfed Camp I on June 30. But they pushed on in a lightweight effort, climbing without oxygen up the mountain's Southeast

Face. On the final night before the assault, the summit party of Moravec, Sepp Larch, and Hans Willenpart made a planned bivouac, another innovation in Himalayan climbing and harbinger of alpine-style tactics to come. On the following morning, July 7, they reached the summit at 11:30 A.M.[97]

"Slightly Stunted Giants"

After the ascent of Everest Eric Shipton predicted a "new era in Himalayan climbing." In years to come climbers would travel to the Himalaya "on their own initiative, and on modest resources" to tackle the hundreds of unclimbed peaks whose summits fell below the arbitrary standard of the 8,000-meter line. In doing so, he wrote, "they will find in the simplicity of their approach the true enjoyment of their endeavour." By the mid-1950s some mountaineers were indeed beginning to turn to the lesser Himalayan peaks (mountains Bill Tilman once referred to as "slightly stunted giants") and, as Shipton predicted, found there a more satisfying style of climbing.[98]

One of the first such efforts was headed up by none other than Sir Edmund Hillary. In 1954 Hillary led a New Zealand–British expedition to the Barun Valley, east of Everest, a region that he had first glimpsed with Shipton on a side trip during the 1951 Everest reconnaissance and returned to for a closer look with George Lowe following the 1952 Cho Oyu expedition. Hillary was elated to find it as appealing a landscape as he remembered from past visits. "High above us on both sides were tremendous rock precipices and jagged ice ridges. But the valley was green and the air was fresh with the scent of pine trees."[99]

Hillary had originally intended to lead his expedition on yet another of the 8,000-meter peaks, Makalu, which overlooked the Barun Valley, but an American party had already secured the permit for 1954 for that mountain. (The California Himalayan Expedition, led by Will Siri, would turn back after reaching 23,200 feet on Maklau's Southeast Ridge.)[100] Hillary's party turned its attention to other peaks in the region, making twenty-three first ascents, nineteen over 20,000 feet, including Baruntse (23,388ft/7,129m), Pethangstse (22,109ft/6,739m), and Chago (22,614ft/6,893m). The expedition's successes were unfortunately overshadowed by Hillary's evacuation from the Barun Valley by stretcher; after injuring his ribs in rescuing an expedition member who had fallen into a crevasse, he developed pneumonia.[101]

Two years later a British expedition set out to climb the blunt-headed obelisk known as Muztagh Tower (23,897ft/7,284m), long an iconic feature of the Karakoram. Martin Conway, on his visit to the Baltoro Glacier in 1892, judged it "the finest mountain in the district." Given its fame, it is striking that for sixty-odd years after Conway's comment no expedition had attempted Muztagh Tower, though many passed it en route to other peaks along the Baltoro. That may have had something to do with the previous fixation on 8,000-meter peaks. But it may also have had something to do with the view of the mountain offered in Vittorio Sella's much-reproduced 1909 photograph, taken from

an angle that made it look virtually impregnable. The prospect of undertaking high standard ice and rock climbing on the tower's upper reaches made the ascent of some of the
neighboring giants seem inviting by comparison.[102]

The 1956 British expedition to Muztagh Tower, led by John Hartog, intended to
tackle the obelisk via its Northwest Ridge. It was only when he had studied aerial photographs taken in 1954 by Ardito Desio on his K2 reconnaissance flight that Hartog realized that the famous Sella photograph of 1909 was misleading in one important respect:
Muztagh Tower had two summits, not one, and they were linked together by a col of about
400 yards length. What remained unclear was which summit was the higher of the two.
The British route would take them first to the West Summit.

A month's effort went into placing and supplying four camps on the mountain.
On July 6 Joe Brown and Ian McNaught-Davis set off for their summit attempt. When
they reached the West Summit it became clear that the true summit still lay ahead of
them, across the col to the east. When they attempted to cross over to the true summit,
ten feet higher than the one that they had already reached, Brown fell through a cornice.
Only good luck kept him from plummeting to the glacier 7,000 feet below. That brought
an end to the day's climb, and the two retreated, bivouacking about 300 feet below the
West Summit.

The following day, July 7, as Brown and McNaught-Davis continued their descent,
they met Hartog and Tom Patey around 9:30 A.M., heading for their own summit attempt.
Hartog and Patey reached the West Summit at 2:30, four hours earlier than Brown and
McNaught-Davis. From there they made their way gingerly across the knife-edge leading
to the eastern summit, having to surmount a ten-foot-high smooth slab of rock en route.
From the top they could see all the great nearby peaks of the Karakoram and in the distance,
standing alone, Nanga Parbat. They began their descent at 4:30 but were still far above their
high camp at 7:30, so they too were forced to bivouac; Hartog suffered frostbitten feet as
a result. A few days later, on July 12 and July 13, all four climbing members of the French
party led by Guido Magnone summited via the mountain's southeastern ridge.[103]

The ascent of Muztagh Tower by the British and French expeditions represented
the most difficult technical climbs yet achieved in the Himalaya. The two climbs were the
first documented instance of a major Himalayan peak having been climbed to its summit
by more than a single route (the mystery of Mallory and Irvine's disappearance on Everest
leaving open the question of whether that mountain had been climbed by both northern
and southern routes). Also impressive was the success of both expeditions in getting all their
members to, or at least within shouting distance, of the summit. Anthony Rawlinson wrote
in the *Alpine Journal* the year after the dual ascents of Muztagh Tower that "the beginnings
are discernible of a new trend" in Himalayan climbing, "towards fine peaks though they are
neither the highest nor the easiest, and to objectives chosen by the same kind of criteria as
we follow in the Alps; the challenge of technical difficulty is being taken up."[104]

The Austrians Climb Broad Peak

On June 9, 1957, every single member of a four-man Austrian expedition made it to the summit of Broad Peak (26,401ft/8,047m) in the Karakoram, the world's twelfth-highest mountain. All four then made it safely back to Base Camp. Unlike some of the more unhappy expeditions of the golden age of Himalayan mountaineering, the Austrians had no authoritarian leaders to obey, no nationalist or family agendas to fulfill. They climbed the mountain for its own sake, and succeeded wonderfully. For Hermann Buhl, the most famous of the four climbers, it was the second time he would make a first ascent of an 8,000-meter peak (something that no other climber had yet accomplished).[105] It could not have worked out any better than it did for all involved. And yet the Broad Peak expedition would prove one of the most contentious of a decade that would see no shortage of occasions when mountaineers were at odds with one another.

Though he returned to Austria a popular hero after his solo ascent of Nanga Parbat in 1953, Buhl found it hard to enjoy his celebrity. It took him a long time to recover from the frostbite that cost him two toes from his right foot. Worse, he found himself embroiled in a dispute with Karl Herrligkoffer over what had actually happened on Nanga Parbat and in legal difficulty because he went ahead and published his own account in violation of his expedition contract. The dispute proved all the more galling to Buhl because his former partner, Kuno Rainer, with whom he had racked up many achievements in the Alps (including the first complete traverse of the Aiguilles de Chamonix), sided with Herrligkoffer. In 1954 Herrligkoffer set off on another expedition, at first hoping to climb Gasherbrum I but then switching to Broad Peak. Herrligkoffer invited Rainer to join the effort but not, of course, Buhl.[106]

Herrligkoffer's expedition failed in its attempt to climb Broad Peak, and Buhl had the satisfaction of choosing the mountain for his next Himalayan venture. Marcus Schmuck, a Salzburg climber, had no grudge to settle with Herrligkoffer, but he shared Buhl's ambition to climb Broad Peak. The two men had climbed together in 1956 in the Alps (making the sixth ascent of the West Face of the Dru) and seemed to form a solid friendship. Influenced by the success of Herbert Tichy's small expedition to Cho Oyu, Buhl and Schmuck decided to tackle Broad Peak in *Westalpenstil,* or the style of the western Alps. What that meant in the context of Himalayan mountaineering was a lightweight expedition that did without high-altitude porters. It was not quite the same as what would later be judged true "alpine style," in which climbers moved in a continuous push up the mountain, carrying their camp with them. But it certainly represented a modification of the traditional siege tactics of larger expeditions (such as Herrligkoffer specialized in), with their elaborately planned schemes for ferrying and stockpiling supplies in a pyramid of camps stretched ever higher on the mountain.[107]

Muztagh Tower, 1909. Photograph by Vittorio Sella.
© 2005—Fondazione Sella, Biella, Italy. Courtesy, Fondazione Sella, Biella, Italy.

To satisfy the Austrian Alpine Club, which donated about a quarter of the costs, Schmuck was designated expedition leader, with Buhl to be climbing leader once they were on the mountain. The division of leadership irritated Buhl, who had a far more illustrious climbing record than Schmuck, but club leaders were concerned about his reputation for controversy as well as the fact that he had failed to reimburse them for his share of the 1953 expedition expenses. Since both men would be equally involved in climbing Broad Peak, the division of authority meant that their decision making would be by consensus—if consensus could be achieved. The leaders selected two other young Austrian climbers to round out the roster: Fritz Wintersteller, like Schmuck an electrician from Salzburg, and Kurt Diemberger, a medical student from Vienna.

The Austrians, accompanied by their Pakistani liaison officer, Qader Saaed, and sixty-five porters, left Skardu for Broad Peak on April 18, 1957. They had not reached the mountain before the first conflicts emerged between Buhl and Schmuck over issues of the day-to-day management of the porters, with Buhl comparing Schmuck in one of his diary entries to Herrligkoffer.[108] Coming from Buhl there could be no more damning judgment. It seems misplaced, since his main complaint was not that Schmuck was too authoritarian but rather that he was too easygoing in his treatment of the porters. Buhl seems to have transferred his resentment over his treatment at Herrligkoffer's hands on Nanga Parbat to a new target, an unfortunate beginning for the Broad Peak venture.

Long before they reached Base Camp, the expedition divided into two teams: Buhl and Diemberger and Schmuck and Wintersteller. The pairings made sense, insofar as each of the two most experienced climbers would share a rope with a less experienced partner. The problem was that the two pairs of climbers each came to view the others as rivals rather than partners.

Other problems developed on the approach march. The porters, who had been complaining about lack of blankets and other amenities, refused to carry past the unsuitably named Concordia junction of the Baltoro and Godwin-Austen glaciers. The four climbers, along with Qader Saaed and two mail runners, ferried loads the remaining twelve miles to Base Camp at 16,000 feet.

On May 13, three and a half weeks after setting off from Skardu, the four Austrians began to push a route up the mountain's western face toward the West Ridge, which they hoped would lead them to the summit. On their first day of climbing they put in Camp I at 19,000 feet. Nicknamed Tooth Camp for a rock spire just below its site, it was followed soon after by the establishment of Camp II at just under 21,000 feet. The Austrians ferried their own supplies up to the higher camps, a necessary modification of alpine style (they needed both the supplies and the acclimatization to higher altitudes gained from the repeated trips up and down the mountainside). They also made use of the fixed ropes left on the mountainside from the Herrligkoffer expedition and uncovered and appropriated a supply dump left by the same expedition. Apart from delays caused by the weather, the party made good progress. Expedition diaries, however, recorded increasing tensions among the mountaineers. "Ate well, slept badly, brooded too much," Buhl noted in his diary on May 15.[109]

On the evening of May 25 the weather improved, and early the next morning the Austrians headed back up the mountain from Base Camp. By May 28 they had Camp III, their assault camp, dubbed the Eagle's Nest, established at just under 23,000 feet. They were now in position to go for the summit. But Buhl was tiring. "I must confess," he wrote in his expedition report on May 28, "I do not sense the same excitement, enthusiasm or anticipation as in the days leading up to my route to the summit of Nanga Parbat." His misgivings increased on their summit day, when they started out much later than he wished. "To be honest," he wrote later that day, "I don't have much drive today and don't feel I have to reach the peak at all costs."[110]

Buhl's frost-damaged feet—his "Nanga Parbat toes," as he called them—caused him considerable pain. As he lagged behind, the customary pairings broke down. At 6:30 P.M. Diemberger and Wintersteller were in the lead, reaching what they hoped was the summit. In the gathering gloom, however, they could see another high point along the summit ridge and could not be sure if it was higher or lower than the point on which they stood. It was too late in the day to find out, and after building a cairn to mark their high point (on what, indeed, turned out to be a false summit, later known as the Forepeak), Wintersteller and Diemberger turned back to rejoin Buhl and Schmuck.

The entire party retreated to Base Camp, where for the next seven days they ate, slept, and quarreled, regaining strength if not regard for one another. All agreed on one thing: they would have to climb Broad Peak again to guarantee that they had truly accomplished its first ascent. Accordingly, on June 7 they headed back up the mountain, reaching the Eagle's Nest the following day.

Their second summit bid came on June 9. This time they got an earlier start, setting off between 3:30 and 4:00 A.M. (as with so many aspects of the expedition, there is a dispute as to whether Schmuck and Wintersteller or Buhl and Diemberger started first).[111] They followed slightly different routes, and by midmorning Schmuck and Wintersteller were in the lead. Diemberger on his own might have kept up with the lead climbers, but Buhl again lagged, suffering the effects of frostbite and exhaustion, and Diemberger remained close by him. Schmuck and Wintersteller broke trail to the Forepeak, reaching it around 4:00 P.M. This time they could clearly see that Broad Peak's true summit still lay ahead of them. Wintersteller and Schmuck reached their goal an hour later, overjoyed but exhausted. They headed down at 5:50 P.M.

Meanwhile, Buhl had reached his limit, still short of the false summit. Diemberger asked permission to go on without him. As Buhl would later write, re-creating his feelings at that moment on the mountain, Diemberger, "the young tiger, is not going to miss out on an 8000er just because of me. I must honestly confess that all my ambition has deserted me. My eight-thousander is Nanga Parbat and what I experienced there could never be repeated anyway."[112] While Buhl sat down to await his expedition mates' return, Diemberger set off alone. He climbed the Forepeak and then pushed on to reach the true summit of Broad Peak just as Schmuck and Wintersteller were beginning their descent. To his annoyance they did not wait for him to join them but hurried down past him. Diemberger stood on the top alone and consoled himself with the view.

With evening approaching, Diemberger began his descent. Before he had reached the Forepeak, however, he had a surprise. En route he spied Buhl, who had gathered his willpower and hobbled up the slope after all. Diemberger waited for Buhl to climb up to him, then turned around and climbed back to the summit with his partner—a generous gesture that may have been unprecedented in Himalayan climbing and has seldom been repeated since. When the two men reached Broad Peak's summit, it marked the first time that an entire expedition had succeeded in making the first ascent of an 8,000-meter mountain. At 7:30 P.M. Buhl and Diemberger headed down the summit ridge, Diemberger for the second time, determined not to spend the night in an unsheltered bivouac. Guided by a full moon, they reached the tents at Camp III sometime after midnight. Schmuck and Wintersteller made it back to Base Camp the next day; Buhl and Diemberger, both suffering from the rigors of their climb, took an additional day, and unlike the first two did not carry all their personal gear down from the high camps.[113]

In an entry in his expedition report, written upon return to Base Camp, Buhl noted, "Broad Peak has been climbed, and by the most idealistic, shortest route. Without high porters, by all four participants, what more could we ask for?"[114]

What more indeed? But the triumph on Broad Peak on June 9 did not mend the divisions between the two climbing teams. The Austrians squabbled over what to write on the postcards they were sending home to friends and supporters, with Buhl and Diemberger fuming that the achievement of the "whole team" was undercut by Schmuck and Wintersteller's emphasis on their own role as the first rope that day (according to long-established custom, all climbers who make it to a summit on the day of a first ascent are credited equally for the ascent, regardless of the order in which they reach the top). The two pairs now went separate ways. While Buhl and Diemberger headed back up Broad Peak to recover the gear they had left up at Camps II and III, Schmuck and Wintersteller struck off on their own, and in a remarkable two-day effort (one that was carried out in what was truly alpine style), made the first ascent of Skil Brum (24,146ft/7,360m) via its Southwest Face on June 19.

On no previous first ascent of an 8,000-meter peak had the mountaineers felt the urge to go off and climb yet another mountain, so Wintersteller and Schmuck were setting a precedent. Still, there was no need for Diemberger and Buhl to attempt any further climbs of their own before returning to Austria. Both were worn out from their exertions on Broad Peak, especially Buhl. And what was left for them to prove? They had already taken part in a great feat of mountaineering. Buhl could have gone home with his existing reputation as one of the world's greatest mountaineers enhanced; Diemberger would have his own newborn fame to enjoy and had many years to come in which to embellish his record. But the fact that Schmuck and Wintersteller, their bitter rivals and the first rope to reach the summit of Broad Peak, were off to make yet another daring first ascent was apparently too great a challenge to ignore. Buhl and Diemberger packed their rucksacks and headed south, crossing the Upper Baltoro Glacier to attempt Chogolisa (25,111ft/7,654m).

And they came close to success. On June 27, their third day on the mountain, they were headed for the summit along its Northeast Ridge, unroped and making good time. But at 24,000 feet the weather turned against them, the wind blowing so fiercely it wiped out their footprints behind them. Fearful of losing the trail they would need to follow on their descent and through a misstep breaking through a cornice, they turned back short of the summit. It was a prudent decision—but it proved in vain. A cornice suddenly crumbled beneath Diemberger, who was the lead climber on the descent. He managed to leap to safety. When he looked back behind him to check on Buhl, there was no one there. All he could see were Buhl's footprints leading to the edge.[115]

The successful and innovative Austrian Alpenverein Karakoram expedition thus ended with the death of one of the heroes of the golden age of Himalayan mountaineering. His death was the result of a misstep on a dangerous mountain, but in some measure it was also the result of the poisonous rivalry that had consumed his final expedition.

The Americans Climb Hidden Peak

In the winter of 1957 Gary Yortin of Willimansett, Massachusetts, a fan of James Ramsey Ullman's books, wrote to ask a favor of the author: "I am fifteen and I love mountain climbing. I have read "Tiger of the Snows" twice and I think it's the best book I ever read. My greatest dream is to go to the Himalayas. . . . my friends and I wish to start a climbing club. But our problem is we have no equipment. I felt that you would please tell us, or give us the address of a store were [sic] we could possibly by [sic] axes, pitons, and hammers. I would appreciate it very much if you would help us if you can."[116]

Ullman's reply has not survived. In 1957 there was not much help he could provide Yortin except, perhaps, to suggest he contact Recreational Equipment Incorporated (REI), a Seattle-based retail cooperative specializing in outdoor and mountaineering gear. The REI store, managed by a young climber named Jim Whittaker, was run out of a twenty-by-thirty-foot second-floor office, upstairs from the Green Apple Pie restaurant on Seattle's Pike Street. Most of the axes, pitons, hammers, and other climbing gear it offered for sale had to be imported from Europe.[117]

Thanks to the publicity generated by the first ascents of Annapurna and Everest, an increasing number of young Americans in the 1950s had aspirations to climb mountains themselves. But outside of a few locales in the shadow of great mountains, like Seattle, and a few mountaineering clubs at schools like Harvard, Dartmouth, and Stanford, the infrastructure simply did not exist in the United States to attract, train, and equip new generations of climbers. As a result the slopes of America's greatest mountains were seldom visited. The North American continent's highest mountain, Mount McKinley—later known as Denali—(20,320ft/6,194m) in Alaska, saw at most one or two attempted climbs a year.[118]

While following the success of other countries' Himalayan expeditions with some interest, the American public paid comparatively little attention to their own mountaineers' exploits. Americans who could identify Sir Edmund Hillary as conqueror of Everest vastly outnumbered those who would have been able to come up with the name of a single prominent American mountaineer. The 1953 American K2 expedition generated headlines in the United States as a survival rather than a mountaineering epic—"We Met Death on K2" was the title the editors of the *Saturday Evening Post* gave Bob Bates's two-part article about the expedition, framing the story in a way unlikely to encourage emulation.[119] To most Americans in the 1950s—the occasional young enthusiast like Ullman's correspondent Gary Yortin notwithstanding—mountaineers remained an exotic and not entirely respectable category of human being, either foreigners or thrill-seeking eccentrics.

Nick Clinch would exaggerate, but not by much, when he described the experience of recruiting mountaineers for an American expedition to the Karakoram in the mid-1950s as akin to "a criminal conspiracy": "There were many competent mountaineers who would be eager to participate in such an undertaking, but everyone was rightly afraid of the repercussions if the public, employers, clients, patients, business associates and immediate family should learn that such an irrational and irresponsible act was even being contemplated. . . . to become a member just was not worth the risk to one's reputation."[120]

The mountain Clinch was conspiring to climb was Gasherbrum I, better known as Hidden Peak. At 26,469 feet (8,068 meters), Hidden Peak was the eleventh-highest mountain in the world, the last eight-thousander unclimbed in the Karakoram, and one of only three still left unclimbed. The only full-scale attempt to climb the mountain had been by a French expedition in 1936.

A recent graduate of Stanford Law School, where he had been a member of the Stanford Alpine Club, Clinch had been working since the fall of 1955 to organize an expedition. Nothing came easily. The American Alpine Club's endorsement was given grudgingly, as some of its leaders seemed reluctant to sponsor an expedition organized by a brash young westerner (although Charlie Houston, among others, proved supportive). Fund-raising was a particularly demoralizing task. In Europe mountaineers could rely on sympathetic and well-heeled sponsors like the Mount Everest Foundation or the Swiss Foundation for Alpine Research, but in the United States they had to go begging to friends, corporate sponsors, and the general public. "Money is slowly dribbling in," Clinch wrote to Swiss mountaineer Jürg Marmet in January 1958, "but what I wouldn't give for an American mountaineering foundation right now."[121]

Recruitment was another headache. A number of climbers expressed interest in coming along, but few made firm commitments. One who did so was Andrew Kauffman, a Foreign Service officer stationed at the American embassy in Paris and past president of the Harvard Mountaineering Club, who had accompanied Clinch on a previous expedition to the rugged Coast Range of British Columbia in 1954. A few months before their departure to Pakistan, Clinch wrote to Kauffman to go over last-minute details. He made it clear that the burden of organizing the expedition had not dampened his enthusiasm for tackling Hidden Peak: "[T]his will be the most fantastic thing in the history of American climbing if we can pull it off. And brother I intend to."[122]

In the end six American climbers set off for Pakistan in the spring of 1958: Clinch and Kauffman were joined by Tom McCormack, Bob Swift, expedition doctor Tom Nevison, and (a late and welcome addition to the party) K2 veteran Pete Schoening. They would be joined later in the summer by two other Americans, Gil Roberts and Dick Irvin. In addition, there would be two Pakistani climbers on the expedition, Lieutenant Mohd Akram and Captain S. T. H. Rizvi.

When they flew to Rawalpindi in May, they met the members of another expedition headed for the Upper Baltoro Glacier. Riccardo Cassin, who had accompanied Ardito Desio on the 1953 reconnaissance of K2 but who had been excluded from the 1954 expedition, was leading a Club alpino italiano expedition to Gasherbrum IV (26,000ft/7,925m). This expedition included an impressive array of climbing talent, including K2 veteran Walter Bonatti (who had in the meantime dazzled the climbing world with his solo ascent of the Southwest Pillar of the Petit Dru in 1955). It also included mountain photographer Fosco Maraini, who was struck by the contrast between the Italians, four of whom were professional mountain guides, and the "nice, quiet, well-mannered, harmless Americans": "My own companions, when I came to think of it, seemed far harder, tougher nuts than these mere youths . . . the Americans, to use the word in its purest sense, were dilettanti; they were doctors, schoolmasters, technicians, agriculturists who had left their desks and offices for a glorious adventure, and a slightly crazy one. Our men were essentially mountaineers, professional climbers: the ice-wall, the glacier, the arête were their whole life, they were career and family, bread and passion."[123]

From Rawalpindi the two parties flew to Skardu and prepared to depart for the march to the Upper Baltoro and their respective mountains. The Americans set off wearing matching ten-gallon cowboy hats and humming the march from *Bridge on the River Kwai*, followed by 116 porters, including 6 Balti high-altitude porters (the Italians, more lavishly supplied, traveled with 500 porters). The American expedition set up Base Camp at 17,000 feet on June 6 on the Abruzzi Glacier to the southwest of Hidden Peak. Only Schoening, who had been to K2, and Swift and Irvin, who had been to Rakaposhi, had ever seen mountains like the ones that now surrounded them. "For years I had looked with wonder at Vittorio Sella's famous photograph of the Muztagh Tower," Clinch would recall, "and now that mountain formed the background for my friends."[124]

Clinch was expedition director, and Schoening, once they were on the slopes, leader. But every important decision taken on the mountain was arrived at by consensus or majority vote. The easiest decision was the composition of the summit party: Kauffman and Schoening won unanimous support. The most difficult choice was route. They identified five possible routes up the mountain, some more and some less direct, some requiring rock climbing, others mostly a long slog up snow slopes. In the end they agreed upon the long slog, which involved climbing a snow-covered rock rib rising from the Abruzzi Glacier to the mountain's southeast plateau and then following the plateau five miles until reaching Hidden Peak's summit pyramid. One of the advantages of the route was that its lower section had been climbed before, by André Roch and Hans Ertl in 1934; accordingly, the Americans dubbed the rib leading to the plateau the Roch Arête (it would later be renamed the IHE Ridge, or International Himalayan Expedition Ridge).

The Americans employed conventional siege tactics. They would be using supplementary oxygen at the higher elevations (the first American expedition ever to do so) and needed to have their high-altitude porters carry supplies to the southeast plateau. That meant fixing ropes all the way up Roch Arête and some distance beyond. They put in four camps up the ridge: Camp I at 18,500 feet, Camp II at 21,000 feet, Camp III at 22,000 feet, and Camp IV at 22,500 feet where the ridge joined the Southeast Plateau.

When they reached the plateau they regretted not bringing skis, which could have been of immense service on the gently rising slopes to the summit pyramid and also would have been a first in the ascent of an 8,000-meter peak. By July 4, when Camp V was established halfway up the southeast plateau at 23,500 feet, all was in readiness.

Kauffman and Schoening awoke at 3:00 the next morning, and they set off for the summit in good weather at 5:00 A.M. They manufactured makeshift snowshoes by stamping their crampon points through nine-by-nine-inch plywood panels salvaged from food boxes, but these soon proved more trouble than they were worth, so they shed them and instead plowed through the soft snow, which rose to their knees or higher. Ten hours of plodding—what Clinch would describe as "a long walk in the sky"—brought them to the summit, the most challenging section coming at the end, as they gingerly climbed an avalanche-prone couloir to the summit ridge. From below their anxious comrades, following their progress through binoculars, could see them when they reached the top at 3:00 P.M. Around them were the glories of the Karakoram: K2, Broad Peak, and Gasherbrum IV (where they spotted the tents of the Italian expedition).

Like their predecessors on K2 in 1953, the Americans on Hidden Peak were not enthusiastic about the idea of flag waving on mountain summits. But they did bring flags for the summit photo—the British, French, Pakistani, and Swiss flags as well as the Stars and Stripes and the United Nations flag to emphasize, as Clinch would write, "that our expedition not only stood on the shoulders of its predecessors but also was the result of a tremendous international effort." Five hours more brought them back to Camp V, and the next day the Americans began the evacuation of the mountain. Before they hiked out, Schoening and Clinch took a side trip to the foot of K2 to pay their respects to Art Gilkey's memorial cairn, feeling it "important that in our moment of success we remember our predecessors to the Karakoram."[125]

They were back in Skardu two months after setting out. It was, all in all, a model

Gasherbrum I (Hidden Peak), from the southwest, showing the 1958 American route of ascent.

D.Molenaar

Gasherbrum 1
Hidden Pk

The Plateau

IV

III

V

II

1958 route

I Base Camp

Abruzzi Glacier

expedition, notwithstanding the fact that the organizer and most of the participants were beginners in Himalayan climbing, or, as Maraini put it, "dilettanti." An 8,000-meter peak had been climbed in record time, in exemplary style, and safely.

Despite all this, the Hidden Peak expedition was virtually ignored in the United States. When news of the climb reached the outside world three weeks later, the *New York Times* ran two brief inside-page wire service accounts, the first understating the height of Hidden Peak by 2,000 feet, and neither report noting that this was the first 8,000-meter peak climbed by Americans. *National Geographic* commissioned an article by Andy Kauffman on the expedition, and then failed to run it.[126]

Kauffman, who had taken an unauthorized leave of absence from his State Department post as second secretary of the U.S. embassy in Paris to make the climb, returned to find his job in jeopardy. He wrote to various friends and supporters in the Foreign Service suggesting that his supposed dereliction of duty might actually be of benefit to the U.S. government. "As a result of my action," he wrote in one such letter, "my position in the Foreign Service has become a rather nebulous one." However, he added: "our success has earned us the congratulations of virtually all European sport and climbing circles, which are extensive, and I think we demonstrated, at considerable cost, what we set out to prove, namely that Americans are not quite as soft physically as many Europeans believe they have become." In the end Kauffman did not lose his job, although he was dispatched from Paris to a hardship posting in Calcutta as punishment.[127]

The expedition's success in climbing Hidden Peak failed to lift American mountaineers out of obscurity. Clinch's expedition book, *A Walk in the Sky*, written the following year, would not find a publisher until 1982. As he would remember: "In the late 1950s the warehouses were full of remaindered books about climbing expeditions and there was not much room for another one, especially about a trip where no one had gotten hurt."[128]

Women's Expeditions

In *The White Tower*, James Ramsey Ullman's 1945 best seller about a downed American pilot making a first ascent of an unclimbed peak in wartime Switzerland, the protagonist is reunited with a childhood girlfriend and climbing partner, Carla Dehn, who goes with him partway—but only partway—up the mountain. Her chief role in the novel is to serve as romantic interest for the protagonist, a relationship consummated with a sex-in-the-sleeping-bag scene in an Alpine hut. One reader, Alma Booker of Pittsburgh, wrote to Ullman in 1947 to take exception to Carla's limited role: "This is not to be a letter of praise for your really breathtaking novel, 'The White Tower,' for I imagine you must have received countless numbers of those. This is to protest your heroine, Carla Dehn, and the way you treated her. Now, why did you have to stop her from getting to the mountaintop? It is rather hard to take after admiring her all through the book for her abilities as a magnificent climber, who gave less trouble than some of the men and who climbed as easily as the hero, but without his aches and pains. Can it be that you meant to take a whack at feminism?"[129]

If Ullman's novel had a political agenda, it was to take a "whack" at Nazism; it is unlikely that he had strong feelings one way or the other about feminism, a political movement with virtually no public adherents in the 1940s. But the fact that Carla Dehn stayed below tending the hut fires while her boyfriend climbed to glory was not accidental, either. For Ullman, and no doubt for most of his readers, mountaineering, like so many other high-profile endeavors, was still assumed to be a male pursuit. In 1947 women accounted for just 45 of the 326 members of the American Alpine Club. The few prominent American women climbers of the era—the Miriam Underhills and Barbara Washburns—did not undermine this assumption, because they climbed in the company of their husbands.[130]

So it was quite an innovation in Himalayan climbing in the years after World War II when women began appearing on expeditions without their husbands—and sometimes without any male climbers other than Sherpas. Annalies Lohner had been the pioneer, accompanying the Swiss Garhwal expedition of 1947 sponsored by the Swiss Foundation for Alpine Research, although there were some who questioned her participation. "I must admit," Swiss climber Ernst Feuz would later write, the foundation "was not exactly eager that a woman should be included. We hesitated to take the responsibility of exposing her to danger and fatigue which would require great stamina for months on end." In the end, however, the men overcame their hesitations regarding Lohner and were "happy that the success of the expedition proved us right."[131]

The most important figure in women's Himalayan climbing in the 1950s was without doubt the French Claude Kogan who, at five feet tall and about 100 pounds, kept up on the mountain slopes with some of the greatest male climbers of her generation. She too had begun her climbing career in the company of her husband, Georges Kogan, joining him on an impressive series of climbs from the Alps to Peru between 1944 and 1951. But when her husband died of illness in 1951 she continued to climb without him on ever-more challenging peaks. In 1953 Kogan made a first ascent of Nun (23,408ft/7,135m), the southern peak of the Nun Kun massif in India's Punjab Himalaya, with Pierre Vittoz. In 1954 she accompanied the French-Swiss expedition led by Raymond Lambert to Gauri-shankar and Cho Oyu, where she had the unhappy task of informing Herbert Tichy that he had a rival for the summit. On Cho Oyu, after the Tichy party's first ascent, she and Lambert reached 25,000 feet—not high enough to reach the summit, but sufficient to set a new altitude record for women. (The previous record had been set in 1934 by Hettie Dyhrenfurth, when she reached 24,000 feet climbing to a summit of Kia Sangri.) The following year Kogan set a new record for women's ascents by climbing Ganesh Himal, or Ganesh I (24,373ft/7,429m). As a result of these accomplishments, she became the first woman ever invited to give an address to the Alpine Club in London.[132]

Another innovation of the mid-1950s was the first all-women's Himalayan expedition. Three Scottish women set off in the spring of 1955 to explore the Jugal Himal region along the Nepalese-Tibetan border, an area previously unvisited by Westerners. As Monica Jackson explained a little apologetically in her expedition report for the *Alpine Journal,* she and her companions, Elizabeth Stark and Evelyn Camrass, had not consciously set out to organize an all-women's expedition: "[I]t was not until our plans had already begun to take shape that it occurred to us that we might be creating a precedent." In addition to setting precedent, they discovered five previously unmapped mountains in the Jugal Himal, one of which they climbed and named for their Sherpa sirdar: Gyalgen Peak (22,000ft/6,706m). They also left a name on a previously unmapped glacier, which became Ladies Glacier. They seem to have gotten along well among themselves and with their male Sherpa companions: "Our expedition was above all a happy one," Jackson would write. "We had no leader and divided the responsibilities between the three of us."[133]

There were several other all-women's expeditions to the Himalaya in the next few years. Claude Kogan organized the most important of these, a twelve-woman international expedition that attempted Cho Oyu in the postmonsoon season of 1959; in another first for Himalayan mountaineering, the expedition included three Sherpanis (Sherpa women) among its climbing party—the daughters and a niece of Tenzing Norgay. In its preparatory stages, Kogan's expedition received more than the usual attention from the press, although the coverage did not focus on the real challenges of climbing Cho Oyu or the women's qualifications for meeting them. Noting that Kogan made her living off the slopes as a designer of "ultra-chic swim suits that sell for a $35 minimum," the *New York Times*'s male reporter commented that she was heading for a place "where a woman in a swim suit would not survive thirty seconds." Kogan tried to keep the reporter's attention on mountaineering, with little success: "I'm not a suffragist," she told him, "but I don't see why a group of women, animated by the love of climbing, shouldn't try a great peak." "Will the girls fight among themselves?" the reporter then asked. "Twelve women," Madame Kogan replied (with, one imagines, a slightly exasperated sigh), "can understand each other the moment there is no man around."[134]

On October 2, a little over two months later, Kogan, Belgian climber Claudine van der Stratten, and Sherpa Ang Norbu were killed in an avalanche that swept down upon them in their high camp on Cho Oyu; another Sherpa, Chuwang, was killed in an avalanche as he attempted to come to their aid. Kogan and van der Stratten were the first women climbers to lose their lives in the Himalaya.[135]

The Chinese Climb Everest

Sports in China in the 1950s were intimately bound to Communist propaganda and rule: mass participation in physical exercise and competitive games was seen by Mao Zedong's regime as a way of promoting public health, a socialist work ethic, and national prestige. Mountaineering had not existed as a sport in China until the Communists came to power. In 1955 three young Chinese men traveled to the Caucasus Mountains in the Soviet Union to an alpine training camp. After three weeks of training they were sent on to the Pamirs, where along with Soviet mountaineers they made a first ascent of Peak October (22,244ft/6,780m). Among their number was a young Russian-speaking interpreter named Zhou Zheng, who would remain a central figure in Chinese mountaineering for the rest of the century.[136]

The following year Chinese mountaineers shifted their efforts to mountains lying within their own country's borders. A joint Chinese-Soviet expedition set off for Muztagh Ata (24,756ft/7,546m) in the first attempt on the mountain since Eric Shipton and Bill Tilman's 1947 effort and, on July 31, 1956, put thirty-one climbers (nineteen of them Russian and twelve of them Chinese) on its summit. That triumph was followed two weeks later by a first ascent of nearby Kongur (25,324ft/7,719m) by six Soviet and two Chinese climbers. And on June 13, 1957, a Chinese expedition, this time including no Soviet climbers, made a second ascent of Minya Konka (24,789ft/7,556m), which had first been climbed by an American expedition in 1932. Four climbers died in the attempt, three on the descent from the summit.[137]

The Chinese were now ready to tackle the greatest prize lying within their territory, the north side of Everest, last visited by the British in 1938, or perhaps by the Soviets in 1952, if rumors of their fatal expedition were true. Planning for a joint Soviet-Chinese expedition on Everest began in the spring of 1958. In preparation for the expedition, a reconnaissance expedition including climbers from both countries visited Everest in December 1958. The Chinese also carried out extensive aerial photographic reconnaissance, and built a nearly 200-mile road leading from Lhasa to Rongbuk Monastery, completed in March 1959.[138]

Had Chinese climbers reached the summit of Everest in 1959, their ascent would have coincided with the tenth-anniversary celebrations of the establishment of the People's Republic of China, a propaganda coup. Plans for the summit bid had to be postponed when an armed uprising broke out in March in Tibet against the Chinese occupation. By the time the revolt was crushed, the Dalai Lama, along with 80,000 other Tibetans, had fled into exile. The Everest expedition was rescheduled for the following year. Political developments again intervened to change plans for the expedition. Before the year 1959 was out, tensions between the Soviet Union and the People's Republic of China had led to the Sino-Soviet split. Soviet mountaineers, who had acted as mentors to their Chinese counterparts in the past, withdrew from the expedition. The Chinese would have to go it alone on the mountain they referred to by its Tibetan name, Chomolungma (or Qomolongma).[139]

The two leading Chinese climbers, Zhou Zheng and Shi Zhanchun, were sent to Europe to purchase mountaineering equipment to replace the materials the Soviets were no longer willing to provide. They returned to China with six tons of gear, including oxygen apparatus, ice axes, crampons, ropes, tents, and sleeping bags. These lavish expenditures, at a time when many Chinese peasants were starving due to the failure of Mao Zedong's abortive "Great Leap Forward" economic policies, suggest the high priority placed on the expedition's success by the Chinese Communists. If Chinese mountaineers could get to the summit of Everest, they would simultaneously strengthen Chinese claims to Tibet, demonstrate to Moscow that China could do quite well on its own without further Soviet aid or tutelage, and remind Kathmandu of the importance of good relations with their powerful neighbor to the north.[140]

Shi Zhanchun was appointed leader of the Everest expedition. In February 1960 an advance party arrived at Rongbuk Glacier to begin setting up Base Camp, and on March 19 the main party arrived by truck from Lhasa over a newly constructed road. Base Camp consisted of twenty large tents, capable of housing the over 200 expedition members. It was equipped with many features missing from the prewar British Base Camps, including electrical generators, a radio station, a clinic, and a canteen.

Just as their Base Camp bore a new look, so the expeditionary ideals of Chinese mountaineering in the Himalaya bore little resemblance to their Western counterparts. Western expeditions set off for the region with a mixture of ambitions, including a desire for national glory. But in addition to nationalist agendas, Western mountaineers tended to be imbued with a romantic desire to escape the strictures of a standardized mass society, embracing the challenges of climbing as a chance for individuals to return to a more elemental truth. Chinese mountaineering, on the other hand, was intended to express the values of the collective over the individual and set out with great zeal to subdue mountains with the bureaucratized rationality of a modern industrial society. As the official expedition account boasted, in the rhetorical style customarily devoted to announcing Five-Year Plans and the like, "thorough consideration and meticulous preparations were made against all possible difficulties which might crop up during the ascent, including even the smallest detail such as the use of matches at altitudes." Framing the entrance to the Chinese Everest Base Camp was an arch of pine branches bearing placards with slogans that many Western mountaineers would have found distasteful, if not blasphemous: "Heroes rise into Heaven with a loud laugh at Qomolongma down below," and "Man will triumph over Nature."[141]

In line with bureaucratic ideals, a strict division of labor was intended to prevail on the Chinese expedition. There was an advanced party of climbers whose task was to set up the lower camps, to be followed by a second wave of elite climbers, who would make the final ascent. Both were supported by "road builders" who cut steps on the icy slopes of the North Col, laid ladders across crevasses, and fixed ropes. The advanced party had established three camps, the highest at 21,000 feet, by the time the main party commenced climbing at the end of March.

But Everest was not easily subdued by bureaucratic fiat. For all the elaborate preparations made by the Chinese and the resources lavished on their expedition, they made very slow progress up the mountain. The Chinese would be following the long-established Mallory-Irvine route all the way to the Second Step on the Northeast Ridge. But they lagged behind their predecessors on the British expeditions in moving up the mountain. It was five weeks before they had a camp on the North Col. Their first summit team made it as far as the Second Step, but could not surmount it.

The Chinese found many reminders of earlier Everest expeditions, including an oxygen bottle still containing "English air" after more than two decades. They also found human remains, coming across one body on the glacier below the North Col and another at the base of the Northeast Ridge. The lower body, dressed in a "faded green suit of English cloth," was that of Maurice Wilson, the English mystic who had died in his one-man attempt on the mountain in 1934 and had been buried in a crevasse by the British expedition of 1935. The upper body, wrapped in a sleeping bag and tent, was a mystery, although there has been speculation that it might have been Andrew Irvine. The Chinese reburied both bodies, though Wilson's ever-dwindling remains would be heaved up by the glacier several times in the decades to come.[142]

By mid-May the Chinese were running the traditional race against the arrival of the monsoon. On May 17 a new summit team left Base Camp, heading up the mountain. It included three Chinese climbers, Wang Fuzhou, Liu Lianman, and Qu Yinhua, as well as a Tibetan named Gongbu, who had at first been assigned to the expedition's road-building crew before being promoted to the assault party.[143]

At 9:30 on the morning of May 23 the four climbers set out for the summit from their high camp at 27,900 feet. (Their late start that day was one of many puzzling aspects of the climb that went uncommented on in official Chinese reports, and was probably due to the inexperience of the climbers.) Gongbu led the way up slopes of ice and scree, bringing them in two hours to the foot of the Second Step. It took them a long time (three hours in one account, five hours in another) to surmount it. Liu Lianman made four separate attempts to climb the ten-foot face of the Second Step, falling off each time. Qu Yinhua then tried to climb the crack along the left-hand side of the Second Step, taking off boots and socks to gain traction. But this too failed. It was getting late and they were running out of oxygen. "What was to be done?" Wang and Qu wrote in their account of the climb. "Turn back like the British climbers had done before? No! Certainly not! The whole Chinese people and the Party were watching us."[144]

Liu suggested they form a human ladder, and Qu, still barefoot, climbed to Liu's shoulders. From there he drove in a piton and scrambled to the top, pulling his companions up the rest of the way. It was 5:00 P.M. when they all sat on top of the Second Step and took stock of their situation. Liu was too exhausted to proceed further. According to the official account, the three Chinese mountaineers (all card-carrying Communists) held a party meeting to discuss what to do next. They decided that Liu should remain where he was, while the other two proceeded with Gongbu in the attempt to reach the summit. They left Liu with their food and their one remaining oxygen bottle.

From the top of the Second Step it would take another eleven hours to reach the summit, leaving behind the Northeast Ridge and moving out onto the North Face for the final approach. According to Wang Fuzhou's account:

> It was midnight when we reached the end of the 100-meter long slope. The valleys down below were filled with black shadows. Above us towered the summit of Qomolongma,

silhouetted vaguely against the starry sky. We turned another rock wall and traversed a small slope. The air had become so thin that we felt suffocated and had to pause a long while every few steps. Ahead of us was yet another steep ice slope. Thinking that its top must be the highest point, we quickened our steps in great excitement. "The top!" cried Gongbu who was leading. Qu and I hurried up and joined him, only to see a higher spot not far to the southwest. With a fresh burst of energy that came from nowhere, we got there. Again Gongbu shouted, "The top! Another step and we're down in Nepal!"

Wang Fuzhou took out his notebook and wrote: "Wang Fuzhou, Gongbu and Qu Yinhua of the Chinese Mountaineering Team topped the world's highest peak at 4:20 A.M., May 25, 1960." Gongbu tore the page from the book and placed it under a rock at the northeast corner of the summit. They gathered nine stones to present to Mao Zedong and left behind a plaster bust of the party chairman wrapped in the five-starred Chinese flag. After fifteen minutes on the summit, they began their descent.[145]

They were reunited with Liu Lianman at the top of the Second Step. Liu, resigned to dying on the mountainside, had refrained from using any of the remaining oxygen and had written a farewell note to his comrades. The others revived him, and together they struggled down to Camp VII and safety. Qu, who had taken off his boots and socks at the Second Step, lost all his toes to frostbite as well as six fingers. Wang lost the toes of his right foot. They were welcomed home as conquering heroes, with rallies in their honor in Lhasa and Beijing.

The Chinese claim to have climbed Everest was greeted with understandable skepticism in the West, given the propagandistic trappings of the official reports. Expedition leader Shi Zhanchun declared in his article for the *Alpine Journal* that without "the leadership of the Communist Party and the unrivalled superiority of the socialist system . . . we, the ordinary workers, peasants and soldiers, could never have succeeded." The lack of photographic evidence from the summit was troublesome (the Chinese claimed it was too dark to take any pictures until they were well down the side of the mountain). Then there was the fact that on the same day of the claimed Chinese ascent an Indian expedition attempting to climb by the Southeast Ridge had been defeated by fierce winds. And finally there was the inherent implausibility of the account of the climbing of the Second Step, for no Western mountaineer had ever taken off shoes and socks to gain traction on a rock face at over 27,000 feet.[146]

But over the next two decades, and especially in the 1980s when Western mountaineers had the opportunity to meet their Chinese counterparts, opinion shifted. As British climbing journalist Peter Gillman would note in a 1981 article: "Later ascents of Everest . . . began to make the Chinese claim appear more credible. Other expeditions have reached the top in semi-darkness with their oxygen supplies exhausted; several climbers have survived bivouacs near the summit, and further analysis of the highest Chinese pictures suggested that it was taken at 8700 metres . . . *above* the Second Step, with the way to the summit clear."[147] Another piece of evidence that Westerners found particularly compelling was Qu Yinhua, who would take off his boots and show his toeless feet.

For all the celebration of collective socialist values by the party's mountaineering officialdom, the Chinese ascent of Everest by Mallory's route actually represented a tremendous individual achievement on the part of the three mountaineers. The oldest of the three, Gongbu, was twenty-seven when he stood at the summit of the mountain. Wang Fuzhou and Qu Yinhua were twenty-five. None had climbed for more than two years prior to their ascent. In contrast, when Tenzing Norgay got to the top of Everest, he was thirty-nine years old, had been climbing for two decades, and was on his seventh Everest expedition. The Chinese mountaineers survived virtually without food or water for two days and made the final stage of the climb without artificial oxygen. In terms of their climbing skills, the Chinese lagged behind their Western counterparts. In terms of sheer physical stamina and daring, Wang Fuzhou, Gongbu, and Qu Yinhua were in a class with the best Himalayan climbers.

New Decade, New Names

There were several first ascents of smaller Himalayan mountains in 1960 worthy of note, not simply for the climbing accomplishments they represented but for the new names involved. In Nepal, Jimmy Roberts led a British-Indian-Nepalese Services Himalayan expedition to Annapurna II (26,039ft/7,937m). On May 17, 1960, Captain Richard Grant of the Royal Marines, Lieutenant Christian Bonington of the Royal Tank Regiment, British Army, and Lance Corporal Ang Nyima of the Gurkha Rifles reached the summit for a first ascent. Annapurna II would be the highest unclimbed peak that Lieutenant Bonington would ever ascend, but he would go on to other and greater achievements in the years to come after he shed his army rank and became known to the world as Chris Bonington.[148]

In the Karakoram, Nick Clinch organized his second expedition to the region to attempt unclimbed Masherbrum (25,659ft/7,821m). Willi Unsoeld and George Bell made the first ascent on July 6, 1960 via the Southeast Face, and Clinch and Pakistani Army captain Jawed Akhter Khan followed two days later. Once again, as on Clinch's previous expedition to Hidden Peak, the American press was not in the least impressed; the *New York Times* restricted its coverage to a single three-paragraph wire story on page sixty, noting in passing that a "Dr. William E. Sunsoeld [*sic*] of Corvallis, Oregon," was in the first party to reach the top.[149]

The Swiss Climb Dhaulagiri

By 1960 only two eight-thousanders remained unclimbed, and only one of them was accessible to Western mountaineers: Dhaulagiri (26,794ft/8,167m), the world's seventh-highest mountain. Ten years before Dhaulagiri had been the first 8,000-meter peak to be visited by a postwar expedition intent on reaching its summit. The Herzog expedition's failure to find a route up the mountain did not discourage subsequent attempts: between 1953 and 1959 six different expeditions tried to reach Dhaulagiri's summit. None were successful, and two climbers died in the attempts.[150]

The Swiss, who had been on the mountain on three earlier expeditions, tried again in 1960. Max Eiselin, a Lucerne climber, had joined a 1958 Swiss expedition led by Werner Stäuble on an unsuccessful attempt to climb Dhaulagiri's Northwest Ridge. Now he was coming back as leader of his own thirteen-member expedition to attempt the Northeast Ridge. Eiselin had two criteria for choosing climbers: one was that they had to be "really tough men" who had proven they could endure bad weather and emergency bivouacs; the other was that they display "good comradeship" for, in Eiselin's opinion, "[i]t was all too easy for one selfish man to ruin a complete expedition."[151] Among those he recruited was Austrian Kurt Diemberger, veteran of the 1957 Broad Peak expedition.

The expedition is chiefly remembered for its use of an STOL (short takeoff and landing) utility transport airplane. The four-seater Pilatus PC6 Porter, equipped with skis for glacier landings and nicknamed the Yeti, was flown from Switzerland to Nepal in short hops. From its base in Pokhara, the Yeti ferried climbers and supplies directly to Dhaulagiri's Dambush Pass at 17,060 feet. It also made a higher landing at the foot of the Northeast Ridge at 18,700 feet, setting a still-existing altitude record for landing by a fixed-wing aircraft. But the plane's performance on the mountain discouraged future expeditions from following Eiselin's example. The Yeti was incapacitated for three weeks in April and early May by engine trouble, and then crash-landed on the Dambush Pass two days after its engine was repaired.[152]

Thanks to the Yeti, the climbers did get an early start on the mountain in April, though, as might have been predicted, some suffered bouts of severe altitude sickness from being deposited so suddenly so high on the mountainside. Once acclimatized, they made good progress and even had time to make ascents of two neighboring peaks, Little Tukucha Peak (18,766ft/5,720m) and Dambush Peak (19,520ft/5,950m).

Kurt Diemberger, Ernst Forrer, Albin Schelbert, and four Sherpas pushed a line of camps up the mountain's Northeast Spur, making use of fixed ropes left in place from the previous year's unsuccessful attempt on the mountain by an Austrian party. By early May they had established Camp V, the assault camp, at 24,300 feet. From there they launched an initial summit bid on May 4, setting out under ideal conditions of clear blue skies and no wind. By midday they reached the mountain's false summit at 25,600 feet. Another 1,400 vertical feet would bring them to the true summit. But then Dhaulagiri's weather, always prone to sudden changes for the worse in the afternoon, brought an ice storm that forced their retreat. This experience convinced them of the necessity of a higher assault camp. Starting from a camp over 25,000 feet, they could reach the true summit by midday and descend before the afternoon storms hit.

Suffering from a bad cough and frost-nipped toes, Diemberger had gone back to

Camp II at 18,860 feet to recover, leaving three climbers and two Sherpas at the high camp. Eiselin, worried about Diemberger's fitness, told him to rest and then to join a scheduled second summit party. But on May 9, without a word to the expedition leader, Diemberger took off for Camp IV, determined to be in on the first ascent. This was not the "good comradeship" that Eiselin had set forth as a precondition for selection to the expedition team. "Oh well, it was all a question of tactics," he wrote enigmatically of Diemberger's disobedience in the expedition account. When Diemberger reached Camp IV he insisted on his right to reach the summit in the first team: "On Broad Peak they beat me to it," he told Ernst Forrer, "although I had done all the hard work." The others did not argue, and by the evening of May 12 Diemberger, Forrer, Peter Diener, Albin Schelbert and Sherpas Nima Dorje and Nawang Dorje were at Camp VI at 25,600 feet, in position for a summit bid the following day. The six men crowded into one two-man tent. No one got much sleep.[153]

The next morning, May 13, they arose to the welcome sight of a sunny and windless day. They were off by 8:00 A.M., with Forrer and Nima Dorje the lead rope. As they toiled upward Diemberger thought of the Herzog expedition trying in vain to pick out a route on Dhaulagiri back in 1950: "Down in the depths, 10,000 feet below us, incredibly far off, lay the 'French Col.' That's where it had all started, ten years before."[154] Despite the slow pace of climbing without oxygen and the care it took to maintain their balance on the narrow ridge, it took just four and a half hours for all six climbers to reach the summit.

They spent an hour at the top, until a rumble of thunder in the distance signaled it was time to descend. With this climb Diemberger became the second man, after Hermann Buhl (and also the last), to be able to claim the distinction of making first ascents of two 8,000-meter mountains. The six climbers were the largest group yet to stand together on the summit of one of the Himalayan giants.[155]

In 1950, when Lionel Terray and Jacques Oudot stood on the French Col and gazed up at what they judged the "absolutely unclimbable" North Face of Dhaulagiri, not a single one of the fourteen 8,000-meter peaks had been climbed; ten years later, all but Shisha-pangma in Tibet had seen their first ascent. Scores of other peaks, only slightly lower than the magic 8,000-meter line, were climbed for the first time in the same decade. As Wilfrid Noyce would write in the *Alpine Journal* at the start of the new decade: "A generation or two ago it would have seemed incredible that by 1960 it would be positively difficult to pick an unclimbed twenty-five or twenty-six thousander off the map. Yet such, only seven years after the first ascent of Everest, is the predicament of those anxiously seeking their share in the Golden Age of Himalayan Mountaineering."[156] With first ascents becoming a thing of the past, the next generation of climbers would have to redefine what it meant to achieve distinction in the Himalaya.

CHAPTER NINE

New Frontiers, New Faces
1961–1970

I n 1961 Chris Bonington made the three-week hike from Kathmandu to the Solu
Khumbu region on an expedition that would make the first ascent of Everest's neighbor Nuptse (25,770ft/7,855m). "These were the days before trekkers and tourists,"
Bonington wrote with obvious nostalgia a quarter of a century later. "There were a
few little tea shops on the pathside for the porters carrying loads and trade goods,
but all you could buy were cups of tea and perhaps a few dry biscuits." Along the entire
route to the mountain his party encountered just one other non-Nepalese visitor—Peter
Aufschnaiter, Heinrich Harrer's companion on his escape to Tibet in 1944. It was "that
first bloom of Himalayan climbing," Bonington recalled, when virtually "no mountain in
the Himalaya had been climbed by more than one route and very few had had a second
ascent."[1]

Before another decade had passed, Chris Bonington had advanced from an obscure
if promising junior member of the Nuptse expedition to Britain's best-known mountaineer.
The time involved in traveling from Kathmandu to Everest was drastically cut by the
construction of an airstrip at Lukla, at 9,200 feet, a long one-day or easy two-day hike
from Namche Bazar. The number of outsiders from Europe and the Americas seen both in
Kathmandu and along Nepalese trails increased dramatically, as Nepal acquired a reputation
among the young, the hip, and the culturally and spiritually disaffected of the West as a
place where the meaning of life's mysteries might be revealed to seekers. Western mountaineers increasingly spoke of their own endeavors in the Himalaya not in the traditional terms
of conquest or national glory but as a kind of transcendent personal experience. The old-
style expeditions, bound up with national prestige and enjoying official sponsorship—still
the predominant form of Himalayan mountaineering venture at the start of the 1960s—by
decade's end were viewed by many mountaineers as embarrassing relics. Their place was
taken by new-style expeditions—either small, informal affairs or, if larger, dependent upon
the personal charisma of celebrity climbers to attract public interest and financial solvency.
Sherpas shed many of the remaining vestiges of colonial subordination to emerge as equals

to the Western climbers, both in their own eyes and in the eyes of the "sahibs" (a term beginning to fall into disfavor) they accompanied to the mountains. And mountaineers began to move off the ridges and onto the faces of 8,000-meter peaks. In all these ways and more, the 1960s proved an era of radical change in Himalayan mountaineering.[2]

Himalayan Scientific and Mountaineering Expedition

Among the first in the field in the new decade was Sir Edmund Hillary, who led a nine-month expedition to the Everest region that set off in September 1960. This was Hillary's first trip back to the Himalaya since his ill-fated 1954 expedition. He had not given up on adventure or exploration, taking part in several expeditions to Antarctica in the meantime. Nepal was rarely far from his thoughts, and in conversation with Griffith Pugh at Antarctica's McMurdo Base, the two Everest veterans hatched the idea for an extended Himalayan expedition devoted to both scientific research and climbing. The twenty-two-member team Hillary assembled for this new venture was a decidedly international affair, a mixture of New Zealand, Australian, British, Indian, and American climbers and scientists, including familiar faces, like Hillary, Pugh, Michael Ward, and George Lowe, and some newcomers, like American glaciologist Barry Bishop.[3] The expedition made its Base Camp about eleven miles south of Mount Everest, at nearly 15,000 feet in Mingbo Valley, beneath Ama Dablam (22,348ft/6,812m).

With funding from the World Book Encyclopedia, the Himalayan Scientific and Mountaineering Expedition had several missions. The first (and more whimsical) consisted of a search for the Yeti, or Abominable Snowman. Many Sherpas swore they had seen one of these famously elusive creatures—or, more often, knew someone who had. And some Western visitors to Nepal came to believe them. On the 1951 Everest reconnaissance expedition, Eric Shipton and Michael Ward had come across and photographed tracks in the snow on the Menlung Glacier that certainly looked like they could have been made by a large, erect, hairy creature. Several expeditions to Nepal in the 1950s set out with the express intent of sighting or capturing a Yeti. Hillary was personally skeptical about the creature's existence, but the search for it had great publicity value, as far as expedition sponsors were concerned, so off he went on the hunt in the fall of 1960 to Nepal's Rowaling Valley and the Khumbu region. In any event, no Yetis were encountered.[4]

The second and more substantive scientific mission of the expedition was a study of human adaptation to high altitude. Expedition members constructed an insulated Quonset, known as the Silver Hut, to provide living and laboratory quarters at 18,765 feet on a snowfield below the Ama Dablam col. Some of them would remain there for five months. Never before had Westerners attempted to stay at so high an altitude for so long a time. Hillary said he hoped it would be proven that Everest could be climbed without oxygen, though few of his fellow climbers believed it could be done.[5]

The final mission of the expedition was mountaineering. In particular, Hillary hoped to make an attempt on Makalu in the spring of 1961. But before that happened, four of the climbers who were wintering in Nepal set off on a lightweight effort of their own to climb the mountain that towered over the Silver Hut. Ama Dablam, whose classically proportioned peak had led to its being called the Matterhorn of the Himalaya, had beaten off attempts in 1958 and 1959 by British climbers. Everest veteran Alf Gregory, who led the 1958 expedition, confessed to despair in his report for the *Alpine Journal* that mountaineers would ever find a "feasible way of climbing the mountain." Barry Bishop, Walter Romanes, Mike Gill, and Michael Ward proved otherwise, despite the challenges of some highly technical climbing on rocky overhangs at high altitude in winter.[6]

The four climbers were understandably pleased with their achievement. As Bishop wrote to his friend Arnold Wexler in the United States: "I guess the big news is that Ama Dablam has been climbed. Mike Ward ('53 Everest, etc.) Wally Romanes & Mike Gill of N.Z., and I reached the summit on [March] 13th after a three-week battle. We worked up the S.W. (or Gregory) ridge, disproving [the] view that the route, and mt., was impossible. Just goes to show one should never go on record saying a peak is impossible."[7]

Hillary, who had been out of the country gathering supplies for the Makalu attempt scheduled for that spring, had known nothing in advance about the attempt on Ama Dablam. He thought that any climbing on the mountain would be restricted to its lower flanks, and purely for the purpose of the scientific measurement of acclimatization.[8] The unauthorized climb angered Nepalese authorities, who threatened to shut down the entire project. Hillary had to travel to Kathmandu and spend several days smoothing things over.

That unpleasantness settled, Hillary turned his attention to Makalu, a mountain he had hoped to climb ever since his first visit to the Barun Valley in 1951 with Eric Shipton. But Makalu was not a lucky mountain for Hillary. He suffered a mild stroke in early May after having climbed to 21,000 feet and had to be evacuated, turning over leadership of the expedition to Mike Ward. Illness, frostbite, and accidents dogged the remaining climbers, who never reached the summit.[9]

In June 1961 the expedition came to an end and its members scattered. Upon returning to the United States, Bishop took up a position as a staff photographer and writer for *National Geographic* magazine, contributing an article entitled "Wintering on the Roof of the World." Among his readers were some who had interests other than simple armchair mountaineering. The U.S. Air Force had been using South Asia as a base for aerial reconnaissance of the Soviet Union for several years—the U-2 spy plane shot down by the Soviets in 1960 had taken off from a secret base in Peshawar, Pakistan. The Soviets, in turn, were known to be increasing their own reconnaissance flights over the Himalaya in 1961. These concerns may have prompted navy captain Ralph N. Styles, chief of the Defense Department's "Production Center Planning Group," to write to Bishop in November 1962 requesting an interview: "Your article appearing in the October 1962 issue of the National Geographic Magazine has stimulated much interest in your experiences in the Himalayas of the past year. In light of the current situation in that part of the world, we are particularly interested in your observations as they concern climatology. To further our understanding in that region, I should like to extend an invitation to you to come to the Pentagon and discuss informally some of the details of your recent experiences."[10]

This may not have been an entirely unexpected request. The U.S. Air Force had contributed funding to the Hillary expedition. Moreover, the National Geographic Society had forged close ties with U.S. military intelligence during the Second World War (its maps often proved more accurate and up-to-date than anything in official files). In the cold war years Melville Grosvenor, society director, routinely allowed *National Geographic* reporters to be debriefed by the U.S. Central Intelligence Agency on return from exotic locales— a practice that made some editors at the magazine uncomfortable, fearing the consequences if their reporters came to be viewed abroad as CIA agents or assets. Bishop, with the blessings of the society's leadership, briefed the Pentagon on his experiences, doing his best to answer such questions as "Can 200mph aircraft operate in valleys and passes?" and "How are conditions for aerial photography and aerial reconnaissance?"[11] The politics of the cold war as well as those of regional conflicts in South Asia would continue to cast their shadow across Himalayan mountaineering throughout the 1960s.

There was another, happier legacy of Hillary's 1960–61 expedition. As part of a bargain with the Sherpa villagers of Khumjung, who allowed Hillary to borrow their prize "Yeti scalp" for testing in the United States, he agreed to secure the funds to build them a school. For Hillary this began a lifetime of philanthropic efforts on behalf of Sherpa communities in Nepal. Over the next forty years the organization he founded, the Himalayan Trust, would raise funds for the construction of two dozen schools, a dozen clinics, two hospitals, two airfields (including the one at Lukla, constructed in 1964), and two dozen bridges, as well as sponsoring projects promoting clean water and reforestation.[12]

From Base Camp of the Hillary Scientific and Mountaineering Expedition, Barry Bishop had written to a friend in the Washington headquarters of the National Geographic Society in November 1960 to request news of the outside world: "Even with an occasional 'listen' to Voice of America over the short-wave, it's amazing how isolated one is here, and how small the periphery of our lives! We did hear, however, the Nixon-Kennedy debates— and the November 8th results, which must have caused quite a stir in the hierarchy of The Society!"[13]

The Republican-leaning Grosvenor family, hereditary rulers of the National Geographic Society, may not have welcomed the election of Democrat John F. Kennedy that November. But a few years later they would develop a common interest with the president in seeing the first Americans set foot on the summit of Mount Everest—including, as it turned out, Barry Bishop.

Kennedy had run for the White House promising to "get the country moving again." Not since Teddy Roosevelt had such an outspoken enthusiast for the virtues of the strenuous life—or "vigor," in the term favored by Kennedy—occupied the White House.[14]

In contrast to the grandfatherly crew who had made up President Eisenhower's Cabinet in the 1950s, Kennedy's Cabinet was relatively youthful and physically active (among their number were two avid mountaineers, Secretary of Defense Robert S. McNamara and Secretary of the Interior Stewart Udall, plus Attorney General Robert Kennedy, who was always eager to try new and risky physical pursuits). They would, in John Kennedy's signature campaign slogan, seek to lead America to a "New Frontier."

Rhetorical style merged with official policy in international affairs, with physical vigor often the watchword. Winning hearts and minds in the cold war would require Americans to prove that they could face up to the challenges of hardship and self-sacrifice in the struggle against the Communist foe, showing their willingness to "bear any burden, pay any price" in the defense of the Free World. The U.S. Army Special Forces—the Green Berets—trained to live off the land and fight in the backcountry, became the darlings of Kennedy's military program. Foreign aid, thought of in the Eisenhower years in terms of mammoth development projects like dams and roads, was given an adventurous spin under Kennedy, with his proposal for a Peace Corps. This agency proved one of his most popular initiatives and attracted a contingent of young, idealistic, and hardy volunteers (and no-where hardier than in Nepal, where the Peace Corps effort was headed by Bob Bates, with Willi Unsoeld serving as deputy director). Peace Corps recruitment efforts appealed both to youthful idealism and to the desire to experience exotic locations: one advertisement for service in Nepal described the country as "The Land of Yeti and Everest."[15]

Norman Dyhrenfurth's New Frontier

Norman Dyhrenfurth had his own long-standing interest in the challenges posed by the land of the Yeti and Everest. Son of mountaineer and geologist Günther Dyhrenfurth, he was raised in Switzerland and emigrated to the United States shortly before World War II. Following military service, Dyhrenfurth embarked on a successful career as a documentary filmmaker. He retained close ties with the European climbing community and served as official photographer on the 1952 Swiss expedition to Everest. He felt a mystical bond with Everest, confessing to a "strong feeling" of having lived in sight of the mountain at the Buddhist monastery of Tengboche in a previous incarnation. Someday he wanted to lead his own expedition to climb the mountain.[16]

Permits for Everest were hard to come by, but Dyhrenfurth took every opportunity he could to return to Nepal. In 1953 he wrote to his old friend James Ramsey Ullman, inviting him along on a mountaineering expedition to the Solu Khumbu in 1954 for an attempt on Ama Dablam or some other mountain yet to be determined (he also mentioned that the expedition would include "a determined effort to hunt and kill a yeti"). For reasons of political expediency, Dyhrenfurth explained, it would *not* be organized as an American expedition: "In view of the fact that Americans are not particularly well-liked in either India or Nepal (as a matter of fact, they are quite strongly disliked), I have decided to get the necessary authorization from Nepal through the political department in Berne." That expedition never got off the ground, but in 1955 Dyhrenfurth did make it back to Nepal to lead an unsuccessful attempt to climb Everest's neighbor Lhotse. He returned twice more in the next few years, in 1958 as leader of yet another Yeti-hunting expedition, and in 1960 as filmmaker on the Swiss expedition to Dhaulagiri.[17]

Dyhrenfurth's passion for leading an expedition to Everest remained undiminished. What had changed by 1960 was his estimation of the advantage of doing so under American auspices. The only two successful climbs of Everest thus far that he knew of—the British in 1953 and the Swiss in 1956—had required large and well-equipped siege operations under quasi-official national sponsorship (the 1960 Chinese expedition had, of course, been wholly state sponsored, but Western mountaineers questioned whether it had actually reached the summit). When Dyhrenfurth mentioned to Nick Clinch, organizer of previous expeditions to Hidden Peak and Masherbrum, that he hoped to raise several hundred thousand dollars for an American Everest expedition, Clinch told him frankly, "You'll never get that kind of money in this country. . . . Nobody gives that much of a damn about mountains or mountaineering."[18] So Dyhrenfurth decided he would have to find a way to make Americans—and the American government in particular—give a damn. He would succeed brilliantly.

American Mount Everest Expedition

In a prospectus written in the summer of 1960 for the American Mount Everest Expedition (or AMEE), Dyhrenfurth used a justification for climbing the mountain considerably more contemporary in its concerns than Mallory's familiar "because it is there." Noting Chinese claims to have reached the summit of Everest that spring and to have left behind a bust of Mao Zedong, Dyhrenfurth suggested Americans needed to prove they too were up to the challenge of ascending the world's highest mountain: "Most mountaineers of the Free World agree that the struggle for the Himalaya should remain a purely idealistic, non-political pursuit. And yet, there can be no doubt that the ascent of [Everest] by an American team would go a long way toward winning new friends in many places."[19]

Kennedy's election-year rhetoric could not have been better suited for Dyhrenfurth's purpose if he had written the candidate's speeches himself. What was the summit of Everest but the ultimate New Frontier? Six months after Kennedy took office, Dyhrenfurth wrote to the White House asking for an appointment with the president, to outline his plans for the Everest expedition. White House science adviser Jerome B. Wiesner replied on Kennedy's behalf, regretting that the president would not have time to see Dyhrenfurth in the foreseeable future. He suggested various government agencies that Dyhrenfurth might contact for funding, but added that private groups, like the National Geographic Society were "traditionally the most logical source of interest and support for activities such as yours." He also passed along Kennedy's "best wishes . . . for success in your 1963 assault." If this was intended as a polite brush-off, Dyhrenfurth chose not to take it as such. "Yesterday I received a most encouraging letter from the White House," he announced in Expedition Letter #1, which went out on August 1, "wherein the President expressed his personal interest in the expedition."[20]

Dyhrenfurth spent the next month in northern Canada on a filmmaking job on behalf of the Atomic Energy Commission (AEC). On his return he wrote again to Kennedy: "Dear Mr. President: I have just returned from the Canadian Arctic where I was a member of an expedition responsible for the permanent installation of the world's first isotope-powered automatic weather station." After conversations with several "top men" in the AEC's Division of Isotopes Development, he had decided to volunteer the services of AMEE to install "the world's highest nuclear-powered automatic weather station on the upper slopes of Mount Everest—to be specific, at an altitude of 26,000 feet on the South Col." The Everest weather station would have "several beneficial effects," Dyhrenfurth argued: "It would for the first time provide the Indian and Nepalese governments with routine weather observational data from the Upper Himalaya. Additionally, such an installation would be decidedly advantageous in enhancing the scientific prestige of the United States among the Asian peoples. Last but not least, Mount Everest, the 'third Pole' of our planet, is a symbol everywhere, and to place the world's highest weather station within 3,000 feet of its summit cannot fail to prove dramatically this country's intent to use atomic energy for the economic and social well-being of mankind."[21]

There was more salesmanship than science to the proposal. There is no evidence that the government of Nepal had any idea that Dyhrenfurth was offering its national territory for such a purpose (and it seems unlikely that the Communist Chinese would have been pleased to watch Americans install such a device on the Nepalese-Tibetan border). Dyhrenfurth may have hoped that, with Kennedy's interest piqued, such details would sort themselves out—in any case, the important thing was to link the climbing of Mount Everest to American international prestige.

The president's schedule remained too full for a meeting with Dyhrenfurth, and not just because he was busy with crises in Berlin and Cuba and Vietnam. Kennedy was a shrewd politician who spent political capital carefully. He gained nothing by prematurely endorsing a private venture like the American Mount Everest Expedition, which might end only in an embarrassing failure. Dyhrenfurth eventually had to settle for a meeting with Secretary of the Interior Stewart Udall.[22]

Udall, it turned out, was a good alternative. A westerner and avid conservationist, he was genuinely interested in the expedition as a mountaineering venture and useful in opening doors to official largesse. A number of government agencies wound up providing funding for the expedition in the form of grants for scientific studies, including one on high-altitude physiology paid for by the U.S. Air Force Office of Scientific Research and the National Aeronautics and Space Administration, and another on psychological problems encountered by men living under hardship conditions, funded by the Office of Naval

Research ("We want to learn the best criteria for selecting men for prolonged submarine duty, Arctic duty, and space exploration," a Navy official explained to *Newsweek*). The expedition also acquired some important private backers, including *Life* magazine, which bought the rights to a postexpedition account.[23]

Dyhrenfurth's greatest coup came when he persuaded the National Geographic Society (NGS) to sign on as a sponsor. Unlike the Royal Geographical Society, which had been involved in the British Everest expeditions from the beginning, the National Geographic Society had never before lent its name or made its resources available to a foreign mountaineering expedition. In the spring of 1962 it agreed to put up much-needed operating funds for the expedition, lent Dyhrenfurth the services of Barry Bishop, and made a commitment to covering the story in *National Geographic* magazine and producing a film about the climb for subsequent television broadcast. In the end, the society provided over a quarter of the $400,000 cost of the expedition (in 2008 the equivalent would be approximately $2,650,000).[24]

The promise to deliver scientific data useful on spacecraft and submarines served the expedition well in grant proposals. For public consumption, the appeal was kept simpler. Other nations had climbed or claimed to climb Everest. How could Americans do otherwise? As James Ramsey Ullman defined the issues in an AMEE press release sent out late in 1961: "Strident nationalism and jingo flag-waving have no place on the great peaks that tower above all mankind. But still the fact remains that the first American go at Everest *will* be an event. If we succeed, it will—no question about it—be a feather in our cap, a booster to our prestige, a refutation beyond argument of our detractors' taunt that we are a nation gone soft and gutless. If we do not . . . we will at least have entered the arena, joined the rest of the world in one of its great enterprises, abandoned our 'isolationism' in mountaineering, as we have long since in other fields."[25]

To guarantee that "the first American go at Everest" would be a success, Dyhrenfurth assembled the largest expeditionary team in American mountaineering history, twenty members strong. He would function as both expedition leader and filmmaker. Will Siri, leader of the 1954 Sierra Club expedition to Makalu, signed on as deputy leader and as a member of the expedition's scientific contingent; Willi Unsoeld, who had summited Masherbrum in 1960, would be climbing leader. Jim Whittaker of REI became equipment coordinator. Tom Hornbein, another Masherbrum veteran, was given responsibility for ordering oxygen equipment (and designed a new breathing mask for the expedition to use). Hornbein was a doctor, but the day-to-day medical responsibilities on the expedition would fall to Gil Roberts and Dave Dingman. Barry Bishop of the National Geographic Society would serve as expedition photographer, while Dan Doody would assist Dyhrenfurth as film cameraman. Dick Emerson, Jim Lester, Maynard Miller, and Barry Prather were all part of the science and social science contingent. Jimmy Roberts, recently retired as British military attaché in Kathmandu, would serve as transport officer. Al Auten, Jake Breitenbach, Barry Corbet, Lute Jerstad, and Dick Pownall would round out the team of climbers. Finally, James Ramsey Ullman would accompany the expedition as far as Everest Base Camp and serve as expedition publicist and historian.

Thirteen of the twenty members of the expedition were from the western United States, either by origin or adoption, which was becoming the norm on American Himalayan expeditions. Nine had worked as professional guides in the Tetons or the Cascades (Willi Unsoeld, who was familiar with both ranges, was in the habit of referring to himself in the third person as "the old guide"); several were connected with the retail end of selling climbing gear; and Dyhrenfurth had aspirations to be a professional expedition organizer, even if he still depended on nonmountaineering documentary filmmaking to pay the bills. In that sense, many expedition members could no longer be described as the *dilettanti* of the earlier American expeditions to the Himalaya, but rather were men whose lives and careers were defined in some significant measure by their involvement with mountaineering. On the other hand, only eight members, including Dyhrenfurth, had prior Himalayan experience. No members of the 1953 K2 expedition were part of the team, and only one member (Gil Roberts) of the 1958 Hidden Peak expedition would be going along.[26]

The "American go at Everest" would be a success in the eyes of the general public in the United States so long as one American got to the summit of the mountain. That meant that the expedition should make its main effort via the Southeast Ridge, the one proven way to get to the top of Everest. But Dyhrenfurth had other audiences in mind whose good opinion he also valued as he planned his expedition. As far as the international climbing community was concerned, climbing Everest by the Southeast Ridge was old news. The British had done it in 1953. The Swiss had repeated the British route in 1956 but had added a note of distinction to their expedition's record by also making the first ascent of neighboring Lhotse. What could the Americans do to match the achievements of their predecessors? Dyhrenfurth's initial idea was to pursue a three-peak or "grand slam" strategy of having his expedition be the first to climb Everest, Lhotse, and Nuptse, the three peaks enclosing the Western Cwm, on a single expedition.[27]

The mountaineers Dyhrenfurth had recruited had their own ideas. Reaching the top of Lhotse and Nuptse did not stir anyone's enthusiasm the way climbing Everest did.[28] And that suggested an alternative strategy, quietly discussed among expedition members in the months before their departure, though not shared with the broader public. In place of the "grand slam," why not a new route on Everest?

This idea first surfaced in a conversation between Dyhrenfurth and Tom Hornbein in Hornbein's San Diego home. Dyhrenfurth suggested the expedition attempt a traverse of Everest in which climbers would ascend the mountain via the standard Southeast Ridge route, and then descend down the as-yet-unclimbed West Ridge to the Western Cwm. The traverse would thus run from east to west. Hornbein was skeptical: "Wasn't it enough to climb by the regular way?"[29]

But the more Hornbein thought about it, the more the idea of a traverse appealed to him. At a shakedown climb on Mount Rainier in the fall of 1962, he talked it over with a number of other expedition members. There was one major problem with the proposal as initially conceived by Dyhrenfurth: "Can you imagine," Hornbein asked, "dragging yourself over the summit of Everest from the Col side, running on the dregs of your oxygen, and then plunging down an unknown route?" Should the route down the West Ridge prove unclimbable for any reason, there would be no possibility of retreat, since the climbers would be in no condition to climb back up to the summit and descend the known Southeast Ridge. The obvious solution was to turn Dyhrenfurth's proposal around. Why not attempt a west-to-east traverse, establishing a new route up the West Ridge, and then descend along the easier Southeast Ridge?[30]

Four against Everest

While the American Mount Everest Expedition considered its options, another American was carrying out his own expedition to Everest, an adventure very different in scope and philosophy than Dyhrenfurth's. A forty-three-year-old Tufts University philosophy professor named Woodrow Wilson Sayre, grandson of the president whose name he bore, was not seeking a White House endorsement—or for that matter any approval—for his own effort. Instead he recruited one friend, Boston attorney Norman Hansen, and one Tufts student, Roger Hart, to join him on a clandestine attempt to climb Everest in the spirit of Earl Denman's 1947 solo attempt. They were subsequently joined by Swiss climber Hans Peter Duttle, an acquaintance of Hart. Together they traveled to Kathmandu, then made the trek up to the Everest region. Like Denman fifteen years earlier, they intended to attempt the mountain from the north side, notwithstanding the fact that Tibet had in the meantime fallen under Chinese control.

Having secured permission from Nepalese authorities to attempt unclimbed Gyachung Kang (26,088ft/7,952m) on the Nepalese-Tibetan border, Sayre's little party left its Nepalese liaison officer at "Base Camp" below the mountain and slipped off for their real objective, crossing the Nup La into Tibet. Carrying all their own supplies, they followed the old British route up to the North Col in an oxygenless attempt that got them to an altitude of 25,500 feet on the North Face before they had to turn back. Although Sayre cracked a rib and injured an arm in falls on the mountain, and although he and all his companions were severely malnourished before they were done, they managed to cross back safely into Nepal and were picked up in the Sherpa village of Khumjung by a helicopter dispatched by the U.S. embassy in Kathmandu.[31]

Norman Dyhrenfurth, by chance in Kathmandu on expedition business, came on the helicopter ride to pick up the Sayre team. At that point, like everyone else, he thought that Sayre had simply gotten lost on an attempt to climb Gyachung Kang. When Sayre confided to him where he and his friends had really been, Dyhrenfurth was aghast. If Chinese authorities learned of Sayre's intrusion into Tibet, they might create an international incident. The Nepalese Foreign Ministry might then cancel the legitimate and authorized American expedition to Everest to placate their powerful northern neighbor. Dyhrenfurth did his best to persuade Sayre to say nothing of his venture into Tibet, and when that failed he called on the White House, the State Department, and even the Central Intelligence Agency to pressure Sayre into silence.[32]

Sayre maintained the fiction of the Gyachung Kang climb for the duration of his stay in Nepal but back in the United States made arrangements to publish the true story in *Life* magazine and later as a book. The American mountaineering establishment, alerted by Dyhrenfurth to Sayre's transgression, shunned the maverick climber (which did not, however, seem to bother him very much). Sayre's account of his climb ran in *Life* magazine in the spring of 1963 under the title "Commando Raid on Everest." His book *Four against Everest,* published the following year, went on to sell 20,000 copies and became a minor mountaineering classic, as well as an early 1960s harbinger of antiestablishment rebellions yet to come: "The Sayre Expedition on Mount Everest was Mad, Ill-Equipped and Admirable," read the headline of Brooks Atkinson's review of *Four against Everest* in the *New York Times* in January 1964.[33]

The Official Expedition Heads for Everest

Finally it was time for the American Mount Everest Expedition (the "second American expedition to Everest," as Sayre sardonically referred to it) to make its own attempt. Dyhrenfurth and a few others flew to Kathmandu in mid-January 1963, followed by the rest in early February. On February 20 a long line of 900 porters, accompanied by 30-odd high-altitude Sherpas (whose numbers would expand en route with some temporary hires) and the 20 members of the AMEE set off on the march from the village of Banepa outside Kathmandu en route for Everest. James Ramsey Ullman, the oldest member of the expedition at fifty-five, had to turn back after the first day due to a chronic problem of poor circulation in his right leg. He would instead serve AMEE in Kathmandu, along with Dyhrenfurth's wife, Sally, in the expedition press office.

On the approach march the climbers continued to refine their plans for Everest. The grand slam strategy remained one option. But the West Ridge proposal had a strong core of supporters. The West Ridgers, as they came to be called, included four of the seven climbers who had previous Himalayan climbing experience—Tom Hornbein, Willi Unsoeld, Dick Emerson, and Barry Bishop. Hornbein was such an enthusiastic proponent of the West Ridge that he even suggested it should take priority over any attempt to climb the mountain by the standard Southeast Ridge route. The opposing faction, the South Colers, included the expedition leader and his deputy as well as Jim Whittaker and Lute Jerstad. The debate between the two groups remained cordial for the moment, although Dyhrenfurth made it clear that as expedition leader he would never agree to "throw everything into a West Ridge attempt and thus possibly jeopardize success over the conventional

Col route." The expedition's financial backers expected AMEE to put a man on top of the mountain for all the reasons of national prestige that Dyhrenfurth and Ullman had hammered home in their press releases. Apart from any of the considerations that might be valued by mountaineering purists, the expedition's marketing strategy would make it difficult to abandon or downplay an attempt on the Southeast Ridge. Still, once that reality had been acknowledged by all, Dyhrenfurth was willing to commit the expedition to making a "serious stab at the West Ridge" as well.[34]

Base camp was established March 21 at 17,800 feet. The next day Jim Whittaker, Willi Unsoeld, Lute Jerstad, and Sherpa Nawang Gombu began putting a route up the Khumbu Icefall. On March 23 Jake Breitenbach, Dick Pownall, Gil Roberts, Ang Pema, and Ila Tsering took over the job of working in the icefall, improving the route. Meanwhile, some of the West Ridgers, finding themselves with a day off, decided that they would like to get a closer look at their objective. As Barry Corbet recorded in his diary: "Emerson, Hornbein and I walked 500 ft. up a nearby ridge where we had a direct view of the West Ridge. It looks horrendous—5,000 ft of rock and almost no snow and very steep. I've downgraded our chances of success by quite a bit, but it's a fantastic and alluring objective. I'm more prepared to fail but enjoy the struggle more than before. Success at all costs no longer seems important although I think it is to Norman. By 'at all costs' I mean prostituting all our manpower to the South Col route, not German do-or-die."[35]

The work party in the icefall worked its way up close to the high point reached the day before. They were on two ropes, one linking Dick Pownall, Ang Pema, and Jake Breitenbach, the other Gil Roberts and Ila Tsering. Suddenly there was a loud roar as a section of an ice cliff collapsed. Roberts and Ila Tsering were spared, but a pile of icy debris fell on the other roped climbers. As Roberts and Ila Tsering scrambled to the aid of their companions, they were able to dig out Pownall and Ang Pema, but of Jake Breitenbach there was no sign, only a rope leading down under tons of ice. He probably died instantly. A rescue party from Base Camp helped the survivors down, while Whittaker, Unsoeld, and Jerstad dug futilely in the debris for any sign of their comrade. The news was radioed from Base Camp to Kathmandu the next day, and the U.S. State Department informed Mary Louise Breitenbach back home of her husband's death.[36]

Everest was proving once again it was a dangerous mountain. Between 1952 and 1962, seven expeditions had attempted to climb the mountain (not counting Sayre's commando raid). Nine climbers had reached the summit in those years; three others had died in the attempts. The Americans were only two days into their own climb and already they had had their first fatality. They had no way of knowing how many more would die before they were done with the mountain, and the mountain with them. It had been just short of ten years since Art Gilkey had been killed on K2, the last and best-known American fatality in the Himalaya and, like Gilkey, Breitenbach was just twenty-seven years old when he died. He had been added to the expedition when Jim Whittaker's brother Lou dropped out. Barry Corbet, Breitenbach's close friend and partner with him in a skiing and mountaineering equipment store in Jackson, Wyoming, wrote in his diary, "Stupid goddamned gentlemen's sport that kills people in their prime."[37]

There was talk of abandoning the expedition, or at least abandoning the West Ridge attempt, in order to minimize the amount of time they would have to spend on the mountain. Some of the AMEE climbers never recovered their enthusiasm for climbing Everest. Nonetheless, three days later, the expedition returned to work on fixing the route up the icefall, and by March 29 had reached the Western Cwm. The following day Camp I was set up and occupied at 20,200 feet at the entrance of the cwm, followed by Camp II at 21,350 feet. Camp II, halfway up the cwm, was located at the site of the 1953 British Camp IV and functioned for the Americans as Advanced Base Camp, from which two routes would now branch off, one to the West Ridge and one to the South Col. Future camp designations would reflect the separate routes on which they were established: thus the next camp to go in on the traditional South Col/Southeast Ridge route would be designated Camp III, while the next camp to go in on the new West Ridge route would become Camp 3W.

Beginning on April 3 one expedition became two, as the South Colers headed up the Lhotse Face and the West Ridgers climbed to the top of the West Shoulder, the snowy hump that would lead them to Everest's North Face and West Ridge. "From now on," Hornbein would write, "we would be competing for manpower and equipment to accomplish our separate goals." Expedition psychologist Jim Lester noted an interesting difference between the two parties working their way up the separate routes: "The West Ridge advocates seemed to care less about rewards in the outside world and to be less sensitive to the possibility of objective failure, more willing to risk failure in favor of possible internalized or self-given rewards." One of the rewards they enjoyed was the sense of moving onto untrodden ground, with views that no climber on the mountain had ever before enjoyed. On April 11 Hornbein, Unsoeld, and Bishop stood on the West Shoulder and looked over into Tibet. As Hornbein wrote: "Our eyes climbed a mile of sloping sedimentary shingles, black rock, yellow rock, grey rock, to the summit. The North Col was a thousand feet below us across this vast glacier amphitheatre. As we stood where man had never stood before, we could look back into history. All the British attempts of the 'twenties and 'thirties had approached from the Rongbuk Glacier, over that Col, on to that North Face. The Great Couloir, Norton, Smythe, Shipton, Wager, Harris, Odell, our boyhood heroes. And there against the sky along the North Ridge, Mallory's steps."[38]

They could also see, although they did not have time to explore, a possible variation on their route. From where the West Shoulder joined the West Ridge above them, there was a crack running diagonally upward across the face to a couloir running up the mountainside that became known as the Hornbein Couloir. The West Ridge itself, from what they could see of its jagged and rotten rock, did not look promising. If they made their way upward to the left of the West Ridge by means of the couloir, they might avoid some difficult technical climbing challenges and then return to the ridge nearer the summit where, they hoped, the going would be easier.

Willi Unsoeld (left) and Tom Hornbein reconnoiter
the West Ridge of Everest, April 1963. Photograph
by Barry Bishop. Reprinted by permission of
the National Geographic Society.

They would not have a chance to test this hypothesis anytime soon. While the
West Ridgers were contemplating the view into Tibet, Dyhrenfurth was having second
thoughts about trying to push two separate routes up the mountain simultaneously. By the
time Hornbein, Unsoeld, Dingman, and Bishop returned to Advanced Base Camp for a
rest day on April 13, they found that the South Col contingent had voted in their absence
to increase the size of the summit parties on their side of the mountain to two four-man
teams. Rather than a simultaneous bid for the West Ridge and the South Col, for which
Hornbein had been pushing, there would now be sequential bids—first the South Col and
then, and only then, the West Ridge. That meant that for the next ten days (or perhaps

more), no Sherpas could be spared for carrying supplies for the West Ridge effort. The West Ridgers, their numbers depleted by Breitenbach's death and the poor acclimatization of several others, would have to make do carrying all their own supplies up to the West Shoulder, except on the rare occasions when they could find a spare Sherpa. As Hornbein would later write, with a rueful humor, his minority party "found ourselves preserved of the basic freedoms of speech, and the right to the pursuit of happiness (the West Ridge), but no inalienable right to Sherpas."[39]

Dyhrenfurth did offer the West Ridgers a consolation prize: they could join the South Col effort. With multiple summit teams, their strongest climbers would have a good shot at making it to the top. Hornbein and Unsoeld declined, with Unsoeld declaring, "Our chances for the summit are tremendously decreased but surely mountaineering is more than a matter of summits—even when the summit is that of Everest."[40] Barry Bishop, however, agreed to switch to the South Col. He had to consider the best interests of the National Geographic Society and that meant going on the route most likely to produce a summit photograph for *National Geographic* magazine (as it turned out, he had already taken the most famous of the expedition's photos, showing Hornbein and Unsoeld making their way up the crest of the West Shoulder from Camp 3W on April 11).

Dyhrenfurth's change in plans certainly paid off in the remarkable progress the Americans made in climbing the Lhotse Face and traversing to the South Col, a goal they reached on April 16. This put them in a position to make their first summit bid nearly a month before the British expedition had been able to do so in 1953. The first summit team would consist of two sahibs and two Sherpas. One of the pairs was an obvious choice: Jim Whittaker and Nawang Gombu (Gombu, a nephew of Tenzing Norgay, was a veteran of both the 1953 Everest expedition and the 1960 Indian attempt).[41] The other pairing came as a surprise, for it would consist of Dyhrenfurth himself with his personal Sherpa, Ang Dawa.

Although Dyhrenfurth had listed himself back in a 1961 circular letter to expedition members as one of those who had "hopes to go high" on the mountain, he had not spoken before of any intention to be part of a summit team.[42] He was now proposing to go higher on a mountain than any other forty-five-year-old had ever done before. Like John Hunt, whom he often cited as a model, Dyhrenfurth believed in leading from the front. But he was setting himself a climbing task far more challenging than anything Hunt had undertaken in 1953. Although the forty-two-year-old Hunt had carried a load almost to the level of Camp IX, the British high camp on the Southeast Ridge, he had not spent the night there. Dyhrenfurth, in contrast, planned not only to stay at the American high camp but to set off the next morning, laden with camera gear as well as oxygen tanks, and continue on as high as he could—perhaps to the South Summit, perhaps higher. Unlike Hunt, of course, Dyhrenfurth was the expedition filmmaker as well as leader. The other cameraman on the American expedition, twenty-nine-year-old Dan Doody, had acclimatized poorly. If there was going to be footage of the climbers on summit day for the expedition film, it could be shot only by Dyhrenfurth.

The second four-man team, scheduled to follow a day later in the tracks of the first team, consisted of Bishop, Jerstad, Pownall, and Girmi Dorje. There would also be a two-man team following them, consisting of Dingman and Prather. This third team's objective would be the summit not of Everest but of Lhotse. The decision to climb Lhotse was another surprise, a vestige of the old grand slam strategy, and to the West Ridgers further evidence that Dyhrenfurth no longer saw their route as important to the expedition's success.

On April 27 the first team left Advanced Base Camp, spending the night at Camp III at the top of the cwm. Two more days brought them to Camp V on the South Col. On April 30 they climbed the Southeast Ridge to 27,450 feet, where they established Camp VI, the assault camp (this was higher than the Swiss camp of spring 1952 but lower than the British camp of 1953).

The next day, May 1, dawned windy but clear. From below, those watching the plume of snow blowing off the summit assumed that there would be no climbing that day, but at Camp VI the climbers decided not to wait. Whittaker and Gombu set off at 6:15 A.M., followed by Dyhrenfurth and Ang Dawa an hour later. The latter pair, laden with camera equipment, soon tired in the stiff cold wind and turned back—but only as far as Camp VI, where they halted to await the return of the others. The two lead climbers pressed steadily on until, just before 1:00 P.M., they paused a few steps short of the summit.

This time there would be no "who got there first" controversy. Whittaker urged Gombu to go ahead of him; Gombu urged Whittaker to do the same. Instead, as Whittaker would write, they compromised. "Side by side we staggered the last few feet until, at 1:00 P.M., we stood together at the highest point on earth." Whittaker removed a four-foot aluminum stake with an American flag wrapped around it from his pack, unfurled the flag, and planted the stake in the summit snow. With that gesture Dyhrenfurth's expedition fulfilled the official goal set forth in its fund-raising appeals, providing for the United States, as promised, "a feather in our cap, a booster to our prestige, a refutation beyond argument of our detractors' taunt that we are a nation gone soft and gutless." None of that was on Jim Whittaker's mind at the moment: "I did not feel expansive or sublime; I felt only, as I said later, 'like a frail human being.' People—mostly nonclimbers—talk about 'conquering' mountains. In my mind, nothing could be further from the truth. The mountain is so huge and powerful, and the climber so puny, exhausted, and powerless."[43] The two climbers looked around for Mao Zedong's bust but could find no sign of it.

After twenty minutes they began their descent, Gombu in the lead. Before they reached the Hillary Step, the cornice along the ridge suddenly dissolved between the roped climbers, leaving a gaping hole that started just behind Gombu and stopped just before it reached Whittaker. Having barely missed sharing the fate of Hermann Buhl on Chogolisa, Whittaker remembered thinking calmly in his state of hypoxia-tinged exhaustion, "Gee. I guess I had better move over a foot or two."[44] It took the two climbers five hours to reach Camp VI, where they found Dyhrenfurth and Ang Dawa waiting for them and where they would all spend the night.

Everest from the southwest, showing the routes of ascent taken by the
1963 American expedition.

While all this had been going on, the second summit team of Bishop, Jerstad,
Pownall, and Girmi Dorje had climbed to Camp V to be in position for their own summit bid, which they hoped to make on May 2. They were shocked to discover that there
was far less oxygen stockpiled on the South Col than they had been led to expect. There
would only be enough for one two-man team, Bishop and Jerstad, to go on to the summit.
May 1, the day the second team was scheduled to move up to Camp VI, was blustery on

the South Col. Bishop and Jerstad assumed that Whittaker and the others up at Camp VI would not make any attempt in such unfavorable conditions, so they stayed put. May 2 brought better weather, and Bishop and Jerstad set out eagerly at 10:00 A.M. to make the climb to Camp VI. But their plans abruptly changed when they looked up the Southeast Ridge and saw Whittaker and Gombu descending toward them. When the two parties met on the slope, Bishop and Jerstad knew they would have to abandon their own summit bid, for Whittaker and Gombu were in poor condition, and Dyhrenfurth and Ang Dawa, they said, were even worse. All four climbers returned to the South Col. When Dyhrenfurth and Ang Dawa reached them an hour and a half later, they were blue in the face from hypoxia. Dyhrenfurth collapsed into Lute Jerstad's arms, crying, "I'm at the end of my rope."[45]

There was nothing to do but get the exhausted climbers down off the South Col as quickly as possible. The Lhotse team of Barry Prather and Dave Dingman had also abandoned their effort. Prather had developed pulmonary edema at Camp IV and retreated down the Lhotse Face; Dave Dingman was carrying oxygen up to the South Col to support the second team's summit attempt on Everest when he met the others descending the mountain and turned back himself.

Dyhrenfurth stopped to spend the night of May 2 at Camp IV on the Lhotse Face, but Whittaker and Gombu, feeling stronger as they descended, made it all the way down to Advanced Base Camp. A report of their success was radioed to Base Camp and from there to Kathmandu. The morning papers in the United States would carry the news of the first American ascent of Everest the next day. The expedition had agreed beforehand that the identities of those who reached the top would be kept a secret until after all the summit attempts had been completed to prevent any single climber or summit team from winning the accolades that should belong to all who reached the top. That condition proved a challenge to the reporters who announced the news of AMEE's success to the public. In its coverage *Newsweek* magazine proclaimed, enthusiastically but vaguely, that the United States "had a new hero last week" (it just didn't know his name). However, the magazine felt confident that whoever he turned out to be, he was: "young, vigorous, talented, a New Frontiersman on a Himalayan scale. . . . And proud the nation was of this first American to plant Old Glory atop Mount Everest, the highest mountain in the world."[46]

President Kennedy no longer hesitated to link his own administration's prestige with Dyhrenfurth's expedition. "These American climbers," he declared in his official congratulations (not knowing, of course, that one of them was a Sherpa), "pushing human endurance and experience to their farthest frontiers, joined the distinguished group of British and Swiss mountaineers who have performed this feat. I know that all Americans will join me in saluting our gallant countrymen."[47] Reporters continued to badger Ullman in Kathmandu for the names of the summiters. He held out for a week, but, realizing the news would leak out sooner or later, finally gave in on May 9. And, as expected, Jim Whittaker's name became the one most Americans would associate with the expedition's success, then and thereafter.

In the United States there was nothing but praise to be heard for the gallant men of the AMEE. Meanwhile, at Base Camp on Everest, there were bitter recriminations. Dyhrenfurth blamed the West Ridgers in general and Hornbein in particular for the oxygen shortage on the South Col route. "If I had known Tom was going to be so fanatical about the West Ridge," he declared, "I would have increased our budget, ordered three hundred oxygen bottles, and hired fifty Sherpas. If only Tom had been honest with me about his ambitions back in the States." Faced with accusations of dishonesty and fanaticism, Hornbein restrained his own temper (it helped that Unsoeld laid a comforting—or perhaps a warning—hand on his shoulder). Dyhrenfurth, he could see, "was exhausted, possibly disappointed, perhaps suffering the lingering effects of oxygen lack, and his restraint was gone."[48]

The oxygen shortage on the South Col and the Southeast Ridge, as Dyhrenfurth would later concede, was the fault not of poor planning but of excessive use by those on the South Col and the Southeast Ridge. Sherpas who carried loads to Camp VI had insisted on using oxygen on their descent from the high camp, when they were supposed to have used it only on the carry up. And several climbers, including Dyhrenfurth, had used oxygen at both the South Col and the high camp during the day and while "sitting," instead of restricting their oxygen use to climbing and sleeping, as originally planned. The oxygen shortage was the most contentious issue on the entire expedition, leading to some dissatisfaction with Dyhrenfurth's leadership, particularly among those who felt their own summit chances had been jeopardized. Barry Bishop diplomatically kept his thoughts to himself in the Base Camp discussion but was less restrained in a letter he wrote home to Arnold Wexler on May 9, recounting the events of the past week: "On May 2nd we started up to [Camp] VI, only to find that Dyhrenfurth & Ang D. had used O2 *continually* & exhausted all the tanks intended for 2nd team & 2) both Dyhrenfurth & Ang D. were in a *complete* state of collapse so we (2nd team) had to escort them down. I'm not saying I [illegible —fussed?], but the summit was so close, we could taste it, we were going strong, & May 3rd was a *perfect day.* Now we find there is only enough O2 for one 2-man try via S. Col."[49]

If Whittaker and Gombu's ascent had marked the end of the American Mount Everest expedition, it would have been an event that pleased the public but left many of the climbers dissatisfied and at odds. But because Dyhrenfurth had gotten his expedition to and up the mountain so early in the season, there remained time for subsequent attempts. And this time, instead of following the tried and true, the AMEE climbers would be making mountaineering history with an assault launched via two separate routes on the same day, with climbers from the Southeast Ridge rendezvousing with climbers from the West Ridge at the summit, and then descending together to the South Col. As Bishop told Wexler in his letter of May 9: "Lute Jerstad & I have the nod & we'll move up the 11th for an 'all or nothing' try on the 18th. Plans call for Unsoeld & Hornbein to try for top the same day—via the W. Ridge. Talk about a long shot!"[50]

The longest shot and the greatest risk on summit day would, of course, fall to the West Ridgers. For if they failed to meet Jerstad and Bishop at the summit on the appointed day, they would face the choice of either descending the route they had just climbed on the West Ridge (which, due to the challenging terrain, might prove difficult or impossible) or continuing on to traverse the mountain via the Southeast Ridge—an easier route, in theory, but one on which they had never before set foot. And by the time they attempted it, they would be running out of oxygen and it would be getting dark.

Unsoeld and Hornbein climbed back up through the icefall on May 6 to resume the attempt on the West Ridge (Corbet, Auten, and Emerson were already on the West Shoulder, ferrying supplies with the aid of a temperamental winch system). Bishop and Jerstad would head up the Western Cwm on May 12 to get into position on the South Col. Back in April the West Ridgers had chosen a site for their proposed Camp 4W at 25,100 feet, where the snow of the West Shoulder met the rock of the West Ridge. On May 14 they returned to 4W, leaving a supply cache. On May 15, after more carries by the five West Ridge climbers and their five Sherpas, Hornbein and Unsoeld spent the night there. The next day they set out across the North Face (and into Tibet), following the crack stretching diagonally upward that they had spotted in April, dubbed the Diagonal Ditch, to the base of Hornbein's Couloir.

Camp 4W was crowded that night, as Corbet, Auten, and four Sherpas joined them. And, as ill luck would have it, they were hit by the worst storm they had yet seen on the mountain. High winds sent the tents holding Corbet, Auten, and the Sherpas careening down the mountain. Tragedy was averted only by chance, when the tumbling tents and climbers wound up deposited in a shallow depression 100 feet below Camp 4W instead of being dropped down the North Face to the glacier 8,000 feet below. In the morning the climbers retreated to Camp 3W to regroup and reassess their situation. Time and supplies had been lost, but Hornbein was not quite ready to call it quits. He suggested to his companions that instead of two summit attempts by two climbers on consecutive days, they had time for only one shot. And instead of establishing two additional camps, one at the bottom of and one above the Hornbein Couloir, they would have to get by with just one. Accordingly, on May 20, Camp 4W was reoccupied. On the following day, Corbet and Auten left early to find the route and final campsite, followed by Hornbein, Unsoeld, Emerson, and five Sherpas. All climbed back across the Diagonal Ditch to the base of the Hornbein Couloir, where Emerson halted. The rest climbed up the couloir to the base of the Yellow Band, where they established Camp 5W on a small snow platform at 27,250 feet. (Some of Hornbein's companions referred to this stretch of the climb as "Hornbein's avalanche trap," and it is possible that the windstorm that had played such havoc with Camp 4W a few days earlier had been a blessing in disguise, scouring the couloir of unstable snow.)[51] Camp 5W was about 200 feet lower than Camp VI, the assault camp on the Southeast Ridge, where Jerstad and Bishop arrived that same day. On the night of May 21 there were four Americans bedding down for the night in two assault camps on opposite sides of Everest. Nothing like it had ever been seen in the history of Himalayan mountaineering.

Hornbein and Unsoeld awoke at 4:00 A.M., May 22, and set out at 7:00 A.M. Just before they left, they tied into the rope that would be their link on the way to the summit. Hornbein took pleasure in the familiar ritual of tying the bowline around his waist: "This knot tied me to the past, to experiences known, to difficulties faced and overcome. To tie it here in this lonely morning on Everest brought my venture into context with the known, with that which man might do. To weave the knot so smoothly with clumsily mittened hands was to assert my confidence, to assert some competence in the face of the waiting rock, to accept the challenge."[52]

They took nothing with them but oxygen, a little food, their personal effects, and their walkie-talkie. They did not expect to see their tent or sleeping bags again. The slope in the Yellow Band was steep, about fifty-five degrees. Their crampons gripped poorly in the granular snow, necessitating much laborious step-cutting. It took four hours to do the first 400 feet. Near the top of the couloir, cutting through the last bit of the Yellow Band, they encountered a sixty-foot high cliff. Hornbein took the lead on the pitch and came to within eight feet of the top when, exhausted, he had to give up and drop back down to the start of the pitch beside Unsoeld. Protected until the last eight feet by Hornbein's piton, taking off his mittens for a better grip, and with his oxygen on full flow, Unsoeld was able to complete the pitch and belay Hornbein to the top of the step. It was the hardest climbing they would do that day. Resting for a moment, they called Base Camp on their walkie-talkie. From below, Jim Whittaker reminded them of the importance of leaving a retreat open—good advice, but no longer an option. "There are no rappel points, Jim, absolutely no rappel points," Unsoeld radioed back. "There's nothing to secure a rope to. So it's up and over for us today."[53]

They were committed to reaching the summit and descending via the Southeast Ridge. Now they had to cut back across the down-sloping rotten slabs of the North Face to regain the West Ridge. As they had hoped, the upper reach of the West Ridge proved less treacherous rock than the Yellow Band. Rock gave way to snow as they neared the summit. At 6:15 P.M., just over eleven hours after setting out, they looked up and could see the flag that Whittaker and Gombu had left on the summit three weeks before. They walked together the last few feet to the top, arms linked. "Now some people have suggested it was to avoid the argument as to who got there first," Unsoeld would later tell audiences at the slide shows he did about the climb, "but there are other reasons to link arms with your buddy." Once at the top, Unsoeld wrapped a *kata* (a Buddhist prayer scarf) around the flagstaff and buried a crucifix in the snow next it.[54]

They knew from the footprints in the summit snow that Barry Bishop and Lute Jerstad had been there earlier that day, that they were too late for the planned rendezvous, and that they were on their own for the descent down the other side to Camp VI. Hornbein and Unsoeld started down, then stopped for a moment to contact Advanced Base Camp on the walkie-talkie. After informing their friends below of their achievement, Unsoeld signed off by quoting Robert Frost's poem about "promises to keep" and "miles to go before

Lute Jerstad approaches the summit of Everest, with Jim Whittaker's flag still flying,
May 22, 1963. Photograph by Barry Bishop. Reprinted by permission of
the National Geographic Society.

I sleep."[55] It was 6:35 P.M. They knew some of what to expect on the route from others'
accounts, and they could follow Jerstad and Bishop's tracks, at least until darkness fell. By
7:15 they were at the South Summit. By 7:30 it was too dark to see even their own feet, let
alone any trail left by Bishop and Jerstad. The batteries in their one flashlight were failing.
They called out and yodeled in the night, hoping to alert Dave Dingman and Girmi Dorje,
the support party waiting at Camp VI. But Camp VI was more than 1,000 feet below, and
no one there could possibly hear them. Someone else did, however, and called back. They
followed the sound of the voices for two hours down 400 feet of the Southeast Ridge until
they came to where Bishop and Jerstad waited, huddled on the slope.

The two South Colers had had a long hard day of their own, which started badly
when their butane cookstove flared up and nearly set fire to their tent. They had toiled to the
summit without benefit of breakfast or fluids, buoyed by the sight of Whittaker's flag, which
reminded Jerstad of Iwo Jima, "the flag raising and everything."[56] They reached the summit at
3:30 and, after shooting the first motion picture film ever taken on top of Everest, began their
own descent at 4:15. Now, at 9:30 P.M., they were utterly exhausted, and Bishop in particular
was in bad shape. The four climbers, still hoping to reach the safety of Camp VI that night,
picked their way down the slope, but by midnight decided it was too dangerous to continue.
All they could do was settle down on a sloping rock outcrop and wait for daylight.

Their bivouac that night at over 28,000 feet was roughly 2,000 feet higher than Buhl's on Nanga Parbat in 1953. Like Buhl, they were blessed with a windless night. Hornbein remembered to take off his crampons so they would not conduct the cold to his feet; the others failed to do so. Unsoeld offered to warm Hornbein's feet against his stomach, and Hornbein took him up on it. But when Hornbein in turn offered to warm his companion's feet, Unsoeld declined. His feet, he said, were feeling fine.

At 6:00 A.M. on the morning of May 23 they set off down the mountain. Dave Dingman and Girmi Dorje were coming up from Camp VI, looking for Bishop and Jerstad. Dingman was immensely relieved to spot two figures coming down toward them—and then astonished to see that it was Hornbein and Unsoeld, not Bishop and Jerstad, as he had expected. Dingman was slow to realize what this meant: that not only had Everest been climbed by a new route, it had been traversed. Unsoeld and Hornbein declined Dingman's offer of oxygen. They could make it down to Camp VI on their own; it was Bishop and Jerstad following behind them who needed it more.

All four men made it off the mountain (with Hornbein and Unsoeld having the unique experience of being the first to down-climb the Southeast Ridge and Lhotse Face without having previously ascended them). The news was radioed to Base Camp and then to Kathmandu, and from there sent on to the rest of the world in time to make the papers in the United States later the same day. President Kennedy proclaimed that the collective achievement of the American Everest climbers commanded "the admiration of all who respect the superb stamina, courage and physical prowess required by such a feat," while congratulatory messages poured in from Edmund Hillary, Tenzing Norgay, John Hunt, and many others.[57] From Namche Bazar, Bishop and Unsoeld were evacuated by helicopter to a hospital in Kathmandu, where they were treated for frostbitten feet: Bishop lost all his toes, Unsoeld all but one. Jerstad recovered from a milder case of frostbite without serious damage, and Hornbein, amazingly, was left unscathed.

The American triumphs on Everest in 1963 fell ten years after the first ascent by the 1953 British expedition. By the time John Hunt returned to Kathmandu from Everest Base Camp in 1953, he had been knighted by the queen of England. By the time Norman Dyhrenfurth made the same trip in 1963, he felt he had been demoted from expedition leader and Bara Sahib to just another one of the crowd of American climbers who had not managed to summit Mount Everest. In early May, when the National Geographic Society saw how much interest the American expedition was generating at home, they rushed their own press representatives to Kathmandu. In promoting the society's interests (in which AMEE tended to be depicted as a National Geographic Society initiative rather than Norman Dyhrenfurth's achievement), they deeply offended the expedition's leader. Matt McDade, a society publicist, sent a telegram to his Washington superiors later that month to alert them of Dyhrenfurth's discontent: "Confidential from McDade it is of utmost importance natgeosoc remember this Dyhrenfurths American Mount Everest expedition resulting from many years dreams planning hard work stop Dyhrenfurth feels as leader he has been virtually ignored Natgeo Washington re White House Reception and Editorial Planning Coverage Expeditions Stop Dyhrenfurth should be kept personally apprised by cable and consulted."[58]

Dyhrenfurth's sense of resentment grew in the months that followed. But at least he finally got his meeting with the president. In a ceremony in the White House Rose Garden on July 8, Kennedy presented the National Geographic Society's Hubbard Medal for exploration to Dyhrenfurth and replicas of the medal to the other AMEE members (of the surviving members, only Willi Unsoeld, still recovering from frostbite in Kathmandu, was absent). "In giving this Medal today to the Leader of the Expedition," Kennedy proclaimed, "I carry on a great tradition, as do they in demonstrating that the vigorous life still attracts Americans."[59]

Five of the expedition's Sherpas were also in attendance at the ceremony. Nawang Gombu presented the president with a Buddhist friendship scarf, much to the president's evident delight (although his Secret Service contingent, seeing Gombu reach into his pocket in this unscripted gesture, stiffened and reached for their weapons). The wire service photographers had been snapping photos throughout the ceremony, but this provided the image that proved irresistible to photo editors the next day; the picture of the smiling six-foot-two-inch president lowering his head to allow five-foot-two-inch Gombu to place the scarf around his neck ran in both the *New York Times* and the *Washington Post*. For John F. Kennedy it was one more opportunity to celebrate the themes of the New Frontier: stoicism, self-sacrifice, courage, vigor; for Americans it was one of the last days of triumphant good feelings, unalloyed by bad news at home or abroad, that the 1960s had to offer.

In September 1963 *Life* magazine carried Ullman's account of the American ascents of Everest as its cover story. Barry Bishop's account ran in *National Geographic* magazine in October. The following year Ullman's expedition book, *Americans on Everest,* was published. And in September 1965 the National Geographic's expedition film, also entitled *Americans on Everest,* ran as an hour-long special on CBS television and earned the highest ratings up until that time for any televised documentary.[60]

When the first American reached the summit of Everest, it was front-page news in the *New York Times,* even though no one yet knew the climber's name. When Tom Hornbein and Willi Unsoeld made the first ascent of Everest's West Ridge and went on to complete the first traverse of the mountain, the account of their climb was relegated to page twenty-eight of the same newspaper. As far as most Americans were concerned, Jim Whittaker was the greatest hero of the expedition, the only one whose name became widely known. Whittaker himself was bemused by the mantle of fame that had dropped upon his shoulders. "[I]t was, I suppose a more innocent era," Whittaker wrote many years later, "in which an individual could somehow embody a sense of hope for a nation. At any rate, we had little to say in the matter. Gradually, it began to dawn on me that my life had changed forever." It was Whittaker who helped Bobby Kennedy make the widely publicized first ascent of the newly named Mount Kennedy in the Canadian Yukon, a year

Nawang Gombu presents President John F. Kennedy with kata;
right, Kennedy presents the National Geographic Society's
Hubbard Medal to Norman Dyhrenfurth, July 8, 1963.
Reprinted by permission of the National Geographic Society.

and a half after John F. Kennedy's assassination, and that too cemented his reputation as America's best-known mountaineer.[61]

As far as the international mountaineering community was concerned, however, it was Tom Hornbein and Willi Unsoeld whose achievement outshone all others on the American Mount Everest expedition. Bill Tilman, reviewing Ullman's expedition book for the *Alpine Journal,* seemed impatient with the chapters devoted to the South Col ascents. He reserved his praise for Unsoeld and Hornbein, "the moving spirits on the West ridge who from the start chose to be beaten if necessary . . . rather than succeed by the South Col route. In spite of having to make do with the scrapings of the barrel in the way of Sherpas and support parties, they stuck to their resolution through thick and thin and brought it to a triumphant conclusion." The West Ridge climb, he concluded, lifted the

1963 American Everest expedition to "a plane level with that of the first ascent of the mountain in 1953."[62]

The Changing Face of American Climbing

"Our flag flies atop Mt. Everest!" the Eddie Bauer company proudly declared in an advertisement in 1965, and it was apparent that it was not the Stars and Stripes the clothing manufacturer had in mind: "*Every member* of the American Mt. Everest Expedition 1963 was outfitted from head to toe with Eddie BAUER 100% northern goose down insulated parkas, pants, underwear, mitts, booties and sleeping bags."[63]

The greatest commercial beneficiary of the Everest climb turned out to be Jim Whittaker's employer, Recreational Equipment Incorporated, which increased its membership from 50,000 to a quarter of a million between 1965 and 1972. From its lone Seattle outlet, REI expanded its marketing empire across the country in the 1970s; by century's end, REI had grown to a chain of forty-six retail outlets plus a catalogue order business, which together brought in half a billion dollars a year. In the same years REI's flagship store in Seattle grew from its humble origins above a restaurant into a gleaming $30 million palace of outdoor consumption, with Whittaker's Everest ice ax on display. New retailers also entered the market, including Eastern Mountain Sports, which opened its first store in Wellesley, Massachusetts, in 1967, and spread its retail outlets westward just as REI was spreading eastward.[64] Baby-boom consumers were at the heart of this retail explosion. In the later 1960s Vibram-soled hiking boots, popularly known as "waffle-stompers," became a badge of a generational identity. Outdoor clothing designers began bringing out form-fitting parkas for women. Mountain climbing—or at the very least the appearance of being ready at any moment to climb a mountain—became chic on American campuses.

And some of those boots and parkas were actually put to the use for which they were originally designed. From the White Mountains to the Cascades, the number of signatures on the pages of the summit registers increased dramatically in the 1960s and the decades that followed. Many of the new climbers picked up their skills informally, through trial and error or from friends. Others turned to climbing schools. In 1965 K2 veteran Paul Petzoldt founded the National Outdoor Leadership School (NOLS) to teach mountaineering; by the time Petzoldt died in 1999, NOLS had 50,000 graduates. Outdoor organizations also grew dramatically in the 1960s: the Sierra Club expanded from its tradi-tional California base into a national organization of tens of thousands of members. Even the American Alpine Club, with a staid reputation and cumbersome application process that discouraged younger climbers from joining, expanded its membership by one-third between 1965 and 1970.[65] If, as Nick Clinch had complained at the start of the decade, no one in America gave "that much of a damn about mountains or mountaineering," that was certainly no longer the case by the decade's end.

The Changing Face of Himalayan Climbers

Everest may have continued to generate the most headlines, but dozens of other Himalayan peaks had their first ascents in the early 1960s, including eight mountains over 23,000 feet in 1962, six in 1963, and eleven in 1964. Many of these peaks fell to Western climbers, including the ascent of Jannu (25,294ft/7,100m) in the Kangchenjunga region in 1962 by a strong French party led by Jean Franco and including Lionel Terray. Increasingly, how-ever, expeditions from Europe and the United States shared the slopes with climbers from other continents. The Japanese accounted for a disproportionate number of first ascents, including that of Saltoro Kangri (25,396ft/7,741m) in the Karakoram.[66]

India's climbers were also emerging as a significant force in Himalayan mountain-eering. In 1958 an Indian expedition climbed Cho Oyu, the mountain's second ascent. Soon afterward the Indian government created the quasi-official Indian Mountaineering Federa-tion, which sponsored regular expeditions to Himalayan peaks. Indians were unsuccessful in their bids to climb Everest in 1960 and 1962, but in 1961 an Indian expedition reached the summit of Annapurna III, the last unclimbed peak in the Annapurna massif. Among the summiters was naval captain Mohan Singh Kohli, who would become one of his country's best-known mountaineers. In 1964 an Indian expedition would make the second ascent of Nanda Devi (although the three summiters were all Sherpas). In 1965 Kohli led a third Indian expedition to Everest; this time the Indians were successful, putting nine climbers on top of the mountain in three separate summit bids. One of the members of the first summit party was Nawang Gombu, who became the first man to climb Everest twice, having been to the summit two years before with Jim Whittaker. When Gombu and Indian climber A. S. Cheema reached the summit on May 20, they found the four-foot flagpole erected by Whittaker in 1963 still standing, although the American flag had long since vanished. They replaced it with the Indian and Nepalese flags they had carried to the summit.[67]

The last of the unclimbed 8,000-meter peaks fell to non-Westerners in 1964. Lying 100 miles west-northwest of Mount Everest, Shishapangma (26,286ft/8,013m) is the world's fourteenth-highest mountain and the only 8,000-meter peak to lie entirely within Tibet. Although visible from Kathmandu, Shishapangma had never been attempted or even reconnoitered by Western climbers. The Chinese sent a massive expedition with 195 climbers to attempt the mountain in the spring of 1964, and on May 2 ten of them (including Wang Fuzhou, who had climbed Everest in 1960), reached the summit via the Northwest Face and North Ridge, leaving behind the inevitable bust of Mao Zedong.[68] This would be the last significant Chinese climbing achievement for over a decade, as the country descended into the chaos of the Cultural Revolution.

Spies and Mountaineers

The American success on Everest in 1963 succeeded in raising the profile of mountaineers with the American public and with the American government. The next great American venture in the Himalaya, to the Indian Garhwal, would have no difficulty at all in attracting official sponsors. But this time no one would be seeking publicity of the sort that accompanied the AMEE to Nepal—quite the contrary.

"You do not send armies to mountain peaks," Indian prime minister Jawaharlal Nehru had declared in 1961, but even as he spoke Indian troops were reinforcing their mountain outposts along the border with China.[69] Throughout the 1960s the Himalayan region proved a flashpoint of both regional and cold war tensions. A Chinese-Indian rapprochement in the mid-1950s came to an end in 1959 when China cracked down on Tibetan resistance and the Dalai Lama fled to exile in India. With a common enemy in India, Pakistan and China developed an informal alliance in the early 1960s, while U.S.-Pakistani relations deteriorated. India and China would fight a war over the mountainous Ladakh region in 1962; India and Pakistan would fight their second war for control of Kashmir in 1965. Neither conflict was conclusive; both cast a shadow over the prospects for mountaineering.

In October 1964 Chinese scientists detonated a nuclear device at a test site in Xinjiang province, bringing Communist China into the club of nuclear powers—much to the dismay of American policy makers. Shortly after this news became known in Washington, Barry Bishop had a conversation over cocktails with the U.S. Air Force chief of staff, General Curtis LeMay. (In addition to being the leading figure in the creation of the U.S. Strategic Air Command, LeMay also found time to serve as a trustee of the National Geographic Society.) The two men discussed the implications of the Chinese achievement for American national security. Bishop raised the possibility of monitoring future tests by means of a nuclear-powered remote-sensor spying device, clandestinely placed atop a Himalayan peak. Bishop's inspiration for the scheme is not clear, but it may have been Norman Dyhrenfurth's off-the-cuff suggestion to President Kennedy several years earlier to place a nuclear-powered weather station atop Everest's South Col.[70]

The idea found favor in Washington and eventually in New Delhi. The Indians were also understandably nervous about the development of a Chinese nuclear capability (particularly since it would take Indian scientists ten more years to detonate their own nuclear device). So the U.S. Central Intelligence Agency found a receptive audience when it proposed placing a listening device atop an Indian mountain to monitor Chinese nuclear and missile testing.[71]

Bishop was given leave by the National Geographic Society to plan and lead an expedition to place the device. He contacted Indian mountaineers, including M. S. Kohli, who would lead the successful Indian expedition to Everest in 1965. Bishop originally planned to mount the device atop Kangchenjunga, but Kohli felt it was too high and difficult a mountain to expect a heavily laden party to climb, and then assemble the listening device. Instead the Americans and Indians agreed to place the device atop Nanda Devi.

Bishop assembled a team for the climb that included Lute Jerstad, Tom Frost, Sandy Bill, and Rob Schaller. Bishop would not accompany the party, and Schaller wound up sidelined by illness. The American climbers were paid $1,000 a month, a very good paycheck at the time, and sworn to secrecy. An Indian team was assembled by Kohli. They set off in the postmonsoon season of 1965 but failed to reach the summit due to the early arrival of winter conditions. Rather than haul the cumbersome sensor device back down the mountain, they stored it on the side of Nanda Devi at an altitude of about 23,750 feet.

The following May an Indian climbing team, accompanied by an American nuclear expert, returned to Nanda Devi to retrieve the device. Over the winter the CIA had decided to install it on yet another peak, Nanda Kot. But when the climbers reached the site where the device had been stored the previous October, it was gone, apparently swept away along with its plutonium fuel by an avalanche.

Alarm bells sounded at CIA headquarters. No one was quite sure what would happen if the plutonium that powered the listening device was carried by glacier melt all the way to the Ganges, a river exalted in Hindu myth and the principal water source for many of India's most populous cities—but the potential for environmental, human and, of course, political disaster was enormous. A new team of American climbers, including Tom Frost, Robert Schaller, and Dave Dingman, was dispatched to Nanda Devi to join the search. Schaller took the opportunity to climb to the summit of the mountain, setting an altitude record for a solo American climb. The team, however, failed to find any trace of the nuclear device. But the CIA remained determined to carry through with the project, and in 1967 Frost, Schaller, Barry Corbet, and Barry Prather succeeded in planting a listening device atop Nanda Kot.[72]

The story of the Nanda Devi fiasco, like so many official secrets, began to emerge in the midst of the Watergate scandal of the early 1970s. Muckraking columnist Jack Anderson was the first to break the story in 1974, drawing on revelations by a former CIA agent, Victor Marchetti, though the version he offered was vague and in key elements misleading. In Anderson's telling, the nuclear listening device was "triumphantly planted" on an unnamed mountain described as "one of the loftiest peaks in the Himalayas" sometime "in the late 1960s," but was later swept away by a blizzard and was already polluting the Ganges with radiation. Anderson's vague grasp of detail, and the nation's preoccupation in 1974 with the Nixon administration's death throes in the Watergate crisis, undercut the impact of his story.[73]

Behind the scenes, the Nanda Devi events had provoked an intense private discussion among leading mountaineers on three continents. Ken Wilson, the English editor of the influential climbing magazine *Mountain,* apparently stumbled on the story in 1973, perhaps tipped off by Alex Bertulis, an American Alpine Club director. Wilson made inquiries of Robert Schaller, who urged him to kill the story: "After some years of political turmoil Westerners are finally being permitted access to the Himalayas. A 'sensational' story at this time, no matter how outdated or untimely, would certainly close the Eastern door not only to Americans, but also many European mountaineers as well." Wilson bristled at the idea that he would be the one responsible for the consequences if the Nanda Devi story were revealed. "I don't hold your view that the passage of time has made this an unimportant historical detail," he replied to Schaller. "I find it fairly scandalous that a group of America's leading mountaineers should place the whole area of Himalayan expedition climbing in jeopardy in order to satisfy the whims of the CIA."[74]

Before he went ahead with the story, Wilson decided to consult with Soli Mehta, editor of the *Himalayan Journal.* "Not having been born yesterday," Mehta told Wilson: "I was aware of the equipment in the Nanda Devi sanctuary for a long time. . . . The truth, Ken, is that by its sheer presence, the equipment has put, is putting and will be putting a number of expeditions out-of-bounds as far as the Sanctuary is concerned." But Mehta, like Schaller, urged Wilson to kill the story, lest it "harden attitudes towards all mountaineering in the Garhwal and any other place even remotely connected with defence strategy." Wilson was persuaded, and *Mountain* made no mention of the Nanda Devi affair.[75]

In 1978 the editors of the newly founded *Outside* magazine in the United States decided to go with the Nanda Devi story when it was uncovered by investigative journalist

Howard Kohn. He did not name names, but he did name the mountain, and he got most of the details correct. (Among the minor details that were wrong, he described an American climber summiting Nanda Devi in the fall of 1965, instead of, as actually happened, the following year.) Kohn's "Nanda Devi Caper" story was widely noticed, and it created political difficulties for the United States in India.[76]

No trace of the missing nuclear fuel rod ever turned up. And within a year or two of the placement of the second listening device atop Nanda Kot, it had become obsolete: satellite surveillance allowed the CIA to keep tabs on the Chinese nuclear program. The only positive aspect of the entire "caper" was that thirty years after Charlie Houston's near miss on Nanda Devi, another American climber, Rob Schaller, finally reached the mountain's summit—only Schaller was forced by circumstance to do everything he could to ensure that no one would ever learn of his achievement.

Mid-1960s Hiatus

Beginning in 1961, border tensions with India had led Pakistan to cut down on the number of mountaineering expeditions to the Karakoram. The higher peaks like K2 and the Gasherbrums were the first to be put off limits. Each year the restrictions grew in intensity. The last significant climbs in the Karakoram in the 1960s were the Japanese first ascent of the highest peak of Baltoro Kangri (23,989ft/7,312m) in 1963 and the Austrian first ascent of Momhil Sar (24,090ft/7,343m) in 1964.[77]

India also made it increasingly difficult for mountaineering expeditions to approach its disputed border regions (and, of course, the Nanda Devi Sanctuary was off limits for other reasons). The Chinese were being increasingly aggressive in patrolling the Tibetan-Nepalese border; in 1963 they arrested a Japanese mountaineer and his Sherpa guide who had strayed into Tibetan territory, releasing them after five days at the request of Nepalese authorities.[78]

The greatest blow to Himalayan mountaineering came in March 1965, when the government of Nepal announced that once the current climbing season came to a close, it would initiate a ban on mountaineering expeditions. Far more than either India or Pakistan, Nepal depended on the revenues generated by foreign mountaineering expeditions. It was no longer Darjeeling but Kathmandu where expeditions came to hire Sherpas. So the decision to ban expeditions could not have been taken lightly by Nepalese authorities. No reason was given for the ban, but it came just days before Chinese foreign minister Chen Yi was scheduled to visit Kathmandu.[79]

The resulting hiatus in Himalayan climbing in the later 1960s marked a generational turning point: the climbers who had scored the greatest successes of the golden age of Himalayan climbing would now, with few exceptions, be relegated to executive or emeritus roles in the climbing world. Meanwhile, a new generation waited in the wings, its members honing their skills in the Alps, Alaska, Yosemite, and elsewhere, dreaming of the day when they would be able to make their own mark in the Himalaya.[80]

The Invention of the Trekking Industry

The attention paid in the Western press to mountaineering triumphs in the golden age of Himalayan mountaineering began to attract a trickle of nonmountaineering tourists to the region, particularly to Nepal. The British travel agency Thos. Cook & Son brought a small party of tourists by plane from Calcutta to Kathmandu for two days in 1955, the first organized tour group. But few tourists ventured far from the city limits. Although there was much to see in the city, including palaces, temples, and bazaars, there was little in the way of basic amenities. In the 1950s there was but one place for tourists to stay in Kathamandu, the Royal Hotel, which occupied the premises of a crumbling old Rana palace and featured what one disgruntled guest referred to as "early Cro-Magnon plumbing." By the beginning of the 1960s the struggling Nepalese tourist industry attracted only 5,000 to 6,000 tourists annually.[81]

In 1964 Jim Lester, a veteran of the American Everest expedition, wrote to James Ramsey Ullman, mentioning in passing a new commercial venture in Nepal: "Did you happen to see Jimmy Roberts' ad in Holiday? He is trying to develop a guiding service for hikers who want to walk in to Tengboche! All the jokes we made about the lemonade concession at Namche, etc., etc., may yet turn out to be prophetic."[82] Roberts, transport officer for the American expedition in 1963, named his new guiding service Mountain Travel Nepal. And it soon became clear just how prophetic the jokes about lemonade stands on the path to Everest would prove.

Roberts's first advertisement in the American tourism magazine *Holiday* for his travel agency brought him three customers for a guided tour—or "trek"—of the Solu Khumbu in the spring of 1965. The price for the trip was $15 a day, all expenses included. The three Americans who signed on for the trip, all of them middle-aged women, were the vanguard of a great army of Western trekkers about to descend upon Nepal. Between 1964 and 1974, the number of foreign tourists visiting the country jumped ninefold to 90,000, with Americans the single largest contingent. A dozen years after Roberts's first trek, over seventy trekking agencies were registered for business in Nepal.[83]

The choice of the term *trekking* to describe a guided hiking trip, with its suggestion of genuine adventure radically different from the soft and inauthentic experiences associated with mere tourism, was a stroke of marketing genius on the part of Roberts and his imitators. From the beginning there was a link between the popularity of trekking and the glamour of mountaineering. Trekkers were literally following in the footsteps of the mountaineers as they hiked through the Solu Khumbu to Tengboche Monastery or Everest Base camp. Some famous mountaineers, including Eric Shipton, found a profitable sideline in leading trekking groups in Nepal. Others, including Barry Bishop and Lute Jerstad, got involved in the business end of the emerging trekking industry.

Guidebook publishers also found a lucrative market in promoting new forms of "adventure travel," including trekking. Two youthful British wanderers, Tony and Maureen

Wheeler, brought out a homely ninety-four-page pamphlet in 1973 entitled *Across Asia on the Cheap,* which they later turned into the Lonely Planet series. Over the next thirty years Lonely Planet grew to a library of 650 separate titles that sold millions of copies. Lonely Planet's guides to the more remote corners of the world were called "travel survival kits" by the company, accentuating the hardships involved in the journeys they described.[84]

Of course, for all the talk of adventure and survival, the influx of affluent trekkers into the Nepalese backcountry predictably served to tame the very hardships that made up part of the appeal of trekking. "Shangri-la" would come to bear an increasing resemblance to every other part of the globe touched by Western consumer culture. Even the hardiest of trekkers, after all, might want to stop for a cold soda after a long day's hike, as enterprising Nepalese villagers were quick to realize. And the truly hard-core trekkers increasingly shared the trails with other tourists who sought an ever-increasing level of creature comforts. The first Sherpa-owned hotel opened for business in Namche Bazar in 1971. This was followed in 1973 by the Japanese-financed Everest View Hotel, located at an altitude of 13,000 feet on a hill above Khumjung, just a dozen miles from Everest. Tourists bound for the world's highest public accommodation flew directly by helicopter or Pilatus Porter aircraft from Kathmandu to an airstrip at Sangboche at 12,500 feet. Unfortunately, having undergone none of the acclimatization available to those who hiked in from lower altitudes, many of the guests at the Everest View Hotel wound up suffering from altitude sickness during their stay (despite the oxygen bottles thoughtfully placed in each room for guest use—available for an extra $10 a night).[85]

Life in the Khumbu got easier for the Sherpas as well as for their visitors. The trekking and tourist industries offered Sherpas new economic opportunities as shopkeepers and hoteliers as well as expanding opportunities for those who worked as guides. Guiding for trekking companies offered steadier work, easier conditions, and a greater likelihood of living to a ripe old age than a career as a high-altitude porter or climber on mountaineering expeditions. Increased employment opportunities drove up the price of skilled Sherpa labor, as Western expedition organizers would discover to their dismay when Nepal finally lifted the ban on mountaineering.[86]

The Climbing Counterculture

The social and cultural changes associated with the 1960s in the West came as a shock to some elders of the climbing community, as they tended to do for the older generation as a whole. Kenneth Mason had retired as professor of geography at Oxford University in 1953 but lived on in Oxford for another decade before moving to Sussex. "During those last years in Oxford we saw great changes," he complained in an aside in the unpublished memoir he wrote in retirement. "Strange long-haired youths of dirty aspect with little respect for authority became common sights."[87]

"Strange long-haired youths of dirty aspect" were also increasingly to be found in Nepal in the later 1960s. An international "Hippie Trail" grew up, followed by young seekers who journeyed overland by bus or car from London and Amsterdam to India and Nepal. Many never got beyond "Freak Street" in Kathmandu.[88] But some reached the mountains as trekkers or as pilgrims to locations like Tengboche Monastery. In fact, by decade's end, it was becoming increasingly difficult to tell the younger mountaineers from their hippie counterparts.

Among the signature elements of the hippie subculture of the 1960s was a fascination with the religions of South Asia, a phenomenon that drew on several sources. In the 1950s Beat poets like Allen Ginsberg and Gary Snyder, and novelist Jack Kerouac, had become interested in Tibetan and Zen Buddhism, and references to concepts like "karma" and "dharma" became a defining feature of their writings. Not a few journeys along the Hippie Trail began with a close reading of Kerouac's *On the Road* or *Dharma Bums*. By the mid-1960s the Beatles, reigning stars of Western pop culture, were popularizing a vague and eclectic mixture of Hinduism and other Eastern beliefs that they picked up as disciples of their Indian guru, the enterprising Maharishi Mahesh Yogi. At the same time, George Harrison apprenticed himself musically to one of the masters of the Indian sitar, Ravi Shankar, and many of the Beatles' most popular songs began to carry a distinct Indian inflection. "After I had taken LSD," Harrison later recalled of his spiritual wanderings in the mid-1960s, "a lingering thought stayed with me, and the thought was 'the yogis of the Himalayas.' I don't know why it stuck. I had never thought about them before, but suddenly this thought was in the back of my consciousness: it was as if somebody was whispering to me, 'Yogis of the Himalayas.' That was part of the reason I went to India. Ravi and the sitar were excuses; although they were a very important part of it, it was a search for a spiritual connection."[89]

Where the Beatles led, the hippie masses were quick to follow. India was close to Nepal, and Nepal close to Tibet, and all three countries became enshrined in hippie lore as the common geographical center of spiritual enlightenment. Before the 1960s were over, the exiled Dalai Lama was well on his way to making the transition from cold war martyr to countercultural folk hero, while the *Tibetan Book of the Dead,* a guide to dying and reincarnation, became an unlikely Western best seller (the book also provided the inspiration for the name of one of the most durable of the era's rock bands, the Grateful Dead). For young Westerners, the dominant image of the Himalayan region shifted in the course of the decade from a place where one set off on arduous struggles to place a flag atop a summit to the scenic backdrop to a quest for ancient wisdom and inner peace.[90]

Of course, long before the smell of hashish and incense drifted past the intersection of Haight and Ashbury streets in San Francisco, a good many mountaineers of outwardly conventional appearance and careers had succumbed in their own fashion to the appeal of the mysterious East. James Ramsey Ullman noted in a passage in his *Americans on Everest* that the spirit of "'up and at it' men of action" was only a part of the motivation of the American climbers who went to Everest in 1963: "[M]ingled with this was far more than one might expect in a group of steak-and-milk-fed young Americans of Buddhism's mystic and reverent om. Everest was not merely an adventure of the body but of the mind and soul . . . a heightening of human experience; an extension beyond the demands of normal living, of man's scope and capabilities."[91]

Mountaineering has always had its romantic side, attractive to those who were at odds with their own culture, a romanticism on display in both nineteenth-century Alpine climbing and twentieth-century Himalayan climbing. Ullman's description of the Everest climbers may well have drawn upon some of his own ambivalent feelings about the state of American society in the mid-twentieth century; for all the flag waving of *Americans on Everest,* he was not uncritical of the shortcomings of the United States. Many mountaineers felt that in overcoming the challenges they encountered en route to a summit, they were leaving behind the trivial distractions of a sedentary, materialist world for something truer and purer. They were forging a mystical bond with the particular mountain they were climbing—or, more broadly, with the natural world itself: as Herbert Tichy felt in approaching the summit of Cho Oyu, he was at last able to perceive "the essentials of the universe." In the Himalaya there was the added dimension of climbing in the company of Sherpas, a people who were a product of the mountain environment, and as such seemed to Westerners to embody the same values and experiences they associated with the act of mountain climbing: purity, authenticity, transcendence, a cleansing of the doors of perception.[92]

In the 1960s Himalayan mountaineers did not need to imbibe their Buddhism secondhand through the works of Beat writers or British musicians. They could see Buddhism's living embodiment in the Sherpas, a people they were coming to admire not only for their physical performance at high altitude but also for their apparent sense of spiritual harmony. In Lionel Terray's climbing memoir, *Conquistadors of the Useless,* published in France in 1961 and translated into English two years later, he praised the Sherpas' "goodheartedness, gaiety, tact and sense of poetry." Sherpa life seemed a utopia to disenchanted Westerners. Whenever Terray spent time in the company of Sherpas, he wrote, "dreams of a better world have always seemed to me suddenly less foolish." Four years later Tom Hornbein offered an equally enthusiastic endorsement of life in the Sherpa communities he observed on the approach march to Everest: "It seemed to me that here man lived in continuous harmony with the land. . . . He used the earth with gratitude. . . . In this peaceful coexistence [with nature], man was the invited guest. It was an enviable symbiosis."[93] It may be that one of the hidden influences for the "back to the land" impulse among young Americans in the later 1960s was the rapturous descriptions they could read of Sherpa life and values in popular accounts of Himalayan expeditions.

Buddhist religion and Sherpa agrarianism thus fit in well with the countercultural sensibilities of youthful Western visitors, who came to regard the Sherpa homeland as Woodstock on the Dudh Kosi. It probably also helped that Nepal was a land where marijuana grew wild by the trailside. Opium and hashish were also plentiful, inexpensive, and perfectly legal to possess and consume in Nepal in the 1960s (under pressure from the U.S.

government, Nepalese authorities finally outlawed the sale of marijuana in 1973, a ruling that drove up prices in Kathmandu but did nothing to reduce availability). There are no indications that any of the "steak-and-milk-fed young Americans" on the 1963 Everest expedition availed themselves of such substances. But by the time American mountaineers returned to Everest in the mid-1970s, many inhibitions had fallen by the wayside. Expedition books began casually to mention drug use by participants, even naming those who indulged. The Sierra Club magazine *Ascent* ran a parody account of an expedition to the mythical peak of Poontanga, which included this aside: "The amazing ration of golden, crystal-like powder [one expedition member] discovered while shopping for medication in Kathmandu has been the mission's great success story. Inhaled through either nostril on a regular basis, it miraculously eliminates the headaches and colds so frequent above 17,000 feet, not to mention what it has done for our morale."[94]

Sex, drugs, and rock and roll aside, the climbing counterculture had its own concerns, among them a reaction against the trend toward ever more elaborate methods of "rock engineering" that had characterized high-level climbing in places like Yosemite and the Alps in the 1950s. In the 1930s the climbing establishment in the United States and Britain had condemned the use of pitons as unsportsmanlike, something only Germans would be so crass as to employ. In the 1950s the pendulum swung dramatically in the opposite direction, as the most exciting innovations in rock climbing involved the use of more sophisticated levels of mechanical aid. Ropes and slings hung from pitons or bolts driven into rock provided a boost that allowed climbers to move up an otherwise impossible pitch on a rock face. Artificial climbing was celebrated for the sense of mastery it offered to those who employed the technology and the technique.[95]

But in the 1960s a rebellion began against the rock engineers. For some young climbers, "artificial" now became a pejorative; the growing use of words like "clean" and "free" to describe preferred climbing styles suggested other values coming to the fore. Sixties innovators scorned the use, or at least the overuse, of pitons and expansion bolts, which resulted in the "scarring" of rock faces. Instead of driving a piton into a rock face for protection, the clean climber leading a pitch jammed a nonscarring metal chockstone (or "chock") in a crack, to be retrieved by the last climber on the rope. And instead of relying on weight-bearing ropes and slings to master difficult pitches, the rock climbing purist's highest ideal was to free-climb a route, relying on nothing but the natural features of the rock to aid upward ascent.[96]

A climber from Italy's South Tyrol named Reinhold Messner codified the new ethos in his manifesto "The Murder of the Impossible," published in 1971 in *Mountain* magazine. "Rock faces are no longer overcome by climbing skill," Messner complained, "but are humbled, pitch by pitch, by methodical manual labour." In place of mechanical aids that "polluted the pure spring of mountaineering," Messner urged on climbers a new ethos of voluntary simplicity: "[T]ake a rope with you and a couple of pitons for your belays, but nothing else."[97] What began as a revolt against pitons would soon be extended in the Himalaya to other forms of "artificial" aid, including bottled oxygen.

Nepal Ends Climbing Ban

In 1968 Nepal announced the end of its ban on mountaineering expeditions. Starting the following year forty-odd peaks, including all the eight-thousanders within its borders, would again be available to climbers. That was good news, but mountaineers were less happy about the fine print accompanying the announcement. As before, the number of annual expeditions allowed to attempt any given mountainside was to be strictly limited to one expedition per season. Since Everest had only one side within Nepal's borders, that meant at most two expeditions a year could attempt the mountain, and a long queue immediately developed for the limited slots available. The regulations also required that expeditions have the endorsement of a national climbing club and the approval of their own governments to qualify for a permit, and these were no longer quite as cheap as they had previously been. To climb Everest would now cost expeditions $1,000—before the ban it had been $640. Permits for smaller peaks cost $800. As before the climbing ban, all expeditions were required to be accompanied by a government-appointed liaison officer, whose services were to be paid for by the foreign expedition and who had to be equipped with a complete set of expedition gear, even though in practice he seldom climbed above Base Camp. In a new requirement, Sherpas and other Nepalese employed on expeditions had to be engaged through a single central agency, the Himalayan Society, and new and higher pay scales were imposed. (The central agency requirement was abandoned in 1975, but the higher pay scales remained in effect.) These regulations provoked much grumbling in Western mountaineering circles about "mountain bureaucrats," but there was no escaping them, and in years to come India, Pakistan, and eventually China would model their own mountaineering rules on the Nepalese system.[98]

Eleven full-scale expeditions and two reconnaissances headed for the Nepalese Himalaya in 1969. Two of the expeditions attempted 8,000-meter peaks, a German expedition on Annapurna, and an American expedition on Dhaulagiri. The Germans were unsuccessful; the Americans met disaster.[99]

The eleven-member American expedition was led by Boyd N. Everett Jr., a Wall Street securities analyst. Expedition members established their Base Camp on the mountain's southeast glacier on April 20. They planned to attempt the mountain's Southeast Ridge, the route that Gaston Rébuffat had first explored and rejected as impossible in 1950. But they never reached the ridge. While the advance party was building a log bridge across a crevasse at the top of the glacier, an ice cliff collapsed above them, letting loose an avalanche. Seven of the climbers—expedition leader Everett, David Seidman, Vin Hoeman, Paul Gerhard, Bill Ross, and Sherpas Pemba Phutar and Panboche Tenzing—were swept away without a trace. Lou Reichardt, the only survivor of the advance party, offered a grim account of the first disaster to accompany the renewal of Himalayan mountaineering:

> It began with the noise of an avalanche, not rare that day, then a mutual realization that it might hit us. A moment to duck, but only a change of slope angle for shelter. A roar.

> A pelting on my back and head of ice. A struggle to remain in a fetal position with an air pocket, then a slackening in intensity of the avalanche. Curiosity compelled me to raise my head. I got sharply whacked on the skull as a reward for my effort.
>
> Then there was silence. No screams, just silence. First came the realization that I was not hurt. It couldn't have been that bad! Then there was a search for the familiar; friends, tents, cache, and gear; then the discovery that nothing was there—no tents, no cache, no ice axe, and no friends.[100]

After a fruitless search for bodies, the chastened survivors left behind a memorial stone along the trail to the glacier and headed home, but not before the Americans vowed to return to the mountain for another attempt.

Five months later an Austrian expedition led by Richard Hoyer attempted the first ascent of Dhaulagiri IV (25,134ft/7,661m), but on the day of their summit bid, November 9, the entire summit party of five Austrians, including Hoyer and one Sherpa, disappeared. They were almost certainly the victims of avalanche, just as the Americans had been earlier in the year. The year 1969 had been the most costly in the history of Nepalese climbing to date.[101]

New Faces: Chris Bonington

Chris Bonington first approached Annapurna in 1960, when he was on an expedition to climb its sister peak, Annapurna II, twenty miles to the east. The Annapurna II team, including Bonington, reached the summit via a ridge on the mountain. In fact, most first ascents on the Himalayan giants had been via ridgelines, for on mountains of any height it is the ridges that usually offer the easiest and least dangerous path to the summit. Annapurna itself proved an exception, having been first climbed by way of its North Face by Maurice Herzog's expedition in 1950. Herzog and his companions decided to attempt a route up the face only after running into impassable obstacles on the mountain's Northwest Spur. As it turned out, the North Face offered a relatively gentle slope, on which, once past its heavily glaciated lower half, the French team found an uncomplicated route to the summit.

Although Annapurna's North Face had been climbed, no one as of 1960 had yet dreamed of climbing its far more demanding South Face, a steep 11,000-foot wall of rock and ice. But a decade would make a big difference. The ascent of all fourteen 8,000-meter peaks, combined with the American success in 1963 in establishing a new and difficult route up Everest's West Ridge (in part a face climb up the Hornbein Couloir), broke a psychological barrier. Increasingly, when climbers assessed Himalayan mountains, they sought routes offering greater challenges than a long snow plod up another ridgeline.

The climbing bans of the later 1960s put off, for the near future anyway, any bold new experiments in Himalayan route finding. While Nepal and Pakistan were off limits, climbers elsewhere—in Yosemite and on the North Face of the Eiger—were mastering the techniques and the confidence necessary for surmounting big mountain faces. It was only a matter of time and opportunity before these would be applied to Himalayan mountain faces.

Ten years would also make a big difference in Chris Bonington's life. In the course of the 1960s Bonington would emerge as "the public face of British mountaineering." Thanks to television, he would become better known to the general public than practically any of his predecessors in that role, with the possible exception of Mallory (who enjoyed the advantage of an early and dramatic death). He would not, however, enjoy the near-universal admiration that had come his predecessors' way from within the climbing community. Instead, he would find himself under attack, somewhat contradictorily, for exercising an authority based on an inherited sense of social superiority and for excessive entrepreneurialism. "Got a bloody plum in his mouth," one working-class climber proclaimed on encountering Bonington for the first time in Chamonix in 1955. Some years later a climbing journalist would criticize the "zeal" with which Bonington pursued an income from his mountaineering activities: "In climbing, as in many other sports, the gentlemen have given way to the players."[102]

Whether gentleman or player, Bonington was not a child of privilege. Born in Hampstead in 1934, he was raised by his mother on a secretarial salary after his father abandoned the family. Compared to the leading British climbers and expedition leaders who preceded him, Bonington's origins were among the most modest (and he was certainly the only one whose mother belonged to the British Communist Party).[103]

So when Bonington began climbing as a teenager (inspired in part by reading Bill Murray's history of Scottish mountaineering), his participation in the sport represented the same broadening of the social basis of British climbing that was taking place in Manchester and Glasgow. The difference was that Bonington had educational and professional aspirations not often found among the climbers associated with Creagh Dhu or the Rock and Ice Club. In 1954 he went to the Royal Military College, Sandhurst, and two years later, as a newly minted British tank commander, was assigned to occupation duty in Germany. He was by his own account an indifferent soldier, but learned some valuable lessons from military service nonetheless. "At Sandhurst we had been warned of the dangers of 'familiarity breeding contempt,' but in the close confines [of a tank], one had no choice," Bonington would later write. "One's crew were soon familiar with one's personal habits, weaknesses and character. It was no good erecting a stockade of discipline, of stiff upper lip; one had to earn [the crew's] friendship, and, at the same time, maintain their respect."[104] Much of Bonington's subsequent career as expedition leader revolved around striking the proper balance between authority and friendship.

The other good thing that came out of military service was finding himself stationed near the Alps, where he could polish his climbing skills and credentials. In 1958 he climbed the Southwest Pillar of the Dru with a party that included Hamish Macinnes and Don Whillans. His growing reputation, in and out of the circles of military climbers, led to his invitation to join the service expedition that set off to climb Annapurna II in 1960.

Bonington made his second Himalayan expedition, to Nuptse, in 1961, following his return to civilian life. After a brief and unhappy stint as a management trainee in a company that retailed margarine to London grocers, he gave up any aspirations to a conventional career and fashioned a calling for himself as a freelance mountaineering journalist and photographer. His big breakthrough came in 1962, when he made the first British ascent of the North Face of the Eiger along with Ian Clough. He came out of that climb with the personal congratulations of British prime minister Harold Macmillan and, more important, his first book contract.[105]

Bonington had undeniable gifts as a showman as well as a climber. He made several widely viewed live climbs on British television, most famously a 1967 ascent of the rock stack in the Orkney Islands of northeastern Scotland known as the Old Man of Hoy (this was his second time on the Old Man; he had completed its first ascent the previous year with Tom Patey and Rusty Baillie). He was a well-spoken and bearded man, given to wearing bulky woolen sweaters; his public image resembled that of a rumpled but wiry academic—and this in an era when many of his climbing peers were best known off-mountain for busting up pubs. His televised climbs inspired a famous Monty Python skit in which John Cleese interviewed a helmeted and roped Graham Chapman as the latter pulled himself along the "North Face of Uxbridge Road" in a direct ascent of a horizontal gutter: a breathless Chapman explained to Cleese he was "doing a layback up this gutter, guttering and philosophizing."[106]

In the mid-1960s Bonington, like many mountaineers, desperately wanted to get back to the Himalaya. Since that was not an option, he began planning an expedition to Alaska with his friends Nick Estcourt and Martin Boysen. Deciding they needed a fourth climber for their team, they invited Dougal Haston to join them.

The Scottish-born Haston, six years Bonington's junior, was then director of the International School of Mountaineering in the small Alpine village of Leysin, Switzerland, near Geneva. Haston had learned his climbing from the hard men of the Creagh Dhu in the 1950s, moving on to the Alps in the 1960s. There he had been part of a well-publicized winter first ascent of a new direct, or *direttissima,* route on the North Face of the Eiger in 1966, catapulting himself into the front ranks of British Alpinists. Bonington had photographed the Eiger direct ascent for the *Daily Telegraph Magazine* and afterward climbed with Haston on several occasions, including the first winter ascent of the North Face of the Argentière. Haston was not as well known to the general public as Bonington, being more of the pub-wrecking than the literary persuasion, but he enjoyed a cult celebrity within the climbing world. He combined a fearless flamboyance with a brooding romanticism, which made him a kind of quintessential 1960s figure. Like many of the era's rock stars, Haston also seemed marked for an early death—which only added to his charisma.[107]

When news arrived in the fall of 1968 of the reopening of Nepal to climbing expeditions, Bonington and the others quickly decided to switch destinations. On their climb of Argentière in 1967, at least according to Haston's memory, he and Bonington had wistfully speculated about what it might be like to attempt the South Face of Annapurna. Bonington obtained a slide of the face taken on the 1964 British expedition to Machapuchare.

The view of the face revealed by the slide was intimidating but also tantalizing, and Bonington and his mates thought they saw a possible route up the center. "What we were actually
contemplating was a new concept of Himalayan climbing," Haston wrote. "Previously it
had been the lines of least resistance that had been taken; our dream was the hardest face
on the mountain."[108]

As always, there were numerous obstacles to overcome before the climbers got
anywhere near the mountain. This time, at least, funding would not be one of them: The
Mount Everest Foundation provided total support. "Suddenly we seemed to be coming
under the wing of the Establishment," Bonington noted ruefully, "something which all of
us regarded with some distrust, having been very much outside those circles."[109]

Permission to climb Annapurna came from Kathmandu in July 1969, too late to
mount an expedition until the following year. In the meantime, Bonington rounded out
his team. British climbers Ian Clough and Mick Burke, both of whom had climbed with
Bonington before in the Alps, were added to the list. So was one outsider, American climber
Tom Frost, added at the suggestion of Bonington's literary agent, who thought it might
be easier to sell an expedition book in the United States if there was an American along.
Apart from the commercial advantage of his nationality, Frost's credentials were impressive,
with rock-climbing skills honed on the granite faces of Yosemite. And, although it wasn't
publicly spoken of as yet, he had also been to the Himalaya much more recently than any
of the others, climbing on Nanda Devi in 1966 and on Nanda Kot in 1967 on the CIA-
organized missions to those mountains. The one reservation some of Bonington's other
climbers had about Frost was his Mormonism: "[T]he rest of us were a pretty irreligious
bunch," Haston commented, "prone to breaking many commandments."[110]

Bonington recruited a doctor, base manager, and a support climber for the expedition. He needed one more top-rank climber to round out the lead party. His final choice
proved a surprise: Don Whillans. Whillans was, to be sure, one of the most experienced Himalayan climbers Great Britain had at the time, having been part of expeditions to Masherbrum, Trivor, and Gaurishankar. But he had not reached the summit of any of those peaks,
and by the later 1960s was increasingly regarded in climbing circles as an embarrassment:
a paunchy, over-the-hill alcoholic. He was also known to bear a grudge toward Bonington
dating back to 1962, when Bonington succeeded in climbing the Eiger with Ian Clough
after an earlier failed attempt with Whillans. But Bonington still thought highly of his
abilities and invited him to join the expedition as his deputy.[111]

Finally all was in readiness. In March 1970 the expedition flew to Kathmandu and
then on to the central Nepalese town of Pokhara, which by now had its own asphalt-covered
landing strip. Theirs was not the only expedition en route to Annapurna. An eight-member
party from the British Army Mountaineering Association, led by Bruce Niven, was headed
to the mountain's North Face to repeat the French 1950 route. There were many signs of
the changes that had taken place since that first ascent twenty years earlier. As Bonington
noted, when Herzog's expedition reached Annapurna "their biggest problem was finding

a route onto the mountain. We didn't even need a map to find ours. There was nothing unknown about the terrain; the mystery was entirely that of the climbing, whether we could contend with the complex difficulties of the Face at altitude."[112]

En route to the mountain, Bonington would report, they encountered scores of Westerners, ranging from clean-cut trekkers to "hippies, dressed in various interpretations of the local garb, looking far gone on pot." The climbers themselves bore little resemblance to their predecessors in the 1950s and early 1960s. Haston described the expedition as looking "like a bunch of freaks in search of a drug scene, with long hair and tattered jeans."[113]

One other difference, apparent to Bonington after nearly a decade's absence from the Himalaya, was the change that had taken place in the appearance and attitude of the Sherpas. Pasang Kami, a veteran of Jimmy Roberts's trekking ventures, was in Bonington's opinion "much more sophisticated than the high-altitude Sherpas I had known on my two previous expeditions, who had spoken very limited English and were essentially simple villagers." Pasang addressed the sahibs "as an equal" and reminded Bonington of a "with-it" Chamonix guide: "I think Pasang probably represents the start of a new breed of Sherpa, partly spawned by their new role in Nepal, where the bulk of the work is confined to conducting parties of tourists on treks round the valleys. The ideal qualifications for this job are organizing ability, command of languages, and a good manner. Pasang had cultivated all three."[114]

While the others made their way to the mountain with the baggage and porters, Whillans went ahead to scout out the South Face. He thought he saw a good route up the face (he also thought he saw a yeti, though some of the others suspected the sighting had something to do with the whiskey bottle he brought with him). Whillans had lost some of his bulging waistline on the approach march to the mountain, but he was by no means as fit as the other climbers. In one of the shrewder decisions he would make as expedition leader, Bonington decided to pair Haston and Whillans as climbing partners, trusting in Haston's drive to compensate for Whillans's still-uncertain physical condition, and in Whillans's experience and mountain judgment to determine the best route to the summit.[115]

The climb began in earnest on March 29, when Whillans, Haston, Mick Burke, and Sherpa Kancha moved up to establish Base Camp at the foot of the South Face. Haston described the task ahead of them with admirable brevity in his autobiography: "The Face seemed to break down into distinct sectors: lower icefall and moraine; upper icefall; couloir leading to the ice ridge and séracs above; rock band and summit cliffs."[116] The climbers would put in six camps on the face, the highest at 24,000 feet, in the midst of the rock band.

The dangers from avalanche and collapsing ice towers were ever present, reflected in the names the climbers attached to features they encountered along the way, such as the Sword of Damocles and the Terrible Traverse. Parts of the climb consisted of relatively straightforward, if steep, ascents of snowfields. But on the ice ridge and the rock band there were difficult technical challenges to be overcome that slowed the climbers' progress and taxed their energies.

Although the route they followed up the face would usher in a new era in Hima-layan climbing, the siege tactics they used to climb it were little different from those em-ployed on Himalayan mountains for the past half century. Pairs of climbers moved up the mountain in turn to take the lead in pushing the route, while others alternated between recuperating in the lower camps and carrying loads of supplies to stock the higher camps. Tom Frost recalled that of sixty days he spent on the mountain, forty-three were devoted to "ferrying loads or snow slogging," eleven to rest, and "only *six* doing technical climbing." For all the comparisons the expedition would garner with Yosemite Big Wall techniques, the climbers rarely found themselves climbing on bare rock: rather, snow and ice defined most of the terrain they crossed. And for all the comparisons with the Eiger direct ascent, the route the climbers took by no means matched the direttissima ideal; it veered leftward on the face at two key points to avoid natural obstacles.[117]

There were significant innovations in equipment on the expedition, including the use of jumars. These mechanical ascenders were attached to the climber's harness by a sling and to a fixed climbing rope; they had a ratcheting device that slid up the rope but under tension would hold fast. They provided protection against slips and aid in climbing difficult stretches. Jumars had been in use for years in Yosemite and the Alps but were new to Hima-layan expeditions. The climbers were also equipped with a "sit harness" designed by Don Whillans that would become standard equipment for climbers in years to come and bring Whillans a tidy income. At some of the higher camps they used a box-shaped tent, with a strong internal frame, also designed by Whillans. Known as a Whillans box, it was less prone than the traditional ridge tents to collapse under accumulated powder snow.[118]

Like John Hunt on Everest, Bonington led his Annapurna expedition from the front, spending a total of thirty-one days at or above 20,000 feet. That was more time at high altitude than anyone on the expedition but Haston, Whillans, and Frost, who each surpassed him only by a day or two.[119] He wrestled constantly with logistics, trying to ensure that enough supplies reached the highest camps to support the lead climbers (a problem later in the climb, as insufficient food made it up the mountain side).

Bonington would get high marks from the other climbers as a master of logistics. Where he would run into problems was in his management of the climbers themselves. As April and the early weeks of May were consumed in pushing a route up to the final great obstacle of the rock band, and as the monsoon season steadily advanced, the chance that more than a single team would be able to make a summit bid just as steadily dwindled. In choosing a summit team, Bonington could please only two of the eight climbers in the lead party; five others, not counting himself, were going to go away disappointed.

Although he did not consider himself a part of the traditional climbing establishment in Britain, Bonington recognized that in many ways he was a product of the older expedi-tionary culture. "If you go right back to where I started from," he would tell an interviewer in the 1980s, "say Annapurna II in 1960, it was like one of the pre-war expeditions, and we were all servicemen steeped in the kind of morals of the Second World War and it was a very cohesive expedition." By 1970, the "morals of the Second World War," with their emphasis on teamwork, self-sacrifice, and a willing if not automatic respect for authority, were in decline, to say the least. The members of the South Face expedition had agreed in writing to obey him as leader, but Bonington "always had a feeling that this was something that would be ignored in the stress of the moment if ever my own commands were far out of line with the consensus of the expedition."[120]

Bonington tested the limits of his authority in a radio conversation with the other climbers on the evening of May 13. All camps on the mountain were linked by portable radio, and there were twice-daily calls in which climbers could report their progress, request supplies, and receive their instructions from the expedition leader. Without warning, Bonington announced his decision to have Haston and Whillans move up to the lead position at Camp V to finish the route through the rock band, thus putting them in position to make the first summit bid. The problem was that in doing this he disrupted the pattern of rotation of lead pairs, which should have fallen to Boysen and Estcourt. Mick Burke, from Camp V, objected, arguing that Haston and Whillans should by rights take their turn load-carrying from Camp IV to Camp V. Bonington, searching for a compromise, agreed to have them spend a day in load-carrying before moving further up the mountain. But Whillans, silent through the early part of the discussion, now weighed in: "Dougal and I left that place Camp V a week ago. Camp V isn't even consolidated and the progress of all towards Camp VI is so poor that it's had me and Dougal depressed all the way up the mountain. I don't know what Mick thinks he's playing at but Camp V is short and we want to get the route pushed out and unless they get their finger out, push it out and establish Camp VI or at least find a site, they should make way for somebody else to try. He's had a week and progress seems poor." That undiplomatic sally provoked an outraged response from the others, and Bonington had to call a quick end to the conversation: "We've managed to be a happy expedition up to now—let's keep it that way. Over and out."[121]

As Whillans and Haston moved to the front and the other climbers descended, Bonington dealt with the continued fallout from his decision and Whillans's blunt intervention. Tom Frost, who had led a difficult pitch through the rock band, was among those who felt betrayed: "Up to now we've kept roughly in turn, though Don and Dougal have done less carrying than anyone else and have definitely nursed themselves for the summit. I'd rather risk failure and yet have everyone feeling that they had a fair share of the leading which, after all, is the real reason why we have all come together on this climb." For Bonington, the feelings of individual climbers would have to take second place to the success of the expedition. "Look at Hillary and Tensing on Everest," he told Frost. "[T]hey were nursed by John Hunt for their summit bid, and I think we must do the same if we are to be successful."[122]

A 1953 precedent was not persuasive to climbers on a 1970 expedition. And, as Frost's comment suggests, the problem was not that Haston and Whillans had been "nursed" by Bonington but that they had, in effect, nursed themselves by shirking the physically draining and less glamorous tasks of load-carrying to preserve their own strength for the summit bid. In an appendix to Bonington's expedition book, Nick Estcourt offered a statistical breakdown of each climber's contribution to the expedition. In the category "Days Carrying Loads," Estcourt and Boysen had the most, twenty-two days each. Haston, on the other hand, scored only ten, and Whillans a mere seven. Until Whillans and Haston took over the final push up the rock band and on to the summit, Whillans had spent the least time of any of the eight lead climbers above Camp III. Estcourt's conclusion was not intended as a compliment: "Don, the wily old mountaineer, had timed things just right."[123]

Apart from the resentments generated, Bonington's decision was doubtless the right one. Boysen and Estcourt were worn out by mid-May. Not only were Haston and Whillans fresher, they were a more dynamic team. They made their climb to Camp V and then pushed on to establish Camp VI at 24,000 feet. Over the next few days they found a gully that led them up through the remainder of the rock band. They had planned to put in Camp VII at the top of the rock band, but weather conditions were deteriorating, and they were desperately short of food (Whillans seemingly surviving on cigars). Finally, at 7:00 A.M. on May 27, Haston and Whillans set out on their summit bid. They carried a tent, in case they wanted to set up Camp VII after all, but in the event did not stop. Although they had decided to climb without oxygen, they experienced no great breathing difficulties. Whillans led throughout the climb, and at 2:30 P.M. they stood on the summit of Annapurna, with the view obscured by clouds. They descended rapidly to Camp VI and called on the radio to Bonington. From below, where all was covered in clouds, it had seemed like an unlikely day for a summit bid. "Did you manage to get out today?" Bonington asked. "Aye," Haston replied. "[W]e've just climbed Annapurna."[124]

On their descent, Haston and Whillans passed Frost and Burke heading up to Camp VI for their own summit bid. But their effort two days later was unsuccessful. And on that same day, May 29, Ian Clough, who had climbed the North Face of the Eiger with Bonington in 1962, was killed in an ice avalanche below Camp II while descending the mountain. He was the first climber to be killed on Annapurna, the mountain that over the next several decades became known as one of the deadliest of all the Himalayan giants.[125]

At the conclusion of his expedition book, Bonington quoted Maurice Herzog's famous ending line from the first account of climbing Annapurna, "There are other Annapurnas in the lives of men." For Bonington, the aphorism had lost none of its truth, either "in the realm of mountaineering" or in "one's own progress through life." He ended his book with a prediction: "Our ascent of Annapurna was a breakthrough into a new dimension of Himalayan climbing on the great walls of the highest mountains in the world—this represents the start of an era, not the end. Climbers will turn to other great faces, will perhaps try to reduce the size of the party, escape from the heavy siege tactics that we were forced to employ and make lightweight assaults against these huge mountain problems."[126]

New Faces: Reinhold Messner

On June 27, 1970, one month to the day after Dougal Haston and Don Whillans reached the summit of Annapurna, there was another breakthrough moment in Himalayan climbing when Reinhold Messner, along with his younger brother Günther, stood atop Nanga Parbat in Pakistan. They too had made it to the summit by a previously unscaled route, the 14,763-foot high Rupal Face. The day's triumph marked the beginning of Reinhold Messner's career as one of the greatest Himalayan climbers; Messner would later call it the "defining experience of my life."[127]

Born in 1944 in the German-speaking region of the Italian Tyrol, Reinhold Messner was introduced by his father to Alpine climbing by the time he had turned five years old. With his brother Günther he explored the Dolomites as a teenager before moving on to climbs in the western Alps. By the time he was twenty-five he had made fifty first ascents in the Alps as well as a score of solo climbs of difficult routes, and wanted to move on to bigger mountains.[128]

He got his opportunity when Dr. Karl Herrligkoffer invited him to join the Sigi Löw Memorial Expedition to Nanga Parbat scheduled for the summer of 1970 (Löw had died in 1962 after successfully ascending the Diamir Face of the mountain on another Herrligkoffer expedition). Herrligkoffer's goal was an attempt on the last unclimbed face of the mountain, the Rupal Face.[129]

As an admirer of Hermann Buhl, Messner of course knew all about the 1953 expedition and Herrligkoffer's bitter quarrel with his lead climber, but the offer was too good to decline. He would have the chance of solving the last great problem on the mountain that had for so long fascinated German-speaking climbers. And, as it turned out, he would be able to do so in the company of his longtime climbing partner and brother Günther, who received an invitation soon after from Herrligkoffer to fill out the ranks of the eleven-member expedition.

For six weeks in May and June 1970, the climbers laid siege to the lower reaches of the Rupal Face. Camp V, the high camp, went in at 24,100 feet, at the base of the feature on the face known as the Merkl Gully. As always on his expeditions, Herrligkoffer was determined to make all the key decisions from his command post at Base Camp. But, as had been the case in 1953, the higher the climbers got on Nanga Parbat, the more tenuous was Herrligkoffer's control. Messner, like Buhl before him, had his own ideas on how to climb the mountain. On June 26 he, his brother, and climber Gerhard Baur set out for high camp to position themselves for a summit bid the following day. As they did so, they climbed out of radio contact with Base Camp.

Herrligkoffer was monitoring radio reports on approaching weather fronts and in his last radio conversation with Messner had arranged to provide a signal on the evening of June 26 to alert the climbers high on the mountain of what to expect the next day. He would send up a colored rocket: red meant bad weather, blue good. If the weather was bad, then Messner, the fastest and strongest of the three, would set off on his own for a quick solo attempt on the summit; if the weather was good, he would do so in the company of his brother and Baur. At 8:00 P.M., as they were approaching Camp V, they saw the rocket; it was red. Messner would climb alone the next morning.

The next morning, shortly after 2:00 A.M., Messner set out alone. Günther and Gerhard Baur remained behind, planning to fix ropes on the lower Merkl Gully in preparation for a later attempt in better weather. But when it became apparent that, red rocket or no, the weather on June 27 was actually going to be fair, and Baur was too ill to fix ropes in the gully, Günther decided on impulse to catch up with his brother. He reached him about 1,000 feet short of the summit. The two brothers climbed on together and reached the top at 5:00 P.M.

But Günther was suffering from the effects of altitude. Climbing alone, Reinhold had not carried a rope, and he feared Günther would not make it down the steep Rupal Face unroped. Instead they descended along the Southwest Ridge, hoping to find a place lower down where they could traverse to the Merkl Gully. They were forced to bivouac about 1,000 feet below the summit, in a notch in the ridgeline known as Merkl Gap.

While Reinhold and Günther climbed to the top of Nanga Parbat on June 27, the next two climbers in line for the summit, Felix Kuen and Peter Scholz, moved up to Camp V. Early the next morning they set off, following the Messner brothers' tracks up the Merkl Gulley. At 6:00 A.M. they heard Reinhold Messner's shouts from above. Four hours later they drew abreast of Reinhold and Günther's bivouac site, about 250 feet away from them on the ridge. What happened next is a matter of controversy and conjecture. According to Messner, he shouted to Kuen and Scholz, asking them to climb over to the ridge and give them the rope that would allow him to get his brother safely down the Rupal Face. They could, he told them, continue to the top up the ridgeline. But Kuen and Scholz remembered things differently. According to their version, Reinhold assured them that everything was all right and did not ask for their aid.

It is possible that Kuen and Scholz simply did not want to give up their rope—or their own chance of ascending the Rupal Face. Or it may be that Messner had decided to add to the glory of the first ascent of the Rupal Face by descending the Diamir Face and thus accomplishing the first traverse of Nanga Parbat, regardless of the condition of his brother. Perhaps the most likely explanation is that on a windy day, separated by 250 feet of mountainside, and possibly suffering the effects of hypoxia, the climbers involved simply misheard or misunderstood one another.[130]

In any case, Kuen and Scholz continued up the Rupal Face, and Reinhold and Günther Messner, ropeless, descended the Diamir Face. It was shorter and not as steep as the Rupal Face, but it had the disadvantage of being terrain that was new to them. And there would be no Camp V for them to stop at and recuperate. They spent a second night bivouacking on the mountainside at the Mummery Spur, at just under 20,000 feet. Both brothers were now in bad shape, weakened by exposure and frostbite, with Reinhold suffering the classic hallucination that a third climber accompanied them. As their third day on the mountain dawned, Reinhold convinced himself that his brother was actually improving. As they approached the bottom of the Diamir Face, Reinhold decided to leave Günther behind to rest while he scouted the glacier ahead; Günther was to join him shortly. But when his brother failed to appear, he climbed back up to find him. Günther was no longer there; instead there was a sign of a recent avalanche.[131]

After searching for his brother for the remainder of the day and into the night, suffering from shock, grief, and exposure, Messner finally set off again down the mountain, reduced to crawling on all fours when he was found and rescued by local villagers. When he rejoined the expedition, which had given him up for dead, he learned that the red rocket on June 26 had been sent by mistake. The weather report Herrligkoffer had received by radio had been for good weather, not for bad. If Messner and his companions had known that, they would have set off for the summit together with a rope, and after summiting might have been able to descend the Merkl Gully in safety.[132]

That, anyway, was Messner's version. Herrligkoffer, for his part, denied ever having authorized a solo ascent of the mountain and accused Messner of having "sacrificed his brother to his mountaineering ambition." Messner and Herrligkoffer would tangle in a series of legal proceedings when they returned to Europe, and Messner would have to withdraw from publication his own account of the climb, *Die Rote Rakete am Nanga Parbat*, published in violation of the expedition contract (another echo of the Buhl-Herrligkoffer conflict in the 1950s). Messner carried a heavy burden of remorse after the expedition; he would become as obsessed with Nanga Parbat as Herrligkoffer had been. He also lost seven toes to frostbite and for a while sounded unsure of whether he would ever again be able to achieve notable climbs: "[I]f you've had frostbite once, you're much more susceptible to further attacks," he told an interviewer from *Mountain* magazine in 1971. "So I've got a considerable handicap. Many of the first ascents I had in mind won't be possible now."[133]

That proved one of the least accurate predictions in the history of mountaineering. Perhaps more than any other single individual, Messner would define the strategy and values of the coming age of extremes in the Himalaya.

CHAPTER TEN

The Age of Extremes
1971–1996

W e entered the mountains as strangers," Charlie Houston wrote of the
members of the 1953 K2 expedition, "but we left as brothers." As
much as any venture in the history of Himalayan mountaineering,
Houston's expedition embodied the highest ideals of expeditionary
culture. It was a true brotherhood of the rope; every member of the
expedition owed his life to Pete Schoening's famed belay at a moment of mortal danger.[1]

Many expeditions failed to achieve the ideal of fellowship displayed by the American K2ers. Nonetheless, at least through the 1960s, the notion of a brotherhood of the rope
served as a kind of bedrock moral principle and social norm from which, most mountaineers would have agreed, the duties and obligations they owed one another derived. "You're
bound together symbolically by the climbing rope," Willi Unsoeld explained to audiences
at his slide shows about the 1963 Everest expedition, "the very umbilical of your connection with each other, and there's a constant awareness of the other members of the team
and a closeness and a cooperation that grows up among mountaineers that is the nearest
thing I've seen to the brotherhood of the battlefield."[2]

In the final decades of the twentieth century that sense of duty and obligation to
others waned. Those who entered the mountains as strangers often departed estranged—and
even more tellingly, seemed to expect little more from the experience. As John Roskelley,
a leading Himalayan climber of the 1970s and 1980s, told an interviewer: "If we're not belaying,
I unrope. That's rule number one. That way I don't kill them and they don't kill me."[3]

The climbing rope, once a symbol of protective solidarity, was becoming instead a
symbol of fatal dependence. Himalayan mountaineers unroped from one another both literally and figuratively, as the old expeditionary culture frayed to the breaking point. Durable
climbing partnerships became scarce. The path to mountaineering fame increasingly took
the form of the solo ascent. Professional guides led groups of amateurs up Himalayan peaks
on a strictly business, cash-paid-in-advance basis. And a culture of blame and recrimination
took root in the mountaineering community.

It had not been unusual in earlier years for multiple accounts of a single expedition to be published: within two years of the completion of the first American Everest expedition, for instance, four separate narratives had been published by its members. These included the official *Americans on Everest* by James Ramsey Ullman, a *National Geographic* article by Barry Bishop, and books by Tom Hornbein and Lute Jerstad. The differences among these works were mostly of emphasis; all were written in a fashion genuinely respectful of the other participants. The American Everest expedition had not been without conflict, but it would take a careful reader to detect animosity. Expedition member Al Auten wrote to Ullman shortly after the publication of *Americans on Everest* to report himself "particularly pleased at the artful way the problems and frictions among the expedition members were handled [in the book]. It would have been foolish to pretend that all was sweetness and light throughout the entire time, but your balance between the problems and their solution was masterful."[4]

Over the next two decades an Ullmanesque "balance" in mountaineering literature came to be replaced by an edgier setting-the-record-straight perspective, especially noticeable in, though by no means restricted to, books about American expeditions. No one reading the following apparently verbatim exchange between two climbers in Rick Ridgeway's account of the next American team to reach Everest, the 1976 Bicentennial expedition, would be left with any illusions that sweetness and light characterized that enterprise:

> You haven't done a damn thing that I can see. . . .
> Fuck you I've done the hardest part of this mountain. . . .
> I have a problem climbing with a guy whose ambitions are about ten times as big as his abilities. . . .
> I'm so fucking impressed. . . .
> He doesn't think I can climb. Prove it, you little turd. . . .
> I can prove you're an asshole [etc.].[5]

It did not matter whether expeditions failed or succeeded (though two Americans summited Everest in 1976, in Ridgeway's book their success somehow seemed secondary to the conflicts preceding their triumph). Galen Rowell's *In the Throne Room of the Mountain Gods,* about the failed 1975 expedition to K2, and Ridgeway's *The Last Step,* about the 1978 expedition that placed four climbers, including Ridgeway, on the summit of the mountain, were both warts-and-all accounts. Ridgeway's K2 account led a British reviewer to complain about the American taste for the confessional: "On this side of the Atlantic, climbing writers usually take it for granted that climbers are extremely self-centered and quarrelsome on the hill, and that the myths about them make better reading than the reality."[6] But on both sides of the Atlantic—and, more important, in the Himalaya—the confessional, the confrontational, and the commercial came to the fore. It was the age of extremes.

The 1971 International Everest Expedition

They did not come any more extreme than the 1971 international Everest expedition. With the Bonington expedition's success on the South Face of Annapurna in 1970, the Southwest Face of Everest, rising 7,000 feet from the Western Cwm to the summit, became the next great problem in Himalayan climbing. In newspaper accounts, it was sometimes described as "Everest's worst face." It certainly posed more difficult technical challenges than any route yet attempted on Everest, particularly its upper third, where the snow slopes hit the rock band.[7]

Several prominent climbers, acting independently, nourished plans in the late 1960s to tackle the challenge of the Southwest Face if and when Nepal opened its mountains again to expeditions. Among them was Norman Dyhrenfurth. Inspired by memories of his father's international expedition to Kangchenjunga in 1930, he began planning a similar attempt on the Southwest Face. There was also a group of British and Norwegian climbers that hoped to attempt the face, and they recruited Jimmy Roberts as leader. When the Roberts group and Dyhrenfurth learned of one another's plans, they merged efforts. Dyhrenfurth applied his considerable energies to fund-raising, signing on the BBC and *The Times* as major sponsors. Thinking big, as he had in planning for the 1963 American Everest expedition, he also added a goal. The international Everest expedition would attempt not one but two routes: in addition to the Southwest Face, climbers would try to find a West Ridge direct route to the summit, eliminating the detour onto the North Face that Tom Hornbein and Willi Unsoeld had made in their 1963 effort.

When Nepal finally lifted the ban on expeditions in 1969, the Japanese got first crack at the Southwest Face, sending two reconnaissance parties that year and a full-scale expedition in 1970. Their attempt failed (although four Japanese climbers did reach the summit via the Southeast Ridge).[8]

Finally, in 1971, the first-ever international expedition to Everest, the so-called Cordée internationale, got its chance. With two separate routes to attempt, the expedition needed a full complement of climbers, twenty-one in all, recruited from ten nations. Among those accepting Dyhrenfurth's invitations were Wolfgang Axt of Austria, Carlo Mauri of Italy, Pierre Mazeaud of France, Harsh Bahuguna of India, and Michel and Yvette Vaucher of Switzerland. Naomi Uemera of Japan had the most recent experience on Everest, reaching the summit on the 1970 expedition. Ten others were in the party, including a seven-man BBC crew, bringing the total to thirty-one. If it was not quite the largest expedition yet to tackle Everest from the south (the Japanese brought thirty-nine climbers for their 1970 effort), it was certainly the most diverse—the first, for instance, in which Japanese climbers joined a Himalayan expedition with Europeans and Americans.[9]

Most of Dyhrenfurth's recruits had never before climbed together. Among the exceptions were Don Whillans and Dougal Haston, fresh from their triumph on Annapurna's South Face and expected to lead the effort on the Southwest Face. (Another prominent

British climber, Chris Bonington, had also been invited to join the expedition as climbing leader. Although he had long been intrigued by the Southwest Face, something about Dyhrenfurth's plans spooked Bonington. He initially declined to join, then changed his mind and accepted the invitation, and finally withdrew.[10])

On the American expedition in 1963 Dyhrenfurth had unapologetically advocated a get-a-man-to-the-top-by-any-route strategy in order to ensure that, come what may, Old Glory flew for the first time from the top of the world's highest mountain. This time, he was committed to attempting two daring and innovative routes. That was fine with the climbers from Britain, America, Japan, and India—that is, the ones from countries whose expeditions had already reached the top of Everest by the Southeast Ridge. The problem was that Dyhrenfurth underestimated the continuing appeal of the standard route to those who came from countries that had yet to fly their own flags from the summit (or, in the case of Switzerland's Yvette Vaucher, the chance to become the first woman to climb to the summit).

Starting from Base Camp, established on March 23, the expedition surmounted the Khumbu Icefall and placed Advanced Base Camp on the Western Cwm on April 5. At first everyone seemed to get on well, despite the mix of nationalities. "There continues to be complete harmony among the team members," Dyhrenfurth noted in his diary on April 4, "not the slightest indication of any friction whatsoever."[11]

Two teams then went to work on their separate objectives: Whillans and Haston, along with a group of American, Japanese, German, and Austrian climbers, devoted their efforts to the Southwest Face, while Mauri, Mazeaud, the Vauchers, Axt, Bahuguna, and several others turned to the West Ridge. As had happened in 1963, tensions developed over the distribution of resources between the two routes, with the "Latins," as they came to be called (Mauri, Mazeaud, and the Vauchers), suspecting a plot by the Anglo-Americans and their allies to hoard supplies at their expense. Their sense of grievance was exacerbated by a belief that they were wasting their time on the wrong side of the mountain; instead of fighting their way up to the West Ridge, they would have preferred the familiar slog up Lhotse Face to the South Col and the Southeast Ridge. When Dyhrenfurth suggested in mid-April to the Latins that they could speed up delivery of supplies for the West Ridge effort by doing some of the load-carrying from Camp I to Advanced Base Camp, he only added insult to injury, as they considered the task beneath them. Dyhrenfurth went down to make a carry from Camp I to inspire the others, to no avail. The "complete harmony" that had prevailed below the Khumbu Icefall seemed to belong to a different expedition than the one now squabbling in the Western Cwm.

On the West Ridge route, events took a deadly twist on April 18. Harsh Bahuguna and Wolfgang Axt, descending from the ridge for a rest at Advanced Base Camp, were caught at about 23,000 feet in a blizzard. Proceeding along fixed ropes with Axt in the lead, the two men were not roped to each other as they traversed across the icy slope. Out of sight of his partner, Bahuguna apparently lost his footing, injured himself, and was unable to proceed. Axt heard his partner scream but did not turn back to help. Expecting an easy descent in good weather, he had not carried a rope or extra carabiners. Exhausted and beginning to freeze himself, he decided the best thing he could do for Bahuguna was to hurry down to the Western Cwm, where he could alert others to his partner's plight.

But help came too late. When a rescue party fought its way through the blizzard and reached the trapped Indian climber, they found him already near death, his face covered in ice. After a failed attempt to lower Bahuguna to a more sheltered spot, they reluctantly decided they would have to abandon the effort; there was no way to move him safely down the slope of the mountain without endangering all their lives. "Sorry, Harsh old son, you've had it," Whillans said to the dying climber, as the rescuers prepared to descend. Bahuguna's death provided a grim statistic: he was the twenty-eighth man to die attempting the mountain, at a time when only twenty-eight men had reached the summit.[12]

"Next morning," John Cleare reported in the official account for the *Alpine Journal:*

> Axt was last to enter the silent cook-tent. The night before he had been on sleeping pills on doctor's orders and knew nothing of the tragedy.
> "How is Harsh?" he asked.
> "Harsh is dead," said Dyhrenfurth.
> Axt broke down and wept.[13]

For the next week and a half, the climbers were confined to their tents by the blizzard; John Cleare described it as "the worst weather for some seventy years" in the Nepal Himalaya. Through an occasional break in the clouds, the climbers in Advanced Base Camp could catch glimpses of Bahuguna's body on the slope above, hanging frozen from his rope anchor. Morale plummeted.[14]

The blizzard ended, but not the discord. Dyhrenfurth faced a mutiny in the ranks, as the Latins informed him they were giving up on the West Ridge and would concentrate instead on reaching the summit via the Southeast Ridge. Disheartened but unwilling to impose his own will, he went along at first, only to find that the shift of route did little to placate the mutineers. Dyhrenfurth finally decided that the expedition could no longer support efforts on two separate routes and closed down the South Col effort. This only served to confirm in the minds of the Latins their dark suspicions of a Dyhrenfurth-BBC plot to keep them from the summit. On May 1 they stalked off the mountain and returned to Kathmandu, where in a two-hour press conference they denounced those who remained to climb the Southwest Face. Pierre Mazeaud, a Gaullist parliamentarian in his nonclimbing life, unburdened himself of a rhetorical flourish that became perhaps the best-remembered moment of the expedition: "They expect me, Pierre Mazeaud, Member of the French Assembly, aged forty-two, to work as a Sherpa for Anglo-Saxons and Japanese. Never! It is not me but France they have insulted!" For the first time, climbers on Everest found themselves depicted in popular media coverage more as comic than heroic figures.[15]

Further departures followed, this time the result of an epidemic of illness that swept through the climbers at Advanced Base Camp. Dyhrenfurth blamed the mysterious virus that felled many of his climbers on the hippies they had encountered en route at Tengboche; he was among those who had to be evacuated from the mountain, leaving Jimmy Roberts in command of the remnants of the expedition.[16]

The ten-nation climbing party had, in essence, been reduced to an Anglo-Japanese effort. Through all the turmoil, Whillans and Haston, supported by Naomi Uemera and Reizo Ito, continued to push the route up the Southwest Face, climbing well past the high point of the previous Japanese expedition. The lower half of the face was a steep but relatively uncomplicated snow slope. At about 26,500 feet the face was cut by the rock band, 600 to 1,000 feet high, through which no obvious route led to the snowfield and summit rocks above. In early May, while the Latins were holding their press conference in Kathmandu, Whillans and Haston were trying to find a way around the rock band to the right (they had looked to the left earlier, but decided that way was impassable). They found a chimney that looked promising, but bad weather and supply shortages, particularly lack of rope, dogged their efforts. Finally, on May 21, Whillans turned to Haston and suggested wearily, "How about buggering off?" Haston agreed.[17]

Unlike the fiasco that had played itself out on the ridges, the effort on the Southwest Face could be counted an honorable failure, not least for the climbers' fidelity to their original goal. Back at Camp II, Whillans told John Cleare that he and Haston could easily have broken off the climb on the Southwest Face, traversed to the Southeast Ridge, and bagged the summit for themselves. "But how many bloody times has Everest been done by that route?" he asked contemptuously.[18]

Dead Ends and New Initiatives

Everest was proving a forlorn hope, if not an acute embarrassment, to some of the world's best mountaineers. Before 1971 was over, a postmonsoon Argentine expedition had failed to climb the mountain via the Southeast Ridge. In 1972 yet another international expedition attempted the Southwest Face, this one led by the famously quarrelsome Dr. Karl M. Herrligkoffer. Don Whillans went along on the eighteen-member expedition, as did Himalayan newcomer Doug Scott. And, true to form for a Herrligkoffer expedition, the effort soon broke down into hostile factions. It failed to reach Whillans and Haston's high point of the previous year on the Southwest Face.

Bonington had been offered the chance to join Herrligkoffer's expedition and, once more sensing disaster, had pulled out before the party left for Nepal. But he remained eager for his own chance to tackle the Southwest Face. Learning that an expedition scheduled to attempt Everest in the postmonsoon season of 1972 had been cancelled, he obtained permission from Nepal to lead an expedition in its place. This would be a British-only group, and Bonington solicited funding to remedy the fact that "[n]o Briton has stood on the summit of Everest" (since neither Hillary nor Tenzing shared the nationality of the sponsors of the 1953 British expedition).[19] Although his expedition was thrown together at the last moment, Bonington had the connections and credibility to recruit a first-rate team of mountaineers on such short notice, including old climbing companions like Dougal Haston and Mick Burke and newcomers like Doug Scott. Although Don Whillans had been on the last two expeditions to the Southwest Face, and had summited Annapurna on Bonington's 1970 expedition, Bonington did not ask him along this time, fearing Whillans simply would not take orders from him on a mountain and a route that Whillans knew far better than he did.

Even without the pugnacious Whillans, Bonington's expedition was not a happy one. In a decision reminiscent of one he had taken on the 1970 Annapurna expedition, Bonington leapfrogged Dougal Haston and Hamish MacInnes ahead of Doug Scott and Mick Burke, to give what he felt was the stronger team the challenge of finding a way through the rock band. "[Y]ou're no better than Herrligkoffer," a disappointed Scott spat at Bonington, who in turn suggested that Scott head back to Kathmandu if that was how he felt.[20] In the end they patched up their differences, so at least the expedition avoided the walkouts that had plagued earlier attempts.

Haston and MacInnes, following the route of the 1971 expedition, could not find their way through the rock band. The chimney that Whillans and Haston had first identified in 1971 as a possible route on the right side of the rock band was simply too difficult at that altitude and in the conditions prevailing in November. Toward the end, Bonington and others did notice a gully to the left of where they had been climbing that looked like a promising alternative route. But any attempt on it would have to wait for another expedition.

Bonington's 1970 expedition to Annapurna ended with the death of Ian Clough in its final days, and a similar tragedy befell Bonington's Everest expedition. An Australian trekker named Tony Tighe had joined in an unofficial capacity as a volunteer and spent nearly the entire time helping out with chores in Base Camp. On the very last day of evacuation from the mountain, Bonington allowed him to climb through the Khumbu Icefall to get a glimpse of the Southwest Face. A serac collapsed and buried Tighe beneath tons of ice.

Before he left Nepal, Bonington filed a request for a permit to attempt the Southwest Face in the next available spring slot. That was not until 1979. When he got back to London he vowed to John Hunt that he would "never again" attempt the face in the postmonsoon season.[21]

In 1973 the Italians got their turn on Everest. In its lavish excess of manpower and supplies, their expedition dwarfed any previous effort on the mountain—and brought little credit to its participants. Some 64 climbers, mostly drawn from the Italian Army, along with 120 Sherpas and 2,000 porters, were deployed against the mountain. In a dubious innovation, the expedition used helicopters to ferry supplies to the climbers, until one of the helicopters crashed in the Western Cwm. All of this to put five Italian climbers and three Sherpas on the summit via the Southeast Ridge route first climbed twenty years earlier. Sir Edmund Hillary pronounced judgment that the Italian effort had "nothing to do with mountaineering" and, outside Italy, few begged to differ.[22]

Another large expedition, this one Japanese, headed for Everest in the fall of 1973 planning to tackle the Southwest Face. Failing in that, they switched their efforts to the Southeast Ridge, getting two climbers to the summit. The Japanese expedition escaped the derision directed at the Italians because it at least achieved the first successful postmonsoon climb of Everest. The Japanese summit team of Hisahi Ishiguro and Yasuo Kato was also the first to climb directly from South Col to the summit, without establishing an intermediate high camp along the Southeast Ridge.[23]

In 1974 no one at all got to the summit of Everest (it would be the last year in the twentieth century in which that proved the case). A Spanish expedition failed to climb the Southeast Ridge in the spring, and a French expedition attempting the West Ridge in the fall abandoned the effort after avalanches killed one French climber and five Sherpas. With the deaths in 1974, the total number killed trying to climb Everest had reached thirty-four, compared to a total of thirty-eight successful summiters.[24]

Doing More with Less

For the moment, Everest seemed played out, a has-been challenge, a mountain where tedium was too often punctuated with death but offering little in the way of genuine mountaineering accomplishment. The interesting climbs of the early 1970s in the Himalaya were happening elsewhere, usually carried off by much smaller parties than the big national expeditions still trudging their way up the Southeast Ridge. These included a number of attempts on unascended subsidiary peaks of the highest Himalayan mountains, some of which were themselves over 8,000 meters. Thus in 1970 an Austrian expedition made the first ascent of Lhotse Shar (27,559ft/8,400m), lowest of the three Lhotse summits; an Austrian-American party made a first ascent in 1971 of Dhaulagiri II (25,429ft/7,751m); a Japanese expedition made the first ascent in 1973 of Yalung Kang (27,903ft/8,505m), the west summit of Kangchenjunga; and a Spanish expedition made a first ascent in 1974 of Annapurna East (26,279ft/8,010m). Previously neglected 7,000-meter peaks also became attractive to climbers looking for alternatives to standard routes on the biggest mountains. Some of these climbs were accomplished by expeditions employing traditional siege tactics. But others were more innovative, such as the Polish expedition that made an alpine-style first ascent in 1974 of Kangbachen (25,928ft/7,903m), a neighbor of Kangchenjunga.[25]

In the early 1970s, Polish climbers emerged at the cutting edge of Himalayan mountaineering, and by necessity rather than choice they did more with less on expeditions characterized by high levels of teamwork and low levels of material provision. Although they enjoyed a measure of official support from the Polish government, Polish climbers garnered few benefits from their mountaineering achievements, save the privilege of traveling outside the Communist bloc. (As one of the most famous of their number, Wanda Rutkiewicz, told an American interviewer, "Our life [in Poland] is so hard that for us Himalayan climbing is by comparison luxurious.") They certainly did not enjoy a life of ease while home from the mountains: for the most part they supported themselves and their families by manual labor (some of the most well known made their living by painting factory chimneys). And when they set off on expeditions, they got by with secondhand equipment and a minimal number of porters and Sherpas to support their climbs.[26]

The Poles were responsible for a significant innovation in Himalayan climbing, adding a third season to supplement the traditional two-season schedule of pre- and post-monsoon expeditions. Andrej Zawada proved a key figure in the rising popularity of winter ascents in the region. In February 1973, along with Tadeusz Piotrowski, Zawada reached the summit of Noshaq (24,581ft/7,492m), the highest mountain in Afghanistan and second highest in the Hindu Kush. Zawada then turned his attention to the Himalaya. In the winter of 1974–75 he led a bold attempt to climb Lhotse, becoming the first to climb above the 8,000-meter level in winter, though failing to reach the summit. Five years later the accumulated Polish experience in winter climbing paid off in spectacular fashion when Zawada led the first successful winter attempt on Everest. On February 17, 1980 Leszek Cichy and Krzysztof Wielicki reached the summit of Everest via the Southeast Ridge, braving temperatures of fifty degrees below zero to do so. The next winter, inspired by the Poles, no fewer than seven expeditions set off to do winter climbs in Nepal, including two on Everest.[27]

Changabang

In between organizing large-scale Everest efforts, Chris Bonington also experimented with a less-is-more approach. In 1974 he led an expedition to Changabang (22,520ft/6,864m), the northernmost peak on the Nanda Devi Sanctuary Wall. Changabang, "a shark's tooth of pale grey granite cleaving the sky" in Bonington's description, was so situated that it was visible only to those who ascended the wall surrounding the Nanda Devi Sanctuary. And though a number of famous mountaineers, including Longstaff, Tilman, Shipton, and Smythe, had admired the mountain from afar, none had suggested a route to its summit. The Bonington expedition would thus be that increasingly rare phenomenon, a mountain reconnaissance and climbing expedition rolled into one.[28]

Though harboring reservations about "international" expeditions (well founded, given the record of the 1971 and 1972 Everest expeditions), Bonington led a joint British-Indian effort to Changabang, with four climbers from each country. The British climbers, Bonington, Dougal Haston, Doug Scott, and Martin Boysen, represented a formidable array of climbing talents, and few Indian climbers were their equals in technical ability. But the Indian Garhwal had only just been reopened to Western climbers, and Bonington felt it was important politically to bring at least one Indian mountaineer with him to the summit.

After establishing Base Camp at the foot of the Rhamani Glacier on the mountain's southern side, they soon decided that the West Ridge, which they had picked out on old photographs as a likely prospect, was impossibly steep. The South Ridge was equally unappealing. Instead, with Martin Boysen and Doug Scott in the lead, they climbed the steep ridge that led to Shipton's Col, from which they could descend to the far side of the mountain. Once over the col, an obstacle beyond the ability of the porters and some of the Indian climbers to cross, the expedition was transformed into a small and self-contained unit of six climbers, carrying all their own supplies.

On June 5 the four British climbers, Bonington, Boysen, Scott, and Haston, along with Indian military officer Balwant Sandhu and Sherpa Tashi Chewang, set off from their high camp at 1:00 A.M., ascending to the col between Changabang and neighboring Kalanka to the northeast. As the hours passed they watched the yellow glow of the rising sun illuminate neighboring Nanda Devi. "Dawn, a beautiful dawn—like the morning of life," Sandhu would recall of the morning of their summit day. "No cloud and no wind and a lot of big mountains and some cold. Where on earth are my toes?" Surmounting the col, they then followed the knife-edged East Ridge to the summit of Changabang. By 5:00 P.M., with clouds closing in, all six were at the top (although, unsure of where on the ridge was actually the highest point, Haston and Scott went a few more rope lengths to the south to make sure they had actually reached it). Sandhu took out his regimental flag for the summit photo; the British had neglected to bring the Union Jack. Back at their high camp twenty hours after setting out, Bonington felt a sense of elation: "Changabang might not have been the biggest or the hardest unclimbed peak in the world but it had given us three days of intensity of effort and living that would sustain us for a long time."[29]

Everest 1975

Everest returned to the headlines in 1975. The mountain had now been climbed by two or possibly three routes: the Southeast Ridge, the West Ridge, and, assuming the Chinese were telling the truth about what had happened in 1960, the Northeast Ridge/North Face. No more than two of these had ever been climbed in a single year. In 1975, for the first time, Everest would be climbed by three routes in a single year, and also for the first time by one of its faces.

The Japanese were the first to reach the summit that year, by the standard Southeast Ridge route. What made this expedition different than all the others that had attempted the standard route was that, apart from its Sherpa contingent, it was made up of women climbers. Junko Tabei, the climbing leader, reached the summit on May 16 with Sherpa Ang Tsering. The thirty-eighth climber to reach the summit of Everest, Tabei was thirty-five years old and in stature (only five feet tall and weighing ninety-two pounds) closer to the Sherpa climbers than most of the Western males who had preceded her up the Southeast Ridge. She was almost certainly the only Everest summiter to raise the money for her share of expedition costs giving piano lessons.[30]

Twelve days later another woman, a Tibetan by the name of Phantog, reached the summit of Everest via the Northeast Ridge/North Face, one of nine climbers in a Chinese expedition to do so. Although Chinese claims to have reached the summit in 1960 were still widely discounted in Western mountaineering circles, this time there could be no doubt. Not only did the Chinese document the climb with photographs and film, they also left lasting physical evidence of it in an aluminum ladder bolted to the upper section of the Second Step on the Northeast Ridge and a metal tripod erected on the summit.[31]

While the Chinese expedition was climbing Everest, one of its members, Wang Hongboa, made a discovery. At 26,900 feet he came across a corpse that he described as "an old English dead" to a Japanese climber four years later (Wang died the day after this exchange before he could be questioned any further). According to the account by Japanese climber Ryoten Hasegewa, who communicated with Wang by means of the written characters common to Japanese and Chinese, Wang said "there was a hole" in the corpse's cheek "and his mouth was open. And when [Wang] touched his clothing, which was already worn to tatters, it flew into pieces and they danced on his breath." As the report of Wang's discovery spread in the next few months, first to Japan and then around the world, it raised hopes among Western mountaineers that Mallory and Irvine's bodies might someday be found and perhaps yield clues revealing whether they had reached the summit before they died.[32]

The most celebrated ascent of Everest in 1975 was pulled off by another Chris Bonington expedition. Though he had not been scheduled to return to the mountain until 1979, at the end of 1973 he learned that a Canadian expedition had dropped plans for a postmonsoon attempt in 1975 and snatched up the newly available permit. Remembering his vow never again to attempt the Southwest Face in the autumn, he intended to climb the Southeast Ridge in the first lightweight alpine-style ascent of Everest. But shortly before departing for Changabang in 1974, his climbing partners Doug Scott and Dougal Haston persuaded him to mount another full-scale Southwest Face expedition.

Bonington decided the effort would require more climbers and equipment than he had scraped together in 1972. Barclays Bank made that possible with a pledge of £100,000 underwriting the expedition. While some degree of commercialism had been built into virtually every Everest expedition since the 1920s, the corporate sponsorship of the 1975 Southwest Face expedition broke new ground. Heretofore, businesses had funded climbing expeditions to the extent that they thought it would improve the sales of their products— thus the usual sources for sponsorship were newspapers (and later television networks) and manufacturers of outdoor gear and clothing. Barclays, in contrast, would gain no direct profit if Bonington's team reached the summit—only the indirect benefits of the prestige that would accrue to the sponsor of a daring and successful Everest climb.[33]

With money in the bank, Bonington recruited the largest British expedition to take the field since 1953, assembling an elite team of eighteen climbers with vast Himalayan experience. Dougal Haston, Doug Scott, and Hamish MacInnes were all on their third trip to the Southwest Face. MacInnes, the deputy leader and the oldest member of the party at forty-four, had made his first trip to the Everest region in 1953. Pete Boardman, a newcomer to the Himalaya, was the youngest member of the expedition, at twenty-four. He was the first British climber on a major Himalayan expedition too young to remember the day Hillary and Tenzing reached the summit of Everest.

The climbers were accompanied to the mountain by thirty-eight Sherpas and a four-man BBC crew. Remembering blowups on previous expeditions, Bonington was careful not to reveal who he considered the likeliest team for the initial summit bid, though Haston and Scott were clearly among the top contenders. He was also determined to get a much earlier start on the mountain than in 1972. By August 22 the expedition had reached Base Camp, and Dougal Haston and Nick Estcourt were already at work finding a route through the Khumbu Icefall.[34]

Despite the danger of avalanche from the heavy snow left by the monsoon, they made rapid progress. By September 13 Camp V was in place below the rock band, near the high mark of the 1972 expedition. Remarkable too was the absence of overt conflict among the leading climbers. Bonington had either grown more adept at managing rival ambitions or, since everyone knew what had happened on Annapurna and the last few Everest efforts, the climbers themselves were determined not to emerge as villains in the next expedition book. As expedition doctor, Charles Clarke harbored no summit ambitions of his own, which made him a shrewd observer of the others. As he noted in his diary in early September: "No splits, no factions, no nastiness, but it's all there in their hearts."[35]

Until the climbers reached the rock band, expedition strategy was fairly simple: all they needed to do was pick the least likely avalanche path as they fixed ropes up the face. Once at the rock band, Estcourt and Paul Braithwaite tackled the left-hand gully that Bonington and the others had picked out in 1972 as worth a try. And this time, in a single day of inspired climbing on treacherous rock, they successfully surmounted the rock band, a climbing achievement that John Hunt would compare in significance to "the original lead across the Hinterstoisser Traverse or the exit gulley above the Spider, on the North Face of the Eiger."[36]

The route was now open to the summit. Haston and Scott established Camp VI, the assault camp, at 27,300 feet at the top of the rock band on September 22. From there, they fixed rope the following day along an eastward traverse, to the foot of a gully that looked like it would lead to the South Summit. On September 24 they set off at 3:30 A.M., following the fixed rope to its end, then moving onto virgin ground roped together. They lost an hour as they fiddled with Haston's oxygen gear to remove an ice blockage. And they lost more time swimming upward against the deep snow that filled the gully that led to the top of the Southwest Face where it ended in the Southeast Ridge: "Classic wind slab avalanche conditions," Haston noted laconically.[37]

At 3:00 P.M., eleven and a half hours after setting off, Haston and Scott reached the South Summit. There they rested, brewed some tea, and considered halting until nightfall,

Dougal Haston on the summit of Everest at sunset with the head of
Rongbuk Glacier below on right, Cho Oyu beyond, and Shishapangma
on the far horizon. Photograph by Doug Scott. Reprinted by
permission of the Alpine Club Library.

when freezing temperatures might make the snow above easier to climb. But they decided
they could not trust the weather to continue fair, and so instead set out again, up the Hillary Step, which was plastered in deep snow.

They reached the summit at 6:00 P.M. on September 24, fifteen and a half hours
after leaving Camp VI, and just thirty-three days after the expedition's arrival at Base
Camp. Haston and Scott became the first British climbers known to stand atop Everest
(leaving open the faint possibility of their having been preceded by Mallory and Irvine).
They found the Chinese tripod, bedecked with red ribbons, and took photographs of
themselves beside it. When they headed down it was far too late to reach Camp VI before
darkness set in.[38]

The climbers bivouacked on the South Summit in a snow hole they dug to protect
themselves from the wind. They had no oxygen, no food, and, after their stove ran out
of fuel, no water. At 28,700 feet it was the highest bivouac yet attempted. "I don't think
we were ever worried about surviving, for we had read of other climbers who had spent
the night out on Everest without much gear, although lower down," Scott would recall.
"However, they had all subsequently had some fingers and toes cut off."[39] To avoid that
fate, they spent the night rubbing hands and feet. At first light they set off, and by 9:00 A.M.
on September 25 they were back in their sleeping bags at Camp VI.

With his prize secured, Bonington might have ordered an immediate descent

The Everest Southwest Face expedition returns to Heathrow Airport,
London, 1975. From left: Pete Boardman, Chris Bonington, Pertemba,
Dougal Haston, and Doug Scott. Reprinted by permission of
Hulton Archives/Getty Images.

and evacuation from the mountain. He had originally planned on sending only a single team to the summit. But the expedition's success in reaching the summit so quickly meant there was still time for others to have their shot. And so another four-man team, Boysen, Burke, Boardman, and Sherpa sirdar Pertemba, was already moving up to high camp to take its turn while Haston and Scott made their summit bid. Bonington was worried about Mick Burke; he had been too long at high altitude and was moving slowly. On September 25, however, he climbed well, and the others at Camp VI decided he could come along with them the next day. On the morning of September 26 four climbers set out for the summit. Boysen, who had problems with his oxygen set and lost a crampon, turned back early. Burke, carrying a movie camera, lagged behind. Boardman and Pertemba, however, moved expeditiously up the face and the Southeast Ridge, summiting shortly after 1:00 P.M. Boardman, recording his impressions of the summit on a small tape recorder he had carried with him, noted slyly, "Well, I can't see a Barclays Bank branch anywhere."[40]

On their descent they met Burke resting a few hundred yards from the summit. He asked if they would walk back to the summit with him so that he could film them for the BBC, but Boardman was worried about getting Pertemba safely down to Camp VI. Burke decided to continue on by himself, following the well-consolidated trail to the summit. He would meet the waiting climbers back at the South Summit to complete the descent together. Boardman and Pertemba reached the South Summit and waited there for Burke for an hour and a half in worsening conditions and increasing anxiety, until Boardman finally decided that to stay any longer would put their own survival at risk. They descended through a blizzard, nearly losing their way, and twice swept by avalanches. At 7:30 P.M. they reached Camp VI, where Boysen awaited them. When Boardman reached the safety of the tent, he burst into tears.

Mick Burke's body was never found, though he is presumed to have reached the top before he disappeared, possibly taking a fatal misstep onto an overhanging cornice on his descent. He was the third climber in five years to die in the final days of a Bonington expedition.[41]

Bonington's expedition won him the rank of commander of the British Empire (CBE); his account of the climb, *Everest: The Hard Way,* his sixth book and the finest of all his many expedition accounts, was a best seller.

In the years that followed, there would be impressive mountaineering achievements on Everest, some of them by full-scale expeditions on the Bonington model (including the Yugoslav expedition that completed the West Ridge route in 1979 and—perhaps in a category by itself—the gargantuan 252-person Chinese-Japanese-Nepalese expedition that simultaneously carried out the first north-south and south-north traverses of Everest in 1988). Some of the best new routes on the mountain would fall to smaller parties, like the 1984 Australian expedition that made the first complete ascent of the Great Couloir on the North Face. Large or small, however, after the 1975 Bonington climb, mountaineering expeditions to Everest rarely attracted much attention from the general public, unless involving a major loss of life.[42]

American Climbers in the 1970s

American mountaineers had a long tradition of companionable Himalayan expeditions. The expeditions to K2 in 1938 and 1953, to Hidden Peak in 1958, and to Masherbrum in 1960 were models of cooperation in the pursuit of a common goal. Tom Hornbein had been doctor on the Masherbrum expedition, and his own summit ambitions had gone unfulfilled. But as he wrote some years later, "We climbed it, and that I failed to reach the summit seemed hardly to matter for I had worked hard; our success was mine, and the depth of companionship would be hard to equal."[43] Not every expedition fit that mold: the 1939 K2 expedition certainly proved an exception, and the 1963 Everest expedition had known some contentious moments. But climbers who came of age in the United States before and immediately after the Second World War shared a common ethic and sense of community. Despite the occasional squabbles, they were, more or less, a band of brothers.

In the 1970s a different familial dynamic came to the fore. A generation gap developed in American Himalayan climbing after the 1963 Everest expedition. The stars of that venture drifted away from mountaineering expeditions, blocked in any case from an early return to Nepal by the climbing ban clamped down in 1965. Economic pressures contributed to the gap: apart from the professional guides who found seasonal employment in the Cascades or the Tetons, American climbers could not expect to support themselves by the fruits of their climbing. There was no American Chris Bonington, enjoying a steady income from books, television appearances, and paid lectures. Jim Whittaker returned from Everest to the life of a corporate executive, albeit one running an outdoor-oriented retail company. Tom Hornbein returned to his medical career. Willi Unsoeld returned to the Peace Corps, then to a stint with Outward Bound, and finally to a teaching position at Evergreen State College. Barry Bishop returned to work for the *National Geographic.* By the time some of these veterans made their next Himalayan ventures in the mid-1970s, they had moved on to quasi-emeritus status; though still vigorous climbers, they no longer expected to play the leading role in forcing challenging new routes up unclimbed ridges or faces. And a younger generation of hard men, eager to make their own mark in Himalayan climbing, displayed scant patience for these elders. When given a choice between "depth of companionship" and reaching the summit themselves, there was no question which they valued more.

After Nepal reopened its borders to mountaineers in 1969, an American expedition headed to Dhaulagiri and disaster, when two Sherpa and five American climbers died in an avalanche. The surviving Americans vowed to return, and in 1973 they did so. That year sixteen climbers, the largest American effort in the Himalaya in a decade, set off to attempt the third ascent of Dhaulagiri (a Japanese party had in the meantime made a second ascent).[44]

The Americans initially intended to tackle Dhaulagiri's unclimbed Southeast Ridge but, finding it too difficult, switched their efforts to the twice-climbed route on the Northeast Ridge. In terms of subsequent mountaineering history, the expedition was notable chiefly for the emergence of the two strongest American Himalayan climbers of the decade to come: Lou Reichardt and John Roskelley. Reichardt's previous experience on the mountain, his status as sole survivor of the 1969 avalanche, along with his native strength and endurance, made him the most likely candidate for the summit team from the beginning. In the jockeying for position as his summit partner, John Roskelley soon emerged as front-runner. Roskelley, a native of Spokane, Washington, was on his first Himalayan expedition; prior to Dhaulagiri, he had never climbed on any mountain outside of North America, or above 14,000 feet. Strength and endurance helped win Roskelley a place on the summit team, as did an intimidating self-assurance. "I was strong," Roskelley would write in a self-portrait for a later expedition book, "but so are many others who participate in sports. The difference was that I didn't know I could be beaten." On May 12 Reichardt, Roskelley, and Sherpa Nawang Samden reached the summit, where they placed American, Nepalese, and National Geographic Society flags, along with a Buddhist prayer scarf.[45]

K2 was another mountain where Americans had unfinished business. Three American expeditions had tried and failed to climb it between 1938 and 1953, and the bodies of two Americans and three Sherpas from those expeditions were lying somewhere on the mountain. After 1960, when a German-American expedition made an unsuccessful attempt, no mountaineers approached K2 for fourteen years.

In 1974 Pakistan reopened the Karakoram to climbing expeditions. Bob Bates, veteran of two of the three American K2 expeditions, was among the first to take advantage of the opportunity. Along with Ad Carter, editor of the *American Alpine Journal,* he returned to K2 on a reconnaissance. They identified a possible route up the mountain's previously untried Northwest Ridge.[46]

The following year America's best-known mountaineer, Jim Whittaker, led a full-scale expedition to K2. His ten-member climbing team included his twin brother, Lou Whittaker, his wife, Dianne Roberts, Jim Wickwire (who had come up with the idea for the expedition), and photographer Galen Rowell, among others. From the start everything went wrong. Bad weather, porter strikes, and illness delayed their progress. Family dynamics also played into what was turning into a fiasco. Brothers Jim and Lou had a long-standing feud, dating back to Lou's abrupt decision to withdraw from the 1963 American Mount Everest expedition for business reasons. Jim Whittaker had hoped that the 1975 expedition would secure reconciliation, but when Lou Whittaker raised questions about Dianne Roberts's qualifications for high-altitude climbing, their estrangement only deepened.[47]

Others in the climbing party decided that they had been invited along only to be glorified porters to get the Whittaker clan to the summit of K2; Galen Rowell described the division in the expedition as consisting of the "Big Four" (the Whittakers plus Wickwire) versus the "Minority Five" (everybody else). Meanwhile, the Northwest Ridge was proving exceedingly difficult, and after climbing no higher than 22,000 feet, the attempt was abandoned.[48]

A group of very disgruntled climbers returned to the United States. Galen Rowell's subsequent account, *In the Throne Room of the Mountain Gods,* was notable for its splendid photographs of K2 and other mountains, its interesting meditations on Himalayan mountaineering history, and as harbinger of "climb and tell" books to come. In the mountaineering literature of the 1970s, bruised feelings and simmering resentments were beginning to replace frostbite and hypoxia as the signature ailments of high-altitude mountaineering. "Dianne and I developed a strong antagonism for each other," Rowell wrote in a typical passage. "Each of us felt the other was overly competitive. We each yearned to be in the centre of things, to always be there when something happened. Dianne considered me a hopeless chauvinist."[49]

Jim Whittaker also had to contend on his return with rumors that the expedition had been devised by the Central Intelligence Agency to plant a listening device on K2 (an unfounded accusation, but one that seemed plausible to some critics in the suspicious post-Watergate climate of the mid-1970s, since expedition doctor Rob Schaller had been involved in the Nanda Devi caper in 1965). And there were charges of ill treatment and mismanagement of porters, which led to an investigation by the American Alpine Club and still more ill will. As Whittaker would write, "it was a sour end to a difficult expedition."[50]

The following year another big American expedition took the field, this time bound for Everest. Although there was also a husband and wife team on the eleven-member 1976 Bicentennial American expedition to Everest (climbers Gerry and Barb Roach), as well as a couple of girlfriends traveling with the climbers, family ties did not play a role in that expedition's quarrels. Instead, the climbers had to contend with an obtrusive seven-member camera crew from CBS television producing a documentary about the climb. There had been a time, not long before, when the press had treated mountaineers with some of the deference they paid to important official figures, like astronauts and presidents. That was before Watergate. If presidents of the United States were no longer awarded reverential treatment by the press, so much the less a bunch of scruffy climbers. From the beginning, CBS treated the climbers as if they were an assortment of not-ready-for-prime-time extras on a film lot. Before the climb, expedition members gathered in Boulder, Colorado, to sort supplies and get in some physical training. A CBS crew was on hand at the University of Colorado track to film the climbers while they jogged. When they showed up in gym clothes and sneakers, the director wasn't pleased. He had them dress up in their high-altitude boots and strap on their backpacks before they ran around the track. "You guys are train-ing for the world's highest mountain," he told them. "We have to make it *look* that way."[51] When the expedition arrived in Kathmandu at the end of July, its members were forced to disembark from the plane three times to give the film crew sufficient footage.

Once on the mountain, the climbers came to regard the film crew as morons who risked their own safety and those of anyone around them. The CBS director asked expedi-tion leader Phil Trimble to cross and recross treacherous crevasses on a precarious ladder so he would have the scene from different angles. With the film crew around, feeding them leading questions, the climbers had the feeling they were being assigned scripted characters to enact: the jock, the feminist, and so forth. Conflict made good television, and cameras and tape recorders were always switched on to capture any disagreement between the climbers. What went unfilmed was the day that one of the climbers and the head cameraman faced off in camp with ice axes, intent on dismembering one another, before being separated by others.[52]

For all that, on October 8 at 4:15 P.M., Chris Chandler and Bob Cormack stood atop Everest, the sixth and seventh Americans ever to do so. They feared given the lateness of the hour that they would be forced to bivouac on the way down, as the last Americans on the summit of Everest had done, but they managed to make their way back in darkness to their tent. "What I did on Everest that day scared the bejesus out of me," Cormack would recall.[53]

Afterward some climbers had the feeling that having been the tenth expedition to climb Everest by the Southeast Ridge had not proven very much beyond the fact that given sufficient numbers and resources, Everest's standard route was no longer much of a challenge for mountaineers. According to expedition member Gerry Roach: "It was not man against the mountain so much as expedition against the mountain, and the expedition seemed to be propelled more by dollars than individual initiative. The true initiative, it seemed to me, lay in coming up with the dollars."[54]

Nanda Devi 1976

Nanda Devi had always held a special mystique for American mountaineers; it had danced on the horizon just beyond their reach. There was the famous story of Charlie Houston's bout of food poisoning back in 1936, a stroke of ill fortune that denied him his place on the summit team with Bill Tilman and Noel Odell on the mountain's first ascent. And then there were whispered stories about the CIA's botched mission to plant a nuclear listening device on the mountain in the mid-1960s, and about the climbers who had disappeared from sight for months at a time and could never lay claim to their achievements on the mountain. Like so much of the Himalaya, from the mid-1960s through the early 1970s Nanda Devi remained off limits, but in 1974 India reopened the region to mountaineers. In 1975 a French-Indian team completed the fifth ascent of the mountain by the standard South Ridge route, and in the following year a Japanese expedition climbed both Nanda Devi and neighboring Nanda Devi East. Yoshinori Hasegawa and Kushige Takami traversed the ridge linking the eastern peak to the main summit, a significant and long-sought mountaineering achievement.[55]

Nanda Devi also had special personal meaning for Willi Unsoeld. Back in 1949, happily bumming his way from the Alps to the Himalaya, Unsoeld had caught a glimpse of Nanda Devi and been so struck by its beauty that he made up his mind that if he ever had a daughter he would name her after the mountain. On the same trip he also formed a mountaineering philosophy that sounded outrageously naive at the time, but by the 1970s was becoming commonplace. Writing about his unsuccessful, somewhat haphazard but enjoyable attempt to reach the summit of Nilkanth (21,640ft/6,596m) in the Indian Garhwal in 1949, Unsoeld declared in the 1956 *American Alpine Journal* that the "benefits of such marginal-existence travel as this outweigh in many respects the rewards of a comfortably supported expedition. Certainly the impact of the country and its people is much more stark and provoking than when the traveler is insulated from its effects by a well-padded pocketbook . . . the quality of the mountain experience enjoyed by members of small expeditions has much to recommend it over that gained by the gigantic Himalayan task forces which have attracted so much popular attention in recent years."[56]

Five years after Unsoeld's first glimpse of the sacred goddess of the Garhwal, his wife, Jolene, gave birth to a daughter whom they named Nanda Devi Unsoeld. Devi had an idyllic and mountain-centered childhood in the guide camps of the Tetons and in Nepal, when her father was deputy director of the Peace Corps. "Marginal-existence travel" became her philosophy as well, linked to a sixties-bred commitment to the ideals of social justice.[57]

In 1975 Devi Unsoeld came up with the idea for an expedition to her namesake mountain. She suggested to Ad Carter, veteran of the 1936 expedition, that he and her

Nanda Devi Unsoeld, Pakistan, 1974. Courtesy of the Henry S. Hall Jr.
American Alpine Club Library.

father lead a fortieth-anniversary attempt on Nanda Devi in 1976. Devi wanted to do it in
a spirit true to the original, which had been carried out with a material austerity typical of
expeditions in which Bill Tilman was involved. Like her father, she was nothing if not an
idealist when it came to mountaineering. "[G]etting to the top of a mountain has little to
do with my climbing," she told a reporter in 1976. "I'm much more concerned about how
the climb goes in terms of relationships that develop among the climbers."[58]

Carter was excited at the prospect, as was Willi Unsoeld when the idea was broached
to him. Carter and Willi Unsoeld agreed to serve as coleaders. To fill out the team they
invited a diverse group of American climbers to join, including Dhaulagiri veterans Lou
Reichardt, John Roskelley, and Andy Harvard. Two Indian climbers, Kiran Kumar and
Nirmal Singh, were also invited, making the expedition a joint American-Indian enterprise.
And there would be two women climbers: in addition to Devi, the expedition would include
Marty Hoey, a Rainier guide who was in a relationship with another expedition member,
Peter Lev. If either Devi Unsoeld or Marty Hoey reached the top, they would establish a
new altitude record for American women climbers.[59]

For John Roskelley, unlike Devi Unsoeld, getting to the top of the mountain was not
a secondary concern. He was not prepared to accept anything, or anybody, who interfered
with his desire to reach the summit. Marty Hoey's participation thus troubled Roskelley,
who did not believe that women were equal to men as climbers, and who particularly objected to the idea of couples taking part in expeditions. He was also unhappy about Devi
Unsoeld's participation, but since the expedition had been her idea to begin with, he was
not in a good position to argue against her going along. Willi Unsoeld, on the contrary,

thought it would be a good thing to prove that "men and women can do this sort of thing together without problems." As far as he was concerned, it "was time to place the 'hard man' image of mountaineering behind us." Roskelley backed down, though grudgingly, "[s]uddenly aware that I was standing in the way of a great American experiment."[60]

From the start the expedition carried too much symbolic weight for its own good. For the Unsoelds, the process of climbing the mountain was as important as the goal; they favored a lightweight and loosely run expedition in which decisions were made by Quaker-style consensus and everyone, including the women and the Indians, theoretically should have an equal chance to reach the summit. Unsoeld was not enthusiastic about the use of fixed ropes, believing they fragmented a climbing party since climbers depended on the ropes for safety instead of on one another. He thus wanted to fix as little of the route as possible. He certainly wanted to climb the mountain, and by a new route if possible (strategy discussions centered on a yet-to-be-determined line up the Northwest Face, and onto the North Ridge), but he also wanted a happy expedition, in which everyone came away feeling fulfilled.

For others, such concerns were beside the point. Roskelley favored a traditional siege-style, fixed-rope operation in which decisions were made by the expedition leader and passed down in hierarchical fashion to those who would carry out the drudge work of ferrying supplies that would enable the two or three fittest members of the party to reach the top. And there was no doubt in his mind who at least one member of that summit team should be.

A great gulf in life experience and ambition separated Willi Unsoeld and John Roskelley. Unsoeld's place in mountaineering history was secured by his first ascent of Masherbrum in 1960 and his partnership with Tom Hornbein on the West Ridge in 1963. Roskelley had, as yet, only a single Himalayan summit to his credit, and that climbed by the standard route. Unsoeld was a university professor. Roskelley had no professional career or income; he wanted to find a way to support himself as a professional mountaineer. Unsoeld, suffering from an arthritic hip, knew he was on his last major Himalayan expedition. Roskelley saw Nanda Devi as a stepping-stone to bigger and better mountains. In addition to everything else, there was Unsoeld's professorial delight in debate for its own sake, and Roskelley's blunt outspokenness. The result—a divided and unhappy expedition—was more or less foreordained.

One of Unsoeld's sons, Krag Unsoeld, had originally planned to join the expedition along with Devi, but after meeting Roskelley for the first time in the Unsoeld home in Olympia, Washington, promptly withdrew. Another expedition member, Marty Hoey, would never set foot on the mountain. On the approach march she suffered an attack of what may have been cerebral edema. Bottled oxygen revived her and she was willing to go on, but Roskelley, Lou Reichardt, and expedition doctor Jim States insisted she would only jeopardize her own life and that of others if she continued. The decision for her to leave was probably the right one, but the acrimonious debate that preceded it left everyone on edge.[61]

From that point on the expedition began to settle into two factions, one consisting of Roskelley, States and, on climbing issues, Reichardt. The other grouping, larger but less cohesive, consisted of the Unsoelds and almost everyone else. John Evans, who arrived at the mountain later than the others, stayed out of the fray. When the expedition established its first camp below the Northwest Ridge, Ad Carter suddenly resigned, saying only that his job as organizer was completed. The decision came as a shock to everyone: the expedition had been his idea to begin with, along with Devi Unsoeld. But after witnessing several bruising Willi Unsoeld–John Roskelley confrontations, and in addition feeling he was not up to the physical challenge of climbing to Advanced Base Camp, Carter lost enthusiasm for going any further. Another climber in the second team, Elliot Fisher, left soon after.

Once the real climbing began, Willi Unsoeld came to agree that the route would require fixed ropes. Just where they would be fixed was another question; at one point Roskelley spent a day refixing the ropes that Unsoeld had fixed the previous day, in what may have been intended (and certainly was interpreted) as a calculated insult to Willi's judgment as a climber. Roskelley and Reichardt found a way up the formidable rock buttress high on the Northwest Ridge that was the key to the route. Camp IV, their high camp, went in above the buttress, and on September 1 Roskelley, Reichardt, and States reached the top of Nanda Devi.[62]

Now the others had a chance to try for the summit, but not all of them were up to it. Willi Unsoeld hoped to get the Indian climbers to the top, but though they showed a lot of determination, their technical skills were deficient. And several climbers were suffering from the usual collection of expedition ailments: hacking coughs, stomach trouble, and failure to acclimatize. In John Evans's case, what seemed like a lack of acclimatization turned out to be a serious case of hepatitis, which would necessitate his evacuation from the mountain. Devi Unsoeld's health was complicated by a hernia, though it did not seem to bother her or interfere with her performance on the mountain. It certainly did not dampen her spirits; her yodel, which she learned from her father, was often heard on the slopes. Adding to Devi's sense of well-being was her relationship with Andy Harvard. The two had become inseparable on the climb and planned to marry on their return to the United States. High on the mountain Kiran Kumar, who was a High Brahmin, sanctified their planned union with a Sanskrit ceremony. That pleased the porters, who had come to regard Devi Unsoeld as a goddess returning to her home mountain.

Devi's health became yet another issue dividing the climbers. Jim States, the expedition doctor, advised her against making a summit attempt, though how strongly he advised against it remains a subject of dispute. Roskelley told Willi Unsoeld he should forbid Devi to climb any higher than Camp III. Willi, not inclined by this point to take advice from Roskelley, was determined to let Devi make up her own mind. She decided to go on.

Devi Unsoeld climbed to Camp IV with Andy Harvard and Peter Lev on September 3. There she remained at 24,000 feet for the next four days. A few months later Harvard described what happened at Camp IV in a letter to Lou Reichardt: "[Devi] was exhausted

Nanda Devi from the southwest, showing the 1936 and 1976 routes of ascent.

Nanda Devi Unsoeld at Camp III
on Nanda Devi, 1976.
Photograph by John Evans.
Courtesy of John Evans.

on arrival, but so was everyone. . . . When she didn't bounce back after a day, I started to worry. I was strong enough to go up with Pete, but I was more interested in Devi than the summit at the time. After two days, we (she, Peter & I) decided she should go down."[63]

On the third day, Willi climbed up to join them (he had been back at Camp III, working with the Indians to improve their skills for a summit bid, but had finally decided they would not be able to make it). Devi was buoyed by her father's arrival, though still feeling too weak for a summit attempt. She hoped the others would push on to the top while she waited for them in Camp IV. But when her condition did not improve by the following day, everyone agreed she needed to return to a lower altitude. She had a bad night on September 7, troubled by gas attacks. On the morning of September 8, at about 10:00, Willi was outside the tent making preparations for their departure. Peter Lev and Andy Harvard were inside, Harvard sitting next to Devi with his arm around her. She suddenly tucked her harmonica in his pocket and asked him to take care of it. Then she murmured some endearments. And then she said, "I'm going to die," vomited, and collapsed. Harvard, Lev, and Willi, who rushed into the tent, all tried to bring her back with mouth-to-mouth resuscitation, but to no avail. Willi implored, "Don't leave Devi."[64]

What killed her is unknown and unknowable, though it could have been anything from a ruptured intestine to appendicitis to a pulmonary embolism (only the latter altitude-related). In his letter to Reichardt, Harvard wrote that until the morning of her death Devi "showed no signs of anything that suggested urgency; no altitude symptoms at all save tiredness." She had been alert and in good spirits and eating well. "On the morning she died, she expected to climb down unassisted (but accompanied), and no one doubted she could."[65]

The three men, shocked and grieving, zipped Devi into a sleeping bag and carried her to the edge of the mountain. They did not want to leave her body in the tent, possibly to be found by later expeditions, nor did they want anyone to risk their lives at a later date trying to retrieve the body. Andy Harvard would describe his final sight of Devi in a letter to Ad Carter: "I kissed her, told her goodbye, and we lowered her over the edge. The thousands of feet she slipped through on the way to the glacier were made up of nothing but wind, and the wind just took her away." "[A]s she disappeared from view," Unsoeld would later tell audiences, "I yodeled a final yodel, which she had so often answered."[66]

When the porters learned of Devi's death, they saw it as confirmation of her identity as a goddess: the mountain for which she had been named had simply reclaimed her. There were others who attributed her death to darker causes. On the trip back to Delhi, according to the memory of several expedition members, John Roskelley confronted Willi Unsoeld, angrily accusing him of "killing his daughter." Later, some in the mountaineering community would blame her death on feminist ideology. Galen Rowell was quoted in *Outside* magazine as suggesting that "Devi was staying in a high camp because she, as a woman, must stay up there and succeed as a woman . . . a male in the same situation who was sick would say 'God, I better get the hell out of here.'"[67]

Rowell was not on the expedition. But John Evans was, and he offered a very different perspective on the issue of Devi Unsoeld's decision to climb to Camp IV. Shortly after the expedition came home, John Roskelley decided to write a book about it. He wrote to Evans (and other members) asking them to comment on a number of questions, including Devi Unsoeld's death. Evans replied in a letter on the first day of January 1977:

> I was enormously impressed with Devi in every way, particularly, I suppose, in her climbing ability which I guess I'd expected to be on the weak side. While her decision to move to the high camp came off as ill-considered in retrospect I doubt that any of us (at least myself) would have behaved much differently. Of course I wasn't party to her medical conferences with Jim [States], so it may be that she did go against his recommendations in a pretty questionable way—but my recollection of my discussions with Jim at the time is that his concern was only moderate, probably not substantially

greater than his concern for me, which certainly wouldn't have dissuaded me from going up. In other words, I don't think she deserves particular criticism for pushing on. I feel she simply took a calculated risk that was not significantly different from those we all assume every time we go to the big peaks.[68]

A Woman's Place: Annapurna 1978

In the 1970s women began to make up a significant proportion of the membership of Himalayan expeditions. Their numbers varied from country to country, as did the willingness of male counterparts to accept their participation as equals on the slopes. Somewhat surprisingly, given the social conservatism of their country's culture, Polish climbers took the lead in the 1970s in breaking down gender barriers in Himalayan climbing. When Polish climber Wanda Rutkiewicz and British climber Alison Chadwick-Onyszkiewicz (the latter married to a Polish climber) summited what was then the world's highest unclimbed mountain, Gasherbrum III (26,089ft/7,952m), in 1975 on a Polish expedition, their feat entered the record books. Gasherbrum III was the highest mountain in which women shared with men in making the first ascent.[69]

If the 1975 K2 and 1976 Nanda Devi expeditions proved nothing else, they suggested that in American climbing circles, men were not nearly as accepting of women as their Polish counterparts. The presence of women on American expeditions to the Himalaya remained a source of controversy and division throughout the decade.

In what was intended as a lighthearted footnote to his account of the 1963 American Everest expedition, James Ramsey Ullman noted that although 3 of the 100 applicants for the expedition had been women, none were chosen. "There was no anti-female plank in the expedition's platform," he wrote, "for there are many first-rate women climbers. But it was felt that Everest itself would present sufficient hazards without our courting the possible added one of petticoat fever."[70]

The opposition that American women climbers met in the 1970s would take on a very different tone than Ullman's chivalrous comments. "Petticoat fever" was, after all, a disorder experienced by men. Women would not be invited to join the American Mount Everest expedition—but not due to any shortcomings on their part. Male weakness, not female weakness, was the issue. Men simply could not be trusted to behave well around women. There was a gentlemanly quality to this argument, implying no hostility to the opposite sex—even though the net effect of Ullman's formula was to rationalize women's exclusion from mountaineering expeditions, as they were routinely excluded from many other endeavors in those days.

The year that Americans first climbed Everest, 1963, also happened to be the year that Betty Friedan's *The Feminine Mystique* appeared. By the 1970s much had changed. Women were demanding equality with men in many spheres, from politics to business to academia, and making significant gains. In 1972 the U.S. Congress passed Title IX of the

Educational Amendments, banning sex discrimination in educational programs, including athletics. Title IX would lead to a dramatic increase in women's sports participation in general. But mountain climbing was not a college sport, and no Title IX provision mandated that women be welcomed on Himalayan expeditions. And the male climbers who opposed their participation no longer felt bound by the courtly code that shaped James Ramsey Ullman's attitude and comments. The "anti-female plank" of the 1970s would be expressed openly, and sometimes crudely, as a desire to protect a traditionally male enclave from female interloping. The issue this time wasn't "petticoat fever," it was, in the minds of male defenders of the gendered status quo, female weakness and inexperience. Women who climbed in the Himalaya, their male critics argued, were out to prove themselves equal in an endeavor that was simply beyond their capabilities, and their insistence on doing so undermined sound mountaineering judgment and threatened the physical safety of themselves and other climbers.

As of 1972, no woman of any nationality had yet reached the summit of an 8,000-meter peak. That year Wanda Rutkiewicz and Alison Chadwick-Onyszkiewicz met American climber Arlene Blum when all three were in the Hindu Kush on expeditions attempting Noshaq. In a chance conversation carried out at 21,000 feet, when Rutkiewicz was heading jubilantly down from the summit and Blum was heading up, Rutkiewicz suggested they organize a joint Polish-American women's expedition to Annapurna I. They were unable to obtain a permit from Nepal for their target year, 1975, and went on to other projects. But when Blum was returning from the Everest Bicentennial expedition in 1976 (during which she set an altitude record for American women, having climbed to 24,500 feet), she arranged in Kathmandu for a permit for an American women's expedition to attempt Annapurna in the 1978 postmonsoon season.[71]

There was a kind of "movement" quality to this expedition, very different from, say, the slick professionalism and media and corporate sponsorship of the typical Bonington expedition. Much of the $80,000 cost of the project, formally known as the American Women's Himalayan expedition, came through sales of T-shirts with the slogan "A Woman's Place is on Top . . . Annapurna." The expedition organizers had hoped to prove this the case not only for American women but for Sherpanis (female Sherpas) as well, none of whom had climbed on a big Himalayan expedition since Claude Kogan's all-women expedition to Cho Oyu in 1959. Unable to find any Sherpanis with high-altitude experience, the American women decided to provide climbing training for a few of them prior to their expedition. Their agent in Kathmandu, Mike Cheney, warned them, however, that any attempt to bring along Sherpanis could create "big trouble" with the expedition's male Sherpas. Though two Sherpanis were recruited, they did not climb above Base Camp.[72]

The ten American climbers set off from Pokhara for Annapurna in mid-August 1978. The route they would follow on Annapurna's North Face was known as the Dutch Rib, first climbed the previous year by an expedition from the Netherlands.[73] Blum carried out her own reconnaissance a few months later. This variation ran up and along a precipitous crest of a steep rib of ice to the left of the 1950 Herzog route on the lower half of the North Face before rejoining the original route on the upper half, reducing the danger of avalanche from the Sickle Glacier.

The expedition set up Base Camp at 15,000 feet on August 28 and found very different conditions prevailing than in 1977. Fierce storms and snow accumulation had raised the danger of avalanche considerably. For the next six weeks the climbers worked their way up the rib, and then above the Sickle, putting in five camps, the highest at 24,200 feet. Six Sherpas accompanied the expedition on the mountainside, fewer than the normal complement on large Everest expeditions but about average for Annapurna (the 1970 North Face Annapurna expedition had been accompanied by six Sherpas, the 1977 Dutch expedition to the South Face by eight). Three of the six Sherpas on the expedition were incapacitated by high-altitude sickness, so the expedition members did most of the load-carrying at high altitude. After some debate the team agreed to the request by two of the Sherpas to be included on the initial summit team. On October 15 Irene Beardsley Miller, Vera Komarkova, and Sherpas Mingma Tsering and Chewang Rinjee set out from Camp V for the summit at 7:00 A.M., reaching it eight and a half hours later. Along with American and Nepalese flags, they unfurled a banner with the expedition slogan, "A Woman's Place is on Top" and a "Save the Whales" pin. Theirs was the fifth ascent of Annapurna, the first by women, and set a new altitude record for American women climbers.

Two days later, on October 17, a second summit team, of Vera Watson and Alison Chadwick-Onyszkiewicz, headed off for high camp from Camp IV. Their objective was to make the first ascent of the middle summit of Annapurna I without Sherpas or oxygen. They did not check in to Base Camp by radio that evening from Camp V as planned. On October 19 two Sherpas found Chadwick-Onyszkiewicz's body. She had fallen 1,000 feet from the route between Camps IV and V. She was tied to a rope that led into a crevasse, which must have been the final resting place of her companion. Neither body could be recovered. Chadwick-Onyszkiewicz and Watson were the first women to die on Annapurna —the tenth and eleventh climbers to die there since 1970.[74]

Notwithstanding the tragedy with which it ended, the Annapurna women's expedition returned home to an enthusiastic reception from its T-shirt-wearing supporters, as well as many others. President Jimmy Carter sent a cable lauding their "extraordinary accomplishment," and an invitation to a White House reception followed. A well-received documentary film was released to theaters and then shown on television, and Blum's *Annapurna: A Woman's Place* proved a best seller.[75]

But the expedition was not without its critics in the mountaineering establishment. Among them was Galen Rowell, who had clashed with Dianne Roberts on the 1975 K2 expedition, later describing her in his expedition book as a "rabid feminist." In early 1979 he wrote a letter to the *National Geographic* magazine urging it not to print a forthcoming article by Blum about the Annapurna expedition. It may have been the first time that one American climber had ever tried to suppress the publication of an expedition report by

Arlene Blum chipping the names of Alison Chadwick-Onyszkiewicz and
Vera Watson in a memorial stone facing Annapurna's summit.
Courtesy of Arlene Blum.

another—an expedition, moreover, of which he had no firsthand knowledge. He sent the
letter not under his own name but that of his girlfriend, Melinda Sanders (as Rowell later
explained to Blum, he "thought a woman's signature would carry more weight").[76]

According to the Rowell/Sanders letter, it was "bald-faced racism" to claim that
the 1978 Annapurna expedition was a "women's achievement." The real work of getting
to the summit, Rowell/Sanders argued, had been done by the two male Sherpas who had
accompanied the two successful women summiters. Not only that, but the "escapade" had
been a "co-educational, cohabiting expedition in which women slept with men, who were
plied into sexual relations with booze." Rowell/Sanders professed shock that the expedition
had concluded "with one woman marrying a Sherpa."[77]

Nothing came of this attack (nor did the Annapurna women learn until some
years later its real source). The *National Geographic* went ahead with publication of Blum's
article. Editor in chief Gil Grosvenor wrote back to Sanders to defend the expedition, noting, "almost every Himalayan expedition uses Sherpas" and expressing puzzlement over the
implication there had been something wrong in the Annapurna expedition doing so. As
for "questions of personal propriety," the National Geographic Society had heard nothing
to substantiate such charges.[78]

Two years passed, and the controversy, which never went public, seemed forgotten.
Then in the summer of 1981, it broke out again, this time into the open, with a story in

Outside magazine by David Roberts entitled "Has Women's Climbing Failed?" Although he discussed several other expeditions where women had died (citing, for instance, John Roskelley and Galen Rowell's judgment that Devi Unsoeld had contributed to her own death on Nanda Devi), the main target of the piece was the 1978 Annapurna expedition. Roberts quoted Galen Rowell once again, accusing the Annapurna women of being hypocrites as well as zealots: "[T]he climb was touted as being an all-women's climb. Yet they had the Sherpas always carrying more weight, and climbing without oxygen, while the women climbed with oxygen, and at times the Sherpas actually broke the trail and were first up the rope."[79]

In Roberts's view, his article simply set forth American mountaineers' traditional dislike of politicized expeditions—his criticism of feminist-inspired expeditions was no different than the criticisms earlier generations had offered of excessively nationalistic expeditions. For their part, the Annapurna women and their defenders in the climbing community felt that they were being held to a new and arbitrary standard of mountaineering purity. Roberts made no attempt to prove, statistically or otherwise, that women were more prone to die on mountaineering expeditions than male climbers, or that when they did die, the fatalities were the product of politically inspired recklessness rather than the traditional dangers of high-altitude mountaineering. "One could write a similar article citing numerous tragedies in men's climbs, and indeed on Mr. Roberts' climbs," Arlene Blum and Irene Beardsley wrote in a response to *Outside*'s managing editor, John Rasmus. Nor did Roberts set out any comparisons that proved that the women on Annapurna had relied on their Sherpas to break trail or carry out other difficult and dangerous tasks any more than was typical of other expeditions. All of the charges in *Outside*'s indictment, Blum and Beardsley argued, "apply equally well to men's expeditions. Roberts could have written an article called, 'Has Men's Climbing Failed?' or 'Has Climbing Failed?'"[80]

K2 1978

By the end of 1977, Mount Everest had been climbed by fourteen expeditions on four separate routes. K2, in comparison, had been climbed only twice and by a single route: by the Italians in 1954 and by a Japanese party in 1977.[81] Americans had been there four times and never reached the summit.

In 1978, for the first time Pakistani authorities gave their approval to two expeditions attempting K2 in a single year. An eight-member British expedition led by Chris Bonington went first, hoping to put a new route up the mountain's West Ridge. Bonington had assembled his usual group of friends for the attempt, including Doug Scott and Nick Estcourt. On their twelfth day on the mountain, Scott and Estcourt were crossing a steep snow slope at 22,500 feet when they were struck by an avalanche. Scott, who had been leading, survived; Estcourt did not. He was the fourth climber to die on a major Bonington expedition in the 1970s. The expedition came to an abrupt end.[82]

The second expedition to tackle K2 in 1978 was American. Once again Jim Whittaker was the leader and Jim Wickwire the principal organizer. The American expedition had originally hoped to climb the mountain via the West Ridge, but when they learned of Bonington's plans shifted their attention to the Northeast Ridge, which had been attempted unsuccessfully by a bold but underequipped Polish expedition in 1976.[83] Their ten-member team included some veterans of the 1975 expedition: Dianne Roberts and Robert Schaller. Others were not invited back. Among the newcomers were Rick Ridgeway, Lou Reichardt, and John Roskelley.

As soon as the expedition reached K2, some predictable dynamics emerged. Roskelley once again objected to the presence of women on the expedition, including Whittaker's wife, as well as Cherie Bech (who was on the expedition with her husband, Terry Bech, but who in the course of the expedition fell in love and started sharing a tent with Chris Chandler). "People always criticize me for being down on women on expeditions," Roskelley told Rick Ridgeway, after Ridgeway expressed his own doubts about Cherie Bech's qualifications, "but I've never yet been on a big mountain with one that's worth a damn." For the second time in two years, Roskelley was challenging the authority of one of the heroes of the 1963 American Everest expedition, and for the second time the ostensible issue was a female family member. "Everybody here knows the only reason [Dianne is] along is because she's your wife," Roskelley shot at Whittaker in one argument. Whittaker was incensed at Roskelley's impertinence: "I'd been guiding on Mt. Rainier since a year before he was born."[84]

The odd thing was that, unlike the 1976 Nanda Devi climb, there was no basic difference in expeditionary strategy involved to divide Roskelley and Whittaker. Unlike Unsoeld on Nanda Devi, Whittaker ran a traditional (and very well-equipped) expedition. Like Roskelley, he was fully committed to the idea of employing siege tactics and to climbing the mountain by a new and challenging route. There was never any question of switching to the standard, and twice-climbed, route up the Abruzzi Ridge. As for the woman question, Dianne Roberts's presence on the K2 expedition was already a given when Roskelley was invited to participate, just as Devi Unsoeld's presence had been a given on the Nanda Devi expedition. It seemed as though Roskelley needed to feel himself at odds with expedition leaders to sharpen his climbing edge. Perhaps John Roskelley, hater though he was of hippies and feminists and the like, proud though he was to be a "down-to-earth, Spokanite redneck," was actually more a child of the sixties than he imagined. He was only a half decade older than Devi Unsoeld, both of them born at the height of the baby boom. He did not have much of the gentle idealism that was one legacy of the 1960s, and that Devi possessed. But in his rage, his in-your-face confrontational style, and his distrust of the older generation's authority (as personified in Ad Carter, Willi Unsoeld, and now Whittaker), he certainly embodied other aspects of the decade.[85]

In any event, in the now-familiar pattern, the expedition split into two factions, an "A Team," this time composed of Reichardt, Roskelley, Wickwire, and Ridgeway, and a "B

Team" of Chandler and the Bechs, with Whittaker trying without much luck to mediate between the two. The B Team never had a chance. By the end of August the expedition had its first resignation, when Chris Chandler announced he was leaving.[86]

Despite the squabbling, the expedition proved a success. At the end of July Roskelley and Ridgeway led a traverse across a knife-edged ridge, putting them high on the Northeast Ridge, in position for a summit bid. The A Team itself divided over how best to reach the summit from the ridge. Roskelley and Ridgeway wanted to push a direct route all the way up the ridge, continuing the route the Poles had first attempted in 1976, while Wickwire and Reichardt favored a traverse across the East Face to the Abruzzi Ridge to complete the climb. Both routes ran into difficulties, but in the end the Abruzzi Ridge proved the more feasible.

On summit day, September 6, high on the Abruzzi Ridge, Jim Wickwire looked down on the site of the 1953 American expedition's Camp VIII; below it he could pick out the place where Pete Schoening had saved the lives of his comrades with his famous belay. At 5:15 P.M. he and Reichardt, arm in arm, stepped onto the summit of K2. Reichardt's oxygen set malfunctioned so he abandoned it en route to the summit; Wickwire had climbed with oxygen. Reichardt was eager to descend as soon as possible, while Wickwire lingered to shoot more photographs. Reichardt made it back to their high camp, but Wickwire was forced to bivouac that night at 28,000 feet, in temperatures that dipped to minus thirty-five degrees Fahrenheit. His oxygen ran out soon after he settled in, and the stove he carried with him malfunctioned, leaving him unable to melt snow for water. The next morning, nearly snow-blind and badly weakened, he made his way down the mountain. On the way he encountered John Roskelley and Rick Ridgeway, who had abandoned their attempt at completing a direct route and were following the Reichardt-Wickwire traverse to the Abruzzi Ridge. Wickwire assured them he was all right, and they headed on up the mountain to the summit. When Roskelley and Ridgeway made it back to high camp that day, Wickwire brewed them some tea. All the mountaineers descended safely, though once off the mountain Wickwire developed pneumonia and had to be evacuated by helicopter.[87]

Reichardt entitled his expedition report for the *American Alpine Journal* "K2: The End of a 40-Year American Quest." But although they had succeeded where so many others had not, the expedition would chiefly be remembered for the dissension and antagonism that divided its members. Few of the climbers emerged from Rick Ridgeway's subsequent book, *The Last Step,* as heroic role models on the order of a Charlie Houston or a Pete Schoening. Instead, those who failed to reach the summit were depicted as inadequate climbers; some of those who did reach the summit came off as less than adequate human beings.[88]

The most sympathetic portrait to appear in the book was that of Ridgeway's climbing partner, John Roskelley. Ridgeway and Roskelley not only reached the summit together, they also agreed on most of the issues dividing the expedition. Ridgeway quoted himself telling Roskelley, "You're one of the best climbers in the country, and as far as Himalayan

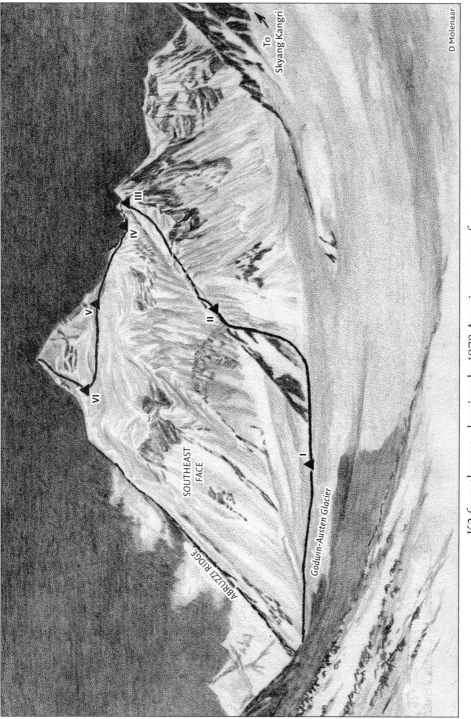

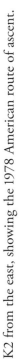

K2 from the east, showing the 1978 American route of ascent.

type-climbing goes, you're far and away the best in the United States." He was so good, in fact, Ridgeway thought he should someday be able to make a living out of it. "Look at Messner," he concluded. "He's doing fine—house, plenty of dough, goes on trips all the time."[89]

Roskelley brought up Reinhold Messner's example on another occasion, when both he and Ridgeway were feeling fed up with their expedition mates: "Messner would never put up with this. That's why he's the best. He's been screwed on too many of these big expeditions."[90]

The Age of Messner

In the 1970s and 1980s everybody in the climbing world seemed to be talking about Reinhold Messner—and with good reason.

In 1971, after returning from Nanga Parbat, still distraught over the loss of his brother Günther, tied up in legal wrangling with Karl Herrligkoffer, and missing seven toes, Reinhold Messner informed readers of *Mountain* magazine that his best climbing days were behind him. The following year, when his climbing partner turned back on their summit day, he made a solo first ascent of the South Face of Manaslu.[91]

At regular intervals over the decade that followed, Messner dramatically redefined the notion of the possible in high-altitude Himalayan climbing. His succession of achievements, high ideals, and relentless self-promotion combined to make him the best-known Himalayan mountaineer of his generation, his fame rivaled only by that of Chris Bonington.

But there were striking differences between their careers. Bonington defined "the essence of climbing" as "teamwork." He realized his finest achievements as expedition leader rather than as a star climber. Messner, in contrast, was seldom happy on expeditions and never became an expedition leader himself. His career instead took the form of being the first postexpeditionary mountaineering celebrity. His popularity with the general public grew out of a carefully crafted image as a lone wolf, a rebel against convention and authority, and a supreme individualist. In one of his many books (he would turn them out at a rate of more than one a year over three decades), Messner described himself as "a tormented child of a generation which has to ask itself what sense there is in following an unloved profession in a world which through a materialistic mentality daily becomes more hateful."[92]

Messner's trademark would become solo ascents of Himalayan peaks, but in the early years of his career he did some of his most significant climbing in partnership with Austrian climber Peter Habeler. Their brotherhood of the rope would prove, for a time, as celebrated as that of Shipton and Tilman. They climbed together in the Alps in 1966, then in Peru in 1969. Five years later they teamed up to attempt the North Face of the Eiger, an ascent they accomplished in a mere ten hours, half the previous record.[93]

The next year, 1975, they made their first Himalayan venture together, traveling to

Pakistan to attempt Hidden Peak (Gasherbrum I), which had not been climbed since its first ascent in 1958. Messner and Habeler intended not only to put up a new route on the mountain's Northwest Face but also to do so in the first true application of alpine style on an 8,000-meter peak. That meant climbing in one continuous push from Hidden Peak's base to its summit, with no artificial oxygen, no fixed ropes, and no assistance carrying supplies up the mountain from the dozen porters who had accompanied them to Base Camp. On August 8, following two weeks of reconnaissance and acclimatization, they set off on their attempt. After the first day's climb they bivouacked at 19,350 feet. The next day they surmounted a band of ice-covered broken rocks, bivouacking above it at 23,300 feet. On summit day, August 10, they set off at 8:00 A.M. Their climb was very much in the tradition of "une affaire de cordée," though they climbed unroped. "[W]e felt like a roped party," Messner would write. "There was something synchronous about the way we thought, the way we did things. A short glance was enough to ascertain the other's intentions and frame of mind, to know and do what the other wanted."[94] At 12:30 P.M. they reached the summit. Messner's hero, Hermann Buhl, had been the first person to climb two 8,000-meter peaks; on this day Messner became the first to have climbed three.

Two days later Messner and Habeler were back in Base Camp, where they were applauded by a party of Polish climbers there to climb Gasherbrums II and III. The Poles were only the first among many mountaineers around the world to congratulate Messner and Habeler on the boldness and vision of their alpine-style ascent, widely understood as signaling a new era in Himalayan climbing. Habeler appreciated the attention. Messner took it as confirmation that he was a man with a mission. "This expedition had not only showed me that an eight thousander can be climbed by two exactly in the same way as an alpine peak," Messner wrote in his expedition book, *The Challenge,* "but it had also given me an answer to the question of mankind's fundamental existence." He did not elaborate.[95]

A few days after Hillary and Tenzing reached the summit of Everest in 1953, Bill Tilman wrote a letter to the editor of *The Times* offering a prediction: "I shall be surprised if after the present excitement is forgotten a few discordant voices are not heard suggesting that someone, relying only on his unaided heart and lungs, should climb Everest for the first time." A quarter century later, on May 8, 1978, Messner and Habeler would fulfill Tilman's prophecy and once again stun the mountaineering world. They called their attempt "Everest by fair means." Unlike their oxygenless climb on Hidden Peak, this was not an alpine ascent. Messner and Habeler had joined a larger Austrian expedition attempting the Southeast Ridge route as a necessary compromise: buying their way into this already-scheduled expedition allowed them to jump the long queue that still existed for Everest permits. By agreement with the others, they would function as their own two-man operation, with first shot at the summit.[96]

Things did not at first go smoothly. Messner and Habeler abandoned their attempt to put up a new route along the South Pillar, the right-hand edge of the Southwest Face, when they discovered it was bare of snow and covered with ice. They shifted their effort to the standard Southeast Ridge route. But even there they ran into problems. Habeler suffered from food poisoning and had to retreat from their camp on Lhotse Face back to Base Camp. Messner decided to keep going in a solo attempt but was caught in a blizzard on the South Col, and he too was forced to retreat. Habeler, meanwhile, was having second thoughts about the oxygenless part of their plan and asked the other Austrians if he could join them. But they rebuffed him, not wanting to spare the oxygen or a place on a summit team to him. And so on May 7 Messner and Habeler returned to the South Col and at 5:30 the next morning set off on their summit attempt. The day was bitterly cold and windy, and new-fallen snow made trail breaking difficult. They stopped briefly at 27,900 feet to brew some tea, taking advantage of the tent and supplies left there by the Austrians, who had reached the summit several days earlier.

When they reached the Hillary Step, Messner climbed it first, then stood on top to film Habeler following behind. They had roped up below the obstacle, but Messner failed to belay his partner. "I was not too happy about it," Habeler later told an interviewer, "and I shouted something about the need for a belay, but perhaps he didn't hear me."[97] Having no alternative, Habeler surmounted the slippery step unbelayed. Now there was only the summit ridge left to climb. Messner and Habeler found themselves having to stop every ten steps, gasping for breath, but forced themselves to press on. Finally, at 1:15 P.M., they stood on top of Mount Everest. The two men, without oxygen, had climbed all the way from the South Col to the summit in under eight hours, a time that rivaled several earlier climbs leaving from high camps on the Southeast Ridge.

They made their way down to the South Col separately. Habeler, in the lead, did a standing glissade on the last long stretch of ridgeline, tumbling at the end, injuring his ankle and losing ice ax and goggles. Messner arrived soon after, on his feet but suffering a painful attack of snow blindness. Despite their injuries, they descended the next day without incident. On the hike out from Base Camp a few days later, they met Sir Edmund Hillary in Khunde, who offered his congratulations, representing but the first of many accolades that were to come their way. In concluding his letter to *The Times* in 1953, Tilman had written that "the difficult can be done at once, but the impossible takes longer." Messner and Habeler had accomplished what many of their peers had thought truly impossible.[98]

Despite their triumph, all was not well with the Messner-Habeler partnership. As the missed signals at the Hillary Step suggested, there was nothing "synchronous" about the way they thought and acted as they made their way toward the top of Everest. Though briefly roped together, they climbed as if they were unroped, two solo climbers who happened to find themselves in the same general vicinity at 29,000 feet. Afterward Habeler decided to write a book about the climb, his first. It came out before Messner's, and whatever remained of their "affaire de cordée" completely unraveled. Habeler praised his partner, but also described him as lonely, tormented, perhaps guilt-ridden over his brother's death, and a bit of a publicity hound. Messner felt himself maligned, and the partnership was at an end.[99]

Messner was ready to go solo in any case. And by solo he meant climbing a mountain entirely on his own, not just completing a climb without his intended companion as he had on Manaslu in 1972. No one yet had ever climbed a major Himalayan peak from base to summit alone—it was considered another of those impossible goals. And yet, before 1978 was out, Messner went on to do a solo ascent of the Diamir Face of Nanga Parbat, the route he had descended with Günther in 1970. He climbed K2 the following year oxygenless, though not solo.[100]

He wished to make a solo attempt on Everest but knew that the mountain presented challenges beyond its height to any would-be soloist. When asked by an interviewer in 1976 if he ever thought about attempting such a climb on Everest, Messner was ambivalent: "I'm sure it would be possible, but I think it would be a little bit crazy. The [Khumbu] icefall and that long glacier would have to be negotiated."[101]

But the opening of Tibet to foreign climbers changed Messner's calculations. Following the death of Mao Zedong in 1976, new Chinese leaders began opening their country to Western influences and Western capital. Tibet, whose value to the Chinese government had been chiefly a matter of prestige and strategic location since its conquest in the 1950s, now held promise as an economic resource. Why should Nepal and Pakistan be the only countries to benefit from the desire of well-heeled foreign mountaineers to risk their lives on high peaks?[102]

And so in 1979 the Chinese government announced it would open access to foreign expeditions to Everest's north side (as well as to seven other mountains, including Shishapangma). A Sino-Japanese expedition made a reconnaissance of the north side of Everest that fall, followed by a full-scale expedition the following spring.[103]

The north side of Everest was far better suited to the kind of solo attempt that Messner envisioned than the south side, for there was no Khumbu Icefall to negotiate. In April 1980 Messner flew to Beijing and received permission from the Chinese Mountaineering Association (in exchange for a considerable fee) to attempt the North Ridge/North Face route later that summer. He was in a hurry to do the climb, having learned the previous fall that Japanese mountaineer Naomi Uemura planned his own solo attempt on Everest in the winter of 1980–81, and Messner feared the prize would be snatched from him.[104]

Messner set off for Everest in June, accompanied only by his new American girlfriend, Nena Holguin. They established a camp at the site of the old British Camp III below the North Col. For the next six weeks, while Nena tended the home fires, he made tentative ventures up the col to acclimatize as well as a side trip to the foot of Shishapangma. By mid-August the worst of the monsoon season avalanche danger had passed. On August 17 he climbed to near the top of the col, depositing a rucksack, bivouac tent, sleeping bag, stove, and enough food and fuel to last him for a week. He spent the night back at Base Camp with Nena and then set off the following morning on his summit push. That night he slept on the Northeast Ridge, the next night on the North Face. On August 20, in a heavy fog that allowed him to see only a few feet ahead, he headed for the summit via the

Reinhold Messner indicating his solo route on Mount Everest, 1980.
Reprinted by permission of Hulton Archives/Getty Images.

Great Couloir, then rejoined the Northeast Ridge just short of the summit. At 3:00 P.M. he was on his hands and knees, still pulling himself upward, uncertain of his position because of the surrounding clouds, when suddenly he found himself staring at the old Chinese tripod. He reached out and grasped it "like a friend." Fifty-nine years after the first British reconnaissance, Everest had been climbed solo and oxygenless. For most of that time, no one but delusional characters like Maurice Wilson, who had died in his own solo attempt in 1934, had believed it could be done. Messner recognized a kindred spirit in the much-derided Wilson. "So long as Wilson was able to remain on his legs he climbed upwards like one possessed," Messner wrote admiringly, "born aloft by belief and by God."[105]

On his return trip from Everest, Messner was asked in Beijing which flag he had brought with him to the summit: "I am my own homeland," he replied, "and my handkerchief is my flag." And when it came to singing the praises of his self-proclaimed homeland, Messner proved the most zealous of patriots. In *The Crystal Horizon,* his book chronicling his Everest solo, he quoted liberally from his girlfriend Nena's letters and diary. "Sometimes I feel myself crushed by this man!" Nena declared in one diary entry that Messner shared with readers. "But I know that is exactly what I want: a strong man."[106]

Messner was often mocked for such self-glorification, but he shrugged off criticisms. In a 1983 article for *Mountain* magazine entitled "The Risk Market: Reflections on Fame and the Boom in Professional Mountaineering," he boasted of his status as a successfully marketed commodity:

It is true what my critics say: my market value increases with every new supreme achievement, with every new record and with every razor edged situation that I survive. Moreover, my market value increases with every outside criticism. Therefore, the frequently
raised contention that I am the most highly criticised mountaineer does not disturb me
in the least . . . I have on offer just about everything that a mountaineer needs in order
to indulge himself in his dreams: signed and dated posters, books with route suggestions
and route descriptions and accounts of risk-filled situations. I allow my person to be
used for advertising, I give lectures and I make films—all for an appropriate fee. My
death is the only thing that cannot be made to sell—at least not by me.[107]

One of Messner's mountaineering critics remarked, "Messner sees Everest as an
8,000 metre extension of himself." Like Narcissus in the ancient Greek myth, Messner was
entranced by the image of himself he saw reflected in nature. He was not alone in his preoccupation with self. As much as his 1971 manifesto "The Murder of the Impossible" helped
define the idealistic hopes of a generation of Alpine and Himalayan climbers, his 1983 "Risk
Market" manifesto exemplified the self-promotion of mountaineering's age of extremes.[108]

Fallen Giants, 1977

Eric Shipton died at home at the age of sixty-nine on March 28, 1977. Shortly before his
death he had told an interviewer that his chief regret in life was having "spent so much
time mucking about Mount Everest." If he had it all to do over, he said, he would have
"gone to more peaks under 25,000 feet that could be climbed with a few classic tools
by a few friends." In an obituary of Shipton in the *Alpine Journal,* Dr. Charles Warren,
veteran of three British expeditions to Everest in the 1930s, wrote that Shipton's death
came as a shock: "One had got into the habit of thinking of Eric as the grand old man of
mountain exploration who went on forever." He also commented, perhaps with an eye on
contemporary climbing icons, "Never at any time was he willing to sell his soul for a mess
of mass-media pottage."[109]

A little over seven months after Shipton's death, on November 1, 1977, seventy-
nine-year-old Bill Tilman set out from Rio de Janeiro as a member of a six-man crew on
a small boat, *En Avant,* a vessel that had already carried him across the Atlantic from England. He and the others on board set their course for the Falkland Islands and then to
Antarctic waters. It proved Tilman's last adventure. *En Avant* was never seen again, and
the fate of its crew remains a mystery. Tilman was saluted with an obituary in the pages of
the *Himalayan Journal* by Noel Odell, with whom he had reached the summit of Nanda
Devi in 1936. Another kind of tribute came two years later on Kangchenjunga, when a
small lightweight climbing party consisting of Doug Scott, Pete Boardman, Joe Tasker, and
Georges Bettembourg reached the summit. "I've so forgotten myself as to shake hands,"
Doug Scott said dryly to his climbing partners, evoking the memory of Tilman and Odell
on the summit of Nanda Devi in 1936.[110]

The Crowded Himalaya

The Himalaya were growing crowded. When Habeler and Messner hiked in to make their solo attempt on Hidden Peak in 1975, they met a French party returning from Paiju Peak, a British party returning from Trango Tower, an Italian party returning from Grand Cathedral Peak, a Swiss party returning from Sia Kangri, and an American party returning from K2, plus the Polish party camped at the base of Gasherbrum II. At the end of the 1970s the Nepalese government lifted the restrictions that had permitted only one or two expeditions to attempt a given mountain annually. The results, particularly on Everest (a mountain that expeditions could now approach from Tibet as well as Nepal) were dramatic: in the 1960s there had been 6 Everest expeditions (including the unauthorized attempt by Woodrow Wilson Sayre); in the 1970s there were 23 Everest expeditions; in the 1980s there were about 140. Increasing numbers of climbers were returning on an annual or even semiannual basis to the Himalaya. In his climbing career Charlie Houston made four expeditions to the Himalaya in eighteen years; by the 1980s some top climbers made that many expeditions every two years, and in 1982 Reinhold Messner became the first to climb three 8,000-meter peaks in a single year.[111]

The opening of Pakistan's Karakoram Highway at the end of the 1970s, linking Rawalpindi to Kashgar in China, provided easier access to a number of Himalayan mountains, including Nanga Parbat and Rakaposhi, as well as a link by road to Skardu, traditional stepping-off place for expeditions to the Baltoro region. As it passes into China, the highway provides access to Muztagh Ata and the Kongur massif in the western Kunlun mountains. It also proved a boon to Pakistan's nascent mountain-trekking industry, which would soon acquire its own Lonely Planet guidebook.[112]

The opening of previously closed or highly restricted regions brought new opportunities for mountaineers in the Himalaya. Sikkim opened to expeditions in 1976, Tibet in 1979, and Bhutan in 1983. Bhutan alone offered nineteen mountains over 7,000 meters, and only one of them, Chomolhari (24,000ft/7,315m), had ever been climbed. John Roskelley, on his first visit to Bhutan in 1985, remarked to Rick Ridgeway, "Nineteen expeditions to the Himalayas and I've finally found Shangri-la."[113]

All of this came at a price. Shangri-la was being corrupted by its own success in attracting outsiders. Anthropologist Sherry Ortner, a regular visitor to the Solu Khumbu since the mid-1960s, recorded in her field notes on a visit in 1976, "We trekked from Thami to Lukla in 2 days. There were a million tourists. Both the trail and Lukla itself were awful, essentially *polluted* with tourists."[114]

In addition to the sheer number of visitors "polluting" the region in an aesthetic or spiritual sense, there was also more tangible physical pollution. The American backpacking motto of the 1960s, "Pack it in/Pack it out," had never been particularly enforced on Himalayan expeditions. Already in 1963, when the American Mount Everest expedition reached the South Col, the area was being described as the "world's highest junkyard" for the collection of discarded oxygen bottles and other detritus that had been left behind by the six previous expeditions to climb that high. Twenty years later the junkyard phenomenon had spread far beyond the South Col and Everest Base Camp. Norwegian climber Hans Christian Doseth wrote to *Mountain* magazine in 1984 complaining about garbage left by British, Japanese, and Spanish expeditions in the Garhwal Himalaya. "Their former Base Camps looked like a rubbish tip; plastic bottles, tin cans and other shit left all over the place. How can climbers leave their camps like that? It is incredibly selfish, irresponsible, and the ultimate form of mountaineering imperialism. Do we behave like that when we are camping back home?"[115]

Litter was not the only environmental problem attributed to mountaineers. Climbing expeditions and trekkers were stripping the approach route to Everest of rhododendron and juniper for firewood. When the British hiked up to Everest Base Camp in 1953 their porters carried up hundreds of loads of juniper in addition to the piles of cut juniper waiting for them up there left by the two Swiss expeditions of the previous year. When Hillary first visited the Khumbu, he would recall in the 1970s, "the whole place was a deep green, clothed in juniper right up the valley and beside the glacier." By 1976 he found "you have to look pretty hard to even see a single bush anywhere."[116]

There was also a growing problem of human remains, a macabre form of mountain litter. By the 1980s scores of bodies had disappeared or been abandoned on Himalayan mountainsides. Some fell into crevasses and were carried down the mountain by the glaciers, to emerge years later at the mountain's base. Those at least could be buried. But other bodies became more or less permanent fixtures of the mountainscape, frozen in place at high altitudes, sometimes beside frequently traveled routes. German climber Hannelore Schmatz, the fourth woman to climb Mount Everest, died high on the Southeast Ridge in 1979 while descending from the summit; her head and upper torso were visible for years afterward, unnerving summit climbers, who felt she was watching them as they passed by her unblinking gaze.[117]

With the number of expeditions increasing so rapidly, there was a dramatic increase in the number of climbing deaths in the Himalaya in the 1980s. Like soldiers in wartime who had seen too many battle casualties, experienced climbers tended to develop a fatalistic, jaded attitude toward the incidence of death and its physical remains. British climber Andy Fanshawe, en route to Chogolisa in the summer of 1986, stopped by K2 Base Camp to see if he could cadge some extra food. The doctor at the British corner of Base Camp kept the skeletal hand of a Balti porter who had died in an earlier climbing season in a tin with some Kit-Kat candy bars—it was the "four finger snack," the doctor remarked lightly to Fanshawe. Someone else joked that Renato Casarotto, an Italian climber who had fallen to his death in a crevasse on the mountain only a few days earlier, "had failed to qualify in the K2 long jumping championships."[118]

By the 1980s, among serious Himalayan mountaineers, the chances were good that they had lost one or more friends or expedition mates to climbing accidents. And that was certainly true for Sherpa climbers. Between 1953 and 1983, 116 Sherpas from the Solu Khumbu region lost their lives on mountaineering expeditions. Of these, 28 were from Khumjung and Khunde, 14 from Namche Bazar.[119]

En route to Everest to attempt the Southwest Face in 1975, Pete Boardman noted in his diary that there was "a tinge of guilt about this expedition." Many Western climbers in the 1970s reported similar feelings. "Nobody ever thinks that it is right that a foreign power subjugates another," Boardman continued, "and so it is that I feel guilty about being waited on by Sherpas and having all the appendages and contrivances of the Western World carried on the backs of a string of Tamang porters." In his expedition book about the 1976 American Bicentennial expedition, Rick Ridgeway revealed both the reluctance of American climbers to carry loads through the Khumbu Icefall and the troubled consciences that resulted: "[T]hough none of us would admit it, we knew we were paying others to risk their lives for us. It was as if we had adopted that attitude—although none of us would have blatantly stated it—so common to Westerners in Asia, that attitude that says, 'Life is cheap here. They don't value it as we do.'" Everest-bound with a Canadian expedition in 1982, Robert Patterson was bothered by the thought that "here we were, decked out in matching Adidas track suits and sneakers, each of us carrying camera gear worth more than most [Nepalese] would earn in a lifetime." He felt guilty "just being there, off on a quest based mainly on self-gratification, while they were in a daily struggle for survival."[120]

One solution was to forgo large expeditions, with their accompanying retinue of low- and high-altitude porters, which seemed inevitably to summon up memories among the "sahibs" of colonial subjugation ("We round a corner," Pete Boardman wrote of the approach march to Everest in 1976, "and there is the British Raj in all its glory neatly lined up, tents erected, crowds kept at a distance. . . . a Bonington Everest Expedition is one of the last great imperial experiences that life can offer").[121]

Alpine-style ascents were less likely to invoke memories of the Raj. Western climbers in small, informal expeditions could, ideally, tread lightly across the landscape, blending in with the indigenous population rather than keeping it at a distance. As British climber Joe Tasker wrote in the *Alpine Journal* in 1977: "Small parties going into an area will do much less damage to the personality of a people and the ecology of a region. . . . Without being swamped by an invasion, the natives of an area can experience other cultures and the member of the expedition has the opportunity for informal and democratic interaction which is a healthy development from the anonymous servant role, a legacy which expeditions have inherited from a colonial past."[122]

Though good intentions clearly motivated such sentiments, the irony was that Sherpas much preferred the earlier expeditionary model—not because they craved servitude but because they sought employment. "The alpine system is ethically great for [Western mountaineers]," Khadga Bickram Shah, president of the Nepal Mountaineering Association, declared in the early 1990s, but "economically the worst for us." Despite its risks, high-altitude climbing support on an expedition remained the best-paid economic opportunity available to most Sherpas, offering ten to fifteen times the annual per capita Nepalese income of $160 for two months of work.[123]

New Faces: Joe Tasker and Pete Boardman

Joe Tasker and Pete Boardman were the first of the British generation born after the war to emerge as stars in Himalayan climbing. Casual acquaintances since the early 1970s, each made his way to the Himalaya independently of the other in 1975. Boardman traveled in luxury as part of the Everest Southwest Face expedition. Tasker's venture, in contrast, would not remind anyone of the balmier days of British imperialism. With climbing partner Dick Renshaw, Tasker bought an ailing van, loaded it with climbing gear, and drove to India. The entire expedition, including the cost of the van (abandoned in Kabul on the return trip), was £1,600, less than one-fiftieth of the cost of the Southwest Face expedition. Tasker and Renshaw put a new route up Dunagiri's South Ridge for the mountain's second ascent, the first since 1939. Apart from a prolonged and harrowing descent, during which Renshaw suffered severe frostbite on his fingers, their chief problem was in dealing with Indian authorities who regarded their threadbare two-man expedition with suspicion. "[W]e had come overland on the 'hippy-trail,'" Tasker would write, "we wore jeans like hippies and stayed in the cheap sort of doss-house where hippies generally stayed."[124]

Boardman had made it to the top of Everest and returned to England to go on the lecture circuit. But he felt little enthusiasm for his new role as climbing celebrity. He was bothered by the sense that he had reached the top of Everest only by means of an experiment in "vertically integrated crowd control," as he would describe the Bonington expedition. At the end of each lecture he would be faced with the usual questions and compliments: "What does it feel like on top? What do you have to eat? How do you go the toilet when you're up there? Don't you think you've done it all now you've been to the top of Everest? What marvelous courage you must have!" All he could think while going through this ritual was "Everest is a bloody bore." When Boardman learned of the Dunagiri climb, he envied Tasker and Renshaw the "adventurous uncertainty" of their expedition.[125]

With Renshaw sidelined by frostbite, Tasker was looking for a new climbing partner. He came to Boardman with a proposal to tackle the West Wall of Changabang, which he had photographed from Dunagiri's summit. Changabang had been climbed for the first time in 1974 by Bonington's British-Indian expedition. Its members had briefly considered an attempt on the mountain's West Ridge before switching to the easier East Ridge. They had not even considered the West Wall as a possibility: Martin Boysen had described it in 1974 as "an enormous sweep of vertical and overhanging rock, plated here and there by ludicrously steep ice." When Chris Bonington heard of Boardman and Tasker's plans, he told them, "[I]f you do get up it'll be the hardest route in the Himalayas." *Mountain* magazine editor Ken Wilson offered a succinct and skeptical appraisal of their chances of success: "It doesn't look like a married man's route."[126]

In early September 1976 Boardman and Tasker hiked in from the village of Latat through the Rishi Gorge into the Nanda Devi Sanctuary. On September 8 they reached their Base Camp, at 15,000 feet on the Rhamani Glacier. Although this was not quite the shoestring operation of Tasker and Renshaw's 1975 Dunagiri climb, Boardman and Tasker were keeping to a tight budget: upon arriving at Base Camp their Indian liaison officer, dismayed by the quality of provisions, promptly quit.

Tasker and Boardman intended to bring big-wall techniques developed in Yosemite to bear on the West Wall. From Camp I, at 18,000 feet at the foot of the wall, they would push a route up the wall, fixing ropes as they went so they could descend to their camp at night and then return the next morning to continue the climb. Some nights they would not retreat but sleep in insulated suspension hammocks. When they reached the halfway point, at about 20,000 feet, they would establish Camp II. They would pull the ropes up behind them that they had fixed below and then repeat the process of pushing a route up the top half of the wall until they were in position to make their bid for the 22,520-foot summit.

They were beaten back on their initial attempt, in part because they could not get their stove working properly and, without the means to melt snow, were becoming severely dehydrated. In addition to the steepness of the West Wall and the technical problems of surmounting overhanging rock, the daily struggle to eat, drink, and sleep was the key to victory: "Some people judge mountaineers by their speed, and by the difficulty of the rock they can climb," Boardman wrote in his expedition account. "But on Changabang the real test was more how efficiently you could put a brew on, warm your fingers or take your boots off."[127]

On October 14, five weeks after they had first moved out onto the wall, they fought their way through to a snow ramp just short of the summit, where for the first time they could walk together, roped: "The leader and the second could share the climbing movement, no longer were we jumaring past the verticality of each other's achievement." Leading the way up a gully, Boardman encountered "a perfect pitch [of] mixed rock and ice-climbing at its finest" and offered one of the last great passages in modern climbing literature celebrating the experience of a roped ascent:

> I felt in perfect control and knew the thrill of seeing the ropes from my waist curl down through empty space. I was as light as the air around me, as if I were dancing on tip-toes, relaxed, measuring every movement and seeking a complete economy of effort. Speak with your eyes, speak with your hands, let it all flow from your heart. True communication, true communion, is silent. Chekhov once said that when a man spends the least possible movement over some definite action, that is grace. This was my lonely quest, until the jerk of the rope reminded me that I must stop and secure myself—and that I had a companion. Looking back at Joe, I realized how late it had grown. . . . Our awareness of each other, and our strength, flowed between us in waves. Now, when Joe arrived, I realized with an almost physical sense of shock that he was tired.[128]

From left: Dick Renshaw, Doug Scott, Pete Boardman, and Joe Tasker,
en route to K2, 1980. Photograph by Doug Scott. Reprinted by
permission of the Alpine Club Library.

They bivouacked that night in sleeping bags above the gully, at 22,000 feet. At 1:30 P.M.
on October 15 they stood atop Changabang and gazed over at Nanda Devi. A storm was
heading their way, and they did not linger. At Base Camp Boardman teased Tasker (a constant element of their relationship), welcoming him to mountaineering's "hall of heroes."
"No thanks," Tasker replied, having heard Boardman's stories of the lecture circuit, "it
sounds like a real rat race."[129]

Whatever reluctance they may have expressed, Boardman and Tasker were now
ensconced in that hall of heroes, forever linked with the emergence of the small expedition
as the preferred style of Himalayan endeavor, though they would go on expeditions both
large and small over the next few years. In 1978 the two climbers were invited on the next
big Bonington expedition, this time to attempt the West Ridge on K2, a venture that was
cut short when Nick Estcourt died in an avalanche. The following year both climbers were
part of a team ascending Kangchenjunga's North Ridge, and Boardman also took part in an
ascent of Gaurishankar. In 1980 Tasker and Boardman were part of another unsuccessful K2
bid, but in 1981 both reached the summit of Mount Kongur on a Bonington expedition.
Both men published their first books in those years: Boardman's account of the Changabang climb, *The Shining Mountain,* appearing to acclaim in 1979, Tasker's *Everest: The
Cruel Way,* an account of a failed winter attempt of Everest's West Ridge, appearing the
following year.[130]

In the spring of 1982 Boardman and Tasker were back on Everest, on a Bonington expedition intending to climb the Northeast Ridge to the summit. On May 17, from a camp below the North Col, Bonington watched Tasker and Boardman through a telescope as they moved up the Northeast Ridge in the previously unclimbed section called the Pinnacles, at an altitude of about 27,000 feet. If all went well, they would be in position for a summit bid the next day. Bonington had a glimpse of them at about 9:00 P.M.: "One figure was silhouetted in the fading light on the small col immediately below the Second Pinnacle, whilst the other figure was still moving to join him." They were not seen alive again.[131]

Keeping Score

Asked by an interviewer in 1986 to identify the next great Himalayan challenge, Doug Scott suggested dryly: "The big one would be the West Face of K2 in winter, solo . . . without shoes."[132] An interest in scoring "firsts" was not an innovation of that era, of course. Since the beginnings of Himalayan climbing, altitude records had been carefully noted, as well as highest peaks summited, culminating in the race to scale the eight-thousanders in the 1950s. But with all the obvious firsts already achieved, the top Himalayan mountaineers required new measures of achievement. They displayed considerable ingenuity in devising ways of distinguishing themselves from their predecessors and the common herd of climbers.

The most common form of record making was that based on identity: becoming the first female or first climber of this or that nationality to reach the summit of this or that peak. Everest, as always, was the most desired destination. Thus Bachendri Pal became the first Indian woman to climb Everest in 1984, Stacy Allison the first American woman to do so in 1988, and Rebecca Stephens the first British woman to do so in 1993. In 1989 Ricardo Torres became the first Mexican (and the first Latin American) to reach Everest's summit, and in 1995 Nasuh Mahruki the first Turk (and the first Muslim) to do so. There were also family firsts: in 1990 Marija and Andrej Stremfelj were the first married couple to reach Everest's summit together, followed two years later by the first pair of brothers to climb the mountain together, Alberto and Felix Inurrategui.[133]

And then there were records based on stunts. As in nonmountaineering "extreme sports" like BASE jumping, paragliding, snowboarding, and extreme skiing, risk served as its own justification in mountaineering stunts, no longer linked to the goal of reaching a summit. The grandfather of all Everest stuntmen was Yuichiro Miura, "the man who skied down Everest" in 1970, as the book and Academy Award–winning documentary film chronicling the attempt were entitled (even though he skied only down the Lhotse Face from below the South Col and tumbled rather than skied the last 600 or so feet of his descent). Others followed in (or sometimes above) his tracks. Jean Marc Boivin made the first hang-gliding descent from Everest in 1988, while Leo Dickinson made the first flight in a hot-air balloon over Everest in 1991.[134]

The most closely watched race in Himalayan mountaineering in the 1980s was the competition among top climbers to become the first to reach the summit of all fourteen

8,000-meter peaks. This too had something of a stunt quality to it; critics pointed out that the competition involved nothing more than reaching a summit, rather than opening up new and challenging routes up a mountain. Not surprisingly, Reinhold Messner took the lead early on and held it until he climbed the fourteenth on his list, Lhotse, in 1986. Polish climber Jerzy Kukuczka, Messner's closest competitor in the race, climbed his fourteenth in 1987, just eight years after having climbed his first.[135]

Climbing in China

China's decision to open its borders to foreign mountaineers in 1980 made available new mountains and new routes on previously climbed mountains. Foreign mountaineers were particularly eager to climb Shishapangma, which had been climbed by only a single route and a single expedition, the Chinese ascent of the Northwest Face in 1964. German climbers Michl Dachler, Wolfgang Schaffert, Günther Sturm, and Fritz Zintl reached its summit on May 7, 1980, also by the Northwest Face.[136]

Minya Konka (now known by its Tibetan name Gongga Shan) in Sichuan province had first been climbed in 1932 by Americans Terris Moore and Richard Burdsall. Two American parties set off to reach its summit in 1980, both unsuccessfully. One of the expeditions, seeking to follow the Moore-Burdsall route up the Northwest Ridge, ended in disaster when it was caught in an avalanche that left Jonathan Wright dead and Kim Schmitz with a broken back. Galen Rowell, Ned Gillette, and Jan Reynolds were more successful on their own venture to China that year, making the first ski ascent (and the third ascent ever) of Muztagh Ata.[137]

The opportunity to climb new routes on Everest's Tibetan ridges and faces was, of course, much prized by foreign mountaineers. In the spring of 1980 the Japanese had climbed both the Northeast Ridge and a new route on the North Face to the summit. And in the fall Reinhold Messner made his solo, oxygenless ascent of the North Face. Another Westerner made his way to Tibetan Everest that fall, but not to the north. Instead, American Andy Harvard made a solo reconnaissance of Everest's East or Kangshung Face, the first person to do so (at least officially) since Mallory had made his own reconnaissance in 1921 and declared "it was not for us." Rounding a slope on the approach to Everest's east through the Kama Valley, Harvard "suddenly faced an immense mass of ice and rock thrusting toward the vault of the sky." The sight of "the virtually unknown East Face of Everest" stopped him in his tracks. He spent the next few days delighted with the opportunity "to explore an unknown corner of the world alone." After two days at the foot of the mountain, Harvard spotted a possible route on the face, "a subtle but definite ridge line." It would be a formidable challenge, requiring climbers to surmount a 3,500-foot-high ice and rock buttress midway up to the summit. But Harvard judged it "not impossible, not suicidal."[138]

He would be back the following fall with an American expedition that would make the first attempt on the East Face. Organized by Richard Blum, the seventeen-member expedition was notable also for including among its members Sir Edmund Hillary and Kurt Diemberger. Though the expedition succeeded in surmounting the ice and rock buttress that led midway up the face, illness, accidents, and disunity hampered the effort. Expedition member John Roskelley left in a huff, for he had wanted to switch to the surer success of a North Face route. In a gesture reminiscent of the infamous 1971 international Everest expedition, he denounced his expedition mates to reporters on his return to the United States.[139]

The year also saw the first ascent of Kongur (25,324ft/7,719m) in China's Xinjiang province. Chris Bonington, Joe Tasker, Pete Boardman, and Al Rouse reached the summit on July 12, 1981, via the mountain's Southwest Rib. Shortly after their success, a Japanese team attempted the mountain by its northern side: three of its members, Yoji Teranishi, Mitsunori Shiga, and Shin'e Matsumi, set out for a summit bid and were never seen again.[140]

In 1982 the Chinese opened access to K2's northern routes. A Japanese Alpine Club expedition led by Masatsuga Konishi climbed the main spur of the North Face of K2 that year. On August 14 Yukihiro Yanagisawa, Naoe Sakishita, and Hiroshi Yoshino reached the summit, in the mountain's sixth ascent and the first from the north. Yukihiro Yanagisawa died on the descent.[141]

In 1983 Americans returned to Everest's Kangshung Face on an expedition led by Jim Morrissey. They made rapid progress up the buttress (now known as the Lowe Buttress for American climber George Lowe, who had led some of the most difficult sections in 1981). They were aided by the fixed ropes left from the 1981 expedition and also by the use of a mechanical winch for ferrying supplies, one of the few times in expedition history when such a device actually proved useful. A month into the climb they stood atop the Lowe Buttress. Ten days later, on October 8, they were ready for their summit bid. Carlos Buhler, Kim Momb, and Lou Reichardt climbed a snowfield above the buttress and then, after reaching a point on the Southeast Ridge below the South Summit, continued on to the top. They were followed the next day by three more American climbers.[142] This was the second time that Americans had pioneered in putting a daring new route up the mountain. It completed a cycle of exploration begun in 1921 when Mallory got his first glimpse of the Kangshung Face. With its ascent, all three of Everest's great faces, North, Southwest, and East, had finally been surmounted.

Foreign mountaineers formed close personal bonds with their Chinese counterparts. Zhou Zheng, a leading figure in the Chinese Mountaineering Association, grew particularly close to a circle of older American mountaineers; he took to calling Bob Bates "Uncle Bob" and sent him the manuscript of his history of Chinese mountaineering, *Footprints on the Peaks,* for suggestions. China's opening to the world in the 1980s proved a great gift to mountaineers in many ways. But there was one difficulty with mountaineering in China; it was hard not to be reminded that China's greatest mountains lay in a conquered and harshly ruled province. "There is a sadness in Tibet today," Andy Harvard would write after his 1980 visit to Everest's Kangshung Face, "that has not been erased by the new schools, hospitals, tractors, and roads furnished by . . . the People's Republic of China." The Rongbuk Monastery, well known to Westerners from expedition accounts and films from the 1920s and 1930s, lay in ruins in the 1980s; it had been destroyed sometime in the early 1970s during the frenzy of the Cultural Revolution. Other rural monasteries known from expedition accounts, like Xegar, the "Shining Crystal Monastery," had met the same fate.[143]

In Lhasa, staging point for Tibetan expeditions, there was less physical damage but ample evidence of Chinese authoritarianism. In 1987 two American climbers returning from a visit to Everest, Blake Kerr and John Ackerly, were put under house arrest in Lhasa for three days when Chinese authorities objected to the Tibetan flag Ackerly displayed on his shoulder bag. This was in the midst of a series of street protests by Tibetans against Chinese rule that left at least fifteen Tibetans dead (Kerr, a medical doctor, treated some of the wounded for injuries sustained by gunshots and beatings). Ultimately, the protests would lead to the imposition of martial law.[144]

Damnable Paths in the Himalaya

Once the loneliest place on earth, the Godwin-Austen Glacier was crowded with tents in July and August 1986, as nine expeditions gathered there at Base Camp. Twenty-seven climbers from the various expeditions would make it to the summit, including the first woman to climb K2, Wanda Rutkiewicz. Other climbers, mostly Poles, would put up daring new routes on K2's South Face and Southwest Pillar. But their achievements were overshadowed by the deaths of thirteen climbers in eight separate accidents, seven of whom died while descending from the summit. Because the deaths were spread out over an entire climbing season, and climbs on K2 rarely attracted the headlines given climbs on Everest, the general public paid little attention. But to the mountaineering community the carnage seemed to set a new benchmark for climbing disasters.[145]

The following summer, Soli Mehta, editor of the *Himalayan Journal*, wrote to American mountaineer Andy Kauffman reflecting on recent events in Himalayan climbing, including the deaths on K2: "The truth is that life has become cheap everywhere in the world—international terrorism—politics and violence on the sports field—the ugly face of competitive life—is all of a piece with the inexcusable attitudes we witness in the mountains these days. 'Because it is there' I'm afraid is now replaced by 'Screw you Jack, I'm alright.' It is all very sad and I don't think that this trend will falter in its damnable path until the new breed of climbers wake up and ask some very searching questions to themselves, and we can only pray that they offer honest answers."[146]

Some of the climbers who died on K2 in the summer of 1986, like Maurice and Liliane Barrard and Renato Casarotto, fell to their deaths, in accidents that no one could have prevented. Alan Rouse, on the other hand, was abandoned at high camp on the shoulder of the Abruzzi Ridge when he grew too weak to attempt a descent, provoking unflattering comparisons between the decisions of Rouse's companions and the heroic self-sacrifice of the 1953 American K2 expedition in attempting Art Gilkey's rescue. Trevor Braham, writing in the *Alpine Journal* in the aftermath of the disaster, echoed Mehta's concerns. Braham decried the decline of a "mountaineering tradition" of mutual support: "[T]he high-altitude climber no longer expects to give or receive any support from other members of his group. He is the sole judge of whether he should be there, and the responsibility for his survival is his own."[147]

Rouse and most of the others on K2 that summer were professional, or at least highly experienced, mountaineers. Further complicating the question of mountaineering ethics in the years that followed was a trend just becoming visible in the mid-1980s, the rise of commercial climbing. Increasingly, climbers with little or no previous high-altitude experience were appearing on the slopes of some of the most dangerous mountains in the world, depending for their survival not on their own skills but on those of the professional mountaineers they were paying to guide them to the summit.

Commercial guides in the 1990s liked to claim a lineage extending back to the 1880s in the Himalayas, when W. W. Graham brought Swiss guides with him to climb in the vicinity of Kangchenjunga, though in that instance the mountains in question were as new to "guides" as to "client." There were also occasions where climbers had been invited along on Himalayan mountaineering expeditions less for any skills they could contribute than for their ability to bankroll the expedition, like Dudley Wolfe on the 1939 K2 expedition. But the main point of that expedition remained the first ascent of K2; getting Dudley Wolfe to the summit was not a concern of Fritz Weissner's.[148]

Guided climbing on Himalayan peaks grew in a natural progression out of the trekking industry. Mountaineers were already taking groups of trekkers to altitudes higher than any mountaintop in Europe simply by walking them up to Everest Base Camp. Adding a peak to a trek was the next obvious step. In 1977 Galen Rowell and Kim Schmitz led thirteen American clients on what may have been the first guided climb of a mountain over 7,000 meters, up India's Nun Kun, with the two leaders and three clients actually reaching the summit. The precedent established, it was not long before clients began inquiring about the possibility of attempting 8,000-meter peaks, including Everest. Dick Bass, the fifty-five-year-old owner of the Snowbird ski resort in Utah, became the first paying client to reach the summit of Everest in the spring of 1985, guided by David Breashears. Bass was a proficient skier and climbed unroped on what was his fourth attempt on Everest. Despite the fact that he was paying to be there, he was probably as qualified as some of the 189 climbers who had preceded him to the summit. In reaching the top of Everest, he also became the first to climb the "Seven Summits," the tallest mountains on the seven continents. Bass, Breashears, and Sherpa Ang Phurba had an uncrowded summit to enjoy; they were the only ones high on the mountain that day.[149]

Everest would not remain uncrowded for long, as marketplace values triumphed over mountaineering tradition. In the 1990s Nepalese authorities opened Everest to anyone who could pay the ever-increasing fees charged for expedition permits (between 1991 and 1996 the fees would increase sevenfold, to $70,000 for a party up to seven, and another $10,000 for each additional climber). Plenty were willing to do so, especially Americans.[150]

In one four-day period in October 1990, thirty-one people climbed to the summit via the Southeast Ridge route, more than the total that had climbed the mountain between 1953 and 1970. The spectacle of the crowded summit prompted an anxious editorial in *Mountain* magazine: "No doubt the summit was compensation for those who were frustrated by the congested conditions on the mountain, but this year's successes should not lull the [Nepalese] Ministry of Tourism into believing that there is safety in numbers on Everest. One can only speculate what might have happened if the mountain had been hit by a storm of the ferocity that stopped most expeditions in their tracks last October."[151]

But commercial guides scoffed at such fears. On May 12, 1992, thirty-two people, six of them paying clients of New Zealand guide Rob Hall, made it to Everest's summit. *Outside* magazine took notice and interviewed some of the guides involved. "Plenty of people in the world are physically and financially capable of climbing Mount Everest," Chuck Cross of Mountain Travel-Sobek declared. "If the guides are diligent," Skip Horner of Alpine Ascents International added, "you have good high-altitude Sherpas, and you have plenty of oxygen, the mountain can be climbed safely." Horner acknowledged that commercial climbing made some mountaineers uneasy. "We would have all loved to have been on the expedition that put the first American on Everest, or to be Edmund Hillary," Horner told *Outside,* "but we weren't and we're not. It would be better to be on top alone, but that's just not the way it is anymore."[152]

Into Thin Air

In the spring of 1996 eleven expeditions set up Base Camp below the Khumbu Icefall, including at least six commercial operations (one of these had Lhotse rather than Everest as its goal). Two of the commercial Everest expeditions were American ventures, one led by Scott Fischer and the other by Peter Athans and Todd Burleson. New Zealander Rob Hall guided another of the Everest-bound expeditions. There were still more commercial expeditions operating on the Tibetan side.

Jon Krakauer, a reporter from *Outside* magazine assigned to write a story about guided climbing, had signed on with Hall's expedition. Hall was perhaps the most respected of all the commercial guides on Everest. But earlier Krakauer had considered going with American guide Scott Fischer. Fischer had impressive credentials of his own: three previous attempts on Everest, finally reaching the summit without the use of bottled oxygen in 1994. He had learned his basic mountaineering technique as a student of Paul Petzoldt.

Adventure Consultants Everest expedition, Everest Base Camp, 1996.
Jon Krakauer is third from left in front row, Rob Hall is fifth from left
in front row, Beck Weathers is fourth from left in back row.
Reprinted by permission of Time and Life Pictures/Getty Images.

He was a careful climber and solicitous not only of his own clients' safety but of others
he encountered on his climbs. On K2 in 1992, he and Ed Viesturs had risked the success
of their own summit bid by helping an ailing climber down from high camp. And, after
going back on a second attempt and making it to the summit, they put themselves in
jeopardy to help another stricken climber (Gary Ball, who was Rob Hall's climbing and
business partner) to safety. If anyone seemed to exemplify the survival of the old ideals of
the expeditionary culture in the new era of commercial climbing, it was Fischer. But he
was not above a little boasting when dealing with clients. "We've got the big E figured out,
we've got it totally wired," he would tell Krakauer in 1994. "These days, I'm telling you,
we've built a yellow brick road to the summit."[153]

Everest was certainly wired in one sense; five of the expeditions had their own
Web sites. The Fischer expedition Web site was cosponsored by NBC broadcasting and
was maintained on Everest by expedition member and New York City socialite Sandy Pittman. She helped provide Internet users with virtually up-to-the-minute reports on the
progress the expedition was making toward the summit, plus interviews with the climbers
and photographs. (She also brought along two laptops, five cameras, a CD-Rom player
and, according to some reports, a cappuccino machine.) There was a fax and a telephone
in a communications tent in Everest Base Camp that, via satellite transmission, allowed
climbers to stay in regular touch with family, friends, and businesses at home. The days

of hand-scrawled, coded messages carried down the mountainside by mail runners was as much a part of the distant past as hobnailed boots.[154]

Most clients who signed up with the commercial expeditions that spring were neophytes; whatever previous high-altitude experience they had was on guided climbs (like Sandy Pittman, who had paid guides to lead her up six of the Seven Summits). Krakauer, an experienced mountaineer, was an exception—although, even in his case, all his experience was on mountains below 14,000 feet. The most experienced client was Pete Schoening, veteran of K2 and Hidden Peak, who was hoping to make his first ascent of Everest with Scott Fischer's expedition, along with his nephew Klev Schoening. More typical was Hall client Beck Weathers, a wealthy pathologist who had climbed his first mountain at age forty, nine years earlier.

After several weeks of acclimatization, involving ever-higher forays onto the mountain, Fischer's and Hall's expeditions left Base Camp on May 6 for their summit bid. By the evening of May 9, the members of the two commercial expeditions, plus a third Taiwanese expedition (which, by prior agreement, was supposed to have delayed its own attempt another day to avoid overcrowding), were all in place on the South Col, readying themselves for a midnight departure for the summit.

What happened in the next twenty-four hours became one of the most famous episodes in mountaineering history—as well known as the story of Mallory and Irvine's disappearance and that of Hillary and Tenzing's triumph. Three separate years—1924, 1953, and 1996—define three distinct eras in the history of Himalayan mountaineering: the age of empire, the golden age, and the age of extremes.

The disaster that unfolded on May 10 had been predicted by *Mountain* magazine in 1990: there was no safety in numbers at the summit of Everest. Because the climbers were of widely mixed abilities, they moved at the pace of the slowest of their party. A bottleneck developed at the Hillary Step. Ropes that were supposed to have been fixed to the summit had not been put in place. Climbers stood around in the cold, using up their oxygen. Deadlines for turning around and heading back down the mountain were ignored by the guides, because the summit seemed so close, and perhaps also because their professional self-interest lay in seeing as many clients make it to the top as possible. And then the weather turned bad, with clouds and the snow whipped up by seventy-mile-an-hour winds reducing visibility and slowing the climbers' descent as darkness fell. Some of the hypoxic, exhausted climbers could not find their tents even when they had reached the South Col.

In the night of May 10–11, there were acts of exemplary heroism. Rob Hall refused to leave the side of his ailing client Doug Hansen at the Hillary Step, though he could have made it to the South Summit and revived himself with the oxygen stored there. Alerted by radio of Hall and Hansen's predicament, Hall's associate guide Andy Harris climbed back up from the South Summit carrying oxygen canisters for the two men stranded at the Hillary Step—and lost his own life as a consequence. Anatoli Boukreev, a guide on the

Fischer expedition, made some controversial decisions on May 10 (descending to the South Col while his clients were still struggling to the summit), but in the early hours of May 11 he braved the blizzard on the South Col to find and rescue three of the missing climbers. The leaders of two other commercial expeditions and an expedition making an IMAX film suspended their own summit attempts to come to the aid of the survivors.

There were also instances of gross indifference to human suffering. A South African expedition leader refused to lend his radio for the rescue effort. Three Indian climbers were trapped high on the Northeast Ridge on May 10, and early the next morning a Japanese party intent on the summit walked past them, though they were still alive. By the time the Japanese descended, one of the climbers was dead, another missing, and a third barely alive and tangled in his rope. They removed the rope from the survivor but made no effort to help him down the mountain. He too would die. "Above eight thousand meters," one of the Japanese climbers offered by way of self-justification, "is not a place where people can afford morality."[155]

Perhaps the best-remembered part of the story is Rob Hall's last communications from the mountainside before he died. Doug Hansen died or was lost during the night, and Hall finally set off to save himself. Somehow in the early morning hours of May 11 he had made his way down alone from the Hillary Step to the South Summit, where he radioed Base Camp at 4:43 A.M. Over the next fourteen hours, his friends at Base Camp urged him to rouse himself to make the effort to descend to the South Col. Hall had one lucky break; on the South Summit he came across the two oxygen bottles cached there, and by early morning was sounding more alert in his radio transmissions, though still unwilling or unable to descend any further. A rescue party of Sherpas set out but was driven back by the winds. Twice Hall talked to his pregnant wife back in New Zealand by radio patched through to her by satellite phone. The first time, early in the morning, there was still reason to think he might be rescued. The second time, shortly after 6:20 P.M., neither could have any illusions. "I love you," Hall said in farewell. "Sleep well my sweetheart. Please don't worry too much."[156]

The final toll for May 10–11 was eight dead: on the mountain's south side Hall, Harris, Hansen, Yasuko Namba (another Hall client, who died on the South Col), and Scott Fischer, and on the north side the three Indian climbers Tsewang Smanla, Tsewang Paljor, and Dorje Morup.[157]

Because the mountain was "wired," the general public followed the events almost as they were happening. By May 11 Internet reports were carrying the bad news around the world. By May 14 readers of the *New York Times* were reading Hall's last words to his wife on the newspaper's front page. A debate over the ethics of high-risk mountaineering began almost at once on the Web sites devoted to the climb. On *Outside* magazine's Web site, one woman who described herself as a friend of Beck Weathers (who survived, albeit with severe frostbite) wrote in to complain about the climbers' risk taking: "The pregnant wife left behind [by Rob Hall] cannot be comforted by her husband's bravery when she goes

Tengboche Monastery, 1950. Photograph by Betsy Cowles.
Courtesy of the Henry S. Hall Jr. American Alpine Club Library.

through the delivery of her child alone and has no father to greet and help raise this infant." Hall and Fischer had their defenders as well: "Rob and Scott Fischer died looking after their clients—they were the consummate professionals up until the end." The extravagant coverage of the disaster elicited a comment from another correspondent: "Although I do not doubt these climbers are brave . . . I really question the wisdom of these gala climbs. If the climbers are summiting for the 'personal challenge,' why all the media coverage? Why the Web page?"[158] Perhaps unconsciously he had echoed the most famous question-and-answer exchange in mountaineering history: "Why do you want to climb Everest?" "Because it is there." Why the Web page? Because a lot had happened to the world, and to mountaineering, since Mallory's time—and not all of it for the better.

Gather Courage

In the waning days of 1950 Charlie Houston, Bill Tilman, and their companions returned home from their Everest reconnaissance. They had been the first Westerners ever to travel in the Solu Khumbu, the first to stay in Namche Bazar, the first to meet the monks of Tengboche, and the first to see the southern exposure of Mount Everest from the ground up in Nepal. Houston's report for the *American Alpine Journal* made clear how blessed he felt in having had this opportunity:

> We had been for five weeks in an area never previously visited by Europeans or Americans. We had marched some 175 miles along rough valley trails, over three 10,000 foot passes, across rude bridges to reach the foot of the highest mountain on earth. There we had found a small community, centered in religion, self-sufficient, self-respecting, happy and healthy. Surrounded by scenery beyond description, this small lamasery and attendant village seemed to us a beautiful oasis in a troubled world. In all our travels we met nothing but friendliness and courtesy, and some of the people we met were extraordinarily kind to us. Our eyes were opened to a different way of life, a different religion. It was hard to return from this happy primitive land to a world in which our first news was of the U.N. reverses in Korea and of political unrest along many borders. It seemed at least debatable that we were returning to civilization. As we came back to the worries, the pleasures and the responsibilities placed upon us by our own way of life, we could not forget the motto over the public school in our favorite town of Dankhuta: "Gather courage, don't be a chicken-hearted fellow."[159]

This book has argued that the history of Himalayan climbing is intimately bound up with the "way of life" that climbers who came to the region from abroad had temporarily left behind (and to which, as in this instance, they were sometimes reluctant to return). Houston and Tilman, like Mallory and Irvine before them and Fischer and Hall after them, displayed the virtues and defects that came with being people of their own times. But a critical view of their history need not be a cynical one. To understand the story of these Himalayan mountaineers as involving something more than heroic adventure is not to deny the heroism they sometimes displayed, nor does it lessen the inspiration their adventures can still offer. As the villagers of Dankhuta so wisely advised visitors, Gather courage, don't be a chicken-hearted fellow.

Notes

CHAPTER ONE: *When Men and Mountains Meet*

1. For accessible introductions to Himalayan geology and tectonics, see Peter Molnar and Paul Tapponier, "The Collision between India and Eurasia," *Scientific American* 236 (Apr. 1977): 30–41; Peter Molnar, "The Geologic History and Structure of the Himalaya," *American Scientist* 74 (1986): 144–54; the Geological Survey of India's *Geology and Tectonics of the Himalaya*.

2. For a recent and invaluable study of the interaction of man and nature in the Himalaya, see Zurick and Karan, *Himalaya: Life on the Edge of the World*.

3. Burrard and Hayden, *A Sketch of the Geography and Geology of the Himalaya Mountains;* Mason, *Abode of Snow*.

4. See Kreutzmann, "The Karakoram Highway."

5. Smythe, *The Kangchenjunga Adventure*, 18.

6. Willy Merkl, "Die Deutsche-Amerikanische himalaja Expedition 1932," *Zeitschrift des Deutschen und Österreichischen Alpenvereins* (1933): 65. For the 1938 Schäfer expedition, see Kater, *Das "Ahnenerbe" der SS;* Hale, *Himmler's Crusade;* Pringle, *The Master Plan*.

7. Thapar, *A History of India,* 1:59; Mason, *Abode of Snow,* 56. For Aurel Stein's work in the region, see Meyer and Brysac, *Tournament of Shadows,* 352–78, 381–93.

8. For a full account of Jesuit exploration in the Himalaya, see Wessels, *Early Jesuit Travellers*.

9. See De Filippi, *An Account of Tibet.* Visiting the Tsug Lag Khan, the main Buddhist temple in Lhasa, in the late 1940s, the German mountaineer Heinrich Harrer was startled to find a bell inscribed "Te Deum Laudamus" hanging from the ceiling: a relic, no doubt, of the Jesuit mission. See Harrer, *Seven Years in Tibet,* 232.

10. For the geographical and cartographic construction of "British India," see Edney, *Mapping an Empire*.

11. Ibid., 135; Keay, *The Great Arc,* 39. For Bogle, see Markham, *Narratives of the Mission of George Bogle to Tibet;* Woodcock, *Into Tibet;* Lamb, *British India and Tibet*.

12. Keay, *The Great Arc,* 36.

13. Ibid., 42–47; Mason, *Abode of Snow,* 63–64.

14. For the official, in-house history of the Indian Survey, see Phillimore, *Historical Records of the Survey of India*.

15. Quoted in Meyer and Brysac, *Tournament of Shadows,* 20. For Moorcroft, see Alder, *Beyond Bokhara;* Keay, *When Men and Mountains Meet,* 17–47.

16. Keay, *The Great Arc,* 116; Tilman, *The Ascent of Nanda Devi,* 10.

17. Keay, *The Great Arc,* 163–64.

18. Hooker, *Himalayan Journals.* See also Huxley, *Life and Letters of Joseph Dalton Hooker;* Desmond, *Sir Joseph Dalton Hooker.*

19. For their own fairly impenetrable account of their adventures (which ended, sadly, in the murder of Adolf in Kashgar in 1857), see Hermann, Adolf, and Robert von Schlagintweit, *Results of a Scientific Mission to India and High Asia.* See also C. F. Meade, "The Schlagintweits and Ibi Gamin (Kamet)," *Alpine Journal* 33 (Mar. 1920): 70–75; Helga Alcock, "Three Pioneers: The Schlagintweit Brothers," *Himalayan Journal* 36 (1978–79): 156–61; Finkelstein, "'Conquerors of the Künlün'?" If anyone has priority over the Schlagintweits in the matter of sporting ascents, it would be the Gerard brothers, Alexander and James, who in 1817, according to their own unconfirmed reports, reached a height of 19,300 feet on Leo Pargial in the Zanskar range. See Unsworth, *Hold the Heights,* 229–30; Mehta and Kapadia, *Exploring the Hidden Himalaya,* 113.

20. Vigne, *Travels in Kashmir.* According to Ian Cameron, Vigne was "the first European to see the mountains as we see them today: not as an inanimate barrier, but as a manifestation of nature at its most magnificent." Cameron, *Mountains of the Gods,* 84–88. See also Keay, *When Men and Mountains Meet,* 80–104.

21. Keay, *When Men and Mountains Meet,* 193–94. Montgomerie awaits his biographer, but see R. H. Vetch, "Montgomerie, Thomas George (1830–1878)," rev. Elizabeth Baigent, *Oxford Dictionary of National Biography* (Oxford: Oxford University Press, 2004). The only local Balti name of any authenticity for K2 is Chogori, meaning Great Mountain, but by the time it came to light "K2" had evidently taken permanent hold of the world's imagination. See Curran, *K2,* 25–31.

22. Mason, *Abode of Snow,* 78.

23. H. H. Godwin-Austen, "On the Glaciers of the Mustakh Range," *Journal of the Royal Geographical Society of London* 34 (1864): 35.

24. Curran, *K2,* 35.

25. Godwin-Austen, "On the Glaciers of the Mustakh Range," 40. Remarkably, Godwin-Austen also still awaits his biographer. Meanwhile, for short sketches of his life, see Kenneth Mason, "Austen, Henry Haversham Godwin- (1834–1923)," rev. Elizabeth Baigent, *Oxford Dictionary of National Biography* (Oxford: Oxford University Press, 2004); T. H. Holdich, "Lieut.-Colonel Henry Haversham Godwin Austen," *Geographical Journal* 63 (1924): 175–76.

26. Keay, *When Men and Mountains Meet,* 201–11.

27. T. G. Montgomerie, "On the Geographical Position of Yarkund, and Some Other Places in Central Asia," *Journal of the Royal Geographical Society* 36 (1866): 157–58. For a complete history of the pundits and the clandestine exploration of Central Asia, see Waller, *The Pundits.* See also Hopkirk, *Trespassers on the Roof of the World;* Meyer and Brysac, *Tournament of Shadows,* 202–22; Mason, *Abode of Snow,* 84–95; Michael Ward, "The Survey of India and the Pundits," *Alpine Journal* 103 (1998): 59–79.

28. Montgomerie, "On the Geographical Position of Yarkand," 158; Mason, *Abode of Snow,* 92. For the Forsyth mission to Kashgar, see Forsyth, *Autobiography and Reminiscences of Sir Douglas Forsyth;* Waller, *The Pundits,* 144–68.

29. See T. G. Montgomerie, "Journey to Shigatze, in Tibet, and Return by Dingri-Maidan into Nepaul, in 1871, by the Native Explorer No. 9," *Journal of the Royal Geographical Society* 45 (1875): 330–49. See also Kenneth Mason, "Kishen Singh and the Indian Explorers," *Geographical Journal* 62 (Dec. 1923): 433–38. For a succinct summary of Hari Ram's expeditions, see Waller, *The Pundits,* 177–84. Remarkably, Hari Ram does

not figure in Walt Unsworth's otherwise definitive history of Everest exploration, *Everest*, but see Ward, *Everest*, 21–23.

30. Fleming, *Bayonets to Lhasa*, 67. For Younghusband, see Seaver, *Francis Younghusband*; French, *Younghusband*.

31. Francis Younghusband, "The Muztagh Pass in 1887," *Geographical Journal* 76 (Dec. 1930): 522; Keay, *The Gilgit Game*, 180. For Younghusband's full account of his 1887 journey, see "A Journey across Central Asia, from Manchuria and Peking to Kashmir, over the Mustagh Pass," *Proceedings of the Royal Geographical Society* 10 (Aug. 1888): 485–518. See also his travel memoir, *The Heart of a Continent*.

32. David Matless, "Younghusband, Sir Francis Edward (1863–1942)," *Oxford Dictionary of National Biography* (Oxford: Oxford University Press, 2004).

33. Stephen, *The Playground of Europe*. For recent histories of Alpine mountaineering, see Fleming, *Killing Dragons*; Ring, *How the English Made the Alps*; Braham, *When the Alps Cast Their Spell*.

34. The classic and still indispensable study of the origins of the mountain aesthetic is Nicolson, *Mountain Gloom and Mountain Glory*. See also Schama, *Landscape and Memory*; Macfarlane, *Mountains of the Mind*.

35. Ruskin, *Sesame and Lilies*, 53–54. For the social history of Alpine mountaineering, see Hansen, "British Mountaineering"; Veyne, "L'alpinisme"; Robbins, "Sport, Hegemony and the Middle Class."

36. Macfarlane, *Mountains of the Mind*, 87–88.

37. Petrarch, "The Ascent of Mont Ventoux," in Thompson, *Petrarch*. For Antoine de Ville, see Gribble, *The Early Mountaineers*, 29–35. For Gesner, see his *On the Admiration of Mountains*. For Simler, see Coolidge, *Josias Simler et les origines de l'alpinisme*; Lunn, *A Century of Mountaineering*, 27–28.

38. Matthews, *The Annals of Mont Blanc*, 336–40; Fleming, *Killing Dragons*, 10–11; Unsworth, *Hold the Heights*, 26. Peter Hansen understands Windham's sortie to Chamonix as "an early example of the global dispersal of British tourists which shaped Britain's national identity as an expansive imperial power" ("British Mountaineering," 19).

39. For three different versions of the first ascent of Mont Blanc, see Matthews, *The Annals of Mont Blanc*; Fleming, *Killing Dragons*, 38–51; and Engel, *A History of Mountaineering in the Alps*.

40. See Macfarlane, *Mountains of the Mind*, 158. For the early climbing history of the Chamonix Valley, see Bernstein, *Ascent*.

41. For Smith, see Hansen, "Albert Smith, the Alpine Club, and the Invention of Mountaineering"; and Schama, *Landscape and Memory*, 498–502.

42. Hansen, "British Mountaineering," 113–15.

43. Coolidge, *The Alps in Nature and History*, 239. For Whymper's own account of the Matterhorn disaster, see his classic *Scrambles amongst the Alps*. For the most recent of many retellings, see Conefrey and Jordan, *Mountain Men*, 27–48.

44. Freshfield, *Travels in the Central Caucasus and Bashan*; Slingsby, *Norway*; Whymper, *Travels amongst the Great Andes of the Equator*. See also Smythe, *Edward Whymper*, 237–40.

CHAPTER TWO: *The Age of Empire, 1892–1914*

1. Maurice de Déchy, "Mountain Travel in the Sikkim Himalaya," *Alpine Journal* 10 (Aug. 1880): 1–11; W. W. Graham, "Travel and Ascents in the Himalaya," *Proceedings of the Royal Geographical Society* 8 (Aug. 1884): 429; W. W. Graham, "Travel and Ascents in the Himalaya," *Alpine Journal* 12 (Aug. 1884): 37–39.

2. Graham, "Travel and Ascents" (*Alpine Journal*), 39, 45, 48–50. The literature surrounding Graham's disputed claims is enormous. See especially Mumm, *Five Months in the Himalaya*, 103–14; Waddell, *Among*

the Himalayas, 388–93; Mason, *Abode of Snow,* 93–95; Unsworth, *Hold the Heights,* 232–37. For Graham's own popular account of his expedition, see "Up the Himalayas: Mountaineering on the Indian Alps," *Good Words* 26 (1885): 18–23, 97–105, 172–78. How exactly Graham offended the worthies of the Alpine Club is unclear, but his nomination for membership was rejected by a heavy majority of forty-nine to seven. As Unsworth notes, he "had obviously blotted his social copybook somehow" (*Hold the Heights,* 392n12).

3. William Martin Conway, "Some Reminiscences and Reflections of an Old-Stager," *Alpine Journal* 31 (June 1917): 155–56. For a life of Conway, see Evans, *The Conways.* See also Conway's own memoirs, *Mountain Memories* and *Episodes in a Varied Life.*

4. Evans, *The Conways,* 132–34; Manton Marble to William Martin Conway, n.d. [1891?], Conway Papers, Add. 7676/G44, Cambridge University Library.

5. W. L. [illegible]-Dyer to William Martin Conway, Dec. 5, 1891, Conway Papers, Add. 7676/P145, Cambridge University Library. For the history of the Royal Geographical Society, see Cameron, *To the Farthest Ends of the Earth.*

6. Mummery, *My Climbs in the Alps and Caucasus,* 326; Conway, *Mountain Memories,* 123–24.

7. Conway, *Mountain Memories,* 126; A. F. Mummery to William Martin Conway, Aug. 29, 1891, Conway Papers, Add. 7676 P/137, Cambridge University Library.

8. Crowley, *Confessions,* 152. For Eckenstein, see David Dean, T. S. Blakeney, and D. F. O. Dangar, "Oscar Eckenstein, 1859–1921," *Alpine Journal* 65 (May 1960): 63–79.

9. Conway, *Mountain Memories,* 127; McCormick, *An Artist in the Himalayas,* 19. For Zurbriggen, see his memoir, *From the Alps to the Andes.* Bruce awaits his biographer, but see Kenneth Mason, "Bruce, Charles Granville (1866–1939)," rev. Peter H. Hansen, *Oxford Dictionary of National Biography* (Oxford: Oxford University Press, 2004). See also Bruce's own memoirs, *Twenty Years in the Himalaya* and *Himalayan Wanderer.* For a history of the Gurkhas, see Tuker, *Gorkha.*

10. M. E. Grant-Duff to Lansdowne, Oct. 7, 1891, Conway Papers, Add. 7676 P/141, Cambridge University Library; Lansdowne to M. E. Grant-Duff, Dec. 14, 1891, Conway Papers, Add. 7676 P/143, Cambridge University Library; Bruce, *Himalayan Wanderer,* 76–77.

11. Conway, *Climbing and Exploration,* 136.

12. Conway, *Mountain Memories,* 145; Conway, *Climbing and Exploration,* 350–60; Eckenstein, *Karakorams and Kashmir,* 148–61. Though Uzum Brakk (21,069ft/6,422m) is still known colloquially as Conway's Ogre, the name Ogre pure and simple, for reasons no one understands, now applies to Baintha Brakk (23,897ft/7,284m), the highest summit in the group.

13. Eckenstein, *Karakorams and Kashmir,* 198; C. G. Bruce to Lord Aberdare, Aug. 15, 1892, Conway Papers, Add. 7676 P/181/2, Cambridge University Library. In his expedition account Conway attributed Eckenstein's departure to illness. As Eckenstein had "never been well since reaching Gilgit," he wrote, "I now decided that he had better return to England" (*Climbing and Exploration,* 416).

14. *The Times,* Aug. 16, 1892; Evans, *The Conways,* 141.

15. C. G. Bruce to Lord Aberdare, Aug. 15, 1892, Conway Papers, Add. 7676 P/181/2, Cambridge University Library. In German-speaking Switzerland, the Aletsch glacial junction that Conway had in mind is actually called Konkordiaplatz, which explains why his Place de la Concorde has come to be known today as Concordia.

16. C. G. Bruce to Lord Aberdare, Aug. 15, 1892, Conway Papers, Add. 7676 P/181/2, Cambridge University Library; Conway, *Mountain Memories,* 155; Conway, *Climbing and Exploration,* 454–55.

17. Conway, *Climbing and Exploration,* 524. For Conway's first account of the ascent of Pioneer Peak, see *The Times,* Oct. 27, 1892. See also Zurbriggen, *From the Alps to the Andes,* 93–99; Bruce, *Himalayan Wanderer,*

100–2. Latest measurements of Conway's "Pioneer Peak," really not an independent peak at all but a high point on a ridge, put it at 21,489 feet (6,550 meters).

18. Douglas Freshfield to Martin Conway, Aug. 24, 1892, Conway Papers, Add. 7676/N12, Cambridge University Library; Manton Marble to Martin Conway, Mar. 14, 1893, Conway Papers, Add. 7676/G/50, Cambridge University Library; *National Observer,* Dec. 15, 1894. For Conway's address to the Royal Geographical Society, see *Proceedings of the Royal Geographical Society* n.s. 14 (1892): 753–770. See also, in addition to his book, W. M. Conway, "Climbing in the Karakorams," *Alpine Journal* 16 (Aug. 1893): 413–22.

19. Martin Conway to Elgin, Dec. 27, 1895, Conway Papers, Add. 7676P/272a, Cambridge University Library; Rosebery to Martin Conway, May 24, 1895, Conway Papers, Add. 7676/P244, Cambridge University Library.

20. Mummery, *My Climbs in the Alps and Caucasus,* viii.

21. W. E. Davidson to Edward Whymper, Mar. 16, 1895, Blakeney Collection, Add. Mss. 63112, British Library.

22. Mummery, *My Climbs in the Alps and Caucasus,* 2nd ed., xxi; Collie, *Climbing on the Himalaya and Other Mountain Ranges,* 43–54.

23. C. G. Bruce, "The Passing of Mummery," *Himalayan Journal* 3 (Apr. 1931): 4; Mummery, *My Climbs in the Alps and Caucasus,* 2nd ed., xxxiii–xxxiv.

24. Collie, *Climbing on the Himalaya and Other Mountain Ranges,* 71; Bruce, "The Passing of Mummery," 8.

25. Mummery, *My Climbs in the Alps and Caucasus,* 2nd ed., xxxvi.

26. Ibid., xxxviii–xxxix.

27. Geoffrey Hastings to [?] Mummery (copy), Sept. 8, 1895, Conway Papers, Add. P/267a, Cambridge University Library.

28. J. N. Collie to Geoffrey Winthrop Young, n.d. [May 1942], typescript copy, Graham Brown Papers, Acc. 4338, box 215/1, National Library of Scotland. For Collie's immediate account of the expedition, see his "Climbing on the Nanga Parbat Range, Kashmir," *Alpine Journal* 18 (Feb. 1896): 17–32. See also Mill, *Norman Collie;* Unsworth, *Tiger in the Snow.* For press coverage of the death of Mummery, see *The Times,* Nov. 12, 1895.

29. Mummery, *My Climbs in the Alps and Caucasus,* 2nd ed., xxix. For an approach to mountaineering in terms of neoimperialism, see Ellis, *Vertical Margins.*

30. Workman and Workman, *In the Ice World of Himálaya,* 1.

31. Ibid., 97.

32. Mason, *Abode of Snow,* 132; Middleton, *Victorian Lady Travellers,* 86. For the Workmans' exploration of the Chogo Lungma Glacier, see their *Ice-Bound Heights of the Mustagh.* See also William Hunter Workman, "Some Obstacles to Himalayan Mountaineering and the History of a Record Ascent," *Alpine Journal* 22 (Aug. 1905): 489–506.

33. Bruce, *Twenty Years in the Himalaya,* 87–106; Neve, *Thirty Years in Kashmir,* 172–83; Neve, *A Crusader in Kashmir,* 60; Mason, *Abode of Snow,* 111. For the Neve brothers, see also Neve, *Beyond the Pir Panjal.*

34. Mason, *Abode of Snow,* 131; Middleton, *Victorian Lady Travellers,* 84.

35. In order to establish their claim to this "highest camp" record, the Workmans had to go out of their way to discredit Tom Longstaff's assertion that he had bivouacked at 23,000 feet on Gurla Mandhata (25,242ft/ 7,694m) in 1905. When the subject then came up for discussion before the Royal Geographical Society in November 1907, Longstaff surrendered his own claim but suggested that the surveyor W. H. Johnson had camped at 22,000 feet in the Kunlun mountains of Tibet in 1864. This too the Workmans vigorously disputed in

print. See T. G. Longstaff, "Six Months' Wandering in the Himalaya," *Alpine Journal* 23 (Aug. 1906): 222–23; Fanny Bullock Workman, "Highest Camps and Climbs," *Appalachia* 11 (June 1907): 257–59; "An Exploration of the Nun Kun Group and Its Glaciers: Discussion," *Geographical Journal* 31 (Jan. 1908): 41; the Workmans' *Peaks and Glaciers of Nun Kun*, 76–79.

36. Workman and Workman, *Peaks and Glaciers of Nun Kun*, 88. Bullock Workman's high-altitude record for women appeared briefly threatened in 1908 when her compatriot Annie Peck (whose previous record she had bested) claimed to have reached 24,000 feet on Huascarán in the Peruvian Andes. Outraged and incredulous, Bullock Workman enlisted the help of the Société générale d'études et de travaux topographiques of Paris and dispatched to Peru at her own $13,000 expense a three-man survey team under the direction of Etienne de Larminant of the Service geographique de l'armes. With the help of the Peruvian government, de Larminant carried out a complete triangulation of the Huascarán massif and fixed the height of the lower north summit (which Peck had climbed) at 21,812 feet (6,650 meters). Vindicated but still not satisfied, Bullock Workman saw to the prominent publication of de Larminant's findings and undertook herself to discredit Peck's claims in *Scientific American* and in a reserved chapter of her and her husband's account of their 1908 expedition to the Karakoram. For Peck's original claim, see "The Conquest of Huascarán," *Bulletin of the American Geographical Society* 41 (June 1909): 355–65. For Bullock Workman's reply, see "Miss Peck and Mrs. Workman," *Scientific American* 102 (Feb. 12 and 26, Apr. 16, 1910). Correspondence and publications relating to the subsequent controversy are in the archives of the American Alpine Club Library. For good secondary accounts, see Miller, *On Top of the World*, 122–24; Olds, *Women of the Four Winds*, 57–60. For a fictional rendering of the encounter between Annie Peck and Fanny Bullock Workman, see Waterman and Waterman, *A Fine Kind of Madness*, 37–48.

37. Kenneth Mason, "A Note on the Topography of the Nun Kun Massif in Ladakh," *Geographical Journal* 56 (Aug. 1920): 124–28. For their 1908 expedition to the Karakoram, see Workman and Workman, *The Call of the Snowy Hispar*.

38. Workman and Workman, *Two Summers in the Ice-Wilds of Eastern Karakoram*. Accompanying the Workman expedition to the Siachen in 1912 were two trained surveyors: Grant Peterkin of the Royal Geographical Society and Surjan Singh of the Indian Survey. The topographical results were therefore, as Kenneth Mason wrote, "in an entirely different category to those of the Workmans' earlier ventures" (*Abode of Snow*, 139). Of the many maps that supplemented the Workmans' books, only Peterkin's map of the Siachen has stood the test of time.

39. Middleton, *Victorian Lady Travellers*, 89. For other biographical portraits of Fanny Bullock and William Hunter Workman, see Rittenhouse, *Seven Women Explorers*, 79–101; Michael Plint, "The Workmans: Travellers Extraordinary," *Himalayan Journal* 49 (1991–92): 47–57; Robinson, *Wayward Women*, 30–31; Stetoff, *Women of the World*, 57–68; Tarbell, "Mrs. Fanny Bullock Workmen [*sic*]"; Tingley, "Fanny Bullock Workman."

40. Curran, *K2*, 65. Judging from a photograph in *Two Summers in the Ice-Wilds of Eastern Karakoram* (facing p. 216), Bullock Workman had a habit of inscribing in enormous characters her initials and dates of passage—F.B.W. AUG 25 1912—on virginal mountain walls in the Karakoram: sure evidence if any were needed of her essentially touristic sensibility.

41. Symonds, *The Great Beast*, 37; Crowley, *Confessions*, 151.

42. Crowley, *Confessions*, 279.

43. Ibid., 281.

44. Ibid., 312.

45. For more reliable original accounts of the 1902 K2 expedition than Crowley's, see Jacot-Guillarmod, *Six mois dans l'Himalaya*; Heinrich Pfannl, "Eine Belagerung des Tschogo-Ri (K2) in der Mustagh-kette des Hindukusch," *Zeitschrift des Deutschen und Österreichischen Alpenvereins* 25 (1904).

46. Crowley, *Confessions,* 420, 425.

47. Ibid., 433. For Freshfield's 1899 circumnavigation of Kangchenjunga, see his *Round Kangchenjunga.* See also Morrow and Morrow, *Footsteps in the Clouds,* an account of a commemorative repeat of the circumnavigation a century later.

48. Crowley, *Confessions,* 440, 444; Smythe, *The Kangchenjunga Adventure,* 33; Symonds, *The Great Beast,* 80. For Jacot-Guillarmod's version of events, see his "Au Kangchinjunga."

49. See Crowley's "Plan to climb Mount Everest, next year, after the fiasco of the present imbeciles" (facsimile) in *Confessions,* plate 15. Nothing so drove Crowley to distraction as the pseudo-science (as he saw it) of acclimatization. "To talk of acclimatization," he wrote, "is to adopt the psychology of the man who trained his horse gradually to live on a single straw a day, and would have revolutionized our system of nutrition, if the balky brute had not been aggravating enough to die on his hands." No. The only thing for it at great altitude, Crowley believed, was "to lay in a stock of energy, get rid of all your fat the exact moment when you have a chance to climb a mountain, and jump back out of its reach, so to speak, before it can take its revenge" (*Confessions,* 320). Crowley thus anticipated today's high-altitude mantra of "get in, get up, get out."

50. Bates and Houston, *Five Miles High,* 184–85.

51. Whymper, *A Right Royal Mountaineer.* For a recent biography, see Tenderini and Shandrick, *The Duke of the Abruzzi.*

52. De Filippi, *The Ascent of Mount St. Elias;* De Filippi, *Ruwenzori.*

53. Younghusband, *Everest,* 6. For the official account of the duke's K2 expedition, see De Filippi, *Karakoram and Western Himalaya.*

54. Watson, "Picturing the Sublime," 125; Clark, *The Splendid Hills,* 5.

55. Clark, *The Splendid Hills,* 13; *Proceedings of the Royal Geographical Society* 12 (Feb. 1890): 97.

56. *Proceedings of the Royal Geographical Society* 12 (May 1890): 288; Freshfield, *The Exploration of the Caucasus.*

57. Adams, "Vittorio Sella."

58. Tenderini and Shandrick, *The Duke of the Abruzzi,* 104.

59. Tilman, *Mount Everest.*

60. On this point, see Ellis, *Vertical Margins,* 135–36.

61. De Filippi, *Karakoram and Western Himalaya,* 218.

62. Ibid., 231; Filippo De Filippi, "H.R.H. the Duke of the Abruzzi's Expedition to the Karakoram," *Alpine Journal* 25 (Nov. 1910): 339.

63. De Filippi, *Karakoram and Western Himalaya,* 248–49; Curran, *K2,* 69.

64. For Longstaff's 1909 expedition, see his *This My Voyage,* 160–92; T. G. Longstaff, "Glacier Exploration in the Eastern Karakoram," *Geographical Journal* 35 (June 1910): 622–53. Owing to a sighting error in Longstaff's triangulation that resulted in an altitude estimate of almost 30,000 feet, Teram Kangri briefly displaced Everest as the highest mountain in the world until 1910, when the Indian Survey accurately fixed its height at 24,489 feet. See Longstaff, *This My Voyage,* 173; Mason, *Abode of Snow,* 137.

65. Younghusband, *Everest,* 6.

66. Clark, *An Eccentric in the Alps,* 100–1; *The Times,* July 9, 1953; Bruce, *Himalayan Wanderer,* 124–25; Unsworth, *Everest,* 12–13; Ward, *Everest,* 24.

67. Curzon to Freshfield, July 2 and 9, 1899, Oriental and India Office Collection, Mss. Eur. F111/181, British Library; Ronaldshay, *Life of Lord Curzon,* 2:166–67.

68. For the 1904 mission to Lhasa, see Younghusband, *India and Tibet;* Fleming, *Bayonets to Lhasa.*

69. Rawling, *The Great Plateau*, 212–13. See also C. H. D. Ryder, "Exploration and Survey with the Tibet Frontier Commission, and from Gyangtse to Simla via Gartok," *Geographical Journal* 26 (1905): 369–95.

70. Unsworth, *Everest*, 14–15; Hansen, "Vertical Boundaries," 62.

71. D. W. Freshfield to James Bryce, Dec. 2, 1906, Bryce Papers, Bodleian Library. See also Hansen, "Vertical Boundaries"; Hansen, "British Mountaineering," 431–33; T. S. Blakeney, "The First Steps towards Mount Everest," *Alpine Journal* 76 (May 1971): 43–44.

72. Longstaff, *This My Voyage*, 92. For the 1905 attempt on Gurla Mandhata, see Longstaff, "Six Months' Wandering in the Himalaya."

73. For the ascent of Trisul, see T. G. Longstaff, "A Mountaineering Expedition to the Himalaya of Garhwal," *Geographical Journal* 31 (Apr. 1908): 361–88; T. G. Longstaff, "Mountaineering in Garhwal," *Alpine Journal* 24 (May 1908): 107–33; Longstaff, *This My Voyage*, 84–113; Mumm, *Five Months in the Himalaya*; Bruce, *Himalayan Wanderer*, 165–84. In 1931 Edward Norton of Everest fame wrote that "Longstaff's feat in conquering Trisul . . . by a climb of 6000 feet up and down in one day, constitutes a *tour de force* worthy of more remark than it has received in all the quarter of a century during which he held the world's record for the highest summit conquered" (*Himalayan Journal* 3 [Apr. 1931]: 133–36).

74. C. W. Rubenson, "Kabru in 1907," *Alpine Journal* 24 (Nov. 1908): 310–21. See also C. W. Rubenson, "An Ascent of Kabru," *Alpine Journal* 24 (Feb. 1908): 63–67.

75. Bruce, *Twenty Years in the Himalaya*, 28.

76. The most extensive biographical profile of Kellas is in German: P. Geissler, "Alexander M. Kellas, ein Pioneer des Himalaja," *Deutsche Alpenzeitung* 30 (1935): 103–10. See also John B. West, "A. M. Kellas: Pioneer Himalayan Physiologist and Mountaineer," *Alpine Journal* 94 (1989–90): 207–13; Scott, "Kellas, Alexander Mitchell (1868–1921)."

77. "The Late Dr. Kellas's Early Expeditions to the Himalaya," *Alpine Journal* 34 (Nov. 1922): 408–10.

78. A. M. Kellas, "The Mountains of Northern Sikkim and Garhwal," *Geographical Journal* 40 (Sept. 1912): 249.

79. Kellas, "The Mountains of Northern Sikkim and Garhwal," 258–60.

80. A. M. Kellas, "A Fourth Visit to the Sikhim Himalaya," *Alpine Journal* 27 (May 1913): 125–52; Noel, *Through Tibet to Everest*, 89–90. See also J. B. L. Noel, "A Journey to Tashirak in Southern Tibet, and the Eastern Approaches to Mount Everest," *Geographical Journal* 53 (May 1919): 289–303. For the Sherpa photographs purporting to be of glaciers descending from Everest and Makalu, see the *Geographical Journal* 53 (May 1919): 289–303.

81. C. G. Bruce, "Mount Everest," *Geographical Journal* 57 (Jan. 1921): 3–4; Longstaff, *This My Voyage*, 152; Hansen, "Vertical Boundaries," 71; *Alpine Journal* 24 (1908): 189–90; Curzon to Morley, June 11, June 20, 1909, Oriental and India Office Collection, Mss. Eur. D573/43(e), British Library.

CHAPTER THREE: *"Because It Is There," 1921–1924*

1. Robertson, *George Mallory*, 122–23.

2. T. H. Holdich to Edwin Montagu (draft), Dec. 19, 1918, Mount Everest Expedition Archives, 1/1, Royal Geographical Society; Edwin Montagu to Lord Chelmsford, Jan. 17, 1919, Oriental and India Office Collection, L/P&S/10/777, British Library; J. E. Shuckburgh, Minute, Apr. 25, 1919, Oriental and India Office Collection, L/P&S/10/777, British Library.

3. *Geographical Journal* 53 (May 1919): 289; Younghusband, *The Heart of Nature*, 212. For contemporary press coverage of Noel's lecture, see *The Times*, June 1, 1920.

4. *Punch,* Mar. 19, 1919; *Daily News,* June 3, 1920; Bell, as reported in Chelmsford to India Office, telegram, July 24, 1920, Oriental and India Office Collection, L/P&S/10/777, British Library; Bell, *A Portrait of the Dalai Lama,* 243–45.

5. Expedition Committee Memorandum, Apr. 26, 1920, Mount Everest Expedition Archives, 1/1, Royal Geographical Society; Younghusband, *The Epic of Mount Everest,* 24; Resolutions of the Joint Everest Committee, Jan. 12, 1921, Mount Everest Expedition Archives, 1/13, Royal Geographical Society.

6. *Morning Post,* Jan. 1, 1921; *Lady's Pictorial,* Jan. 22, 1921.

7. Douglas Freshfield to Lord Curzon, Oct. 18, 1906, Oriental and India Office Collection, Eur/F111/183, British Library; Howard-Bury, *Mount Everest,* 15.

8. Younghusband, *The Epic of Mount Everest,* 27.

9. "As with so many aspects of his life, Mallory failed to make the significant contributions to climbing which were expected of him," writes Walt Unsworth, "and far from being the greatest mountaineer of his day, he was not really in the leading cadre" (*Everest,* 43). For biographies of Mallory see, among others, Pye, *George Leigh Mallory;* Robertson, *George Mallory;* Green, *Mallory of Everest;* and, most recently, Gillman and Gillman, *The Wildest Dream.*

10. Robertson, *George Mallory,* 17.

11. R. L. G. Irving, "George Herbert Leigh Mallory," *Alpine Journal* 36 (Nov. 1924): 383.

12. Mallory, *Boswell the Biographer.*

13. Gillman and Gillman, *The Wildest Dream,* 32; Robertson, *George Mallory,* 37.

14. Holroyd, *Lytton Strachey,* 1:441–42.

15. Young, *Mountains with a Difference,* 25; Robertson, *George Mallory,* 51.

16. R. L. G. Irving, "Five Years with Recruits," *Alpine Journal* 24 (Feb. 1909): 367–81, 453; Gillman and Gillman, *The Wildest Dream,* 51; Young, Sutton, and Noyce, *Snowdon Biography,* 36–37.

17. Breashears and Salkeld, *Last Climb,* 37; Pye, *George Leigh Mallory,* 57. For the most complete statement of his mountaineering philosophy, see Mallory, "The Mountaineer as Artist."

18. Virginia Woolf, *Mr. Bennett and Mrs. Brown* (London: Hogarth, 1924), 4–5. For a book-length reflection on the significance of Woolf's remark, see Stansky, *On or about December 1910.*

19. Graves, *Good-bye to All That,* 62. The classic and still indispensable evocation of these turbulent years in British history is Dangerfield, *The Strange Death of Liberal England* (New York: Smith and Haas, 1935).

20. Pye, *George Leigh Mallory,* 73; Breashears and Salkeld, *Last Climb,* 40.

21. Gillman and Gillman, *The Wildest Dream,* 122; Mallory, *War Work for Boys and Girls;* Robertson, *George Mallory,* 103.

22. Gillman and Gillman, *The Wildest Dream,* 139.

23. Robertson, *George Mallory,* 106–7, 111; Gillman and Gillman, *The Wildest Dream,* 139–40.

24. George Mallory, "Mont Blanc from the Col du Géant by the Eastern Buttress of Mont Maudit," *Alpine Journal* 32 (Sept. 1918): 148–62.

25. Robertson, *George Mallory,* 121; George Mallory to Herbert Mallory, Oct. 14, 1918, Mallory Papers, F/GM/III/i, Magdalene College Library; George Mallory to Ruth Mallory, Nov. 12, 1918, Mallory Papers, F/GM/III/i, Magdalene College Library.

26. Robertson, *George Mallory,* 143.

27. George Mallory to Gilbert Murray, June 14, 1920, *Alpine Journal* 105 (2000): 161; Robertson, *George Mallory,* 130, 148.

28. Robertson, *George Mallory,* 148; Younghusband, *The Epic of Mount Everest,* 26; George Mallory to Geoffrey Winthrop Young, Feb. 10, 1912, Mount Everest Expedition Archives, 3/5, Royal Geographical Society.

29. George Mallory to Mount Everest Committee, Feb. 22, 1921, Mount Everest Expedition Archives, 3/4, Royal Geographical Society.

30. Statement of A. F. R. Wollaston, n.d. [1921], Mount Everest Expedition Archives, 3/1, Royal Geographical Society; George Mallory to Francis Younghusband, Mar. 11, 1921, Mount Everest Expedition Archives, 3/4, Royal Geographical Society; Gillman and Gillman, *The Wildest Dream,* 179.

31. George Mallory to Geoffrey Winthrop Young, Mar. 9, 1921, Mount Everest Expedition Archives, 3/3, Royal Geographical Society; George Mallory to Arthur Hinks, Mar. 27, 1921, Mount Everest Expedition Archives, 3/4, Royal Geographical Society; Arthur Hinks to George Mallory, Mar. 29, 1921, Mount Everest Expedition Archives, 3/4, Royal Geographical Society; George Mallory to Francis Younghusband, Mar. 31, 1921, Mount Everest Expedition Archives, 3/4, Royal Geographical Society.

32. Robertson, *George Mallory,* 150; Gillman and Gillman, *The Wildest Dream,* 183.

33. George Mallory to Ruth Mallory, May 17, 1921, Blakeney Collection, Add. Mss. 63119, British Library; George Mallory to Ruth Mallory, May 24, 1921, Mallory Papers, F/GM/III/i, Magdalene College Library.

34. Macfarlane, *Mountains of the Mind,* 240–41; George Mallory to Ruth Mallory, June 5, 1921, Mallory Papers, F/GM/III/i, Magdalene College Library.

35. Robertson, *George Mallory,* 154; Gillman and Gillman, *The Wildest Dream,* 187.

36. Howard-Bury, *Mount Everest,* 183–86; Robertson, *George Mallory,* 155.

37. Howard-Bury, *Mount Everest,* 188.

38. Ibid., 192.

39. Ibid., 197–98; George Mallory to Ruth Mallory, June 28, 1921, Blakeney Collection, Add. Mss. 63119, British Library.

40. Robertson, *George Mallory,* 158; George Mallory to Ruth Mallory, July 6, 1921, Blakeney Collection, Add. Mss. 63119, British Library; George Mallory to Rupert Thompson, July 12, 1921, Mallory Papers, F/GM/III/i, Magdalene College Library.

41. George to Ruth Mallory, July 28, 1921, Mallory Papers, F/GM/III/i, Magdalene College Library; George Mallory to Ruth Mallory, Aug. 9, 1921, Mallory Papers, F/GM/III/i, Magdalene College Library; Howard-Bury, *Mount Everest,* 230.

42. Howard-Bury, *Mount Everest,* 238; Robertson, *George Mallory,* 172; George Mallory to Ruth Mallory, Aug. 22, 1921, Blakeney Collection, Add. Mss. 63119, British Library.

43. Gillman and Gillman, *The Wildest Dream,* 195.

44. George Mallory to Geoffrey Winthrop Young, Sept. 9, 1921, Mount Everest Expedition Archives, 3/3, Royal Geographical Society.

45. Howard-Bury, *Mount Everest,* 258; George Mallory to Francis Younghusband, Oct. 13, 1921, Mount Everest Expedition Archives, 3/4, Royal Geographical Society.

46. Howard-Bury, *Mount Everest,* 259; George Mallory to Francis Younghusband, Oct. 13, 1921, Mount Everest Expedition Archives, 3/4, Royal Geographical Society; Robertson, *George Mallory,* 172; George Mallory to Ruth Mallory, Sept. 29, 1921, Mallory Papers, F/GM/III/i, Magdalene College Library.

47. *The Times,* Oct. 11, 1921.

48. Robertson, *George Mallory,* 177.

49. Charles Howard-Bury to Arthur Hinks, Dec. 1, 1921, Mount Everest Expedition Archives, 13/1/70, Royal Geographical Society; George Mallory to Francis Younghusband, Jan. 14, 1922, Mount Everest Expedition Archives, 3/4, Royal Geographical Society.

50. Unsworth, *Everest,* 72.

51. Ibid., 76. See also P. J. H. Unna, "The Oxygen Equipment of the 1922 Everest Expedition," *Alpine Journal* 34 (May 1922): 235–50. For a general introduction to the subject of oxygen and high-altitude physiology, see Houston, *Going Higher;* Hornbein and Schoene, *High Altitude.*

52. Gillman and Gillman, *The Wildest Dream,* 206–7; Robertson, *George Mallory,* 183; Finch, *The Making of a Mountaineer,* 293.

53. Robertson, *George Mallory,* 183; George Mallory to Ruth Mallory, Mar. [4?] and 16, 1922, Blakeney Collection, Add. Mss. 63119, British Library.

54. George Mallory to Ruth Mallory, Apr. 6, 1922, Blakeney Collection, Add. Mss. 63119, British Library; George Mallory to Ruth Mallory, Apr. 26, 1922, Mallory Papers, F/GM/III/ii, Magdalene College Library; Gillman and Gillman, *The Wildest Dream,* 209.

55. Bruce, *The Assault on Mount Everest,* 47; Murray, *The Story of Everest,* 208. See also Macdonald, "The Lama and the General"; Hansen, "The Dancing Lamas of Everest," 721–24.

56. Noel, *Through Tibet to Everest,* 152.

57. Somervell, *After Everest,* 61–62.

58. George Mallory to Ruth Mallory, May [18], 1922, Mallory Papers, F/GM/III/ii, Magdalene College Library; *The Times,* June 16, 1922.

59. *The Times,* June 16, 1922; George Mallory to Ruth Mallory, May 26, 1922, Mallory Papers, F/GM/III/ii, Magdalene College Library.

60. George Mallory to Ruth Mallory, May 26, 1922, Mallory Papers, F/GM/III/ii, Magdalene College Library; Finch, *The Making of a Mountaineer,* 327.

61. Unsworth, *Everest,* 96; George Mallory to Ruth Mallory, June 1, 1922, Mallory Papers, F/GM/III/ii, Magdalene College Library.

62. Bruce, *The Assault on Mount Everest,* 282; George Mallory to Ruth Mallory, June 9, 1922, Mallory Papers, F/GM/III/ii, Magdalene College Library.

63. George Mallory to Francis Younghusband, June 11, 1922, Mount Everest Expedition Archives, 3/4, Royal Geographical Society; Breashears and Salkeld, *Last Climb,* 118; Bruce, *The Assault on Mount Everest,* 286.

64. Charles Bruce to Francis Younghusband, June 11, 1922, Mount Everest Expedition Archives, 18/1, Royal Geographical Society.

65. *New York Times,* Jan. 18, 1923; Lee Keedick to Gerald Christy, Feb. 17, 1923, Mount Everest Expedition Archives, 25/4, Royal Geographical Society; Arthur Hinks to George Mallory, Feb. 27, 1923, Mount Everest Expedition Archives, 3/4, Royal Geographical Society.

66. Robertson, *George Mallory,* 216.

67. *The Times,* Mar. 27, 1924; George Mallory to Geoffrey Winthrop Young, Oct. 18, 1924, Mount Everest Expedition Archives, 3/3, Royal Geographical Society.

68. Robertson, *George Mallory,* 221.

69. Mount Everest Committee financial report, Nov. 26, 1923, Blakeney Collection, Add. Mss. 63122, British Library. For a full page of Everest Committee product endorsements (Bovril, Morawattee Tea, Ingersolls watches), see *The Times,* Dec. 10, 1924. See also Ellis, *Vertical Margins,* 140.

70. Noel, "Photographing *The Epic of Everest*," 368; Ellis, *Vertical Margins*, 142; *Weekly Dispatch*, Feb. 17, 1924. For more on Noel and "the affair of the dancing lamas," see Unsworth, *Everest*, 142–57; Ellis, *Vertical Margins*, 172–73; Hansen, "The Dancing Lamas of Everest."

71. Robertson, *George Mallory*, 223, 226; Gillman and Gillman, *The Wildest Dream*, 245; Norton, *The Fight for Everest*, 208.

72. Norton, *The Fight for Everest*, 208, 217; George Mallory to Ruth Mallory, Apr. 12, 1924, Mallory Papers, F/GM/III/iv, Magdalene College Library; Younghusband, *The Epic of Mount Everest*, 191–92.

73. Norton, *The Fight for Everest*, 219–20.

74. Unsworth, *Everest*, 111; Robertson, *George Mallory*, 232.

75. Noel, *Through Tibet to Everest*, 226; Robertson, *George Mallory*, 241.

76. A. W. Vincent to Arthur Hinks, Oct. 12, 1924, Mount Everest Expedition Archives, 31/1, Royal Geographical Society. For the India Pavilion, see Greenhalgh, *Ephemeral Vistas*, 61–62.

77. Noel, *Through Tibet to Everest*, 233; George Mallory to Ruth Mallory May 16, 1924, Mallory Papers, F/GM/III/iv, Magdalene College Library.

78. George Mallory to Ruth Mallory, May 27, 1924, Mallory Papers, F/GM/III/iv, Magdalene College Library.

79. Norton, *The Fight for Everest*, 95; Breashears and Salkeld, *Last Climb*, 160.

80. Norton, *The Fight for Everest*, 108.

81. Ibid., 112.

82. Breashears and Salkeld, *Last Climb*, 171.

83. Norton, *The Fight for Everest*, 125.

84. Ibid.; *The Times*, July 5, 1924; *Alpine Journal* 36 (Nov. 1924).

CHAPTER FOUR: *"A Random Harvest of Delight," 1929–1933*

1. Norton, *The Fight for Everest*, 145; Unsworth, *Everest*, 132; Douglas Freshfield to Arthur Hinks, June 29 and July 5, 1924, Mount Everest Expedition Archives, 26/5/9–12, Royal Geographical Society; Somervell, *After Everest*, 135. "Did Mallory and Irvine lay down their lives in vain?" Somervell asked himself fifteen years after the tragedy. "It is a sad thing that they never returned to tell the tale of endeavour, and possibly of conquest. But nobody can hold that lives lost in fighting Nature's greatest obstacles in the name of adventure and exploration are thrown away. *Dulce et decorum est pro patria mori;* and surely death in battle against a mountain is a finer and nobler thing than death whilst attempting to kill someone else" (*After Everest*, 138).

2. *The Times*, Aug. 19, 1924; Norton, *The Fight for Everest*, 148–49; Robertson, *George Mallory*, 254; Breashears and Salkeld, *Last Climb*, 190; Geoffrey Winthrop Young to Francis Younghusband, Aug. 19, 1924, Oriental and India Office Collection, Mss. Eur. F197/115, British Library.

3. Geoffrey Winthrop Young to Douglas Freshfield (copy), Aug. 19, 1924, Mount Everest Expedition Archives, 26/5/14, Royal Geographical Society; Robertson, *George Mallory*, 250–51; *The Times*, Oct. 18, 1924; *Alpine Journal* 36 (Nov. 1924): 274–75; Breashears and Salkeld, *Last Climb*, 194. The finding of Mallory's body on the North Face of Everest in 1999 seems to have confirmed that he died in a fall after dark—his climbing rope was severed, his ankle broken, and his sun goggles in his pocket—but it has done nothing to settle the question of whether he or Irvine reached the summit. For a sampling of the voluminous and competitive literature that the discovery inspired, see Hemmleb, Johnson, and Simonson, *Ghosts of Everest;* Holzel and Salkeld, *The Mystery of Mallory and Irvine;* Breashears and Salkeld, *Last Climb;* Firstbrook, *Lost on Everest;* Anker and Roberts, *The Lost Explorer*.

4. Arthur Hinks to F. M. Bailey, Nov. 5, 1924, Mount Everest Expedition Archives, 27, Royal Geographical Society. According to Unsworth, both Hinks and the Everest Committee suffered from unreasonable "Finch-mania." The person who did have private designs on Everest was one Captain Angus Buchanan, a desert explorer who resented the committee's exclusive access. See Unsworth, *Everest,* 732n14.

5. F. M. Bailey to Arthur Hinks, Nov. 18, 1924, Mount Everest Expedition Archives, 24/2, Royal Geographical Society. For Noel and his "dancing lamas," see Hansen, "The Dancing Lamas of Everest"; Unsworth, *Everest,* 142–57; Ellis, *Vertical Margins,* 135–74.

6. Shipton, *That Untravelled World,* 72.

7. G. L. Corbett, "The Founding of the Himalayan Club," *Himalayan Journal* 1 (Apr. 1929): 1–3; Mason, *Abode of Snow,* 189–92.

8. Mason, *Abode of Snow,* 153; *Alpine Journal* 40 (May 1928): 192–94; Corbett, "The Founding of the Himalyan Club," 3. See also John Martyn, "The Story of the Himalayan Club, 1928–1978," *Himalayan Journal* 35 (1977–78): 1–56; Trevor Braham, "Fifty Years—Retrospect and Prospect," *Himalayan Journal* 35 (1977–78): 57–63. For Mason, see Doug Scott's foreword to the 1987 edition of *Abode of Snow.* Mason's unpublished autobiography (in which he blames postwar nationalist unrest on "agitators encouraged by ignorant visitors from the U.S.A. and sometimes by left-wing politicians from England") is with his papers at the School of Geography and the Environment, Oxford University.

9. *Alpine Journal* 41 (May 1929): 230–33.

10. Mason, *Abode of Snow,* 195.

11. Bauer, *Himalayan Campaign,* xi; Bauer, *Kanchenjunga Challenge,* 16; Paul Bauer to Reichssportsführer Hans von Tschammer und Osten, Dec. 10, 1934, German Alpine Club Archives (translated by Celia Applegate).

12. Bauer, *Himalayan Campaign,* xiv, 2–3.

13. Ibid., xiv–xvi.

14. Paul Bauer, "Report to the Executive Committee of the German-Austrian Alpine Club," Mar. 19, 1929, German Alpine Club Archives; "Die Auslese der Him-Mannschaft: Paul Bauer über das Problem der Mannschafts wahl," *National Zeitung* (Essen), Feb. 9, 1937; Francis Younghusband, foreword to Bauer, *Himalayan Quest,* vii.

15. Styles, *On Top of the World,* 237.

16. For Farmer, see W. S. Ladd, "The Fatality on Kanchenjunga," *American Alpine Journal* 1 (1930): 195–99. See also Farmer's letter to Walter A. Wood of the American Alpine Club, Jan. 30, 1929, archives of the American Alpine Club Library, box 3.

17. *Alpine Journal* 42 (1929): 202.

18. For Bauer's 1929 expedition see, in addition to his own account in *Himalayan Campaign* (the original German edition of which, oddly, won a gold medal at the 1932 Olympic Games in Los Angeles), Smythe, *The Kangchenjunga Adventure,* 36–52; Tucker, *Kanchenjunga,* 25–31; Dyhrenfurth, *To the Third Pole,* 98–103; Paul Bauer, "The Fight for Kangchenjunga, 1929," *Alpine Journal* 42 (Nov. 1930): 185–202.

19. Mason, *Abode of Snow,* 198; Clark, *Men, Myths, and Mountains,* 157.

20. Calvert, *Smythe's Mountains,* 15; Shipton, *That Untravelled World,* 73. Despite their successful collaboration as climbers, Smythe and Graham Brown disliked one another personally and soon fell out altogether over whose contribution to their climbs of the Brenva Face had been the more decisive. For the original rival accounts, see F. S. Smythe, "The First Ascent of Mont Blanc Direct from the Brenva Glacier and Other Climbs in 1927," *Alpine Journal* 40 (May 1928): 58–77; T. Graham Brown, "The First Direct Ascent of Mont Blanc de Courmayeur from the Brenva Glacier and Other Climbs," *Alpine Journal* 41 (May 1929): 34–49. For the entire history of the Smythe/Graham Brown feud, see appendix 4 in Smythe, *The Six Alpine/Himalayan Climbing*

Books (Seattle: Mountaineers, 2000), 924–932. See also Smythe, *Climbs and Ski Runs;* and, for the last word, Graham Brown, *Brenva.*

21. Smythe, *The Kangchenjunga Adventure,* 423; Calvert, *Smythe's Mountains,* 88.

22. Calvert, *Smythe's Mountains,* 92. From Tseram, the nearest village on the Nepalese side of the Kang La, Smythe and Wood Johnson briefly explored the Yalung Valley in hopes of finding evidence of the fate of E. F. Farmer, the American who had vanished on this side of Kangchenjunga the previous year. Farmer's mother had evidently had visions of her son held captive in a monastery at the foot of the Yalung Glacier and had asked Dyhrenfurth to look for him. Smythe and Wood Johnson found the Detsenroba (or Decherol) Monastery, but it was in ruins and uninhabited by Farmer or anyone else. See Smythe, *The Kangchenjunga Adventure,* 154–56; Sale and Cleare, *Climbing the World's 14 Highest Mountains,* 127.

23. "Himalayan Porters," *Himalayan Journal* 16 (1930): 123. The Himalayan Club did not begin officially to award the tiger badges until 1939, but the term had been in casual use since 1924 to describe the Sherpa climbing elite.

24. Smythe, *The Kangchenjunga Adventure,* 282. Reviewing *The Kangchenjunga Adventure,* Edward Norton (of Everest fame) wrote that the ascent of Jonsong Peak scarcely merited the attention it got in the press, for it presented "no serious technical difficulties" and should have been "comfortably within the powers of an expedition equipped for the conquest of Kangchenjunga" (*Himalayan Journal* 3 [Apr. 1931]: 133–36). For Dyhrenfurth's own, highly defensive accounts of the 1930 expedition, see "The International Himalaya Expedition, 1930," *Himalayan Journal* 3 (Apr. 1931): 77–91 and his *To the Third Pole,* 103–9. See also F. S. Smythe, "The Assault on Kangchenjunga, 1930," *Alpine Journal* 42 (Nov. 1930): 202–26.

25. Report by Paul Bauer on "the relations between the German Himalayan expedition of 1929 and the International Himalaya Expedition of 1930," May 6, 1930, German Alpine Club Archives.

26. Bauer, *Himalayan Campaign,* 117–18; Douglas, *Tenzing,* 12.

27. A second Sherpa on Schaller's rope, Tsin Norbu, mysteriously survived this accident. According to Bauer's account (*Himalayan Quest,* 139–47), Pasang fell while negotiating a difficult, snow-strewn gully just below Camp VIII, taking Schaller with him. Norbu then threw a belay around a rock, which failed when the rock cut the rope. But in 1999 an elderly Ang Tsering told Jonathan Neale (then doing research for a book on the 1934 Nanga Parbat expedition) that Tsin Norbu had cut the rope to save himself from being dragged off the mountain. Neale assumes that Bauer suppressed the truth to avoid public controversy. See his *Tigers of the Snow,* 121, 308n35. The dead "Pasang," incidentally, is not to be confused with either Pasang Anju or the famous "Tiger" Pasang Kikuli, both of whom, confusingly, were also on Bauer's 1931 Kangchenjunga expedition. "Pasang," which simply means "Friday"—at birth many Sherpas are given the name of the day on which they are born—is probably the most common of Sherpa porters' names: in 1950 the Himalayan Club register listed sixteen of them. See *Himalayan Journal* 16 (1950): 127–28.

28. Bauer, *Himalayan Campaign,* 150; Paul Bauer, "Kangchenjunga, 1931: The Second Bavarian Attempt," *Alpine Journal* 44 (May 1932): 24.

29. Longstaff, *This My Voyage,* 107–13; Mumm, *Five Months in the Himalaya,* 156–99; Smythe, *Kamet Conquered,* 356–67; "Dr. Kellas' Expedition to Kamet," *Geographical Journal* 57 (Feb. 1921): 124–30.

30. Steele, *Eric Shipton,* 9.

31. Ibid., 11; Shipton, *Upon That Mountain,* 49.

32. Perrin, introduction, 7.

33. Shipton, *Upon That Mountain,* 80; Shipton, *That Untravelled World,* 71. For Tilman, see Anderson, *High Mountains and Cold Seas;* Madge, *The Last Hero.*

34. Steele, *Eric Shipton,* 31; Shipton, *That Untravelled World,* 72–73.

35. Steele, *Eric Shipton,* 36–37.

36. Calvert, *Smythe's Mountains,* 121; Shipton, *That Untravelled World,* 72, 74; Steele, *Eric Shipton,* 40. For firsthand accounts of the Kamet expedition, see F. S. Smythe, "The Kamet Expedition, 1931," *Alpine Journal* 43 (Nov. 1931): 289–308, E. St. J. Birnie, "The First Ascent of Kamet," *Himalayan Journal* 4 (1932): 27–35; Smythe, *The Adventures of a Mountaineer,* 154–83; and, most fully, Smythe, *Kamet Conquered.*

37. Roberts, *Welzenbach's Climbs,* 190.

38. A. M. Kellas, "A Consideration of the Possibility of Ascending the Loftier Himalaya," *Geographical Journal* 49 (Jan. 1917): 45.

39. Roberts, *Welzenbach's Climbs,* 239; Max Mayerhofer to AAVM, Dec. 9, 1930, German Alpine Club Archives.

40. Knowlton later claimed she would have climbed even higher than 20,000 feet had the men on the expedition allowed her to. See her obituary in the *New York Times,* Jan. 27, 1989.

41. Knowlton, *The Naked Mountain,* 78; Neale, *Tigers of the Snow,* 63–68.

42. Knowlton, *The Naked Mountain,* 99.

43. Willy Merkl, "Die Deutsche-Amerikanische himalaja Expedition 1932," *Zeitschrift des Deutschen und Österreichischen Alpenvereins* (1933): 65 (translation by Celia Applegate).

44. Styles, *On Top of the World,* 179.

45. Knowlton, *The Naked Mountain,* 148.

46. Ibid., 283. For other firsthand accounts of the 1932 expedition, see Willy Merkl, "The Attack on Nanga Parbat," *Himalayan Journal* 5 (1933): 65–75; Herbert Kunigk, "The German/American Himalayan Expedition, 1932," *Alpine Journal* 44 (Nov. 1932): 192–200; Elizabeth Knowlton, "Nanga Parbat, 1932," *American Alpine Journal* 2 (1933): 17–31; Fritz Wiessner, "Nanga Parbat in Retrospect," *American Alpine Journal* 2 (1933): 31–35. See also Bauer, *The Siege of Nanga Parbat,* 35–50; Herrligkoffer, *Nanga Parbat,* 23–44.

47. Knowlton, "Nanga Parbat, 1932," 31.

48. Zebhauser, *Alpinismus im Hitlerstaat,* 146–47, 150–51 (translations by Celia Applegate).

49. Skuhra, *Sturm auf die Throne der Götter,* 169.

50. Sir William Goodenough to William Wedgwood Benn, Mar. 23, 1931, Oriental and India Office Collection, L/P&S/12, British Library; J. C. Walton to Sir William Goodenough, Apr. 2, 1931, Blakeney Collection, Add. Mss. 63120, British Library; J. C. Walton to A. Hinks, Aug. 9, 1932, Blakeney Collection, Add. Mss. 63120, British Library; Unsworth, *Everest,* 158–60.

51. Francis Younghusband to William Goodenough, Aug. 10, 1932, Mount Everest Expedition Archives, 46, Royal Geographical Society; Calvert, *Smythe's Mountains,* 129; Longland, "Ruttledge, Hugh (1884–1961)"; Salkeld, "Ruttledge, Hugh (1884–1961)." For Ruttledge, see also J. Longland, T. H. Somervell, and R. Wilson, "Hugh Ruttledge, 1884–1961," *Alpine Journal* 67 (1962): 393–99; Eric Shipton, "Hugh Ruttledge," *Geographical Journal* 128 (1962): 124–25; Kenneth Mason, "Hugh Ruttledge, 1884–1961," *Himalayan Journal* 23 (1961): 177–79; *The Times,* Nov. 9, 1961.

52. Unsworth, *Everest,* 163.

53. Ruttledge, *Everest 1933,* 21–44.

54. Shipton, *That Untravelled World,* 81; W. R. Wager, "Chumunko: An Episode of the 1933 Mount Everest Expedition," *Cambridge Mountaineering* (1934).

55. For Lady Houston, see Day, *Lady Houston;* Davenport-Hines, "Houston, Dame Fanny Lucy (1857–1936)."

56. *The Times,* Apr. 4, 1933. For firsthand accounts of the Houston Mount Everest expedition, see L. V. Stewart Blacker, "The Mount Everest Flights," *Himalayan Journal* 6 (1934): 54–66; Blacker, "The Aërial Conquest of Everest"; Fellowes, *First over Everest!;* Douglas and Clydesdale and McIntyre, *The Pilots' Book of Everest.* For a more recent celebratory account by Clydesdale's son, see Douglas-Hamilton, *Roof of the World.* See also Lewis, "No Mountain Too High."

57. Ruttledge, *Everest 1933,* 93; *The Times,* Apr. 24, 1933 (supplement); Mason, *Abode of Snow,* 217.

58. Shipton, *That Untravelled World,* 77.

59. Hugh Ruttledge to Charles Bruce, May 19, 1933, Mount Everest Expedition Archives, 46, Royal Geographical Society; Unsworth, *Hold the Heights,* 349.

60. Shipton, *Upon That Mountain,* 126; Steele, *Eric Shipton,* 50; Sir William Goodenough to Hugh Ruttledge (telegram), June 27, 1933, Mount Everest Expedition Archives, 46, Royal Geographical Society.

61. Ruttledge, *Everest 1933,* 161; H. Ruttledge to S. Spencer, Feb. 27, 1935, Blakeney Collection, Add. Mss. 63120, British Library.

62. Jack Longland, "Hugh Ruttledge," *Alpine Journal* 67 (Nov. 1962): 395; Steele, *Eric Shipton,* 64; Frank Smythe to Sir Francis Younghusband, 14 July 1933, Oriental and India Office Collection, F197/115, British Library. For Warren and Kirkus's ascent of Bhagirathi III, see C. F. Kirkus, "Central Santopant'h," in Pallis, *Peaks and Lamas,* 38–47; C. Warren, "The Gangotri Glacier and Leo Pargial, 1933," *Alpine Journal* 46 (Nov. 1934): 306–20.

63. Shipton, *That Untravelled World,* 77, 81. For Shipton's Tibetan wanderings in 1933, see his "Lashar Plain," *Alpine Journal* 46 (May 1934): 129–31.

CHAPTER FIVE: *"Himalayan Hey-Day," 1934–1939*

1. Ortner, *Life and Death on Mt. Everest,* 177–78; Tilman, *The Ascent of Nanda Devi,* 6.

2. Charles S. Houston, "Nanda Devi," *Himalayan Journal* 45 (1987–88): 50–52.

3. W. W. Graham, "Travels and Ascents in the Himalaya," *Alpine Journal* 12 (Aug. 1884): 40; Hugh Ruttledge, "Nanda Devi," *Himalayan Journal* 5 (1933): 28–32; Tilman, *The Ascent of Nanda Devi,* 19.

4. Shipton, *Nanda Devi,* vii; Shipton, *That Untravelled World,* 84.

5. Shipton, *Upon That Mountain,* 147; Shipton, *That Untravelled World,* 85.

6. Shipton, *That Untravelled World,* 85; Anderson, *High Mountains and Cold Seas,* 125.

7. Shipton, *Upon That Mountain,* 147; Shipton, *Nanda Devi,* 64.

8. Shipton, *That Untravelled World,* 90.

9. Ibid., 91.

10. Shipton, *Nanda Devi,* 147, 300. From the moment of its publication in 1936, *Nanda Devi* was recognized as "one of the revolutionary texts of mountain literature." As Jim Perrin observes, "it has a magical, fresh quality, a get-through-by-the-skin-of-your-teeth spontaneity, a candour, a clear rationale, an excited commitment, an elation about the enterprise undertaken, which no previous mountaineering book had approached" (introduction, 7, 10). In 1951 *Nanda Devi* was one of the 100 books chosen to represent the achievements of British literature at the Festival of Britain.

11. To say as Jonathan Neale, for instance, does, that "the new Reich sports leader, von Tschammer und Osten, enthusiastically provided everything Merkl needed" is inaccurate and misleading. See Neale, *Tigers of the Snow,* 90.

12. Roberts, *Welzenbach's Climbs*, 241; R. Finsterwalder to the Notgemeinschaft der deutschen Wissenschaft, Feb. 28, 1934, German Alpine Club Archives (translated by Celia Applegate). "It was no easy thing getting them to agree to [*Misch*]," Finsterwalder later wrote, "but recommenders were unanimous on his scientific, personal, mountaineering, and national merits" (R. Finsterwalder to [?] Ficker, Mar. 19, 1934, German Alpine Club Archives [translated by Celia Applegate]).

13. Bechtold, *Nanga Parbat Adventure,* 9; Zebhauser, *Alpinismus im Hitlerstaat,* 190. Forwarding Dyhrenfurth's letter of resignation from the Swabian chapter of the Alpine Club to the central office in Innsbruck, the local chairman commented marginally: "Professor Dyhrenfurth seems to have sold himself to international Jewry. . . . This is what comes of a German who marries a Jew" (Zebhauser, *Alpinismus im Hitlerstaat,* 190 [translated by Celia Applegate]).

14. Bechtold, *Nanga Parbat Adventure,* 30; Roberts, *Welzenbach's Climbs,* 244–46. For Finsterwalder's map, see Mierau, *Die Deutsche Himalaja-Stiftung,* 53. See also Finsterwalder, Raechl, Misch, and Bechtold, *Forschung am Nanga Parbat.*

15. Zebhauser, *Alpinismus im Hitlerstaat,* 108–9; Roberts, *Welzenbach's Climbs,* 247–48.

16. Roberts, *Welzenbach's Climbs,* 250–51.

17. Herrligkoffer, *Nanga Parbat,* 58. Many years later, G. O. Dyhrenfurth suggested that Merkl called a halt on the Silver Saddle to prevent Aschenbrenner and Schneider from reaching the summit and thus grabbing the glory for Austria, a suggestion that Schneider himself refuted. See Roberts, *Welzenbach's Climbs,* 255, 264n10.

18. Over sixty years later, an aged Ang Tsering told Jonathan Neale that Aschenbrenner and Schneider, once unroped from their Sherpas, took flight down the mountain on skis. See Neale, *Tigers of the Snow,* 162–65. No other source, official or unofficial, public or private, confirms this shameful detail, and given the thoroughness of the subsequent investigation and the closeness with which it scrutinized the actions of Aschenbrenner and Schneider in particular, we are inclined to doubt it.

19. Roberts, *Welzenbach's Climbs,* 259. For official accounts of the 1934 disaster, see Bechtold, *Nanga Parbat Adventure,* 53–76; Fritz Bechtold, "The German Himalayan Expedition to Nanga Parbat, 1934," *Himalayan Journal* 7 (1935): 27–37; Fritz Bechtold, "Nanga Parbat 1934," *Zeitschrift des Deutschen und Österreichischen Alpenvereins* 66 (1935): 1–15. For an authoritative account based on expedition records and Ang Tsering's immediate description of the final days on the mountain, recorded at Base Camp on July 20, 1934, see Mierau, *Die Deutsche Himalaja-Stiftung,* 44–63. For a highly fanciful account based on the aged Ang Tsering's memories and the author's sympathetic imagination, see Neale, *Tigers of the Snow.*

20. Roberts, *Welzenbach's Climbs,* 248; Paul Bauer, "Aufreten der deutschen Bergsteiger im Ausland," Nov. 1934, in Mierau, *Die Deutsche Himalaja-Stiftung,* 65–68 (translated by Celia Applegate).

21. Paul Bauer to Hans von Tschammer und Osten, Dec. 4, 1934, German Alpine Club Archives (translated by Celia Applegate).

22. Paul Bauer to Hans von Tschammer und Osten, Dec. 12, 1934, German Alpine Club Archives (translated by Celia Applegate).

23. Mierau, *Die Deutsche Himalaja-Stiftung,* 70, 80; Erinnerungsprotokoll der Sitzung beim Reichssportführer, Mar. 11, 1935, German Alpine Club Archives (translated by Celia Applegate).

24. Mierau, *Deutsche Himalaja-Stiftung,* 79–80, 84–85; Philip Borchers to Paul Bauer, July 10, 1935, German Alpine Club Archives; Paul Bauer to Philip Borchers, July 20, 1935, German Alpine Club Archives.

25. Bauer, *The Siege of Nanga Parbat,* 103.

26. Herrligkoffer, *Nanga Parbat,* 70; For the 1936 German expedition to Sikkim, see Bauer, *Himalayan Quest;* Paul Bauer, Günther Hepp, Adolf Göttner, and Karl Wien, "Die Deutsche Himalaja-Kundfahrt 1936," *Zeitschrift des Deutschen und Österreichischen Alpenvereins* 68 (1937): 21–29; Karl Wien, "The Ascent of Siniolchu and Simvu North Peak," *Himalayan Journal* 9 (1937): 58–73.

27. Shipton, *Upon That Mountain,* 171–72; Jack Longland, "Hugh Ruttledge," *Alpine Journal* 67 (Nov. 1962): 395; Unsworth, *Hold the Heights,* 350; Shipton, *That Untravelled World,* 95.

28. Eric Shipton, "The Mount Everest Reconnaissance," *Geographical Journal* 87 (Feb. 1936): 98–99.

29. Douglas, *Tenzing,* 43–44. We have relied on this excellent biography for the details of Tenzing's life. For Tenzing's own imaginative version of his life story as told to James Ramsey Ullman, see Tenzing Norgay, *Tiger of the Snows.*

30. Douglas, *Tenzing,* 53, 57–58; Tenzing Norgay, *Tiger of the Snows,* 27–32.

31. Braham, *Himalayan Odyssey,* 18–19.

32. Tenzing Norgay, *Tiger of the Snows,* 29–30; Douglas, *Tenzing,* 59–60.

33. Tenzing Norgay, *Tiger of the Snows,* 32–33.

34. Ang Tharkay, *Mémoires d'un Sherpa.*

35. Shipton, "The Mount Everest Reconnaissance," 101; Unsworth, *Everest,* 244.

36. Shipton, *Upon That Mountain,* 176; Roberts, *I'll Climb Mount Everest Alone.*

37. Roberts, *I'll Climb Mount Everest Alone,* 61, 144. The manuscript of Wilson's (largely unilluminating) diary is now in the archives of the Alpine Club, London.

38. Roberts, *I'll Climb Mount Everest Alone,* 111–12; Unsworth, *Everest,* 198; Shipton, *Upon That Mountain,* 179.

39. Shipton, *That Untravelled World,* 98; Eric Shipton, "The Mount Everest Reconnaissance 1935," *Alpine Journal* 48 (May 1936): 10; Unsworth, *Everest,* 200; *Geographical Journal* 87 (Feb. 1936): 111. The definitive history of the 1935 Everest reconnaissance is now Astill, *Mount Everest,* which appeared after this chapter was written.

40. Shipton, *That Untravelled World,* 99; Steele, *Eric Shipton,* 70.

41. Steele, *Eric Shipton,* 71. For Oliver's ascent of Trisul, see P. R. Oliver, "Dunagari and Trisul, 1933," *Himalayan Journal* 6 (1934): 91–105.

42. *Morning Post,* Oct. 17, 1936. For the 1936 Everest expedition, see Ruttledge, *Everest: The Unfinished Adventure;* and Hugh Ruttledge, "The Mount Everest Expedition, 1936," *Himalayan Journal* 9 (1937): 1–15.

43. Eric Shipton, "More Explorations round Nanda Devi," *Alpine Journal* 90 (Aug. 1937): 97–98; Steele, *Eric Shipton,* 73. The following account of the 1936 Nanda Devi expedition relies mainly on Tilman, *The Ascent of Nanda Devi* and the authors' July 2003 interview with Dr. Charles S. Houston, Burlington, Vermont.

44. Roberts, "Five Who Made It to the Top," 34. See also Burdsall and Emmons, *Men against the Clouds.* One Joseph Rock, "a self-taught botanist with a flair for the dramatic and loose way with the facts," seems to have been largely responsible for the rumor surrounding Minya Konka's height, which he put at 30,250 feet in a highly publicized cable to the National Geographic Society in 1930. See "The Glories of Minya Konka," *National Geographic,* 58 (1930): 385. Theodore and Kermit Roosevelt, the sons of the first President Roosevelt, also spread it about and assigned a height of 30,000 feet in *Trailing the Giant Panda,* their account of their travels in China. See also Jon Krakauer, "A Mountain Higher than Everest?" in his *Eiger Dreams,* 116–29. For the extraordinary climbing and photographic career of Bradford Washburn, see Washburn and Freedman, *Bradford Washburn.*

45. Houston, "Heyday Climbs," in Bonington and Salkeld, *Heroic Climbs,* 154.

46. "We blindfolded him and told him he had to be initiated," Houston later recalled. "We roped him up and made him cut steps up the paths of the hotel gardens. Then we made him climb the stairs to the second story of the annex and rappel out the window blindfolded. Then we made him climb a small boulder in the garden and belay while we tried to pull him off. We ended up by having him bivouac on a chair tied to one

of the trees on the main street. We tied him snugly and took off his blindfold. I don't think I'll ever forget his look of astonishment and horror when he looked around at the considerable crowd—fifty or a hundred people—who were watching all this, and realized that some of the leading lights of the Alpine Club were there" (Roberts, "Five Who Made It to the Top," 35).

47. Ibid., 34; Tilman, *The Ascent of Nanda Devi*, 28–29. That Pasang Kikuli should have been overlooked by the Everest expedition is perplexing, as he was one of the outstanding Sherpas of his time and had already been twice to Everest, twice to Kangchenjunga, and once to Nanga Parbat, where he was one of the five porters to survive the high camps. "But their loss was our gain," Tilman noted, "and he turned out to be a treasure" (*The Ascent of Nanda Devi*, 29).

48. Tilman, *The Ascent of Nanda Devi*, 54.

49. Charles Houston, letter to the authors, Aug. 9, 2006.

50. Tilman, *Ascent of Nanda Devi*, 64–66.

51. Ibid., 66–67. "It is really just like a picnic," Houston wrote home of the Sherpas, "for they pitch camp, blow up air mattresses, lay out sleeping bags and pajamas, cook, wash up, etc. etc. It will certainly spoil one for Alaska, especially the packing part" (Charles Houston to "family," July 19, 1936, Nanda Devi scrapbook in the possession of Charles Houston). See also Houston's "Introductory Memoir," 8–9.

52. Tilman, *Ascent of Nanda Devi*, 91, 96.

53. Ibid., 131.

54. Bill Moyers, interview with Charles Houston, on NOW, the weekly newsmagazine from public television, Dec. 10, 2004.

55. Charles Houston, letter to the authors, Aug. 9, 2006.

56. Tilman, *Ascent of Nanda Devi*, 181.

57. Ibid., 185–86; Houston, "Heyday Climbs," 157; Moyers, interview with Houston.

58. N. E. Odell, "Nanda Devi," *Climbers Club Journal* 5 (1937): 122; Tilman, *Ascent of Nanda Devi*, 196–98.

59. Tilman, *The Ascent of Nanda Devi*, 198; Roper, *Fatal Mountaineer*, 17. The ascent of Nanda Devi received a fair bit of press coverage, including pictorial spreads in the *New York Times Magazine* (Nov. 22, 1936) and the *Illustrated London News* (Dec. 5, 1936). And Tilman's *The Ascent of Nanda Devi* was a great success that later inspired a classic parody, *The Ascent of Rum Doodle*, by W. E. Bowman. But when the Americans tried to sell their story to *Life*, the magazine showed no interest. "[Our] main chance at notoriety," Adams Carter recalled, "came from the makers of Camel cigarettes, who had celebrities like [baseball star] Rogers Hornsby endorsing their product" (Roberts, "Five Who Made It to the Top," 37).

60. Tom Longstaff to Charles Houston, Feb. 5, 1937, Nanda Devi scrapbook in the possession of Charles S. Houston; C. R. Cooke, "The Ascent of Kabru," *Himalayan Journal* 8 (1936): 107–17; J. Hunt and C. R. Cooke, "A Winter Visit to the Zemu Glacier," *Himalayan Journal* 10 (1938): 49–70.

61. Y. Hotta, "The Ascent of Nanda Kot, 1936," *Himalayan Journal* 10 (1938): 71–78; Kinichi Yamamori, "Japanese Mountaineering in the Himalaya Before and After World War II," *Japanese Alpine News* 7 (May 2006): 41–66; F. S. Smythe, "Garhwal 1937," *Alpine Journal* 50 (1938): 60–81.

62. Rudolf Schwarzgruber, "The German Garhwal-Himalaya Expedition, 1938," *Alpine Journal* 51 (1939): 79–84; André Roch, "Garhwal 1939: The Swiss Expedition," *Alpine Journal* 52 (1940): 34–52; S. B. Blake and Jakub Bujak, "The Polish Ascent of Nanda Devi, East Peak, 1939," *Alpine Journal* 53 (1941): 31–45; Klarner, *Nanda Devi*.

63. Shipton, *That Untravelled World*, 71.

64. Aimone di Savoia-Aosta and Desio, *La spedizione geografica italiana al Karakoram;* G. O. Dyhrenfurth, "Internationale Himalaya-Expedition 1934," *Die Alpen* 11 (1935): 67–112. See also Dyhrenfurth, *To the Third Pole,* 188–89. Dyhrenfurth had no surveyor along on this expedition, and Kenneth Mason later questioned his altitude claims, all of which were based on notoriously unreliable aneroid readings. See Mason, *Abode of Snow,* 249n1.

65. Dyhrenfurth, *To the Third Pole,* 190; Ségogne, *Himalayan Assault;* N. R. Streatfeild, "The French Karakoram Expedition, 1936," *Himalayan Journal* 9 (1937): 100–4.

66. The dead Sherpas were Pasang Nurbu, Jingmay Sherpa, Gyalgen III Monjo, Chong Karma, Ang Tsering II, Mingma Tsering, Karmi Sherpa, Nima Tsering I, and Nima Tsering II. See Kenneth Mason, "In Memoriam: The Porters Who Died on Nanga Parbat, 1937," *Himalayan Journal* 10 (1938): 191–92. See also Paul Bauer, "Nanga Parbat, 1937," *Himalayan Journal* 10 (1938): 145. For full-length accounts of the 1937 disaster, see Bauer, *Himalayan Quest,* 97–150; Bauer, *The Siege of Nanga Parbat,* 103–43.

67. Bauer, *The Siege of Nanga Parbat,* 108.

68. Nursang's "forcible appeals" to his fellow Sherpas in Darjeeling to accompany him to Nanga Parbat reminded Bill Tilman of "the exhortation of Frederick the Great to his wavering troops: 'Come on you unmentionable offscourings of scoundrels. Do you want to live for ever?'" (*Mount Everest 1938,* 27).

69. Bauer, *The Siege of Nanga Parbat,* 150, 156.

70. Paul Bauer, "Nanga Parbat 1938," *Himalayan Journal* 11 (1939): 103. In Merkl's pocket Bauer found a poignant last letter from Welzenbach dated from Camp VII, July 10, [1934]: "We have lain here since yesterday, when Uli got lost on the way. We are both ill. An attempt to make VI failed due to general exhaustion. I, Willo, have probably got bronchitis, angina and influenza. Bara Sahib [Merkl] has a feeling of exhaustion, and frost-bitten feet and hands. We have neither of us eaten a hot meal for six days, and have drunk almost nothing. Please help *us soon here* in Camp VII" (Bauer, *The Siege of Nanga Parbat,* 162).

71. Lutz Chicken, "Nanga Parbat Reconnaissance, 1939," *Himalayan Journal* 14 (1947): 53–58. See also Harrer's famous memoir, *Seven Years in Tibet.*

72. Tilman, *Mount Everest,* 1.

73. Stewart, "Tenzing's Two Wrist-Watches," 185; *The Times,* June 19, 1936; *Mountaineering Journal* 4 (Summer 1936): 147; Frank Smythe to Sir Percy Cox, Sept. 7, 1936, Blakeney Collection, Add. Mss. 63120, British Library.

74. Eric Shipton, *Blank on the Map;* Steele, *Eric Shipton,* 77; F. Spencer Chapman, "The Ascent of Chomolhari, 1937," *Himalayan Journal* 10 (1938): 126–44; F. Spencer Chapman, "Chomolhari," *Alpine Journal* 49 (Nov. 1937): 203–9; Tilman, *Mount Everest,* 4–6.

75. Tilman, *Mount Everest,* 17; H. W. Tilman, "Mount Everest, 1938," *Alpine Journal* 51 (May 1939): 4.

76. Shipton, *Upon That Mountain,* 185; Steele, *Eric Shipton,* 92; Anderson, *High Mountains and Cold Seas,* 158.

77. Steele, *Eric Shipton,* 93.

78. Fritz Wiessner, "K2–1938–1953," 12 (unpublished book manuscript in the Kauffman Collection, American Alpine Club Library); Kauffman and Putnam, *K2,* 24.

79. Bates and Houston, *Five Miles High,* 29. A notable absence from the party was Walter Abbot Wood Jr. of the American Geographical Society, a world-class Alpinist and future president of the American Alpine Club who had led notable expeditions to the Canadian Yukon. Why Houston did not invite Wood is unclear, though Brad Washburn's memories of him as "a big name" with "a pile of money" who was used to calling his own shots are certainly suggestive of a likely incompatibility. See Washburn and Freedman, *Bradford Washburn,* 69. For whatever reason, Houston, Bates, and Wiessner all felt that Wood would simply not "fit in."

See Charles Houston to Bob Bates, Nov. 22, 1937, K2 1938 scrapbook in the possession of Charles Houston. Interestingly, Wood would later preside over the American Alpine Club's formal inquiry into the conduct of Wiessner's 1939 K2 expedition.

80. Ringholz, *On Belay!* 89.

81. Obituary of Jimmy Roberts, http://www.actionasia.com/actionasia/Articles/index.jsp?aid=816.

82. Houston, "Heyday Climbs," 158.

83. Charles Houston, "A Reconnaissance of K2, 1938," *Himalayan Journal* 11 (1939): 117; Bates and Houston, *Five Miles High,* 111–12.

84. Bates and Houston, *Five Miles High,* 185.

85. Ibid., 203, 264; Houston, "Heyday Climbs," 159.

86. Bates and Houston, *Five Miles High,* 266; Houston, "A Reconnaissance of K2, 1938," 124.

87. Bates and Houston, *Five Miles High,* 278.

88. Ringholz, *On Belay!* 111; Edward Groth to "the leader and members of the American Karakoram Expedition," [May, 1938], K2 scrapbook in the possession of Charles Houston; Houston, "Heyday Climbs," 159.

89. Kauffman and Putnam, *K2,* 33.

90. Ibid., 73.

91. Sheldon, "Lost behind the Ranges," 126.

92. K2 diary of Jack Durrance (typescript copy), Kauffman Collection, box 2, folder 2/8, p. 39 (entry for July 2, 1939), American Alpine Club Library.

93. Ibid., pp. 69–70 (undated "Medical Notes"). The typescript entry actually reads: "Sleepless nights combined with emotional upset that I had been selected to make summit dash with Fritz," and Kauffman and Putnam take this as evidence that Durrance "really wanted no part of it—just to do his duty and let it go at that" (*K2,* 99). "Emotional upset" is an odd phrase to apply in this case, however, and having considered the passage in the context of his obvious jealousy of Wolfe, we have concluded that Durrance surely meant to write, or did write in the manuscript original, "that I had *not* been selected," and we have taken the liberty of restoring this crucial negative qualifier in brackets.

94. That it was Tony Cromwell and not Jack Durrance who ordered the clearing of the lower camps came to light only recently, when Durrance shared his expedition diary with Kauffman and Putnam. See the entry for July 18, 1939: "Dawa danced up here yesterday aft. with notes from Tony & Chap = 'Salvage all the tents + sleeping bags you can, we have ample food'" (K2 diary of Jack Durrance, typescript copy, Kauffman Collection, American Alpine Club Library).

95. Unpublished English translation of Wiessner, *K2: Tragödie und Sieg am zweithöchsten Berg der Erde,* typescript copy, Kauffman Collection, box 2, folder 2/5, pp. 31–32, American Alpine Club Library. See also Chappel Cranmer and Fritz Wiessner, "The Second American Karakoram Expedition to K2," *American Alpine Journal* 4 (1940): 9–19.

96. Conefrey and Jordan, *Mountain Men,* 136; Wiessner, "The K2 Expedition of 1939," 65.

97. Conefrey and Jordan, *Mountain Men,* 137; K2 diary of Fritz Wiessner (typescript copy), Kauffman Collection, folder 2/6, p. 18 (entry for July 22, 1939), American Alpine Club Library.

98. K2 diary of Fritz Wiessner (typescript copy), Kauffman Collection, folder 2/6, p. 19 (entry for July 23, 1939), American Alpine Club Library; Kauffman and Putnam, *K2,* 124; Roberts, "The K2 Mystery," 43.

99. Until 2002, that is, when the American journalist Jennifer Jordan stumbled on what was left of Wolfe's body a mile and half down the Godwin-Austen Glacier. See Kevin Fedarko, "The Mountain of Mountains," *Outside* (Nov. 2003): 98.

100. Mason, *Abode of Snow*, 263.

101. Edward Groth memorandum, Sept. 13, 1939, in Kauffman and Putman, *K2*, appendix E, 188–89.

102. Report on the 1939 American Alpine Club Karakoram expedition, Mar. 16, 1940; Fritz Wiessner to Walter Wood, Apr. 3, 1940; Alfred Lindley to Fritz Wiessner, Apr. 8, 1940; Alfred Lindley to Walter Wood, Apr. 8 [13?], 1940; Robert Underhill to Walter Wood, May 1, 1940, all in Kauffman Collection, American Alpine Club Library; American Alpine Club Council minutes, May 18, 1940, American Alpine Club Library.

CHAPTER SIX: *The Golden Age Postponed, 1940–1950*

1. Rudolf Schwarzgruber's report on the German Garhwal-Himalaya expedition in the same issue offered profuse thanks to the British authorities for aiding their endeavor. Among those receiving thanks was Oxford geographer Kenneth Mason, who had provided the German party with his firsthand observations on the region. Rudolf Schwarzgruber, "The German Garhwal-Himalayan Expedition, 1938," *Alpine Journal* 51 (May 1939): 79. Also see in the same issue H. W. Tilman, "Mount Everest, 1938," 3–17; C. S. Houston, "The American Karakoram Expedition to K2, 1938," 54–69; Fritz Bechtold, "Nanga Parbat, 1938," 74. In the Axis nations, British and American mountaineering efforts in the Himalaya were also given extensive coverage in mountaineering journals. The Austrian Alpine Club's journal reprinted Houston's account of the K2 expedition, C. S. Houston, "Die Amerikanische Karakorum Expedition zum K2 1938," *Österreichischen Alpenzeitung* Sept.–Oct. 1939. Ichiro Yoshizawa, director of the Japanese Alpine Club, wrote to Houston from Tokyo in the spring of 1939 to say that he was translating Houston's article for the club's journal. Letter from Ichiro Yoshizawa, in Tokyo, to Houston, June 3, 1939, K2 scrapbook in the possession of Charles Houston.

2. Tilman, *When Men and Mountains Meet*, 9.

3. For what may have been the original use of the term see R. Scott Russell, "The Karakoram Expedition, 1939," *Alpine Journal* 52 (May 1940): 208. After the war the Swiss climber Marcel Kurz would publish a work entitled *Chronique Himalayenne; L'âge d'or, 1940–1955*. For the Mount Everest Committee's plans for future Everest expeditions, see Anderson, *High Mountains and Cold Seas*, 166–67. For the American plans, see Houston and Bates, *K2*, 47. For the Italians, see A. Desio, "The 1954 Italian Expedition to the Karakorum and the Conquest of K2," *Alpine Journal* 60 (May 1955): 3. For the Germans, see Baume, *Sivalaya*, 62, 187. And for the New Zealanders, see Temple, *The World at Their Feet*, 37.

4. Conefrey and Jordan, *Mountain Men*, 191.

5. E. L. Strutt, "Memorable Days," *Alpine Journal* 53 (May 1941): 11. The climbing journals were hard put to fill their pages during the war, given the lack of new expeditions and ascents to report. The *Himalayan Journal* suspended publication for the duration. The *Alpine Journal* continued to appear throughout the war but became a kind of old-timers' club periodical, recycling stories of prewar climbing and historical notes. See, for example, R. L. G. Irving, "When We Were Very Young," *Alpine Journal* 54 (May 1944): 257–67.

6. Charles Houston, "Norman R. Streatfeild," *Alpine Journal* 53 (May 1941): 67. The American Alpine Club donated two ambulances to the British war effort. "The Gift of an Ambulance," *Alpine Journal* 52 (May 1940): 298.

7. Apart from Ullman, American authors writing about mountaineering appealed to a small circle of initiates. See, for example, Thorington, *A Survey of Early American Ascents in the Alps*. Ullman played a singularly important role in the popularization of mountaineering in the United States. Tom Hornbein, later to become famous for his 1963 ascent of Everest's West Ridge, read *High Conquest* as a teenager growing up during the Second World War in St. Louis, Missouri. For Hornbein, the book "was like the magic mirror through which I could climb into a fantasy world of high mountains and audacious human aspiration." *High Conquest* "was kind of a bible for a fair number of my generation of climbers." Tom Hornbein, e-mail to the authors, Mar. 22, 2005.

8. Ullman, *High Conquest*, 199. For a contemporary review of Ullman's book highlighting his argument about the Germans on Nanga Parbat, see R. L. Duffus, "On Mountaineers and the Peaks They Have Climbed," *New York Times*, Oct. 26, 1941, BR9. For an interesting reflection on Ullman's role in creating a lasting set of stereotypes about 1930s German climbing ventures, see Rowell, *In the Throne Room of the Mountain Gods*, 113–17.

9. Other members of the expedition were eager to return home to support the German war effort. As Heinrich Harrer, in 1939 a committed Nazi, would later write, "Only Aufschnaiter was for staying in Karachi. He had fought in the First World War and could not believe in a second" (*Seven Years in Tibet*, 19). A veteran of the First World War and the India Army, Mason was too old to serve in uniform in the new conflict. Instead, he made his contribution to the war effort directing the British Interservices Topographical Department production center at the School of Geography at Oxford, where he oversaw the production of a collection of regional studies and naval intelligence handbooks to inform both military operations and peacetime planning. See Mason's unpublished autobiography, 557–58, a manuscript that can be found in the School of Geography and the Environment Library, Oxford University. Also see Clout, "Place Description, Regional Geography, and Area Studies," 256–59.

10. Kenneth Mason to H. E. C. Tyndale, Feb. 5, 1945, Graham Brown Papers, Acc. 4338, box 215, folder 1, National Library of Scotland.

11. Ibid. Mason would echo the language of the letter in the opening lines of his chapter "The Second World War and After" in his history of Himalayan mountaineering: "The War was like a gigantic avalanche that sweeps everything before it. All were engulfed in the catastrophe" (*Abode of Snow*, 285). Also see Mason's comments on Aufschnaiter and other Germans in *Abode of Snow*, 285–86, and in his unpublished autobiography, 437–38.

12. In addition to Harrer's *Seven Years in Tibet* also see Aufschnaiter's posthumously published memoir, Brauen, *Peter Aufschnaiter's Eight Years in Tibet*. For Finsterwalder, see Von Walther Hofmann, "Richard Finsterwalder und die Alpenvereinskartographie," *Jahrbuch des Österreichischen Alpenvereins 1964* 88:132–37; Konecny, "Die Anfange der Photogrammetrie in Hannover," 4–5. For Bauer's wartime record, see Zimmerman, *Paul Bauer*, 208.

13. Charles Houston, "Norman R. Streatfeild," *Alpine Journal* 53 (May 1941): 67–68; R. H. B. [Robert Bates], "Norman R. Streatfeild," *American Alpine Journal* 4 (1941): 282–83. Bill Tilman notified Houston of Streatfeild's death and told him the story about the film showing. Tilman's letter hasn't survived, but Houston relayed this information to Bob Bates in a letter dated July 7, 1940, K2 scrapbook in the possession of Charles Houston.

14. For Tilman's wartime experiences, see part 2, chapters 8–17 of *When Men and Mountains Meet;* the Monte Serva climb is described on 201. Also see Anderson, *High Mountains and Cold Seas*, 185–218; Madge, *The Last Hero*, 141–69.

15. Hunt, *Life Is Meeting*, 63–64. In a talk to the Alpine Club in 1945, Smythe gave a more modest assessment of his inspirational qualities. He recalled the day he led a unit of trainees on a forced march in the Scottish hills through galelike winds, each man laden with a seventy-pound pack. The winds grew so strong that Smythe, at the head of the column, was knocked off his feet. "As I lay recovering my wind, which had been knocked completely out of me," he recalled, "I saw the section in single file manfully toiling up towards me. Then came another gust which lifted every man off his feet. As they slowly struggled upright there was a momentary lull and in it I heard the voice of the sergeant: ''E can 'ave 'is Everest, every —— inch of it!'" The sergeant's actual expletive was left to the imagination in Smythe's account. See F. S. Smythe, "Some Experiences in Mountain Warfare Training," *Alpine Journal* 55 (May 1946): 237. The second half of his talk was reprinted in *Alpine Journal* 55 (Nov. 1946): 345–51. Smythe went on to train troops in Wales and in the Canadian

Rockies before serving with the Eighth Army in Italy. On Smythe's role in mountain warfare training, see Lane, *Military Mountaineering,* 22.

16. "Correspondence," *American Alpine Journal* 5 (1944): 311. Smythe would never return to Everest. While organizing an expedition in India in 1949 he was taken seriously ill and died shortly after returning to England. "Francis Sydney Smythe, 1900–1949," *Alpine Journal* 57 (Nov. 1949): 230–35.

17. Houston, *Going Higher,* 177.

18. Charles Houston to Bates et al., Oct. 25, 1942, from U.S. Naval Air Station, Miami, Florida, typescript copy, K2 scrapbook in the possession of Charles Houston.

19. Bob Bates, "For the AAC Library," note dated July 16, 1998, Bates Papers, American Alpine Club Library; Bob Bates, "H. Adams Carter, 1914–1995," *American Alpine Journal* 38 (1996): 371; G. C. Marshall to W. Cameron Forbes, n.d. [Dec. 1940], Bates Papers, folder "Efforts to Persuade the US Army to Establish Mountain Troops 1940–1941," American Alpine Club Library. According to Bates, Ad Carter met with Secretary of War Stimson sometime during 1940 to convince him of the need for mountain troops. Bates climbed with James V. Conant, president of Harvard University, in New Hampshire in the fall of 1940, and according to Bates, "We talked about the need for mountain troops all day. Two days later Conant was seeing [Army Chief of Staff] Marshall in Washington, and he said he would give him good arguments for having mountain troops." Bob Bates, memorandum dated June 22, 1998, Bates Papers, folder "Efforts to Persuade the US Army to Establish Mountain Troops 1940–1941," American Alpine Club Library. Also see H. Adams Carter, "Suggestions about Mountain Troops," Oct. 1940, in the same folder.

20. "John Case sent me a frantic telegram asking me to give up all and flee to the Wind Rivers for the training school. I debated strenuously for several hours but finally phoned him that it was no go, I had to stay here. I hated to give it up, was severely tempted, but am glad I decided as I did. Shortly afterwards I was put in charge of the Low Pressure Chamber here and have been doing nothing else but that ever since." Letter from Charlie Houston to Bob Bates, Sept. 18, 1942, K2 scrapbook in the possession of Charles Houston. On the history of the Tenth Mountain Division, see Albert H. Jackman, "The Tenth Mountain Division," *American Alpine Journal* 6 (1946): 187–92; Burton, *The Ski Troops;* Jenkins, *The Last Ridge;* Shelton, *Climb to Conquer;* and the 1996 documentary *Fire on the Mountain,* directed by Beth and George Gage. Also see the firsthand account of Tenth Mountain Division veteran (and later president of the American Alpine Club) William Putnam, *Green Cognac.*

21. Bates, *The Love of Mountains Is Best,* 183–241; Jenkins, *The Last Ridge,* 23–24; William P. House, "Mountain Equipment for the U.S. Army," *American Alpine Journal* 6 (1946): 231; William P. House, "Nylon Climbing Rope," *Appalachia* 13 (June 1947): 411–12; Washburn and Freedman, *Bradford Washburn,* 156–67.

22. The *American Alpine Journal* 4 (1940) drew its readers' attention to the innovation in a brief note, "Equipment," 147. On American mountaineers and the development of cold weather gear, see Bates, *The Love of Mountains Is Best,* 183–215; Putnam, *Green Cognac,* 19–22, 209; William House, "Surplus Army Outdoor Equipment," *Appalachia* 13 (June 1947): 383–89; House, "Mountain Equipment for the U.S. Army," 231; Jenkins, *The Last Ridge,* 149.

23. Spenser, *Flying the Hump.*

24. Scott, *God Is My Co-pilot,* 98. Also see "Scott Flies over Mount Everest," *New York Times,* July 22, 1942, 21. The authors are grateful to Nick Clinch for pointing out the mislabeled photograph in Scott's book. Another American pilot flying a mission in China claimed to have glimpsed a "Super-Everest" in western China's Amne Machin range in 1944, whose height he estimated at 30,000 feet. An aerial survey in 1948, sponsored by the Boston Museum, failed to find any peaks in the region higher than 18,000 feet. Brooks Atkinson, "Peak Much Higher Than Everest Is Believed Seen by Flier in China," *New York Times,* Mar. 27, 1944, 21; "Traveling over the Top of China in Search of a Super Mount Everest," *New York Times,* Apr. 24, 1948, 8. Also see

Dyhrenfurth, *To the Third Pole,* xviii–xix. The mountain, first ascended in 1980, is actually 20,610 feet (6,282 meters) in altitude.

25. Unsworth, *Everest,* 235.

26. Hillary, *Nothing Venture,* 28, 31–36, 59, 69–72. Also see Hillary, *View from the Summit,* 37–57. After his ascent of Everest in 1953, Hillary secured a contract for publishing his memoirs. He initially intended to call them *Battle against Boredom,* which aptly summed up his feelings about the life he would have led had he not discovered mountain climbing. The publisher apparently felt that was not a particularly marketable title. Johnston, *Reaching the Summit,* 9.

27. Tilman, *Two Mountains and a River,* 1–2. Also see Anderson, *High Mountains and Cold Seas,* 220; Madge, *The Last Hero,* 113. H. W. Tilman, "Notes: The Problem of Everest," *Himalayan Journal* 13 (1946): 133.

28. Keay, *India,* 499–505; Shipton, *That Untravelled World,* 183; Douglas, *Tenzing,* 155; Steele, *Eric Shipton,* 122; Unsworth, *Everest,* 267; Ward, *Everest,* 169; "Six Men with Nylon Ropes to Attack Everest," *News Chronicle,* Dec. 8, 1945, Newspaper Clippings Archive, vol. 30, Alpine Club; "A Projected Mount Everest Expedition," *Alpine Journal* 55 (1945–46): 314–15. The viceroy's prohibition on expeditions did not stop mountaineers from various countries fantasizing about a return to Everest. There is a suggestive although mysterious reference in a letter from Bob Bates to a friend in 1947 mentioning one such instance: "The date of the S. African Everest Expedition is surprising & doesn't tally with what [Noel] Odell suggested on his visit here. I'm afraid the S.A.'s are indulging in a little wishful thinking." Bob Bates to "Schnackel" [Christine Reid?], Nov. 13, 1947, "Papers Found in K2: The Savage Mountain," Appalachian Mountain Club Library.

29. Tenzing had also been on a 1937 Doon School expedition to Bandarpunch. In 1950 he would climb with the school expedition to Bandarpunch for a third time, and this time made the summit. The Doon School is credited with inspiring several generations of young Indian students with a love of mountaineering. See R. L. Holdsworth, "Bandarpunch Again," in Ali, *For Hills to Climb,* 48–55; Kohli, *Mountaineering in India,* 15; C. W. F. Noyce, "An Expedition to Sikkim," *Alpine Journal* 55 (May 1946): 323; J. O. M. Roberts, "A Reconnaissance of Saser Kangri, Eastern Karakorams, 1946," *Alpine Journal* 56 (May 1947): 149–56; Mason, *Abode of Snow,* 299–300; Braham, *Himalayan Odyssey,* 42; Lane, *Military Mountaineering,* 23–24; Douglas, *Tenzing,* 110. Wilfred Noyce described his wartime training assignment in C. W. F. Noyce, "An Aircraft Mountain Centre in Kashmir," *Alpine Journal* 55 (May 1945): 74–76. Fritz Kolb, an Austrian mountaineer who was interned by British authorities in India from 1939 through 1944, was one of the very first to venture back to the Himalaya immediately after the war. He took a walking tour to the Pindari Glacier below Nanda Devi in May 1945, which he describes in *Himalaya Venture,* 71–90.

30. Unlike his wartime experiments, which focused on the impact of sudden oxygen deprivation, Houston's 1946 experiments measured the impact of a gradual exposure to oxygen deprivation and the extent to which the negative effects of hypoxia could be prevented or offset through careful acclimatization. Four volunteers went through five weeks of testing in a decompression chamber designed to subject them in stages to the stress of subsisting on the oxygen available at ever-higher elevations, to a simulated elevation of 29,000 feet, the approximate height of the summit of Everest. Two of the volunteers were able to exercise on a stationary bicycle for twenty minutes at that simulated altitude without the aid of supplementary oxygen, reinforcing Houston's already firm belief that Everest and other high peaks in the Himalaya could be climbed without oxygen. "High Altitude Tests Are Begun in Florida," *New York Times,* June 29, 1946, 21; Houston, *Going Higher,* 177–78, 195–200; Charles S. Houston, "Operation Everest, 1946," *American Alpine Journal* 6 (1946): 311–15; Houston and Riley, "Respiratory and Circulatory Changes during Acclimatisation to High Altitude"; Ward, *Everest,* 167–69.

31. Orville Prescott, "Books of the Times," *New York Times,* Sept. 5, 1945, 21. Henry A. Perkins, an American Alpine Club member since 1903, wrote to Ullman in 1946 to take issue with his definition of "bergschrund" in the novel, pointing out that it was "not a glacial crevasse, in the ordinary sense, and does not

mark the foot of an icefall." Letter from Henry A. Perkins to James Ramsey Ullman, May 12, 1946, Ullman Papers, box 71, folder 9, Department of Rare Books and Special Collections, Princeton University Library.

32. "The 'White Tower's' Author Shows How to Master a Strenuous Sport," *Life,* Dec. 31, 1945, 66–71; James Ramsey Ullman, "Men and Mountains," *Life,* Dec. 31, 1945, 71.

33. J. E. F. [Joel Fisher], "Book Reviews," *American Alpine Journal* 6 (1946): 15.

34. See appendix B, "Annual Meetings and Membership Statistics," in Fay, *A Century of American Alpinism,* 177–81.

35. Kenneth A. Henderson, "Robert Lindley Murray Underhill, 1889–1983," *American Alpine Journal* 26 (1984): 344–47. For Underhill's climbing career, see Waterman and Waterman, *Yankee Rock and Ice,* 21–22; Unsworth, *Hold the Heights,* 257–59, 314. For Underhill's role in introducing new alpine techniques to the United States, see Middendorf, "The Mechanical Advantage," 158. Also see Underhill, *Give Me the Hills.* The American Alpine Club annually awards a Robert and Miriam Underhill Prize for outstanding mountaineering achievement. Robert Underhill to Henry Hall, June 24, 1946, Himalaya Library Archives, box K2, folder 1939 American Karakoram Expedition, K2, American Alpine Club Library. To join the AMC required formal nomination from two already-enrolled members, a requirement that would be dropped only in the late 1970s, after which anyone willing to pay dues was accepted as a member. For the change in policy, see Any Nichols, "Open Door: The AMC and Change," *Appalachia* 44 (Feb. 1978): 4. For further evidence of anti-Semitism in the AMC in its earlier years, see Susan Schwartz's biography of climber Hans Kraus (a climbing partner of Fritz Wiessner and an influential figure in the climbing history of New York's Shawagunks), who came to the United States in 1938 as refugee from Austria and who was one-quarter Jewish. According to Schwartz, a "leading Shawagunks climber of the era [i.e., the 1940s], Bonnie Prudden, recalled being approached by some Appalachian Mountain Club members trying to enlist her support to expel Jewish members from the club" (*Into the Unknown,* 56).

36. Bill Ullman, son of James Ramsey Ullman and one of the two "beautifully Jewish" boys Underhill described, remembers the visit to Lake of the Clouds Hut in 1946. Of his father, he writes: "JRU was pretty much the model of an Edwardian gentleman. . . . He took good manners seriously (alas for us children); his grammar and diction were faultless." Bill Ullman, e-mail to the authors, May 15, 2006. When Ullman died in 1971, he was eulogized in the American Alpine Club's journal as American mountaineering's "most distinguished man of letters." Samuel C. Silverstein, "James Ramsey Ullman, 1908–1971," *American Alpine Journal* 17 (1972): 237. Information on Ullman's ethnic and educational background was provided by Bill Ullman.

37. Alpine Club List of Members and Rules, 1945, American Alpine Club Library. Of course, not all mountaineers in either the United States or Britain belonged to their respective Alpine Clubs. In the United States mountaineers could also be found in regional groups like the AMC, the Sierra Club, the Colorado Mountain Club, the Mazamas, and the Washington State–based Mountaineers. In 1951 the Sierra Club counted 6,802 members, the Colorado Mountain Club 855, the Mazamas 876, and the Mountaineers 2,037. *Accidents in North American Mountaineering* 1, no. 4 (1951): 3. In Britain Alpine Club numbers were supplemented by the membership of scores of local and regional climbing groups. The British Mountaineering Council (BMC), established in 1944 as a federation of the country's climbing clubs, spoke for an estimated 6,000 climbers in the early years after the war. Clark and Pyatt, *Mountaineering in Britain,* 234. Also see "Mountaineering at Home," *The Times,* Mar. 10, 1951; Newspaper Clippings Archive, vol. 30, Alpine Club; Chris Bonington, "In Retrospect," *Mountain* 1 (Mar. 1969), 19. Even with these additions, the numbers of mountaineers in the Anglo-American world were minuscule by continental standards.

38. Jean-Charles Meyer, "Un siècle au service de la montagne," *La montagne et alpinisme,* no. 1 (1974): 190; Maraini, *Karakoram,* 11; Italian Alpine Club, *1863–1963,* 290.

39. Gaston Rébuffat, along with Edouardo Frendo, made the second ascent of the Walker Spur of the Grandes Jorasses in 1945; in 1948 Rébuffat and Bernard Pierre made the second ascent of the Northeast Face

of Piz Badile. Lionel Terray and Louis Lachenal made the second ascent of the North Face of the Eiger in 1947, and in 1949 made the sixth and speediest ascent of Piz Badile. See Rébuffat, *Starlight and Storm*, 3–67; A. K. Rawlinson, "Crescendo, 1939–1956," *Alpine Journal* 62 (Nov. 1957): 99; Frison-Roche and Jouty, *A History of Mountain Climbing*, 124–25; Bonington, *The Climbers*, 162–76. H. G. Nichol, "Thomas Duncan Bourdillion," *Alpine Journal* 61 (Nov. 1956): 358. Eric Shipton, writing a decade after Bourdillion's death in 1956, would say that the young British climber had been "fired by an almost missionary zeal to put British Alpine achievement back on the map" (foreword to Bonington, *I Chose to Climb*, 14). From the perspective of the late 1960s Chris Bonington would write: "It is difficult now to envisage the climbing scene at the end of the war. . . . In the Alps, British mountaineers were still in the clutches of pre-war Alpine Club traditions which had checked the advances of the Continental countries and which persisted in advocating the use of guides" ("In Retrospect," 18, 20). A parallel leap in technique was taking place in the decade after the war in the United States among Californians like John Salathé, Mark Powell, Royal Robbins, and Warren Harding, young climbers who were making a specialty of breathtaking ascents on the granite cliffs of Yosemite, some of whom would later go on to make American first ascents of the classic Alpine routes. Jones, *Climbing in North America*, 175–200; Middendorf, "The Mechanical Advantage," 162–63.

40. Reflecting on the British triumph on Everest in 1953, Denman regretted that "the ascent of Everest had become a matter of vital national prestige. From being a tremendous ideal, the mountain had fallen into the grip of nationalism, one of the greatest curses of our age. The individual no longer mattered. The important factor was the nationality of the individual" (*Alone to Everest*, 249).

41. Tenzing Norgay, *Tiger of the Snows*, 52.

42. Denman, *Alone to Everest*, 230; Tenzing Norgay, *Tiger of the Snows*, 53; Douglas, *Tenzing*, 111–17. Earl Denman, "A Lone Attempt to Climb Everest," *Appalachia* 17 (June 1951): 369–79. Denman would return to Darjeeling in 1948, somewhat better equipped and determined to try again on Everest, but this time he could not persuade Tenzing or any other Sherpa to accompany him, to his great disappointment. Denman, *Alone to Everest*, 242. Denman would find a latter-day admirer in Reinhold Messner, who also desired to climb Everest solo, and had better luck in the quest. Messner, *The Crystal Horizon*, 85.

43. As described by Walt Unsworth, the Swiss Foundation for Alpine Research, founded in 1940, was "similar to the British Royal Geographical Society or the American National Geographic Society, except . . . more closely linked with government—it works directly under the [Swiss] Department of Internal Affairs" (*Everest*, 282). In addition to funding expeditions, the Swiss Foundation published an annual report on mountaineering from 1946 through 1968, entitled *Berge Der Welt*. Starting in 1953 the annual report also appeared in English as *The Mountain World*. Mme. A. Lohner et al., "The Swiss Garhwal Expedition of 1947," *Himalayan Journal* 15 (1949): 19. Annalies Lohner would later marry one of the other climbers in the group, Alfred Sutter; the romance began on the expedition.

44. Lohner et al., "The Swiss Garhwal Expedition of 1947," 18–45; "Himalayan Climb," *Life*, Dec. 15, 1947, 145–152; Tenzing Norgay, *Tiger of the Snows*, 54–57; Douglas, *Tenzing*, 118–23; Braham, *Himalayan Odyssey*, 78–96; Mason, *Abode of Snow*, 293–94. The other first ascents by the expedition were of Kalindis Parbat, Nanda Gunthi, White Dome, and Balbala.

45. Tenzing Norgay, *Tiger of the Snows*, 58. Also see Douglas, *Tenzing*, 119. The praise Tenzing received in the official expedition account showed that, even on this relatively egalitarian expedition, prewar conventions of European-Sherpa relations had not disappeared. The Swiss climbers valued the Sherpas, including Tenzing, as much as personal body servants as they did as climbing companions. "Tenzing, my man, was an absolute gem," Mme. Lohner would report. "Neat and full of initiative, he spoiled me dreadfully. Hardly had we arrived [at Base Camp] than I found my bedding roll and washing water laid out ready, and my box transformed into an elegant washstand" ("The Swiss Garhwal Expedition of 1947," 20).

46. H. W. Tilman, "Rakaposhi," *Alpine Journal* 56 (May 1948): 329–40; Tilman, *Two Mountains and a River,* 51–94; Mason, *Abode of Snow,* 299–300.

47. E. E. Shipton, "Mustagh Ata," *Alpine Journal* 56 (May 1948): 317–29; Shipton, *Mountains of Tartary,* 102–24. *Mountains of Tartary* was reprinted in Shipton, *The Six Mountain-Travel Books,* 455–587. Also see Tilman, *Two Mountains and a River,* 131–43; Steele, *Eric Shipton,* 129.

48. Among those forced to flee was a sixteen-year-old Sikh, M. S. (Manmohan) Kohli, who had spent his childhood years in his ancestral home in Haripur, in the North West Frontier Province of India, which became part of Pakistan. In 1947 he and his family fled across the newly established Pakistani-Indian border to escape the communal violence that had engulfed his homeland. In 1965 he would lead the first successful Indian expedition to the summit of Everest. Kohli, *Miracles of Ardaas,* 11, 45–57.

49. Keay, *India,* 511–54; Mason, *Abode of Snow,* 301. For a firsthand account of the partition and fighting in Kashmir by a Pakistani medical officer who later served as liaison officer for the 1953 and 1954 K2 expeditions, see Ata-Ullah, *Citizen of Two Worlds,* 182–203.

50. H. W. Tobin "Editorial," *Himalayan Journal* 14 (1948): 7.

51. John Martyn, "The Story of the Himalayan Club, 1928–1978," *Himalayan Journal* 35 (1977–78): 26–28. Also see Trevor Braham, "Recollections of a Former Editor," 19–23, and Harish Kapadia, "The Journey of the Journal," 24–32, both in *Himalayan Journal* 50 (1992–93).

52. During the Second World War Tibet initiated a modest opening to the West. The U.S. intelligence agency the OSS sent missions to Lhasa and provided the Dalai Lama's government with its first long-range radio transmitters. But the U.S. government was reluctant to take any formal steps toward acknowledging Tibet's independence, since to do so might offend the Nationalist Chinese government which, like the Communist government that came to power in 1949, claimed sovereignty over Tibet. Grunfeld, *The Making of Modern Tibet,* 82–83. A handful of foreigners were permitted to visit Tibet in the postwar years. John Nichols Booth, a Unitarian minister from the United States, made a solitary trek to Phari Dzong in 1948, a journey that he described in *Fabulous Destinations,* 208–39. In the summer of 1949 the Dalai Lama invited CBS radio reporters Lowell Thomas and his son, Lowell Thomas Jr., to visit Lhasa, where they met and reported on Harrer and Aufschnaiter's escape to Tibet, the first time that the general public had learned of the adventure. The Dalai Lama's invitation to Thomas and his son were part of an effort by the Tibetan government to gain American support for Tibetan independence, now that the Communists were replacing the Nationalists as the ruling power in China. Thomas, *So Long Until Tomorrow,* 163, 171; Thomas Jr. *Out of This World,* 29–30. Also see Harrer, *Seven Years in Tibet,* 220, 242–43. Lowell Thomas Jr. had planned to make a return trip to Lhasa in 1950 and invited Charlie Houston to accompany him. Houston was eager to visit the country, and he had also been asked to make a delivery of cortisone to the ailing operator of a clandestine anti-Communist radio transmitter in Tibet. The plans fell through because of the Communist invasion. Michael Ward, "The Exploration of the Nepalese Side of Everest," *Alpine Journal* 97 (1992): 216. The Dalai Lama, *My Land and My People,* 80–99; Avedon, *In Exile from the Lands of Snows,* 3–61; Goldstein, *The Snow Lion and the Dragon,* 43–60.

53. The last Western expedition to climb in Tibet before the Chinese invasion (albeit without the permission of the Tibetan government) was a small Anglo-Swiss party organized by Kenneth Berill and Alfred Tissières in 1950 to 24,130-foot (7,355-meter) Abi Gamin in the Garhwal. Crossing over into Tibet, they made their attempt from the Northeast Ridge, and on August 22 Tissières, René Dittert, Gabriel Chevalley, and Dawa Tondup reached the summit. Kenneth Berrill, "Abi Gamin, 1950," *Himalayan Journal* 17 (1952): 80–96. The next time Mustagh Ata was attempted was by a joint Soviet-Chinese expedition in 1956. Thirty-one climbers from the two Communist nations reached the summit after a prolonged siege. See Zhou and Liu, *Footprints on the Peaks,* 55–68; Rowell, *Mountains of the Middle Kingdom,* 10–11.

54. Tilman, *Nepal Himalaya.* 7, 1. Tilman's enumeration actually understated the mountaineering possibilities; instead of fourteen mountains over 25,000, there were "at least" twenty-three over that height, according to Walt Unsworth's estimate in the 1970s (*Encyclopedia of Mountaineering,* 261).

55. Ward, "The Exploration of the Nepalese Side of Everest," 216; M. P. Ward and P. K. Clark, "Everest, 1951: Cartographic and Photographic Evidence of a New Route from Nepal," *Geographical Journal* 158 (Mar. 1992): 47; Ward, *Everest,* 171.

56. On the travel arrangements from India to Kathmandu, see S. Dillon Ripley, "Peerless Nepal—A Naturalist's Paradise," *National Geographic* 97 (Jan. 1950): 5. Also see Tilman's description in *Nepal Himalaya,* 9–13.

57. Robert Trumbull, "Shangri-La Greets Traveler in Nepal," *New York Times,* July 17, 1950, 11; "Air Transportation to Nepal," *Appalachia* 15 (Dec. 1949): 507. To Lionel Terray, who first visited the city in 1954, Kathmandu was "a weird and wonderful place, a kind of Eden, out of this world, and out of all time" (Franco and Terray, *At Grips with Jannu,* 144). Also see Noyce, *South Col,* 42–44; Thomas, *So Long Until Tomorrow,* 208–9.

58. Trumbull, "Shangri-La Greets Traveler in Nepal," *New York Times,* 11; Robert Trumbull, "Nepal Reinforces Border with Tibet," *New York Times,* July 31, 1950, 9; Robert Trumbull, "Nepalese Capital an Air Hub in Sky," *New York Times,* Dec. 24, 1951, 3. When a foreign promoter suggested to King Tribhuvan in the early 1950s that it might be possible for Nepal to attract large numbers of tourists someday soon, he is reputed to have replied, "I can see why tourists want to visit a place like Calcutta, where there are things to do. But why would they want to come to Nepal, where all we have is mountains?" (William Borders, "Himalayas Lure Tourists to a Forbidding Kingdom," *New York Times,* May 29, 1978, 10).

59. An early postwar visitor, the American S. Dillon Ripley, would write in 1950, "If I ask a man if he is a Nepalese, I probably get a blank stare" ("Peerless Nepal," 4). Joshi and Rose, *Democratic Innovations in Nepal,* 38–39; Whelpton, *A History of Nepal,* 61–85.

60. Joshi and Rose, *Democratic Innovations in Nepal,* 57–58. The Nepalese living in India seemed to prefer working with the Americans, rather than with the British intelligence agents, perhaps assuming that they cherished fewer pretensions to colonial supremacy in the region. Smith, *OSS,* 290.

61. United States ambassador to India Henry Grady presented his credentials to the Nepalese government as minister to Nepal in May 1948. Diplomatic ties were raised to exchange of ambassadors in 1951, although the United States did not establish an embassy in Katmandu until 1959. Joshi and Rose, *Democratic Innovations in Nepal,* 60.

62. Grunfeld, *The Making of Modern Tibet,* 84. On Ripley's expeditions, see Ripley, *A Naturalist's Adventure;* Francis Leeson, "A Note on the US Expedition to Nepal," *Himalayan Journal* 15 (1949): 46–53. Ripley would go on to a distinguished career as an ornithologist, serving for twenty years as director of the Smithsonian Institution. But there may have been factors in addition to the interests of pure science bringing him to Nepal. Communists in India certainly suspected that was the case; they denounced Ripley's "bird hunt" as "an excellent opportunity for making political contacts." Ripley had served in American intelligence during World War II in the China-Burma-India theater, including a stint as chief of OSS counterintelligence in Southeast Asia. Ripley, *A Naturalist's Adventure,* 206; Smith, *OSS,* 314–15; Bart Barnes, "Smithsonian Visionary Ripley Dies; Secretary Enlivened Museums 'to Reach Out to People,'" *Washington Post,* Mar. 13, 2001, A01.

63. Tilman, *Nepal Himalaya,* 4; Baume, *Sivalaya,* 153, 165; Diemberger, *Summits and Secrets,* 194–95. Heim was a veteran of a 1930s expedition to Tibet. See Heim and Gansser, *The Throne of the Gods.* Steele, *Eric Shipton,* 140.

64. Tenzing Norgay, *Tiger of the Snows,* 84; H. W. Tilman, "The Nepal Himalaya," *Alpine Journal* 57 (May 1950): 305–12; Tilman, *Nepal Himalaya,* 68, 100.

65. René Dittert, "The Swiss Himalayan Expedition," *Himalayan Journal* 16 (1950): 25–37; Dittert and Chevalley, *Forerunners to Everest,* 15.

66. Lucien Devies was the most powerful figure in French mountaineering in the early postwar years, holding the posts of president of the Club alpin français, the Federation française de la montagne, and the Groupe de haute montagne. Defrance and Holblan, *Lucien Devies.*

67. Terray, *Conquistadors,* 235.

68. Roberts, *True Summit,* 83–84; Terray, *Conquistadors,* 101–2. Terray's climbing partner, Louis Lachenal, who had fled to Switzerland during the war to avoid compulsory labor service, had an even more pronounced antipathy to war and military service. Roberts, *True Summit,* 54–55.

69. Roberts, *True Summit,* 33. Herzog, who approved of the oath, admitted that "[m]ountaineers don't care for ceremonies" but claimed that his fellow climbers gave the impression of being both "awkward and impressed" during the oath taking (*Annapurna,* 25). Herzog's leadership style was less rigid than the Devies oath would suggest. "His flexible and friendly nature enabled him to get his way with individualists who would have rowed with an overt authoritarian," Terray would later write (*Conquistadors,* 237).

70. Terray wrote that this route "had only been followed once before by westerners, a group of American ornithologists" (*Conquistadors,* 258). S. Dillon Ripley and his party had actually explored the Karnali river valley, farther west. The French were the first Westerners to explore the Kali Gandaki.

71. Herzog, *Annapurna,* 35–36. In *Annapurna* Herzog often failed to identify individual speakers, as though the expedition spoke with a single voice, as mediated through his own memory.

72. It is possible that they were feigning ignorance. Unlike the Sherpas of the Solu Khumbu region, the Bhotias living in the Annapurna region did not benefit economically from the foreign expeditions that came to climb their mountains. Later expeditions would sometimes be attacked by mobs of local villagers who pillaged their supplies and forced them to pay extortion to secure the right to climb. See Kohli, *Sherpas,* 31–34.

73. Herzog, *Annapurna,* 42; Terray, *Conquistadors,* 242, 245.

74. Herzog, *Annapurna,* 43–44.

75. Ibid., 69.

76. Ibid., 68–69. Also see G. O. Dyhrenfurth and Norman Dyhrenfurth, "Dhaulagiri," *Mountain* 63 (Sept.–Oct. 1978): 32.

77. Herzog, *Annapurna,* 42.

78. The Miristi Khola was a formidable obstacle in itself. On the return march from Annapurna in June, a porter fell to his death on its steep slopes, as Louis Lachenal noted in his expedition diary. Herzog made no mention of the death in his expedition book. Viesturs and Roberts, *No Shortcuts to the Top,* 211–12.

79. "Without quite knowing why," Rébuffat would later write, he and Lachenal decided from the first that the Northwest Spur would not work; instead they set out to find "the rational and proper route," which they felt would lie on the North Face (*Mount Blanc to Everest,* 83).

80. Chris Bonington, who led an expedition to Annapurna's South Face two decades later, described the mountain's northern exposure as resembling "the North Face of Mont Blanc writ large" (*The Climbers,* 186).

81. Herzog, *Annapurna,* 191. Lachenal showed similar enthusiasm, writing in his journal on May 31, "This morning, one more time, I set out not to descend again until after I have made the summit" (Roberts, *True Summit,* 91).

82. Herzog, *Annapurna,* 197. It was a prudent choice and perhaps saved his life, but it also meant that Ang Tharkay chose obscurity over the fame that would come to his fellow Sherpa Tenzing Norgay three years later on Everest. As Ed Douglas suggested in his biography of Tenzing, "Had Tenzing and not Ang Tharkay been at Camp V on Annapurna on June 2, 1950, he would—almost certainly—have agreed to go with Herzog and Lachenal to the top" (*Tenzing,* 131). Also see Ang Tharkay's autobiography, *Mémoires d'un Sherpa,* and the chapter devoted to Ang Tharkay in Kohli, *Sherpas,* 78–86.

83. Herzog, *Annapurna,* 204–6.

84. Roberts, *True Summit,* 224–25. For the expurgated version, see Lachenal, *Carnets du vertige.* The un-expurgated edition was published by Editions Guerin in 1996. It is hard not to come away from this exchange of views feeling that Lachenal is the more sympathetic character of the two, and in *True Summit* David Roberts writes that "Lachenal's instinct to turn around . . . was the right one." (223). But Herzog had not insisted that Lachenal continue on with him to the summit and risk either his feet or his life. Herzog hazarded his own life that day and in choosing to do so showed that his instincts were more closely aligned than Lachenal's to the demands of Himalayan climbing. Edmund Hillary would conclude after Eric Shipton made a cautious decision to turn back below the Western Cwm on the Everest reconnaissance expedition in 1951 that "the only way to attempt this mountain was to modify the old standards of safety and justifiable risk," which is precisely what Herzog did on Annapurna. Hillary, *High Adventure,* 48–50. For an account of the Annapurna climb more sympathetic to Herzog than Roberts's version, see Messner, *Annapurna,* 18–23, 58–64, 68–78. Herzog, *Annapurna,* 206–7.

85. Herzog, *Annapurna,* 208.

86. Ibid., 209.

87. Terray, *Conquistadors,* 287, 288.

88. Ibid., 86, 295.

89. For accounts of the ascent and descent of Annapurna, see Maurice Herzog, "Annapurna," *Alpine Journal* 58 (Nov. 1951): 155–68; Maurice Herzog, "Annapurna," *La montagne: Revue officielle du Club alpin français* (Oct.–Dec. 1950): 80–106; Herzog, *Annapurna;* Terray, *Conquistadors,* 232–306; Roberts, *True Summit.*

90. "Victoire sur l'Himalaya," *Paris Match,* Aug. 19, 1950, 12–27.

91. "M. Vincent Auriol, president de la Republique, salue l'Expedition Française a l'Himalaya," *La montagne: Revue officielle du Club alpin français* (Oct.–Dec. 1950): 79.

92. Roberts, *True Summit,* 154. Bound by a contract restricting how soon he could publish anything about his experiences on Annapurna, Rébuffat included only a few lines about the expedition in his 1954 memoir *Starlight and Storm.*

93. Herzog, *Annapurna,* 311.

94. James Ramsey Ullman, "Great Climb, Gallant Chronicle," *New York Herald Tribune,* Jan. 18, 1953, section 6, 1. Ullman also wrote a feature story about the Annapurna climb for *Life* magazine, "Trial by Ice," July 9, 1951, 84–94. British reviewers tended to be less enthusiastic than their American counterparts. John Hills, writing in the *London Spectator,* found himself wishing that the practical-minded Louis Lachenal rather than Herzog had written the account: "For Herzog gets into an alarming state of emotional exaltation, unlike anything I have ever met" ("Emotion on the Heights," Dec. 5, 1952, 786). When Kenneth Mason wrote about Herzog in his history of Himalayan climbing, he could barely disguise his disdain. He was particularly annoyed at the French presumption in criticizing the India Survey maps of the Annapurna region: "It is a curious trait among some mountaineers who set out to explore new ground," he growled, "that they expect to have a map of it accurate in detail; they like to have it both ways: to be the first there and to have had surveyors there before them" (*Abode of Snow,* 315). "Himalayan Victory," *Time,* Jan. 12, 1953, 96. A few years after the climb Herzog's enduring celebrity was confirmed in the United States, that least mountaineering-minded country, in an odd place—the daily crossword of the *New York Times.* In a puzzle appearing in April 1953, the clue for 17 across (nine letters) read, "Highest mountain conquered by man," and the clue for 56 down (four letters) read, "Maurice Herzog's playground" (Apr. 25, 1953, 13). The correct answer to 17 across was, of course, "Annapurna," to 56 down, less predictably, "Alps."

CHAPTER SEVEN: *"Don't Be a Chicken-Hearted Fellow," 1950–1953*

1. Shipton, *Upon That Mountain,* 191–92.

2. Ibid., 104.

3. For the past decade or so, Tilman had been complaining to his readers about his increasing infirmity, all the while going on to make pathbreaking climbs and exploratory trips. His report on his trip to the Annapurna Himal was no exception: "However well a man in his fifties may go up to 20,000 ft.," he wrote, "I have come regretfully to the conclusion that above that height, so far as climbing goes, he is declining into decrepitude" (*Nepal Himalaya,* 164). Also see H. W. Tilman, "The Annapurna Himal and South Side of Everest," *Alpine Journal* 58 (May 1951): 101–10.

4. Letter from Shingha to Loy Henderson, Apr. 21, 1950, Himalaya Library Archives, box Mount Everest, 1912–1960, folder 1950, Clippings and articles, American Alpine Club Library. For an obituary of the elder Houston, see "Oscar R. Houston, Lawyer, 86, Dead," *New York Times,* Dec. 21, 1969, 62.

5. Among Cowles's climbing credentials were difficult ascents in the Tetons with Glen Exum, Paul Petzoldt, and Bob Bates. Andy Bakewell had worked with Bob Bates in Alaska in 1941, testing cold-weather supplies for the U.S. Army. See Bates, *The Love of Mountains Is Best,* 164, 170.

6. Tilman, *Nepal Himalaya,* 212. On the natural advantages of climbing Everest from the south, see Murray, *The Story of Everest,* 168–69; Charles Houston, "Towards Everest, 1950," *Himalayan Journal* 17 (1952): 9; Mason, *Abode of Snow,* 327–28; Unsworth, *Everest,* 281. Despite his disparaging remarks about women on expeditions, Tilman would remain friends with Betsy Cowles until his death. Madge, *The Last Hero,* 124.

7. Houston, "Towards Everest," 11; Tilman, *Nepal Himalaya,* 215. According to Houston the slogan was written above the schoolhouse door; in Tilman's account it was chalked on a Hindu shrine close by the school. Also see Robertson, *Betsy Cowles Partridge,* 124.

8. Tilman, *Nepal Himalaya,* 216.

9. Ibid., 224.

10. Houston, "Towards Everest," 12. On their return to the monastery a few days later Tilman discovered that the monks also "had the pleasant custom of fortifying their guests with a snorter [of raksi] before breakfast" (*Nepal Himalaya,* 230). Houston, "Towards Everest," 13.

11. Houston, "Towards Everest," 14.

12. Today the summit of Kala Patar is frequently climbed by trekkers. See Maurice Isserman, "Himalayan Summitry: A Lesser Peak, Not a Lesser Lesson," *Christian Science Monitor,* July 3, 2007, 24.

13. By the time Tilman published *Nepal Himalaya,* the book that described this reconnaissance, he had begun to realize his error: "From the map, we appeared to be due west of the south [i.e., southeast] ridge and were thus seeing it in profile. . . . I now think we were not looking at its true edge, but merely a buttress protruding from the south-west face" (235). Also see Michael Ward, "The Exploration of the Nepalese Side of Everest," *Alpine Journal* 97 (1992): 217; Ward, *Everest,* 172–74; Steele, *Eric Shipton,* 142–43. Sir Edmund Hillary would later express surprise that "such experienced men" as Houston and Tilman "should have made the mistake they did make on that trip" ("Mountain Interview: Sir Edmund Hillary," *Mountain* 45 [Sept.–Oct. 1975]: 31).

14. Elizabeth Cowles to "Dear People," Nov. 23, 1950, Houston Everest Expedition 1950, American Alpine Club Archives, box 5, American Alpine Club Library.

15. Robert Trumbull, "U.S. Expedition Goes 18,000 Feet Up Unexplored Side of Mt. Everest," *New York Times,* Dec. 11, 1950, 1. Houston offered a discouraging analysis to his fellow climbers in subsequent reports in the leading climbing journals, suggesting that the south side of the mountain did not offer "a reasonable route by which to climb Everest." See Charles S. Houston, "South Face of Mount Everest," *American Alpine Journal*

8 (1951): 18; Houston, "Towards Everest," 15. Tilman's assessment was equally pessimistic in his report for the *Alpine Journal:* "[A]lthough we cannot yet dismiss the south side, I think it is safe to say that there is no route comparable in ease and safety—at any rate up to 28,000 ft.—to that by the north east" ("The Annapurna Himal and South Side of Everest," *Alpine Journal* 58 [May 1951]: 109). The Swiss climbers who tackled Everest in 1952 understood Tilman and Houston to say that the south side was "very difficult, if not impossible." See Dittert and Chevalley, *Forerunners to Everest,* 57–58.

16. Elizabeth Cowles to "Dear Friends," Dec. 4, 1950, Houston Everest Expedition 1950, American Alpine Club Archives, box 5, American Alpine Club Library.

17. For an overview of Nepalese political history from the early to mid-twentieth century, see Bernstein, *In the Himalayas,* 48–53. For the events of 1950–51, see Singh, *Impact of the Indian National Movement on the Political Development of Nepal,* 178–92; Joshi and Rose, *Democratic Innovations in Nepal,* 57–102.

18. Houston, "South Face of Mount Everest," 20–21. For other accounts of the Houston-Tilman reconnaissance, see Dr. Charles S. Houston, "Venture into Forbidden Nepal," *Look,* Jan. 1, 1952, 50–54; Elizabeth Cowles, "North to Everest: Eastern Nepal, 1950," *American Alpine Journal* 7 (1951): 1–11; Madge, *The Last Hero,* 119–26; Anderson, *High Mountains and Cold Seas,* 244–49; Robertson, *Betsy Cowles Partridge,* 101–64; Dyhrenfurth, *To the Third Pole,* 32–34. Bill Murray offered a judicious assessment of the importance of the Houston-Tilman reconnaissance: "It was not what they discovered but the fact that they were there at all that was so stimulating an event" (*The Story of Everest,* 142).

19. Ward recounted his early fascination with Everest in his memoir *In This Short Span,* 18. Although he never achieved the fame of some of the climbers with whom he was associated in the next few years, he played a singularly important role in furthering British exploration in the Himalaya for three decades, as well as in contributing to the development of the field of high-altitude physiology. Ward died in 2005. Margalit Fox, "Michael Ward, 80, Doctor on '53 Everest Climb, Dies," *New York Times,* Oct. 25, 2005, C19. Shipton later suggested that the initial plans hatched by Ward and his friends included a possible summit attempt. No other source mentions that possibility. Shipton, *That Untravelled World,* 186. Also see Ward, "The Exploration of the Nepalese Side of Everest," 217–18; M. P. Ward and P. K. Clark, "Everest 1951: Cartographic and Photographic Evidence of a New Route from Nepal," *Geographical Journal* 158 (Mar. 1992): 47–56; Ward, *Everest,* 174–79; Murray, *The Story of Everest,* 143. The 1945 flight over Everest is described in Andrews, *Flight over Everest,* while the 1947 flight is described in K. Neame, "Alone over Everest," *Mountain World* (1955): 131–41.

20. Ward, "The Exploration of the Nepalese Side of Everest," 218; Ward, *Everest,* 179.

21. Secord, a Canadian economist working in London, had made a pioneering reconnaissance of Rakaposhi in the Karakoram in 1938. Murray had led a Scottish Mountaineering Club expedition in 1950 that made the first ascent of the North Ridge of Uja Tirche (20,347ft/6,202m). See W. H. Murray, "Scottish Garhwal and Kumaon Expedition," *Alpine Journal* 58 (May 1951): 49–66; Murray, *The Scottish Himalayan Expedition;* Murray, *The Evidence of Things Not Seen,* 151–90. Although Murray and his companions believed their climb of Uja Tirche to be a first ascent of the mountain, it was discovered years later that there had been an earlier unrecorded ascent of the West Southwest Ridge by a British army surveyor in 1937. Ward, *In This Short Span,* 58; Steele, *Eric Shipton,* 144–45. While Ward was sifting Everest photographs in the RGS archives, a Danish adventurer by the name of Klaus Becker-Larsen was actually heading up the mountain's flanks. Becker-Larsen departed from Darjeeling headed for Everest's north side on March 31. Accompanied by seven Sherpas, he crossed the Nangpa La (18,750ft/5,716m) from Nepal into Tibet, the first European to do so. Larsen followed the old British route up the East Rongbuk Glacier to what had been Camp III, below the North Col. On May 7 he attempted to climb to the North Col, as prelude to a solo attempt on the summit, but the Sherpas who had accompanied him this far had had enough and refused to go any farther. They returned to Nepal across the Nangpa La, a step ahead of the Chinese soldiers who had heard of the Western interloper and come looking for him. Larsen was lucky to escape with his freedom and his life; still, given his lack of any previous

high-altitude experience, he had pulled off an impressive feat. Ward, *Everest,* 183; Messner, *The Crystal Horizon,* 83–85.

22. Murray, *Evidence of Things Not Seen,* 275; Shipton, *The Mount Everest Reconnaissance Expedition,* 18; Shipton, *That Untravelled World,* 185.

23. Shipton, *The Mount Everest Reconnaissance Expedition,* 18–19.

24. Shipton, *That Untravelled World,* 152, 187; Steele, *Eric Shipton,* 65. The New Zealand climbers, all on their first trip to the Himalaya, had originally hoped to attempt Kangchenjunga. But permission for the mountain never came, and instead they decided to attempt some lower but challenging peaks in the Garhwal. Earle Riddiford, Ed Cotter, and Sherpa Pasang did a first ascent of Mukut Parbat (23,760ft/7,242m), the highest peak yet climbed by New Zealanders, and at that point the fifteenth-highest mountain in the world to have been climbed. The group also summited five other peaks over 20,000 feet. The New Zealand expedition is described in H. E. Riddiford, "Expedition to the Garhwal Himalaya, 1951," *New Zealand Alpine Journal* 14 (June 1952): 170–93. Also see Hillary, *High Adventure,* 18–19; Hillary, *Nothing Venture,* 112–29; Bryant, *New Zealanders and Everest,* 31–35.

25. Lowe, *Because It Is There,* 18.

26. Hillary, *High Adventure,* 16; Shipton, *The Mount Everest Reconnaissance Expedition,* 38; Shipton, *That Untravelled World,* 189–90.

27. Hillary got along well with his new British climbing partners, though he and Riddiford were aware of the social distance that existed between themselves and the climbing establishment in England. Having been told he would be reimbursed by the Alpine Club for incidental expenses incurred while on the expedition, Hillary dutifully wrote down everything he spent, including the hot drinks he occasionally purchased along the trail. When he submitted the itemized bill he was informed by the club treasurer, "Gentlemen are expected to pay for their own cups of tea." Hillary wrote back to say they made no claim to that designation (Steele, *Eric Shipton,* 158). Shipton, *The Mount Everest Reconnaissance Expedition,* 39–40; Steele, *Eric Shipton,* 153.

28. Hillary, *High Adventure,* 40–41. Shipton, on the other hand, would later write that he had had to "divert" Hillary's attention from the north side of the mountain to its southern exposure (*That Untravelled World,* 192).

29. Hillary, *Nothing Venture,* 136. Shipton's decision to abandon Everest for two weeks in midexpedition may seem, in retrospect, an odd one. Shipton and his companions had come a long way, at considerable expense, to find a route up the southern side of Mount Everest. Now they were heading off to explore subsidiary glacier systems, all very interesting but beside the point of the expedition that the sponsors thought they were paying for. The decision, however, was utterly characteristic of Shipton, who as contemporaries and later writers would note, always seemed more interested in being an explorer than a mountaineer. It was also fully consistent with his actions on the 1935 Everest reconnaissance, when he delayed his expedition's arrival at the north side of the mountain to explore two previously unexplored ranges in Tibet, Nyonno Ri and Ama Drime. Unsworth, *Hold the Heights,* 350–51. Shipton's decision to explore the region surrounding the southern approach to Everest in 1951 found at least one prominent supporter at the time: Gunther Dyhrenfurth commented, "The area they explored had never been trodden before by human feet: the geographical and mountaineering results were of the first importance" (*To the Third Pole,* 45).

30. Shipton, *The Mount Everest Reconnaissance Expedition,* 48; Hillary, *High Adventure,* 50.

31. Ward, *In This Short Span,* 80. Hillary was among those disappointed in Shipton's decision not to push on into the cwm: "[I]n my heart," he would write a few years later, "I knew the only way to attempt this mountain was to modify the old standards of safety and justifiable risk" (*High Adventure,* 48). Also see Unsworth, *Hold the Heights,* 362. In his own autobiography, published nearly three decades later, Shipton passed over the whole exploration of the icefall and the decision not to push on further very quickly. "It was disappointing not to be able to go to the head of the Cwm," he would write, "though in fact there was little of

importance to be learned by doing so" (*That Untravelled World,* 193). Also see Murray, *Evidence of Things Not Seen,* 276; Ward, *Everest,* 192–94.

32. "Grand View of Everest/First Exploration of the Great Ice-Fall," *Times,* Oct. 7, 1951, Newspaper Clippings Archive, vol. 30, Alpine Club; Shipton, *The Mount Everest Reconnaissance Expedition,* 91. Also see E. P. Hillary, "A New Approach to Everest," *New Zealand Alpine Journal* 14 (June 1952): 194–205; W. H. Murray, "The Reconnaissance of Mount Everest, 1951," *Alpine Journal* 58 (Nov. 1952): 433–52.

33. Steele, *Eric Shipton,* 163; Ward, *In This Short Span,* 90; Hansen, "Coronation Everest," 60.

34. Gunther Dyhrenfurth doubtless had Shipton in mind when he wrote that "in the most friendly spirit the British gave way to the Swiss for the 1952 attempt on Everest" (*To the Third Pole,* 51). Basil Goodfellow of the Himalayan Committee was convinced "that the Swiss, for all their affability, were determined to be the dominant partner," an attitude that, given the fact that they held all the advantages and had little incentive to make concessions, was not surprising. Memo on the Everest Expedition Leadership for 1953, T. J. Blakeney, Nov. 1967, Mount Everest Expedition Archives, box 66, folder 1, Royal Geographical Society; Eric Shipton, "Brief Summary of the British Himalayan Expedition 1952," Blakeney Collection, Add. Mss. 63122, British Library. Also see Steele, *Eric Shipton,* 165–66; Shipton, *That Untravelled World,* 206; Hansen, "Confetti," 316–17; Unsworth, *Everest,* 279–80.

35. As far as the British were concerned, making the second ascent of Everest after the Swiss would in some ways be more humiliating than making no ascent at all. The Himalayan Committee agreed that should the Swiss prove successful in 1952, the British would switch their own expedition in 1953 to Kangchenjunga. John Hunt, letter dated Nov. 28, 1952, Mount Everest Expedition Archives, box 66, folder 2, Royal Geographical Society.

36. "Doctor Will Study Everest Climbers," *New York Times,* Mar. 8, 1952, 19; West, *High Life,* 272; Ward, *Everest,* 165–66. Griffith Pugh is a significant figure in the history of Himalayan climbing who has yet to find a biographer: his obituary was published in *Alpine Journal* 100 (1995): 326–29; his papers are collected in Mandeville Special Collections Library, Geisel Library, University of California, San Diego.

37. Hillary, *High Adventure,* 68. As British consul in Kunming in Yunnan province in China 1949–51, Shipton had witnessed the Communist takeover and the police state that was imposed. Shipton knew that he was already a marked man in the Communist world. The 1951 Everest reconnaissance team had been denounced in the Moscow publication *Soviet Sport* as "cunning agents of British imperialism." "Spies on Everest?" *Manchester Guardian,* Nov. 28, 1951, Newspaper Clippings Archive, vol. 30, Alpine Club; Steele, *Eric Shipton,* 136–38.

38. Hillary, *High Adventure,* 68, 71. Also see Hillary, *Nothing Venture,* 139–40; R. C. Evans, "The Cho Oyu Expedition, 1952," *Alpine Journal* 59 (May 1953): 9–18; G. O. Dyhrenfurth and Norman Dyhrenfurth, "Cho Oyu," *Mountain* 60 (Mar.–Apr. 1978): 40. On the way back, passing Everest, Hillary and George Lowe made one more foray into Communist territory, crossing over the 19,400-foot Nup La into Tibet, crossing the Rongbuk Glacier to its spur, the East Rongbuk, the traditional British route to the North Ridge of Everest. Coming to the remains of Camp I, Hillary had an "eerie feeling," as though "the ghosts of Mallory and Irvine and Smythe were still flitting among the ruins" (*High Adventure,* 94–95).

39. Apart from his leadership of the 1952 Everest expedition, Wyss-Dunant is also famed in mountaineering history for coining the phrase *zone of death* (or *death zone*) in 1953 to describe the effect of prolonged stays at altitudes above 25,500 feet. See Tichy, *Himalaya,* 170–71.

40. Tenzing Norgay, *Tiger of the Snows,* 108; Robert McG. Thomas Jr., "Raymond Lambert, 82, Dies; Paved the Way on Mt. Everest," *New York Times,* Mar. 3, 1997, B10; Douglas, *Tenzing,* 151.

41. Dittert and Chevalley, *Forerunners to Everest,* 19–55; Michael L. Hoffman, "Swiss Off on Bid to Everest," *New York Times,* Mar. 14, 1952, 3; Tenzing Norgay, *Tiger of the Snows,* 109; Robert Trumbull, "Nepalese Capital an Air Hub in Sky," *New York Times,* Dec. 24, 1951, 3; Unsworth, *Everest,* 283. Not all expeditions in

the 1950s left from Kathmandu: In 1956 the Swiss expedition to Everest left from Jaynagar, on the Indian-Nepalese border, but returned via the route to Kathmandu.

42. Dittert and Chevalley, *Forerunners to Everest*, 78.

43. Ibid., 67.

44. The Swiss choice of this route, rather than the one suggested by Shipton, was the "key error" of the expedition, in Edmund Hillary's judgment (*High Adventure*, 103–4).

45. Dittert and Chevalley, *Forerunners to Everest*, 146.

46. Ibid., 147. It is not unusual for the winds sweeping the South Col to be stronger than those felt at the summit. See Krakauer, *Into Thin Air*, 210. Tenzing's grandson, Tashi, writes in his book about his grandfather, "What other Sherpa or Western climber, I wonder, could have matched my grandfather's performance in these conditions?" (Tashi Tenzing, *Tenzing Norgay*, 96). Ed Douglas wrote, "This was Tenzing at the height of his powers, doing things on a big mountain that very few modern climbers, with the best equipment and training, could match" (*Tenzing*, 165).

47. Tenzing Norgay, *Tiger of the Snows*, 118.

48. Raymond Lambert, "The Attack upon the Summit," *Mountain World* (1953): 93; Tenzing Norgay, *Tiger of the Snows*, 119; Dittert and Chevalley, *Forerunners to Everest*, 149.

49. Dittert and Chevalley, *Forerunners to Everest*, 19.

50. Lambert, "The Attack upon the Summit," 94.

51. Based on interviews with Sir Edmund Hillary and John Hunt, both of whom saw the site of the 1952 Swiss camp on their own expedition in 1953, Bradford Washburn estimated that Tenzing and Lambert had pitched their tent and spent the night of May 28 at 27,265 feet. If that is accurate, then the 650 feet Lambert and Tenzing gained would have brought them to a high point of 27,915 feet. Bradford Washburn, "The Location of Camp IX," *Alpine Journal* 108 (2003): 20–21. Raymond Lambert, introduction to Lambert and Kogan, *White Fury*, 12. For the summit bid, see André Roch, "The Swiss Everest Expedition—Spring, 1952," *Alpine Journal* 59 (May 1953): 1–9; Lambert, "The Attack upon the Summit," 89–95; Dittert and Chevalley, *Forerunners to Everest*, 151–53; Dyhrenfurth, *To the Third Pole*, 50–54; Douglas, *Tenzing*, 160–67; Unsworth, *Everest*, 284–91; Ward, *Everest*, 207–16. Also see the photo history of the expedition by André Roch, *Everest 1952*.

52. Dittert and Chevalley, *Forerunners to Everest*, 173. On the march out, when they reached Tengboche Monastery the Swiss met Shipton, Gregory, and Bourdillion returning from Cho Oyu. At Namche Bazar they met Hillary, returning from an excursion to the East Rongbuk Glacier in Tibet. He found the Swiss "disappointed but still generous" with information about their experience (*View from the Summit*, 95).

53. Dittert and Chevalley, *Forerunners to Everest*, 224–25; Douglas, *Tenzing*, 169. As described below, there may have been six unrecorded deaths on a secret Russian expedition on the northern side of the mountain that same fall. Dittert and Chevalley, *Forerunners to Everest*, 254; Michael L. Hoffman, "Swiss Start for Mount Everest Again," *New York Times*, Aug. 29, 1952, 25; Norman Dyhrenfurth, "Mount Everest, 1952," *American Alpine Journal* 8 (1953): 408; Dyhrenfurth, *To the Third Pole*, 54–57.

54. C. E. J. Crawford to Lt. Col. H. W. "Toby" Tobin, Oct. 4, 1952, Mount Everest Expedition Archives, folder "Himalayan Club," Royal Geographical Society; Douglas, *Tenzing*, 173; Tashi Tenzing, *Tenzing Norgay*, 105, 108; Douglas, *Tenzing*, 150.

55. "Russians Plan Climb," *New York Times*, Dec. 24, 1951, 4; "Russian Attack on Everest, Failure with Loss of Six Lives," *The Times*, Sept. 12, 1953, 5. More recent accounts, including Yevgeniy B. Gippenreiter, "Mount Everest and the Russians, 1952 and 1958," *Alpine Journal* 99 (1994): 109–15, and Unsworth, *Everest*, 345–47, have expressed skepticism about whether the alleged expedition or disaster ever happened. Unsworth, for example, argues that Chinese denials that the Soviet expedition took place are persuasive, given chilly Chinese-Soviet relations, "for it would have been a golden opportunity to make political capital at their arch-enemy's

expense." But it could also be argued that, given the Sino-Soviet split, the Chinese might be reluctant to admit they had ever been so dependent on their former ally as to permit it the honor of launching the first major postwar attempt on the north side of the mountain.

56. Hillary, *Nothing Venture,* 142; Steele, *Eric Shipton,* 185–86. T. J. Blakeney, who had been assistant secretary of the Alpine Club in 1952, looking back on the Shipton controversy from a perspective of a decade and a half, offered this comment on the discussion that took place that summer in the Himalayan Committee: "[T]he considerable success achieved by the Swiss on Everest was felt to contrast heavily with the British failure to achieve anything on Cho Oyu. . . . Everest, it seemed to me, was on so much bigger a scale than other mts., that if we were not to have yet another indecisive expedition, like those of the 1930s, new blood was needed." Memo on the Everest Expedition Leadership for 1953, T. J. Blakeney, Nov. 1967, Mount Everest Expedition Archives, box 66, folder 1, Royal Geographical Society.

57. For Hunt's climbing record in the Karakoram, see John Hunt, "The Expedition to Peak 'K36,' 1935," *Alpine Journal* 47 (May 1935): 282–87. Also see Hunt, *Life Is Meeting,* 46, 52–53.

58. Steele, *Eric Shipton,* 188. Also see Hunt, *Life Is Meeting,* 112.

59. Shipton, *That Untravelled World,* 211–12.

60. In 1971 T. J. Blakeney once more reviewed the circumstances of Shipton's downfall, this time in a letter to Claude Elliott, who had been president of the Alpine Club and the Himalayan Committee at the time the events transpired in 1952: "Looking back at it all, my feeling is . . . that the right thing was done, tho' the thing hadn't been handled in the best way. The major error was made at the Comtee [Himalayan Committee meeting] of July 28, when Shipton was induced to accept the leadership, despite his expressed diffidence. As you may recall, it was a small comtee and Kirwan [secretary of the Royal Geographical Society] was v[ery] strong on the side of Shipton being selected, and really the basic trouble lay in the fact that hardly anyone knew [John] Hunt in those days. And, of course, there was some argument (as heavily urged by Kirwan, I remember) in favour of using Shipton, who was well-known to Sherpas, etc." Later that summer, Blakeney continued, "[Harry] Tobin, [Donald George] Lowndes, [Claremont] Skrine (and in the background a bit, [James] Wordie) [set out] to stage a revolt" against Shipton's leadership. Letter from T. J. Blakeney to Claude Elliott, June 7, 1971, Blakeney Collection, Add. Mss. 63122, British Library. "What emerges, from close examination of relevant Himalayan Committee minutes and written submissions from its surviving members," Jim Perrin wrote in a judicious appraisal of the affair many years later, "is a bizarre tale of fudging and mudging, falsification of official minutes, unauthorized invitations, and opportunistic and desperate last-minute seizures of initiative by a particular faction. It is a perfect illustration of the cock-up rather than the conspiracy theory of history, from which little credit redounds on the British mountaineering establishment of the time" (Perrin, introduction, 13). Also see the well-documented account in Cameron, *To the Farthest Ends of the Earth,* 189–95.

61. Hunt, *Life Is Meeting,* 113.

62. Cameron, *To the Farthest Ends of the Earth,* 190.

63. Shipton, *That Untravelled World,* 213.

64. E. E. S. [Eric Shipton], to "Claude" [Elliott], Sept. 14, 1952, Blakeney Collection, Add. Mss. 63122, British Library.

65. Eric Shipton, "Will They Climb Mt. Everest Now?" *Collier's,* Apr. 4, 1953, 11.

66. Johnston, *Reaching the Summit,* 48. Also see "Everest Leader Resigns," *New York Times,* Oct. 9, 1952, 8; Shipton, *That Untravelled World,* 211–14; Ward, *In This Short Span,* 93; Hillary, *High Adventure,* 114; Hunt, *Life Is Meeting,* 114. Murray to Margaret, Oct. 13, 1952, in Murray, *Evidence of Things Not Seen,* 340.

67. B. R. Goodfellow to Earle Riddiford, n.d., 1952, Mount Everest Expedition Archives, box 66, folder 2, Royal Geographical Society. For Hillary's personal plea to Hunt to allow Harry Ayres to accompany the expedition, and Hunt's refusal, see Edmund Hillary to John Hunt, Nov. 2, 1952, and John Hunt to Edmund

Hillary, Nov. 12, 1952, Mount Everest Expedition Archives, box 68, folder "Organization—Hillary and Lowe," Royal Geographical Society. For the "half-commitment to take two Americans," see "Notes for Colonel H. C. J. Hunt," n.d., 1952, Mount Everest Expedition Archives, box 66, folder 2, Royal Geographical Society. Also see the collection of letters exchanged between Henry Hall, president of the American Alpine Club, and Claude Elliott, president of the Alpine Club, in the spring and summer of 1952, contained in box 10, folder "Himalaya, Everest, 1952 and 1953," American Alpine Club Library.

68. In fact, there would be two *Times* correspondents reporting on Everest; Morris on the mountainside and Arthur Hutchinson to assist him in Kathmandu. The expedition also drew a number of reporters from other papers to Nepal, who did their best to pick up what scraps of unofficial information came their way from porters and messengers traveling between Base Camp and Kathmandu. For an account by one of the most persistent of the *Times*'s competitors, see *Daily Telegraph* reporter Ralph Izzard's book, *An Innocent on Everest.*

69. Peter H. Hansen noted the many ways in which the British government aided the expedition in his essay "Coronation Everest," 61–62.

70. Noyce, *South Col,* 17.

71. Ward, *In This Short Span,* 97; Hunt, *The Ascent of Everest,* 95, 269–74.

72. "Equipment for Everest, British Industry's Contribution," *The Times,* June 9, 1953, 4; Hunt, *The Ascent of Everest,* 57–58; Band, *Everest,* 129.

73. West, *High Life,* 272.

74. See Stephen Venables, "The Long Ascent, 1921–1953," in Venables, *Everest,* 166.

75. Noyce, *South Col,* 52.

76. C. E. J. Crawford to Lt. Col. H. W. "Toby" Tobin, Oct. 4, 1952; C. E. J. Crawford to John Hunt, Oct. 21, 1952, both in Mount Everest Expeditions Archives, box 68, folder "Himalayan Club," Royal Geographical Society. For the 1951 pay dispute, see Unsworth, *Everest,* 283.

77. *Times* correspondent James Morris stayed in something calling itself the "Nepal Hotel," which he described as a "defunct palace of incomparable discomfort" (*Coronation Everest,* 27). The incident at the embassy went unmentioned in the official expedition account. Tenzing wrote about it in his own autobiography, *Tiger of the Snows,* 137–38. Also see Tashi Tenzing, *Tenzing Norgay,* 113; Douglas, *Tenzing,* 181. There was further grumbling along the route, culminating in the firing of two Sherpas at Tengboche as troublemakers. Tenzing Norgay, *Tiger of the Snows,* 134.

78. One potential disaster was discovered when they first arrived in the shadow of the mountain: Tom Bourdillion, who was in charge of the oxygen equipment, learned to his horror that nearly a third of the oxygen bottles they had carried in with them had leaked their contents en route. Fortunately, a second shipment of over 100 oxygen bottles brought to Base Camp in early April from Kathmandu by Major Jimmy Roberts did not leak. Hunt, *The Ascent of Everest,* 93; Ward, *Everest,* 252; Morris, *Coronation Everest,* 41.

79. John Hunt, "Everest Men in Readiness," *The Times,* May 13, 1953, 8.

80. For Hunt's pledge, see Hillary, *High Adventure,* 119.

81. John Hunt, "Letters from Everest," *Alpine Journal* 98 (1993): 14; Hillary, *Nothing Venture,* 147; Hunt, *Life Is Meeting,* 114.

82. James Morris, "The Effect of Everest," *Alpine Journal* 98 (1993): 73; Morris, *Coronation Everest,* 83. Because it took so long for Morris's dispatches to make their way into print, other news agencies filled in the gap with reports cobbled together from rumor. Thus the United Press reported in late May that two British teams had tried and failed to climb the mountain, the first consisting of George Band and Michael Westmacott, the

second of Edmund Hillary and Alfred Gregory. "2 Everest Teams Fail in First Tries," *New York Times,* May 26, 1953, 6. "Charles Kenneth Howard-Bury, 1883–1963," *Alpine Journal* 69 (May 1964): 173.

83. Ward, *In This Short Span,* 109; Noyce, *South Col,* 23.

84. James Morris, "Plans for Double Assault on Peak of Everest, Colonel Hunt Picks His Final Teams," *The Times,* May 19, 1953, 6.

85. According to Hillary, Tenzing told John Hunt that a Sherpa should be in the first assault party (*High Adventure,* 161). In *Everest, 50 Years on the Mountain,* the fiftieth-anniversary documentary film released in 2003 by National Geographic, Hunt's preference for placing British mountaineers on the summit instead of Hillary and Tenzing is taken as a given. Hunt, *The Ascent of Everest,* 50. On the 1922 expedition, the high camp was put in at 25,000 feet, and then pushed up to 25,500. In 1924 Mallory and Irvine set off for the top from high camp at 26,800 feet. In 1933 this was pushed up to 27,400. In 1938 it was at 27,200 feet.

86. "I myself have always been surprised [at Hunt's decision]," Chris Bonington would write in 1992. "Had they been allowed to place a top camp, it is very likely Bourdillion and Evans whose names would have gone into the history books as the first men on top of Everest" (*The Climbers,* 196).

87. In a 1975 interview, Hillary commented, "George [Lowe] and I expected to climb together. If we had done [so] in 1953, I honestly think we would have been on top of Everest together" ("Mountain Interview," 31). Also see Hillary, *View from the Summit,* 19. In his history of climbing on Everest, Walt Unsworth argued that "consciously or unconsciously, Hunt never believed that Bourdillion and Evans would reach the summit" and was "simply testing out the enemy's defences before throwing in his crack troops" (*Everest,* 323). Hunt undoubtedly read Unsworth's interpretation of his 1953 decisions and may have been influenced by it in subsequent comments he offered on expedition strategy. He told a television audience in 1991: "I had in mind the prospect, although I didn't say it to them, that the second assault would be the one that would succeed and I regarded [Evans and Bourdillion's] first attempt more as a reconnaissance, but of course if they *could* make it, God bless them" (Ward, *Everest,* 256). Also see Douglas, *Tenzing,* 189–90.

88. Hunt, "Letters from Everest," 16.

89. Ibid., 18.

90. Venables, "The Long Ascent, 1921–1953," 170–71.

91. "I greatly admired what Charles and Tom had done," Hillary would later admit, "but I had a regrettable feeling of satisfaction" that they hadn't made it to the top (*View from the Summit,* 5).

92. Hunt, "Letters from Everest," 19; Edmund Hillary, "A Letter to Jim Rose," *Alpine Journal* 98 (1993): 23; Hillary, *Nothing Venture,* 157; Tenzing Norgay, *Tiger of the Snows,* 154.

93. Two Sherpas who were supposed to carry supplies to the assault camp succumbed to altitude sickness and had to head down from the South Col. So Hillary, Tenzing, and the remaining three support climbers added the additional loads to their already bulging rucksacks, carrying fifty pounds each. Further up the ridge they came to the supplies dumped by Hunt and Da Nymgal two days earlier; adding that to their own packs brought them up to about fifty-five pounds each; Hillary wound up carrying sixty-three pounds. Hillary, "The Summit," in Hunt, *The Ascent of Everest,* 203–4; Ward, *Everest,* 263.

94. Washburn, "The Location of Camp IX," 20–21.

95. Tenzing Norgay, *Tiger of the Snows,* 159.

96. Hillary, *High Adventure,* 201; Hillary, "The Summit," 207. Tenzing thought this was one of the "most dangerous" moments he had ever known on a mountain (*Tiger of the Snow,* 16).

97. Hillary, *High Adventure,* 204.

98. Venables, "The Long Ascent, 1921–1953," 180; Hillary, *High Adventure,* 230. In his first account of the climb, written for *The Times* of London, and then appearing as a chapter in Hunt's *The Ascent of Everest,*

Hillary described Tenzing as resembling a "giant fish when it has just been hauled from the sea." Edmund P. Hillary, "At the Summit of Everest," *The Times*, June 25, 1953, 7. Tenzing would complain in his autobiography that he had been insulted by the image, which suggested to him that he was a helpless creature hauled up the mountain by a stronger Hillary. In his subsequent account in *High Adventure,* Hillary dropped the "giant fish" image, simply writing that Tenzing was left "gasping for breath" at the top of the Hillary Step.

99. Hillary, "The Summit," 210.

100. Ibid. The debate over whether Hillary or Tenzing first reached the summit broke out almost immediately after the news of their achievement reached the rest of the world and would linger on for decades thereafter—which is odd, because Hillary in the passage above from Hunt's 1953 expedition book *The Ascent of Everest* makes it implicitly clear that he was in the lead, cutting steps. And, if that weren't sufficient evidence, Tenzing confirmed in his 1955 autobiography that it was Hillary who got there first (*Tiger of the Snows,* 163).

101. Later on Hillary would write that he did not ask Tenzing to take his photograph because "as far as I knew, he had never taken a photograph before and the summit of Everest was hardly the place to show him how" (*High Adventure,* 210–12). As Ed Douglas wrote, "Some climbers might have taken the chance on Tenzing getting lucky" (*Tenzing,* xvi). Tenzing, who could operate a primus stove, was certainly not incapable of learning how to operate a camera. And Hillary had had an entire day down on the South Col to instruct Tenzing in the intricacies of snapping a camera shutter—that is, had he really cared whether or not he would be immortalized in a summit photograph.

102. Tenzing remembered what Hillary left as a small cloth cat, rather than a crucifix (*Tiger of the Snows,* 165). Ward, *Everest,* 268.

103. Hillary, *Nothing Venture,* 162; Hillary, *View from the Summit,* 18; Lowe, *Because It Is There,* 40.

104. Tenzing Norgay, *Tiger of the Snows,* 169; Hunt, "Letters from Everest," 20. For the first official reports from the expedition by the climbers themselves, see "Everest," *Alpine Journal* 59 (Nov. 1953): 103–6; John Hunt and Michael Westmacott, "Everest, 1953, Narrative of the Expedition," *Alpine Journal* 59 (Nov. 1953): 107–22; "Everest, 1953, Sir John Hunt's Diary," *Alpine Journal* 9 (Nov. 1953): 123–78; Sir Edmund Hillary, "Everest 1953, The Last Lap," *Alpine Journal* 59 (May 1954): 235–37.

105. "The Challenge of Everest, a Brave Chapter in the Story of Human Endeavour," *The Times,* June 2, 1953, 7. Also see "Everest Conquered, Hillary and Tensing Reach the Summit," *The Times,* June 2, 1953, 6. Eric Shipton may have been the first to employ the "second Elizabethan era" theme, writing in an article in *Colliers* magazine in early April, "The 1953 expedition can climb—if weather holds out—until the first week in June. The coronation of Queen Elizabeth II is June 2d. The events, if fate is kind, may coincide. And the climbing of Everest would be a jewel for the diadem of the second Elizabethan era—an adventure worthy of the Drakes and the Raleighs who set alight the reign of the first Elizabeth" ("Will They Climb Mt. Everest Now?" 11–15). For similar editorials, see "A Crown on the Great Day," *Yorkshire Post,* June 2, 1953; "The Conquest of Everest," *Glasgow Herald,* June 2, 1953, both in Mount Everest Expedition Archives, box 85a, clippings folder, Royal Geographical Society. The press coverage of the triumph on Everest is a good illustration of the wave of postwar "imperial nostalgia" popular with the British public in the 1950s and early 1960s, as described by historian John M. Mackenzie in *Propaganda and Empire,* 90. Also see Stewart, "Tenzing's Two Wrist-Watches," 186–87. Another historical analogy occurred to Sir Edwin Herbert, president of the Himalayan Committee. Henry Hall, president of the American Alpine Club, wrote to Herbert a few days after the news arrived from Everest, offering the congratulations of the American climbing community. Hall also passed along a comment from an American publisher eager to publish John Hunt's expedition account: "I just hope that Colonel Hunt will be able to tell the story with the same emotion and feeling that gave Annapurna such distinction." Sir Herbert was evidently irritated by the tactless reminder that the traditional rival across the Channel had been first to surmount an 8,000-meter peak: "I was very interested in your postscript. I am afraid that it would be quite impossible and wholly undesirable for Hunt to emulate the Gallic élan of our French

friends. To have brought the entire party back from Everest, including no less than 28 of them from the South Col (which is in itself higher than Annapurna) is a tremendous achievement, but with no frost-bitten limbs to show for it may seem less heroic than the French effort. The French remind me in this connection of Prince Rupert and his cavalry in the Civil War. They had all the dash and romance but it was Cromwell's Ironsides advancing at the trot who won the battles." Sir Edwin S. Herbert to Henry Hall, June 17, 1953, Himalaya Library Archives, box Mount Everest 1912–1960, folder 1953 Everest Correspondence, American Alpine Club Library. The summit of Annapurna, at 26,453 feet, is actually about 600 feet higher than the elevation of the site of the British camp on the South Col of Everest.

106. Hillary, *Nothing Venture,* 163; Eric Shipton to Geoffrey Winthrop Young, June 6, 1953, Blakeney Collection, Add. Mss. 63120, British Library. Also see Shipton's comments in "Col. Hunt's Aim, A Second Everest Feat Possible," *The Times,* June 3, 1953, 12.

107. Alfred B. Fitt to James Ramsey Ullman, June 1, 1953, Ullman Papers, box 80, folder 1, Department of Rare Books and Special Collections, Princeton University Library.

CHAPTER EIGHT: *The Golden Age of Himalayan Climbing, 1953–1960*

1. Alfred B. Fitt to James Ramsey Ullman, June 1, 1953, Ullman Papers, box 80, folder 1, Department of Rare Books and Special Collections, Princeton University Library.

2. Hunt, *The Ascent of Everest,* 3. James Ramsey Ullman's review in the *New York Times* of the American edition of the book, which was published in January 1954 as *The Conquest of Everest,* celebrated both the climbing of Everest and the expeditionary culture that produced that triumph: "As one finishes John Hunt's book," Ullman concluded, "it is this, above all else, that seems the important and significant thing about the climbing of Everest: that it was a common victory in a common cause. For a few magical minutes on that May morning of 1953, a man of the East and a man of the West stood side by side on the summit of the earth, bound together not only by a nylon rope but by the bonds of brotherhood and high enterprise" ("The Crowded Road to Everest," *New York Times Book Review,* Jan. 24, 1954, BR1–2). Hunt also published a shorter illustrated history of the expedition in 1954, *Our Everest Adventure: The Pictorial History from Kathmandu to the Summit,* along with an abridged children's edition, also entitled *The Ascent of Everest.* Many of the participants of the expedition also published their own accounts, including works previously cited by Sir Edmund Hillary, Tenzing Norgay (in collaboration with James Ramsey Ullman), Wilfrid Noyce, and James Morris. In addition, see Alfred Gregory's photo collection from the expedition, *The Picture of Everest,* and his more recent *Alfred Gregory's Everest.* In an effort to explain the popularity of climbing literature, James Morris would write some years after the Everest expedition, "There is something warmly intriguing, most of us feel, about a man who gives up his job for three or four months, spends half his savings, abandons his wife and adorable children, risks his neck and deserts his television set, just for the sake of reaching a spot that nobody cares two hoots about, consisting merely of a mound of snow on the top of a very cold, high, nasty hill. Reading about such a character and his perversities is like probing a lunatic mind, or reconstructing an inexplicable murder" ("Why They Climb and Climb and Climb," *New York Times,* Apr. 10, 1960, SM25).

3. John Hunt to Himalayan Committee, June 23, 1953, Mount Everest Expedition Archives, box 67, folder 6, Royal Geographical Society.

4. Tenzing Norgay, *Tiger of the Snows,* 172; "Tensing's Own Story/He Tells All," *Daily Express,* July 1, 1953, Newspaper Clippings Archive, vol. 30, Alpine Club.

5. Tenzing Norgay, *Tiger of the Snows,* 172; Douglas, *Tenzing,* 213–14. An enterprising songwriter had already written what became a very popular song in Nepal dedicated to celebrating the exploits of "Tenzing, the gem of the world," who "must have guided Hillary through the confusing trails / Tenzing hoisted the national flag / On the tallest tower of the world." Tashi Tenzing, *Tenzing Norgay,* 146; Douglas, *Tenzing,* 207–8;

Stewart, "Tenzing's Two Wrist-Watches," 188. To the disappointment of the Nepalese nationalists, Tenzing had no intention of moving back to Nepal; he would continue to make his residence in Darjeeling.

6. The *Manchester Guardian* noted editorially that the George Medal was customarily "given in recognition of such acts of gallantry as . . . the arrest by police officers of armed criminals." Its award to Tenzing did not seem commensurate to his achievement, particularly since Hillary had received a knighthood. "Would it not be wiser, since Hillary and he stood on the summit side by side, to honor them in the same way?" ("Everest Honours," *Manchester Guardian,* June 17, 1953). Hillary, *Nothing Venture,* 165–66; Tashi Tenzing, *Tenzing Norgay* 145; Douglas, *Tenzing,* 208, 213–15. Also see "Villagers en Fête for Everest Men," *The Times,* June 22, 1953, 4. In addition to the who-reached-the-summit-first controversy, there was also a nobody-reached-the-summit-at-all conspiracy theory, popular in certain corners of the Indian nationalist movement where it was believed that the whole ascent was fabricated to shore up British prestige in South Asia. For an example from 1954, see S. M. Goswami, *Everest: Is It Conquered?*

7. According to George Band, veteran of the 1953 expedition, Hunt "had a strong social conscience, and his political leanings tended to be left of centre" (George Band, e-mail to the authors, July 10, 2006). For Hunt's views regarding Indian independence, see Hunt, *Life Is Meeting,* 27–28. While Tenzing had no sympathy for Communism, the Nepalese Communist Party may have had some role in the events surrounding the Everest expedition's reception in Kathmandu. The party had been outlawed by King Tribhuvan in 1952 but had shown strength in municipal elections in Kathmandu in 1953, backing an insurgent slate of ostensibly independent candidates (Whelpton, *A History of Nepal,* 91–92). "Next Everest Climb without Oxygen," *Yorkshire Post,* June 16, 1953, Mount Everest Expedition Archives, box 85a, clippings folder, Royal Geographical Society.

8. "Leader's Views Resented/Tensing Voices Protest," *Times of India,* June 23, 1953, Newspaper Clippings Archive, vol. 30, Alpine Club. Also see "Everest Men in Katmandu, Triumphal Entry, Further Controversy over Tensing," *The Times,* June 22, 1953, 6. Hunt later told Tenzing that he had not meant his comment to be belittling at all: "What I actually said was that I considered you a very fine mountaineer but you had not yet had experience of some of the very high standard technical climbing to be experienced in the Alps. What I should have added was that Hillary was exactly in the same position" (Douglas, *Tenzing,* 246).

9. Tashi Tenzing, *Tenzing Norgay,* 151; Douglas, *Tenzing,* 224–25; Tenzing Norgay, *Tiger of the Snows,* 175–77. Tenzing would make it clear in his autobiography in 1955 that "almost together" meant that Hillary was a step ahead of him: "Hillary stepped on the top first. And I stepped up after him" (*Tiger of the Snows,* 163). In later years there would be occasional echoes of the who-got-there-first controversy. On the fiftieth anniversary of the Everest climb a major Indian newspaper ran this commentary: "Who reached the summit first? Hillary said he did; then, as the subcontinent rumbled indignantly at what it saw as a white man's arrogant presumption, conceded they had made the final ascent 'almost together.' Tenzing's dignified comment was that they 'climbed as a team.'" Sunanda K. Datta-Ray, "Mountain Work—How a Sherpa Left His Daughter's Ballpoint Pen on Everest," *Telegraph* [Calcutta], June 7, 2003, http://www.telegraph.com/1030607/asp/opinion/story_2039176.asp.

10. "Everest Party Home, Rousing Welcome at Airport," *The Times,* July 4, 1953, 6; "Everest Heroes Show the Flag in London," *Evening Standard,* July 3, 1953, Mount Everest Expedition Archives, box 85a, clippings folder, Royal Geographical Society; "Everest Heroes Are Home," *Evening News,* July 3, 1953, Mount Everest Expedition Archives, box 85a, clippings folder, Royal Geographical Society; "Tenzing's Family Steals the Show," *New York Times,* July 4, 1953, 13.

11. On Tenzing's experiences in Britain, see Douglas, *Tenzing,* 225–27; Stewart, "Tenzing's Two Wrist-Watches," 189; Hansen and Stewart, "Debate: Tenzing's Two Wrist-Watches," 159–77.

12. John Hunt to Tenzing, Sept. 2, 1953, Mount Everest Expedition Archives, box 67, folder 6, Royal Geographical Society. In later years, when Hillary became known in the Solu Khumbu for his humanitarian work,

Tenzing would show some resentment of Hillary's popularity among Sherpas. Ed Douglas describes an incident in the mid-1970s when both Tenzing and Hillary were separately visiting the region. "Tenzing made a disparaging remark about Hillary" to an acquaintance, overheard by others. "When Tenzing later approached the village of Phortse, some villagers, angered by the gossip they had heard about the incident, came out and threw stones at him" (*Tenzing,* 230). Tenzing's grandson believes that late in life Hillary and his grandfather drew closer. Tashi Tenzing, *Tenzing Norgay,* 173–74.

13. At a meeting of the Himalayan Committee in London in September 1953, Colonel H. W. Tobin, editor of *Himalayan Journal,* "expressed his views that the time had come to attempt to control the increasingly exorbitant terms which Sherpas were demanding in return for their services with Himalayan expeditions, and to regulate the extent to which they should be permitted to retain High Altitude equipment issued to them. It is proposed that the Himalayan Club should initiate a scheme and seek the support of organizations throughout the world who were planning expeditions to the Himalayas." The committee gave its full support for Colonel Tobin's proposal. Minutes of the Meeting of the Himalayan Committee Held at the Alpine Club on the 3 Sept. 1953, Blakeney Collection, Add. Mss. 63122, British Library. A month later the committee met again and once again discussed the Sherpa labor problem. "Colonel Tobin and Mr. [George?] Lowe both spoke of the delicate situation that had arisen in India over Sherpa recruitment, the Himalayan Club already having an agency established, whilst Tenzing and Lakba [Lhakpa Tschering, Tenzing's personal adviser] had set up a rival agency. Furthermore, newspaper funds subscribed in India after the Everest expedition had been handed over to the Himalayan Club, with the idea of their being distributed to the porters of the expedition. Since this would result in the porters getting a sum in excess of their entire Everest pay, it was felt to be a very undesirable step." Minutes of a Meeting of the Himalayan Committee, 6 Oct. 1953, Blakeney Collection, Add. Mss. 63122, British Library. By 1954 the Himalayan Club conceded defeat, recommending that foreign expeditions henceforth directly contact Sherpa sirdars when seeking porters. See Hansen, "Partners," 229. Kohli, *Mountaineering in India,* 22–24; Douglas, *Tenzing,* 233–35.

14. Added together, postexpeditionary lectures, books, and the film had by 1955 earned the expedition's backers a sum five times the cost of climbing the mountain. The surplus went to fund future mountaineering expeditions, administered through the newly established Mount Everest Foundation, which took the place of the Himalayan Committee. "There's Gold in That Thar Hill (29,002 ft.)," *Daily Mail,* Feb. 3, 1955; "Everest Trust Grants," *The Times,* July 31, 1955, both in Newspaper Clippings Archive, vol. 30, Alpine Club. Presumably Lady Hillary did not accompany the expedition menfolk on an evening in Paris in the fall 1953 when Maurice Herzog played host to Hillary, Hunt, and Alf Gregory. Following a formal welcoming ceremony at the Elysée Palace, Herzog took them to a Pigalle nightclub, where, as Hunt would recall, they witnessed their triumph on Everest reenacted "by a troupe of enchanting young ladies" who "were roped together in a sort of fashion, with coils round their elegant middles, but that was as far as equipment—or clothing—went, as they danced and sang against a backcloth of snowy mountains." The act concluded with a musical and dramatic flourish when "the intrepid leader of this *cordee* produced, as though from nowhere, a little Union flag" (*Life Is Meeting,* 123). Also see John Hunt to Maurice Herzog, Dec. 3, 1953, Mount Everest Expedition Archives, box 69, folder "Paris Visit," Royal Geographical Society. The stag party atmosphere continued to be a feature of the lecture tour for many of the participants. George Lowe remembered (perhaps a little hazily) the postexpedition tour as a series of "nightly climbs over glassy peaks of Scotch or Bourbon on the rocks—the alcoholic Western Cwm, the dipsomaniac ice-fall" (*Because It Is There,* 42).

15. "Hitting a New High," Mount Everest Expedition Archives, box 80, folder "Photographs," Royal Geographical Society. Also see "Mountain Climbing TV Thrill," *Chicago Tribune,* Feb. 1, 1954, Mount Everest Expedition Archives, box 85a, clippings folder, Royal Geographical Society; "Everest, Programs, etc, Program—Carnegie Hall, January 29 and 30, 1954," Himalaya Library Archives, American Alpine Club Library; "President Hails Everest Team," *New York Times,* Feb. 12, 1954, 29.

16. "Ambition Unsated," *Centralia Chronicle,* Feb. 5, 1954, Mount Everest Expedition Archives, box 85a, clippings folder, Royal Geographical Society. Although Americans were taken with Hillary, the feelings of affection were not reciprocal. "I can't say that I enjoyed my first visit to the United States," he would later write. "We traveled too much and worked too hard—and we met all the wrong people. We were being lionized by a class of society with which we had little in common. In those days every rich American expected foreigners to want to share the American way of life and they simply couldn't understand it when I told them I was content to remain a New Zealander" (*Nothing Venture,* 173–74). Tenzing's memoir was hailed by Charlie Houston on its appearance as the story of a man "who is great in spirit and in mind and in comprehension of the many values which are found in the sharing of adventure and danger" ("The Mountain and the Man," *New York Times Book Review,* June 5, 1955, BR3). For an assessment of the book's appeal and its historical shortcomings, see Douglas, *Tenzing,* 244–46. Tenzing finally made his own visit to the United States in 1964, when he too took the obligatory ride to the top of the Empire State Building. He also made appearances at Yankee Stadium and the New York World's Fair and climbed Mount Rainier. Philip Benjamin, "'Snow Tiger' Tenzing Lionized at Fair," *New York Times,* July 15, 1964, 25; "Tenzing Reaches Top of Mt. Rainier," *New York Times,* July 26, 1964, 13; Douglas, *Tenzing,* 255.

17. Robert Trumbull, "Six Other Asian Peaks Are Targets of Expeditions This Year," *New York Times,* June 4, 1953, 10.

18. Buhl, *Nanga Parbat Pilgrimage,* 309–10; W. Frauenberger and Hermann Buhl, "The Ascent of Nanga Parbat," *Alpine Journal* 59 (Nov. 1954): 371. Buhl's *Nanga Parbat Pilgrimage* was reprinted in the United States as *Lonely Challenge* in 1956.

19. To Reinhold Messner, who as a boy in the South Tyrol worshipped Buhl, "he was without argument *the* mountaineer of the fifties." Messner and Höfler, *Hermann Buhl,* 11, 103. The two most recent deaths on the mountain were British climbers Jim Thornley and Bill Crace, who made an unauthorized and ill-equipped winter attempt on the mountain in 1950. Bauer, *The Siege of Nanga Parbat,* 183. Tenzing was on the expedition, and he was constantly aware of the presence on the mountain of what he believed to be the ghosts of the German and Sherpa climbers who had died there in earlier attempts: "Even on the clearest day, with the sun bright and the sky blue, a cloud seemed to move down from the heights and bring their coldness into our bones" (Tenzing Norgay, *Tiger of the Snows,* 92; see also Douglas, *Tenzing,* 137–42). Buhl, *Nanga Parbat Pilgrimage,* 299. Buhl's imagery seemed to harken back to recent events in German and Austrian history. *Holocaust* was not yet in common use as a label for Nazi genocide, but it was often used to describe the experience of combat in both world wars of the twentieth century. Buhl, drafted as an eighteen-year-old into the Wehrmacht in 1943, served two years with the mountain troops in Italy before being captured by the Americans.

20. Bauer, *The Siege of Nanga Parbat,* 184. Herrmann Buhl first learned of Herrligkoffer's plan for a Nanga Parbat expedition when Heinrich Harrer showed him an article about it in a German magazine in 1952. "I had never heard the name, nor had Harrer," Buhl would write, "but he seemed to have very definite plans and to be a master at propaganda, if the periodicals were publishing articles about him. For not a single mountaineer had ever heard of Dr. Herrligkoffer" (*Nanga Parbat Pilgrimage,* 286).

21. Bauer, *The Siege of Nanga Parbat,* 185; Messner, *The Naked Mountain,* 73.

22. Herrligkoffer thought he had convinced the Pakistan government to admit a contingent of five Sherpas, including veteran Pasang Dawa Lama, but the Sherpas were delayed so long at the border that they failed to link up as arranged with the expedition in Rawalpindi, prior to its flight to Gilgit.

23. Buhl, *Nanga Parbat Pilgrimage,* 302–3.

24. Sale, *Broad Peak,* 23.

25. Buhl, *Nanga Parbat Pilgrimage,* 318.

26. Ibid., 323.

27. Bauer, *The Siege of Nanga Parbat,* 208–209.

28. Abandoning his ice ax, a vital piece of climbing equipment, seems like a strange decision for Buhl to make, and may have reflected the onset of hypoxia, but the ax also laid to rest any lingering doubts about the climb when it was found on the summit in 1999 (Messner, *The Naked Mountain,* 313). Buhl, *Nanga Parbat Pilgrimage,* 336.

29. The imaginary companion phenomenon is described in Houston, *Going Higher,* 109. Among those reporting similar experiences over the years were Frank Smythe, Achille Compagnoni, Herbert Tichy, Nick Estcourt, and Stephen Venables.

30. As they waited for Buhl's return, his colleagues fastened a memorial plaque for Willy Merkl and the other victims of 1934 to the Moor's Head. "While fixing this plate in its place," Walter Frauenberger wrote (as rather awkwardly translated for the *Alpine Journal*), "I must think continually whether there isn't one name missing, the name of a young comrade from 1953. This thought is tormenting me." He went back later that day to fix the plate more securely, still thinking his somber thoughts about Buhl's fate, and, glancing up the Silver Saddle, he saw a black dot descending on the white slope. Laughing and crying, Frauenberger recalled, "I report to Willy Merkl, Uli Wieland and Willo Welzenbach, whose names are engraved on the plate in front of me, that . . . their bequest has been accomplished." Frauenberger and Buhl, "The Ascent of Nanga Parbat," 383. For accounts of Buhl's climb, see Messner, *The Naked Mountain,* 75–82; Bauer, *The Siege of Nanga Parbat,* 188–211; Karl M. Herrligkoffer, "Nanga Parbat 1953," *Jahrbuch des Deutschen Alpenvereins* (1953): 5–16; Herrligkoffer, *Nanga Parbat;* Thur and Hanke, *Sieg am Nanga Parbat;* Dyhrenfurth, *Das Buch von Nanga Parbat.*

31. Buhl, *Nanga Parbat Pilgrimage,* 345. For a contrasting account of Buhl's reception in Base Camp, see Herrligkoffer, *Nanga Parbat,* 226.

32. See, for example, H. Adams Carter, "Nanga Parbat: The Killer Mountain," *Appalachia* 20 (Dec. 1954): 306–7. Still, Herrligkoffer had little reason to complain: without Buhl's defiance of his orders, he could not have parlayed the third successful ascent of an 8,000-meter peak into a lifetime of leading Himalayan expeditions. He returned to Nanga Parbat in 1961 and 1962 with expeditions attempting the Diamir or western face of the mountain. His climbers met success on the latter expedition, though one of them, Siegried Löw, died in the descent. Karl M. Herrligkoffer, "The Diamir Face of Nanga Parbat," *Himalayan Journal* 25 (1964): 120–31. He returned again in 1970 with an expedition that attempted the last unclimbed face of the mountain, the Rupal Face.

33. Buhl, *Nanga Parbat Pilgrimage,* 351. That Buhl's expanded notion of acceptable risk was becoming the norm was shown in John Hunt's preface to the English-language edition of Paul Bauer's 1955 book on the history of Nanga Parbat expeditions: "Looking back . . . on the era of mountaineering between the wars, I have the impression that whereas the German climbers seemed too thrusting, too bent on achievement in the cause of national prestige, we British were too insistent on prudence. . . . I am inclined to think that, in our dislike of the motive, we wrongly condemned the daring" (preface to Bauer, *The Siege of Nanga Parbat,* 11).

34. Kevin Fedarko, "The Mountain of Mountains," *Outside* 28 (Nov. 2003): 99–100.

35. Bill Shand, a young Californian chemist and mountaineer with extensive climbing experience in the Alps, the Tetons, and elsewhere, wrote to Bates early in 1946, "I was very much interested to hear that you and House and Houston are planning another expedition to the Karakoram, and there is nothing I should like better to do than to join you on the trip" (Bill Shand to Bob Bates, Mar. 31, 1946, Bates Papers, American Alpine Club Library). In a 1952 letter to Hall, Houston wrote that he had been working for "four consecutive years" to win permission for an expedition to K2 (Charles Houston to Henry Hall, May 29, 1952, Himalaya Library Archives, box K2, folder 1953 K2, American Alpine Club Library). Charles Houston to Henry Hall, July 9, 1950, Himalaya Library Archives, box K2, folder 1953 K2, American Alpine Club Library.

36. Charles Houston to Henry Hall, Feb. 27, 1952, Himalaya Library Archives, box K2, folder 1953 K2, American Alpine Club Library. Also see Charles Houston to Henry Hall, May 21, 1952, Himalaya Library

Archives, box K2, folder 1953 K2, American Alpine Club Library. Houston was not the only American planning an expedition to the Himalaya. Out on the West Coast, Al Baxter, William Siri, and others were organizing a group of Stanford Alpine Club alumni and Sierra Club members for what became known as the "California Himalayan Expedition." The group initially hoped to climb Dhaulagiri in 1954, but the permit for that mountain was given to the Swiss, so they shifted their sights to Makalu. If the Americans had succeeded in climbing both K2 in 1953 and Makalu in 1954, it would have established them as contenders equal to the British, the French, and the Germans in the Himalayas. As Siri wrote to Henry Hall in March 1952, "It would appear that mountaineering is finally growing to maturity in this country and perhaps before long a mountain climber here will no longer be regarded as a curiosity and constantly subject to the foolish question as to why men climb mountains" (William Siri to Henry Hall, Mar. 30, 1952, Himalaya Library Archives, box K2, folder 1953 K2, American Alpine Club Library).

37. The expedition wound up costing about $30,000. Although it was sponsored by the American Alpine Club, the club lacked the resources to fund expeditions. Instead, the expedition relied on personal contributions from members and friends, plus advances paid by the *Saturday Evening Post* and NBC television. See appendix 5, "Finances," in Houston and Bates, *K2,* 311–13. Houston and Bates, *K2,* 49. One of those turned down for the expedition was James Ramsey Ullman, who had written to Houston to offer his services. Houston felt he was too old and inexperienced (Charles S. Houston to James Ramsey Ullman, Nov. 19, 1952, Ullman Papers, box 95, folder 2, Department of Rare Books and Special Collections, Princeton University Library). Streather joined the Indian Army in 1945, at age eighteen, in time to see the end of the British Empire in South Asia. He served with the Chitral Scouts on Pakistan's North West frontier, a T. E. Lawrence kind of posting, in command of mounted tribesmen. His first venture in mountaineering came when he served as transport officer for the successful Norwegian expedition to Tirich Mir (25,288ft/7,708m) in the Hindu Kush in 1950 and reached the summit. Lane, *Military Mountaineering,* 25–26, 28.

38. Houston and Bates, *K2,* 76; Ata-Ullah, *Citizen of Two Worlds,* 234. Bob Bates broached the idea with Pakistani authorities of using air transport to drop supplies to the expedition's Base Camp at K2, but to no avail; the Pakistanis were afraid of provoking a hostile reaction from the Chinese government. Bates, *The Love of Mountains Is Best,* 260–61.

39. Ata-Ullah, *Citizen of Two Worlds,* 235, 264.

40. Charles Houston to Oscar Houston, June 9, 1953, K2 scrapbook in the possession of Charles Houston; Houston and Bates, *K2,* 47–48.

41. Houston and Bates, *K2,* 124.

42. Ibid., 122–23.

43. Charles Houston, Ninth Expedition Letter, July 18, 1953, Himalaya Library Archives, folder "K2—Expedition Letters, 1953, Third American Karakoram Exp.," American Alpine Club Library.

44. Houston and Bates, *K2,* 140.

45. Robert H. Bates, "The Fight for K2," *American Alpine Journal* 9 (1954): 12; Houston and Bates, *K2,* 143.

46. Houston and Bates, *K2,* 152. The date for the selection of summit team is given as August 3 in Houston and Bates, *K2,* 158. Dee Molenaar's diary entry gives the date as August 5. Dee Molenaar, "Two Weeks High on K2," excerpt from unpublished manuscript "High and Wide with Sketchpad," 83. The authors are grateful to Dee Molenaar for providing them with a copy of this manuscript. "We did hope to carry the umbrella up, but it was some how abandoned" (Charlie Houston, letter to the authors, Jan. 17, 2006).

47. Houston and Bates, *K2,* 151; Molenaar, "Two Weeks High on K2," 83.

48. "Material from Dee Molenaar about K2," 83, Bates Papers, folder "Efforts to Persuade the US Army to Establish Mountain Troops 1940–1941," American Alpine Club Library.

49. Houston and Bates, *K2,* 187.

50. Molenaar, "Two Weeks High on K2," 85; Houston and Bates, *K2,* 194.

51. "If Bob Craig had been the only survivor he might have made it down alone if he were very careful and found various anchoring ropes still intact along the ridge, along with stoves and food at various camps" (Dee Molenaar, letter to the authors, Jan. 16, 2006).

52. "The belay" became one of the most celebrated moments in the history of mountaineering. See, for example, Krakauer, *Into Thin Air,* 118–19. Also see Nick Clinch and Tom Hornbein, "Peter K. Schoening, 1927–2004," *American Alpine Journal* 47 (2005): 476–78. After the expedition's return, Schoening offered a detailed description of the technique he employed: see Peter Schoening, "Ice-Axe Belay," *Appalachia* 22 (June 1956): 12–14.

53. Streather was recalling the events of that day in an interview with mountaineering journalist Peter Gillman in 1970. See "The End of Hope," in Gillman, *In Balance,* 153. Houston and Bates, *K2,* 199.

54. Conefrey and Jordan, *Mountain Men,* 216.

55. Writing to Bob Gilmore shortly after the expedition returned from the mountain, Houston stated, "[A]n avalanche came down and carried [Gilkey] away." This, he believed, was "the Hand of God" at work because "we should all have died there had we tried to bring him down" (Charles Houston to "Bob," Aug. 28, 1953, Himalaya Library Archives, folder "K2—Expedition Letters, 1953, Third American Karakoram Exp.," American Alpine Club Library). Houston would later decide that Gilkey had actually cut himself loose in a supreme act of self-sacrifice. Bates, on the other hand, remained convinced that Gilkey died as a result of avalanche, arguing that "there was no possible way" that he could have reached the axes that pinned him to the mountainside, "let alone pull them out" (Bates, *The Love of Mountains Is Best,* 282–83). Gilkey's remains were found near K2 Base Camp in 1993 by a British climbing party and returned to his family for burial in Ames, Iowa. Greg Child, "Still the Hairiest," *Outside* 18 (Nov. 1993): 24.

56. Dee Molenaar, "K2 Diary with Sketchbook," typescript copy, Kauffman Collection, box 2, American Alpine Club Library.

57. Molenaar, "Two Weeks High on K2," 87; Curran, *K2,* 95–103.

58. Clinch, *A Walk in the Sky,* 4. For contemporary reaction in the U.S. press, see "Death and Snow Foil U.S. Climbers on Unconquered Himalayan Peak," *New York Times,* Aug. 27, 1953, 1; clippings in K2 scrapbook in the possession of Charles Houston. Houston and Bates, *K2,* 269. Houston arrived back in New York on September 10 and soon after sat down to write a final letter to expedition friends and supporters. Summing up the lessons of their ordeal on K2, he wrote: "Had we not been such a closely knit team we would not have survived. The character, personality and courage of each member of the party supported the others and made possible our descent" (Charles Houston, Tenth Expedition Letter, Sept. 11, 1953, Himalaya Library Archives, folder "K2—Expedition Letters, 1953, Third American Karakoram Exp.," American Alpine Club Library). For other accounts of the K2 expedition, see H. R. A. Streather, "K2: The Third American Karakorum Expedition, 1953," *Alpine Journal* 59 (Nov. 1954): 391–401; Bates, "The Fight for K2," 5–19; Robert H. Bates, "We Met Death on K2," *Saturday Evening Post,* Dec. 5, 1953, Dec. 12, 1953.

59. "Climbers, Beaten by Storms, to Try K-2 Again in 1954," *New York Post,* Aug. 31, 1953, clippings in K2 scrapbook in the possession of Charles Houston. Nor was Houston the only American climber hoping to tackle K2 in 1954. Paul Petzoldt, who had been with Houston on K2 in 1938, was also planning his own return to the mountain. In October 1953 he sent a letter outlining plans for a K2 expedition to Glenn Exum, Willi Unsoeld, James Ullman, Dick Pownall, and several other potential members of the expedition. The Atomic Energy Commission, Petzoldt wrote, "has taken an interest in our expedition and certain individuals there are outlining our scientific studies and will assist us in many ways." In the light of later attempts to plant nuclear-powered listening devices on other Himalayan peaks, Petzoldt's reference to the Atomic Energy Commission is intriguing, but he did not offer any further clues as to the nature of the scientific project under

consideration. In any case, the proposed expedition did not progress beyond the sending of Petzoldt's letter ("Expedition Letter #1," Oct. 19, 1953, Ullman Papers, box 95, folder 1, Department of Rare Books and Special Collections, Princeton University Library). A. Desio, "The 1954 Italian Expedition to the Karakorum and the Conquest of K2," *Alpine Journal* 60 (May 1955): 3; Cassin, *50 Years of Alpinism,* 110.

60. Bonatti, *On the Heights,* 63.

61. Curran, *K2,* 106; also see Conefrey and Jordan, *Mountain Men,* 225. Curran, *K2,* 109.

62. Lacedelli and Cenacchi, *K2,* 34. According to Nick Clinch, "Years ago, Ricardo had dinner at our house and his story through an interpreter was that Desio went to the doctor who gave the expedition medical exams and told him that Cassin was a communist and had to be kept off the trip. The doctor told Cassin that he had a heart problem and could not go" (Nick Clinch, e-mail to the authors, Aug. 7, 2006). Cassin's supposed infirmities in 1954 did not prevent him from going on to climb the North-East Face of the Piz Badile in 1987 at the age of seventy-nine. Reinhold Messner would describe Cassin as "without doubt the best climber of his generation" and describe the route he climbed on the Walker Spur of the Grandes Jorasses in 1938 as "the most beautiful route in the Alps" (Messner, *The Big Walls,* 42). Also see Cassin, *50 Years of Alpinism,* 114–16; Conefrey and Jordan, *Mountain Men,* 225; Mantovani and Diemberger, *K2,* 52.

63. Dyhrenfurth, *To the Third Pole,* 213. The estimate in today's dollars is from Lacedelli and Cenacchi, *K2,* 20.

64. Bonatti would call his offer to Mahdi a "subtle but necessary deception." But Bonatti himself was being deceived at the same time. Compagnoni apparently had held out to him the possibility of taking "the place of one of us" [Compagnoni or Lacedelli] if Bonatti should prove stronger when they were all gathered at Camp IX. It seems highly unlikely that Compagnoni had any intention of sacrificing his own place on the summit team to Bonatti. See Bonatti, *The Mountains of My Life,* 87, 89, and the essay by Bonatti's translator Robert Marshall "What Really Happened on K2," reprinted in the Modern Library edition of Bonatti's book, especially 370.

65. Bonatti, *The Mountains of My Life,* 91.

66. Lacedelli and Cenacchi, *K2,* 62–63.

67. For accounts of the climb, see Desio, "The 1954 Italian Expedition to the Karakorum and the Conquest of K2," 3–16; Desio, *Ascent of K2;* Bonatti, *The Mountains of My Life,* 85–105; Curran, *K2,* 111–17; Ata-Ullah, *Citizen of Two Worlds,* 267–79; "Italians Conquer the 'Unclimbable Peak,'" *Life,* Oct. 11, 1954, 28–35.

68. Bonatti, *The Mountains of My Life,* 317. The postexpedition controversy revolved around three main issues: (1) had the two lead climbers deliberately gone farther than agreed upon before establishing Camp IX (and if so, why)? (2) had Lacedelli and Compagnoni any idea that Bonatti and Mahdi were bivouacking on the slope below them (and if so, why hadn't they made any effort to aid them)? and (3) when forced to bivouac, did Bonatti tap the oxygen supply meant for the summit attempt—for his own survival or, worse, in an attempt to sabotage the first team? Lacedelli's account on the fiftieth anniversary of the climb suggests that Compagnoni plotted the site of Camp IX to prevent Bonatti from joining them. He also suggests that the two lead climbers did not realize that Bonatti and Mahdi were bivouacked nearby. And Lacedelli dismissed the idea that Bonatti could have tapped the oxygen tanks that night, since he did not have a face mask. In addition to Lacedelli and Cenacchi, *K2,* see Samantha Sacks, "The Revision of History," *Alpinist* 14 (Winter 2005–6): 58.

69. Mantovani and Diemberger, *K2,* 48, 62.

70. Charles S. Houston to the editor, *New York Times,* Aug. 21, 1954, 16. The Genoa celebration is described in Italian Alpine Club, *1863–1963,* 303.

71. Charles Houston, letter dated Oct. 20, 1954, Houston personal papers, K2 scrapbook in the possession of Charles Houston. Houston apparently cherished the hopes of still another return engagement with K2, securing permission from the Pakistan government for a 1958 expedition, but then failed to put together an

expedition. A reference to the aborted 1958 K2 expedition can be found in a letter from Lawrence G. Coveney to Andrew J. Kauffman, Apr. 12, 1958, Kauffman Collection, box 1, folder 1/1, American Alpine Club Library. In 1960 Major William Hackett, who had won a silver star while serving in the Tenth Mountain Division in Italy, led a German-American Karakoram expedition to K2, reaching 23,900 feet on the Abruzzi Ridge before being turned back by adverse weather. Hackett and Conrad, *Climb to Glory,* 197–217.

72. Most recently, in the fall of 1953 Tichy had climbed "five or six 20,000-foot peaks" in northwestern Nepal. Expedition reports, *American Alpine Journal* 9 (1955): 178. It was on that expedition, in conversation with Sherpa Pasang Dawa Lama, that the idea for the Cho Oyu expedition was born.

73. Tichy, *Cho Oyu,* 19–20.

74. Ibid., 95.

75. Ibid., 95–97; Herbert Tichy, "Cho Oyu, 1954," *Alpine Journal* 60 (Nov. 1955): 241.

76. Lambert and Kogan, *White Fury,* 118; Tichy, *Cho Oyu,* 116. Most accounts of the Cho Oyu events in 1954 side with Tichy in the dispute with Lambert's party. The exception is Roger Frison-Roche and Sylvain Jouty, who found it "unfortunate that the fraternal mountaineering spirit was not sufficiently strong to spur Tichy, however good his reasons, to agree to join forces with Lambert and Kogan" (*A History of Mountain Climbing,* 222).

77. When Pasang reached the summit on October 19, he had climbed 14,000 feet in three days. Tichy, *Cho Oyu,* 125–26.

78. Ibid., 245.

79. Ibid., 246.

80. Ibid., 247. In addition to being the first time an 8,000-meter peak had been climbed by so small an expedition, this was also the first successful postmonsoon ascent of an 8,000-meter peak.

81. Tichy, *Himalaya,* 8. Also see the account of the Cho Oyu climb in Bonington, *Quest for Adventure,* 211–27. Pasang Dawa Lama had reached the summit of Chomolhari (23,996ft/7,314m) in Bhutan with F. Spencer Chapman in 1937. G. O. Dyhrenfurth, "Some Hints for Himalayan Aspirants," *Alpine Journal* 68 (May 1963): 36–37. But, as Tichy noted, he still dreamed of climbing a "very high" mountain (*Cho Oyu,* 140). In 1958, on an Indian expedition to Cho Oyu, Pasang Dawa Lama and S. Gyatso would make the second ascent of the mountain by the same route, the first time that the summit of the same 8,000-meter peak had twice been reached by the same climber. See expedition reports, *American Alpine Journal* 11 (1959): 323–24; G. O. Dyhrenfurth and Norman Dyhrenfurth, "Cho Oyu," *Mountain* 60 (Mar.–Apr. 1978): 40–41; Fanshawe and Venables, *Himalaya Alpine-Style,* 152–53. Also see the chapter on Pasang Dawa Lama in Kohli, *Sherpas,* 102–13.

82. Patey, *One Man's Mountains,* 263. As Jim Perrin notes, local climbing cultures often derive their character from the quality of rock available to them. As he writes of the gritstone formations of northern England: "In its outward show it is the unkindest of rocks, brutally steep, abrasive, studded all over with razor crystals of quartz and feldspar. . . . It demands a style based on confidence and agility, on both sophistication of technique and aggression in approach, on ingenuity and faith in friction" (*The Villain,* 53–54).

83. Brown, *The Hard Years,* 21–33, 60–66; Ron Moseley, "The Petit Dru by the West Face," *Alpine Journal* 60 (May 1955): 25–30. For Don Whillans's early years in Manchester and as a climber, see Whillans and Ormerod, *Don Whillans,* 1–95; Perrin, *The Villain,* 8–107, 147–50. In the mid-1960s a British journalist took a look back at the past two decades of climbing history, arguing that the key event in the democratization of rock climbing in Britain occurred when "[t]he Government eased hire-purchase restrictions on motorcycles. Overnight, mountains became accessible and climbing them became cheap. For the cost of a gallon of petrol, the student or apprentice or office clerk could go straight from work on Friday, his tent stowed on the pillion, and camp at the foot of his first climb, door to door, within a few hours. . . . The standard climbs got so

overcrowded you had to queue." Anthony Greenbank, "The Hard Ones: Britain's New-Style Climbers," *Sunday Telegraph,* June 27, 1965, Newspaper Clippings Archive, vol. 31, Alpine Club.

84. Brown, *The Hard Years,* 100. On the continent, in contrast, it was not unusual for Himalayan climbers to come from working-class backgrounds. Although many of those from less privileged backgrounds worked as professional guides in the Alps, there were also a fair number of manual laborers in their ranks: two of the four members of the Austrian Alpenverein Karakoram expedition who climbed Broad Peak in 1957, for instance, were Salzburg electricians. Marcus Schmuck, the expedition leader, went back to work at his electrician's trade six days after his return from Broad Peak. Sale, *Broad Peak,* 32.

85. John Kempe, "Kangchenjunga Reconnaissance, 1954," *Alpine Journal* 59 (Nov. 1954): 428–31; Douglas Side, "Towards Kangchenjunga," *Alpine Journal* 60 (May 1955): 95; Braham, *Himalayan Odyssey,* 65–75.

86. G. C. Band, "Kangchenjunga Climbed," *Alpine Journal* 60 (Nov. 1955): 211.

87. Ibid., 217.

88. Ibid., 220.

89. Ibid., 224–25.

90. Brown, *The Hard Years,* 113.

91. Streather's ascent of Kangchenjunga made him the first climber to have ascended two peaks over 25,000 feet. Hardie, *In Highest Nepal,* 9–10. The expedition's one casualty was Sherpa Pemi Dorje, who died on May 26 of cerebral thrombosis and was buried near Pache's grave. For accounts of the climb, see Band, "Kangchenjunga Climbed," 207–26; Charles Evans, "Kangchenjunga," *American Alpine Journal* 10 (1956): 54–59; Evans, *Kangchenjunga.*

92. "Success on Kangchenjunga," *American Alpine Journal* 10 (1956): 114–15.

93. Jean Franco, "Makalu," *Alpine Journal* 61 (May 1956): 13–28; Franco, *Makalu.*

94. Yasuji Yamazaki, "Modern Mountaineering in Japan," *Alpine Journal* 71 (Nov. 1966): 251–53; Kinichi Yamamori, "Japanese Mountaineering in the Himalaya," *Japanese Alpine Centenary, 1905–2005,* 42–43, Tsunemichi Ikeda, "From the Japanese Alps to the Greater Ranges of the World," *Japanese Alpine Centenary, 1905–2005,* 32–33. The authors are grateful to Tamotsu Nakamura for providing copies of the articles from *Japanese Alpine Centenary* before their publication. Also see Yuko Maki and Toshio Imanishi, "The Ascent of Manaslu," *Himalayan Journal* 20 (1957): 12–25; Yoda, *Ascent of Manaslu in Photographs;* G. O. Dyhrenfurth and Norman Dyhrenfurth, "Manaslu," *Mountain* 62 (July–Aug. 1978): 38–39; Baume, *Sivalaya,* 140–42; Clark, *Men, Myths, and Mountains,* 209–10.

95. Eggler, *The Everest-Lhotse Adventure,* 158–75. There had been an attempt on Lhotse the previous year by a Swiss-American expedition, led by Norman Dyhrenfurth, a veteran of the 1952 Swiss expedition. It had ended in near disaster and acrimony, hampered by storms and poor decisions by some of the mountaineers. Fred Beckey, a leading American climber, was accused by Dyhrenfurth of panicking for choosing to abandon a sick teammate high on the mountainside (he was later rescued). Dyhrenfurth's official expedition report gave no hint of the controversy, but he would make his charges publicly some years later. See Norman G. Dyhrenfurth, "Lhotse, 1955," *American Alpine Journal* 10 (1956): 7–20; G. O. Dyhrenfurth and Norman Dyhrenfurth, "Lhotse," *Mountain* 66 (Mar.–Apr. 1979): 40–41; Jon Krakauer, "Warning! Fred Beckey Is Still on the Loose!" *Outside* 17 (July 1992): 52–53.

96. Eggler, *The Everest-Lhotse Adventure,* 186–99. Also see Albert Eggler, "On Lhotse and Mount Everest," *Alpine Journal* 61 (Nov. 1956): 239–52; Jürg Marmet, "Everest-Lhotse, 1956," *American Alpine Journal* 10 (1957): 38–42.

97. F. Moravec, "Gasherbrum II," *Mountain World* (1958–59): 11–125; Moravec, *Weisse Berge—Schwartze Menschen;* Baume, *Sivalaya,* 230–31.

98. Steele, *Eric Shipton*, 200. Three years later Charlie Houston would offer a similar prophecy to the readers of the *American Alpine Journal:* "The large expedition is a complicated and expensive affair available only to a few, and can be organized only for the greatest peaks. It has probably passed its vogue. We may expect now to see many small parties, lightly outfitted and planned on an amateur basis" ("Expedition Philosophy—1956," *American Alpine Journal* 10 [1956]: 90). One of the first parties to set off "on their own initiative and on modest resources" was a pair of climbers from the Glasgow climbing club Creagh Dhu. Hamish MacInnes and John Cunningham displayed the élan typical of Creagh Dhu when they traveled to Nepal on the heels of the 1953 Everest expedition—without visas or permission to climb anything. They hiked into Everest Base Camp, accompanied as far as Namche by a single Sherpa. From there they were on their own. MacInnes and Cunningham at first envisaged launching a postmonsoon assault on Everest itself, but in the end decided instead to climb its neighbor Pumori. They gave up after reaching a height of 22,000 feet on the mountain. They would estimate their total expedition expenses, outside of airfare, as £50 each (Hamish MacInnes, "The Creagh Dhu Himalayan Expedition," *Alpine Journal* 60 [May 1955]: 58–61). Wilfrid Noyce, "Large and Small Giants of the Himalaya," *Appalachia* 23 (Dec. 1957): 454.

99. Hillary and Lowe, *East of Everest,* 24.

100. William W. Dunmire and William Unsoeld, "Makalu, 1954: California Himalayan Expedition," *American Alpine Journal* 9 (1955): 7–24.

101. George Lowe, "The Barun Expedition, 1954," *Alpine Journal* 60 (Nov. 1955): 227–38; Fanshawe and Venables, *Himalaya Alpine-Style,* 179; Hillary, *View from the Summit,* 123. Although Hillary would go on to lead other expeditions, after the Barun expedition he would never again have the same ease of acclimatization or enormous physical strength he had shown on Everest in 1951 and 1953.

102. Conway, *Climbing and Exploration in the Karakoram-Himalayas,* 5; J. M. Hartog, "The Climbing of the Muztagh Tower," *Alpine Journal* 61 (Nov. 1956): 253–54; David Brower, foreword to Brower et al., *Summit,* 5. Joe Curran noted that from the southeast perspective on the Upper Baltoro Glacier from which Sella took his famous photograph, "both summits of the peak are in line and the mountain appears as a slender tooth, the epitome of the impossible" (*K2,* 66). Guido Magnone suggested that it was "not the highest mountains that are destined to make [the basin of the Baltoro Gacier in the Karakoram] a Mecca for mountaineers of the whole world, but rather the formidable bristle of spikes and towers which stand at the entrance of the glacier" ("The Muztagh Tower," *Himalayan Journal* 20 [1957]: 40).

103. Hartog, "The Climbing of the Muztagh Tower," 263–68; Magnone, "The Muztagh Tower," 49–50.

104. Hartog, "The Climbing of the Muztagh Tower," 253–70; Tom Patey, "The Mustagh Tower," reprinted in Patey, *One Man's Mountains,* 135–47; Brown, *The Hard Years,* 115–32; Magnone, "The Muztagh Tower," 40–50. A. K. Rawlinson, "Crescendo, 1939–1956," *Alpine Journal* 62 (Nov. 1957): 110. Sir Anthony Keith Rawlinson was an Alpine Club stalwart, who would later serve as its president. There were several other notable Himalayan expeditions attempting smaller peaks in 1957–58. In 1957 a British party led by Joe Walmsley got within 300 feet of the summit of Masherbrum (25,659ft/7,821m). J. Walmsley, "Masherbrum 1957," *Alpine Journal* 63 (Nov. 1958): 169–84. One member, Bob Downes, died of pulmonary edema. The expedition was also notable for the presence of one of its strongest members, Don Whillans, on his first Himalayan expedition. Perrin, *The Villain,* 176–79. An Oxford University Mountaineering Club expedition, led by 1953 K2 veteran Tony Streather, carried out a reconnaissance and attempted to climb Haramosh (24,270ft/7,397m). An avalanche brought an end to the effort, and two of the climbers lost their lives in the rescue effort that followed. See Barker, *The Last Blue Mountain.* Streather played a heroic role in the doomed rescue effort. The year 1957 also saw Eric Shipton's last Himalayan expedition, when he led the Imperial College Karokaram expedition in a three-month effort surveying the Bilafond, Lolofond, Siachen, Teram Shehr, and K12 glaciers. E. E. Shipton, "The Imperial College Karakoram Expedition, 1957," *Alpine Journal* 63 (Nov. 1958): 185–93. And on June 21, 1958 Mike Banks and Tom Patey reached the summit of Rakaposhi (22,550ft/7,788m) despite blizzard conditions; it was a mountain that had previously turned back attempts by mountaineers of the quality of

Campbell Secord and Bill Tilman. Mike Banks, "Struggle for Rakaposhi," *Alpine Journal* 61 (May 1957): 449–57; Lt. Cmdr. F. R. Brooke, "The Ascent of Rakaposhi," *Alpine Journal* 63 (Nov. 1958): 159–68; Tom Patey, "Rakaposhi—The Taming of the Shrew," reprinted in Patey, *One Man's Mountains,* 158.

105. Buhl, though the first to participate in two first ascents, was not the first to climb two 8,000-meter peaks: that distinction went to Sherpa Gyalzen Norbu, who shared in the first ascent of Manaslu in 1955 and climbed Makalu in 1956 on the day after its first ascent. Kurt Diemberger would climb Broad Peak with Buhl in 1957 and share in the first ascent of Dhaulagiri in 1960.

106. "Expeditions," *Alpine Journal* 60 (Nov. 1955): 176.

107. Hermann Buhl, "The West Face of the Dru," in Messner and Höfler, *Hermann Buhl,* 160–70. Greg Child discusses the etymology of the term *alpine style* in his encyclopedia *Climbing,* 39. Kurt Diemberger attributed the choice of expedition strategy to Hermann Buhl: "No one had yet succeeded in climbing an eight-thousander without using high-altitude porters; this is what Hermann [Buhl] wanted to attempt. His plan was that from base camp onwards there would only be climbers on the mountain; they would do everything, load-carrying, establishment of camps and, finally, the assault on the summit. And it was all to be done without the use of oxygen; we were all to achieve high altitude acclimatization during our load-carrying up to the high camps" (*Summits and Secrets,* 116). Reinhold Messner and Horst Höfler followed Diemberger's lead in attributing the idea of climbing Broad Peak in lightweight style to Buhl alone (*Hermann Buhl,* 21). Richard Sale, in contrast, in his revisionist account of the Broad Peak expedition, argues that both Buhl and Marcus Schmuck had been planning such an expedition when they decided to collaborate (*Broad Peak,* 30–31).

108. Sale, *Broad Peak,* 59.

109. Ibid., 83. The individual climbers harbored resentments of others who they thought were failing to pull their weight, and Schmuck, Wintersteller, Buhl, and Pakistani liaison officer Qader Saaed all seemed to find Diemberger personally abrasive. Sale's *Broad Peak* offers numerous examples: see, for instance, 53, 59, 68–69, 77–78, 94–95, 96–97, 115–16.

110. Messner and Höfler, *Hermann Buhl,* 177.

111. Buhl wrote that Schmuck and Wintersteller set off first, despite the fact that "we had agreed to set off together." "Hermann Buhl's Report, 9 June 1957," in Messner and Höfler, *Hermann Buhl,* 179. Wintersteller said that he and Schmuck left at 4:00 A.M., *after* Buhl and Diemberger departed, and cites a photograph that Schmuck took of him at Camp III that morning, with the tracks of the other, already departed, climbers visible in the foreground. Fritz W. Wintersteller (son of the climber), letter to the authors, Dec. 30, 2005.

112. "Hermann Buhl's Report, 9 June 1957," 180.

113. In 1975, descending from Everest's summit, Pete Boardman met Mick Burke heading up the mountain and declined to return to the top with him. Burke would disappear on his own descent. In 1996 commercial guide Rob Hall, descending from the summit of Everest, met his client Doug Hansen some forty feet below the summit, turned around, and escorted Hansen to the top. Hall's generosity had fatal consequences, for neither man would survive the climb. Diemberger himself downplayed his act of generosity on Broad Peak, saying simply, "I wanted to be with him up there, so I turned around and went back up with him" (O'Connell, *Beyond Risk,* 72). For accounts of summit day, see Marcus Schmuck, "Karakorum-Expedition des OAV 1957 zum Broad Peak," *Jahrbuch des Deutschen Alpenvereins* (1957): 24–41; Schmuck, *Broad Peak;* Kurt Diemberger, "Broad Peak: The Austrian Karakoram Expedition 1957," Malcolm Barnes, ed., *Mountain World* (1958–59): 126–41; Diemberger, *Summits and Secrets,* 121–28; Sale, *Broad Peak,* 127–49; Bonington, *Quest for Adventure,* 253–58. In writing this section, the authors benefited from the opportunity to read Bill Buxton's unpublished paper "Broad Peak and the 1957 Austrian Karakoram Expedition." It would be two decades before Broad Peak would have its second ascent, by a Japanese expedition that placed Kazuhisa Noro, Takashi Ozaki, and Yoshi-yuki Tsuji on the summit on August 8, 1977. Baume, *Sivalaya,* 243.

114. "Hermann Buhl's Report, 9 June 1957," 182.

115. Diemberger, *Summits and Secrets,* 128–35; Bonington, *Quest for Adventure,* 258–61.

116. Gary Yortin to James Ramsey Ullman, Feb. 20, 1957, Ullman Papers, box 80, folder 1, Department of Rare Books and Special Collections, Princeton University Library.

117. Whittaker describes his early days as REI manager in his autobiography *A Life on the Edge,* 63–69. Another important outlet for mountaineering gear in the 1950s was the Ski Hut in Berkeley, California, managed by Allen Steck. See Middendorf, "The Mechanical Advantage," 163. In equipping the 1953 American expedition to K2, the organizers were able to buy American tents and packs but had to turn to Europe for crampons and ice axes. Bates, "The Fight for K2," 7. Before REI came along, it was even harder to find mountaineering equipment in the United States. Dee Molenaar, a member of the American K2 expedition in 1953, made his first climb on Rainier in 1939 carrying a garden tool for an ice ax and homemade nailed boots. Timothy Egan, "Old Men of the Mountains," *Washington Magazine* 3 (May–June 1987): 54.

118. John Roskelley, growing up in eastern Washington in the early 1960s, was fortunate to live in one of the few places in the country with an active mountaineering group. In 1965 he joined the Spokane Mountaineers, taking their basic climbing course. Safety was stressed, while the cutting-edge techniques practiced further south in the Yosemite valley went unmentioned. According to Roskelley: "A. F. Mummery, in 1879, had equipment as good as and better knowledge of technique than we did" (*Stories Off the Wall,* 27). For Dartmouth College's contributions to mountaineering, see Engle, *Talus.* Five members of the 1963 American Everest expedition—Barry Bishop, Jake Breitenbach, Barry Corbet, Dave Dingman, and Barry Prather—attended Dartmouth College in the 1950s, though only Breitenbach ('57) and Corbet ('58) finished their degrees. Engle, *Talus,* 102–3. For the Stanford club, see Rawlings, *The Stanford Alpine Club.* While most of the climbing sponsored by university clubs in the 1950s focused on nearby peaks, in the White Mountains or the Sierras, some club members went further afield: see, for example, Craig Merrihue, "Harvard Karakoram Expedition, 1955," *Harvard Mountaineering* 13 (May 1957): 49–57. Curiously enough, one of the major student climbing clubs of the era was located at the University of Iowa. Lloyd Athearn, "The Risks of Mountaineering Put in Perspective," *American Alpine News* 11 (Summer 2004): 10; Jones, *Climbing in North America,* 242. By 2000 the number attempting Denali (the former Mount McKinley) had increased to over 1,200 annually.

119. Robert H. Bates, "We Met Death on K2," *Saturday Evening Post,* Dec. 5, Dec. 12, 1953. American climbing expeditions in the Himalaya that did not involve death were virtually ignored. The *New York Times* carried a single wire-service story on the 1954 Makalu expedition: "Americans, Defeated in Himalayan Climb, Make Scientific Success of Expedition," *New York Times,* June 28, 1954, 21.

120. Clinch, *A Walk in the Sky,* 7.

121. Ibid., 14–15; Nick Clinch to Dr. Jürg Marmet, Jan. 14, 1958, Kauffman Collection, box 1, folder 1/1, American Alpine Club Library. Loans and contributions from the American Alpine Club and individual members paid for about half the $30,000 cost. The rest had to be contributed by the participants. Public interest and contributions were virtually nil. At one point, Clinch would recall, "in a desperate attempt to raise money, I decided to 'wave the flag' a little," planting an article in the *Los Angeles Times* that stressed the benefits for American prestige should they succeed in climbing Hidden Peak. When nothing happened, Clinch decided that "I might as well stick to my principles and struggle along with a clear conscience," since a descent to jingoism wasn't going to work anyway. Clinch, *A Walk in the Sky,* 18.

122. For Kauffman's career as a climber and in the State Department, see obituaries Bart Barnes, "Leading Mountain Climber, Andrew J. Kauffman II," *Washington Post,* Jan. 3, 2003, B7; William L. Putnam, "Andrew John Kauffman, II 1920–2003," *American Alpine Journal* 45 (2003): 478–79. Nick Clinch to Andrew Kauffman, Jan. 11, 1958, Kauffman Collection, box 1, folder 1/1, American Alpine Club Library.

123. Bonatti, *The Mountains of My Life,* 113–36; Maraini, *Karakorom,* 51. (The "agriculturalist" Maraini mentioned was rancher Tom McCormack.) Nick Clinch had a conversation with another of the Italian party, the expedition doctor, Donato Zeni, that made him feel better about the amateur status of his own party. "You are

very lucky," Zeni told him. "You are a party of friends climbing for fun. If you climb the mountain, fine; if you don't nothing happens. We are a national expedition. If we climb the mountain we are heroes; if we don't . . . " (Zeni then made a cutting gesture across his throat to demonstrate figuratively his fate in the event of failure). Clinch, *A Walk in the Sky*, 136.

124. On August 6, 1958 Walter Bonatti and Carlo Mauri reached the summit of Gasherbrum IV by its technically difficult North Ridge, climbing without oxygen. Fosco Maraini, "The Italian Expedition to Gasherbrum IV," *Alpine Journal* 64 (Nov. 1959): 155–67; Bonatti, *On the Heights*, 173–74; Cassin, *50 Years of Alpinism*, 117–28; Clinch, *A Walk in the Sky*, 91.

125. Clinch, *A Walk in the Sky*, 34, 63, 176. They also carried a Lone Star flag of Texas (Clinch, born in Illinois, was living in Texas at the time of the expedition) and a green "Free Hungary" flag, in solidarity with the recently suppressed Hungarian Revolution. For accounts of the climb, see Nick Clinch, "We Conquered Hidden Peak," *Saturday Evening Post*, Jan. 31, 1959, 15–17, 62–64; Clinch, *A Walk in the Sky*, 154–76; Peter K. Schoening, "Ascent of Hidden Peak," *American Alpine Journal* 11 (1959): 165–72. Clinch, *A Walk in the Sky*, 194.

126. "Pakistan Peak Scaled: Eight-Man U.S. Team Climbs 24,470-foot Mountain," *New York Times*, July 22, 1958, 6; "Pakistan Peak Scaled: Gasherbrum I Is Conquered by 2 of 8-man U.S. Team," *New York Times*, July 26, 1958, 3. The *New York Times*'s obituary of Peter Schoening continued the neglect of this landmark in the history of American mountaineering; while offering a detailed account of his role in the 1953 K2 expedition, it made no mention at all of his first ascent of Gasherbrum I. Douglas Martin, "Peter Schoening, 77, Legend of a Mountaineering Rescue," *New York Times*, Sept. 27, 2004, B7. San Francisco papers, noting the local angle, gave the story more play: "Yank Expedition First to Climb 26,470 Foot Pakistan Peak: Four Bay Area Grads on Team," *San Francisco Examiner*, July 26, 1958, 1. Nick Clinch is the source for the *National Geographic*'s failure to run Kauffman's article about the expedition, in an e-mail to the authors, Dec. 9, 2006.

127. Andrew John Kauffman to Gwen Barrows, Aug. 3, 1958, Kauffman Collection, box 1, folder 1/2, American Alpine Club Library. Bill Putnam provided information on Kauffman's Calcutta posting in an e-mail to the authors, Mar. 8, 2006.

128. Clinch, *A Walk in the Sky*, vii. In contrast to the indifference of the American public, the European mountaineering community understood the importance of Clinch's expedition to Hidden Peak as well as of the expedition he led to Masherbrum two years later. As two well-known British climbers and writers would write, "Clinch himself did not reach the summit of Hidden Peak but masterminded the first ascent, two years later of Masherbrum and was a member of that expedition's second successful summit party. His contribution to American mountaineering is thus profound, though he was never to gain the same acclaim as his country-men who were to climb Everest and K2 in the following decades" (Fanshawe and Venables, *Himalaya Alpine-Style*, 57).

129. Letter from Alma Booker to James Ramsey Ullman, Sept. 25, 1947, Ullman Papers, box 54, folder 11, Department of Rare Books and Special Collections, Princeton University Library.

130. The figures on American Alpine Club (AAC) membership are drawn from "Proceedings of the Club/Year 1947," *American Alpine Journal* 7 (1948): 21; American Alpine Club, *Bylaws and Register of the American Alpine Club 1947*. Unlike its British counterpart, which would not admit women as members until 1974, the AAC had admitted women since its founding. Miriam Underhill, an AAC member and one of the best-known women mountaineers, had been climbing in the Alps for over a decade as a single woman before she met and married her husband, Robert. But she achieved her best-known climbing achievement, the first winter ascent of all of New Hampshire's 4,000-foot mountains, in the company of her husband. See Underhill, *Give Me the Hills*. Barbara Washburn, on the other hand, made it clear in the title of her autobiography that she would never have become a mountaineer at all if she hadn't happened to marry one: Washburn, *The Accidental Adventurer*.

131. Mme. A. Lohner et al., "The Swiss Garhwal Expedition of 1947," *Himalayan Journal* 15 (1949): 19. There were physiological arguments for as well as against women climbing in the Himalaya. British climber Nea Morin, a former president of the Ladies Alpine Club, recalled: "At this time Himalayan climbing for women was still in its infancy, but I had once heard a novel theory put forward claiming that women ought to do well at high altitudes since their brains were smaller and would therefore require less oxygen!" (*A Woman's Reach,* 215). Morin would be the only woman member of a six-member British team that attempted to climb Ama Dablam (22,348ft/6,812m) in 1959. J. H. Emlyn Jones, "Ama Dablam, 1959," *Alpine Journal* 65 (May 1960): 1–10. Among other distinctions, Morin helped translate Maurice Herzog's *Annapurna* for publication in English.

132. Bernard Pierre, "Nun-Kun," *American Alpine Journal* 9 (1954): 29–31; Pierre, *A Mountain Called Nun Kun;* Frison-Roche and Jouty, *A History of Mountain Climbing,* 306. Also see Buffet, *Première de cordée.*

133. Monica Jackson, "The Scottish Women's Himalayan Expedition," *Alpine Journal* 61 (May 1956): 60, 62. Also see Jackson and Stark, *Tents in the Clouds;* Norie Kizaki, "Pilgrimage: Gyalgen Peak 50 Years Later," *Shesends* 9 (Summer–Fall 2005): 12–13, 27. A new edition of the expedition book was published in 2000 by Seal Press with a foreword by Arlene Blum.

134. For women's expeditions, see, for example, Dunsheath, *Mountains and Memsahibs;* Ann Davies, "Women's Overland Himalayan Expedition, 1958," *Alpine Journal* 64 (May 1959): 83–90; Deacock, *No Purdah in Padam.* Robert Daley, "Dozen Women Hope to Climb 26,867 Peak," *New York Times,* July 26, 1959, S6.

135. Baume, *Sivalaya,* 126. The *New York Times'*s obituary was respectful, perhaps in atonement for the flippancy of its preexpedition coverage. See Robert Daley, "The Mountain Is Still the Master," *New York Times,* Oct. 29, 1959, 50. Not so the unofficial expedition book produced by British freelance reporter Stephen Harper. Harper had attempted to accompany the expedition to the mountain but Kogan, for reasons that remain unclear, had banned him from Base Camp. He retreated to Namche Bazar, but when he heard of the disaster made his way back to the mountain and got his scoop. And his book, *Lady Killer Peak,* provided ample testimony to the subordinate position still occupied by women in the mountaineering world of the 1950s. "This is the story," he wrote in his preface, "of one man, twelve women and a killer peak—told by the man. It is a story of women obsessed, hypnotized by the strange inexplicable urge to battle against rock and ice and thin air until the highest places of the earth lie conquered beneath their tiny, feminine feet. It is also a story of women's rebellion against man's natural assumption of command decision, and of feminine rivalries that contributed to the loss of four lives. From it emerges a verdict that even the toughest and most courageous of women are still 'the weaker sex' in the White Hell of a blizzard and avalanche torn mountain."

136. Brownell, *Training the Body for China,* 56–60; Zhou and Liu, *Footprints on the Peaks,* 54–58.

137. Zhou and Liu, *Footprints on the Peaks,* 60–68; Michael Ward and Peter Boardman, "The History of the Exploration of the Mustagh Ata-Kongur Massif," in Bonington, *Kongur,* 189–90; Lane, *Military Mountaineering,* 47–48; Shi Chan-Chun, "The Second Ascent of Minya Konka," *Alpine Journal* 63 (Nov. 1958): 194–202. Shi Chan-Chun (or Shi Zhanchun), the author of this account of climbing Minya Konka, would be a central figure in Chinese mountaineering from its origins in the mid-1950s for the next three decades. According to Chris Bonington, who would get to know him well in later decades, Shi Zhanchun "was the party official who had been put in charge of mountaineering in 1956 when it was decided that the Chinese should climb their own mountains. He had started as a bureaucrat but had come to enjoy and love the mountains and consequently had taken an active part in the expeditions, co-leading the first Russian/Chinese expedition to Mustagh Ata in 1956 and then leading the Chinese Everest expeditions of 1960 and 1975" (*Kongur,* 26). Shi Zhanchun's account of the climbing of Minya Konka for the *Alpine Journal* was, by the standards of Chinese mountaineering, a fairly nonpolitical narrative, with no mention of Mao Zedong's thoughts intruding. On the other hand, parts of it were clearly plagiarized from Richard Burdsall and Arthur Emmons's account of their first ascent of the mountain. Burdsall and Emmons wrote of the view from the summit, "The horizon

surrounded us in one unbroken ring. . . . The panorama of tremendous snow peaks, which had so dominated the sky at our 19,800-foot camp, had now dwindled to a series of mere white patches against the brown plain" (*Men against the Clouds*). Shi Zhanchun's account of the Chinese summit day declared, "Around us stretched the horizon in one unbroken ring. The tremendous snow peaks that had dominated the sky-line as we made our way up had now dwindled to a series of white patches against the brown of the lower plains" (201).

138. Shih Chan-Chun, "The Conquest of Mount Everest by the Chinese Mountaineering Team," *Alpine Journal* 66 (May 1961): 28–40; Zhou and Liu, *Footprints on the Peak*, 70–72.

139. Zhou and Liu, *Footprints on the Peaks*, 72. Soviet officials offered a somewhat different version of these events. According to a statement released in the 1970s, a joint Soviet-Chinese reconnaissance of the Everest North Face actually took place in 1959, with plans for a full-scale expedition the following year. Unsworth, *Everest*, 346.

140. Zhou and Liu, *Footprints on the Peaks*, 73; "Insurmountable Dreams Become Reality," *China Daily*, May 22, 2003, http://www.china.org.cn/english/travel/65177.htm. A Reuters dispatch in the spring of 1960 reported that Nepal's government feared a Chinese ascent of Everest would lead to an attempt to claim the mountain as Chinese territory. "Nepalese See a Ruse by Reds on Everest," *New York Times*, May 29, 1960, 9.

141. Shih Chan-Chun, "The Conquest of Mount Everest by the Chinese Mountaineering Team," 29; Zhou and Liu, *Footprints on the Peaks*, 76–77.

142. The discovery of Wilson's body was reported in 1960 in the June 15 issue of *Soviet Sport* and was cited in an editor's note following Shih Chan-Chun's article in the *Alpine Journal*. The most recent reported sighting of Wilson's body came in 1999. "How Many Bodies on Everest?" *Mountain* (Apr. 1980): 14; Dipesh Risal, "Death on the High Himal," *Himal* (Nov.–Dec. 1992): 25; Hemmleb and Simonson, *Detectives on Everest*, 83, 181–86.

143. "Insurmountable Dreams Become Reality."

144. Wang Fu-chou [Wang Fuzhou] and Chu Yin-hua [Qu Yinhua], "How We Climbed Chomolungma," in Gillman, *Everest*, 75. This article originally appeared in *Mountain Craft* 52 (Summer 1961): 9–11.

145. Zhou and Liu, *Footprints on the Peaks*, 82.

146. Shih Chan-Chun, "The Conquest of Mount Everest by the Chinese Mountaineering Team," 35–36; B. R. Goodfellow, "Chinese Everest Expedition, 1960," *Alpine Journal* 66 (Nov. 1961): 313–15; Hugh Merrick, "Everest: The Chinese Photograph," *Alpine Journal* 67 (Nov. 1962): 310–12; "Everest Climbers of '33 Say Chinese Claim Unsure," *Guardian*, Sept. 5, 1962, Newspaper Clippings Archive, vol. 31, Alpine Club. For the 1960 Indian expedition, see Brigadier Gyan Singh, "Indian Mount Everest Expedition," *Alpine Journal* 66 (May 1961): 15–27. Singh, *Lure of Everest*; Kohli, *Mountaineering in India*, 46–62.

147. Peter Gillman, "Backtracking on Everest," in Gillman, *In Balance*, 134.

148. Bonington, *I Chose to Climb*, 106–24; Bonington, *Mountaineer*, 58. Ang Nyima had previously distinguished himself by climbing to Camp IX on Everest in the 1953 British expedition, carrying supplies for Tenzing and Hillary's summit bid.

149. "Pakistan Peak Climbed," *New York Times*, Aug. 21, 1960, 60. Tom Hornbein, expedition doctor, wrote one of the expedition reports: Thomas F. Hornbein, "The Ascent of Masherbrum," *Alpine Journal* 67 (May 1962): 9–25. Also see William Unsoeld, "Masherbrum—1960," *American Alpine Journal* 12 (1961): 209–29. Unsoeld had been on two previous trips to the Himalaya: one a decidedly casual attempt in 1949 to climb Nilkanta (21,640ft/6,595m) in the Indian Garhwal, the second the 1954 Sierra Club–sponsored attempt on Makalu. For the earlier journey, see William Unsoeld, "Nilkanta, Garhwal Himalaya, 1949," *American Alpine Journal* 10 (1956): 75–80.

150. A Swiss expedition to Dhaulagiri made it to 25,400 feet in 1953, an Argentine party to 26,250 feet in 1954 (the leader of this expedition, Francisco Ibanez, died in a hospital in Kathmandu of frostbite sustained on the mountain). There were four more parties on the mountain in the next five years: a Swiss-German effort

in 1955, an Argentine expedition in 1956, another Swiss attempt in 1958, and an Austrian attempt in 1959 (the last expedition also sustained a fatality when one of its members, Heini Roiss, fell into a crevasse). None of the later expeditions reached the height achieved by the 1954 expedition. High winds and heavy snows proved the main factors defeating expeditions on the peak some called the Mountain of Storms. André Roch, "Dhaulagiri, 1953," *Alpine Journal* 59 (May 1954): 302–6; J. O. M. Roberts, "Round about Dhaulagiri," *Alpine Journal* 60 (Nov. 1955): 248–56; Fritz Moravec, "Dhaulagiri, 1959," *Alpine Journal* 65 (May 1960): 11–17; Eiselin, *The Ascent of Dhaulagiri*, 1–10; Harvard and Thompson, *Mountain of Storms*, 2–3; G. O. Dyhrenfurth and Norman Dyhrenfurth, "Dhaulagiri," *Mountain* 63 (Sept.–Oct. 1978): 32–34.

151. Eiselin, *The Ascent of Dhaulagiri*, 14.

152. The use of airplanes to supply expeditions had precedent in the Himalaya and elsewhere; the Germans had partially supplied themselves by parachute drops during the 1938 Nanga Parbat expedition, and American climbers in Alaska had used aircraft to reach remote mountains and for aerial resupply. This experiment in aerial resupply tended to overshadow the actual climb on the mountain in most accounts, including the official expedition book by Eiselin. Richard Sale and John Cleare described Eiselin's expedition book as a "curious read," in which the actual ascent of Dhaulagiri appeared to be "merely a sideshow in the 'Yeti' story" (*Climbing the World's 14 Highest Mountains*, 188). Eiselin devoted three pages in his concluding chapter of the book to the summit bid but the better part of three chapters to the flight of the Yeti from Europe to Nepal, another chapter to aerial reconnaissance, and still another to the mechanical problems and eventual crash of the plane.

153. Eiselin, *The Ascent of Dhaulagiri*, 133, 154. In Diemberger's own account of the climb, he wrote that he and others left on May 9 "on our second drive for the summit, taking with us the good wishes of all those remaining down on the col" (*Summits and Secrets*, 221). The night was notable for another clash between the assumptions of Western climbers that Sherpas remained the ever-submissive servants of years gone by and the new assertiveness they were increasingly displaying in the 1950s. In the early evening, Sherpa Nima Dorje brewed tea and soup for the others on the butane-gas cooker. According to Peter Diener's recollection: "Kurt [Diemberger] told Nima to go on cooking all through the night, but he had had enough and refused. When Kurt again ordered him to do so, he got up without a word, took his foam rubber mat and sleeping-bag, and went outside into the cold night. . . . He was fed up with the constant demands of his Sahibs" (Eiselin, *The Ascent of Dhaulagiri*, 156–57). Diemberger's own account is somewhat at odds with Diener's; he wrote that it was both Ernst and he who asked Nima Dorje to make tea, "knowing how anxious he always was to help," and were then horrified when he left the tent to sleep outside (*Summits and Secrets*, 222).

154. Diemberger, *Summits and Secrets*, 224.

155. Michel Vaucher and Hugo Weber repeated the ascent ten days later. For accounts of the climb, see Norman G. Dyhrenfurth, "The Mountain of Storms—Dhaulagiri 1960," *American Alpine Journal* 12 (1961): 231–48; Dyhrenfurth and Dyhrenfurth, "Dhaulagiri," 4–35; Kurt Diemberger, "Dhaulagiri, the White Mountain: A Chronicle of the 1960 Expedition," *Himalayan Journal* 22 (1959–60): 38–50; Max Eiselin and Ernst Forrer, "The Ascent of Dhaulagiri: Report of the Swiss Himalayan Expedition 1960," *Mountain World* (1960–61): 131–40; Diemberger, *Summits and Secrets*, 194–226; Eiselin, *The Ascent of Dhaulagiri*, 154–59; Sale and Cleare, *Climbing the World's 14 Highest Mountains*, 189–90.

156. Wilfrid Noyce, "Ascent of Trivor," *Alpine Journal* 66 (May 1961): 9. Noyce's recent ascent of Trivor (25,354ft/7,728m) would be his last successful climb; he would be killed on a British-Soviet expedition in the Pamirs in 1962. A. D. M. Cox, "Cuthbert Wilfrid Frank Noyce, 1917–1962," *Alpine Journal* 67 (May 1962): 384–88.

CHAPTER NINE: *New Frontiers, New Faces, 1961–1970*

1. Dennis Davis and Tashi Sherpa reached the summit of Nuptse on May 16, 1961 by its South Face, followed the next day by Bonington, Les Brow, Jim Swallow, and Ang Pemba (J. Walmsley, "Nuptse," *Alpine Journal* 66 [Nov. 1961]: 209–34; Bonington, *I Chose to Climb*, 128–44). Bonington, *The Everest Years*, 15.

2. Some expeditions, including Bonington's 1975 Everest Southwest Face expedition, would still make the two-week hike from Kathmandu to help acclimatization or because they were approaching the mountain during the monsoon season when landing at the airport was untenable. For an overview of the changing face of Himalayan climbing in the later 1960s and early 1970s, see Mike Cheney, "Events and Trends 1970–6, Nepal Himalaya," *Alpine Journal* 83 (1978): 218–27. Sherry Ortner describes the many changes that affected Sherpas in the 1960s and in subsequent years, including the declining usage of the term *sahib,* especially among the younger generation of Sherpas. *Life and Death on Mt. Everest,* 215.

3. For Hillary's Antarctic exploration, see Johnston, *Reaching the Summit,* 89–113; Hillary, *No Latitude for Error.* Bishop made his mark as an up-and-coming American climber when he made a first ascent of the West Buttress of Mount McKinley (later Denali) in 1951. He would become the National Geographic Society's in-house expert on mountaineering. For Bishop's background, see the obituary by his son Brent Bishop, "Barry Bishop," *American Alpine Journal* 69 (1995): 361–63.

4. For the popularity of Yeti hunting in the 1950s, see Bishop, *The Myth of Shangri-La,* 236–37. For Sir Edmund Hillary's somewhat embarrassed preexpeditionary explanation for the Yeti search, see Hillary, "Abominable—and Improbable?" *New York Times,* Jan. 24, 1960, SM13. Hillary's search party included Marlin Perkins, host of the popular American television show *Wild Kingdom.* All that they found were some ambiguous footprints and an ancient scalp that on examination by experts in Chicago was pronounced that of a Himalayan blue bear. Doig, *High in the Thin Cold Air,* 5, 130–32.

5. James Morris, who covered the 1953 expedition for *The Times* of London, noted in a humorous piece for the *New York Times* on the eve of the 1960 expedition that Hillary "has gay plans for climbing Everest again, without oxygen this time" ("Why They Climb and Climb and Climb," *New York Times,* Apr. 10, 1960, SM25). For an example of the scientific studies conducted by the expedition, see Pugh, "Cardiac Output in Muscular Exercise." John West, a veteran of the Silver Hut experiment, would return to lead the American Medical Research Expedition to Everest in 1981. He described the 1960–61 expedition in *Everest,* 11–13. Also see Houston, *Going Higher,* 178–79.

6. Alfred Gregory, "Ama Dablam," *American Alpine Journal* 11 (1959): 326. On the other hand, J. H. Emlyn Jones ended his own expedition report on the 1959 climb with the prediction that the mountain could be climbed by the route they attempted ("Ama Dablam, 1959," *Alpine Journal* 65 [May 1960]: 1–10; also see Morin, *A Woman's Reach,* 213–46). M. B. Gill, "The Ascent of Ama Dablam," *Himalayan Journal* 23 (1961): 30–36; "Asian Peak Conquered," *New York Times,* Mar. 20, 1961, 2.

7. Barry Bishop to Arnold Wexler, Mar. 3, 1961, Bishop Papers, folder "MSS Bishop, Barry corresp. w/ Arnold Wexler," American Alpine Club Library. Wexler was a veteran climber with a long record of first ascents in the Canadian Rockies and elsewhere. His greatest contribution to mountaineering was in helping to develop the idea of the "dynamic belay," a technique in which a belayer allowed some rope slippage to lessen the impact of holding a falling climber. John Christian, "Arnold Wexler," *American Alpine Journal* 72 (1998): 411. Also see Leonard and Wexler, *Belaying the Leader.*

8. Hillary, *Nothing Venture,* 245.

9. Lead climber Pete Mulgrew suffered an attack of pulmonary embolism and had to be rescued from the mountain. During the evacuation he suffered severe frostbite that cost him both legs below the knees. Doig, *High in the Thin Cold Air,* 204–25; Hillary, *Nothing Venture,* 246–50; Michael Ward, "The Descent from Makalu, 1961," *Alpine Journal* 68 (May 1963): 11–19.

10. Barry Bishop, "Wintering on the Roof of the World," *National Geographic* 122 (Oct. 1962): 503–47; "Soviet Planes Reported Photographing Pakistan," *New York Times*, May 29, 1961, 4; Letter from Ralph N. Styles to Barry Bishop, Nov. 19, 1962, Bishop Grant File, microfiche 502 1.3, 2 of 8, National Geographic Society.

11. According to Robert M. Poole, former executive editor of *National Geographic*, during World War II and the cold war "the organization began to look less like a journalistic enterprise than an extension of government" (*Explorer's House*, 184, 216–17). See memo from Barry Bishop to Melvin Payne [National Geographic Society executive vice president], Nov. 19, 1962, microfiche 502 1.3, 2 of 8, National Geographic Society. At the end of the memo, Bishop added this request: "I am supplying this information in order that you will know what is involved. This is the only copy of this memo so please destroy after reading."

12. Hillary led a new expedition to the region in 1963, with both mountaineering and philanthropic aims. During the expedition Americans David Dornan and Tom Frost and New Zealanders Mike Gill and Jim Wilson made the first ascent of Kangtega (22,240ft/6,779m) via its East Face. See Hillary, *Schoolhouse in the Clouds*; J. G. Wilson, "The Himalayan Schoolhouse Expedition, 1963," *Alpine Journal* 69 (May 1964): 23–33; David B. Dornan, "The Himalayan Schoolhouse Expedition," *American Alpine Journal* 14 (1964): 31–36. Also see John C. Devlin, "Hillary to Help School in Nepal," *New York Times*, May 23, 1962, 4; James Brooke, "In Sherpa Country, They Love 'Sir Ed,'" *New York Times*, May 29, 2003, 14.

13. Barry Bishop to "Bob" [Cochran], Nov. 30, 1960, Bishop Grant File, microfiche 502 1.3, 3 of 8, National Geographic Society.

14. Kennedy's rhetorical commitment to "vigor" was intended in part to obscure his own lifelong physical ailments. Doctor Hans Kraus, rock-climbing partner of Fritz Wiessner and a member of the American Alpine Club since 1946, secretly treated Kennedy's severe back problems in his White House years. Unlike Kennedy's other doctors, Kraus prescribed exercise rather than drugs as his primary treatment. Schwartz, *Into the Unknown*, 163–207. Kennedy was interested in Kraus's climbing experiences and questioned him closely and often about mountaineering topics. Jim McCarthy, e-mail to the authors, Apr. 5, 2006.

15. Hoffman, *All You Need Is Love*, 123, 209. While Bates and Unsoeld ran the Peace Corps effort in Nepal, Charlie Houston headed it up in India from 1962 through 1965. Unsoeld's first biographer, Lawrence Leamer, was a Peace Corps volunteer in Nepal in 1964, serving under Unsoeld. See Leamer, *Ascent*, 9–15, 102–15.

16. Norman G. Dyhrenfurth, foreword to Ullman, *Americans on Everest*, xx.

17. Norman Dyhrenfurth to James Ramsey Ullman, Nov. 23, 1953, Ullman Papers, box 53, folder 8, Department of Rare Books and Special Collections, Princeton University Library. Ullman was interested in Dyhrenfurth's plans for a 1954 expedition, but when it was delayed for a year (and switched its purpose to that of climbing Lhotse), he could no longer go. Ullman did, however, travel to Kathmandu in 1954 in connection with research for his book with Tenzing Norgay, *Tiger of the Snows*. Norman G. Dyhrenfurth, "Lhotse, 1955," *American Alpine Journal* 10 (1956): 7–20; Norman G. Dyhrenfurth, "The Mountain of Storms—Dhaulagiri 1960," *American Alpine Journal* 11 (1961): 231–48.

18. Dyhrenfurth, foreword, xx.

19. Norman Dyhrenfurth, "American Everest Expedition, 1961," typescript copy n.d. [1960], Ullman Papers, box 92, folder 6, Department of Rare Books and Special Collections, Princeton University Library. U.S. Army major William D. Hackett, who led an unsuccessful German-American expedition to K2 in 1960, had already applied for a permit to climb Everest in 1961; for awhile he and Dyhrenfurth cooperated, but Hackett soon dropped out of the planning. "US Expedition to Try to Climb Mount Everest," *New York Times*, Oct. 10, 1960, 23; "US Climbers Eye Everest," *New York Times*, Jan. 24, 1961, 16; Ullman, *Americans on Everest*, 19–20. With the Nepalese authorities dragging their feet on the climbing permit, plans for a 1961 expedition proved unrealistic. Permission finally arrived from Kathmandu in May 1961 for a 1963 American expedition to attempt one or more of the three peaks of the Everest massif—Everest itself, Lhotse, and Nuptse. In the

meantime, Indian mountaineers would make their second unsuccessful attempt to climb Everest in 1962. Hari Dang, "Mount Everest, 1962," *Alpine Journal* 68 (May 1963): 1–10.

20. Jerome B. Wiesner to Norman Dyhrenfurth, July 27, 1961, Ullman Papers, box 92, folder 4, Department of Rare Books and Special Collections, Princeton University Library; "Expedition Letter #1," Aug. 1, 1961, Ullman Papers, box 53, folder 3, Department of Rare Books and Special Collections, Princeton University Library.

21. "Expedition Letter #2," Sept. 23, 1961, Ullman Papers, box 53, folder 3, Department of Rare Books and Special Collections, Princeton University Library.

22. "Expedition Letter #3," Dec. 29, 1961, Ullman Papers, box 53, folder 3, Department of Rare Books and Special Collections, Princeton University Library. Not that Dyhrenfurth gave up on the quest to see Kennedy after these early rebuffs. In March 1962 he was still at it, writing to Senator Warren Magnuson of Washington, an expedition supporter, "A few words from [Kennedy] at a brief meeting—with the press or at least the wire services in attendance—would certainly get us off the launching pad." Letter from Norman Dyhrenfurth to Warren Magnuson, Mar. 11, 1962, Ullman Papers, box 53, folder 3, Department of Rare Books and Special Collections, Princeton University Library.

23. Udall also arranged the permit that allowed expedition members to train on Mount Rainier in the fall of 1962. The Udall family connection to Himalayan mountaineering continued into the next generation. Mark Udall, Stewart Udall's nephew, became a Himalayan mountaineer with a solo ascent of Kangchenjunga among his achievements; he was elected to Congress from Colorado's Second District in 1998 (William Faries, "Forged by the Wild," http://www.open-spaces.com/article-v3n2-faries.php). "Freud on Everest," *Newsweek*, Dec. 13, 1962, 33. The notion that climbing mountains could yield benefits for space exploration had been kicking around for several years. Sir Edmund Hillary may have been the first to employ it as justification for a trip to the Himalaya. According to a news report on the 1960 expedition he led to the Makalu region, Hillary explained to reporters that "a human passenger in a space capsule would be subjected to pressure comparable to that experienced on a mountain at 17,000 feet" ("Hillary to Climb Himalayan Peak," *New York Times*, June 6, 1960, 9). *Life* wasn't the only magazine Dyhrenfurth attempted to interest in the story. He wrote to *Playboy* publisher Hugh Heffner in January 1962 suggesting that the magazine do an article about the expedition prior to its departure. Jack Kessie, managing editor of *Playboy*, sent back a discouraging reply two months later: "Yes, we certainly do consider the first American attempt on Mount Everest worthy of note; it is simply that PLAYBOY is not the proper magazine to offer publicity for that event. We are not generally regarded as an outdoor men's magazine but rather specialize in entertainment for the urban-bred male. Mountain climbing is simply not a sport that receives much coverage from PLAYBOY." Jack Kessie to Dyhrenfurth, Mar. 26, 1962, Ullman Papers, box 53, folder 2, Department of Rare Books and Special Collections, Princeton University Library.

24. Not all American mountaineers were convinced that Dyhrenfurth's elaborate fund-raising strategy was a good idea. Charlie Houston, for one, was concerned with the expedition's ever-expanding mission and budget. "Without arguing the pros and cons of big expeditions versus little ones, a field which has been plowed too many times already," he wrote to Dyhrenfurth, "I would point out that what you are engaged in is a vicious and self-perpetuating cycle. A 'big' expedition necessitates 'big' money, which in turn necessitates contacts with radio, television, and the press. This leads inevitably to dealing in big terms and with big people. And this too requires the publicity, the development of the expedition personnel, the 'make work' scientific programs, and all the rest." He pointed out that in 1936 his Nanda Devi expedition had put two men on the summit for under $8,000. "I have always settled for a comfortable minimum, and have avoided the luxuries of Delco generators, twenty different kinds of chocolate, six pairs of boots, and the like. We estimated that one pound of equipment cost one dollar to deliver at base camp from the United States, and if that pound was not essential for safety we did not take it, placing comfort last. . . . The reason for this is not the cult of poverty, or a fetish of hardship, but rather the realities of a large versus small expedition." None of Houston's expeditions had

made any pretense of engaging in scientific research while attempting their mountains. In his experience, he wrote, "it is not possible to combine 'first-rate' scientific work with a major mountaineering objective. One may do one thing or the other, but trying to do both is certain to lead to failure in one." Charles Houston to Norman Dyhrenfurth, Mar. 30, 1962, Ullman Papers, box 53, folder 2, Department of Rare Books and Special Collections, Princeton University Library.

25. James Ramsey Ullman and Norman G. Dyhrenfurth, "Americans to Attempt Everest," *Summit* 7 (Dec. 1961): 2. Also see James Ramsey Ullman to "Editor," Jan. 19, 1962, Ullman Papers, box 53, folder 2, Department of Rare Books and Special Collections, Princeton University Library.

26. "Maybe the old guide's too far along for this kind of thing," Willi Unsoeld confided to Tom Hornbein at the very start of the expedition's march from Kathmandu to Everest in February 1963. The "old guide," at thirty-six, was four years older than Hornbein. Hornbein, *Everest,* 27. For a differing view of the composition of the 1963 team, stressing their essential amateurism, see Roper, *Fatal Mountaineer,* 61. Some other Himalayan veterans turned down Dyhrenfurth's offer to join the expedition because of career concerns. This was the case with George Bell, a veteran of the K2 expedition, who had made the first ascent of Masherbrum in 1960 with Willi Unsoeld and had also been on Dyhrenfurth's 1955 Lhotse expedition. Dyhrenfurth offered him the position of "climbing leader," which he had to decline. Norman Dyhrenfurth, e-mail to the authors, Jan. 22, 2006.

27. For preexpeditionary publicity touting the grand slam strategy, see James Ramsey Ullman, "Everest—1963," *Appalachia* 28 (June 1962): 15–17.

28. As Walt Unsworth wrote, Dyhrenfurth's grand slam strategy "was the sort of package he felt he could sell to the American public. In the end, his problem was that he couldn't sell it to his climbers" (*Everest,* 367).

29. Hornbein, *Everest,* 33. Both Dyhrenfurth and Hornbein remember the conversation, but neither can date it exactly. It almost certainly took place before Dyhrenfurth wrote a letter to James Ramsey Ullman in February 1962 that included this paragraph: "Although we are planning on a close look at Lhotse Shar during the acclimatization phase, and another good look at the feasibility of traversing Everest and descending toward the West shoulder and from there back down to Advance Base, *these plans are to be kept confidential for the time being.*" Norman Dyhrenfurth to James Ramsey Ullman, Ullman Papers, box 53, folder 9, Department of Rare Books and Special Collections, Princeton University Library.

30. Hornbein, *Everest,* 35.

31. Gyachung Kang would have its first ascent two years later by a Japanese expedition led by Kazayoshi Kohara. Yukihiko Kato, Kiyoto Sakaizawa, and Sherpa Pasnag Putra reached the summit on April 10, 1964. "Japanese Team Conquers 25,910-Foot Himalaya Peak," *New York Times,* Apr. 19, 1964, 6. Sayre's expedition was reported on the slopes of Gyachung Kang by American newspapers, and then reported as missing when it slipped off into Tibet. "U.S. Team Starts Nepal Climb," *New York Times,* May 28, 1962, 22; "3 American Climbers Missing in Attempt on a Nepalese Peak," *New York Times,* June 21, 1962, 6; "Three US Climbers Are Found Safe in Nepal," *New York Times,* June 23, 1962, 1.

32. Dyhrenfurth described his role in rescuing Sayre in "Expedition Letter #8," Aug. 10, 1962. The authors are grateful to Dyhrenfurth for providing them with a copy of this document. In the letter he did not mention where Sayre's party had been prior to its rescue, writing, "The less said about their 'exploits' the better, we are all hoping that it will never appear in print." In a memorandum that Dyhrenfurth sent to President Kennedy a few weeks earlier, he had outlined the dire consequences he feared if Sayre's account of his foray into Tibet were to be published: "1. Immediate cancellation of the American Mount Everest Expedition by the Foreign Ministry of Nepal. Having worked on the project for over two years, this would be a serious blow to me personally, as well as to American Mountaineering as a whole. Ours is not just a mountaineering venture, but a serious scientific endeavor for which considerable backing has been obtained from the National Geographic Society, the National Science Foundation, the U.S. Air Force, the Atomic Energy Commission, and other

groups and individuals. 2. A serious curtailment, if not discontinuance, of all future Himalayan exploration by all nations. 3. Abrupt worsening of diplomatic relations between the United States and Nepal. This would undo much of the good work carried out in Nepal by our Technical Aid people over the past ten years. 4. A possible take-over of Nepal by the Chinese Communists, who have been looking for some pretext for quite some time." Norman Dyhrenfurth to John F. Kennedy, July 25, 1962, Dyhrenfurth Grant File, microfiche 502 1.1199, 2 of 38, National Geographic Society. Dyhrenfurth's fears seem exaggerated in retrospect, but in the context of the cold war tensions of the era were more understandable. His stake in a successful outcome of the American Mount Everest expedition may also have played into a feeling of resentment against Sayre's impudent attempt to steal the glory of being the first American to climb the mountain.

33. Woodrow Wilson Sayre, "Commando Raid on Everest," *Life,* Mar. 22, 1963, 58–66; Sayre, *Four against Everest;* Brooks Atkinson, "Critic at Large: The Sayre Expedition on Mount Everest Was Mad, Ill-Equipped, and Admirable," *New York Times,* Jan. 5, 1964, 28. Doug Scott would write in the foreword to a 1999 edition of Hornbein's account of the 1963 expedition that the "four young climbers who . . . attempted Everest in 1962 . . . made a significant contribution to style, although the event was ahead of its time " (foreword to *Everest,* vi). Among those Dyhrenfurth contacted in 1962 in his attempt to block publication of Sayre's story was American Alpine Club president Carlton P. Fuller. Fuller wrote back: "When [Kennedy's national security adviser] Mac Bundy (an old friend of mine) writes you, hoping that Sayre's mountaineering friends will restrain him, he is unaware that Sayre belongs to no mountaineering clubs and has few if any mountaineering friends" (Carlton P. Fuller to Norman Dyhrenfurth, Oct. 16, 1962, Dyhrenfurth Grant File, microfiche 502 1.1199, 3 of 38, National Geographic Society). Sayre's book came out the year after Dyhrenfurth's expedition succeeded in climbing Everest, and he had some pointed criticisms of the latter effort as well as some interesting predictions about the future of Himalayan climbing: "Personally, I was disappointed that in the year following our expedition at least one team of the Dyhrenfurth expedition didn't try [to climb Everest] without oxygen. I think it will not be too long now before [an oxygenless ascent] is made. In spite of its inevitability, when it is made, this will be one of the top climbing achievements of all times" (*Four against Everest,* 41). Fourteen years later Sayre would be proven right when Reinhold Messner and Peter Habeler made their successful oxygenless ascent of Everest via the Southeast Ridge route.

34. Ullman, *Americans on Everest,* 63–64.

35. Barry Corbet field notes, typescript copy, Ullman Papers, box 53, folder 12, Department of Rare Books and Special Collections, Princeton University Library. Also see Hornbein, *Everest,* 75.

36. "Mt. Everest Climber Dies; Wife Notified in Wyoming," *New York Times,* Mar. 26, 1963, 9. Breitenbach's body would be found by a Japanese expedition at the foot of the icefall in the fall of 1969 and buried near Tengboche Monastery. Norman Dyhrenfurth and Barry Bishop attended the burial.

37. Ullman, *Americans on Everest,* 111. Jake Breitenbach's name would live on in another setting. On Mount Rainier, when search and rescue parties found a dead climber, they would radio back to headquarters, "We've got a Breitenbach here" to spare the feelings of any family members of the missing climber who might be listening in. Whittaker and Gabbard, *Lou Whittaker,* 57, 87.

38. Hornbein, *Everest,* 86; Leamer, *Ascent,* 124. In his book on the climb Tom Hornbein noted in passing that none of the West Ridge advocates, with the exception of Willi Unsoeld, had played competitive sports, while the opposite was true for most of those who made up the South Col contingent (Hornbein, *Everest,* 40; also see Roper, *Fatal Mountaineer,* 41; Whittaker, *A Life on the Edge,* 51–53). Hornbein, *Everest,* 94.

39. Hornbein, *Everest,* 100–1.

40. Ullman, *Americans on Everest,* 154. Ullman does not make clear the source of the quotation, but he had access to all the climbers' diaries in writing his own account.

41. See the chapter on Nawang Gombu in Kohli, *Sherpas,* 114–24.

42. Norman Dyhrenfurth, "Expedition Letter #2," Sept. 23, 1961, Ullman Papers, box 53, folder 3, Department of Rare Books and Special Collections, Princeton University Library.

43. Whittaker, *A Life on the Edge,* 110, 111.

44. Ibid., 111.

45. Ullman, *Americans on Everest,* 202.

46. "Old Glory on Everest," *Newsweek,* May 13, 1963, 52.

47. "Americans Reach Everest Summit," *New York Times,* May 3, 1963, 1. Planning began immediately for the president to greet the triumphant expedition on its return to the United States in a White House ceremony. Secretary of the Interior Stewart Udall personally telephoned National Geographic Society president Melville Grosvenor to offer his congratulations on the success of the expedition and to say, according to the memo in Grosvenor's files, that "he thought the President would want to see Mr. Dyhrenfurth and his team when they returned." L. J. Grant memo for file, May 3, 1963, Dyhrenfurth Grant File, microfiche 502 1.1199, 6 of 38, National Geographic Society.

48. Hornbein, *Everest,* 123, 124.

49. Dyhrenfurth offered an apology to Hornbein in a letter sent to all AMEE members after the expedition. "To make a long story short," he concluded, "Tom's overall oxygen logistics were absolutely correct, but there was, as so frequently is the case at high altitudes, a certain lack of communication as well as full understanding on our part. . . . There is nothing like a few weeks and months back at sea level to regain one's proper perspective" (Norman Dyhrenfurth, "Post-Expedition Letter #3," Oct. 10, 1963; the authors are grateful to Norman Dyhrenfurth for providing them with a copy of this document). Barry Bishop to Arnold Wexler, May 9, 1963, Bishop Papers, folder "MSS Bishop, Barry corresp. w/ Arnold Wexler," American Alpine Club Library.

50. Barry Bishop to Arnold Wexler, May 9, 1963, Bishop Papers, folder "MSS Bishop, Barry corresp. w/ Arnold Wexler," American Alpine Club Library.

51. Tom Hornbein, e-mail to the authors, June 2, 2006.

52. Hornbein, *Everest,* 159.

53. Ibid., 163.

54. Pielmeier, *Willi,* 24. The crucifix had been given to Unsoeld by Andy Bakewell, the Jesuit priest who had been with the Houston-Tilman party on the first approach to the south side of Everest thirteen years earlier. Unsoeld was given to such gestures on mountaintops—though also willing to mock his own piety. When he summited Masherbrum with George Bell in 1960 he had also buried a crucifix, while kneeling in prayer. He prayed so long, in fact, that Bell grew impatient, eventually interrupting his devotions with the query, "Well, Willi, shall we go down—or up?" William Unsoeld, "Masherbrum—1960," *American Alpine Journal* 12 (1961): 225.

55. Ullman, *Americans on Everest,* 261. Unsoeld's choice of these particular verses had a connection to John Kennedy, as he explained in a letter to Ullman written from his hospital bed in Kathmandu following the expedition. "[S]orry not to be able to give you a direct quote of what I said to Maynard [Miller] from the top. However, here's the background: I had recently read 'The Making of a President—1960' by [Theodore] White while at Camp II. In it [Adlai] Stevenson is quoted as using this last verse of 'Stopping By Woods on a Snowy Evening': 'The woods are lovely, dark and deep, / But I have promises to keep, / And miles to go before I sleep, / And miles to go before I sleep.' A footnote gave this verse as one of Kennedy's campaign favorites, too. I was impressed by it at the time I read it and do dimly recall using part of it just as we were leaving the summit." Willi Unsoeld to James Ramsey Ullman, Aug. 2, 1963, Ullman Papers, box 53, folder 2, Department of Rare Books and Special Collections, Princeton University Library.

56. Barry Bishop, "How We Climbed Everest," *National Geographic* 124 (Oct. 1963): 484; McCallum, *Everest Diary,* 154. Ullman's account of the Bishop-Jerstad climb offered a more elaborate patriotic image to

describe the moment when Jim Whittaker's flag came in view: "After three weeks [Whittaker's] aluminum Maypole still stood firm and tall. And from it—wrapped once or twice around the pole, but not ripped or shredded, only slightly tattered along its edges—Old Glory streamed out above the summit of the world" (*Americans on Everest,* 256). Like those climbing the Southeastern Ridge, the West Ridgers found the sight of Whittaker's flag encouraging, because it signaled their proximity to the summit. But there is a notable absence of the standard patriotic imagery in the West Ridgers' subsequent accounts of their own part of the climb. "I don't know how everyone on the expedition felt, in terms of nationalism, but I do know how those of us on the West Ridge felt about it," Tom Hornbein recalled to the authors. "It just wasn't part of our scheme of things. We even had some quiet discussions about not taking flags to the top, but that wasn't a viable option. We had an American flag, we had a National Geographic flag, and what not. But to some extent it seemed to me almost a desecration." Authors' interview with Tom Hornbein, June 4, 2002.

57. "Kennedy Sends Message," *New York Times,* May 26, 1963, 26. In addition to previously cited sources on the climb, see Norman G. Dyhrenfurth, "Americans on Everest, 1963," *Alpine Journal* 60 (May 1964): 1–22; Norman G. Dyhrenfurth and William F. Unsoeld, "Mount Everest, 1963," *American Alpine Journal* 14 (1964): 1–29.

58. A week after Hornbein, Unsoeld, Bishop, and Jerstad reached the summit on May 22, Hillary, Tenzing, Hunt, and other veterans of the 1953 expedition gathered in London to celebrate the tenth anniversary of their climb. It proved the last gathering of the Everest veterans of the 1920s and 1930s, for also in attendance were Howard Somervell and Eric Shipton, while Colonel Howard-Bury, too ill to attend, sent a message of congratulations ("Tenth Anniversary of the First Ascent of Everest," *Alpine Journal* 68 [Nov. 1963]: 303–4). Matt McDade telegram, n.d. [May 1963] Dyhrenfurth Grant File, microfiche 502 1.1199, 9 of 38, National Geographic Society.

59. In a letter to Ullman written shortly after the expedition returned to the United States, Dyhrenfurth gave vent to feelings of being denied due recognition for organizing AMEE: "As you know, I have for the past eleven years given up any appearance of a 'normal' life in order to devote all of my time—as far as I was financially able to—to Himalayan exploration. . . . John Hunt has always been my idea of a good expedition leader, but compared to what I had to go through in order to get this expedition going, Hunt's job was quite easy. He did not enter the picture until late in the fall of 1952, after the funds had been raised, and the team fairly well selected. . . . Usually an expedition leader writes the official accounts, including the expedition book. In our case, since I asked you to come along as our 'historian,' the LIFE account is being written by you, as well as the book. This means that most people will soon forget that I was even on the Expedition. They will only remember the LIFE article by James Ramsey Ullman and the book about the American Everest Expedition, again by JRU. It is for this reason that it is important for me, not for reasons of personal vanity, but for reasons of my future career, that my name appear on the jacket of the book. Just how, I don't know. Whether it should say, 'by James Ramsey Ullman, with a Prologue by NGD, Leader of the American Mount Everest Expedition,' is something to be decided upon in the next few months. But I believe you will understand why I must insist that my name appear on the book alongside of yours. Even in the case of John Hunt's book, you realize that most Americans have completely forgotten just who John Hunt is, or was; all they remember is Hillary" (Norman Dyhrenfurth to James Ramsey Ullman, Aug. 5, 1963, Ullman Papers, box 53, folder 9, Department of Rare Books and Special Collections, Princeton University Library). "Kennedy Gives Medal to Conquerors of Everest," *New York Times,* July 9, 1963, 3. Also see the account of the Rose Garden ceremony by Marian Ullman in an expedition newsletter, Ullman Papers, box 91, folder 1, Department of Rare Books and Special Collections, Princeton University.

60. James Ramsey Ullman, "At the Top—And Out of Oxygen," *Life,* Sept. 20, 1963, 73–92; Bishop, "How We Climbed Everest," 474–507. The *New York Times* somewhat mischievously assigned Woodrow Wilson Sayre to review Ullman's book (Sayre's 1962 foray into Tibet had been roundly denounced in *Americans on Everest*): Woodrow Wilson Sayre, "Peak Performance," *New York Times,* May 17, 1964, BR7. The choice of

reviewer provoked an outraged letter to the editor from the American Alpine Club's president: see Carlton P. Fuller, letter to the editor, *New York Times Book Review,* July 5, 1964, BR20. For the National Geographic documentary, see Jack Gould, "TV Review: First Films from Top of Mount Everest Shown," *New York Times,* Sept. 11, 1965, 55.

61. "2 US Teams Set Everest Records," *New York Times,* May 24, 1963, 28; Whittaker, *A Life on the Edge,* 119. In one of his postexpeditionary circular letters, Norman Dyhrenfurth ended with a note on "Individual vs. Team Effort," complaining, "In spite of our original noble resolve, the press, local enthusiasm, and enterprising chambers of commerce have thwarted our attempts at presenting AMEE's accomplishments as a team effort. This should come as a surprise to no one, but it is disappointing just the same. A number of people in very high government positions commented to me during a recent trip to Washington that they were disappointed by the recent emphasis on one individual [i.e., Jim Whittaker] rather than the team. However, this is something over which none of us have any control" (Norman Dyhrenfurth, "Post-Expedition Letter #4," Mar. 2, 1964; the authors are grateful to Norman Dyhrenfurth for providing them a copy of this document). Martin Arnold, "Kennedy Puts Flag Atop Mount Kennedy," *New York Times,* Mar. 25, 1961, 1; Robert F. Kennedy, "Our Climb Up Mount Kennedy," *Life,* Apr. 9, 1965, 22–27. Whittaker and Bobby Kennedy subsequently became very close, and Whittaker named one of his sons Bobby. In March 1968 Whittaker became part of the "Kennedy Machine" working to win Kennedy the Democratic presidential nomination; in June he served as one of Kennedy's pallbearers in St. Patrick's Cathedral. Richard Reeves, "The Making of a Candidate, 1968: The Kennedy Machine Is Moving," *New York Times,* Mar. 31, 1968, SM25; Whittaker, *A Life on the Edge,* 122–36.

62. W. Tilman, "Americans on Everest," *Alpine Journal* 71 (May 1966): 163–64. His judgment would be echoed by a younger British climber a few years later. "After 1961, the most important Himalayan achievement was undoubtedly the traverse of Everest by the Americans. Once again this was the victory of a superbly organized heavy-weight expedition, yet the actual traverse by Unsoeld and Hornbein was a magnificent individual performance." Chris Bonington, "In Retrospect," *Mountain* 1 (Mar. 1969): 22.

63. See back cover of *Appalachia* 30 (June 1965).

64. Whittaker, *A Life on the Edge,* 150, 204; Timothy Egan, "Is Hiker's Shop a Paradise Lost?" *New York Times,* Sept. 26, 1996, C1; Waterman and Waterman, *Yankee Rock and Ice,* 227.

65. According to statistics kept by the Washington State climbing group the Mountaineers, in the 114 years between 1855 and 1969 14,797 climbers attempted to reach the summit of Mount Rainier. In the next eight years, 1970–78, 26,332 made the attempt. Wayne King, "Mountain Climbing Gains Popularity Despite Danger," *New York Times,* June 29, 1981, A13. Petzoldt's association with NOLS ended in 1978 in a tangle of legal and financial disputes. Ringholz, *On Belay!* 181–208. Also see Christopher S. Wren, "Paul Petzoldt Is Dead at 91; Innovator in Rock Climbing," *New York Times,* Oct. 9, 1999, 15. The Sierra Club grew from 29,000 members in 1965 to over 100,000 in 1970. The American Alpine Club grew from 672 members in 1965 to 880 in 1970. Isserman and Kazin, *America Divided,* 124–25; "Secretary's Report for the Year 1965," *American Alpine Journal* 15 (1966): 246; "Secretary's Report for the Year 1970," *American Alpine Journal* 17 (1971): 502. The AAC's difficulties in recruiting younger climbers in the 1960s are illustrated in a letter Nick Clinch sent to AAC president Bob Bates in 1961, recounting a meeting that Clinch had had with students from the University of Colorado: "The talk centered around the American Alpine Club. . . . The young climbers seem to feel that a large number of AAC members are antagonistic to the type of climbing that they do. I explained that the club was composed of many different types of mountaineers but that we did not disapprove of difficult rock climbing—most of the club members did rock climbing of a high standard for their day. However, rock climbing was not an end in itself. This has always been the main breach between the AAC and younger climbers." Nick Clinch to Bob Bates, Feb. 27, 1961, Bates Papers, American Alpine Club Library.

66. D. F. O. Dangar, "The Highest Mountains, 1962–1967," *Alpine Journal* 73 (Nov. 1968): 241–43. On April 27, 1962, Rene Desmaison, Paul Kellar, Robert Paragot, and Sherpa Gyalzen Mitchung reached the

summit of Jannu, followed the next day by seven other climbers, including Terray (Franco and Terray, *At Grips with Jannu*). Tsunahiko Shidei, "The Ascent of Saltoro Kangri," *Alpine Journal* 68 (1964): 73–80. For other significant Japanese first ascents in the early 1960s, see Akira Takahasi, "The Ascent of Big White Peak," *Himalayan Journal* 25 (1964): 43–50; Seihei Kato, "The Ascent of Baltoro Kangri, 1963," *Himalayan Journal* 25 (1964): 132–35; Shoichiro Uyeo, "The Ascent of Annapurna South Peak (Ganesh)," *Alpine Journal* 70 (Nov. 1965): 213–17. These and other climbs of the less than 8,000-meter peaks are chronicled in Neate, *High Asia*.

67. For the second ascent of Cho Oyu, see "Expeditions 1958: Nepal," *Himalayan Journal* 21 (1958): 164–66. For the first ascent of Annapurna III, see Kohli, *Last of the Annapurnas*, 89–96. For the ascent of Nanda Devi, see Nawang Gombu, "The Second Ascent of Nanda Devi," *American Alpine Journal* 15 (1966): 90–92; Major N. Kumar, "Nanda Devi: Indian Mountaineering Expedition, 1964," *Mountain World 1964/1965*, 52–56. For the Indian expeditions to Everest, see Unsworth, *Everest*, 361–62, 393–94; M.S. Kohli, "Nine on the Summit of Everest," *Alpine Journal* 71 (May 1966): 1–14; "2 Man Expedition Plants Indian Flag Atop Mount Everest," *New York Times*, May 21, 1965, 8.

68. Chou Cheng, "The Ascent of Shisha Pangma," *Alpine Journal* 69 (Nov. 1964): 211–16; *Mountaineering in China*; Zhou and Liu, *Footprints on the Peaks*, 99–102; Sale and Cleare, *Climbing the World's 14 Highest Mountains*, 198–99.

69. Paul Grimes, "India Reinforcing her China Border," *New York Times*, Nov. 29, 1961, 6.

70. Poole, *Explorer's House*, 239.

71. The CIA was already active in the region. Since 1959 it had been secretly training Tibetan refugees at the Mountain Warfare Training Center at Camp Hale, Colorado (home of the Tenth Mountain Division during World War II), then returning them to bases in Nepal where they staged raids into their homeland. They were supplied by airdrop, at first from East Pakistan then, after Pakistan and China reconciled in the early 1960s, from Thailand. Kohli and Conboy, *Spies in the Himalayas*, 15–16; Galen Rowell, "Selling Shangri-la," *Outside* 5 (Oct.–Nov. 1980): 39.

72. For a full account of the CIA/Nanda Devi affair, see Kohli and Conboy, *Spies in the Himalayas;* for Schaller's solo ascent of the mountain, see 131–32.

73. Jack Anderson, "Filling in the Blanks on the CIA," *Seattle Post-Intelligencer*, May 5, 1974.

74. Robert T. Schaller to Kenneth Wilson, May 21, 1973, Kauffman Collection, box 2, folder 2/23, American Alpine Club Library; Ken Wilson to Robert T. Schaller, May 31, 1973, Kauffman Collection, box 2, folder 2/23, American Alpine Club Library.

75. Soli Mehta to Ken Wilson, June 27, 1973, Kauffman Collection, box 2, folder 2/23, American Alpine Club Library; Kenneth Wilson to "Alex" [Bertulis], Aug. 16, 1973, Kauffman Collection, box 2, folder 2/23, American Alpine Club Library.

76. Howard Kohn, "The Nanda Devi Caper," *Outside* 3 (May 1978): 23–29. Galen Rowell had made a passing reference to rumors of the affair the previous year, noting the CIA's role in placing a "surveillance device" on an unnamed Indian mountaintop "before the advent of satellites" (*In The Throne Room of the Mountain Gods*, 315). William Borders, "Desai Says U.S.-Indian Team Lost Atomic Spy Gear," *New York Times*, Apr. 18, 1978, 11.

77. Seihei Kato, "The Ascent of Baltoro Kangri, 1963," *Himalayan Journal* 25 (1964): 132–35; Rudolf Pischinger, "The First Ascent of Momhil Sar," *Alpine Journal* 70 (May 1965): 69–73. An expedition led by G. O. Dyhrenfurth had made the first ascent of the lower eastern peak of Baltoro Kangri in 1934. "Alpine Notes," *Alpine Journal* 68 (Nov. 1963): 306.

78. "Chinese Reds Seize Two Climbers," *New York Times*, Dec. 28, 1963, 4.

79. "Nepal to Ban Climbers from Himalayan Peaks," *New York Times*, Mar. 20, 1965, 7; "The Nepalese Ban," *Alpine Journal* 70 (Nov. 1970): 329. Concern about border violations was not entirely paranoia on the

part of the Chinese. In 1964 a British expedition led by Michael Ward had been planning an attempt on Shishapangma. Although the mountain lies in Tibet, it is only fifty miles from Kathmandu and could be approached via the Langtang Glacier in Nepalese territory. The British counted on the fact that the Chinese were unlikely to have border guards on the mountain itself. But the attempt was abandoned when news came of the Chinese success in reaching Shishapangma's summit. Ward, *In This Short Span,* 214–18. The last major climb before the ban went into effect was the first ascent of Gangapurna (24,458ft/7,455m) via its South Face and East Ridge by a German expedition in May 1965. Günther Hauser, "The German Himalayan Expedition, 1965," *Alpine Journal* 71 (May 1966): 89–97.

80. One result of the climbing bans in South Asia was that mountaineers began to pay more attention to some previously neglected mountain ranges. The five highest mountains to have a first ascent in 1967, for example, were all found in the Hindu Kush, including Kurt Diemberger and Dietmar Proske's ascent of the North Face of Tirich West IV (24,075ft/7,338m). Diemberger, *Summits and Secrets,* 267–72. Also see D. F. O. Danger, "The Highest Mountains, 1962–1967," *Alpine Journal* 73 (Nov. 1968): 244.

81. Robert Trumbull, "Shangri-La Greets Traveler in Nepal," *New York Times,* July 17, 1950, 11. Rowell, *Many People Come,* 43. The plumbing critic was James Ramsey Ullman, in *Americans on Everest,* 50. Also see Bernstein, *In the Himalayas,* 66–74. The Royal was managed by Boris Lissanevitch, a White Russian exile who had moved to Kathmandu in 1951 and talked his way into the good graces of Nepal's King Tribhuvan. Several generations of Western climbers stayed at the Royal Hotel (Lissanevitch offered climbing expeditions steep discounts on his rates) and did their drinking at the hotel's Yak and Yeti bar (where he made back the money he offered in the discounts). Lissanevitch was a fixer who knew everybody in Kathmandu, and a useful person for foreign expeditions to consult on any last-minute problems they faced before heading off to the mountains. He also made appearances in several novels set in Kathmandu, such as Ullman, *And Not to Yield,* 214. Also see Lionel Terray's appreciative portrait of Lissanevitch in Franco and Terray, *At Grips with Jannu,* 146.

82. Letter from Jim Lester to James Ramsey Ullman, Nov. 16, 1964, Ullman Papers, box 53, folder 14, Department of Rare Books and Special Collections, Princeton University Library. By the time Roberts died in 1997, there were over 350 trekking agencies operating in Nepal, but his Mountain Travel remained the leader in the field. Douglas, *Chomolungma Sings the Blues,* 165–66.

83. Tomoroy, *A Season in Heaven,* 206; Bernstein, *In the Himalayas,* 113; Nancy L. Ross, "Top of the World in Nepal," *New York Times,* Sept. 5, 1965, X21; Elizabeth Knowlton, "Camping Out in High Style," *New York Times,* Sept. 5, 1965, X21.

84. Unsworth, *Adventure Travel for All,* 40; Ward, *Everest,* 252; Kohli, *Sherpas,* 277–92; Rowell, "Selling Shangri-la," 38–41; Rowell, *Many People Come,* 47–48; Stevens, *Claiming the High Ground,* 360–61; M. S. Kohli, "Himalayan Tourism and Environment," *Himalayan Journal* 38 (1980–81): 150–54; A. D. Moddie, "Himalayan Tourism: A Mongol Needing Eco-Civilizing," *Himalayan Journal* 40 (1982–83): 7–15; Tad Friend, "The Parachute Artist," *New Yorker,* Apr. 18, 2005, 78–91.

85. Eventually the flights were shifted to the lower-altitude Lukla airstrip, requiring a three-day trek to the hotel and thus cutting business considerably. Scott Schamadan, "A Room with a View," http://www.frugalfun .com/room-with-a-view.html; Douglas, *Chomolungma Sings the Blues,* 188–89; Rowell, *Many People Come,* 60; Doug Scott, "The Himalaya and the Pace of Change," *Mountain* 111 (Sept.–Oct. 1986): 32; Bonington, *Everest,* 66.

86. Although nostalgic for the early pretourist days of Himalayan mountaineering, Chris Bonington acknowledged the improvements that tourism brought to the Sherpas: "The tourists going into Sola Khumbu or into Nepal are bringing in money. Materially the people are much better off; you could say that maybe some of them are confused, as in fact an awful lot of young westerners are confused, but it's all part of progress. . . . to say that we should actually reduce the numbers of people going in, the Sherpas wouldn't thank you for that because they have built up an economy around tourists and significantly they have built up the economy

themselves. It's the Sherpas who are actually exploiting the tourists" (Jim Curran and John Porter, "Bonington: The Mountain Interview," *Mountain* [Nov.–Dec. 1989]: 24). "Sherpas Avoiding Strenuous Climbs," *New York Times,* Jan. 6, 1974, 6.

87. Kenneth Mason autobiography, typescript copy, 643, Mason Papers, School of Geography and the Environment, Oxford University. In his memoirs Mason recalled the beatings he had received as a schoolboy in Sutton six decades earlier. His bitterness was not for his own mistreatment but for the way the younger generation of the 1960s had apparently been spoiled in comparison: "If every silly ass that grows a beard and sits down in the London roads to demonstrate had been well and truly beaten when young, he too might have learnt sense" (72). Also see John Morris, "Lieut-Colonel Kenneth Mason, M.C. (1887–1976)," *Alpine Journal* 82 (1977): 271–72.

88. Tomoroy, *A Season in Heaven,* 207. Sherry Ortner goes so far as to argue that "starting in the late 1960s, Nepal became probably the single biggest magnet in the world for the countercultural lifestyle," a judgment that probably overstates the case a little (the Bay Area is at least a rival claimant) but underscores the appeal of Nepal to hippies. Ortner, *Life and Death on Mt. Everest,* 186.

89. The Beatles, *The Beatles Anthology,* 233.

90. Isserman and Kazin, *America Divided,* 264.

91. Ullman, *Americans on Everest,* 21, 239.

92. On nineteenth-century romanticism and Alpine climbing, see Fleming, *Killing Dragons,* 83–85; Hansen, "British Mountaineering," 215–74; on twentieth-century romanticism and Himalayan climbing, see Ortner, *Life and Death on Mt. Everest,* 35–42, 186–88. Ullman would participate in the march on Montgomery in April 1965 led by Martin Luther King Jr. demanding voting rights for southern blacks. Among Ullman's many correspondents was Unitarian minister and mountaineering enthusiast John Nicholls Booth. In 1964 Booth sent Ullman a letter chronicling his battles with the John Birch Society in Southern California, who were crusading to remove "subversive" literature from local library shelves. "Who knows," Booth wrote, "the rightists may next be demanding the elimination of the works of Ullman in the interests of preserving American freedom and patriotism. After all, that subversive novelist sees some merit in foreigners and has a kind word for non-American humanity" (John Nicholls Booth to James Ramsey Ullman, Oct. 20, 1964, Ullman Papers, Department of Rare Books and Special Collections, Princeton University Library). Herbert Tichy, "Cho Oyu, 1954," *Alpine Journal* 60 (Nov. 1955): 139, 246.

93. Terray, *Conquistadors,* 214, 256; Hornbein, *Everest,* 45.

94. For an account of drug use see, for instance, Ridgeway, *The Last Step,* 84. Geoffrey Childs, "Poontanga," *Ascent* (1976): 40.

95. In a 1957 article for the journal of the Appalachian Mountain Club, Robert Swift, an experienced Yosemite and Himalayan climber (he would be part of expeditions to both Rakaposhi and Hidden Peak), had celebrated the "mechanical sense which can be satisfied by developing and collecting climbing hardware." "Driving a knife-blade piton into a hairline crack," Swift declared, "may provide an additional means of deriving pleasure from rock." "Class VI Climbing in Yosemite Valley," *Appalachia* 23 (Dec. 1957): 452.

96. Middendorf, "The Mechanical Advantage," 167–68; Clark, *Men, Myths, and Mountains,* 222–23; Yvon Chouinard, "Modern Yosemite Climbing," *Alpine Journal* 71 (Nov. 1966): 224.

97. Reinhold Messner, "The Murder of the Impossible," *Mountain* 15 (May 1971): 27.

98. The rules also stipulated that the Nepalese liaison officer would provide the climbers with a Nepalese flag to be raised on summits alongside their own national flag. The problem was that many expeditions were no longer interested in carrying any flags to the summit, including those of their own nation; if strictly enforced (which it wasn't) the requirement would have meant that mountaineers had to perform the traditional summit flag-raising ritual with a flag not their own (Rob Collister, "Small Expeditions in the Himalaya,"

Himalaya Journal 36 [1978–79]; 171). For complaints about the effect of the new rules on climbing expeditions to Nepal, see "Discussion," in Clarke and Salkeld, *Lightweight Expeditions to the Great Ranges*, 27; Scott, "The Himalaya and the Pace of Change," 37. Also see J. O. M. Roberts, "Nepal," *Alpine Journal* 74 (1969): 230–33; Cheney, "Events and Trends," 218–19, 225–26.

99. Although the Germans failed in their attempt to climb Annapurna's East Ridge, they made the first ascent of 24,556-foot (7,485-meter) Roc Noir (Khangsar Kang) in the Annapurna Sanctuary. Roberts, "Nepal"; Cheney, "Events and Trends," 218–19, 225–26; "Nepal," *Alpine Journal* 75 (1970): 197–98; "Climbs and Regional Notes: Nepal, German Annapurna Expedition," *Alpine Journal* 75 (1970): 197–98; Joseph Lelyveld, "Mountaineering Resumes in Nepal," *New York Times,* Apr. 27, 1969, 9.

100. Harvard and Thompson, *Mountain of Storms,* 14. Also see "7 Climbers, 5 from U.S. Reported Killed in Nepal," *New York Times,* May 1, 1969, 2; William A. Read, James D. Morrissey, and Louis F. Reichardt, "American Dhaulagiri Expedition—1969," *American Alpine Journal* 17 (1970): 19–26; Michael S. Shor, "Boyd Everett Jr., 1933–1969," *American Alpine Journal* 16 (1969): 499–500.

101. "Nepal," 196–97. The carnage continued the next year. In the spring of 1970 a thirty-member Japanese expedition made a two-prong attack on Everest, attempting the Southeast Ridge and the Southwest Face. The attempt on the Southwest Face failed, but Teruo Matsuura and Naomi Uemura climbed the Southeast Ridge to the summit on May 11. One Japanese climber died of a heart attack, and a Sherpa was killed in the icefall by a collapsing serac. A second team summited the following day. A Japanese skiing expedition on Everest at the same time saw six Sherpas die in an avalanche in the icefall before Y. Miura descended on skis from the South Col. Kotani and Yasuhisa, *Japan Everest Skiing Expedition.*

102. Bonington is described as "the public face of British mountaineering" in Child, *Climbing,* 32. The "plum" comment can be found in Whillans and Ormerod, *Don Whillans,* 147–48. The charge of excessive showmanship was made by Peter Gillman in a *London Sunday Times Magazine* article, reprinted in Gillman, *In Balance,* 45. (Gillman would later apologize for the comment.)

103. Reflecting his mother's influence, Bonington attended some Young Communist League meetings as a teenager after the war but found them "bloody dreary." Curran, *High Achiever,* 13–14, 28. Bonington passes quickly over his childhood experiences in his autobiography, Bonington, *I Chose to Climb,* 16–17.

104. Bonington, *I Chose to Climb,* 48. Also see Curran, *High Achiever,* 47–55. Bonington spent the last years of his military career as an instructor in an army Outward Bound school in Wales.

105. Willis, *The Boys of Everest,* 63–72; Curran, *High Achiever,* 91–92. Bonington first attempted the climb with Don Whillans, but the two were diverted by the need to rescue another party in trouble on the face. Bonington returned several weeks later with Clough and completed the climb.

106. *Monty Python's Flying Circus,* episode 33. Among many other distinctions, Chris Bonington was probably also the most parodied of Himalayan mountaineers. His friend Tom Patey, with whom he climbed the Old Man of Hoy, mocked Bonington's commercial success in a famous ballad entitled "Onward Christian Bonington." It included the verse: "He has climbed the Eigerwand, he has climbed the Dru— / For a mere ten thousand francs, he will climb with you." Reprinted in Patey, *One Man's Mountains,* 274. Bonington contributed a good-humored preface to this volume, published posthumously after Patey's climbing death in Scotland in 1970. For the Old Man of Hoy ascent, see Bonington, *The Next Horizon,* 221–34; Curran, *High Achiever,* 118–19.

107. Gillman, Haston, and Bonington, *Eiger Direct;* Bonington, *The Next Horizon,* 154–98; Willis, *The Boys of Everest,* 101–35. The *direttissima* ideal first emerged in the Alps and was later applied to the Himalaya. As Haston would define it, "The idea, was to climb as directly as possible towards the summit." As a climbing aesthetic, it meant ignoring the natural lines of the mountains, which often led a climber a crooked path, and straightening the route out (Haston, *In High Places,* 43; Child, *Climbing,* 71). J. Marshall, C. J. S. Bonington, and D. Scott, "Dougal Haston: A Tribute," *Alpine Journal* 88 (1978): 136; Haston, *In High Places,* 87–91.

Haston had also taken part in the BBC televised ascent of the Old Man of Hoy in 1967. One of Haston's students at the International School of Mountaineering recalled him holding court nightly in the Club Vagabond, a local dive, in the early 1970s: "[T]here he was, the star. Dougal really was, physically and emotionally, and to his admirers, very much like Jim Morrison and Mick Jagger. He was the Mick Jagger and he was the Jim Morrison of the climbing world. He had that sort of face, the high cheekbones, very drawn like he had been taking drugs and booze for a long time, or hanging out at 27,000 feet too long. He just lived life with that passion that was very much admired in those days" (Chic Scott, quoted in Connor, *Dougal Haston,* 119–20). Doug Scott suggested in an obituary that Haston's involvement in a fatal drunk-driving accident in Scotland in 1965 left him "morose, cryptic, elusive, hard-drinking and aggressive." His driven style of climbing, Scott thought, was an attempt to "purge himself of the guilt he felt." Scott et al., "Dougal Haston: A Tribute," *Alpine Journal* 83 (1978): 138.

108. In Bonington's account of the climb, the Argentière conversation went unmentioned; rather, he recalled conversations with Estcourt and Boysen, plus some timely encouragement from Jimmy Roberts, as the origin of the idea to tackle the South Face (Bonington, *Annapurna South Face,* 6). Haston, *In High Places,* 112.

109. Bonington, *Annapurna South Face,* 31.

110. Haston, *In High Places,* 114.

111. Jim Perrin points out that Whillans's apparent decline as a climber must have been all the more galling to him because of the great success his onetime partner Joe Brown had enjoyed in the Himalaya with the first ascent of Kangchenjunga. Brown was prospering as owner of a string of climbing stores in Wales and continued to put up new and challenging routes on rock, something Whillans had not done in a long time (*The Villain,* 254). To make certain that Whillans was still capable of climbing at a high standard, Bonington arranged to pick Whillans up at his Lancashire home and drive him up to Scotland for a tryout. Whillans arrived late, having spent the evening in the pub downing eleven pints of ale. This was not an encouraging sign, but on the subsequent climb in Scotland Whillans redeemed himself in Bonington's eyes. Bonington, *Annapurna South Face,* 10–13; Perrin, *The Villain,* 255–56.

112. Captain Henry Day, the climbing leader, and Captain Gerry Owens of the North Face expedition reached the summit on May 20, the second ascent of the mountain (M. H. W. Day, "Annapurna—North Face Route," *Alpine Journal* 76 [1971]: 88–98; G. F. Owens, "Annapurna I, 1970," *Himalayan Journal* 30 [1971]: 106–11; Lane, *Military Mountaineering,* 102–4). Bonington, *Annapurna South Face,* 145.

113. Bonington, *Annapurna South Face,* 58–59; Haston, *In High Places,* 116.

114. Bonington, *Annapurna South Face,* 54.

115. Ibid., 138; Curran, *High Achiever,* 128.

116. Haston, *In High Places,* 117.

117. Tom Frost, "Can a Technical Climber Find Happiness in the Himalayas?" *Mountain* 12 (Nov. 1970): 29. Whillans, no purist, was untroubled by the variations on the direct route. "All this *direttissima* business is a load of cobblers as far as I'm concerned," he declared with characteristic bluntness in 1972. "If you have a route you want to do, get on and do it. Why hang labels on it?" "Don Whillans," *Mountain* 20 (Mar. 1972): 27.

118. Perrin, *The Villain,* 258–60; Bonington, *The Climbers,* 216; Middendorf, "The Mechanical Advantage," 164. John Hunt would describe the advent of jumar-assisted climbing on fixed ropes as "the most revolutionary change in climbing big mountain faces during the past twenty years" (foreword to Bonington, *Everest,* ix). The development of new ice-climbing tools, like the inclined pick ice hammer known as the Terrordactyl invented in the mid-1970s by Hamish MacInnnes, would also revolutionize big wall and winter climbing in the Himalaya. See Raphael Slawinski, "Degrees of Freedom," *American Alpine Journal* 44 (2002): 74–77.

119. For statistics on each climber's time above 20,000 feet, see Nick Estcourt, "Appendix I, Diary and Statistics," in Bonington, *Annapurna South Face,* 306. Bonington would tell Nicholas O'Connell, "You want to be right behind the lead climbers." O'Connell, *Beyond Risk,* 132. Also see Bonington, *Mountaineer,* 57–58, 98–99; Curran, *High Achiever,* 194.

120. Jim Curran and John Porter, "Chris Bonington: Thirty Years of Climbing," *Himalayan Journal* 46 (1988–89): 5; Bonington, *Quest for Adventure,* 175.

121. The entire May 13 radio conversation is reproduced in Bonington, *Annapurna South Face,* 233–40.

122. Ibid., 245–46.

123. Estcourt, "Appendix I, Diary and Statistics," 306–7. Asked in an interview shortly after the climb about charges that he had been malingering, Whillans complained that "this business of being wise after the event is beginning to crop up more and more after expeditions" ("Don Whillans," 27).

124. Bonington, *Annapurna South Face,* 290. For other accounts of the climb, see Christian Bonington, "Annapurna South Face," *Alpine Journal* 76 (May 1971): 19–34; Tom Frost, "Annapurna South Face," *American Alpine Journal* 17 (1971): 229–33. Also see Willis, *The Boys of Everest,* 146–92.

125. "British Climber Is Killed in Accident on Annapurna," *The Times,* June 1, 1970, 4; "Wife of Dead Climber to Have Baby," *The Times,* June 2, 1970, 6; "Climber Tells of Briton's Death under Ice Fall," *The Times,* June 6, 1970, 6. As of 2004, a total of 53 climbers had died on Annapurna, compared to 130 who had reached the summit. For a chart illustrating expeditions and deaths on the mountain, see Messner, *Annapurna,* 162–68. Also see Sale and Cleare, *Climbing the World's 14 Highest Mountains,* 41.

126. Bonington, *Annapurna South Face,* 303.

127. Messner, *The Naked Mountain,* 11.

128. Messner, *Free Spirit,* 23–27, 121; also see Faux, *High Ambition,* 33–50.

129. Herrligkoffer led a reconnaissance to the Rupal side of the mountain in 1963, followed by two full-scale and unsuccessful expeditions in 1964 and 1968. The 1964 and 1968 expeditions ended in fierce quarrels, in 1964 between Herrligkoffer and the expedition's Pakistani liaison officer, and in 1968 between the climbers and their expedition leader. Sale and Cleare, *Climbing the World's 14 Highest Mountains,* 74–75. By the late 1960s others hoped to break Herrligkoffer's monopoly on Nanga Parbat attempts. Jimmy Roberts wrote to Bob Bates in 1968 to tell of a proposal for an international (British-American-Norwegian-Pakistani) expedition to Nanga Parbat in 1970 (he hoped to head off a rival American bid by American Boyd Everett). He mentioned in passing to Bates, "Then, there is this German Herrligkoffer who used to make almost yearly trips to the mountain. We know he is still interested in the Rupal face. But as his last expedition, in 1964, ended in a first class row with the Government of Pakistan we hope, perhaps, we may take precedence over him." Jimmy Roberts to Bob Bates, Feb. 21, 1968, Bates Papers, folder "American Alpine Club," American Alpine Club Library. But Herrligkoffer would again get the nod in 1970, and Roberts abandoned the plan.

130. For an evenhanded discussion of the many questions left from the controversy, see Sale and Cleare, *Climbing the World's 14 Highest Mountains,* 76–77.

131. Günther Messner's remains were found by two climbers at 14,000 feet on Nanga Parbat in the summer of 2005. Barbara McMahan, "Mountain Gives Up Its Tragic Secret," *Guardian Weekly,* Aug. 26–Sept. 1, 2005, 8; Greg Child, "Es Ist Mein Bruder!" *Outside* (Jan. 2006).

132. For Messner's version of the climb and its aftermath, see *The Naked Mountain,* 170–252. Also see "Interview with Mountaineer Reinhold Messner," http://observer.guardian.co.uk/osm/story/0,,1315445,00 .html. For critical accounts from other veterans of the climb, see Kienlin, *Die Überschreitung;* Hans Saler, *Zwischen Licht und Schatten.*

133. On the legal battles between Messner and Herrligkoffer, see Faux, *High Ambition,* 86–90. "Reinhold Messner," *Mountain* 15 (May 1971): 28, 30.

CHAPTER TEN: *The Age of Extremes, 1971–1996*

1. Houston and Bates, *K2*, 269. More than four decades afterward, Jim Curran would write that "the 1953 American K2 expedition became a symbol of all that is best in mountaineering" (*K2*, 103).

2. Pielmeier, *Willi*, 34. For discussions of the symbolic significance of the climbing rope, see Roper, *Fatal Mountaineer*, 59–60, 133; Roberts, *True Summit*, 59, 66, 224–25.

3. David Roberts, "The Direct Style of John Roskelley," *Outside* 8 (July–Aug. 1983): 93. This trend was not restricted to mountaineers, of course. For an influential study of the decline of "social connectedness" among Americans in the late twentieth century, as measured by the waning of political involvement, card playing, participation in bowling leagues, and much else, see Putnam, *Bowling Alone*.

4. Al Auten to James Ramsey Ullman, Sept. 16, 1964, Ullman Papers, box 53, folder 4, Department of Rare Books and Special Collections, Princeton University Library.

5. Ridgeway, *The Boldest Dream*, 172.

6. John Porter, "Books," *Mountain* 79 (May–June 1981): 50.

7. Ronald Faux, "Strong Team in New Try on Everest's Worst Face," *The Times*, July 29, 1975, 1. As Walt Unsworth has noted, it would be more accurate to describe the Southwest Face in the 1960s and early 1970s as "the last great unsolved problem on Everest that was available to western mountaineers" (*Everest*, 459). The North and the East (or Kangshung) faces of Everest offered climbing challenges as great or greater than those posed by the Southwest Face. John Harlin, an American famed as both a Yosemite and an Alpine climber, was the first to seriously consider the possibility of attempting the face. A veteran of the Stanford Alpine Club, John Harlin had been the first American to climb the North Face of the Eiger, via the established route in 1962. Harlin became an influential figure in European climbing circles, introducing Yosemite "big wall" strategies to Alpine climbing. Shortly before he fell to his death on the 1966 Eiger Direct climb, Harlin discussed his plan to tackle the Everest Southwest Face with Chris Bonington. Bonington was intrigued. See "3,000 Foot Alps Fall Kills American," *New York Times*, Mar. 23, 1966, 19; Bonington, *Everest*, 7; Bonington, *The Everest Years*, 20; James Ramsey Ullman, "John Elvis Harlin, II, 1935–1966," *American Alpine Journal* 15 (1967): 447–48; Ullman, *Straight Up*. Also see Gillman, *In Balance*, 17.

8. Hiromi Ohtsuka, "Japanese Mount Everest Expedition, 1969–1970," *Himalayan Journal* 32 (1972): 100–12. Also see "Mt. Everest," *American Alpine Journal* 17 (1970): 183; "Mt. Everest: Japanese Visits, 1969," *Alpine Journal* 75 (1970): 199; "Mt. Everest (8848m)," *Alpine Journal* 76 (1971): 231.

9. Norman Dyhrenfurth, "Everest Revisited: The International Himalayan Expedition 1971," *American Alpine Journal* 18 (1972): 13. The phrase *Cordée internationale* appeared in John Cleare, "Thirteen Nations on Mount Everest," *Alpine Journal* 77 (1972): 9. Cleare's count of "thirteen nations" included the participation of the Nepalese liaison officer, a Polish member of the BBC crew, and an Australian journalist.

10. Bonington later described the misgivings that led to his withdrawal: "The idea of trying to persuade climbing stars from ten different countries, almost all of whom desperately wanted to reach the top themselves, to work unselfishly together to put someone of a different nationality on the summit, seemed an impossible task" (*The Everest Years*, 23). Also see Perrin, *The Villain*, 272–73.

11. Cleare, "Thirteen Nations on Mount Everest," 13.

12. Perrin, *The Villain*, 277. For statistics on deaths on Everest compared to summiters, see the lists provided on the Web site http://www.everestsummiteersassociation.org.

13. Cleare, "Thirteen Nations on Mount Everest," 16. Axt was, by all accounts, devastated by Bahuguna's death. The fact that he did not go back to aid his partner would long be held against him, particularly among Indian climbers, though in reality there was little he could have done by himself to rescue Bahuguna. In 1995 Himalayan Club president A. D. Moddie would bitterly label the preceding quarter century of Himalayan

climbing "the age of Axt, leaving a fellow climber, Bahuguna to hang and freeze to death, without even a look back" ("Climbing and the Himalayan Environment," *Himalayan Journal* 51 [1995], 3).

14. Cleare, "Thirteen Nations on Mount Everest," 9.

15. Dyhrenfurth, "Everest Revisited," 15. Mazeaud charged at the press conference that Dyhrenfurth had maliciously sabotaged the Southeast Ridge party. If the ridge route had succeeded, "we should draw all public interest from the climbers on the face route. If Yvette [Vaucher] reaches the summit and becomes the first woman to climb Everest the public loses interest in what happens on the face" ("Frenchman Plans Own Everest Expedition," *The Times,* May 7, 1971, 8).

16. Robert Fisk, "Everest Doctor Tells of Expedition's Strange Virus Disease," *The Times,* June 1, 1971, 4; Cleare, "Thirteen Nations on Mount Everest," 18.

17. *The Times* headlined its account of the end of the Southwest Face attempt in this fashion: "How Don Whillans, the Everest climber, put thoughts into words which will probably not be recorded in Alpine Club history" (June 3, 1971, 1). Also see Alpine Club honorary secretary Michael Westmacott's letter to the editor, "Spoken on Everest," *The Times,* June 7, 1971, 15.

18. Perrin, *The Villain,* 279.

19. Clark, *Men, Myths, and Mountains,* 214.

20. Bonington, *The Everest Years,* 30.

21. Ibid., 30–33; Curran, *High Achiever,* 139–40; Connor, *Dougal Haston* 172; Scott, *Himalayan Climber,* 34; John Hunt, foreword to Bonington, *Everest,* vii; Bonington, *Everest,* 13.

22. McDonald, *"I'll Call You in Kathmandu,"* 119; Doug Scott, "Himalaya—An Alpine Playground," *Mountain* 77 (Jan.–Feb. 1981): 42–43; Rowell, *Many People Come,* 139; "Two Italians Reach Summit of Mt. Everest," *New York Times,* May 6, 1973, 13.

23. "2 Japanese Are First atop Everest in Autumn," *New York Times,* Oct. 30, 1973, 49.

24. Unsworth, *Everest,* 597–98, 682, 690.

25. British Alpinist Dennis Gray argued in the pages of the *Alpine Journal* in 1971 that there were more interesting things to accomplish in the Himalaya than the second, third, or fourth ascent of the 8,000-meter giants. Calling for a new "Himalayan ethic," Gray argued that climbers "should be trying to do more, much more, with much less [for] it is how a mountain is climbed which is paramount, not that it is conquered." In his opinion, "the best peaks in the whole Himalayan chain have yet to be attempted or climbed." "The Himalayan Ethic—Time for a Rethink?" *Alpine Journal* 76 (1971): 156, 159. For Gray's climbing credentials see his memoir, *Rope Boy* (London: Victor Gollancz, 1970). Ronald E. Fear, "Dhaulagiri II," *American Alpine Journal* 18 (1972): 21–25; Higuchi, "The First Ascent of Yalung Kang," *Alpine Journal* 80 (1974): 17–28; Anglada, "Spanish Annapurna Expedition, 1974," *Himalayan Journal* 32 (1975): 203–4; Kazimierz W. Olech, "The First Ascent of Kangbachen (7902m)," *Alpine Journal* 80 (1975): 29–36.

26. "Interview with Wanda Rutkiewicz, June 1988." This unpublished interview was conducted by Arlene Blum; the authors are grateful to her for sharing it with us. Kukuczka, *My Vertical World,* 2.

27. Andrej Zawada, "Winter at 8250 Metres," *Alpine Journal* 82 (1977): 28–35; Mike Cheney, "Events and Trends 1970–6, Nepal Himalaya," *Alpine Journal* 83 (1978): 221–22; Doug Scott, "Himalayan Climbing: Part Two of a Personal Review," *Mountain* 101 (Jan.–Feb. 1985): 30–31; Marek Brniak and Józef Nyka, "Two Polish Ascents of Everest," *American Alpine Journal* 23 (1981): 51–52; "Poles Climb Everest in Winter," *Mountain* 72 (Mar.–Apr. 1980): 14; "Nepal Winter," *Mountain* 79 (May–June 1981): 3. Joe Tasker paid tribute to the Polish climbers who, "somehow setting their own standards outside the mainstream of the climbing world, were the ones who applied themselves directly to the problems of climbing in winter in the Himalayas. . . . They seem to have an aptitude for choosing bold, dangerous climbs which are often completed under duress and against great hardship" (*Everest,* 12).

28. Bonington, *Changabang,* v, 28.

29. Ibid., 101–7.

30. "Woman Scales Mount Everest," *New York Times,* May 17, 1975, 1; "Japanese Woman Overcame Injury to Climb Everest," *New York Times,* May 18, 1975, 3; Birkett and Peascod, *Women Climbing,* 102–10. Also see Junko Tabei's essay "Garbage on the Goddess Mother of the World," in Macdonald and Amott, *Voices from the Summit,* 23–29.

31. "Chinese Expedition Again Ascends World's Highest Peak," *China Reconstructs* 24 (Sept. 1975): 26–39; Zhou and Liu, *Footprints on the Peaks,* 106–12.

32. Henry Scott-Stokes, "Scaling Everest to Find a Legend," *New York Times,* Feb. 26, 1980, C1; "How Many Bodies on Everest?" *Mountain* 72 (Apr. 1980): 14; Anker and Roberts, *The Lost Explorer,* 26–27.

33. Barclays' sponsorship proved controversial among its shareholders, who felt the bank's directors were squandering their money on frivolous pursuits in the midst of economic hard times. Some mountaineers also questioned the arrangement, including Ken Wilson of *Mountain* magazine (who had joined the 1972 Bonington expedition to Everest). He asked editorially if the 1975 effort was "really worth the expenditure of £100,000 . . . when the country and indeed the world are in such dire economic straits?" Bonington, *Everest,* 26–27.

34. Ibid., 61; Connor, *Dougal Haston,* 176–77. On August 24 the first death on the expedition came when a young deaf and dumb Sherpa named Mingma wandered off and drowned in an icy stream below Base Camp. Bonington, *Everest,* 76–77.

35. Bonington, *Everest,* 115. Also see "Rapid Progress on Everest Climb," *The Times,* Sept. 5, 1975, 6.

36. Hunt, foreword, ix. Also see Scott, *Himalayan Climber,* 34, 37.

37. Bonington, *Everest,* 165.

38. Ronald Faux, "Two British Climbers Scale Everest by South-West Face," *The Times,* Sept. 26, 1975, 1.

39. Bonington, *Everest,* 170.

40. Ibid., 179. Also see Peter Boardman and Ronnie Richards, "British Everest Expedition SW Face," *Alpine Journal* 81 (1976): 3–14.

41. "Cameraman Dies in New Everest Assault," *The Times,* Sept. 30, 1975, 1; "Everest Man 'Had to Be Left Behind,'" *The Times,* Oct. 18, 1975, 2; Martin Boysen, "Mick Burke, 1941–1975," *Alpine Journal* 81 (1976): 268. Also see Willis, *The Boys of Everest,* 273–83.

42. Cheney, "Events and Trends," *Alpine Journal* 83 (1978): 223. For the Yugloslav West Ridge expedition, see Tony Skarja, "The Complete West Ridge of Everest," *American Alpine Journal* 23 (1980): 429–36. For the Chinese-Japanese-Nepalese expedition, see Zhou and Liu, *Footprints on the Peaks,* 159–66. For the 1984 Australian climb, see Unsworth, *Everest,* 487–88.

43. Hornbein, *Everest,* 29.

44. Ichiro Yoshizawa, "Dhaulagiri," *American Alpine Journal* 17 (1971): 438.

45. Roskelley, *Nanda Devi,* 4. Robert Roper, referring to a number of expeditions in which Roskelley was involved, offers a good general description of the emerging dynamics of "factionalized seventies-style expeditions." They worked, he said, "something like this: the hard-men get out early, impressing everyone, including themselves, and establishing their superiority. They self-select for the summit in two main ways: first by showing how physically and mentally superior they are, and second, by generating an intense esprit, a feeling within their little group alone that everyone senses and comes to resent. Feeling excluded and implicitly put down, those not accepted in the lead faction pull back—after a while they'd sooner cut their own throat than ask to be included" (*Fatal Mountaineer,* 106–7). Harvard and Thompson, *Mountain of Storms,* 139; Louis F. Reichardt, "Dhaulagiri 1973," *American Alpine Journal* 19 (1974): 1–10.

46. H. Adams Carter, "Balti Place Names in the Karakoram," *American Alpine Journal* 20 (1975): 52–60; Curran, *K2,* 122.

47. Whittaker, *A Life on the Edge,* 91, 168–69; Whittaker and Gabbard, *Lou Whittaker,* 104–6.

48. James Wickwire, "The Northwest Ridge of K2," *American Alpine Journal* 20 (1976): 359–67; Wickwire and Bullitt, *Addicted to Danger,* 64–71; Rowell, *In the Throne Room of the Mountain Gods,* 312; Curran, *K2,* 127.

49. Rowell, *In the Throne Room of the Mountain Gods,* 53. The phrase *climb and tell* was coined by Christopher Wren, "Climb and Tell; or, It's a Long Way from Annapurna," *New York Times,* Feb. 15, 1987, BR7.

50. Whittaker, *A Life on the Edge,* 174–75; Rowell, *In the Throne Room of the Mountain Gods,* 312–20. Alex Bertulis, who served on the American Alpine Club's board of directors, made the charges of CIA involvement in a letter to AAC president Bill Putnam. See Bertulis to Putnam, Nov. 22, 1975, Kauffman Collection, box 2, folder 2/23, American Alpine Club Library. Whittaker would describe Bertulis as "someone who was bitter that he hadn't been invited to join the expedition" (*A Life on the Edge,* 175). Actually, he had been invited, and then disinvited. For more on Bertulis, see Wickwire and Bullitt, *Addicted to Danger,* 57, 74; Rowell, *In the Throne Room of the Mountain Gods,* 25–26, 40–44; letter from Leif Patterson to Bertulis, Nov. 25, 1974, Kauffman Collection, box 2, folder 2/23, American Alpine Club Library.

51. Ridgeway, *The Boldest Dream,* 49.

52. Bob Cormack, e-mail to the authors, May 8, 2006; Blum, *Breaking Trail,* 203.

53. Bob Cormack, e-mail to the authors, May 10, 2006; Philip R. Trimble, "The American Bicentennial Everest Expedition," *American Alpine Journal* 21 (1977): 30–33.

54. Unsworth, *Everest,* 464. The ninth successful expedition to reach the summit via the Southeast Ridge, a joint British-Nepalese military expedition, had taken place the previous spring. See Fleming and Faux, *Soldiers on Everest.*

55. In 1951 French climbers Roger Duplat and Gilbert Vignes disappeared near the summit of Nanda Devi while attempting a traverse of the main and east peak. In searching for the missing climbers, Tenzing Norgay and Louis Dubost made the second ascent of the eastern summit. Jean-Jacques Languepin et al., "The French on Nanda Devi," *Himalayan Journal* 17 (1952): 60–63. For the 1975 climb, see Balwant S. Sandhu, "The Ascent of Nanda Devi and Nanda Devi East, 1975: The Indian-French Expedition to Garhwal Himalaya," *Himalayan Journal* 34 (1974–75): 59–66. For the 1976 climb, see Masahiko Kaji, "Nanda Devi, Traverse from East to Main Peak," *American Alpine Journal* 21 (1977): 244–48.

56. Unsoeld told the story of his determination to name a daughter after the mountain to reporter Worth Hedrick in 1976 and then, with characteristic mischief, suggested it was "probably apocryphal." Worth Hedrick, "'The Sweetness of Fear,'" *Weekly of Metropolitan Seattle,* Apr. 7, 1976, 12. The authors are grateful to Jolene Unsoeld for providing a copy of this article. Willi Unsoeld, "Nikanta, Garhwal Himalaya, 1949," *American Alpine Journal* 10 (1956): 75–80.

57. Andrew Harvard, "Nanda Devi Unsoeld, 1954–1976," *American Alpine Journal* 21 (1977): 310–12. "The mountains were very important to Devi," a memorial leaflet sent to Unsoeld family friends noted, "but so was her awareness of the social and economic injustices in our world. As she so often said, 'It is easy to turn your eyes away from the social problems of the world and concentrate on yourself in the mountains. It is good for a short period, but if you feel involved with social problems, you can't like that kind of thing for long. For me, and my family, it's where we recharge our batteries.'" American Alpine Club Archives, box 3, Nanda Devi folder, American Alpine Club Library.

58. Hedrick, "'The Sweetness of Fear,'" 13.

59. Marty Hoey, John Roskelley, Bob Craig, Yevgeniy B. Gippenreiter, and others described or quoted in this book appear as characters in a 1990 made-for-television movie *Storm and Sorrow,* which tells the story of the international expedition to the Soviet Pamirs in 1974 that ended in disaster.

60. Roskelley, *Nanda Devi,* 9; Hedrick, "'The Sweetness of Fear,'" 13. By the time the climb began, Hoey and Lev were no longer a couple, which only increased Roskelley's concerns about the personal dynamics of their relationship on the expedition.

61. Marty Hoey died in a fall on the North Face of Everest in 1982. Her obituary noted that she "was determined to perform well on Everest, spurred on, she freely admitted, by the acute disappointment that lingered from the Nanda Devi episode." James Wickwire, "Marty Hoey, 1951–1982," *American Alpine Journal* 25 (1983): 343.

62. Louis F. Reichardt and William F. Unsoeld, "Nanda Devi from the North," *American Alpine Journal* 21 (1977): 1–23; Roskelley, *Nanda Devi,* 183–88.

63. Letter from Andy Harvard to Lou Reichardt, Dec. 15, 1976, in authors' possession. The authors are grateful to Andy Harvard for providing a copy of this letter.

64. Authors' interview with Andy Harvard, June 19, 2006; Roper, *Fatal Mountaineer,* 2.

65. Letter from Andy Harvard to Lou Reichardt, Dec. 15, 1976.

66. Letter from Andy Harvard to Ad Carter, June 10 [1982], in authors' possession. The authors are grateful to Andy Harvard for providing a copy of the letter. Also see Pielmeier, *Willi,* 36; "Girl Buried on Namesake Peak in India," *Boston Herald American,* Sept. 21, 1976, 38; Roper, *Fatal Mountaineer,* 257–59.

67. Andy Harvard, annotation on copy of his letter to Lou Reichardt, Dec. 15, 1976, in author's possession; authors' interview with Andy Harvard, June 19, 2006; Peter Lev, e-mail to the authors, June 4, 2006; David Roberts, "Arduous Routes," *Outside* 6 (June–July 1981): 85. The number of counterexamples of men ignoring serious medical conditions on mountains are legion, but to cite one famous and lethal instance consider Art Gilkey's belief on K2 in 1953 that the trouble he had been experiencing with his leg for five days was a case of "charley horse."

68. Letter from John Evans to John Roskelley, Jan. 1, 1977, in authors' possession. The authors are grateful to Andy Harvard for providing a copy of this letter, and to John Evans for giving permission to quote this passage. Another expedition member, Lou Reichardt, also commented on the controversy over Devi Unsoeld's decision to climb to Camp IV: "John [Roskelley] came back [from Nanda Devi] saying he hadn't wanted Devi to go higher. But it was clear to me that he didn't want any other people to get to the summit. I think Devi was one of the people I would have cited as absolutely *not* a problem on a mixed expedition. She was strong, but she was also a very sensible woman. You had complete confidence in her judgment" (Roberts, "Arduous Routes," 85).

69. Alison Chadwick-Onyszkiewicz, "Gasherbrum II and III, 1975," *American Alpine Journal* 21 (1977): 36–41; Jordan, *Savage Summit,* 31–33. Wanda Rutkiewicz would go on to be the third woman to reach the summit of Mount Everest and the first to reach the summit of K2. She died in 1992 attempting to climb Kangchenjunga. Had she succeeded, it would have been her ninth 8,000-meter peak.

70. Ullman, *Americans on Everest,* n.28.

71. Blum, *Annapurna,* xxii; Ruth Robinson, "A Team of American Women Seeks to Scale Nepal's Heights," *New York Times,* Oct. 10, 1977, 34.

72. Mike Cheney to Arlene Blum, Feb. 27, 1978. The authors are grateful to Arlene Blum for providing a copy of this letter. Sherpanis would in a few years time begin appearing on expeditions. In 1993 Pasang Lhamu became the first Sherpani to reach the summit of Mount Everest, though she died on the descent. In 2000 an all-woman Sherpani expedition climbed the mountain. Unsworth, *Everest,* 550; http://www.pbs.org/frontlineworld/stories/nepal/lhamu.html.

73. "New and Safe Route," *American Alpine Journal* 22 (1978): 594.

74. Vera Komarkova, "American Women's Himalayan Expedition, Annapurna I," *American Alpine Journal* 22 (1979): 45–58; Blum, *Annapurna,* 199–221; Blum, *Breaking Trail,* 216–36; Fran Allen, "Vera Watson, 1932–1978," *American Alpine Journal* 22 (1979): 345–47; John Fowler, "Alison Chadwick-Onyszkiewicz," *American Alpine Journal,* 22 (1979): 347–48. Following Alison's death on Annapurna, her husband, Janusz Onyszkiewicz, ran into trouble with Polish authorities; a Solidarity activist and adviser to Lech Walesa, he was arrested in Poland's martial law crackdown in December 1981, and again a year and a half later for reading a message at the Warsaw Ghetto Memorial to commemorate the 1943 uprising. Audrey Salkeld, "People," *Mountain* 78 (Mar.–Apr. 1981): 44, (Mar.–Apr. 1982): 42, and (July–Aug. 1983): 46.

75. Grace Lichtenstein, "Himalayan Scaling Called an Inspiration to Women," *New York Times,* Nov. 11, 1978, 8; Mildred Hamilton, "Annapurna Climbers Readjust to Life at Sea Level," *San Francisco Examiner,* Nov. 20, 1978, 22.

76. Blum, *Breaking Trail,* 259. Melinda "Jo" Sanders would be a pioneer in the adventure travel business in China in the early 1980s. http://www.geoex.com/about_us/our_history.asp.

77. Melinda A. Sanders to Gilbert Grosvenor, Jan. 2 [1979], letter in authors' possession.

78. Gilbert Grosvenor to Melinda A. Sanders, Jan. 18, 1979, copy in authors' possession.

79. Roberts, "Arduous Routes," 32.

80. "I still stand by my *Outside* piece. If you disregard the inflammatory cover blurb and subhead [written by an *Outside* editor], it reads—I hope—as a balanced argument about the dangers of anybody climbing for ulterior (nationalistic, feminist, score-settling, etc.) motives" (David Roberts, e-mail to the authors, Nov. 12, 2006). Arlene Blum and Irene Beardsley to John Rasmus, June 11, 1981, copy in authors' possession. The authors are grateful to Arlene Blum for providing a copy of this letter. Also see "Letters," *Outside* 6 (Aug.–Sept. 1981): 8–9. Roberts would return to the topic of women's climbing with an article on the goal of putting an American woman atop Everest. David Roberts, "The Summit of Hype," *Outside* 13 (Oct. 1988): 41–47, 98–102.

81. Tsuneo Shigehiro, Takeyoshi Takatsuka, and Shoji Nakamura reached the summit of K2 just before 7:00 P.M. on August 8, 1977, and were forced to bivouac on their descent. The following day Mitsuo Hirishima, Masahide Onodera, Hideo Yamamoto, and Hunza porter Ashraf Aman also summitted. Though successful, the forty-one-climber enterprise was ridiculed in the mountaineering community. As Jim Curran notes, "Even in 1977, the expedition was seen as a dinosaur" (*K2,* 131).

82. Christian Bonington, "British K2 Expedition," *American Alpine Journal* 22 (1979): 19–23; Curran, *K2,* 132–36; Curran, *High Achiever,* 173–81.

83. For the earlier attempt, see Janusz Kurczab, "Polish K-2 Expedition—1976," *Alpine Journal* 83 (1978): 8–11.

84. Ridgeway, *The Last Step,* 87; Whittaker, *A Life on the Edge,* 191.

85. For Roskelley's attitude toward the 1960s, see Roskelley, *Stories Off the Wall,* 47; Roberts, "The Direct Style of John Roskelley," 93.

86. For the perspective of one "B Team" member from the expedition, see Bremer-Kamp, *Living on the Edge,* 20–40. Sharing a tent with several A Team members high on K2, she was dismayed to hear a discussion of climbing ethics that she described as "every man for himself."

87. Jim Wickwire, foreword to Houston and Bates, *K2,* 18. Wickwire would also lose the tips of two toes to frostbite. For his bivouac, see Wickwire and Bullitt, *Addicted to Danger,* 120–22. When Willi Unsoeld heard the story of Wickwire's encounter with Roskelley and Ridgeway, he was indignant (although, of course, already ill disposed to Roskelley). As he told an audience at Evergreen College the next year: "What do you expect a guy like Wickwire to say? 'Help me.' No, in a pig's eye—'I've got one leg left. I can hobble. It's okay guys, I'll

make it." 'Good. Glad to hear it. We'll see you when we come back . . .' I can't help but comment on that. I think times have changed. We [saw] a similar situation on Everest and an extremely different resolution." Unsoeld was referring to Barry Bishop and Lute Jerstad's decision to abandon their own summit bid to aid Jim Whittaker, Nawang Gombu, Norman Dyhrenfurth, and Ang Dawa in their descent from the South Col. "Somehow the social matrix has been altered," Unsoeld concluded, "and the day of the individual has become rampant, even in Himalayan climbers" (Leamer, *Ascent,* 360).

88. Louis F. Reichardt, "K2: The End of a 40-Year American Quest," *American Alpine Journal* 22 (1979): 1–18. Also see H. Adams Carter, "1978 American K2 Expedition," *Alpine Journal* 69 (1979): 52; Ridgeway, *The Last Step,* 234–82. Ridgeway would pay tribute to Lou Reichardt's climbing abilities but also offered a detailed description of Reichardt blowing his nose in his hand and wiping the results on his pants, with his own reaction at the time: "Boy, this guy sure is weird." Ridgeway, *The Last Step,* 97. It was the kind of detail that inevitably got picked up and repeated in other accounts; see, for example, Roper, *Fatal Mountaineer,* 77.

89. Ridgeway, *The Last Step,* 107. Roskelley was profiled in the influential British climbing magazine *Mountain* in 1980. As the introduction to the article noted, "Himalayan climbing is dominated by the Europeans and Japanese. 30 year old John Roskelley from the Pacific North-West U.S.A. is the equal of anyone in the big mountain game." "Who Is This Man Roskelley?" *Mountain* 75 (Sept.–Oct. 1980): 32.

90. Ridgeway, *The Last Step.* 180.

91. "Reinhold Messner," *Mountain* 15 (May 1971): 28, 30. For the Manaslu climb, see "Manaslu South Face," *American Alpine Journal* 18 (1973): 483–85; Faux, *High Ambition,* 93–99. Like his earlier ascent of Nanga Parbat, Messner's Manaslu climb embroiled him in a postexpedition controversy. Messner's climbing partner Franz Jager turned back below the summit and Messner completed the climb on his own. His decision was seen by some climbers as having contributed to Jager's subsequent death by exposure when he went out to look for Messner. Another climber, searching for Jager, also died. For the controversy, see David Roberts, "Messner and Habeler: Alone at the Top," *Outside* 7 (May 1982): 30; "A Second Talk with Messner," *Mountain* 51 (Sept.–Oct. 1976): 32; Habeler, *The Lonely Victory,* 89–90. That same year saw one of the costliest Himalayan disasters on the slopes of Manaslu, when an avalanche killed four Korean, one Japanese, and ten Sherpa climbers. "Avalanche Kills 15 on Himalaya Climb," *New York Times,* Apr. 15, 1972, 1; Doug Scott, "Himalayan Climbing: Part One of a Personal Review," *Mountain* 100 (Nov.–Dec. 1984): 28.

92. Bonington, *The Everest Years,* 13; Messner, *The Crystal Horizon,* 87. Messner is among the most prolific writers in the history of mountaineering literature, churning out at least forty-eight titles between 1970 and 2006. In comparison, Chris Bonington, no slouch himself at the typewriter, had only eighteen titles to his credit by 2006. Many of Messner's books, especially the later ones, tended to be slapped together or silly (or both), like *The Second Death of George Leigh Mallory,* which consisted of large chunks of Mallory's writings interspersed with sections in which Messner imagined what Mallory would have to say if he could comment from the grave.

93. Faux, *High Ambition,* 60–62, 112–17; Messner, *Free Spirit,* 169. At the foot of the Eiger, Messner met American actor Clint Eastwood, who was there filming a climbing/espionage thriller, *The Eiger Sanction.* As David Roberts would write of a widely circulated photograph showing Messner and Habeler with Eastwood and *Eiger Sanction* actress Heidi Bruhl: "In the photo Bruhl and Eastwood look like admiring fans; Habeler and Messner are the stars" ("Messner and Habeler," 27).

94. Messner, *The Challenge,* 185.

95. Ibid., 195. Also see Faux, *High Ambition,* 118–27.

96. H. W. Tilman, "Letter to the Editor," *The Times,* June 16, 1953, 7; Messner, *Everest,* 10; Habeler, *The Lonely Victory,* 25–29.

97. Unsworth, *Everest,* 473.

98. Tilman, "Letter to the Editor"; Unsworth, *Everest*, 476; Habeler, *The Lonely Victory*, 186, 211; Faux, *High Ambition*, 21–32.

99. The passages that particularly aroused Messner's ire read: "Reinhold has set this all [i.e., their earlier climbing history] out in detail in his books, even if the reader may gain the impression there that he was the leader and I was simply a passenger. However, I don't feel bitter about this—the books sell better that way. The applause of the general public is not so important to me. But Reinhold needs the recognition of that public. He likes to be on public show" (Habeler, *The Lonely Victory*, 19). For Messner's reaction, see Roberts, "Messner and Habeler," 33.

100. There was one recent precedent of a solo climb on a non-Himalayan mountain. In 1977 Polish climber Christopher Zurek made a solo ascent of Noshaq in the Hindu Kush (see Scott, "Himalayan Climbing, Part Two of a Personal Review," 26). Messner, *Solo Nanga Parbat*; Messner, *K2*.

101. "A Second Talk with Messner," *Mountain* 51 (Sept.–Oct. 1976): 33–34.

102. In 1978, in what may have been a test for the opening to foreign expeditions, the Chinese invited fifteen mountaineers from Iran to join them on a "training" expedition on Everest's north side. Unsworth, *Everest*, 602.

103. The spring 1980 expedition, led by Hyoriki Watanabe, simultaneously tackled the North East Ridge and the North Face of Everest, and succeeded on both routes. Yasuo Kato, who had previously climbed Everest from the Nepalese side, reached the summit via the North East Ridge on May 3, and in so doing became the first person ever to have climbed the mountain from both Nepal and Tibet. (Kato would die on the mountain following his third successful ascent of Everest in 1982.) Tsuneo Shigehiro and Takashi Ozaki put a new route up the North Face (making use of the Hornbein Couloir and West Ridge in the upper stretch), reaching the summit on May 10. "Japanese North Face and Northeast Ridge," *American Alpine Journal* 23 (1981): 305–6; Unsworth, *Everest*, 479–80; Messner, *The Crystal Horizon*, 88–90.

104. Messner, *The Crystal Horizon*, 24–25. Uemura's notion of a solo climb was different than Messner's, since it involved a large support team and a film crew to accompany him; he was, in any event, unsuccessful. For an account of Uemura's experiences on Everest in 1969, 1970, 1971, and 1980, see Uemura, *Beyond Mount Everest*.

105. Messner, *The Crystal Horizon*, 244; Faux, *High Ambition*, 158–66; Unsworth, *Everest*, 480–84; Messner, *The Crystal Horizon*, 224. According to Doug Scott, "Messner's three day ascent of the world's highest peak will forever stand as a landmark and reference point in the evolution of Himalayan climbing." Scott, "Himalayan Climbing: Part One," 26. Also see "Messner Solo," *American Alpine Journal* 23 (1981): 306–7.

106. Messner, *The Crystal Horizon*, 261, 145.

107. Reinhold Messner, "Ideas: The Risk Market: Reflections on Fame and the Boom in Professional Mountaineering," *Mountain* 92 (July–Aug. 1983): 44–45.

108. Unsworth, *Everest*, 484. American historian Christopher Lasch offered this description of what he saw as the prevalent personality disorder of his time, in a book that appeared the year of Messner and Habeler's oxygenless ascent of Everest: "Notwithstanding his occasional illusions of omnipotence, the narcissist depends on others to validate his self-esteem. He cannot live without an admiring audience. His apparent freedom from family ties and institutional constraints does not free him to stand alone or to glory in his individuality. On the contrary, it contributes to his insecurity, which he can overcome only by seeing his 'grandiose self' reflected in the attentions of others. . . . For the narcissist, the world is a mirror" (*The Culture of Narcissism*, 10).

109. Rowell, *Many People Come*, 142; Charles Warren, "Eric Earle Shipton (1907–1977)," *Alpine Journal* 88 (1978): 271.

110. Boardman, *Sacred Summits,* 158. For the 1979 climb, see Joe Tasker, "Kangchenjunga North Ridge 1979," *Alpine Journal* 85 (1980): 49–58. For Odell's tribute to his old climbing partner, see Noel Odell, "In Memoriam: Harold William Tilman," *Himalayan Journal* 36 (1978–79): 237. Also see Peter Lloyd and Colin Putt, "Harold William Tilman (1898–1978): A Tribute," *Alpine Journal* 84 (1979): 132–35.

111. Messner, *The Challenge,* 110–35; Rab Carrington, "Some Sobering Thoughts on Nepalese Climbing," *Alpine Journal* 88 (1983): 202. The numbers of expeditions are derived from "Appendix 4: Summary of Expeditions to Mount Everest, 1921–1998," in Unsworth, *Everest,* 585–675. The precise number of expeditions for the 1980s is harder to determine due to the increasing informality of expeditions and their merger or division once on the mountain. Junko Tabei gives a figure of 144 Everest expeditions in the 1980s in Macdonald and Amott, *Voices from the Summit,* 26. By the 1980s climbs on 8,000-meter peaks had become so common that the *Himalayan Journal,* which had noted every such ascent since 1950, decided to stop listing them. M. H. Contractor, "The Continuing Story of the Himalayan Club, 1978–1988," *Himalayan Journal* 46 (1986–87): 153.

112. King, *Karakoram Highway,* 111; "New Chinese Road Opens Remote Area to the West," *New York Times,* June 18, 1978, 37; William Borders, "A Strategic New Link on the Roof of the World," *New York Times,* Jan. 28, 1979, E5; John F. Burns, "Karakoram Highway," *New York Times,* June 22, 1986, XX15.

113. Ridgeway, *Below Another Sky,* 232. Also see M. S. Kohli, "Mountaineering in Bhutan," *Alpine Journal* 90 (1985): 18–20; Neate, *High Asia,* 16–23; F. Spencer Chapman, "Chomolhari," *Alpine Journal* 49 (Nov. 1937): 203–9.

114. Ortner, *Life and Death on Mt. Everest,* 199; emphasis in original.

115. Ullman, *Americans on Everest,* 145; Barry Bishop, "How We Climbed Everest," *National Geographic* 124 (Oct. 1963): 489; letter to the editor, *Mountain* 95 (Jan.–Feb. 1984): 50–51. This had not been a problem for earlier generations of climbers, in part because their numbers were so few and in part, as Bill Tilman noted in his 1946 travel book *When Men and Mountains Meet,* because "Tibetans are such thorough scavengers." On the East Rongbuk Glacier, home to a line of British camps where "there had probably been more tins opened in the last twenty years than anywhere in India," there was, Tilman noted, "not a trace of a tin to be seen." Tilman, *When Men and Mountains Meet,* reprinted in *The Seven Mountain-Travel Books,* 317.

116. Galen Rowell, "Selling Shangri-la," *Outside* 5 (Nov.–Dec. 1980): 85. Also see Kohli, "Himalayan Tourism and Environment"; Lhakpa Norbu Sherpa, "The High Profile Dump," *Himal* (Nov.–Dec. 1992): 28. For a discussion of the extent of deforestation and its sources, see Stevens, *Claiming the High Ground.*

117. In 1985 David Breashears came across parts of the bodies of two Sherpas he had climbed with on Everest the previous year. They had died in a fall on the Southeast Ridge, and their corpses were tethered to the Geneva Spur when it proved impossible to retrieve them. During the winter the frozen bodies were blown loose and shattered at the foot of Lhotse Face. Breashears gathered up the body parts and buried them in a crevasse, refusing to allow a photographer who came upon him in the act to take any pictures (Breashears, *High Exposure,* 187–88). Douglas, *Chomolungma Sings the Blues,* 186; McDonald, *"I'll Call You in Kathmandu,"* 135. By the time of the fiftieth anniversary of the Hillary and Tenzing climb in 2003, 175 climbers had died attempting Everest; 120 bodies remained on the mountain. James Brooke, "Young and Old, and Speedy, They Are All Doing Everest," *New York Times,* May 27, 2003, 1, 4.

118. "I can't say that I find this all that funny now," Fanshawe wrote in defense of the jokers, "but it would be very wrong for onlookers who were not there to pronounce these comments as grotesque. . . . climbers, like them, were dying, and everyone had to come to grips with this horrible truth—or go home" (*Coming Through,* 46–47). Casarotto's body, buried in a crevasse in 1986, was discovered on the Phillipo Glacier at the foot of K2 in the summer of 2004. "Renato Casarotto Remains Found at the Foot of the Magic Line on K2," July 22, 2004, http://www.k2climb.net/story/RenatoCasarottoremainsfoundatthefootoftheMagicLineonK2Jul212004 .shtml.

119. Data on Sherpa mortality rates comes from von Fürer-Haimendorf, *The Sherpas Transformed,* 74. Also see Ortner, *Life and Death on Mt. Everest,* 124–48.

120. Bonington, *Everest,* 58; Ridgeway, *The Boldest Dream,* 180; Patterson, *Canadians on Everest,* 36–37.

121. Bonington, *Everest,* 55–56.

122. Joe Tasker, "Small Expeditions," *Alpine Journal* 82 (1977): 26. The enthusiasm for small expeditions was not universally shared. At a symposium on "lightweight expeditions" sponsored by the Alpine Club in 1984, Don Whillans declared: "The Himalaya are not the Alps, and . . . the real dangers are still there, and I think it extremely foolish to assume that the Himalaya have suddenly become an *alpine* playground." Don Whillans, "The Risks and How I See Them," in Clarke and Salkeld, *Lightweight Expeditions to the Great Ranges,* 46.

123. Kanak Mani Dixit, "Mountaineering's Himalayan Face," *Himal* (Nov.–Dec. 1992): 12; Krakauer, *Into Thin Air,* 60. The falloff in high-altitude employment on serious mountaineering expeditions linked to the embrace by climbers of the alpine style was made up for by the steady increase in the popularity of trekking (and, somewhat later, the rise of commercial guided climbing). Trekking agencies increasingly turned to non-Sherpa Nepalese to meet the demand. To many foreigners, any native Nepalese who brought them tea in the morning or carried their gear on the trail was by definition a "Sherpa," and Gurungs and Tamangs were not quick to disabuse their clients of that misapprehension. Also see A. D. Moddie, "Himalayan Tourism: A Mongol Needing Eco-civilizing," *Himalayan Journal* 49 (1982–83): 9.

124. Tasker was born in 1948, Boardman in 1950. Tasker, *Savage Arena,* 49. For Dunagiri's previous ascent, see André Roch, "Garhwal 1939: The Swiss Expedition," *Alpine Journal* 52 (1940): 34–52.

125. Boardman, *The Shining Mountain,* 12–14.

126. Ibid., 18–19, 51.

127. Ibid., 136.

128. Ibid., 141–43.

129. Ibid., 165. On completing their descent to Base Camp on October 18, they met an American climber, Ruth Erb, who told them of the disaster her expedition had suffered on Dunagiri in which four members, including her husband, were killed in a fall high on the mountain. They helped to retrieve the bodies from where they lay on the glacier and lowered them into a crevasse on the Rhamani Glacier.

130. Joe Tasker, "Small Expeditions," *Alpine Journal* 82 (1977): 23. The Kangchenjunga and Gaurishankar climbs are described in Boardman's posthumously published *Sacred Summits.* Also see Tasker, *Everest;* and his posthumously published *Savage Arena.* Also see "Gaurishankar (23,454ft)," *Mountain* 71 (Jan.–Feb. 1980): 13.

131. Bonington and Clarke, *Everest,* 155; Chris Bonington, "Pete and Joe," *Mountain* 87 (Sept.–Oct. 1982): 36–37; Chris Bonington, "Peter Boardman and Joe Tasker," *Himalayan Journal* 38 (1981–82): 218–21; Chris Bonington, "China 1982," *Alpine Journal* 88 (1983): 190–91. Boardman's body was found on the Northeast Ridge in 1992. Also see the accounts by Joe Tasker's girlfriend, Maria Coffey: *Fragile Edge* and *Where the Mountain Casts Its Shadow.*

132. "Messner Summit," *Mountain* 109 (May–June 1986): 41.

133. http://www.everestnews.com/history/firsts.htm.

134. The acronym BASE stands for Building—Antenna-Span—and Earth. BASE jumping consists of taking standing parachute jumps off fixed high points. Amateur participation in traditional team sports like baseball and touch football declined in the 1990s, while mountain biking, skateboarding, scuba diving, snowboarding, and BASE jumping enjoyed dramatic growth. BASE jumping's "stark metaphor," *Time* magazine declared— "a human leaving safety behind to leap into the void—may be a perfect fit with our times" ("Life on the Edge," Sept. 6, 1999, 28). Miura, *The Man Who Skied Down Everest.* The first ski descent from the summit, via the Southeast Ridge and Lhotse Face, was accomplished by Slovenian climber Davo Karnicar in 2000. Yuichiro

Miura established another record in 2003 when he climbed to the summit of Everest, becoming, at age seventy, the oldest climber to do so. "Everest: Jean Marc Boivin Wings It," *Outside* 14 (Mar. 1989): 91; Dickinson, *Ballooning over Everest,* 108–38.

135. Trip Gabriel, "The Last Crusades of Reinhold Messner," *Outside* 12 (Aug. 1987): 37–42, 98–101. Ed Viesturs became the first American to climb all fourteen in 2005 with the ascent of Annapurna. http://www.nationalgeographic.com/adventure/0508/excerpt3.html.

136. Shishapangma continued to draw foreign mountaineers in the years that followed. Junko Tabei and Reinhold Messner each climbed it in separate parties in 1981, again by the original route. In 1982 Doug Scott, Alex MacIntyre, and Roger Baxter-Jones made a four-day, Base Camp to summit alpine-style of ascent of Shishapangma's Southwest Face. And Americans Mike Browning, Chris Pizzo, and Glen Porzak reached the summit via the Northeast Face in September 1983. "Shishapangma," *American Alpine Journal* 25 (1981): 307–8; "Xixabangma (8013m)," *Mountain* 86 (July–Aug. 1982): 11; Scott and MacIntyre, *The Shishapangma Expedition;* Glenn Porzak, "Shisha Pangma—First American Ascent," *American Alpine Journal* 27 (1984): 19–23; Sale and Cleare, *Climbing the World's 14 Highest Mountains,* 200–1.

137. Jonathan Wright left a widow and an eighteen-month-old daughter, Asia. In 1999 Asia Wright accompanied Rick Ridgeway back to Minya Konka to visit the grave where Ridgeway and the others had buried her father. See Ridgeway, *Below Another Sky,* 3–21. For other accounts of the 1980 avalanche, see Craig Vetter, "Lucky Yvon," *Outside* 9 (Mar. 1984): 42; "Kim Schmitz Retires from Guiding," http://www.exumguides.com/news/schmitz.shtml. Rowell, *Mountains of the Middle Kingdom,* 15–29.

138. Howard-Bury, *Mount Everest,* 230; Andy Harvard, "The Forgotten Face of Everest," *National Geographic* (July 1984): 72–77; Unsworth, *Everest,* 497–98.

139. Geoffrey C. Tabin, "The Kangshung Face of Everest," *American Alpine Journal* 24 (1982): 101–8; Unsworth, *Everest,* 498–500; Breashears, *High Exposure,* 119–38. Kim Momb departed Everest at the same time as Roskelley but did not leave behind the same bad feelings; he would be back for another try on the Kangshung Face in 1983.

140. Bonington, *Kongur.*

141. A second team of four climbers reached the summit on August 15 by the same route. "K2: Japs Climb North Face," *Mountain* 88 (Nov.–Dec. 1982): 11; Sale, *Climbing the World's 14 Highest Mountains,* 64–65. This was Japan's second triumph on K2 in two years; in 1981 a Japanese expedition led by Teruch Matsuura attempted K2 by its West Ridge, previously unsuccessfully attempted by British climbers in 1978 and 1980. Eiho Ohtani and Pakistani climber Nazir Sabir reached the summit, using oxygen, on August 6, 1981. "Mixed Fortunes in Karakoram," *Mountain* 82 (Nov.–Dec. 1981): 11.

142. For the American Kangshung Face expedition, see James D. Morrissey, "Kangshung Face of Everest," *American Alpine Journal* 26 (1984): 1–7; James D. Morrissey, "Conquest of the Summit," *National Geographic* (July 1984): 79–89; Christopher S. Wren, "US Team Finds a Harder Way to Scale Everest," *New York Times,* Oct. 28, 1983, A2. The route was not repeated in the twentieth century, but in 1988 a four-man team climbed a new route to its left. For the 1988 Anglo-American Kangshung expedition, see Venables, *Everest: Kangshung Face;* Webster, *Snow in the Kingdom,* 201–491.

143. Letter from Zhou Zheng to "Uncle Bob," Oct. 28, 1987, Bates Papers, American Alpine Club Library. Bates, along with Tom Hornbein, Nick Clinch, Pete Schoening, and several other Americans were part of an expedition jointly sponsored by the American Alpine Club and the Xinjiang Mountaineering Association to attempt the unclimbed Ulugh Muztag (22,923ft/6,987m) in the Kunlun range in 1985. Five Chinese climbers, Hu Fengling, Zhang Baohua, Ardaxi, Mamuti, and Wu Qiangxing, reached the top on October 21 (Robert H. Bates, "The Ulugh Muztagh," *American Alpine Journal* 28 [1986]: 27–38; also see Zhou and Liu, *Footprints on the Peaks,* 156–59). Harvard, "The Forgotten Face of Everest," 76–77; Rowell, *Mountains of the Middle King-*

dom, 104–7. Harvard provided before (1922) and after (1980) photographs of Xegar Monastery and its ruins; Rowell did the same for the Rongbuk Monastery.

144. Marvine Howe, "2 American Mountaineers Tell of Witnessing Tibet Protests," *New York Times,* Nov. 13, 1987, A6.

145. For accounts of the K2 events of 1986, see "Success and Disaster on K2," *Mountain* 111 (Sept.–Oct. 1986): 8–10; Greg Child and Jon Krakauer, "The Dangerous Summer," *Outside* 12 (Mar. 1987): 35–36. In *K2: The Story of the Savage Mountain,* Curran devotes a chapter to unraveling the charges and countercharges that swirled around the mountaineering community in the aftermath of the summer of 1986, 197–207. Also see Kauffman and Putnam, *K2,* 44.

146. Soli S. Mehta to Andrew Kauffman, July 17, 1987, Kauffman Collection, box 2, folder 2/23, American Alpine Club Library.

147. Jim Curran, who was part of the British expedition co-led by Rouse, thinks the comparison with the attempt to rescue Gilkey is unfair, given that all the climbers trapped for five days at high camp with Rouse in blizzard conditions were near collapse themselves from lack of food and water when they made their descent (*K2: The Story of the Savage Mountain,* 205). Trevor Braham, "Expedition Style—A Himalayan Perspective (1976–1986)," *Alpine Journal* 93 (1988–89): 58.

148. Jon Tinker, "Commercial Expeditions," *Alpine Journal* 102 (1997): 173.

149. Rowell, *Many People Come,* 1–39. In the mid-1980s Swiss climber Stefan Woerner began taking clients to 8000-meter peaks in the Karakoram (Doug Scott, "The Himalaya and the Pace of Change," *Mountain* 111 [Sept.–Oct. 1986]: 35). Jon Krakauer, "Seven Up," *Outside* 10 (July 1985): 12; Breashears, *High Exposure,* 156–63; Bass, Wells, and Ridgeway, *Seven Summits.*

150. New Zealand guide Rob Hall estimated that 80 to 90 percent of his potential market lay with an American clientele. Krakauer, *Into Thin Air,* 87.

151. "Everest a Sell-Out: 31 Reach Summit in Four Days!" *Mountain* 137 (Jan.–Feb. 1991): 8.

152. Bob Howells, "Meanwhile, over on Everest . . . " *Outside* 17 (Aug. 1992): 61, 120. In a postscript for a fortieth anniversary edition of John Hunt's *The Ascent of Everest* published in 1993, Sir Edmund Hillary wrote: "I haven't the slightest doubt that we who were attempting Everest in 1953 were the lucky ones. We were not driven by ideas of fame or fortune (or certainly I wasn't). All we wanted to do was climb a mountain that had been a constant challenge for more than thirty years. But how things have changed! Prima donnas have come and gone; huge expeditions have moved side-by-side with small alpine efforts; the mountain has been cluttered with junk; and many of the expeditions are now outright commercial undertakings at $US35,000 a customer. With a dozen or more expeditions together at Base Camp, the sense of freedom and challenge has long disappeared" ("Postscript to This Edition," 238).

153. Fischer and Viesturs's rescue efforts on K2 are described in Viesturs and Roberts, *No Shortcuts to the Top,* 19–21, 31–34. "False Summit: Everest a Year Later," *Outside* 22 (May 1997): 58. Also see Potterfield, *In the Zone,* 105–64.

154. Peter H. Lewis, "Atop Peaks or beneath Sea, Adventurers Have Company on the Internet," *New York Times,* July 2, 1996, C8; Mary Turner, "Sandy Hill, 51," *Outside* 31 (Sept. 2006): 84–85.

155. Krakauer, *Into Thin Air,* 313; Unsworth, *Everest,* 559.

156. Krakauer, *Into Thin Air,* 306. Also see Maria Coffey's interview with Jan Arnold, "The Ones Left Behind," *Outside* 31 (Sept. 2006): 80–81.

157. Krakauer's *Into Thin Air* is the best-known source for the events of May 10–11, 1996. But also see Breashears, *High Exposure,* 241–76; Boukreev and DeWalt, *The Climb;* Weathers and Michaud, *Left for Dead;* Gammelgaard, *Climbing High.* Also see the special issue of *Outside* magazine devoted to a tenth-anniversary

retrospective, "Return to Thin Air," *Outside* 31 (Sept. 2006). And see, though not in any expectation of historical accuracy, the 1997 made-for-television movie *Into Thin Air: Death on Everest,* in which Scott Fischer is transformed into the villain of the drama.

158. John F. Burns, "Refusing to be Stylish, Everest Kills," *New York Times,* May 14, 1996, 1; "Mountain Climbing Is Sublime; Is It Selfish Too?" *New York Times,* May 19, 1996, E7.

159. Charles S. Houston, "South Face of Mount Everest," *American Alpine Journal* 8 (1951): 20–21.

Bibliography

PAPERS AND MANUSCRIPTS

In addition to the following, we have used papers and unpublished manuscripts in private possession as noted throughout.

Alpine Club, London
Douglas Freshfield Correspondence
Miscellaneous Expedition Reports
A. F. Mummery Papers
Newspaper Clippings Archive
Geoffrey Winthrop Young Correspondence

American Alpine Club Library, Golden, Colorado
American Alpine Club Archives
Robert Bates Papers
Barry Bishop Papers
Henry Hall Correspondence
Himalaya Library Archives ("Vertical Files")
Andrew John Kauffman Collection
Annie Peck Papers
Fannie Bullock Workman and William Hunter Workman Papers

Appalachian Mountain Club Library, Boston
Miscellaneous Papers and Correspondence

Bodleian Library, Oxford University, Oxford
James Bryce Papers

British Library, London
 T. S. Blakeney Collection
 George Nathaniel Curzon Papers
 John Morley Papers
 Oriental and India Office Collection
 Francis Edward Younghusband Collection

Cambridge University Library, Cambridge
 Martin Conway Papers

German Alpine Club Library, Munich
 German Alpine Club Archives
 German Himalayan Foundation Archives

India International Centre, Delhi
 Himalayan Club Collection

Magdalene College Library, Cambridge University, Cambridge
 George Leigh Mallory Papers

National Geographic Society, Washington, D.C.
 Barry Bishop Grant File
 Norman G. Dyhrenfurth Grant File

National Library of Scotland, Edinburgh
 Thomas Graham Brown Papers
 Fanny Bullock Workman and William Hunter Workman Papers

Princeton University Library, Princeton
 James Ramsey Ullman Papers, Department of Rare Books and Special Collections

Royal Geographical Society, London
 Mount Everest Expedition Archives

School of Geography and the Environment, Oxford University, Oxford
 Kenneth Mason Papers

JOURNALS, NEWSPAPERS, AND MAGAZINES

Accidents in North American Mountaineering *National Geographic Magazine*
Die Alpen *National Observer*

Alpine Journal

Alpinist

American Alpine Journal

American Alpine News

Appalachia

Blackwoods Magazine

Boston Herald American

Bulletin of the American Geographical Society

Cambridge Mountaineering

Chicago Tribune

Climber's Club Journal

Collier's

Daily Express

Daily Mail

Daily News

Deutsche Alpenzeitung

L'écho des Alpes

Geographical Journal

Good Words

Guardian Weekly

Harvard Mountaineering

Himal

Himalayan Journal

Illustrated London News

Jahrbuch des Österreichischen Alpenvereins

Japanese Alpine News

Life

Look

Manchester Guardian

La montagne et alpinisme

La montagne: Revue officielle du Club alpin
    français

Mountain

Mountain Craft

Mountaineering Journal

Mountain World

National Geographic Adventure Magazine

National Zeitung

New England Magazine

New Statesman and Nation

News Chronicle

Newsweek

New Yorker

New York Herald Tribune

New York Post

New York Times

New York Times Book Review

New York Times Magazine

New Zealand Alpine Journal

Österreichischen Alpenzeitung

Outside

Oxford and Cambridge Mountaineering

Paris Match

Proceedings of the Royal Geographical Society

Reader's Digest

San Francisco Examiner

Saturday Evening Post

Scientific American

Seattle Post-Intelligencer

Sierra Club Bulletin

Spectator

Summit

Sunday Telegraph

Telegraph (Calcutta)

Time

The Times

Times of India

Washington Magazine

Washington Post

Weekly Dispatch

Yorkshire Post

Zeitschrift des Deutschen und Österreichischen
    Alpenvereins

BOOKS AND ARTICLES

Adams, Ansel. "Vittoria Sella: An Intensity of Seeing, Majesty, and Mood." *Sierra Club Bulletin* 31 (Dec. 1946): 15–17.

Aimone di Savoia-Aosta, Duca di Spoleto, and Ardito Desio. *La spedizione geografica italiana al Karakoram*. Rome: Bertarelli, 1936.

Alder, Garry. *Beyond Bokhara: The Life of William Moorcroft, Asian Explorer and Pioneer Veterinary Surgeon*. London: Century, 1985.

Ali, Aamir, ed. *For Hills to Climb: The Doon School Contribution to Mountaineering: The Early Years*. New Delhi: Doon School Old Boys' Society, n.d.

Alpine Club. *Alpine Club Library Catalogue: Books and Periodicals*. London: Heinemann, 1982.

American Alpine Club. *Bylaws and Register of the American Alpine Club, 1947*. New York: American Alpine Club, 1947.

Amstädter, Rainer. *Der Alpinismus: Kultur—Organisation—Politik*. Vienna: WUV-Universitätsverlag, 1996.

Anderson, J. R. L. *High Mountains and Cold Seas: A Biography of H. W. Tilman*. London: Gollancz, 1980.

Andrews, C. G. *Flight over Everest*. Tararua, New Zealand: Wellington Tramping Club, 1947.

Ang Tharkay, *Mémoires d'un Sherpa*. Paris: Aimiot-Dumont, 1954.

Anker, Conrad, and David Roberts. *The Lost Explorer: Finding Mallory on Mount Everest*. New York: Simon and Schuster, 1999.

Astill, Tony. *Mount Everest, the Reconnaissance 1935: The Forgotten Adventure*. Southampton, England: published by the author, 2005.

Ata-Ullah, Mohammad. *Citizen of Two Worlds*. New York: Harper, 1960.

Avedon, John F. *In Exile from the Lands of Snows: The Dalai Lama and Tibet since the Chinese Conquest*. New York: Harper, 1997.

Bakewell, Michael. *Fitzrovi: London's Bohemia*. London: National Portrait Gallery, 1999.

Ball, John, ed. *Peaks, Passes, and Glaciers: A Series of Excursions by Members of the Alpine Club*. London: Longmans, 1859.

Band, George. *Everest*. New York: Barnes and Noble, 2003.

Bank, Mike. *Commando Climber*. London: J. M. Dent, 1955.

Barker, Ralph. *The Last Blue Mountain*. London: Chatto and Windus, 1959.

Bass, Dick, Frank Wells, and Rick Ridgeway. *Seven Summits*. New York: Warner, 1986.

Bates, Robert H. *The Love of Mountains Is Best: Climbs and Travels from K2 to Kathmandu*. Portsmouth, N.H.: Peter E. Randall, 1994.

Bates, Robert H., and Charles S. Houston. *Five Miles High: The Story of an Attack on the Second Highest Mountain in the World*. New York: Dodd, Mead, 1939. Reprinted with foreword by Jim Wickwire. New York: Lyons, 2000.

Bauer, Paul. *Himalayan Campaign: The German Attack on Kangchenjunga, the Second Highest Mountain in the World*. Oxford: B. Blackwell, 1937.

————. *Himalayan Quest: The German Expeditions to Siniolchum and Nanga Parbat*. London: Nicholson and Watson, 1938.

————. *Kanchenjunga Challenge*. London: W. Kimber, 1955.

————. *The Siege of Nanga Parbat, 1856–1953*. London: Rupert Hart-Davis, 1956.

Baume, Louis C. *Sivalaya: Explorations of the 8000 Metre Peaks of the Himalaya*. Seattle: Mountaineers, 1979.

The Beatles. *The Beatles Anthology*. San Francisco: Chronicle, 2000.

Bechtold, Fritz. *Nange Parbat Adventure: A Himalayan Expedition*. Translated by H. E. G. Tyndale. New York: Dutton, 1936.

Bell, Charles Alfred. *A Portrait of the Dalai Lama*. London: Collins, 1946.

————. *Tibet: Past and Present*. Oxford: Oxford University Press, 1924.

Bernstein, Jeremy. *Ascent: Of the Invention of Mountain Climbing and Its Practice*. New York: Random House, 1965.

————. *Dawning of the Raj: The Life and Trials of Warren Hastings*. Chicago: Ivan R. Dee, 2000.

————. *In the Himalayas: Journeys through Nepal, Tibet, and Bhutan*. Rev. ed. New York: Lyons, 1996.

Birkett, Bill, and Bill Peascod. *Women Climbing: 200 Years of Achievement*. Seattle: Mountaineers, 1990.

Bishop, Peter. *The Myth of Shangri-La: Tibet, Travel Writing, and the Western Creation of Sacred Landscape*. Berkeley: University of California Press, 1999.

Blacker, L. V. Stewart. "The Aërial Conquest of Everest," *National Geographic Magazine* 94 (Aug. 1933): 127–62.

Blum, Arlene. *Annapurna: A Woman's Place*. San Francisco: Sierra Club, 1998.

————. *Breaking Trail: A Climbing Life*. New York: Scribner, 2005.

Boardman, Peter. *Sacred Summits: A Climber's Year*. London: Hodder and Stoughton, 1982.

————. *The Shining Mountain: Two Men on Changabang's West Wall*. New York: Dutton, 1984.

Bonatti, Walter. *The Mountains of My Life*. Translated by Robert Marshall. New York: Modern Library, 2001.

————. *On the Heights*. London: Rupert Hart-Davis, 1964.

Bonington, Chris. *Annapurna South Face*. London: Cassell, 1971.

————. *The Climbers: A History of Mountaineering*. London: BBC, 1992.

————. *Everest: The Hard Way*. New York: Random House, 1976.

————. *The Everest Years: A Climber's Life*. London: Hodder and Stoughton, 1986.

————. *I Chose to Climb*. London: Gollancz, 1966.

————. *Kongur: China's Elusive Summit*. London: Hodder and Stoughton, 1982.

————. *Mountaineer*. San Francisco: Sierra Club, 1996.

————. *The Next Horizon*. London: Gollancz, 1973.

———. *Quest for Adventure.* London: Hodder and Stoughton, 1981.

Bonington, Chris, and Charles Clarke. *Everest: The Unclimbed Ridge.* New York: W. W. Norton, 1984.

Bonington, Chris, and Audrey Salkeld. *Heroic Climbs: A Celebration of World Mountaineering.* Seattle: Mountaineers, 1994.

Bonington, Chris, and Doug Scott. *Changabang.* New York: Oxford University Press, 1976.

Booth, John Nichols. *Fabulous Destinations.* New York: Macmillan, 1950.

Boukreev, Anatoli, and G. Weston DeWalt. *The Climb: Tragic Ambitions on Everest.* New York: St. Martin's, 1997.

Bowman, W. E. *The Ascent of Rum Doodle.* London: Max Parrish, 1956.

Braham, Trevor. *Himalayan Odyssey.* London: Allen and Unwin, 1974.

———. *When the Alps Cast Their Spell: Mountaineers of the Alpine Golden Age.* Glasgow: Neil Wilson, 2004.

Brauen, Martin, ed. *Peter Aufschnaiter's Eight Years in Tibet.* Bangkok: Orchid, 2002.

Breashears, David. *High Exposure: An Enduring Passion for Everest and Unforgiving Places.* New York: Simon and Schuster, 1999.

Breashears, David, and Audrey Salkeld. *Last Climb: The Legendary Everest Expeditions of George Mallory.* Washington, D.C.: National Geographic, 1999.

Bremer-Kamp, Cherie. *Living on the Edge.* Layton, Utah: Gibbs M. Smith, 1987.

Brower, David, et. al., *Summit: Vittorio Sella, Mountaineer and Photographer, the Years 1879–1909.* New York: Aperture, 1999.

Brown, Joe. *The Hard Years.* London: Gollancz, 1967.

Brownell, Susan E. *Training the Body for China—Sports in the Moral Order of the People's Republic.* Chicago: University of Chicago Press, 1995.

Bruce, Charles Granville. *The Assault on Mount Everest, 1922.* New York: Longmans, Green, 1923.

———. *Himalayan Wanderer.* London: Alexander Maclehose, 1934.

———. *Twenty Years in the Himalaya.* London: E. Arnold, 1910.

Bryant, L. V. *New Zealanders and Everest.* Wellington, New Zealand: A. H. and A. W. Reed, 1953.

Buffet, Charlie. *Première de cordée: Claude Kogan, femme d'audace et de passion.* Paris: Robert Laffont, 2003.

Buhl, Hermann. *Nanga Parbat Pilgrimage.* London: Hodder and Stoughton, 1956.

Burdsall, Richard L., and Arthur B. Emmons III. *Men against the Clouds: The Conquest of Minya Konka.* New York: Harper and Brothers, 1935.

Burrard, S. G., and H. H. Hayden. *A Sketch of the Geography and Geology of the Himalaya Mountains and Tibet.* Calcutta: Government of India, 1907–8.

Burton, Hal. *The Ski Troops.* New York: Simon and Schuster, 1971.

Calvert, Harry. *Smythe's Mountains: The Climbs of F. S. Smythe.* London: Gollancz, 1985.

Cameron, Ian. *Mountains of the Gods.* New York: Facts on File, 1984.

———. *To the Farthest Ends of the Earth: 150 Years of Exploration by the Royal Geographical Society.* New York: Dutton, 1980.

Campbell, Robin. "The Brief Mountaineering Career of Aleister Crowley, the Great Beast 666." *Mountain* 11 (1970): 12–14.

Cassin, Riccardo. *50 Years of Alpinism.* Seattle: Mountaineers, 1981.

Child, Greg. *Climbing: The Complete Reference to Rock, Ice, and Indoor Climbing.* New York: Facts on File, 1985.

Clark, Ronald W. *An Eccentric in the Alps: The Story of the Rev. W. A. B. Coolidge, the Great Victorian Mountaineer.* London: Museum, 1959.

———. *Men, Myths, and Mountains.* London: Weidenfield and Nicholson, 1976.

———. *The Splendid Hills: The Life and Photographs of Vittorio Sella.* London: Phoenix House, 1948.

Clark, Ronald W., and Edward C. Pratt. *Mountaineering in Britain: A History from the Earliest Times to the Present Day.* London: Phoenix House, 1957.

Clarke, Charles, and Audrey Salkeld, eds. *Lightweight Expeditions to the Great Ranges.* London: Alpine Club, 1984.

Clinch, Nick. *A Walk in the Sky.* Seattle: Mountaineers, 1982.

Clout, Hugh. "Place Description, Regional Geography, and Area studies." In *A Century of British Geography,* edited by Roy Johnston and Michael Williams. Oxford: Oxford University Press, 2003.

Coffey, Maria. *Fragile Edge: Loss on Everest.* London: Chatto and Windus, 1989.

———. *Where the Mountain Casts Its Shadow: The Dark Side of Extreme Adventure.* New York: St. Martin's, 2003.

Collie, J. Norman. *Climbing on the Himalaya and Other Mountain Ranges.* Edinburgh: David Douglas, 1902.

Conefrey, Mick, and Tim Jordan. *Mountain Men: Tall Tales and High Adventure.* London: Boxtree, 2001.

Connor, Jeff. *Dougal Haston: The Philosophy of Risk.* Edinburgh: Canongate, 2002.

Conway, William Martin. *Climbing and Exploration in the Karakoram-Himalayas.* 2 vols. London: T. Fisher Unwin, 1894.

———. *Episodes in a Varied Life.* London: Country Life, 1932.

———. *Mountain Memories: A Pilgrimage of Romance.* London: Cassell, 1920.

Coolidge, W. A. B. *The Alps in Nature and History.* London: Methuen, 1908.

———. *Josias Simler et les origines de l'alpinisme.* Grenoble: Allier frères, 1904.

Cox, James R. *Classics in the Literature of Mountaineering and Mountain Travel from the Francis P. Farquhar Collection of Mountaineering Literature: An Annotated Bibliography.* Los Angeles: University of California Library, 1980.

Craig, Gordon A. *Germany, 1866–1945.* Oxford: Oxford University Press, 1978.

Crowley, Aleister. *The Confessions of Aleister Crowley: An Autohagiography.* Edited by John Symonds and Kenneth Grant. London: Arkana, 1979.

Curran, Jim. *High Achiever: The Life and Climbs of Chris Bonington.* London: Constable, 1999.

———. *K2: The Story of the Savage Mountain.* Seattle: Mountaineers, 1995.

The Dalai Lama. *My Land and My People.* New York: McGraw-Hill, 1962.

Dana, Francis. "Elders of the Tribe: 7, Fanny Bullock Workman." *Backpack* 2 (Fall 1974).

Das, Sarat Chandra. *Journey to Lhasa and Central Tibet.* London: Murray, 1902.

Davenport-Hines, Richard. "Houston, Dame Fanny Lucy (1857–1936)." *Oxford Dictionary of National Biography.* Oxford: Oxford University Press, 2004.

Day, James Wentworth. *Lady Houston, DBE: The Woman Who Won the War.* London: A. Wingate, 1958.

Deacock, Antonia. *No Purdah in Padam: The Story of the Women's Overland Himalayan Expedition.* London: George G. Harrap, 1960.

Decker, Ronald. "Crowley, Aleister (1875–1947)." *Oxford Dictionary of National Biography.* Oxford: Oxford University Press, 2004.

De Filippi, Filippo, ed. *An Account of Tibet: The Travels of Ippolito Desieri of Pistoia, S.J., 1712–1727.* London: Routledge and Sons, 1931.

———. *The Ascent of Mount St. Elias by H.R.H. Prince Luigi Amedeo di Savoia, Duke of the Abruzzi.* London: Constable, 1900.

———. *Karakoram and Western Himalaya 1909: An Account of the Expedition of H.R.H. Prince Luigi Amedeo of Savoy, Duke of the Abruzzi.* New York: Dutton, 1912.

———. *Ruwenzori: An Account of the Expedition of H.R.H. Prince Luigi Amedeo di Savoia, Duke of the Abruzzi.* London: Constable, 1908.

Defrance, Jacques, and Oliver Holblan. *Lucien Devies: La montagne pour vocation.* Paris: Sports en Société, 2004.

Denman, Earl. *Alone to Everest.* New York: Coward-McCann, 1954.

Desio, Ardito, *Ascent of K2.* London: Elek, 1955.

———. *Victory over K2: Second Highest Peak in the World.* New York: McGraw-Hill, 1956.

Desmond, Ray. *Sir Joseph Dalton Hooker: Traveler and Plant Collector.* Woodbridge, Conn.: Antique Collectors' Club with Royal Botanic Gardens, Kew, 1999.

Dickinson, Leo. *Ballooning over Everest.* London: Jonathan Cape, 1993.

Diemberger, Kurt. *The Kurt Diemberger Omnibus.* Seattle: Mountaineers, 1999.

———. *Summits and Secrets.* London: Allen and Unwin, 1971.

Dittert, René, and Gabriel Chevalley. *Forerunners to Everest: The Story of the Two Swiss Expeditions of 1952.* London: Allen and Unwin, 1954.

Doig, Desmond. *High in the Thin Cold Air: The Story of the Himalayan Expedition Led by Sir Edmund Hillary, Sponsored by World Book Encyclopedia.* Garden City, N.Y.: Doubleday, 1962.

Douglas, Ed. *Chomolungma Sings the Blues: Travels round Everest.* London: Constable, 1997.

———. *Tenzing, Hero of Everest: A Biography of Tenzing Norgay.* Washington, D.C.: National Geographic, 2003.

Douglas, William O. *Exploring the Himalaya.* New York: Random House, 1958.

Douglas and Clydesdale, the Marquis of, and D. F. McIntyre. *The Pilots' Book of Everest.* London: W. Hodge, 1936.

Douglas-Hamilton, James. *Roof of the World: Man's First Flight over Everest.* Edinburgh: Mainstream, 1983.

Drew, Frederick. *The Jummoo and Kashmir Territories: A Geographical Account.* London: E. Stanford, 1875.

Dunsheath, Joyce. *Mountains and Memsahibs.* London: Constable, 1958.

Durand, A. G. A. *Making of a Frontier: Five Years' Experiences and Adventures in Gilgit, Hunza, Nagar, Chitral, and the Eastern Hindu-Kush.* London: Murray, 1899.

Dyhrenfurth, G. O. *Das Buch von Nanga Parbat.* Munich: Nymphenburger Verlagshaus, 1954.

―――. *To the Third Pole: The History of the High Himalaya.* London: Werner Laurie, 1955.

Eckenstein, Oscar. *The Karakorams and Kashmir: An Account of a Journey.* London: T. Fisher Unwin, 1896.

Edney, Matthew H. *Mapping an Empire: The Geographical Construction of British India, 1765–1843.* Chicago: University of Chicago Press, 1997.

Eggler, Albert. *The Everest-Lhotse Adventure.* London: Allen and Unwin, 1957.

Eiselin, Max. *The Ascent of Dhaulagiri.* London: Oxford University Press, 1961.

Ellis, Reuben. *Vertical Margins: Mountaineering and the Landscapes of Neoimperialism.* Madison: University of Wisconsin Press, 2001.

Engel, Claire. *A History of Mountaineering in the Alps.* London: Allen and Unwin, 1950.

Engle, Dean. *Talus: A History of the Dartmouth Mountaineering Club.* Portsmouth, N.H.: Peter E. Randall, 1993.

Evans, Charles. *Kangchenjunga: The Untrodden Peak.* London: Hodder and Stoughton, 1956.

Evans, Joan. *The Conways: A History of Three Generations.* London: Museum, 1966.

Fanshawe, Andy. *Coming Through: Expeditions to Chogolisa and Menlungtse.* London: Hodder and Stoughton, 1990.

Fanshawe, Andy, and Stephen Venables. *Himalaya Alpine-Style: The Most Challenging Routes on the Highest Peaks.* Seattle: Mountaineers, 1996.

Faux, Ronald. *High Ambition: A Biography of Reinhold Messner.* London: Gollancz, 1982.

Fay, Charles Ernest. *A Century of American Alpinism.* Boulder: American Alpine Club, 2002.

Fellowes, P. F. M. *First over Everest! The Houston-Mount Everest Expedition, 1933.* New York: Robert M. McBridge, 1934.

Finch, George Ingle. *The Making of a Mountaineer.* London: Arrowsmith, 1924.

Finkelstein, Gabriel. "'Conquerors of the Künlün'? The Schlagintweit Mission to High Asia, 1854–57." *History of Science* 38 (2002): 179–218.

Finsterwalder, Richard, Walter Raechl, Peter Misch, and Fritz Bechtold. *Forschung am Nanga Parbat: Deutsche Himalaya-expedition 1934.* Hannover: Helwingsche Verlagsbuchhandlung, 1935.

Firstbrook, Peter. *Lost on Everest: The Search for Mallory and Irvine.* Chicago: Contemporary, 1999.

Fleming, Fergus. *Killing Dragons: The Conquest of the Alps.* New York: Atlantic Monthly, 2000.

Fleming, Jon, and Ronald Faux. *Soldiers on Everest: The Joint Army Mountaineering Association—Royal Nepalese Army Mount Everest Expedition, 1976.* London: HMSO, 1977.

Fleming, Peter. *Bayonets to Lhasa: The First Full Account of the British Invasion of Tibet in 1904.* New York: Harper, 1961.

Forsyth, Ethel, ed. *Autobiography and Reminiscences of Sir Douglas Forsyth, C.B.* London: R. Bentley, 1887.

Franco, Jean. *Makalu 8470 Metres: The Highest Peak Yet Conquered by an Entire Team.* London: Jonathan Cape, 1957.

Franco, Jean, and Lionel Terray. *At Grips with Jannu.* London: Gollancz, 1967.

French, Patrick. *Younghusband: The Last Great Imperial Adventurer.* London: Harper Collins, 1994.

Freshfield, Douglas. *The Exploration of the Caucasus; With Illustrations by Vittorio Sella.* London: E. Arnold, 1896.

———. *Round Kangchenjunga: A Narrative of Mountain Travel and Exploration.* London: E. Arnold, 1903.

———. *Travels in the Central Caucasus and Bashan.* London: Longmans, Green, 1869.

Frison-Roche, Roger, and Sylvain Jouty. *A History of Mountain Climbing.* New York: Flammarion, 1996.

Fürer-Haimendorf, Christoph von. *The Sherpas of Nepal: Buddhist Highlanders.* Berkeley: University of California Press, 1964.

———. *The Sherpas Transformed: Social Change in a Buddhist Society of Nepal.* New Delhi: Sterling, 1984.

Gammelgaard, Lene. *Climbing High: A Woman's Account of Surviving the Everest Tragedy.* Seattle: Seal, 1999.

Geology and Tectonics of the Himalaya. Calcutta: Geological Survey of India, 1989.

Gesner, Konrad. *On the Admiration of Mountains: The Prefatory Letter Addressed to Jacob Avienus, Physician, in Gesner's Pamphlet "On Milk and Substances Prepared from Milk," First Printed at Zürich in 1543.* Translated by William Dock. San Francisco: Grabhorn, 1937.

Ghose, Indira. *Women Travellers in Colonial India: The Power of the Female Gaze.* Delhi: Oxford University Press, 1998.

Gillman, Peter. *Everest: Eighty Years of Triumph and Tragedy.* Seattle: Mountaineers, 2000.

———. *In Balance: Twenty Years of Mountaineering Journalism.* London: Hodder and Stoughton, 1989.

Gillman, Peter, and Leni Gillman. *The Wildest Dream: Mallory, His Life and Conflicting Passions.* London: Headline, 2000.

Gillman, Peter, Dougal Haston, and Chris Bonington. *Eiger Direct.* London: Collins, 1966.

Gilmour, David. *Curzon: Imperial Statesman.* New York: Farrar, Straus and Giroux, 1994.

Goldstein, Melvyn. *The Snow Lion and the Dragon: China, Tibet, and the Dalai Lama.* Berkeley: University of California Press, 1997.

Goswami, S. M. *Everest: Is It Conquered?* Calcutta: India, 1954.

Graham, W. W., and Joseph Thomson. *From the Equator to the Pole: Adventures of Recent Discovery by Eminent Travellers.* London: W. Ibister, 1886.

———. "Up the Himalayas: Mountaineering on the India Alps." *Good Words* 26 (1885): 18–23, 97–105, 172–78.

Graham Brown, Thomas. *Brenva.* London: J. M. Dent, 1944.

Graves, Robert. *Good-bye to All That.* 2nd ed. New York: Anchor, 1958.

Green, Dudley. *Mallory of Everest.* Burnley, England: Faust, 1990.

Greene, Raymond. *Moments of Being: The Random Recollections of Raymond Greene.* London: Heinemann, 1974.

Greenhalgh, Paul. *Ephemeral Vistas: The 'Expositions Universelles,' Great Exhibitions and World's Fairs, 1851–1939.* Manchester: Manchester University Press, 1988.

Gregory, Alfred. *Alfred Gregory's Everest.* London: Constable, 1993.

———. *The Picture of Everest.* London: Hodder and Stoughton, 1954.

Gribble, Francis. *The Early Mountaineers.* London: T. E. Unwin, 1899.

Grob, Ernst, and Ludwig Schmader. *Drei in Himalaja.* Munich: Bruckmann, 1938.

Grunfeld, A. Tom. *The Making of Modern Tibet.* Armonk, N.Y.: M. E. Sharpe, 1987.

Gupta, Raj Kumar. *Bibliography of the Himalayas.* Gurgaon: India Documentation Service, 1981.

Habeler, Peter. *The Lonely Victory: Mount Everest, '78.* New York: Simon and Schuster, 1979.

Hackett, June, and Ric Conrad. *Climb to Glory: The Adventures of Bill Hackett.* Beaverton, Ore.: K2, 2003.

Hagen, Toni, G. O. Dyhrenfurth, Christoph von Fürer-Haimendorf, and Erwin Schneider. *Mount Everest: Formation, Population, and Exploration of the Everest Region.* London: Oxford University Press, 1963.

Haines, Charles S. "Re-routing/Rooting the Nation State: The Karakoram Highway and the Making of the Northern Areas, Pakistan." Ph.D. diss., University of Wisconsin–Madison, 2000.

Hale, Christopher. *Himmler's Crusade: The Nazi Expedition to Find the Origins of the Aryan Race.* Hoboken, NJ: John Wiley, 2003.

Hansen, Peter H. "Albert Smith, the Alpine Club, and the Invention of Mountaineering in Mid-Victorian Britain." *Journal of British Studies* 34 (July 1995): 300–24.

———. "British Mountaineering, 1850–1914." Ph.D. diss., Harvard University, 1991.

———. "Confetti of Empire: The Conquest of Everest in Nepal, India, Britain, and New Zealand." *Comparative Studies in Society and History* (Apr. 2000): 307–32.

————. "Coronation Everest: The Empire and Commonwealth in the 'Second Elizabethan Age.'" In *British Culture and the End of Empire,* edited by Stuart Ward. Manchester: Manchester University Press, 2001.

————. "The Dancing Lamas of Everest: Cinema, Orientalism, and Anglo-Tibetan Relations in the 1920s." *American Historical Review* 101 (June 1996): 712–47.

————. "Partners: Guides and Sherpas in the Alps and Himalayas, 1850s–1950s." In *Voyages and Visions: Towards a Cultural History of Travel* edited by Jas Elsner and Joan-Pau Rubiés. London: Reaktion, 1999.

————. "Vertical Boundaries, National Identities: British Mountaineering on the Frontiers of Europe and the Empire, 1868–1914." *Journal of Imperial and Commonwealth History* 24 (Jan. 1996): 48–71.

Hansen, Peter H., and Gordon T. Stewart. "Debate: Tenzing's Two Wrist-Watches: The Conquest of Everest and Late Imperial Culture in Britain, 1921–1953." *Past and Present* 157 (Nov. 1997): 159–90.

Hardie, Norman. *In Highest Nepal: Our Life among the Sherpas.* London: Allen and Unwin, 1957.

Harper, Stephen. *Lady Killer Peak: A Lone Man's Story of Twelve Women on a Killer Mountain.* London: World Distributors, 1965.

Harrer, Heinrich. *Seven Years in Tibet.* London: Rupert Hart-Davis, 1953.

Harvard, Andrew, and Todd Thompson. *Mountain of Storms: The American Expeditions to Dhaulagiri, 1969 and 1973.* New York: New York University Press, 1974.

Haston, Dougal. *In High Places.* Edinburgh: Canongate, 1997.

Heim Arnold, and August Gansser. *The Throne of the Gods: An Account of the First Swiss Expedition to the Himalayas.* New York: Macmillan, 1939.

Hemmleb, Jochen, Larry A. Johnson, and Eric R. Simonson. *Ghosts of Everest: The Search for Mallory and Irvine.* Seattle: Mountaineers, 1999.

Hemmleb, Jochen, and Eric R. Simonson. *Detectives on Everest: The 2001 Mallory and Irvine Research Expedition.* Seattle: Mountaineers, 2002.

Herrligkoffer, Karl M. *Nanga Parbat.* New York: Alfred A. Knopf, 1954.

Herzog, Maurice. *Annapurna: First Conquest of an 8000-Meter Peak.* New York: Dutton, 1952.

Hillary, Sir Edmund. *High Adventure.* New York: Dutton, 1955.

————. *No Latitude for Error.* London: Hodder and Stoughton, 1961.

————. *Nothing Venture, Nothing Win.* New York: Coward, McCann, and Geoghegan, 1975.

————. "Postscript to This Edition." In *The Ascent of Everest,* by John Hunt. London: Hodder and Stoughton, 1993.

————. *Schoolhouse in the Clouds.* London: Hodder and Stoughton, 1964.

————. *View from the Summit.* New York: Pocket, 1999.

Hillary, Sir Edmund, and George Lowe. *East of Everest: An Account of the New Zealand Alpine Club Himalayan Expedition to the Barun Valley in 1954.* London: Hodder and Stoughton, 1956.

Hoffman, Elizabeth Cobbs. *All You Need Is Love: The Peace Corps and the Spirit of the 1960s.* Cambridge, Mass.: Harvard University Press, 1998.

Höfler, Horst, ed. *Nanga Parbat: Expeditionen zum "Schicksalsberg der Deutschen," 1934–1962.* Zurich: AS Verlag and Buchkonzept AG, 2002.

Holborn, Hajo. *A History of Modern Germany, 1840–1945.* New York: Alfred A. Knopf, 1969.

Holroyd, Michael. *Lytton Strachey: A Critical Biography.* 2 vols. New York: Holt, Rinehart, and Winston, 1968.

Holzel, Tom, and Audrey Salkeld. *The Mystery of Mallory and Irvine.* Rev. ed. Seattle: Mountaineers, 1999.

Hooker, Joseph Dalton. *Himalayan Journals; or, Notes of a Naturalist in Bengal, the Sikkim and Nepal Himalayas, the Khasia Mountains, &c.* London: Murray, 1854.

Hopkirk, Peter. *The Great Game: On Secret Service in High Asia.* London: Murray, 1990.

———. *Trespassers on the Roof of the World: The Secret Exploration of Tibet.* London: Murray, 1982.

Hornbein, Thomas F. *Everest: The West Ridge.* Seattle: Mountaineers, 1999.

Hornbein, Thomas F., and Robert B. Schoene, *High Altitude: An Exploration of Human Adaptation.* New York: Marcel Dekker, 2001.

Houston, Charles S. *Going Higher: The Story of Man and Altitude.* 4th ed. Seattle: Mountaineers, 1998.

———. "Introductory Memoir." In *Nanda Devi: Exploration and Ascent,* by Eric Shipton and H. W. Tilman. Seattle: Mountaineers, 2000.

Houston, Charles S., and Robert H. Bates. *K2: The Savage Mountain.* New York: McGraw-Hill, 1954. Reprint, Guilford, Conn.: Lyons, 2000.

Houston, Charles S., and R. L. Riley. "Respiratory and Circulatory Changes during Acclimatisation to High Altitude." *American Journal of Physiology* 149 (1947): 565–88.

Howard-Bury, C. K. *Mount Everest: The Reconnaissance, 1921.* London: E. Arnold, 1922.

Hunt, John. *The Ascent of Everest.* London: Hodder and Stoughton, 1953. Reprint, Seattle: Mountaineers, 1998.

———. *Life Is Meeting.* London: Hodder and Stoughton, 1978.

———. *Our Everest Adventure: The Pictorial History from Kathmandu to the Summit.* New York: Dutton, 1954.

Huxley, Leonard. *Life and Letters of Joseph Dalton Hooker.* London: Murray, 1918.

Isserman, Maurice, and Michael Kazin. *America Divided: The Civil War of the 1960s.* 2nd ed. New York: Oxford University Press, 2004.

Italian Alpine Club. *1863–1963: I cento anni del Club alpino italiano.* Milan: Club Alpino Italiano, 1964.

Izzard, Ralph. *An Innocent on Everest.* New York: Dutton, 1954.

Jackson, Monica, and Elizabeth Stark. *Tents in the Clouds: The First Women's Himalayan Expedition.* London: Collins, 1956.

Jacot-Guillarmod, J. "Au Kangchinjunga: Voyage et explorations dans l'Himalaya du Sikhim et du Népal." *L'écho des Alpes* 8–9 (1914): 389–406, 425–44.

————. *Six mois dans L'Himalaya, le Karakoram, et L'Hindu-Kush: Voyages et explorations aus plus hautes montagnes du monde.* Neuchatel: W. Sandoz, 1904.

Jamling Tenzing Norgay, with Broughton Coburn. *Touching My Father's Soul: A Sherpa's Journey to the Top of Everest.* San Francisco: Harper Collins, 2001.

Japanese Alpine Club. *Japanese Alpine Centenary, 1905–2005.* Tokyo: Japanese Alpine Club, 2006.

Jenkins, McKay. *The Last Ridge: The Epic Story of the U.S. Army's 10th Mountain Division and the Assault on Hitler's Europe.* New York: Random House, 2003.

Johnston, Alexa. *Reaching the Summit: Sir Edmund Hillary's Life of Adventure.* New York: DK, 2005.

Jones, Chris. *Climbing in North America.* Seattle: Mountaineers, 1997.

Jordan, Jennifer. *Savage Summit: The True Stories of the First Five Women Who Climbed K2.* New York: Harper Collins, 2005.

Joshi, Bhuwan Lal, and Leo E. Rose. *Democratic Innovations in Nepal: A Case Study of Political Acculturation.* Berkeley: University of California Press, 1966.

Kater, Michael. *Das "Ahnenerbe" der SS, 1935–1945: Ein Beitrag zur Kulturpolitik des Dritten Reiches.* Stuttgart: Deutsche Verlagts-Anstalt, 1974.

Kauffman, Andrew J., and William L. Putnam. *K2: The 1939 Tragedy.* Seattle: Mountaineers, 1992.

Keay, John. *The Gilgit Game: The Explorers of the Western Himalayas, 1865–1895.* London: Murray, 1979.

————. *The Great Arc: The Dramatic Tale of How India Was Mapped and Everest Was Named.* New York: Harper Collins, 2000.

————. *India: A History.* New York: Grove, 2000.

————. *When Men and Mountains Meet: The Explorers of the Western Himalayas, 1820–1875.* London: Murray, 1977.

Kennedy, Dane. *The Magic Mountains: Hill Stations and the British Raj.* Berkeley: University of California Press, 1996.

Kienlin, Max-Engelhardt von. *Die Uberschreitung: Günther Messners Tod am Nanga Parbat: Expeditionsteilnehmer brechen ihr Schweigen.* Munich: Herbig, 2003.

King, John. *Karakoram Highway, the High Road to China: A Travel Survival Kit.* Hawthorn, Australia: Lonely Plant, 1993.

Klarner, Januscz. *Nanda Devi.* Warsaw: Czytelnik, 1950.

Knight, E. F. *Where Three Empires Meet: A Narrative of Recent Travel in Kashmir, Western Tibet, Gilgit, and the Adjoining Countries.* London: Longmans, Green, 1893.

Knowlton, Elizabeth. *The Naked Mountain.* New York: G. P. Putnam's Sons, 1933.

Kohli, M. S. "Himalayan Tourism and Environment." *Himalayan Journal* 38 (1979–80): 150–54.

————. *Last of the Annapurnas.* Delhi: Ministry of Information and Broadcasting, 1962.

————. *Miracles of Ardaas: Incredible Adventures and Survivals.* New Delhi: Indus, 2003.

————. *Mountaineering in India.* New Delhi: Vikas, 1989.

————. *Sherpas: Himalayan Legends.* New Delhi: UBSPD, 2003.

Kohli, M. S., and Kenneth Conboy. *Spies in the Himalayas: Secret Missions and Perilous Climbs.* Lawrence: University Press of Kansas, 2002.

Kolb, Fritz. *Himalaya Venture.* London: Lutterworth, 1959.

Konecny, Gottfried. "Die Angange der Photogrammetrie in Hannover." http://www.ipi .uni-hannover.de/html/ipiinform/50_jahre_ipi.pdf.n.

Kotani, A., and K. Yasuhisa. *Japan Everest Skiing Expedition.* Tokyo: n.p., 1970.

Krakauer, Jon. *Eiger Dreams.* New York: Lyons, 1990.

————. *Into Thin Air: A Personal Account of the Mt. Everest Disaster.* New York: Villard, 1997.

Krawczyk, Chess. *Mountaineering: A Bibliography of Books in English to 1974.* Metuchen, N.J.: Scarecrow, 1977.

Kreutzmann, Hermann. "The Karakoram Highway: The Impact of Road Construction on Mountain Societies." *Modern Asian Studies* 45 (Oct. 1991): 711–36.

Kukuczka, Jerzy. *My Vertical World.* Seattle: Mountaineers, 1992.

Kurz, Marcel. *Chronique himalayenne: L'âge d'or, 1940–1955.* Zurich: Fondation Suisse pour Explorations Alpines, 1959.

Lacedelli, Lino, and Giovanni Cenacchi, *K2: Il prezzo della conquista.* Milan: Mondadori, 2004.

Lachenal, Louis. *Carnets du vertige.* Paris: Pierre Horay, 1956.

Lamb, Alistair. *British India and Tibet, 1766–1910.* London: Routledge and Kegan Paul, 1986.

Lambert, Raymond, and Claude Kogan. *White Fury: Gaurisankar and Cho Oyu.* London: Hurst and Blackett, 1956.

Lane, Bronco. *Military Mountaineering: A History of Services Mountaineering, 1945–1970.* Cumbria, England: Hay Loft, 2000.

Lasch, Christopher. *The Culture of Narcissism: American Life in an Age of Diminishing Expectations.* New York: W. W. Norton, 1978.

Leamer, Lawrence. *Ascent: The Spiritual and Physical Quest of Willi Unsoeld.* New York: Simon and Schuster, 1982.

Leonard, Richard M., and Arnold Wexler. *Belaying the Leader: An Omnibus on Climbing Safety.* San Francisco: Sierra Club, 1956.

Lewis, Brenda Ralph. "No Mountain Too High." *Aviation* (Nov. 1993): 46–53.

Longland, Jack. "Ruttledge, Hugh (1884–1961)." *Dictionary of National Biography.* Oxford: Oxford University Press, 1981.

Longstaff, Thomas George. *This My Voyage.* New York: Charles Scribners' Sons, 1950.

Lowe, George. *Because It Is There.* London: Cassell, 1959.

Lunn, Arnold. *A Century of Mountaineering.* London: Allen and Unwin, 1957.

Macdonald, Alexander W. "The Lama and the General." *Kailash: A Journal of Himalayan Studies* 1 (1973): 225–33.

Macfarlane, Robert. *Mountains of the Mind: How Desolate and Forbidding Heights Were Transformed into Experiences of Indomitable Spirit.* New York: Pantheon, 2003.

Mackenzie, John. *Propaganda and Empire: The Manipulation of British Public Opinion, 1880–1960.* Manchester: Manchester University Press, 1984.

Madge, Tim. *The Last Hero: Bill Tilman, a Biography of the Explorer.* Seattle: Mountaineers, 1995.

Mallory, George. *Boswell the Biographer.* London: Smith, Elder, 1912.

———. "The Mountaineer as Artist." *Climber's Club Journal* 3 (Mar. 1914): 28–40.

———. *War Work for Boys and Girls.* London: Allen and Unwin, 1916.

Mantovani, Roberto, and Kurt Diemberger. *K2: Challenging the Sky.* New York: Smithmark, 1995.

Maraini, Fosco. *Karakoram: The Ascent of Gasherbrum IV.* New York: Viking, 1961.

Markham, Clements R. *A Memoir on the Indian Surveys.* London: Allen, 1878.

———, ed. *Narratives of the Mission of George Bogle to Tibet.* London: Trübner, 1876.

Märtin, Ralf-Peter. *Nanga Parbat: Wahrheit und Wahn des Alpinismus.* Berlin: Berlin Verlag, 2002.

Mason, Kenneth. *Abode of Snow: A History of Himalayan Exploration and Mountaineering.* New York: Dutton, 1955.

Matthews, C. E. *The Annals of Mont Blanc.* London: T. Fisher Unwin, 1898.

McCallum, John D. *Everest Diary: Based on the Personal Diary of Lute Jerstad.* Chicago: Follett, 1996.

McCormick, A. D. *An Artist in the Himalayas.* London: Unwin, 1895.

McDonald, Bernadette. *Brotherhood of the Rope: The Biography of Charles Houston.* Seattle: Mountaineers, 2007.

———. *"I'll Call You in Kathmandu": The Elizabeth Hawley Story.* Seattle: Mountaineers, 2005.

McDonald, Bernadette, and John Amott, eds. *Voices from the Summit: The World's Great Mountaineers on the Future of Climbing.* Washington, D.C.: National Geographic, 2000.

Mehta, Soli, and Harish Kapadia. *Exploring the Hidden Himalaya.* London: Hodder and Stoughton, 1990.

Messner, Reinhold. *Annapurna: 50 Years of Expeditions in the Death Zone.* Seattle: Mountaineers, 2000.

———. *The Big Walls.* Seattle: Mountaineers, 2001.

———. *The Challenge.* New York: Oxford University Press, 1977.

———. *The Crystal Horizon: Everest—The First Solo Ascent.* Seattle: Mountaineers, 1989.

———. *Everest: Expedition to the Ultimate.* Seattle: Mountaineers, 1999.

———. *Free Spirit: A Climber's Life.* Seattle: Mountaineers, 1991.

———. *K2: Mountain of Mountains.* New York: Oxford University Press, 1982.

———. *The Naked Mountain.* Seattle: Mountaineers, 2003.

———. *The Second Death of George Leigh Mallory: The Enigma and Spirit of Mount Everest.* New York: St. Martin's, 2001.

———. *Solo Nanga Parbat.* New York: Oxford University Press, 1981.

Messner, Reinhold, and Horst Höfler. *Hermann Buhl: Climbing without Compromise.* Seattle: Mountaineers, 2000.

Meyer, Karl E., and Shareen Blair Brysac. *Tournament of Shadows: The Great Game and the Race for Empire in Central Asia.* Washington, D.C.: Counterpoint, 1999.

Middendorf, John. "The Mechanical Advantage: Tools for the Wild Vertical." In *Ascent: The Climbing Experience in Words and Image,* edited by Allen Steck, Steve Roper, and David Harris. Golden, Colo.: American Alpine Club, 1999.

Middleton, Dorothy. *Victorian Lady Travellers.* London: Routledge and Kegan Paul, 1965.

Mierau, Peter. *Die Deutsche Himalaja-Stiftung von 1936 bis 1998: Ihre Geschichte und Ihre Expeditionen.* Munich: Bergverlag Rudolf Rother, 1999.

Mill, Christine. *Norman Collie: A Life in Two Worlds.* Aberdeen: Aberdeen University Press, 1987.

Miller, Luree. *On Top of the World: Five Women Explorers in Tibet.* London: Paddington, 1976.

Mills, Sara. *Discourses of Difference: An Analysis of Women's Travel Writing and Colonialism.* London: Routledge, 1991.

Miura, Yuichiro. *The Man Who Skied Down Everest.* New York: Harper and Row, 1978.

Moravec, Fritz. *Weisse Berge—Schwartze Menschen.* Vienna: Österreichischer Bundesverlag, 1958.

Morin, Nea. *A Woman's Reach: Mountaineering Memoirs.* New York: Dodd, Mead, 1968.

Morris, James. *Coronation Everest.* London: Faber and Faber, 1958.

Morrow, Baiba, and Pat Morrow. *Footsteps in the Clouds: Kangchenjunga a Century Later.* Vancouver, B.C.: Raincoast, 1999.

Mountaineering in China. Beijing: Foreign Languages, 1965.

Mumm, A. L. *Five Months in the Himalaya: A Record of Mountain Travel in Garhwal and Kashmir.* London: E. Arnold, 1909.

Mummery, A. F. *My Climbs in the Alps and Caucasus.* London: T. Fisher Unwin, 1895. 2nd ed., London: T. Fisher Unwin, 1908.

Murray, W. H. *The Evidence of Things Not Seen: A Mountaineer's Tale.* London: Baton Wicks, 2002.

———. *The Scottish Himalayan Expedition.* London: J. M. Dent and Sons, 1951.

———. *The Story of Everest.* London: J. M. Dent and Sons, 1953.

Neale, Jonathan. *Tigers of the Snow: How One Fateful Climb Made the Sherpas Mountaineering Legends.* New York: St. Martin's, 2002.

Neate, Jill. *High Asia: An Illustrated History of the 7,000 Metre Peaks.* Seattle: Mountaineers, 1989.

Neate, W. R. *Mountaineering and Its Literature: A Descriptive Bibliography of Selected Works Published in the English Language, 1744–1976.* Seattle: Mountaineers, 1980.

Neve, Arthur. *Thirty Years in Kashmir.* London: E. Arnold, 1913.

Neve, Ernest F. *Beyond the Pir Panjal: Life and Missionary Enterprise in Kashmir.* London: Church Missionary Society, 1914.

————. *A Crusader in Kashmir: Being the Life of Dr. Arthur Neve, with an Account of the Medical Missionary Work of Two Brothers and Its Later Developments Down to the Present Day.* London: Seeley, Service, 1928.

Nicolson, Marjorie Hope. *Mountain Gloom and Mountain Glory: The Development of the Aesthetics of the Infinite.* Ithaca, N.Y.: Cornell University Press, 1959.

Noel, J. B. L. "Photographing *The Epic of Everest:* How the Camera Recorded Man's Battle against the Highest Mountain in the World." *Asia* 27 (1927): 366–73.

————. *Through Tibet to Everest.* London: E. Arnold, 1927.

Norton, E. F. *The Fight for Everest, 1924.* New York: Longmans, Green, 1925.

Noyce, Wilfrid. *South Col: A Personal Story of the Ascent of Everest.* New York: William Sloane, 1955.

Noyce, Wilfrid, and Ian McMorrin, eds. *World Atlas of Mountaineering.* London: Thomas Nelson and Sons, 1969.

Nunn, Paul. *At the Sharp End.* London: Unwin Hyman, 1988.

O'Connell, Nicholas. *Beyond Risk: Conversations with Climbers.* Seattle: Mountaineers, 1993.

Olds, Elizabeth Fagg. *Women of the Four Winds.* Boston: Houghton Mifflin, 1985.

Ortner, Sherry B. *Life and Death on Mt. Everest: Sherpas and Himalayan Mountaineering.* Princeton: Princeton University Press, 1999.

Pallis, Marco. *Peaks and Lamas.* New York: Alfred A. Knopf, 1949.

Palmer, Dek. *A Price Guide to Books concerning Mountaineering in the Himalayas.* Philadelphia: Northern Liberties, 2002.

Patey, Tom. *One Man's Mountains: Essays and Verses.* London: Gollancz, 1971.

Patterson, Bruce. *Canadians on Everest.* Calgary: Detselig Enterprises, 1990.

Pemble, John. *The Invasion of Nepal: John Company at War.* Oxford: Oxford University Press, 1971.

Perrin, Jim. Introduction to *The Six Mountain-Travel Books,* by Eric Shipton. Seattle: Mountaineers, 1997.

————. *The Villain: A Portrait of Don Whillans.* Seattle: Mountaineers, 2005.

Petzoldt, Patricia. *On Top of the World: My Adventures with My Mountain-Climbing Husband.* New York: Thomas Y. Crowell, 1953.

Phillimore, R. H. *Historical Records of the Survey of India.* Dehra Dun: Survey of India, 1945.

Pielmeier, John. *Willi: An Evening of Wilderness and Spirit, Adapted from the Speeches of Willi Unsoeld.* Seattle: Rain City Projects, 1991.

Pierre, Bernard. *A Mountain Called Nun Kun.* London: Hodder and Stoughton, 1955.

Poole, Robert. *Explorer's House: National Geographic and the World It Made.* New York: Penguin, 2004.

Potterfield, Peter. *In the Zone: Epic Survival Stories from the Mountaineering World.* Seattle: Mountaineers, 1996.

Pringle, Heather. *The Master Plan: Himmler's Scholars and the Holocaust.* New York: Hyperion, 2006.

Pugh, Griffith. "Cardiac Output in Muscular Exercise at 5800m (19,000ft)." *Journal of Applied Physiology* 19 (1964): 441–47.

Putnam, Robert D. *Bowling Alone: The Collapse and Revival of American Community.* New York: Simon and Schuster, 2000.

Putnam, William Lowell. *Green Cognac: The Education of a Mountain Fighter.* New York: AAC, 1991.

Pye, David. *George Leigh Mallory: A Memoir.* Oxford: Oxford University Press, 1927.

Randhawa, M. S. *The Kumaon Himalayas.* New Delhi: Oxford and IBH, 1970.

Rawling, C. G. *The Great Plateau: Being an Account of Exploration in Central Tibet, 1903, and of the Gartok Expedition, 1904–1905.* London: E. Arnold, 1905.

Rawlings, John. *The Stanford Alpine Club.* Stanford, Calif.: CSLI, 1999.

Rébuffat, Gaston. *Mount Blanc to Everest.* New York: Thomas Y. Crowell, 1956.

———. *Starlight and Storm.* New York: Modern Library, 1999.

Ridgeway, Rick. *Below Another Sky: A Mountain Adventure in Search of a Lost Father.* New York: Henry Holt, 2001.

———. *The Boldest Dream: The Story of Twelve Who Climbed Mount Everest.* New York: Harcourt, Brace, Jovanovich, 1979.

———. *The Last Step: The American Ascent of K2.* Seattle: Mountaineers, 1980.

Ring, Jim. *How the English Made the Alps.* London: Murray, 2000.

Ringholz, Raye C. *On Belay! The Life of Legendary Mountaineer Paul Petzoldt.* Seattle: Mountaineers, 1997.

Ripley, S. Dillon. *A Naturalist's Adventure in Nepal: Search for the Spiny Babbler.* Boston: Houghton Mifflin, 1952.

Rittenhouse, Mignon. *Seven Women Explorers.* Philadelphia: J. B. Lippincott, 1964.

Robbins, David. "Sport, Hegemony, and the Middle Class: The Victorian Mountaineers." *Theory, Culture, and Society* 4 (1987): 579–601.

Roberts, David. "Five Who Made It to the Top." *Harvard Magazine* (Jan.–Feb. 1981): 31–40.

———. "K2 at 50: The Bitter Legacy." *National Geographic Adventure Magazine* (Sept. 2004).

———. "The K2 Mystery." *Outside* 9 (Oct. 1984): 39–44, 79–82.

———. *Moments of Doubt and Other Mountaineering Writings.* Seattle: Mountaineers, 1986.

———. *True Summit: What Really Happened on the Legendary Ascent of Annapurna.* New York: Simon and Schuster, 2000.

Roberts, Dennis. *I'll Climb Mount Everest Alone: The Story of Maurice Wilson.* London: R. Hale, 1957.

Roberts, Eric. *Welzenbach's Climbs: A Biographical Study and the Collected Writings of Willo Welzenbach.* Seattle: Mountaineers, 1981.

Robertson, David. *George Mallory.* London: Faber, 1969.

Robertson, Janet. *Betsy Cowles Partridge: Mountaineer.* Niwot: University Press of Colorado, 1998.

Robinson, Jane. *Wayward Women: A Guide to Women Travellers*. Oxford: Oxford University Press, 1990.

Roch, André. *Everest 1952*. Geneva: Editions Jeheber, 1952.

Ronaldshay, Earl of. *The Life of Lord Curzon*. 3 vols. London: Ernest Benn, 1928.

Roosevelt, Theodore, and Kermit Roosevelt. *Trailing the Giant Panda*. New York: Charles Scribners, 1929.

Roper, Robert. *Fatal Mountaineer: The High-Altitude Life and Death of Willi Unsoeld, American Himalayan Legend*. New York: St. Martin's, 2002.

Roskelley, John. *Nanda Devi: The Tragic Expedition*. New York: Stackpole, 1987.

———. *Stories Off the Wall*. Seattle: Mountaineers, 1993.

Ross, Donald, and James J. Schramer, eds. *American Travel Writers, 1850–1915*. Detroit: Gale Research, 1998.

Rowell, Galen. *In the Throne Room of the Mountain Gods*. San Francisco: Sierra Club, 1977.

———. *Many People Come, Looking, Looking*. Seattle: Mountaineers, 1980.

———. *Mountains of the Middle Kingdom: Exploring the High Peaks of China and Tibet*. San Francisco: Sierra Club, 1983.

Ruskin, John. *Modern Painters*. Vol. 4, *Mountain Beauty*. Boston: Dana Estes, 1900.

———. *Sesame and Lilies: Two Lectures Delivered at Manchester in 1864*. London: Smith Elder, 1865.

Ruttledge, Hugh. *Everest 1933*. London: Hodder and Stoughton, 1936.

———. *Everest: The Unfinished Adventure*. London: Hodder and Stoughton, 1937.

Sakai, Toshiaki. "The History of the Academic Alpine Club of Kyoto." http://www.aack.or.jp/english/history.htm.

Sale, Richard. *Broad Peak*. Hildersley, England: Carreg, 2004.

Sale, Richard, and John Cleare. *Climbing the World's 14 Highest Mountains: The History of the 8,000-Meter Peaks*. Seattle: Mountaineers, 2000.

Saler, Hans. *Zwischen Licht und Schatten: Die Messnere-Tragödie am Nanga Parbat*. Munich: A1 Verlag, 2003.

Salkeld, Audrey. "Ruttledge, Hugh (1884–1961)." *Oxford Dictionary of National Biography*. Oxford: Oxford University Press, 2004.

Sayre, Woodrow Wilson. *Four against Everest*. Englewood Cliffs, N.J.: Prentice-Hall, 1964.

Schama, Simon. *Landscape and Memory*. New York: Alfred A. Knopf, 1995.

Schamadan, Scott. "A Room with a View." http://www.frugalfun.com/room-with-a-view.html.

Schlagintweit, Hermann, Adolf Schlagintweit, and Robert von Schlagintweit. *Results of a Scientific Mission to India and High Asia, Undertaken between the Years 1854 and 1858, by Order of the Court of Directors of the Honourable East India Company*. Leipzig: F. A. Brockhaus, 1861–66.

Schmuck, Marcus. *Broad Peak 8047m: Meine Bergfahrten mit Hermann Buhl*. Salzburg and Stuttgart: Das Bergland Buch, 1958.

Schwartz, Susan. *Into the Unknown: The Remarkable Life of Hans Kraus.* Lincoln, Neb.: Universe, 2005.

Scott, Doug. Foreword to *Everest: The West Ridge,* by Thomas F. Hornbein. Seattle: Mountaineers, 1999.

———. *Himalayan Climber: A Lifetime Quest to the World's Greatest Ranges.* San Francisco: Sierra Club, 1992.

———. "Kellas, Alexander Mitchell (1868–1921)." *Oxford Dictionary of National Biography.* Oxford: Oxford University Press, 2004.

Scott, Doug, and Alex MacIntyre. *The Shishapangma Expedition.* Seattle: Mountaineers, 1984.

Scott, Robert L. Jr. *God Is My Co-pilot.* New York: Charles Scribner's Sons, 1944.

Seaver, George. *Francis Younghusband: Explorer and Mystic.* London: Murray, 1952.

Ségogne, Henri de. *Himalayan Assault: The French Himalayan Expedition, 1936.* London: Metheun, 1938.

Sheldon, George. "Lost behind the Ranges." *Saturday Evening Post,* Mar. 16, 1940, 9–11, 123–28.

Shelton, Peter. *Climb to Conquer: The Untold Story of World War II's 10th Mountain Division Ski Troops.* New York: Scribner, 2003.

Sherry, Michael. *In the Shadow of War: The United States since the 1930s.* New Haven: Yale University Press, 1995.

Shipton, Eric E. *Blank on the Map.* London: Hodder and Stoughton, 1938.

———. *Men against Everest.* Englewood Cliffs, N.J.: Prentice-Hall, 1955.

———. *Mountains of Tartary.* London: Hodder and Stoughton, 1950.

———. *The Mount Everest Reconnaissance Expedition.* London: Hodder and Stoughton, 1952.

———. *Nanda Devi.* London: Hodder and Stoughton, 1936.

———. *The Six Mountain-Travel Books.* Seattle: Mountaineers, 1997.

———. *That Untravelled World.* London: Hodder and Stoughton, 1969.

———. *Upon That Mountain.* London: Hodder and Stoughton, 1943.

Sierra Club. *Ascent, 1975–1976: The Mountaineering Experience in World and Image.* San Francisco: Sierra Club, 1976.

Singh, Gyan. *Lure of Everest: Story of the First Indian Expedition.* Delhi: Ministry of Information and Broadcasting, 1961.

Singh, Shiva Bahadur. *Impact of the Indian National Movement on the Political Development of Nepal.* New Delhi: Marwah, 1985.

Skuhra, Rudolf. *Sturm auf die Throne der Götter.* Berlin: Büchergilde Gutenberg, 1950.

Slingsby, William Cecil. *Norway, the Northern Playground: Sketches of Climbing and Mountain Exploration in Norway between 1872 and 1903.* Edinburgh: D. Douglas, 1904.

Smith, R. Harris. *OSS: The Secret History of America's First Central Intelligence Agency.* Berkeley: University of California Press, 1972.

Smythe, Frank. *The Adventures of a Mountaineer.* London: J. M. Dent, 1940.

———. *An Alpine Journey.* London: Gollancz, 1934.

———. *Climbs and Ski Runs: Mountaineering and Ski-ing in the Alps, Great Britain, and Corsica.* London: W. Blackwood and Sons, 1929.

———. *Edward Whymper.* London: Hodder and Stoughton, 1940.

———. *Kamet Conquered.* London: Gollancz, 1932.

———. *The Kangchenjunga Adventure.* London: Gollancz, 1930.

———. *The Valley of Flowers.* London: Hodder and Stoughton, 1938.

Somervell, T. Howard. *After Everest: The Experiences of a Medical Missionary.* London: Hodder and Stoughton, 1936.

Spenser, Otha C. *Flying the Hump: Memories of an Air War.* College Station: Texas A & M University Press, 1994.

Stansky, Peter. "Art, Industry, and the Aspirations of William Martin Conway." *Victorian Studies* (June 1976): 465–84.

———. *On or about December 1910: Early Bloomsbury and Its Intimate World.* Cambridge, Mass.: Harvard University Press, 1996.

Steck, Allen, Steve Roper, and David Harris, eds. *Ascent: The Climbing Experience in Words and Image.* Golden, Colo.: American Alpine Club, 1999.

Steele, Peter. *Eric Shipton: Everest and Beyond.* London: Constable, 1998.

Stephen, Leslie. *The Playground of Europe.* London: Longmans, Green, 1871.

Stetoff, Rebecca. *Women of the World: Women Travelers and Explorers.* New York: Oxford University Press, 1992.

Stevens, Stanley F. *Claiming the High Ground: Sherpas, Subsistence, and Environmental Change in the Highest Himalayas.* Berkeley: University of California Press, 1993.

Stewart, Gordon T. "Tenzing's Two Wrist-Watches: The Conquest of Everest and Late Imperial Culture in Britain, 1921–1953." *Past and Present* 149 (Nov. 1995): 170–97.

Styles, Showell. *On Top of the World: An Illustrated History of Mountaineering and Mountaineers.* London: Hamish Hamilton, 1967.

Symonds, John. *The Great Beast: The Life of Aleister Crowley.* London: Ridder, 1951.

Tarbell, Arthur. "Fanny Bullock Workmen [*sic*], Explorer and Alpinist." *New England Magazine,* n.s., 33 (Dec. 1905): 487–90.

Tashi Tenzing. *Tenzing Norgay and the Sherpas of Everest.* New York: McGraw-Hill, 2001.

Tasker, Joe. *Everest, the Cruel Way.* London: Eyre Methuen, 1981.

———. *Savage Arena.* New York: St. Martin's, 1982.

Temple, Philip. *The World at Their Feet: The Story of New Zealand Mountaineers in the Great Ranges of the World.* Christchurch, New Zealand: Whitcombe and Tombs, 1969.

Tenderini, Mirella, and Michael Shandrick. *The Duke of the Abruzzi: An Explorer's Life.* Seattle: Mountaineers, 1997.

Tenzing Norgay. *Tiger of the Snows: The Autobiography of Tenzing of Everest, Written in Collaboration with James Ramsey Ullman.* New York: G. P. Putnam's Sons, 1955.

Terray, Lionel. *Conquistadors of the Useless.* Seattle: Mountaineers, 2001.

Thapar, Romila. *A History of India.* 2 vols. Harmondsworth, England: Penguin, 1966.

Thomas, Lowell. *So Long until Tomorrow: From Quaker Hill to Kathmandu.* New York: William Morrow, 1977.

Thomas, Lowell Jr. *Out of This World: Across the Himalayas to Forbidden Tibet.* New York: Greystone, 1950.

Thompson, David, ed. *Petrarch: A Humanist among Princes.* New York: Harper and Row, 1971.

Thorington, J. Monroe. *A Survey of Early American Ascents in the Alps.* New York: American Alpine Club, 1943.

Thur, Hans, and H. Hanke. *Sieg am Nanga Parbat.* Munich: Andermann, 1954.

Tichy, Herbert. *Cho Oyu: By Favour of the Gods.* London: Methuen, 1957.

———. *Himalaya.* Delhi: Vikas, 1970.

Tilman, H. W. *The Ascent of Nanda Devi.* Cambridge: Cambridge University Press, 1937.

———. *Mount Everest 1938.* Cambridge: Cambridge University Press, 1948.

———. *Nepal Himalaya.* Cambridge: Cambridge University Press, 1952.

———. *The Seven Mountain-Travel Books.* Seattle: Mountaineers, 1983.

———. *Two Mountains and a River.* Cambridge: Cambridge University Press, 1949.

———. *When Men and Mountains Meet.* Cambridge: Cambridge University Press, 1946.

Tingley, Stephanie. "Fanny Bullock Workman." In *American Travel Writers, 1850–1915,* edited by Donald Ross and James J. Schramer. Detroit: Gale Research, 1998.

Tomoroy, David. *A Season in Heaven: True Tales from the Road to Kathmandu.* Melbourne: Lonely Planet, 1998.

Tucker, John. *Kanchenjunga.* London: Elek, 1955.

Tuker, Francis. *Gorkha: The Story of the Gurkhas of Nepal.* London: Constable, 1957.

Uemura, Naomi. *Beyond Mount Everest.* Tokyo: Bungei-shunju, 1982.

Ullman, James Ramsey. *Americans on Everest: The Official Account of the Ascent Led by Norman G. Dyhrenfurth.* Philadelphia: J. B. Lippincott, 1964.

———. *And Not to Yield.* Garden City, N.Y.: Doubleday, 1970.

———. *High Conquest: The Story of Mountaineering.* Philadelphia: J. B. Lippincott, 1941.

———. *Kingdom of Adventure: Everest.* New York: William Sloane, 1947.

———. *Straight Up: The Life and Death of John Harlin.* New York: Doubleday, 1968.

Underhill, Miriam. *Give Me the Hills.* Riverside, Conn.: Chatham/Appalachian Mountain Club, 1971.

Unsworth, Walt. *Adventure Travel for All.* Milnthorpe, England: Cicerone, 1997.

———. *The Encyclopedia of Mountaineering.* New York: Penguin, 1977.

———. *Everest: The Mountaineering History.* 3rd ed. Seattle: Mountaineers, 2000.

———. *Hold the Heights: The Foundations of Mountaineering.* Seattle: Mountaineers, 1994.

———. *Tiger in the Snow: The Life and Adventures of A. F. Mummery.* London: Gollancz, 1967.

Venables, Stephen. *Everest: Kangshung Face.* London: Hodder and Stoughton, 1989.

———, ed. *Everest: Summit of Achievement*. London: Bloomsbury, 2003.

Veyne, Paul. "L'alpinisme: Une invention de la bourgeoisie." *L'histoire* 11 (Apr. 1979): 41–49.

Viesturs, Ed. *Himalayan Quest: Ed Viesturs on the 8,000-Meter Giants*. Washington, D.C.: National Geographic Society, 2003.

Viesturs, Ed, and David Roberts. *No Shortcuts to the Top: Climbing the World's 14 Highest Peaks*. New York: Broadway, 2006.

Vigne, G. T., *Travels in Kashmir, Ladak, Iskardo, the Countries Adjoining the Mountain Course of the Indus, and the Himalaya North of the Punjab*. London: H. Coburn, 1842.

Waddell, L. Austine. *Among the Himalayas*. London: Constable, 1899.

Waller, Derek. *The Pundits: British Exploration of Tibet and Central Asia*. Lexington: University Press of Kentucky, 1988.

Ward, Michael P. *Everest: A Thousand Years of Exploration*. Glasgow: Ernest, 2003.

———. *In This Short Span: A Mountaineering Memoir*. London: Gollancz, 2003.

Ward, Michael, James Millege, and John West. *High Altitude Medicine and Physiology*. 2nd ed. London: Chapman and Hall Medical, 1995.

Washburn, Barbara. *The Accidental Adventurer: Memoir of the First Woman to Climb Mount McKinley*. Fairbanks, Alaska: Epicenter, 2001.

Washburn, Bradford, and Lew Freedman. *Bradford Washburn: An Extraordinary Life*. Portland, Ore.: WestWinds, 2005.

Waterman, Laura, and Guy Waterman. *A Fine Kind of Madness: Mountaineering Adventures, Tall and True*. Seattle: Mountaineers, 2000.

———. *Yankee Rock and Ice: A History of Climbing in the Northeastern United States*. Harrisburg, Pa.: Stackpole, 1993.

Watson, Wendy. "Picturing the Sublime: The Photographs of Vittorio Sella." In *Summit: Vittorio Sella, Mountaineer and Photographer*. New York: Aperture, 1999.

Weathers, Beck, and Stephen G. Michaud. *Left for Dead: My Journey Home from Everest*. New York: Villard, 2000.

Webster, Ed. *Snow in the Kingdom: My Storm Years on Everest*. Eldorado Springs, Colo.: Mountain Imagery, 2000.

Wessels, C. J. *Early Jesuit Travellers in Central Asia, 1603–1721*. The Hague: Nijhoff, 1924.

West, John. *Everest: The Testing Place*. New York: McGraw-Hill, 1985.

———. *High Life: A History of High-Altitude Physiology and Medicine*. New York: Oxford University Press, 1998.

Whelpton, John. *A History of Nepal*. Cambridge: Cambridge University Press, 2005.

Whillans, Don, and Alick Ormerod. *Don Whillans: Portrait of a Mountaineer*. London: William Heinemann, 1971.

Whittaker, Jim. *A Life on the Edge: Memoirs of Everest and Beyond*. Seattle: Mountaineers, 1999.

Whittaker, Lou, and Andrea Gabbard. *Lou Whittaker: Memoirs of a Mountain Guide*. Seattle: Mountaineers, 1994.

Whymper, Edward. *A Right Royal Mountaineer.* London: William Clowes and Sons, 1909.

———. *Scrambles amongst the Alps in the Years 1860–69.* London: Murray, 1871.

———. *Travels amongst the Great Andes of the Equator.* London: Murray, 1892.

Wickwire, Jim, and Dorothy Bullitt. *Addicted to Danger: A Memoir.* New York: Pocket, 1998.

Wiessner, Fritz. "The K2 Expedition of 1939." *Appalachia* (June 1956): 60–73.

———. *K2: Tragödie und Sieg am zweithöchsten Berg der Erd, mit einem einführenden Teil und einem Kapital über die Erstbesteigung des K2.* Munich: R. Rother, 1955.

Willis, Clint. *The Boys of Everest: Chris Bonington and the Tragedy of Climbing's Greatest Generation.* New York: Carroll and Graf, 2006.

Wilson, Andrew. *The Abode of Snow: Observations on a Tour from Chinese Tibet to the Indian Caucasus, through the Upper Valleys of the Himalaya.* New York: G. P. Putnam's Sons, 1875.

Wilson, Colin. *Aleister Crowley: The Nature of the Beast.* London: Harper Collins, 1987.

Woodcock, George. *Into Tibet: The Early British Explorers.* London: Faber and Faber, 1971.

Workman, Fanny Bullock, and William Hunter Workman. *Algerian Memories: A Bicycle Tour over the Atlas to the Sahara.* London: T. Fisher Unwin, 1895.

———. *Ice-Bound Heights of the Mustagh: An Account of Two Seasons of Pioneer Exploration and High Climbing in the Baltistan Himalaya.* London: Constable, 1908.

———. *In the Ice World of Himálaya.* New York: Cassell, 1900.

———. *Peaks and Glaciers of Nun Kun: A Record of Pioneer-Exploration and Mountaineering in the Punjab Himalaya.* London: Constable, 1909.

———. *Two Summers in the Ice-Wilds of Eastern Karakoram: The Exploration of Nineteen Hundred Square Miles of Mountain and Glacier.* New York: Dutton, 1917.

Workman, William Hunter, and Fanny Bullock Workman. *The Call of the Snowy Hispar: A Narrative of Exploration and Mountaineering on the Northern Frontier of India.* New York: Charles Scribner's Sons, 1911.

Yakushi, Yoshimi. *Catalogue of Himalayan Literature.* Tokyo: Hakusuisha. 1984.

Yoda, Takayoshi. *Ascent of Manaslu in Photographs.* Tokyo: Mainichi Newspapers, 1956.

Young, Geoffrey Winthrop. *Mountains with a Difference.* London: Eyre, 1951.

Young, Geoffrey Winthrop, Geoffrey Sutton, and Wilfrid Noyce. *Snowdon Biography.* London: J. M. Dent, 1957.

Younghusband, Francis Edward. *The Epic of Mount Everest.* London: E. Arnold, 1926.

———. *Everest: The Challenge.* New York: T. Nelson, 1936.

———. *The Heart of a Continent: A Narrative of Travels in Manchuria, across the Gobi Desert, through the Himalayas, the Pamirs, and Chitral, 1884–1894.* London: Murray, 1896.

———. *The Heart of Nature; or, The Quest for Natural Beauty.* London: Murray, 1921.

———. *India and Tibet: A History of the Relations Which Have Subsisted between the Two Countries from the Time of Warren Hastings to 1910; with a Particular Account of the Mission to Lhasa of 1904.* London: Murray, 1910.

Zebhauser, Helmuth. *Alpinismus im Hitlerstaat: Gedanken, Erinnergunger, Dokumente.* Munich: Bergverlag Rother, 1998.

Zhou, Zheng, and Zhenkai Liu. *Footprints on the Peaks: Mountaineering in China*. Seattle: Cloudcap, 1995.

Zimmerman, Ingelies, ed. *Paul Bauer: Wegbereiter für die Gipfelsiege von heute*. Berwang: Steiger Verlag, 1987.

Zurbriggen, Mattias. *From the Alps to the Andes: Being the Autobiography of a Mountain Guide*. London: T. Fisher Unwin, 1899.

Zurick, David, and P. P. Karan. *Himalaya: Life on the Edge of the World*. Baltimore: Johns Hopkins University Press, 1999.

Index

Abbottabad, 38, 39, 46

Abi Gamin, 8, 17, 144, 147

Abominable Snowman. *See* Yeti

Abram, Erich, 316, 318

Abruzzi, Luigi Amedeo, Duke of the, 63–65, 68, 69–74, 76, 207, 210

Ackerley, John, 446

Adams, Ansel, 68

Agassiz, Louis, 30

Agra, 11, 12, 33

Akademischer Alpenverein München, 133–35, 143, 180

Alexander the Great, 11

Alexander's Barge, 11, 199, 210

Allison, Stacy, 443

Allsup, William, 130

Allwein, Eugen, 132, 134, 135, 138, 143, 156

Almora, 4, 16, 76, 129, 131, 158

Alpine climbing, 27–32

Alpine Club, 31, 34, 35, 37, 45, 62, 74, 76, 90, 130, 140, 208, 222, 234, 275; and interwar Everest expeditions, 85, 95, 108, 117, 128, 158, 164, 190; and postwar Everest expeditions, 231, 322

Alpine Journal, 130, 131, 223, 224, 225, 226, 227, 329, 342, 346, 349, 374, 436, 447

Alpine-style climbing, 331, 334, 432, 439

Ama Dablam, 258, 351–52

American Alpine Club, 63, 207, 208, 214, 221–22, 224, 232, 233–35, 278, 336, 341, 376, 379

American Alpine Journal, 227, 326, 416, 429, 453

American Mount Everest Expedition *(1963),* 355–59, 360–75

Anglo-Nepali War, 15

Ang Tharkay, 161, 168, 171, 183, 186, 190, 191, 197, 205, 232, 243, 248, 263, 322

Annapurna I, 9, 24, 239, 241, 255, 269; *1950* expedition, 242–53, 278, 279; *1970* South Face expedition, 387, 389–94; *1978* women's expedition, 424–27

Annapurna II, 347

Annapurna III, 377

Annapurna IV, 255, 260, 327

Annapurna East, 405

Api-Saipal, 9

Appalachian Mountain Club, 67–68, 234

Apsarasas, 56

Arandu, 40

Artificial climbing, 234, 385

Arunachal Pradesh, 10

Arun River, 9, 241, 257, 264

Arun Valley, 100, 104, 257, 264

Aschenbrenner, Peter, 150, 153, 154, 172, 173, 175, 176, 178, 179–80, 300

Askole, 19, 39, 42, 52, 53, 59, 210, 220

Assam Himalaya, 10, 16, 17, 129

Astor, 40, 151

Athans, Peter, 448

Aubert, René, 271, 272

Auden, John, 204

Aufschnaiter, Peter, 135, 138, 143, 203, 225–26, 238, 350

Austrian Alpine Club, 133, 300, 304, 332

Auten, Al, 357, 369, 399
Axt, Wolfgang, 400–2
Ayres, Harry, 231, 277–78

Babusar Pass, 39, 201
Badrinath, 14, 23, 148, 170
Badrinath Range, 145
Bagrot Valley, 40
Bahuguna, Harsh, 400–2
Bakewell, Anderson, 255, 257
Ball, John, 31, 72
Balmat, Jacques, 30
Baltoro Glacier, 6, 19, 21, 39, 42, 43, 199, 208, 328
Baltoro Kangri, 43, 44, 53, 56, 199, 380
Baltoro Kangri V, 199
Baltoro Muztagh, 42, 57
Band, George, 278, 282, 286, 322–26
Bandarpunch, 205, 232
Barclays Bank, 408
Barmal Glacier, 56
Barmal La, 56
Barun Glacier, 266
Baruntse, 328
Barun Valley, 328
Bass, Dick, 447
Bates, Bob, 207–15, 227–28, 305–14, 336, 354, 445
Batura Glacier, 6
Batura Muztagh, 6
Bauer, Paul, 148–49, 156, 172, 179–82, 200, 225–
    26, 300; background, 132–35; 1929 Kangchen-
    junga expedition, 138–39; 1931 Kangchenjunga
    expedition, 143–44; 1938 Nanga Parbat expedi-
    tion, 201–3
Baur, Gerhard, 395–96
Beaufoy, Mark, 30
Bech, Cherie, 428–29
Bech, Terry, 428–29
Bechtold, Fritz, 150, 154, 172, 175, 176, 178, 200,
    201, 223
Beetham, Bentley, 117, 119
Beigel, Ernst, 135, 138
Bell, George, 306, 308, 310, 313, 347
Bell, Mark, 25
Bernard, Willy, 172, 174
Bertholet, Denis, 320
Bertulis, Alex, 379
Bhaghat Kharak Glacier, 170
Bhagirathi, 8

Bhagirathi II, 198
Bhagirathi III, 164, 197
Bhote Kosi River, 9, 24, 185, 257
Bhote Kosi Valley, 268
Bhotias, 77, 184
Biafo glacier, 6, 39, 40, 52, 210
Birnie, E. St. J. (Bill), 147, 158, 161
Bishop, Barry: 1961 scientific expedition, 351–52;
    ascent of Ama Dablam, 352; Pentagon debrief-
    ing, 352–53; 1963 Everest expedition, 357, 360,
    362–72, 399; CIA Nanda Devi operation, 378;
    trekking industry, 381
Blacker, L. V. Stewart, 159–60
Blum, Arlene, 424–27
Blum, Richard, 445
Boardman, Pete, 409–12, 440–42, 443, 445
Bogle, George, 13
Boivin, Jean Marc, 443
Bombay, 33, 46, 68, 69, 111, 145, 146
Bonatti, Walter, 235, 314–18, 337
Bonington, Chris, 387–89; 1960 Annapurna II
    expedition, 347; 1961 Nuptse expedition, 350;
    1970 Annapurna South Face expedition, 387,
    389–94; 1972 Everest expedition, 403–4; 1974
    Changabang expedition, 406–7; 1975 Everest
    Southwest Face expedition, 407–12; 1978 K2
    expedition, 427; 1982 Everest Northeast Ridge
    expedition, 442–43; 1981 Kongur expedition,
    445
Borchers, Philip, 181
Boukreev, Anatoli, 450–51
Bourdillon, Tom, 235, 277, 302; 1951 Everest
    reconnaissance, 263–67; 1952 Cho Oyu recon-
    naissance, 267–68; 1953 Everest expedition,
    278, 280–84, 286–88
Boustead, Hugh, 158, 161
Boysen, Martin, 389, 390–94, 406–12
Braham, Trevor, 447
Brahmaputra River, 2
Braldu Glacier, 6
Braldu Valley, 19, 40, 199, 210
Bramani, Vitale, 228
Breashears, David, 447
Breevort, Meta, 74
Breitenbach, Jake, 357, 361
Brenner, Julius, 135, 143
Bride's Peak. See Chogolisa
British East India Company, 12–13, 15, 17, 18

British Empire Exhibition *(1924)*, 116, 122

Broad Peak, 6, 43, 129, 331–35

Brocherel, Alexis, 66, 70, 72, 77

Brocherel, Emilio, 66, 70, 72

Brocherel, Henri, 66, 72, 77

Brocklebank, Tom, 158, 163

Brown, Joe, 322–26, 329

Brown, T. Graham, 140, 195–96, 208

Bruce, Charles Granville, 54, 74, 78, 82, 83, 86, 144, 149, 157, 166, 204; exploration with Martin Conway, 38–39, 40; with Mummery on Nanga Parbat, 46–50; proposes Everest expedition, 76–77, 81; *1922* Everest expedition, 109, 111, 112, 114; *1924* Everest expedition, 116, 120

Bruce, Geoffrey, 113, 123–24

Bryant, Dan, 183, 189, 262

Buhl, Hermann, 299–305, 320, 331–35

Bullock, Guy, 97, 100, 101, 105, 106, 107, 108

Burdsall, Dick, 207–15, 444

Burke, Mick, 390–94, 404, 407–12

Burleson, Todd, 448

Burrard, Sir Sidney, 4

Burzil Pass, 151

Cacella, Stephen, 12

Calcutta, 13, 16, 21, 33, 62, 64, 75, 97, 111, 119, 130, 135, 139, 158, 168

Campbell, Archibald, 17

Carter, Adams, 192–97, 227–28, 416–19

Casarotto, Renato, 438, 446

Cassin, Ricardo, 314–15, 337

Chadwick-Onyszkiewicz, Alison, 423, 425

Chamberlain, Joseph, 24

Chamlang, 258

Chamonix, 29–30, 31, 235, 242, 322, 388

Chandler, Chris, 415, 429

Chandra Parbat, 198

Changabang, 8, 34, 165

Changtse, 100, 105, 112, 189

Chapman, Freddie Spencer, 204

Charnock, Job, 12

Chaukhamba, 8, 198

Chettan Sherpa, 142

Chevalley, Gabrielle, 273

Chicken, Lutz, 203

Chlingensperg, Rolf von, 201

Chogolisa (Bride's Peak), 43, 72, 335, 438

Chogolisa Saddle, 72

Chogu Lungma Glacier, 18, 40, 53, 66

Chomolhari, 10, 98, 129, 204

Chomolungma. *See* Everest, Mount

Chomoyummo, 80, 99

Chongra Peak, 48, 152, 200

Cho Oyu, 9, 12, 24, 341, 376; *1952* reconnaissance, 267–68, 275; *1954* expedition, 319–21; *1959* expedition, 342

Chumbi Valley, 10, 12, 98, 111, 159

Cichy, Leszek, 406

Clark, Ronald, 66

Clarke, Charles, 409

Clean climbing, 385

Cleare, John, 402–3

Climbing hardware, 132, 148, 208, 214, 228–30, 235, 385, 408

Clinch, Nick, 314, 335–40, 347, 355, 376

Clive, Robert, 13

Clough, Ian, 389, 390–94, 404

Cobham, Sir Alan, 159

Colebrooke, Robert, 14

Coleridge, Samuel Taylor, 30

Colledge, Roy, 268

Collie, Norman, 46–50, 118, 127, 131, 149

Commercial climbing, 118, 447–52

Compagnoni, Achille, 316–18

Concordia, 6, 60, 70, 210

Connolly, Arthur, 22

Conway, William Martin, 27, 34–45, 55, 56, 60, 69, 72, 74, 86, 131, 328

Cooke, C. R., 197

Coolidge, W. A. B., 32, 36

Corbet, Barry, 357, 361–62, 369, 379

Corbett, Sir Geoffrey, 130–31

Cormack, Bob, 415

Counterculture, 382–85

Couzy, Jean, 242, 244–45, 248, 326

Cowles, Betsy, 255–57, 261

Cox, Sir Percy, 204

Craig, Bob, 306, 308, 310, 311, 313

Crampons, 38, 43, 132

Cranmer, Chappell, 215, 216

Crawford, Charles, 14

Crawford, Colin, 109, 112, 115, 136, 163, 189

Creagh Dhu, 322, 388

Cromwell, Tony, 216–22

Crowley, Aleister, 57–63, 136, 322

Croz, Michael, 31

Crystal Peak, 43, 44
Curran, Jim, 71
Curzon, George Nathaniel, 74–76, 86, 111

Daily Express, 296
Daily Telegraph, 158
Dalai Lama, 13, 23, 75, 85, 157, 203, 238, 343, 377, 383
Dambush Peak, 348
Dankhuta, 257, 453
Darjeeling, 4, 9, 16, 64, 77, 97–99, 119, 129, 131, 136, 143, 158–59, 173, 185–86, 189, 224, 298, 323
Das, Sarat Chandra, 23
Datschnolian, Pawel, 274
Dawa Tenzing, 322, 323
De Andrade, Father Antonio, 12
De Déchy, Maurice, 33, 51
De Filippi, Filippo, 66, 70–71, 74, 210
De Goes, Benedict, 12
Dehra Dun, 2, 16, 23, 226, 232
Delhi, 11, 14, 75, 131, 135, 146
Denman, Earl, 235–36, 290, 359
De Noyelle, Francis, 242, 243
De Righi, Alcesti C. Rigo, 61–62, 79
De Saussure, Horace Bénédict, 29–30, 147
De Ségogne, Henri, 182, 199
Desideri, Ippolito, 12
Desio, Ardito, 198, 314–19, 329
Devies, Lucien, 242, 243, 248
Dhaulagiri, 9, 239, 241, 255; *1950* expedition, 242–45; *1960* expedition, 347–49; *1969* expedition, 386–87; *1973* expedition, 413
Dhaulagiri II, 405
Dhaulagiri IV, 387
Dhauli Valley, 147, 166, 168, 194
Diamirai Peak, 49
Diamir Valley, 48, 49
Dibrugheta, 169, 194
Dickinson, Leo, 443
Diemberger, Kurt, 332–35, 348–49, 445
Diener, Peter, 349
Dingman, Dave, 357, 363, 371–72, 379
Dittert, René, 235, 236, 241, 263, 269–74
Dongkya Ridge, 10
Doody, Dan, 357, 364
Doon School, 205, 232
D'Orville, Albert, 12
Doseth, Hans Christian, 438

Douglas, Ed, 185
Douglas, Lord Francis, 31
Douglas-Hamilton, Sir Douglas, 159
Dras River, 70, 209, 306
Drew, Frederick, 53
Drexel, Alfred, 172, 173, 174–75
Dreyer, George, 110
Dudh Kosi River, 9, 24, 257, 269, 384
Dunagiri, 8, 34, 165, 198, 440
Durashi Pass, 169, 194
Durrance, Jack, 216–22
Duttle, Hans Peter, 359–60
Dyhrenfurth, Günther Oskar, 144, 149, 151, 157, 180, 273; *1930* International Himalaya Expedition, 139–43, 199; *1934* Gasherbrum I expedition, 173
Dyhrenfurth, Hettie, 56, 139, 199, 341
Dyhrenfurth, Norman, 273; background, 354–55; *1963* Everest expedition, 355–59, 360–75; *1971* Everest expedition, 400–3
Dzatrul Rinpoche, 111, 186
Dzongri, 33, 142

Eastern Mountain Sports, 376
East India Company. *See* British East India Company
East Rongbuk Glacier, 103–4, 106, 112, 121, 153, 205, 264, 290
Eckenstein, Oscar, 38–41, 57–61, 63, 90, 132
Eddie Bauer Company, 375
Eggler, Albert, 327
Eiselin, Max, 348–49
Ellenborough, Lord, 22
Elliott, Charles, 276–77
Emerson, Dick, 357, 360, 369
Emmons, Arthur, 191, 193
Ertl, Hans, 198, 300, 302, 338
Estcourt, Nick, 389, 390–94, 409–12, 427
Evans, Dr. Charles, 255, 268, 276, 302; *1953* Everest expedition, 278, 282, 284, 286–88, 299; *1955* Kangchenjunga expedition, 322–26
Evans, John, 419–23
Everest, Sir George, 2, 8, 14, 16–17
Everest, Mount (Chomolungma), 9, 12, 23, 24, 44, 153, 254; altitude, 1, 74; prewar exploration, 74–76, 81; postwar planning, 84–87; *1921* reconnaissance, 95–108; *1922* expedition, 108–15; *1924* expedition, 118–26, 223; *1933* expedition,

158–59, 160–64, 166; Houston-Westland expedition, 159–60; *1935* reconnaissance expedition, 182–84, 186–90; Maurice Wilson's death on, 187–88; *1936* expedition, 189–90; *1938* expedition, 203–7, 223; wartime overflights, 230; Earl Denman attempt on, 235–36; *1950* reconnaissance, 255–62; *1951* reconnaissance, 263–67; *1952* Swiss expeditions, 269–74; *1952* (rumored) Soviet expedition, 274; *1953* British expedition, 277–99; *1956* expedition, 327; *1960* expedition, 343–47; *1963* expedition, 355–59, 360–75; *1962* attempt, 359–60; *1965* expedition, 377; *1971* expedition, 400–3; *1972* Herrligkoffer expedition, 403; *1972* Bonington expedition, 403–4; *1973* Italian expedition, 403–4; *1973* Japanese expedition, 404; *1974* Spanish expedition, 405; *1974* French expedition, 405; *1975* Japanese women's expedition, 407; *1975* Chinese expedition, 408; *1975* Southwest Face expedition, 407–12; *1976* expedition, 415–16; *1980* winter ascent, 406; *1982* expedition, 442–43; *1983* expedition, 445; *1996* disaster, 446–52

Everest Committee. *See* Mount Everest Committee

Everest View Hotel, 382

Everett, Boyd N., Jr., 386–87

Fairy Meadow, 153, 173, 200

Fankhauser, Pert, 200, 201

Fanshawe, Andy, 438

Farmer, E. F., 136–38

Farrar, Percy, 95

Federation française de la montagne, 242

Fendt, William, 135, 143

Finch, George, 96, 117, 119, 190; *1922* Everest expedition, 109, 110, 111, 112, 113, 115

Finsterwalder, Richard, 172, 173, 225–26

Fischer, Scott, 448–52

Fisher, Elliot, 419

Fisher, J. Ellis, 207, 221–22

Flory, Leon, 271, 272

Forbes, James David, 30

Forrer, Ernst, 348

Forsyth, T. Douglas, 23

Franco, Jean, 326, 376

Frauenberger, Walter, 300, 302

French Alpine Club, 234, 243

Freshfield, Douglas, 32, 36, 37, 44, 61, 68, 74–76, 86, 130, 136, 142, 182

Frier, Lieutenant R. N. D., 151, 154

Frost, Tom, 378–79, 390–94

Gallotti, Pino, 316, 318

Ganesh Himal (Ganesh I), 241, 341

Gangroti Glacier, 170

Ganilo Peak, 50

Garhwal Himal, 8, 14, 165, 263

Garhwal-Kumaon, 6, 8, 14, 129, 158

Gasherbrum group, 42, 129

Gasherbrum I (Hidden Peak), 6, 43, 182; *1934* expedition, 173; *1936* expedition, 199; *1958* expedition, 335–40

Gasherbrum II, 6, 327–28

Gasherbrum III, 423

Gasherbrum IV, 337

Gaurishankar, 24, 341, 390

Gaylay, 176, 178, 179, 203

Geographical Journal, 36

Gerhard, Paul, 386–87

German Alpine Club, 133, 173, 300

German and Austrian Alpine Club, 133, 143, 156, 179, 180–82

German Himalayan Foundation, 181–82

Ghori Parbat, 198

Gibson, Jack, 205, 232

Gilgit, 26, 40, 149

Gilgit Road, 11, 40, 151, 182

Gilkey, Art, 306, 308, 310, 311, 313, 314, 315, 361

Gill, Mike, 352

Gillette, Ned, 444

Godwin, Major General Henry Thomas, 19

Godwin-Austen, Henry Haversham, 18–21, 36, 40, 42, 43, 53, 209

Godwin-Austen Glacier, 6, 60, 70–71, 210, 220, 305, 307, 446

Golden Throne, 43, 56

Gongbu, 345–47

Gongga Shan (Minya Konka), 191–92, 207, 343, 444

Goodenough, Admiral Sir William, 157

Goodfellow, Basil, 275–76, 278

Gorak Shep, 269

Göttner, Adolf, 182, 200, 201

Graham, R. B., 117

Graham, William Woodman, 33–34, 36, 37, 65, 74, 136, 166, 169

Graven, Alexandre, 236

Great Game, 22, 24, 26, 210

Great Trigonometrical Survey of India, 2, 14, 16, 18, 19, 21, 74

Greene, Raymond, 147, 158, 161, 163

Gregory, Alfred, 268, 278, 287, 288

Grosvenor, Gil, 426

Groth, Edward, 207, 215, 221–22

Grueber, Johann, 12

Gunten, Hans Rudolf, von, 327

Gurkhas, 39, 46, 49, 51, 54, 240

Gurla Mandhata, 9

Gyachung Kang, 359

Gyalgen, 237, 257

Gyalzen Norbu, 326–27

Gyr, Hans, 236, 237

Habeler, Peter, 431–33

Hadow, Douglas, 31, 216

Hadow, Kenneth, 216

Hall, Henry S., 234, 305–6

Hall, Rob, 448–52

Hamid, Abdul, 22–23

Hansen, Doug, 450–51

Hansen, Norman, 359–60

Hardie, Norman, 322–26

Harrer, Heinrich, 135, 203, 226, 238

Harris, Andy, 450

Harrison, George, 383

Harrison, J. B., 208

Hart, Roger, 359–60

Hartmann, Hans, 143–44, 200, 201

Hartog, John, 329

Harvard, Andy, 417–23, 444–45, 446

Harvard Mountaineering Club, 191, 192, 336

Hasegewa, Ryoten, 408

Hasegewa, Yoshinori, 416

Hastings, Geoffrey, 46, 48–50

Hastings, Warren, 13

Haston, Dougal: background, 389; 1970 Anna-purna North Face expedition, 390–94; 1971 Everest expedition, 400, 401, 403; 1972 Everest expedition, 404; 1974 Changabang expedition, 406–7; 1975 Everest Southwest Face expedition, 408–12

Hazard, John de Vere, 117, 119, 121, 123

Hearsey, Hyder Young, 14, 15

Hedin, Sven, 25

Heim, Dr. Arnold, 241

Hendricks, Sterling, 215

Hepp, Günther, 182, 200, 201

Herbert, James, 15

Heron, A. M., 87, 97, 101, 129

Herrligkoffer, Karl, 178, 319, 331; 1953 Nanga Parbat expedition, 299–305; 1970 Nanga Parbat expedition, 395–97; 1972 Everest expedition, 403

Herron, Rand, 150, 151, 153, 154, 155

Herzog, Maurice, 140, 253, 280, 293, 296; 1950 Annapurna expedition, 242–53, 278, 293

Heuberger, Helmut, 319

Hidden Peak. See Gasherbrum I

Higeta, Minoru, 327

Hillary, Sir Edmund: background, 230–31; 1951 Everest reconnaissance, 263–67; 1952 Cho Oyu reconnaissance, 267–68, 275; 1953 Everest expe-dition, 277–94, 302; aftermath of 1953 expedi-tion, 296–99; 1954 Barun Valley expedition, 328; 1961 scientific expedition, 351–52; 1981 Everest Kangshung expedition, 445

Himalayan Club, 130, 138, 142, 143, 147, 149, 150, 186, 216, 238, 281

Himalayan Committee, 231, 255, 262–63, 267, 268, 275–77, 296, 298–99

Himalayan Journal, 131, 231, 237–38, 275, 379, 436, 446

Himalayan Mountaineering Institute, 298

Himalayan Society, 386

Himalchuli, 255

Hinks, Arthur, 87, 159; and 1921 Everest reconnais-sance, 95–97, 108; and 1922 Everest expedition, 109, 110, 111, 114; and 1924 Everest expedition, 117, 118, 122, 127–29

Hippie Trail, 383, 440

Hispar Glacier, 6, 40, 56

Hispar Pass, 40, 44, 52

Hodgkin, R. A., 208

Hoeman, Vin, 386–87

Hoerlin, Herman, 140, 142

Hoey, Marty, 417–18

Holdsworth, R. L., 147

Holguin, Nena, 434–35

Hooker, Joseph Dalton, 17, 136

Hörlin, Herman, 180, 181

Hornbein, Tom, 357–59, 360–75, 384, 399, 412–13, 418

Horner, Skip, 448

Hotta, Yaichi, 197
House, Bill, 208–15, 222, 228, 305
Houston, Charles, 63, 224, 226, 318, 336, 452–53;
    1936 Nanda Devi expedition, 192–97; *1938* K2
    expedition, 207–15, 223; World War II service,
    227, 232; *1950* Everest reconnaissance, 255–62;
    1953 K2 expedition, 305–14; fellowship of the
    rope, 398
Houston, Dame Fanny Lucy, 159
Houston, Oscar, 193, 255–56
Houston-Westland Everest Expedition, 159–60
Howard-Bury, Charles, 85–87, 96, 101, 103, 104,
    107, 108, 184
Hoyer, Richard, 387
Hudson, Rev. Charles, 31
Hunt, Sir John, 136, 189, 197, 226, 275–77, 404;
    1953 Everest expedition, 277–94; aftermath of
    1953 Everest expedition, 295–99
Hunza Valley, 11, 26, 40

Ichac, Marcel, 242, 245
Imanishi, Kinji, 327
Imanishi, Tojio, 327
Imboden, Josef, 33
Imha Khola River, 257
Indian Archeological Survey, 11
Indian Intelligence Department, 39
Indian Mountaineering Federation, 376
Indian Survey, 11, 13, 22–23, 34, 39, 51, 53, 56, 80,
    130, 239
Indus River, 2, 4, 6, 11, 40, 49, 59, 148, 152, 209,
    306
Inurrategui, Alberto, 443
Inurrategui, Felix, 443
Irvin, Dick, 337
Irvine, Andrew, 117–18, 119, 121–27, 290, 345
Irving, R. L. G., 88, 90, 97
Ishiguro, Hisahi, 404
Italian Alpine Club, 234, 314
Ito, Reizo, 403

Jackson, Monica, 342
Jacot-Guillarmod, Jules, 57, 60, 61–62
Jannu, 10, 376
Japanese Alpine Club, 326–27
Jerstad, Lute, 357, 360, 361, 365–72, 378, 381,
    399
Jöchler, Sepp, 319–21

Jogbani, 257, 259, 264
Johnson, William Henry, 21, 23
Jones, J. H. Emlyn, 255
Jonsong Glacier, 79
Jonsong Peak, 79, 143
Josimath, 34, 168, 194
Jugal Himal, 241, 342
Jumars, 392
Jumna River, 8

Kabru, 10, 34, 65, 77–78, 136, 197
Kailas, 8
Kala Patar, 260–61, 262, 264
Kali Gandaki Gorge, 9, 24, 242, 243
Kama Valley, 81, 104–5, 444
Kamet, 8, 15, 17, 87, 109, 129, 130, 135, 157, 158;
    first ascent *(1931)*, 144, 147–48, 197
Kampa Dzong, 99–100, 205
Kangbachen, 62, 241, 405
Kangchengyao, 80, 99
Kangchenjunga, 4, 9, 16, 33, 37, 51, 52, 64, 68,
    78, 80, 87, 100, 129, 172, 179, 192, 224; *1905*
    expedition, 61–63; *1929* expedition, 135, 138–39;
    E. F. Farmer attempt, 136–38; *1930* expedition,
    139–43; *1931* expedition, 143–44; *1955* expedi-
    tion, 321–26
Kangshung Glacier, 289, 290
Kappeler, Robert, 236, 237
Karakoram, 1, 6, 17, 19, 25–26, 39, 56, 129, 153,
    327, 336
Karakoram Highway, 6, 437
Karakoram Pass, 23, 25, 26, 52
Karnali River, 9, 241
Kashmir, 18, 39, 46, 53, 59, 130, 151, 172, 209,
    237, 377
Kathmandu, 12, 14, 23, 24, 81, 97, 186, 239–41,
    255, 269, 281, 292, 296–98, 344, 350, 360, 372,
    380, 381
Kato, Kiichiro, 237
Kato, Yasuo, 405
Kauffman, Andrew, 336–40, 446
Kauffman, Ulrich, 33
Kedarnath, 8, 170, 236
Kellas, Alexander Mitchell, 83, 87, 120, 127, 136,
    144, 149; background and early exploration,
    78–81; *1921* Everest reconnaissance, 97–99; and
    oxygen question, 109–10
Kellas Rock Peak, 189

Kempe, John, 323
Kempson, Edwin, 183, 188, 189
Kempter, Otto, 300, 301, 302
Kerr, Blake, 446
Keynes, John Maynard, 90, 92, 94, 111, 134
Kharta, 81, 104, 105, 185, 206
Kharta Changri, 188
Kharta Glacier, 105, 188
Khartaphu, 188
Khumbu Glacier, 258–59, 269, 282
Khumbu Icefall, 259, 265–66, 282, 327, 448
Khumjung, 359, 382, 439
Kick, Wilhelm, 53
Kipling, Rudyard, 8, 22
Kirkus, Colin, 164, 183
Kirwan, Sir Laurence, 275–76
Klarner, Januscz, 198
Knowles, Guy, 57
Knowlton, Elizabeth, 150, 151, 155
Kogan, Claude, 320, 341, 342, 424
Kohli, M. S., 377, 378
Kohn, Howard, 380
Köllensperger, Hermann, 300
Komorkova, Vera, 425–27
Kongur, 343, 437, 445
Kosi Valley, 241
Krakauer, Jon, 448–52
Kraus, Karl von, 135, 138, 200, 201
K2, 6, 37, 38, 39, 42, 43, 44, 57, 63, 129, 135;
    early exploration, 18–21, 25; *1902* expedition,
    57, 59–61; *1909* expedition, 63, 65, 69–74;
    1938 expedition, 207–15, 223; *1939* expedition,
    215–22, 224; *1953* expedition, 305–14; *1954*
    expedition, 314–18; *1975* expedition, 414; *1978*
    Bonington expedition, 427; *1978* American
    expedition, 428–31; deaths in *1986*, 446–47
Kuari Pass, 14, 76
Kuen, Felix, 396
Kuhn, Emil, 200
Kumaon, 8, 76, 129, 164, 165. *See also*
    Garhwal-Kumaon
Kumar, Kiran, 417, 419
Kunigk, Herbert, 153, 154
Kurz, Marcel, 140
Kyetrak Glacier, 268

Lacedelli, Lino, 315–18
Lachenal, Louis, 235, 248–53, 269, 288

Ladakh, 12, 22, 23, 52, 54, 377
Ladies Glacier, 342
Lambert, Raymond, 235, 248, 283, 288, 290, 320;
    1952 Swiss Everest expeditions, 269–74
Lambton, William, 2, 16
Langtang Himal, 241
Larch, Sepp, 328
Larkya Himal, 9
Latimer, George, 232
Leh, 12, 22, 23, 26
Leininger, Jean, 199
Lerco, Roberto, 42
Lester, Jim, 357, 381
Leupold, Joachim, 135, 143
Lev, Peter, 417–23
Lhakpa La, 105–6, 107, 188, 206
Lhasa, 12, 22, 23, 75, 85, 98, 116, 129, 157, 163,
    226, 230, 231, 343
Lhatse Dzong, 75
Lho La, 189
Lhotse, 9, 101, 105, 264, 267, 270–71, 273–74,
    282, 327, 355
Lhotse Glacier, 264
Lhotse Shar, 405
Life (magazine), 357, 360, 373
Lindley, Alfred, 215
Ling, Bill, 96–97
Lingtren, 103, 189, 262
Little Tukucha Peak, 348
Liu Lianman, 345
Lloyd, Peter, 191, 192, 195–96, 205, 206, 207, 241
Lobenhoffer, Hans, 203
Lobsang Palden Yeshé, Panchen Lama, 13
Lobsang Sherpa, 136–37, 143
Lohner, Annalise, 236, 341
Lonely Planet guidebook series, 382, 437
Longland, Jack, 158, 159, 161, 163, 164, 189, 205
Longstaff, Tom, 66, 71–72, 81, 83, 121, 144, 166,
    169, 170, 197, 204; ascent of Trisul, 77; *1922*
    Everest expedition, 109, 112, 114
Longstaff's Col, 170, 197
Loomis, William Farnsworth, 191, 193, 195–96,
    208
Lowe, George, 263, 268, 328; *1953* Everest expe-
    dition, 277–78, 282, 286, 287, 288, 291, 292;
    aftermath of *1953* Everest expedition, 299; *1961*
    scientific expedition, 351
Lucas, F. G., 54

Luchsinger, Fritz, 327
Luft, Uli, 200, 201, 203
Lukla, 269, 350, 437

Machapuchare, 389
Macinnes, Hamish, 388, 404, 408–9
Magnone, Guido, 326, 329
Mahalungar Himal, 9, 75
Mahdi, 316–17, 318
Mahruki, Nasuh, 443
Maiktoli, 8, 165, 166, 171
Makalu, 2, 9, 105, 160, 258, 266, 352; *1954* expedition, 328; *1955* expedition, 326
Maki, Yuko, 326–27
Mallory, George Leigh, 83, 135, 139, 157, 158, 162, 184, 194, 290; background, 87–95; *1921* Everest Reconnaissance, 95–108; *1922* Everest expedition, 108–15; *1923* American tour, 116–17; *1924* Everest expedition, 118–26; aftermath of disappearance, 127–28
Mallory, Ruth, 83, 92–94, 95, 98–102, 106, 107, 111, 115, 118, 119, 121–23, 127–28
Malubiting, 53
Mana Pass, 12, 23
Manaslu, 9, 255, 326–27
Mandani Parbat, 198
Mangalbare, 241
Maraini, Fosco, 337, 340
Marlung, 320
Marmet, Jürg, 327, 336
Marques, Brother Manuel, 12
Martyn, John, 205
Masherbrum, 6, 18, 20, 43, 208
Mason, Kenneth, 4, 11, 18, 53, 55, 130–32, 139, 149, 221, 225–26, 382
Matterhorn, 31–32
Maurer, Andreas, 33
Mauri, Carlo, 400, 401
Mazeaud, Pierre, 400–2
Mazeno Ridge, 48, 49
McCormack, Tom, 337
McCormick, A. D., 38
McGregor, Sir Charles, 24, 25
McIntyre, David, 159
McMahon Line, 10
McNaught-Davis, Ian, 329
Meade, Charles F., 144, 204
Meade's Col, 147

Mehta, Soli, 379, 446
Merkl, Willi, 11, 148, 300; *1932* Nanga Parbat Expedition, 149–55; *1934* Nanga Parbat Expedition, 157, 171–80; body found, 203
Merrell, George R., 240
Messner, Günther, 395–97
Messner, Reinhold, 385; background, 395; *1970* Nanga Parbat expedition, 395–97; partnership with Peter Habeler, 431–33; *1975* Hidden Peak expedition, 432; *1978* Everest expedition, 432–33; *1978* Nanga Parbat solo, 434; *1980* Everest solo, 434–36
Miar Peak, 40
Middleton, Dorothy, 55
Miller, Irene Beardsley, 425–27
Miller, Maynard, 357
Mintaka Pass, 236
Minya Konka. *See* Gongga Shan
Miristi Khola River, 244–46
Misch, Peter, 172–73
Miura, Yuichiro, 443
Molenaar, Dee, 306, 308, 311, 313
Monserrate, Father Antonio, 12
Mont Blanc, 29–32, 42, 88, 93, 101, 135, 140, 172, 248, 269
Montgomerie, Thomas George, 18, 21, 22–23
Moorcroft, William, 15
Moore, A. W., 32
Moore, Terris, 191–92, 222, 228
Moravec, Fritz, 327–28
Morris, James, 278, 292
Morris, John, 190
Morrissey, Jim, 445
Morshead, Henry, 87, 97, 98, 101, 112, 113, 117, 144
Morup, Dorje, 451
Mountain (magazine), 379, 385, 397, 435–36, 438, 450
Mountaineering Journal, 204
Mountain Travel Nepal, 381
Mountain Travel-Sobek, 448
Mount Everest Committee, 85, 95, 96, 110, 111, 117, 118, 122, 127–29, 157, 158, 159, 160, 163, 164, 183, 186, 188, 190, 191, 204
Mount Everest Foundation, 322, 336, 390
Mughal Empire, 11–12
Muktinath, 9
Müllritter, Peter, 172, 200
Mumm, Arnold, 64, 77, 144, 166

Mummery, Albert Frederick, 35, 37, 38, 51, 64, 65, 75, 149, 153; attempt on Nanga Parbat, 45–50

Munich school of mountaineering, 132–33, 148

Mussoorie, 4, 8, 19

Muztagh Ata, 236–37, 238, 343, 437

Muztagh Pass, 19, 25

Muztagh Tower, 43, 72, 328–29, 337

Naina Peak, 8

Nainital, 4, 8, 17

Namba, Yasuko, 451

Namcha Barwa, 10

Namche Bazar, 257, 269, 320, 350, 382

Nanda Devi, 8, 15, 23, 34, 77, 129, 164, 223, 407; *1934* Shipton-Tilman exploration, 165–71; *1936* ascent, 191–97; *1964* Indian ascent, 377; CIA operations on, 378–80; *1976* Unsoeld expedition, 416–23

Nanda Devi East, 165, 198

Nanda Kot, 8, 15, 197, 378–79

Nanga Parbat, 4, 10, 18, 64, 130, 135, 223, 224–25; Mummery attempt on, 45–50, 65; *1932* expedition, 148–55; *1934* expedition, 157, 171–82; *1937* expedition, 200–1; *1938* expedition, 201–3; *1939* expedition, 203; *1953* German expedition, 299–305, 317; *1970* Messner ascent, 395–97; *1978* Messner solo ascent, 434

Nangpa La, 24, 77, 185, 186, 267, 268, 319

National Aeronautics and Space Administration, 356

National Geographic, 241, 352–53, 357, 364, 373, 413, 425–26

National Geographic Society, 353, 355, 357, 364, 372–73, 378, 426

National Outdoor Leadership School (NOLS), 376

Nawang Gombu, 361, 364–65, 367–68, 370, 373, 377

Negrotto, Federic, 66, 70, 72

Nehru, Jawaharlal, 298, 377

Nepal Gap, 78–79

Nepali Congress Party, 240, 261

Nepal Mountaineering Association, 439

Nepal Peak, 79, 197

Neve, Arthur, 54, 71

Neve, Ernest, 54, 131, 149

Nevison, Tom, 337

Newsweek, 357, 367

New York Herald Tribune, 253

New York Times, 299, 318, 340, 360, 373, 451

New York Times Magazine, 340

Nicholson, James, 16

Nicholson, Nancy, 94

Nilgiri Parbat, 197

Nilgiris, 244–46

Nilkanth, 198, 416

Nima Dorje, 176, 178

Nima Tashi, 176, 178

Niven, Bruce, 390

Noel, John Baptiste, 81, 83, 84, 97, 159; *1922* Everest expedition, 109, 110, 112; *1924* Everest expedition, 118–19, 121, 125, 158; *Climbing Mount Everest,* 111, 118, 122; *The Epic of Everest,* 129

Norton, Edward, 109, 112–13, 117, 120–24, 127–28, 223, 273, 284, 287

Noshaq, 406

Noyce, Wilfrid, 232, 237, 278, 279, 281, 283, 292, 349

Nun Kun, 4, 53–56, 341, 447

Nuptse, 97, 101, 259, 261, 350, 358, 388

Nyönno Ri, 186

Odell, Noel, 189, 436; *1924* Everest expedition, 117, 119, 121, 123–26, 127; *1936* Nanda Devi ascent, 191, 192–93, 195–97, 223; *1938* Everest expedition, 205–6

Oestreich, Karl, 53

Ogre (Uzum Brakk), 40

Oliver, Peter, 190, 205–6

O'Malley, Mary (Cottie Sanders), 89, 92

Ortner, Sherry, 437

Osmaston, Gordon, 191

Oudot, Jacques, 242, 249, 349

Outside (magazine), 379–80, 422, 427, 448, 451

Outward Bound, 413

Oxford University Mountaineering Club, 278

Oxygen, supplemental use of, 109–10, 113–14, 280–81, 385

Paccard, Michael-Gabriel, 30

Pache, Alexis, 61–62, 323

Packard, Bill, 255

Pal, Bachendri, 443

Pallis, Marco, 164

Pamir Range, 25

Pandjh, 24–25

Pangboche, 258

Panmah Glacier, 19

Paradis, Marie, 30

Pasang Bhotia, 206–7

Pasang Dawa Lama, 216, 317, 319–21

Pasang Kami, 391

Pasang Kikuli, 169, 176, 178, 193, 195, 197, 208, 214, 216–21, 308

Pasang Kitar, 216, 218–19, 221, 308

Patey, Tom, 322, 389

Patterson, Robert, 439

Pauhunri, 10, 79, 80, 136, 232

Peace Corps, 354, 413

Peak October, 343

Peary, Robert, 64, 81

Pen-y-Pass, 90, 94, 95

Pertemba Sherpa, 411

Pethangstse, 328

Petigax, Joseph, 53, 66, 72

Petigax, Laurent, 53, 66, 72

Petzoldt, Paul, 208, 210–15, 376, 448

Pfannl, Heinrich, 57–60

Pfeffer, Martin, 200, 201

Phalut, 33, 74

Pindar River, 197

Pinnacle Peak, 56

Pinzo Norbu, 176, 178

Pioneer Peak, 44

Piotrowski, Tadeusz, 406

Pircher, Hans, 143

Pir Panjal, 5, 19, 54, 78

Pitons and carabiners, 132, 148, 208, 214, 230, 235, 385

Pittman, Sandy, 449–50

Pococke, Richard, 29

Pokhara, 9

Polish Mountaineering Club, 198

Polunin, Oleg, 241

Pownall, Dick, 357, 361, 365–66

Prather, Barry, 357, 365, 367, 379

Puchoz, Mario, 315

Pugh, Lewis Griffith, 268, 275, 280, 289, 351

Pulmonary edema, 60, 174, 216, 315, 367

Pumori, 97, 103, 260, 264

"Pundits," 22–24

Pye, David, 92, 94, 108, 110

Pyramid Peak, 241

Queen Mary Peak. See Sia Kangri

Qu Yinhua, 345, 347

Raeburn, Harold, 87, 95, 96, 97, 98, 106, 109, 136

Raechl, Walter, 172

Ragobir Thapa, 48, 49–50, 149

Rainer, Cuno, 300, 301

Rakaposhi, 6, 40, 236

Rakhiot Glacier, 153, 173, 300

Rakhiot Peak, 153, 154, 174, 175, 178, 179, 200, 201, 301

Rakhiot Ridge, 154, 178, 179, 300

Rakhiot Valley, 50, 152

Ram, Hari, 23–24

Ramgamga River, 15

Ramsay, Sir William, 78

Ramthang Peak, 143

Rana regime (Nepal), 9, 240, 261–62, 296

Ranikhet, 4, 8, 147, 168, 193–94, 263

Rataban, 198

Raverat, Jacques, 89

Rawalpindi, 306, 314

Rawling, Cecil, 75–76, 81–82, 83, 84, 97

Rawlinson, Anthony, 329

Rebitsch, Mathias, 201

Rébuffat, Gaston, 235, 242–52, 386

Recreational Equipment Incorporated (REI), 335, 357, 375–76

Reichardt, Lou, 413, 417, 418–19, 428–29, 445

Reich League of German Mountaineers, 156

Reich Sports Ministry, 172, 179, 181–82

Reiss, Ernst, 327

Reist, Adolf, 327

Rennell, James, 13

Renshaw, Dick, 440, 441

Rey, Emile, 166

Reymond, Charles, 61–62

Reynolds, Jan, 444

Rickmers, Willi Rickmer, 131–32, 134, 200

Riddiford, Earle, 263, 265, 268, 275, 278

Ridgeway, Rick, 399, 428–31, 439

Rigele, Fritz, 132

Rikkyo University Mountaineering Club, 197

Rinzing Bhotia, 161, 183, 190

Ripley, S. Dillon, 240–41

Rishi Ganga River, 34, 193

Rishi Gorge, 165–66, 170, 193

Roach, Gary, 415

Roberts, David, 427

Roberts, Dianne, 425, 428

Roberts, Gil, 337, 357, 358, 361

Roberts, Jimmy, 208, 232, 255, 347, 357, 381, 391, 400, 403

Robertson, David, 88, 90

Roch, André, 198, 199, 236, 269, 271

Rock and Ice Club (Manchester), 322

Romanes, Wally, 352

Romanticism, 22, 25, 27–30, 80, 384

Rongbuk Glacier, 101, 103, 111, 121, 189, 190, 206

Rongbuk Monastery, 101, 111, 186, 188, 235, 258, 343, 446

Roskelley, John, 398, 413, 417–23, 428–31, 437, 445

Ross, Bill, 386

Ross, James Clark, 17

Roudebush, Hayward, 38

Rouse, Alan, 445, 447

Rousseau, Jean-Jacques, 27

Rowell, Galen, 399, 414, 422, 425–27, 444, 447

Royal Geographical Society, 36–37, 39, 44, 45, 56, 63, 67; and early Everest exploration, 75, 76, 81; and interwar Everest expeditions, 83–85, 108, 128, 159, 357; and *1953* Everest expedition, 276, 289

Rubenson, Wilhelm, 77–78

Rudolph, Johann, 30

Ruskin, John, 27, 30, 34, 35

Rutkiewicz, Wanda, 406, 423, 424, 446

Ruttledge, Hugh, 165, 166, 172, 199; *1933* Everest expedition, 158–59, 160–64, 188; *1936* Everest expedition, 183, 189–90, 276, 277

Ruwenzori Mountains, 64–65, 68, 77

Ryder, C. D. H., 75

Saaed Qader, 332

Saltoro Kangri, 56, 376

Sandakphu, 4, 74

Sanders, Cottie (Mary O'Malley), 89, 92

Sandhu, Balwant, 407

Santopanth, 8

Santopanth Glacier, 170

Saussure, Horace Bénédict de, 29–30, 147

Savoia, Princess Margherita di, 64

Savoia Glacier, 70, 71, 210, 212

Sayle, Charles, 89, 90

Sayre, Woodrow Wilson, 359–60, 437

Schäfer, Ernst, 1

Schaffert, Wolfgang, 444

Schaller, Robert, 378–80, 414, 428

Schatz, Marcel, 242, 246

Schelbert, Albin, 348–49

Schlagintweit, Adolf, 17–18, 144

Schlagintweit, Hermann, 17–18, 74, 136

Schlagintweit, Robert, 17–18, 144

Schmetterer, Ludwig, 201

Schmied, Ernst, 327

Schmitz, Kim, 447

Schmuck, Marcus, 331–35

Schneider, Erwin, 134, 140, 142, 172–76, 179–82

Schoening, Pete, 306, 308, 310–13, 337–38, 398, 429, 450

Scholz, Peter, 396

Schwarzgruber, Rudolf, 198

Scott, Doug, 404, 406–7, 409–11, 427, 436, 443

Scott, J. S., 241

Scott, Robert F., 81, 127

Scott, Robert L., 230

Seabrook, William, 63

Secord, Campbell, 236, 262, 263, 268, 275

Ségogne, Henri de, 182, 198

Seidman, David, 386

Sella, Vittorio, 61, 66–68, 70, 71, 72, 136, 207, 210, 328–29

Sentinel Peak, 80

Shafat Glacier, 54, 55, 56

Shaksgam Valley, 26, 56, 130

Shekar Dzong, 111, 159

Sheldon, George, 216–18

Shelley, Percy Bysshe, 30

Sherpa Climbers Buddhist Association, 296

Sherpas, 9, 33, 39, 77–79, 115, 138, 143, 166, 321, 350–51, 382, 384, 386, 391, 439. *See also individual Sherpas by name*

Shigatse (Xigaze), 12, 13, 24

Shilla, 21

Shipton, Eric Earle, 35, 130, 140, 191, 197, 198, 231, 253, 254, 273, 279–80, 282, 292; background, 145–46; *1931* Kamet expedition, 146–48; *1933* Everest expedition, 158–59, 160–64; *1934* Nanda Devi exploration, 166–71; *1935* Everest reconnaissance expedition, 182–84, 186–90; *1936* Everest expedition, 189–90; *1938* Everest expedition, 204–7; *1947* Muztagh Ata attempt, 236–37, 238; *1951* Everest reconnaissance, 263–67, 268, 351; *1952* Cho Oyu reconnaissance, 267–

68, 319–20; deposed as leader of *1953* Everest expedition, 275–77; death, 436

Shishapangma, 9, 12, 198, 238, 349, 377, 434, 444

Shivalik Range, 2

Shi Zhanchun, 343–44, 346

Siachen Glacier, 6, 56, 71

Sia Kangri (Queen Mary Peak), 56, 199, 437

Siege tactics, 43, 112, 121, 144, 171, 268, 270, 338, 392

Sierra Club, 357, 385

Sikdhar, Radhanath, 16

Sillem, H., 54, 55

Simla, 4, 8, 25

Simler, Josias, 29

Simon, Felix, 153, 154

Simvu, 78–79, 182, 197

Singalila Ridge, 4, 17, 33, 61, 74, 323

Singh, Goman, 48, 49–50, 149

Singh, Kailian, 23

Singh, Kishan, 23

Singh, Mani, 23

Singh, Nain, 23

Singh, Ranbir, 18

Singh, Ranjit, 18

Siniolchu, 10, 68, 182, 197

Siri, Will, 328, 357

Skanda Purana, 2

Skardu, 11, 59, 70, 210, 237, 306

Skyang Kangri, 60, 71

Slingsby, A. M., 71, 144

Slingsby, William Cecil, 32, 46

Smith, Albert, 31

Smythe, Frank, 9, 32, 173, 192, 226–27, 232, 242, 262, 287; background, 140–41; *1930* Kangchenjunga expedition, 141–43; *1931* Kamet expedition, 144–48; *1933* Everest expedition, 157–58, 160–64; *1936* Everest expedition, 189–90; *1937* Garhwal expedition, 197–98; *1938* Everest expedition, 204–7

Solu Khumbu, 9, 24, 255, 261, 262, 264, 267–68, 381

Somervell, Howard, 109, 110, 112–15, 117, 120–24

Spender, Michael, 183, 188

Spoleto, Duke of, 198

Sports Association of the German State Railroad, 172

Srinagar, 12, 26, 39

Stanley, Henry Morton, 64

Stark, Elizabeth, 342

States, Jim, 418–19

Stäubel, Werner, 348

Stein, Sir Aurel, 11

Stephen, Leslie, 27, 31, 90

Stephens, Rebecca, 443

Stevenson, Robert Louis, 36

Stimson, Henry, 227

Stobard, Tom, 278, 291

Strachey, Lytton, 89, 92

Streatfeild, Norman R., 199, 210, 216, 226

Streather, Tony, 306, 311, 313, 322, 323, 325–26

Stremfelj, Andrej, 443

Stremfelj, Marija, 443

Strutt, E. L., 109, 110–11, 112, 208, 224

Sturm, Günther, 444

Styles, Ralph N., 352

Sunderhunga Col, 166, 170

Suru, 55, 56

Sutter, Alfred, 236

Swift, Robert, 337

Swiss Foundation for Alpine Research, 236, 262, 269, 298, 327, 341

Syndicat des Guides de Chamonix, 30

Tabei, Junko, 407

Takami, Kshige, 416

Talung Glacier, 33

Tang La, 12, 13

Tarshing, 46, 48

Tasker, Joe, 436, 439, 440–43, 445

Taugwalder, Rudolf, 52

Technological innovation, 37, 66, 119, 132, 228–30, 385

Tengboche Monastery, 257–58, 261, 264, 282, 354, 381, 383, 452

Tenth Mountain Division, 228

Tent Peak, 182

Tenzing Norgay, 87, 169, 191, 232, 305, 372, 403; background, 184–86; *1935* Everest reconnaissance expedition, 189; *1936* Everest expedition, 190; *1938* Everest expedition, 205–6; and Denman attempt on Everest, 235–36; *1947* Swiss Garhwal expedition, 236; *1949* Annapurna IV attempt, 241; *1952* Swiss Everest expeditions, 269–73; *1953* British Everest expedition, 278, 281–94, 302; aftermath of *1953* expedition, 296–99

Teram Kangri, 71–72

Terray, Lionel, 235, 242–52, 326, 349, 376, 384

Thoenes, Alexander, 135

Thompson, Rupert, 103

Thomson, J. M. A., 90

Tichy, Herbert, 319–21, 384

Tiger Hill, 16, 186

Tighe, Tony, 404

Tilman, H. W., 16, 35, 69, 145–46, 189, 197, 198, 208, 226, 231, 238–39, 253, 374, 432–33; *1934* Nanda Devi exploration, 168–71; *1935* Everest reconnaissance, 188–89; *1936* Nanda Devi ascent, 191, 192–97; *1938* Everest expedition, 203–7, 223; *1947* Rakaposhi reconnaissance, 236; *1947* Muztagh Ata attempt, 236–37; *1949* Nepal expedition, 241; *1950* Nepal expedition, 255; *1950* Everest reconnaissance, 256–61, 263, 264, 452–53; death, 436

Times, The (London), 36, 42, 96, 118, 127, 160, 263, 278–79, 283, 292, 296, 298, 400

Tingri, 101

Tirsuli, 198

Tissieres, Alfred, 263

Tista River, 10

Tobin, H. W., 130, 138, 142, 143, 237–38, 275, 281

Torres, Ricardo, 443

Traill, G. W., 15–16

Trekking industry, 381–82

Trench, George, 216

Tribhuvan, Bir Bikram Shah Dev, King of Nepal, 240, 261–62

Trimble, Philip, 415

Trisul, 77, 190

Tsangpo River, 10, 13

Tschammer und Osten, Hans von, 156, 172, 173, 174, 179–81, 201

Tukucha, 244, 245

Turkestan, 22–23

Turner, J. M. W., 30

Turner, Samuel, 13

Tyndall, John, 31, 66

Udall, Stewart, 354, 356

Uemera, Naomi, 400, 403, 434

Ullman, James Ramsey, 232–34, 253, 293, 295, 354; *1963* Everest expedition, 357–58, 360–61, 367. Works: *High Conquest,* 224–25, 231; *The White Tower,* 232, 340–41; *Tiger of the Snows,*

299; *Americans on Everest,* 373, 383–84, 399, 423–24

Underhill, Robert, 234

Unsoeld, Krag, 418

Unsoeld, Nanda Devi, 416–23, 427, 428

Unsoeld, Willi, 347, 398, 413, 428; *1963* Everest Expedition, 357–58, 360–64, 368–74, 400; *1976* Nanda Devi expedition, 416–23

Urdukas, 60, 70, 72

Uzum Brakk (Conway's Ogre), 40

Van der Stratten, Claudine, 342

Vaucher, Michel, 400, 401

Vaucher, Yvette, 400, 401

Vibram soles, 228, 237, 376

Viesturs, Ed, 449

Vigne, Godfrey Thomas, 18, 43

Vittoz, Pierre, 341

Wager, Lawrence, 158, 161–63, 287

Wakefield, A. W., 109, 111, 114–15

Walker, James, 21

Waller, James, 208

Wang Fuzhou, 345–47, 377

Wang Hongboa, 408

Ward, Michael, 262–63, 265–66, 268, 278, 283, 289, 351–52

Warren, Charles, 164, 183, 187, 188, 189, 190, 205–6, 436

Washburn, Bradford, 191–92, 207

Washington Post, 373

Watson, Vera, 425

Waugh, Andrew, 16, 19

Weathers, Beck, 450, 451

Webb, William, 14

Wedderburn, E. A. M., 204

Welzenbach, Willo, 132, 148, 149–50, 172–79

Wessely, Victor, 57–60

Western Cwm (Everest), 103, 183, 189, 259, 261, 264–67, 269–71, 282, 362

Westmacott, Michael, 278, 286

Wexler, Arnold, 352, 368

Wheeler, Oliver, 87, 97, 101, 106, 107

Wheeler, Tony and Maureen, 381–82

Whillans, Don, 322, 388, 404; *1970* Annapurna South Face expedition, 390–95; *1971* International Everest expedition, 400–3; *1972* Herrligkoffer Everest expedition, 403

Whittaker, Jim, 335, 413; *1963* Everest expedition, 357, 360, 361, 364–68, 369, 373–76; *1975* K2 expedition, 414; *1978* K2 expedition, 428–31
Whittaker, Lou, 361, 414
Whymper, Edward, 31–32, 35, 46, 66, 144
Wickwire, Jim, 414, 428–29
Wieland, Ulrich, 140, 142, 172, 175, 178
Wielicki, Krzysztof, 406
Wien, Karl, 134, 143–44, 182, 200–1
Wiesner, Jerome B., 355
Wiessner, Fritz, 150, 153–55, 207, 214, 215–22, 224, 228, 305, 447
Wigram, Edmund, 183, 188, 189
Willenpart, Hans, 328
Wills, Alfred, 31
Wilson, Kenneth, 379, 440
Wilson, Maurice, 187–88, 235, 345, 435
Windham, William, 29
Wintersteller, Fritz W., 332–35
Wolfe, Dudley, 216–22, 447
Wollaston, Alexander, 87, 97, 101, 107, 109
Women climbers, 51–52, 53, 56, 150, 199, 340–42, 376, 381, 407–8, 417–18, 423–27, 428
Wood, Walter, 222
Wood-Johnson, George, 158
Woolf, Virginia, 90, 91, 111
Wordsworth, William, 30
Workman, Fanny Bullock, 51–57, 70, 72, 76, 80, 210

Workman, William Hunter, 51–57, 70, 72, 76, 80, 210
World Book Encyclopedia, 351
Wright, Jonathan, 444
Wylie, Charles, 278, 279, 286, 291
Wyn-Harris, Percy, 145, 158, 161–63, 189
Wyss-Dunant, Edouard, 241, 269

Yakub Beg, 23
Yale University Mountaineering Club, 208
Yalung Glacier, 61, 136, 323
Yanagisawa, Yukihiro, 445
Yeti, 351, 353, 354
Young, Geoffrey Winthrop, 50, 83–84, 90, 92–95, 108, 128, 231, 292
Younghusband, Francis, 14, 19, 22, 24–27, 39, 42, 51, 69, 72, 74, 128, 135; and *1904* military mission to Tibet, 75; and interwar Everest expeditions, 84–86, 95, 103, 109, 111, 114, 115–16, 157; on Mallory, 124

Zanskar Range, 4, 8, 144
Zawada, Andrej, 406
Zemu Glacier, 78, 138
Zhou Zheng, 343, 445
Zoji La, 12, 59, 70, 306
Zuck, Stefan, 201, 203
Zurbriggen, Mattias, 38, 39, 40, 43, 52, 53